Forever Young

May God bless and keep you
May your wishes all come tru
May you always do for others
And let others do for you

May you build a ladder to the stars
And climb on every rung
And may you stay forever young.

May you grow up to be righteous
May you grow up to be true
And may you always know the truth
And the light surrounding you

May you always be courageous
Stand upright and be strong
And may you stay forever young.

Forever young, forever young
May you stay forever young.

May your hands always be busy
May your feet always be swift
May you have a strong foundation
When the winds of changes shift

May your heart always be joyful
May your song always be sung
And may you stay forever young.

Forever young, forever young
May you stay forever young.

Songwriter: Bob Dylan 1974
Ram's Horn Music Publisher (SESAC)

God speaks to each of us as He makes us
Then walks with us silently out of the night

These are the words we dimly hear:

You sent out beyond your recall,
Go to the limits of your longing
Embody me.

Flare up like flame
And make big shadows I can move in

Let everything happen to you: beauty and terror
Just keep going. No feeling is final.
Don't let yourself lose me.

Nearby is the country they call life.
You'll know it by its seriousness.

Give me your hand.

Ranier Maria Rilke

THE DIMENSIONS READER

COMMUNITY COLLEGE OF VERMONT

Fifth Edition

COORDINATING EDITORS

KD Maynard
Debby Stewart
Yasmine Ziesler

Copley Custom Textbooks

An imprint of XanEdu Custom Publishing

ISBN 13: 978-1-58152-598-4
ISBN 10: 1-58152-598-2

Acknowledgments:

pp. 6-12: From *Bird by Bird* by Anne Lamott. Copyright © 1994 by Anne Lamott. Used by permission of Pantheon Books, a division of Random House, Inc.

pp. 52–68: As appeared in *Harper's*, June, 1995. Copyright © 1995.

pp. 69–73: From *Narrative of the Life of Frederick Douglass*, originally published in 1845.

pp. 74–82: From *Black Boy* by Richard Wright. Copyright © 1937, 1942, 1944, 1945 by Richard Wright; renewed © 1973 by Ellen Wright. Reprinted by permission of HarperCollins Publishers.

pp. 84–93: From *O Rugged Land of Gold* by Martha Martin. Copyright © 1952, 1953 by Macmillan Publishing Company, copyright renewed © 1980, 1981 by Christine H. Niemi. Reprinted with the permission of Scribner, a division of Simon & Schuster, Inc.

pp. 94–96: From *Teacher* by Sylvia Ashton-Warner. Copyright © 1963 by Sylvia Ashton-Warner. Reprinted by permission of International Creative Management, Inc.

pp. 97–110: From *Hundreds and Thousands: The Journals of Emily Carr*. Copyright © 1966 by Clarke, Irwin and Co. Reprinted by permission of Stoddart Publishing Co. Limited, Toronto.

pp. 111–119: From *Child of the Dark* by Carolina Maria de Jesus, translated by David St. Clair. Copyright © 1962 by E. P. Dutton & Co., Inc., New York and Souvenir Press, Ltd., London. Used by permission of Dutton, a division of Penguin Putnam Inc.

pp. 120–127: From *Anne Frank: The Diary of a Young Girl* by Anne Frank. Copyright © 1952 by Otto H. Frank. Used by permission of Doubleday, a division of Random House, Inc.

pp. 128–132: From *Hanna Senesh: Her Life and Diary* by Hannah Senesh, English translation copyright © 1971 by Nigel Marsh. Used by permission of Schocken Books, a division of Random House, Inc.

pp. 133–142: From *Journal of a Residence on a Georgia Plantation in 1838–1839* by Frances Anne Kemble, edited by John A. Scott, Copyright © 1961 by Alfred A. Knopf, Inc. Used by permission of Alfred A. Knopf, a division of Random House, Inc.

Copley Custom Textbooks

An imprint of XanEdu Custom Publishing
138 Great Road
Acton, MA 01720
800-562-2147

Contents

Section Two: Journals, Memoirs, First-Person Accounts

Section Three: Poetry and Drama

Section Four: Short Fiction

Section Six: The Allegory of the Cave

Preface

"On the shoulders of giants . . . "

Many colleges across the United States have developed first semester seminars to help entering students engage with their new academic environments, and to provide a more consistent "launch pad" as the students take off into their curricular endeavors.

Historical Underpinnings

Back in 1981, Community College of Vermont created its *Dimensions of Learning* course to empower students with the skills and confidence necessary for success in college. Traditionally, *Dimensions of Learning* was the first course a student took at CCV, and its aim was to provide students with what its founders considered to be "the basic of basics" by:

Instilling a sense of self-worth;

Encouraging cognitive development; and

Providing a structure that encourages basic skills mastery.

Dimensions of Learning challenged students with a powerful, thought-provoking curriculum, and at the same time provided them with structured support for developing their academic skills. Study skills, reading strategies, writing techniques, and the steps to critical thinking were all purposefully and sequentially woven into the class activities and assignments to give students—every step of the way—the tools they needed to learn and to be successful in the course.

We are most grateful to Roger Cranse, the author of the "white paper" written in 1982 that framed the *Dimensions of Learning* course. Roger and a team of others first created the "magic" that has stood the test of time and that has influenced hundreds of CCV students. John Christensen and Connie Yandow were early editors of the *Dimensions* anthologies, along with a number of terrific CCV coordinators and faculty who have worked to find a selection that will best serve our students and our course objectives. Lucy Miskin at Copley Publishing has coached us through the process, throughout the years; we greatly appreciate her assistance and her personal interest in our work.

The "New" Dimensions

A group of staff and faculty from CCV spent approximately two years—from 2006 to 2008—reviewing the general education curriculum. The result is a new "gen ed" framework that is debuting in the fall of 2008. One segment of the gen ed program is a required first semester seminar for all degree students. In the past two years, several courses were piloted to address specific needs (such as foundational learning in information literacy, academic deployment of technological skills, and learning online) and to try to carry over the "magic" of the *Dimensions* course we have known and loved.

The result is that CCV will offer two different *Dimensions* seminars: *Dimensions of Freedom* and *Dimensions of Work*, from Fall 2008 onward. The courses carry the same purpose and outcomes: "Beginning with the self and then drawing upon others' experiences, knowledge, and representations of the world, students develop and apply twenty-first century skills necessary for lifelong learning and active participation in a diverse community." The difference between the two offerings will be the underlying theme of the course. Each of the first semester seminar options will include three common skill elements: student development as a learner in a learning community; an introduction to information literacy, quantitative reasoning, and critical thinking skills; and the development of basic online learning skills. In terms of the curriculum, each *Dimensions* course will incorporate the following five pieces: discovering the self, text and context, Plato's *Allegory of the Cave*, Challenges, and Commitment.

The *Dimensions* Anthology

This anthology has been created to meet the needs of both courses, and we expect that some readings—beyond Plato's *Allegory of the Cave*, which will be featured in both courses—can and will be used in either section. Our hope is that students will be tempted by readings that are not assigned to them, and that the anthology will serve them beyond their first semester in college.

Finally, a public word of thanks to Robert Sessions, from Kirkwood Community College in Iowa, who edited an anthology entitled *Working in America: Supplemental Readings*. We have relied on his shoulders, as well, as we compiled this anthology.

Section One:
Being a College Student

*M*ichelle Fairbanks is a forty-five-year-old student who started taking college courses in the fall of 2005. She credits going back to school to her
"three beautiful daughters," two of whom are recent college graduates, and the
third is currently attending college. Michelle plans to graduate in 2010 with a
degree in either education or liberal arts. Both Michelle and her husband of
twenty-two years took Dimensions in the fall of 2007 which "made for some
very interesting class discussions and marked the beginning of his college
career."

Letter to a New Student

Michelle Fairbanks

Dear Friend,

Soon, you will be faced with choosing the classes that will best prepare you for your college degree while at CCV. As a fellow college student, I can understand the careful thought and consideration that goes
into making such choices. If you are looking for a class that offers a great
start to your academic career, will challenge you, and will leave you with
some new skills that will be useful through out your academic career and
life in general, for that matter, then I have the class for you: *Dimensions*.

At the first glance of the course description for this class, you may
find it a bit overwhelming, and perhaps you will doubt your ability to do
the work asked of you. I can relate. I started this class with not much
more than a high school diploma at the age of . . . well, we won't talk
about that . . . and while I knew from the start that it wasn't going to be
easy and it would require a lot of hard work and perhaps longer hours of
me than of most students to get the job done, I am pleased to say I did
well. With your positive attitude and strong work ethic, I know you have
what it takes to do the same.

You might be wondering why you should take this class instead of
another and, I must say, that is a thoughtful question to ask. In all honesty, there are several very good reasons to consider this class. In a very
safe and comfortable setting, you will improve your writing mechanics
and develop the skills to organize a well-written college level paper; you
will develop the ability to think critically; you will be able to experience
giving oral presentations; you will learn how to interpret and understand
various pieces of literature; and you will learn how to contribute to a class
discussion in a fulfilling way. No matter what class you take in college,

2

these skills, and the many more you will learn are what will create and strengthen the foundation for your success.

The oral presentation you will be required to give might provide you another reason to hesitate before signing up for this class. Relax. I, too, was terrified about this. As a matter of fact, I was so full of trepidation that I came close to dropping the class right up to the week before it began. I am so glad I didn't give in, and if you choose to stick with it, I think you will be just as pleased with yourself. Once I started my class and realized that it was filled with students just like me, many with fears similar to my own, it occurred to me that my anxiety over this didn't really matter; we were all there for the same reason: to learn. Very soon it was understood that we respected and valued one another and we were all in the same boat. By the time we were ready to give oral presentations, I had learned (in fact we all had learned) how to research, prepare, organize, and present my project in a professional manner and did much better than I thought I ever would have done. My fears of the unknown have been replaced by confidence in my own growing bank of knowledge as a result of taking this class. Please give this letter some serious thought and consider taking this class. Should you have any further questions or concerns please feel free to contact me and I will be happy to discuss it further.

Your Friend,

Michelle F.

P. S. Just a bit more advice, should you have a teacher that asks you to literally SPELL OUT true or false don't ignore it and write T or F. If the directions say to do it one way do it the way it asks. Reading and following directions accurately, whether it be on a test or otherwise, is a very valuable skill for you to learn as soon as possible. I, for one, lost ten points on my midterm not because I didn't know the answers but because I let myself get so nervous about taking the test and doing well that I missed what it said.

*K*D Maynard is dean of student services at Community College of Vermont, where she has held an assortment of administrative positions.

Why Participate in Class?

KD Maynard

Each CCV student brings a body of knowledge and experience— life, academic, and work experience—to the classroom. When we convene a class, we are essentially bringing together a community of learners. Each learner (and I, as an instructor, am a learner as well!) has a unique educational, sociological, and cultural "lens" through which s/he will experience the materials and exchanges that occur in the classroom and between classes.

This learning community, within our class, requires a "mutual effort in helping each other both understand the course material and the differing interpretive positions we may bring to a more complex understanding of the material" (Knefelkamp). We owe it to ourselves and our classmates to come prepared, to be open to new perspectives, and to share our thoughts and opinions in a constructive manner. Our learning will come not just from our textbooks, but also from each of the people in this room and the contributions they (and you!) bring to our conversations.

As part of a college classroom community, let's agree to the following. We will:

- Work to develop our personal skills so we will be open to the content, the context, and the broader concepts presented in the course;

- Gain an ability to evaluate the methods used to create and express knowledge, recognizing that we, as "constructors" of knowledge, have a responsibility to decide whether we want to accept that knowledge and/or consult other sources;

- Develop communication skills (as a sender and a receiver, in written and oral form) that will promote the learning of ourselves and of others;

- Relate our knowledge and experience to what we learn, to help us and others better understand the material we are learning;

- Strive to offer substantive feedback to our peers, in an appropriate manner; and

- Critique, constructively, the material we encounter, and substantiate the reasons why we might agree or disagree with it—accept it or not.

To help us maximize our learning, I propose that we follow the suggestions given by Lee Knefelkamp in her "Listening to Understand" article in the Spring 2006 edition of the journal *Liberal Education,* put out by the American Association of Colleges & Universities (p. 35). Here's what she has to say:

> . . . we need to develop the capacity of listening for understanding. (Of course, listening for understanding can also be applied to how we read and observe as well as listen and communicate.) Listening for understanding involves:
>
> - Listening for the meaning/standpoint/positionality of both others and the self;
>
> - Listening for the affect that results from the standpoints;
>
> - Staying in communication even when one is confused or fearful or unsure;
>
> - Searching for the appropriate response;
>
> - Acknowledging that understanding does not imply agreement;
>
> - Taking responsibility for one's complexity, personal integration, and skills so that one can respond in appropriate ways to a wide variety of complex situations.

*A*nne Lamott (1954–) is a prolific writer and a political activist based in San Francisco. Noted for her largely autobiographical, narrative style of non-fiction called "particularisim," a term coined by writer Howard Freeman, Lamott is the author of several novels, including Hard Laughter, as well as works of nonfiction such as Bird by Bird: Some Instructions on Writing and Life, and Traveling Mercies: Some Thoughts on Faith.

Short Assignments

Anne Lamott

The first useful concept is the idea of short assignments. Often when you sit down to write, what you have in mind is an autobiographical novel about your childhood, or a play about the immigrant experience, or a history of—oh, say—say women. But this is like trying to scale a glacier. It's hard to get your footing, and your fingertips get all red and frozen and torn up. Then your mental illnesses arrive at the desk like your sickest, most secretive relatives. And they pull up chairs in a semicircle around the computer, and they try to be quiet but you know they are there with their weird coppery breath, leering at you behind your back.

What I do at this point, as the panic mounts and the jungle drums begin beating and I realize that the well has run dry and that my future is behind me and I'm going to have to get a job only I'm completely unemployable, is to stop. First I try to breathe, because I'm either sitting there panting like a lapdog or I'm unintentionally making slow asthmatic death rattles. So I just sit there for a minute, breathing slowly, quietly. I let my mind wander. After a moment I may notice that I'm trying to decide whether or not I am too old for orthodontia and whether right now would be a good time to make a few calls, and then I start to think about learning to use makeup and how maybe I could find some boyfriend who is not a total and complete fixer-upper and then my life would be totally great and I'd be happy all the time, and then I think about all the people I should have called back before I sat down to work, and how I should probably at least check in with my agent and tell him this great idea I have and see if he thinks it's a good idea, and see if *he* thinks I need orthodontia—if that is what he is actually thinking whenever we have lunch together. Then I think about someone I'm really annoyed with, or some financial problem that is driving me crazy, and decide that I must resolve this before I get down to today's work. So I become a dog with a chew toy,

6

worrying it for a while, wrestling it to the ground, flinging it over my shoulder, chasing it, licking it, chewing it, flinging it back over my shoulder. I stop just short of actually barking. But all of this only takes somewhere between one and two minutes, so I haven't actually wasted that much time. Still, it leaves me winded. I go back to trying to breathe, slowly and calmly, and I finally notice the one-inch picture frame that I put on my desk to remind me of short assignments.

It reminds me that all I have to do is to write down as much as I can see through a one-inch picture frame. This is all I have to bite off for the time being. All I am going to do right now, for example, is write that one paragraph that sets the story in my hometown, in the late fifties, when the trains were still running. I am going to paint a picture of it, in words, on my word processor. Or all I am going to do is to describe the main character the very first time we meet her, when she first walks out the front door and onto the porch. I am not even going to describe the expression on her face when she first notices the blind dog sitting behind the wheel of her car—just what I can see through the one-inch picture frame, just one paragraph describing this woman, in the town where I grew up the first time we encounter her.

E. L. Doctorow once said that "writing a novel is like driving a car at night. You can see only as far as your headlights, but you can make the whole trip that way." You don't have to see where you're going, you don't have to see your destination or everything you pass along the way. You just have to see two or three feet ahead of you. This is right up there with the best advice about writing, or life, I have ever heard.

So after I've completely exhausted myself thinking about the people I most resent in the world, and my more arresting financial problems, and, of course, the orthodontia, I remember to pick up the one-inch picture frame and to figure out a one-inch piece of my story to tell, one small scene, one memory, one exchange. I also remember a story that I know I've told elsewhere but that over and over helps me to get a grip: thirty years ago my older brother, who was ten years old at the time, was trying to get a report on birds written that he'd had three months to write, which was due the next day. We were out at our family cabin in Bolinas, and he was at the kitchen table close to tears, surrounded by binder paper and pencils and unopened books on birds, immobilized by the hugeness of the task ahead. Then my father sat down beside him, put his arm around my brother's shoulder, and said, "Bird by bird, buddy. Just take it bird by bird."

I tell this story again because it usually makes a dent in the tremendous sense of being overwhelmed that my students experience. Sometimes it actually gives them hope, and hope, as Chesterton said, is the power of being cheerful in circumstances that we know to be desperate. Writing can be a pretty desperate endeavor, because it is about some of our deepest needs: our need to be visible, to be heard, our need to make sense of our lives, to wake up and grow and belong. It is no wonder if we sometimes tend to take ourselves perhaps a bit too seriously. So here is another story I tell often.

In the Bill Murray movie *Stripes,* in which he joins the army, there is a scene that takes place the first night of boot camp, where Murray's platoon is assembled in the barracks. They are supposed to be getting to know their sergeant, played by Warren Oates, and one another. So each man takes a few moments to say a few things about who he is and where he is from. Finally it is the turn of this incredibly intense, angry guy named Francis. "My name is Francis," he says. "No one calls me Francis—anyone here calls me Francis and I'll kill them. And another thing. I don't like to be touched. Anyone here ever tries to touch me, I'll kill them," at which point Warren Oates jumps in and says, "Hey—lighten up, Francis."

This is not a bad line to have taped to the wall of your office.

Say to yourself in the kindest possible way, Look, honey, all we're going to do for now is to write a description of the river at sunrise, or the young child swimming in the pool at the club, or the first time the man sees the woman he will marry. That is all we are going to do for now. We are just going to take this bird by bird. But we are going to finish this *one* short assignment.

Shitty First Drafts

Anne Lamott

Now, practically even better news than that of short assignments is the idea of shitty first drafts. All good writers write them. This is how they end up with good second drafts and terrific third drafts. People tend to look at successful writers, writers who are getting their books published and maybe even doing well financially, and think that they sit down at their desks every morning feeling like a million dollars, feeling great about who they are and how much talent they have and what a great story they have to tell; that they take in a few deep breaths, push back their sleeves, roll their necks a few times to get all the cricks out, and dive in, typing fully formed passages as fast as a court reporter. But this is just the fantasy of the uninitiated. I know some very great writers, writers you love who write beautifully and have made a great deal of money, and not *one* of them sits down routinely feeling wildly enthusiastic and confident. Not one of them writes elegant first drafts. All right, one of them does, but we do not like her much. We do not think that she has a rich inner life or that God likes her or can even stand her. (Although when I mentioned this to my priest friend Tom, he said you can safely assume you've created God in your own image when it turns out that God hates all the same people you do.)

Very few writers really know what they are doing until they've done it. Nor do they go about their business feeling dewy and thrilled. They do not type a few stiff warm-up sentences and then find themselves bounding along like huskies across the snow. One writer I know tells me that he sits down every morning and says to himself nicely, "It's not like you don't have a choice, because you do—you can either type or kill yourself." We all often feel like we are pulling teeth, even those writers whose prose ends up being the most natural and fluid. The right words and sentences just do not come pouring out like ticker tape most of the time.

9

Now, Muriel Spark is said to have felt that she was taking dictation from God every morning—sitting there, one supposes, plugged into a Dictaphone, typing away, humming. But this is a very hostile and aggressive position. One might hope for bad things to rain down on a person like this.

For me and most of the other writers I know, writing is not rapturous. In fact, the only way I can get anything written at all is to write really, really shitty first drafts.

The first draft is the child's draft, where you let it all pour out and then let it romp all over the place, knowing that no one is going to see it and that you can shape it later. You just let this childlike part of you channel whatever voices and visions come through and onto the page. If one of the characters wants to say, "Well, so what, Mr. Poopy Pants?," you let her. No one is going to see it. If the kid wants to get into really sentimental, weepy, emotional territory, you let him. Just get it all down on paper, because there may be something great in those six crazy pages that you would never have gotten to by more rational, grown-up means. There may be something in the very last line of the very last paragraph on page six that you just love, that is so beautiful or wild that you now know what you're supposed to be writing about, more or less, or in what direction you might go—but there was no way to get to this without first getting through the first five and a half pages.

I used to write food reviews for *California* magazine before it folded. (My writing food reviews had nothing to do with the magazine folding, although every single review did cause a couple of canceled subscriptions. Some readers took umbrage at my comparing mounds of vegetable puree with various ex-presidents' brains.) These reviews always took two days to write. First I'd go to a restaurant several times with a few opinionated, articulate friends in tow. I'd sit there writing down everything anyone said that was at all interesting or funny. Then on the following Monday I'd sit down at my desk with my notes, and try to write the review. Even after I'd been doing this for years, panic would set in. I'd try to write a lead, but instead I'd write a couple of dreadful sentences, xx them out, try again, xx everything out, and then feel despair and worry settle on my chest like an x-ray apron. It's over, I'd think, calmly. I'm not going to be able to get the magic to work this time. I'm ruined. I'm through. I'm toast. Maybe, I'd think, I can get my old job back as a clerk-typist. But probably not. I'd get up and study my teeth in the mirror for a while. Then I'd stop, remember to breathe, make a few phone calls, hit the kitchen and chow down. Eventually I'd go back and sit down at my desk, and sigh for the next ten minutes. Finally I would pick up my

one-inch picture frame, stare into it as if for the answer, and every time
the answer would come: all I had to do was to write a really shitty first
draft of, say, the opening paragraph. And no one was going to see it.

So I'd start writing without reining myself in. It was almost just typing, just making my fingers move. And the writing would be *terrible*. I'd
write a lead paragraph that was a whole page, even though the entire
review could only be three pages long, and then I'd start writing up
descriptions of the food, one dish at a time, bird by bird, and the critics
would be sitting on my shoulders, commenting like cartoon characters.
They'd be pretending to snore, or rolling their eyes at my overwrought
descriptions, no matter how hard I tried to tone those descriptions down,
no matter how conscious I was of what a friend said to me gently in my
early days of restaurant reviewing. "Annie," she said, "it is just a piece of
chicken. It is just a bit of *cake*."

But because by then I had been writing for so long, I would eventually let myself trust the process—sort of, more or less. I'd write a first
draft that was maybe twice as long as it should be, with a self-indulgent
and boring beginning, stupefying descriptions of the meal, lots of quotes
from my black-humored friends that made them sound more like the
Manson girls than food lovers, and no ending to speak of. The whole
thing would be so long and incoherent and hideous that for the rest of the
day I'd obsess about getting creamed by a car before I could write a
decent second draft. I'd worry that people would read what I'd written
and believe that the accident had really been a suicide, that I had pan-
icked because my talent was waning and my mind was shot.

The next day, though, I'd sit down, go through it all with a colored
pen, take out everything I possibly could, find a new lead somewhere on
the second page, figure out a kicky place to end it, and then write a second draft. It always turned out fine, sometimes even funny and weird
and helpful. I'd go over it one more time and mail it in.

Then, a month later, when it was time for another review, the whole
process would start again, complete with the fears that people would find
my first draft before I could rewrite it.

Almost all good writing begins with terrible first efforts. You need to
start somewhere. Start by getting something—anything—down on paper.
A friend of mine says that the first draft is the down draft—you just get
it down. The second draft is the up draft—you fix it up. You try to say
what you have to say more accurately. And the third draft is the dental
draft, where you check every tooth, to see if it's loose or cramped or
decayed, or even, God help us, healthy.

What I've learned to do when I sit down to work on a shitty first draft is to quiet the voices in my head. First there's the vinegar-lipped Reader Lady, who says primly, "Well, *that's* not very interesting, is it?" And there's the emaciated German male who writes these Orwellian memos detailing your thought crimes. And there are your parents, agonizing over your lack of loyalty and discretion; and there's William Burroughs, dozing off or shooting up because he finds you as bold and articulate as a houseplant; and so on. And there are also the dogs: let's not forget the dogs, the dogs in their pen who will surely hurtle and snarl their way out if you ever *stop* writing, because writing is, for some of us, the latch that keeps the door of the pen closed, keeps those crazy ravenous dogs contained.

Quieting these voices is at least half the battle I fight daily. But this is better than it used to be. It used to be 87 percent. Left to its own devices, my mind spends much of its time having conversations with people who aren't there. I walk along defending myself to people, or exchanging repartee with them, or rationalizing my behavior, or seducing them with gossip, or pretending I'm on their TV talk show or whatever. I speed or run an aging yellow light or don't come to a full stop, and one nanosecond later am explaining to imaginary cops exactly why I had to do what I did, or insisting that I did not in fact do it.

I happened to mention this to a hypnotist I saw many years ago, and he looked at me very nicely. At first I thought he was feeling around on the floor for the silent alarm button, but then he gave me the following exercise, which I still use to this day.

Close your eyes and get quiet for a minute, until the chatter starts up. Then isolate one of the voices and imagine the person speaking as a mouse. Pick it up by the tail and drop it into a mason jar. Then isolate another voice, pick it up by the tail, drop it in the jar. And so on. Drop in any high-maintenance parental units, drop in any contractors, lawyers, colleagues, children, anyone who is whining in your head. Then put the lid on, and watch all these mouse people clawing at the glass, jabbering away, trying to make you feel like shit because you won't do what they want—won't give them more money, won't be more successful, won't see them more often. Then imagine that there is a volume-control button on the bottle. Turn it all the way up for a minute, and listen to the stream of angry, neglected, guilt-mongering voices. Then turn it all the way down and watch the frantic mice lunge at the glass, trying to get to you. Leave it down, and get back to your shitty first draft.

A writer friend of mine suggests opening the jar and shooting them all in the head. But I think he's a little angry, and I'm sure nothing like this would ever occur to you.

Preparing for Tests

KD Maynard

Common Types of Tests

- **Multiple Choice** . . . You will be asked to match up related information. Make sure you read and understand the instructions. Work quickly, answering what you can and "flagging" questions you don't know and will go back to later, if you have time. READ ALL CHOICES before you make a decision. Eliminate obvious wrong answers. If you can eliminate at least half of the options, take a guess from the remaining options. Look for familiar phrases from lectures/discussions/readings. If time permits, go back and work on the questions you'd left blank, and check over your answers. Before changing any answers, be sure you have a good reason to do so . . . often, a first response is correct!

- **True/False** . . . These questions can be trickier than you think. You will be asked to recognize specific facts and details. Be sure you understand the directions. Read carefully, and do not analyze for deeper meanings. If the question is confusing, take it apart and look at the parts. If any part of the statement is false, the whole statement is false. Look for "qualifying" words: because, no one, nobody, only, etc.—the answer will typically hinge on these words. Absolute qualifiers (always, never, etc.) may indicate a false statement.

- **Matching** . . . Again, you will be asked to recognize specific facts and details. Read directions carefully. Read BOTH columns before starting. Choose the longest column and work down that one first. This column has more clues and information. Cross off used answers as you go. Do the easiest matches first. Match the more difficult ones through a process of elimination.

- **Fill-in-the-blank** . . . Read the directions carefully and look for clue words (especially before the blanks), such as: a, an, the, these, those, they. If you get stuck, brainstorm for a moment. If you can't think of the exact work or word, write a similar word or phrase. Partial credit is better than none.

- **Short answer** . . . Look carefully at what you are asked to do, and make every effort to include the important information, but not extra details. Include the basics (e.g., what work or writer, etc). Be concise.

- **Essay** . . . Follow these four steps: (1) **Analyze** the question—read it carefully several times, and note any key words, sub-questions, etc. (2) **Organize** your answer before you start writing—jot down the points you'll want to include and think about the order you'll want to use them in. (3) **Write** in a clear, orderly, and formal style. State what you want to say (rephrase the question in your topic sentence); follow your notes; use details to support your points; stick to the subject; summarize by rephrasing important points. (4) **Proofread** your answer to see that you've answered the full question; that it makes sense; and that your spelling, grammar, etc. are OK.

Before the Test

- Keep the test in perspective (one day at a time, one foot in front of the other). . . . Know what portion of your overall grade it will be.

- Listen carefully to your instructor for clues about what to study or what the format of the test will be.

- Form a study group to review material, make up and give mini-quizzes, and discuss questions.

- Review—daily reviews (look over notes, make up study sheet of important terms, etc); weekly reviews (about an hour—look over all notes and readings, make up questions about the material, take notes if you haven't already done so); major reviews (reaffirm hard data, integrate concepts, deepen understanding). Paraphrase material—put it into your own words.

- Pay attention to the test format and rules: is a wrong guess better than a blank? Will you get partial credit—is it to your advantage to write down anything you know? Do you know what questions/portions of the test are more important (get more points)?

- Take good care of yourself: don't push too hard by cramming—you'll burn out. Get good rest, eat well, and stay away from caffeine, sugar, and junk food.

- Arrive early, with extra writing implements and paper. Take a few minutes to look over your notes and take some deep breaths to relax.

During the Test

- Listen carefully to any oral instructions. Know the "ground rules" (i.e., is the test open book, can you consult notes, etc.)

- Use your SQ3R strategy on the test: Scan the test immediately to note what kinds of questions are being asked. Question: what's most important in the test/how many points are given for each section? READ ALL DIRECTIONS AT THE START, CAREFULLY AND SLOWLY. Recite: you won't be able to speak out loud (!), but repeat, in your mind, what you're giving for an answer to see if it "sounds" right. Review when you think you've finished, go back and look over both the directions AND what you've written.

- Find out how long you will have to complete the test, and estimate (as you scan) about how much time you should spend on each section. Check in with yourself periodically to see how well you're keeping to your schedule. Think about time management strategies —you want to be devoting your energy to what is IMPORTANT, and not let it get to the point of being URGENT.

- Make notes in a margin or on the back if you have terms, etc., that you want to make sure you remember. Move on if you can't remember something—it may come back to you. Circle or make a mark on the number of any question you've left incomplete, so you can find it later.

- Answer the shortest and easiest questions first. You'll build confidence, as well as get warmed up for more complex questions. Mark questions you want to return to later.

- Try to leave time to go over the test before you hand it in.

After the Test

- Heave a sigh of relief and reward yourself—regardless of how you think you may have done. Don't waste emotional energy speculating.

- Take time to evaluate your PROCESS of studying and taking the test. Learn from what you did well, and make note of where you could make improvements.

- When you get a test back, go over it carefully to see what you did wrong and why. (Did you know the material, but not follow directions? Did you draw a blank on terms, names, titles, etc.?) Correct your mistakes and highlight important information that might reappear.

- Put your grade in perspective, and do a self-evaluation on what you've learned—about the material and about your process of learning.

Direction Words in Essay Questions

Learn to recognize and respond to the following words:

Analyze—*Analyze* tells you to break something down into its parts and show how the parts relate to each other to make the whole.

Compare—*Compare* tells you to show how two or more things are BOTH similar and different.

Contrast—*Contrast* tells you to show how two or more things are different.

Define—*Define* tells you to explain the meaning of something in a brief, specific manner.

Describe—*Describe* tells you to present a full and detailed picture of something in words to include important characteristics and qualities.

Diagram—*Diagram* tells you to illustrate something by drawing a picture of it and labeling its parts.

Evaluate—*Evaluate* tells you to present both the positive and negative characteristics of something.

Explain—*Explain* tells you to provide facts and reasons to make something clear and understandable.

Justify—*Justify* tells you to provide reasons and facts in support of something.

List—*List* tells you to present information about something as a series of brief numbered points.

Outline—*Outline* tells you to present the most important information about something in a carefully organized manner.

Summarize—*Summarize* tells you to present the main points about something in a brief form.

Trace—*Trace* tells you to present the order in which something occurred.

Active Learning and Reading

KD Maynard

The learning process is best done actively. Active learners are more engaged, interested, and happy. Active learners take responsibility for their learning, and are open to changing both their ideas and their behaviors. Active learners focus on concepts and ideas (the "big picture"), rather than on the "right answer" or "what the teacher wants." Active learners constantly test the new ideas and material that is presented to them, and they try to see how it fits with their existing knowledge and experience base. Active learners *think about* and *react to* what they learn.

Here are some of the things active learners do:

- Ask questions about what they are learning or reading;

- Think about the "so what?" and the "why?" behind assignments, trying to discover the significance of the material;

- Think about how assignments and readings fit into the larger context of a course, semester, degree program, professional goal, and/or life in general;

- Relate what is being learned/read to "real life." Make connections between what they are learning and what they have learned and experienced in the past;

- Seek out "AHA!" moments;

- Look for examples of what they are learning, and look for ways to apply what they have learned to new situations or settings;

- Invite their learning into their everyday life: they talk about it with friends and family, identify examples of what they've learned, and think about where their learning fits into their world.

Active learning is a mental posture, and a way of wrestling with what you're learning or reading. Active learners DO NOT just absorb material and let it flow over them.

Here are some of the things you, as an active learner, might think about while you read or take in new material:

- "What's this writer trying to say here?"

- "Where's s/he coming from?"

- "In other words, s/he means _____."

- "Next s/he's probably going to say _____."

- "Hang on—you haven't convinced me yet . . ."

- "That doesn't make sense—let me go over it again."

- "I totally disagree with _____."

- "Oh yeah, that's like what we were doing in _____ class."

- "That happened to me—I remember when _____."

- "I wonder what _____ (another writer, teacher, friend) might say about that."

Time Management

KD Maynard

Tips for How to Plan Your Time

- Block out your fixed obligations (e.g., class time, work hours, meetings, etc.,) first. Schedule in essential life activities (e.g., sleeping, preparing food/eating/cleaning up, etc.).

- Include time for travel and errands.

- Schedule time for FUN, however you define it (e.g., exercise, TV, socializing, etc.).

- Set realistic goals—don't set yourself up for failure.

- Leave room for some flexibility—leave some times open, and know that they'll get filled!

- Block out 2–3 hours of study time for each hour in class. If your weekly homework takes you less time, use the extra for review, working ahead, or keeping up in another class.

- Don't set yourself up for marathon study sessions at the last moment. Shorter study sessions, spaced throughout the week, are most effective.

- Set clear start and stop times, and stick to them. Use a kitchen timer.

- Expect the unexpected. Always have a Plan B waiting in the wings.

Getting the Most Out of Your Time

- Know your best time of day to study, and make good use of it.

- Study your hardest or most tedious subjects first—get them out of the way.

- Use the in-between times and waiting time: have a book with you, review some notes, or do one small piece of an assignment.

- Always study in the same place, and set it up so you know you're in study mode.

- Get your body ready to study—exercise, eat, drink, or do whatever you need to BEFORE you sit down to study.

- Keep a "parking lot" where you can jot down things you want to do or think about later.

- Don't let yourself get interrupted. Ask your friends or family to respect your study time, don't answer the phone or read email, avoid noise distraction, hang a DO NOT DISTURB sign, and learn to say no.

Questions to Consider if You're Feeling Blocked

- What is ONE task I can accomplish toward my goal?

- Am I working for perfection, or just a "good enough" job?

- Am I finding time for what I feel is MOST important in my life?

- How am I wasting my time, and how can I make better use of the time I have?

- Can I squeeze in just one more small thing?

- If this was my job, would I be earning my pay?

- Do I need to ask for help? How? Where?

*D*ebby Stewart is associate academic dean at Community College of Vermont, where she has played multiple roles: student, faculty, academic coordinator, and her current position.

Sample Rubrics:
Evaluating Your Own and Others' Work

Debby Stewart

A rubric is a tool or set of criteria for evaluating work. Because rubrics can provide you with detailed information on what's expected of the assignment or work you're completing, they can be a powerful incentive for learning, as long as they are timely, concrete, and clear. Rubrics have been used successfully in a wide range of courses to evaluate writing, critical thinking, problem-solving, speaking, analyzing, and reflecting skills. A rubric can even be used as a tool to assess participation in a class. Most online teachers use rubrics to evaluate students' contributions to online discussions. This helps everyone construct the most meaningful discussions possible each week.

In some college courses, you may be asked to help with the creation of a rubric. In general, though, you will usually see a rubric *before* you begin working on a task or assignment. It's important to look carefully at the rubric in order to best understand what's expected of you and how it will be measured. You can save yourself a lot of time and effort by paying close attention at the beginning of the process. In addition, you may be asked to reflect on the rubric at the end of the process as part of a self-assessment that is submitted along with your assignment. This will provide you with valuable insight on how well you met the expectations of the assignment.

Included in this section are examples of rubrics you might find at CCV. Since most teachers will customize a rubric to fit a particular assignment or activity, you may encounter many different rubrics and their variations while you're in college. However, rubrics tend to have some things in common—no matter how different they are. Along with each of the rubrics below, we've included some questions to consider:

21

Attendance and Class Participation: Self Evaluation

This is an example of a rubric that might be used in a variety of on-ground courses to assess how often students participated in specific behaviors. Questions to consider: What point is this instructor making? Why are certain behaviors included here? Are there any missing? Which behaviors are most important here, and how do you know? How might a student decide what grade s/he had earned for attendance and participation?

Rubric for Oral Presentations I

This is an example of a rubric that might be used when an oral presentation is assigned. Questions to consider: Is it possible to do poorly in one area and still do well overall? Why are certain elements included here? Are there any missing? Which elements are most important, and how do you know? If you were a teacher using this rubric, what would you expect to see in students' presentations? If you were developing a list of "don'ts" aligned with this rubric, what presentation advice would you give to other students?

Rubric for Oral Presentations II

This is an example of another rubric that might be used when an oral presentation is assigned. Questions to consider: How is this rubric different from the previous one? What kind of oral presentation might be addressed with this rubric? Is it possible to do poorly in one area and still do well overall? Why are certain elements included here? Are there any missing? Which elements are most important, and how do you know? If you were a teacher using this rubric, what would you expect to see in students' presentations? If you were developing a list of "don'ts" aligned with this rubric, what presentation advice would you give to other students?

Reflective Writing Rubric

This is an example of a rubric that evaluates reflective writing, such as writing you might complete in a journal, letter, or short paper. Often, reflections are written in response to one or more prompts. Questions to consider: Which elements of writing are most valued in this rubric and how might they differ from other types of writing? What is the greatest number of points you can possibly score on this rubric, and how is the scoring balanced between the different elements or categories? What kinds of differences do you see in how this rubric is organized visually? Do these differences make it easier or more challenging for you to use?

Online Discussion Rubric

This is an example of a rubric that might be used in an online class to evaluate students' weekly discussion contributions. Because regular discussion is the heart of the online class—the place where everyone meets, interacts, and connects to weekly topics—the work is usually worth a significant part of a student's total grade. Questions to consider: Which elements of online writing or discussion are most valued in this rubric and how might they differ from other types of writing? How does a performance scored at 3 differ from one scored at 5? Are there expectations that all students must meet in order to earn even 1 point? If a score of 5 points is worth 100 percent, what's the equivalent of a 1, 2, 3, or 4? What kinds of differences do you see in how this rubric is organized visually? Do these differences make it easier or more challenging for you to use?

Evaluating Research Writing

This is an example of a rubric that is used in many classes at CCV, including English Composition and CCV's capstone course, Seminar in Educational Inquiry. This rubric is particularly used in assignments that integrate writing and information literacy skills, such as when students write research papers. Questions to consider: Which elements of writing are most valued in this rubric, and how might they differ from other types of writing? Why does this rubric encourage you to approach your own and others' writing as a reader? What is the greatest number of points you can possibly score on this rubric, and how is the scoring balanced between the different elements or categories? Looking at several specific elements or categories, what distinguishes a 4-point performance from a 2-point performance? What actions or behaviors could result in earning a 0 for the whole paper? Why are these behaviors emphasized above all others? What kinds of differences do you see in how this rubric is organized visually? Do these differences make it easier or more challenging for you to use?

Attendance and Class Participation: Self Evaluation

Name:_____ Today's Date: ___/ ___/ ___

Total absences thus far: _____ out of _____ classes.

Take a moment to honestly and realistically consider your attendance and participation in this course. Select the one answer (with a checkmark) for each item below that you believe best describes your contributions to the class.

	Always	Most of the Time	Sometimes	Rarely	Never
I attended class.					
I arrived on time and stayed for the entire class period.					
I read the entire week's reading assignment before class.					
I completed my assignments on time.					
I came to class with an open mind and was willing to try new things.					
I paid attention during class.					
I did NOT disrupt class or cause others to be distracted.					
I positively contributed to class discussions and activities.					
I asked and answered questions in class.					
I helped my classmates when they needed assistance.					
I asked for help when I needed it.					
I listened to my classmates when they were speaking.					
I challenged myself to do my best in this course.					

Based on my answers above, I believe I deserve the following attendance and participation grade for this course (Circle one):

A   **B**   **C**   **D**   **F**

Rubric for Oral Presentations I

Criteria	A	B	C	D
Organization	• Presents information in well-organized, interesting manner • Focuses on a central idea or narrowed topic • Presentation flows • Has an introduction • Has a well-developed body • Has a conclusion • Lasts 10 minutes	• Presents information in well-organized, interesting manner • May try to cover too much or too little • Presentation flows • Has an introduction • Has a well-developed body • Has a conclusion • Lasts 10 minutes	• Presents information in an interesting manner • Focuses on more than one aspect of topic • May digress from topic and have trouble getting back on track • Has an introduction • Has a body • Ends abruptly • Has to be cut off at the 10 minute time limit	• Presents information in a random and vague manner • Unclear transitions between parts • Focuses on a broad topic, not the main idea • Appears unrehearsed • Lacks an introduction and/or conclusion • Lasts less than 10 minutes
Requirements	• Has a conference (face-to-face, telephone, or e-mail) at least a week before the presentation • Submits a plan at least a week before the presentation • Has prepared materials if needed • Hands materials out in a timely manner • Does a self evaluation	• Has a conference (face-to-face, telephone, or e-mail) at least a week before the presentation • Submits a plan at least a week before the presentation • Has prepared materials if needed • Hands materials out in a timely manner • Does a self evaluation	• Meets all but two of the criteria • Has a conference (face-to-face, telephone, or e-mail) at least a week before the presentation • Submits a plan at least a week before the presentation • Has prepared materials if needed • Hands materials out in a timely manner • Does a self evaluation	• Meets fewer than three of the criteria • Has a conference (face-to-face, telephone, or e-mail) at least a week before the presentation • Submits a plan at least a week before the presentation • Has prepared materials if needed • Hands materials out in a timely manner • Does a self evaluation

Criteria	A	B	C	D
Active Involvement	• Actively involves all members of the class through learning props/activities/handouts/questions • Creatively teaches an aspect of the topic	• Attempts to engage the audience in his/her topic • Involves some of the class members through learning props/activities/handouts/questions	• Makes weak attempt to involve the class through use of some visual aids but may not explain them in an effective way • May read or recite short excerpts from notes or paper	• Does not involve the class in the presentation • Reads from prepared material • Does not provide quality supplementary material for the class
Content	• Demonstrates superb knowledge and understanding of topic • Supports main idea with vivid examples and details • Makes relevant connections for others	• Demonstrates good knowledge and understanding of topic • Supports main idea with clear, factual data • Makes some connections for others	• Demonstrates fair knowledge and understanding of topic • May have difficulty explaining certain aspects of the topic • Has difficulty making connections for others	• Demonstrates minimal knowledge and understanding of topic • Has problems supporting the topic • Offers confusing or no examples • Makes no connections for others
Voice	• Demonstrates great enthusiasm for topic • Speaks clearly and loudly enough to be understood • Varies tone and pitch for animated speaking style	• Demonstrates comfort in speaking • Speaks clearly and with emphasis • May demonstrate a bit of nervousness and/or shaky voice at the beginning only	• Demonstrates some nervousness or discomfort in speaking throughout presentation • Some evidence of verbal "padding" but uses appropriate pace, tone, and volume to be heard clearly most of the time	• May appear nervous or troubled throughout presentation • Voice too quiet or monotone to be heard effectively • May rush through his/her sentences or speak in halting, slow manner or make excessive use of verbal "padding"
Body language	• Makes effective eye contact with whole audience throughout presentation • Uses gestures and body language to emphasize certain points	• Makes good eye contact but limits it to only a few people • Uses gestures and body language to emphasize certain points	• Makes some eye contact but not for duration and not with more than a couple of people • May look stiff or uncomfortable while presenting	• Fidgets, taps feet, or makes other nervous movements • Makes little or no eye contact • Uses distracting or ineffective gestures

Rubric for Oral Presentations II

	Excellent	Good	Fair	Beginning/Developing
Organization	Presents issue in well-organized, interesting manner; focuses on a central idea or thesis; speech flows well, building to strong conclusion	Presents issue in well-organized, interesting manner, but may try to cover too much or too little; speech flows well, building to succinct conclusion	Presents issue in an interesting but general manner; focuses on more than one aspect of the issue; speaker may digress from thesis and have difficulty getting back	Presents issue in a random and vague manner; uses unclear transitions between parts; focuses on broad topic, not central thesis; speech appears unrehearsed
Content	Demonstrates superb knowledge and understanding of the issue; supports ideas with vivid examples and details; acknowledges opposing arguments and ideas but uses them to create powerful counter-arguments; makes relevant connections for others	Demonstrates good knowledge and understanding of the issue; supports ideas with clear, factual data; acknowledges and uses opposing arguments to support his or her own position; makes some connections	Demonstrates fair knowledge and understanding of the issue, but may have difficulty explaining certain aspects of the issue or making connections for the audience; demonstrates some difficulty in acknowledging and using opposing arguments	Demonstrates minimal knowledge and understanding of the issue; has problems supporting his/her main point, and may offer contradictory or confusing examples; has a lot of difficulty acknowledging and/or using opposing arguments
Voice	Demonstrates great enthusiasm for issue; speaks clearly and loudly enough to be understood easily; varies tone and pitch for animated speaking style	Demonstrates comfort in speaking; speaks clearly and with emphasis; may illustrate a bit of nervousness and/or shaky voice at the beginning	Demonstrates some nervousness or discomfort at speaking, but uses appropriate pace, tone, and volume to be heard clearly for much of the time	May appear nervous or troubled, voice too quiet or monotone to be heard effectively; may rush through his/her sentences or speak in halting, slow manner
Body Language	Makes effective eye contact with whole audience throughout the presentation; uses gestures and body language to emphasize certain points	Makes good eye contact but limits it to only a few people; is expressive in his/her gestures although they may be unrelated to key points	Makes some eye contact, but not for duration and not with more than a couple of people; may look stiff or uncomfortable while presenting	Fidgets or engages in other nervous movements; makes little or no eye contact; uses ineffective or distracting gestures

Supplementary Information on Oral Presentations

In some oral presentation assignments, students are asked to submit ideas in writing also. But even when that is not a required part of the assignment, it's helpful to prepare for a presentation by writing about your topic or issue. This is especially true when your issue is politically or socially charged, or when you've been asked to develop a thesis or stance regarding the issue. In college, you will often be asked to create a thesis and support it with evidence. Most of your presentations—oral or written—will do more than *inform* your audience, they will be focused on *persuading* them.

Questions to Consider

- What could you tell people that would get their attention about your issue?

- Write a short summary of the issue (you must encapsulate the issue in 75 words or less).

- Why is this important now? What is the urgency? Why should people care about this issue?

- What do you think should be done regarding this issue? (This is your thesis—your main point—so spend time crafting exactly what it is you want to convince people to do or think with regard to your issue. You should be able to state this in one or two sentences.)

- What are the strongest reasons in support of your opinion? (List all facts, examples, statistics, anecdotes, and other support that could help convince an audience of your peers. Be sure to include source information for your support. Where does it come from?)

- What are the strongest reasons *against* taking the stance you do? (List the facts, examples, statistics, anecdotes, or other material that could most sway your audience in the other direction. Be sure to include source information for your opposition. Where does it come from?)

- How will you address the 2–3 strongest reasons that could be used to oppose your argument? Describe a counter-argument for each one.

- What do you want to leave your audience thinking about? Write a short conclusion that reminds your audience what you want them to think or do.

Reflective Writing Rubric

1. **How thorough is the writer's response? Does s/he respond to every question in such a way as to demonstrate thoughtfulness, depth, and engagement?**

    4 points: The writer responds thoroughly and substantively to the questions.

    2–3 points: The writer responds to the questions, but I feel there could be more detail or substance to the writer's response.

    0–1 point: The writer does not respond to all questions, or may respond only in a cursory manner to questions.

2. **How reflective is the writer's response? Does the writer demonstrate that s/he is open or willing to consider different perspectives, and has made connections between the exercise and him or herself?**

    4 points: The writer really appears to be thinking reflectively in this response; s/he makes connections, considers different perspectives, and demonstrates the willingness to think deeply about communication.

    2–3 points: The writer makes some connections and appears candid and thoughtful in his or her response.

    0–1 point: The writer offers only routine insight in responding to the questions. The writer neglects to make valuable connections or consider other perspectives.

3. **How relevant is the writer's response? Does the writer respond in such a way as to demonstrate knowledge of course content? Does the writer draw from knowledge and skills associated with the course to make connections to the exercise and his/her performance?**

    4 points: The writer demonstrates higher-level thinking skills in the response and makes clear connections between course concepts and skills and his or her performance in the exercise.

    2–3 points: The writer makes some connections between the course content and his/her response, but it isn't always clear that the writer is integrating knowledge and skills associated with the course into a larger context.

    0–1 point: The writer doesn't connect with or demonstrate skills associated with this course, except at a basic or cursory level.

4. **How effective is the writer's response? Is the writing clear, orga-nized, persuasive, and detailed? Does the writing demonstrate the writer has thoughtfully addressed the needs of a reader?**

    4 points: The writing is lively, persuasive, detailed, and organized. There are few if any grammatical/mechanical errors. The response is not only easy to read, but the writer explains his/her thoughts in an appropriate manner for a college-level reader, and supports his/her ideas with examples.

    2–3 points: The writing is clear, organized, and focused. The response may lack some supporting details or examples that would have been helpful to me as a reader, but there are only minor errors in grammar and mechanics, which interfere little with readability.

    0–1 point: The writing may lack focus, clarity, and/or organization. Ideas are left unsupported and/or vague. Errors in grammar and mechanics may make reading the response difficult.

Total Points

What these point values mean:

15–16 points: You have described an exemplary college-level reflection piece.

9–14 points: You have described a passing college-level reflection piece.

5–8 points: You have described a piece that may have some strengths, but is not passing as a finished college-level reflection.

0–4 points: You have described a piece that should be considered only as a first attempt to reflect on this topic in writing.

Online Discussion Rubric

5 Points = Superb work, both in terms of the quality of the answers and the thoroughness of the response. For 5 points, a student will:

- Compose a substantive and thoughtful response in his or her own words to at least one main question, demonstrating both depth and breadth in his/her thinking;

- Thoroughly answer at least one classmate's question, asking for clarification, where needed, and communicating respectfully with him/her;

- Ask a thoughtful, relevant question of his/her own that clearly connects to the week's assignment and generates discussion among his/her peers;

- Respond in a timely and engaging manner so that classmates have the opportunity to read and respond back to him/her;

- Illustrate that s/he has read the assignment and keenly understands the subject material through use of key concepts, vocabulary, and the ability to relevantly connect the topic to other subjects and experiences;

- Communicate clearly and effectively in writing with a minimum of grammatical or usage errors, and support his/her ideas through examples;

- If the student used a source to support his/her response or ask a question, s/he will clearly identify the source and give credit for others' ideas and words (using MLA style formatting).

4 Points = Great work completed in a thoughtful and reflective manner. For 4 points, a student will:

- Compose a relevant and thoughtful response in his or her own words to at least one main question;

- Answer a classmate's question, asking for clarification, where needed, and communicating respectfully with him/her;

- Ask a question of his/her own that clearly connects to the week's assignment though it may not generate much discussion among his/her peers;

- Respond in a timely and engaging manner, so that classmates have the opportunity to read and respond back to him/her;

- Illustrate that s/he has read the assignment and generally under-stands the subject matter through use of key concepts, vocabulary, and the ability to connect the topic to other subjects and experiences;

- Communicate clearly and effectively in writing (though there may be a few grammatical or usage errors, they do not interfere with read-ability);

- Support his/her ideas through examples, though they may not be extensive throughout the response;

- If the student used a source to support his/her response or ask a question, s/he will clearly identify the source and give credit for oth-ers' ideas and words (using MLA style formatting).

3 Points = Good work, but parts of the assignment may be missing, incomplete, or simply lacking in depth. For 3 points, a student will:

- Compose a relevant response in his/her own words to at least one main question; however, the response may not fully address all aspects of the question;

- Answer a classmate's question in a respectful manner, but the response may be limited, cursory, or lacking relevance;

- Ask a question of his/her own that connects only generally to the week's assignment and/or does not promote further discussion on the topic;

- Respond in a manner that allows only some classmates the opportu-nity to read and respond back to him/her. For instance, the student may post his/her response and questions just before the discussion closes;

- Demonstrate that s/he has read the assignment but may have only a basic understanding of the subject matter. Student may have difficulty using and responding to key concepts and vocabulary; student may also have difficulty connecting the topic to other relevant subjects and experiences;

- Communicate his/her ideas in writing, though problems with gram-mar and mechanics make it difficult to fully appreciate his/her points;

- Lack support for his/her ideas, making general statements that are not fully explored in the writing, don't take into consideration other information, and may lack pertinent examples and details;

- If the student used a source to support his/her response or ask a question, he/she will identify the source and give credit for others' ideas and words, though there may be difficulty with using MLA style formatting.

1–2 Points = Incomplete work, either in terms of the amount of the discussion or the quality of the discussion. For 1–2 points, a student will:

- Compose a cursory response to one main question, missing key elements altogether or only addressing them in a very basic manner;

- Answer a classmate's question in a respectful manner, but the response may be limited, cursory, or lacking relevance;

- Ask a question of his/her own that is not related to the week's assignment and/or only minimally connected to the topics being discussed;

- Respond in an incomplete or untimely manner, posting late in the week and/or missing opportunities to contribute to the class dialogue;

- Have difficulty demonstrating that s/he has read the assignment and understands the subject matter;

- Demonstrate difficulty with writing (grammar, mechanics, usage) that greatly interferes with the ability of others to understand and appreciate his/her ideas;

- Lack support for his/her ideas;

- If the student used a source to support his/her response or ask a question, he/she will identify the source and give credit for others' ideas and words, though there may be great difficulty with using MLA style formatting.

0 Points = Awarded when students are not present at all or only to make a personal statement. Also, students who participate in any academic dishonesty will not be awarded points for their discussion contributions.

Evaluating Research Writing

Evaluating your own research writing or providing your classmates with feedback on their papers can seem daunting. Yet it's important to think about your development as a writer. Reflecting on your own and others' work is an important expectation of being in college. The questions below are designed to help you with this process and require only that you approach any paper *as a reader*. This perspective will help you to evaluate either finished or unfinished drafts.

Respond to the following ten questions:

1. **Do you see evidence of a thesis?** (*A thesis is a brief statement that outlines the parameters of the writer's argument—his or her claim, what s/he wants to assert within the context of the paper*).

   4 points: Yes, there's a strong, arguable thesis; I also get a sense of how the writer will construct his/her argument and try to persuade me as a reader to accept it.

   3 points: Yes, there's a thesis, but it's fairly general. It could be made stronger or more engaging.

   2 points: Yes, but the thesis is weak or vague; I had to really search for it, and it may not be arguable or supportable.

   1 point: I'm not sure what the writer intended the thesis to be.

   Comments:

2. **Does the paper have a sense of purpose?**

   4 points: Yes, I have a clear sense of what the writer's goals are for the paper and how s/he intends to support them.

   3 points: Yes, I have a good sense of where the writer is leading me as a reader, but this could be done with more intention and clarity.

   2 points: I think I know what the purpose of the paper is but the writer sometimes takes detours in his or her writing or makes confusing shifts in the writing.

   1 point: I don't know what the writer's purpose is.

   Comments:

3. **Does the paper handle its ideas in a way that illustrates critical and/or creative thinking?**

4 points: Yes, the writer appropriately uses facts, examples, and others' ideas in service to his/her own ideas, always giving credit for source material, but also re-shaping the material in original and interesting ways to fit his/her own purpose in the paper. I get a clear sense that the writer knows this subject well, can form his/her own ideas, and can articulate those ideas in original and/or creative ways. The writer also provides a context for thinking about this topic and why I as the reader should care about it.

3 points: Yes, the writer seems to understand how to draw upon facts, examples, and others' ideas to make his/her strongest points in the paper; however, s/he often forgets to offer analysis of these sources or draw conclusions from them. The writer provides some context for the topic, but I sense that s/he may be tentative about or struggling with certain ideas in the paper.

2 points: Not really. The paper offers generalizations and/or routine insights into the topic. I get a sense that the writer is "reporting" information and simplifying ideas on this topic rather than refining his/her ideas and using source material in support of these ideas.

1 point: No. I don't have a clear sense that the writer has thought about this topic thoroughly and reflectively; there are contradictory statements, vague assertions, over-simplifications, or off-topic remarks. I get a sense that the writer hasn't made up his/her mind about the thesis or purpose of the paper or that the writer has ignored important elements that would convince me s/he has thought critically about the ideas presented here.

Comments:

4. **Are there sufficient examples, details, and support in the paper?**

4 points: Yes, the writer supports his/her point and constructs a convincing argument in a number of varied ways.

3 points: Yes, the writer provides a lot of support but it is not as varied or persuasive as it might be. Sometimes the writer presents information but neglects to tell me as the reader, why the information is relevant.

2 points: No, the writer makes claims that are not supported, provides details or examples that are not fully convincing, and over-relies or under-relies on sources.

1 point: The writer doesn't provide support for his/her opinion or uses irrelevant examples and details in an effort to persuade me as a reader.

Comments:

5. **Does the writer appear to be aware of and meet the needs of an audience?**

4 points: Yes, the writer appears to understand perfectly my needs as a general, college-level reader, using the appropriate tone and providing me with the necessary information to understand his/her point and the larger context of general thinking on this topic/subject area.

3 points: Yes, the writer generally seems to be aware of my needs as a general, college-level reader, but sometimes presents information in a confusing manner or without the background context that would better help me to follow his/her point.

2 points: The writer slips into language that identifies a specific reader that is not me; the writer may also present information in a way that is not suited for a general academic audience, with either too much technical jargon, slang/informalities, or language that is inflammatory in tone.

1 point: I don't have a sense that the writer has thought about my needs as a reader.

Comments:

6. **Does the paper feel organized and coherent?**

4 points: Yes, sentences and paragraphs flow well, building the writer's argument in progression and strength. Nothing seems out of order or irrelevant.

3 points: Yes, the writer develops his or her ideas over the course of the paper, although some parts of the paper may feel less developed than others, and a few parts may feel out of place.

2 points: No, the paper makes a lot of unexpected shifts or detours, contributing to a sense of confusion and lessening the persuasive aspects of the writer's argument.

1 point: I felt lost while reading this paper.

Comments:

7. **Is the language fluent or stilted?**

4 points: The writer uses language that is appropriate to the topic, clear and easy to understand, and engaging to me as a reader. The writer uses direct quotes when truly necessary, and he/she always "bridges" these quotes with his or her own language to create a seamless paper.

3 points: The writer uses language that is suitable for the topic but the paper may feel choppy or disjointed in a few places, sometimes through the placement of direct quotes.

2 points: The writer moves from one source quotation to another, and sometimes the language shifts even when there is no direct quotation, leading me to question the authorship or voice in passages of the paper.

1 point: I had difficulty reading this paper.

Comments:

8. **Are there difficulties with grammar and mechanics? If so, do they substantially interfere with readability?**

4 points: This paper is very readable; I didn't notice grammatical or mechanical problems if they existed.

3 points: I may have noticed some errors in the paper's grammar or mechanics, but they were slight in nature and didn't interfere with the writer's ability to present a convincing argument.

2 points: I found myself distracted because I often had to sort through grammatical errors in order to discern what the writer was saying.

1 point: Problems with the writing made it difficult to read this paper and appreciate what this writer had to say on the topic.

Comments:

9. **Do you see evidence of information literacy skills?**

4 points: Yes, I have a sense that the writer re-shaped his/her topic over time. I also have a sense that the writer consulted a wide variety of academic source materials, considered potential counter-arguments, and then only used those sources that would best support his/her argument and purpose for the paper. In addition, those sources are used accurately, relevantly, and properly in the paper.

3 points: Yes, I have a sense that the writer sought a variety of relevant academic sources in support of his/her general topic; however, I don't always have the sense that the writer uses these sources in the most convincing and thorough manner.

2 points: Not really. I see some evidence that the writer sought out different sources for the paper but had difficulty discerning which sources would best support the paper's argument or purpose. I also see problems in how these sources were used or not used in the body of the paper. The writer may over-simplify, generalize, or ignore important counter-arguments.

1 point: No. This paper is a patch-work of information from sources that feel randomly drawn together or detract from a writer's credibility on the topic. It feels like the writer did a minimal search for information, pulled out pieces that seem loosely related to the topic, and strung them together without considering how they contribute to his/her thesis. The writer may mis-state source information, take material out of context, or dismiss other credible points of view without appearing to have considered them.

0 points for entire paper: No. This paper is plagiarized in part or in whole. Regardless of the writer's intentions, this paper demonstrates serious problems in applying information literacy skills.

Comments:

10. **Is the paper appropriately cited? Are sources properly identified in places where they are summarized, paraphrased, and directly quoted? Are sources properly identified at the end?**

4 points: Yes, whenever others' ideas or language choices are used in the paper, they are properly cited. The writer has clearly identified those ideas and word phrases that belong to others, even when s/he is combining his/her own ideas with those from sources. I find all sources for the paper listed in full and correct form on the Works Cited (MLA)/Reference Page (APA).

3 points: The writer properly uses and cites summary information, paraphrases, and direct quotes. There may be a very few places in the paper where the student fails to cite an idea or fact because s/he imagines it is common knowledge in the field. Or there may be a very few places where the writer paraphrases a source and cites it, but doesn't alter the writer's original language to the degree s/he should. All sources are clearly identified in the paper's body and in the Works Cited (MLA)/Reference Page (APA).

2 points: No, the paper contains multiple statements that should be cited but aren't. The writer may attempt to paraphrase and cite whole excerpts by including a citation at the end of a paragraph. The writer may cite direct quotations but neglect to identify a few facts, examples, and/or details that are drawn from sources. The paper may refer to certain sources that are not included in the Works Cited (MLA)/Reference Page (APA). Or the Works Cited/Reference Page may include sources that were not identified anywhere in the body of the paper.

1 point: The connection between sources and the body of the paper is unclear. I am not sure the writer used sources to support his or her ideas. There may be few citations included in the paper itself and/or the citations are for such general information that I question their usefulness. Sources may or may not be listed on a reference page.

0 points for entire paper: No. This paper is plagiarized in part or in whole. Regardless of the writer's intentions, this paper demonstrates serious problems in understanding the academic process for acknowledging the work and ideas of others.

Comments:

Sub-total Points:

Deducted Points:

How well does the paper meet the guidelines of the assignment? You may deduct 1–5 points from the sub-total if the paper does NOT meet the assignment guidelines, including minimum page limit, required number of sources and in-text citations, formatting details, and required elements (such as annotated bibliography, abstract, outline, table of contents, or other).

Total Points:

What these point values mean:

35–40 points: A paper of distinction for a college-level writer

25–34 points: A passing-level paper for a college-level writer.

15–24 points: A paper that may demonstrate certain strengths but is not passing as a finished document for a college-level writer.

1–14 points: A paper that should be considered only as a first attempt to think in writing about the given topic.

0 points: A paper that is plagiarized and not considered passing for a college-level writer. Plagiarism may result in an academic incident report and failure to pass the course.

Framing an Argument

Debby Stewart

Many times in life you will be asked to take a stance on an issue or topic; however, it's not enough—in most situations—to simply present your opinion. You'll be called upon to present a *well-reasoned* and *fully-supported* opinion. In college, we often call such opinions an argument or persuasive presentation. Whether your argument is delivered orally or in writing, it's helpful to begin by brain-storming or writing informally about your topic or issue. This process will help you frame your argument to be most effective. This is especially important when your issue is politically or socially charged, or when you've been asked to develop a thesis or stance and support it with evidence. Most of your college presentations—oral or written—will do more than *inform* your audience, they will be focused on *persuading* them.

Questions to Consider in Developing or Framing an Argument:

- Who is your audience? Who will be listening to or reading your argument, and what do they know about your topic already? What assumptions might they make about the topic? What might they *not* know?

- What could you tell your audience that would get their attention about your issue?

- Write a short summary of the issue (try to encapsulate the issue in 75 words or less).

- Why is this important now? What is the urgency? Why should people care about this issue?

41

- What do you think should be done regarding this issue? (This is your thesis—your main point—so spend time crafting exactly what it is you want to convince people to do or think with regard to your issue. You should be able to state this in one or two sentences.)

- What are the strongest reasons in support of your opinion? (List all facts, examples, statistics, anecdotes, and other support that could help convince an audience of your peers. Be sure to include source information for your support. Where does it come from?)

- What are the strongest reasons *against* taking the stance you do? (List the facts, examples, statistics, anecdotes, or other material that could most sway your audience in the other direction. Be sure to include source information for your opposition. Where does it come from?)

- How will you address the 2–3 strongest reasons that could be used to oppose your argument? Describe a counter-argument for each one.

- What do you want to leave your audience thinking about? Write a short conclusion that reminds your audience what you want them to think or do.

Writing at CCV

Debby Stewart

It's likely that no matter what your first course is at CCV, you will be assigned to write a paper at some time during the semester. That's because CCV knows effective communication skills—writing and speaking—are critical both in the classroom and in the workplace. However, if you've been away from college for a long time or this is your first college experience, you may be unsure of how to write a paper, especially a research paper.

Rest assured that CCV has support for you! Ask an advisor about writing/learning labs or *eTutor,* which are free services to students. Ask also about special workshops on topics like research paper writing. In addition, many students learn to write their first college-level papers in English Composition, a course that is best taken early. Don't be afraid to talk to your academic advisor about your learning needs; he or she can be a valuable resource for you.

Also, feel free to talk to the faculty who assigned the paper. You might ask about written guidelines for the assignment, sample papers, or an evaluation rubric. Don't be embarrassed about asking for clarification. By asking questions, you'll not only help other students to think about the assignment more carefully, but you may also help the faculty to articulate his or her assumptions. Below are just a few questions you might raise with your teacher, either before, during or after class:

- What are the requirements for the paper?

- When is it due? What are the consequences if it is late?

- What kind of documentation style should I use?

- How many sources and what kinds of sources would be ideal for this assignment?

- How will you evaluate the paper?

- Do you have any examples of the kind of work you are expecting?

Plagiarism: What It Is and How to Avoid It

Whenever you're writing a paper, especially a paper that involves using sources to support your ideas, it's important also for you to think about plagiarism and how to avoid it. *Plagiarism is the presentation of the language, ideas, or thoughts of another person as one's own work in the preparation of a paper, laboratory report, oral presentation, or any other type of presentation.* Many people understand that buying a paper or purposely using someone else's ideas or language as one's own is academic dishonesty. However, it's also important to understand that plagiarism can result from carelessness or misunderstanding the rules.

Below are some general tips for appropriately giving credit to sources in a paper.

1. **Keep track of all sources.** Whenever you are consulting a source that you may or may not use in your final paper, be sure to copy down the bibliographic information about the source. This varies depending on the type of source it is, but, in general, you need the author(s), title, publisher, and date. If it is a Web source, you will also need the address and the date of access.

2. **Take careful notes.** You must be very careful when writing notes from your source. Make sure you include the page number and indicate, with quotation marks, whether or not the passage is a direct quote. If you are paraphrasing a passage from the source, be sure that you are really putting it in your own words and that you are also changing the way the words are arranged. Perhaps you want to highlight the words that appear in both the original passage and in your notes. If there are too many of the same words in both, you're probably in danger of plagiarizing the passage.

In addition, it's a good idea to keep copies of your work. You will want to double-check your notes once the paper is completed. It's easy for mistakes to happen and a source to get omitted from your final draft, resulting in plagiarism. If you photocopy pages from a book or print Web pages from your source, be sure to keep them also.

3. Avoid "cutting and pasting" from an Internet source into your paper.
    Though it may save you time in re-typing quoted material, the poten-
    tial consequences outweigh any gain. First, there's the problem of over-
    using direct quotes, especially long or extended quotes. It's so easy to
    cut and paste from the Internet that many student writers over-rely on
    this kind of material, which leads to papers that are choppy, confusing
    and disjointed. Secondly, and more importantly, it's easy to forget—in
    the revising process—which is the borrowed material and which is
    your own, often resulting in plagiarism. Since instructors readily use
    the Internet to check the writing in papers, carelessness here can result
    in a failed assignment and/or a failed class, which is too high a price
    to pay for the ease of cutting and pasting.

4. Understand the system of documentation that's appropriate for your
    paper. Most CCV instructors require students to use MLA or APA style
    of documentation. MLA is often used for papers in writing, humani-
    ties, and history courses. APA is often used for papers in the social
    sciences or education. You can easily find information about these
    documentation styles at a CCV site and online.

    An important thing to know here is that both of these styles use par-
    enthetical citations. In other words, footnotes or endnotes are not
    needed. A parenthetical citation is when you include a brief reference
    to the source right in the text of your paper—every time you use a
    direct quote, paraphrase, or idea. A Works Cited or References page
    is added at the end, which lists your sources in full detail.

5. Understand when and how to appropriately cite sources in your
    paper. What you include in a parenthetical citation depends on
    which style (MLA or APA) you're following. In general, when using
    MLA style, you include the author's last name and the page number.
    When using APA style, you include the author's last name, the pub-
    lication date, and the page number (if it is a direct quote). Again,
    information on MLA and APA styles of documentation is readily
    available.

    Whatever style of documentation you use, it is probably most impor-
    tant to know when you must cite a source, and this is the same for all
    styles. You must cite the following types of material from a source:

Direct Quotes

This is when you use quoted material in your paper. The quote
should include the exact words of the author or source framed by quotation marks. Then designate the source at the end of the sentence. For

example, if you were to use a direct quote from George J. Demko's book, *Why in the World: Adventures in Geography*, it would look like:

> *"It's hard to think of any place that is untouched by human contact, even the cruelest, most hostile environments, such as the glaciers of Antarctica and the broiling, waterless Sahara. All places bear the imprimatur of human visits and habitations, or the vestiges of such connections" (Demko 13).*

Or you might preface the quote, connecting it to the point you were making in your paper:

> *George Demko, former director of the United States Office of the Geographer, might agree that humans have impacted, sometimes significantly, the areas we have come to see as wilderness. After all, he writes, "It's hard to think of any place that is untouched by human contact, even the cruelest, most hostile environments, such as the glaciers of Antarctica and the broiling, waterless Sahara"(13).*

Note that the second example is more effective than the first because it gives a context for the quote. It lets the reader know a little more about the author of your source, which can be helpful to establish his or her credibility. Even more importantly, however, is the way the second example reinforces the paper's thesis or main point. Many writers forget to make these connections, thinking that a quote speaks for itself. Only rarely is this true. It is very important in a paper to provide more than facts or quotes; most teachers are looking to you, as the writer of the paper, to interpret or analyze the information you're including. How does a particular fact or figure support your point?

Also, this quote demonstrates why you should use direct quotes sparingly in your papers. For a paper to be most effective, it's important to get a sense of the writer's voice. When direct quotes from different sources are used frequently in a paper, it's difficult to keep that sense of the one writer's voice.

The examples above raise another question for writers: when should a quote be separated from the body of your paragraph? Quoted material should be included in your paper as a **block quotation** when it is longer than four manuscript lines. Quotes of this length are indented *without* the normal quotation marks since the indenting signals the reader that it is a direct quote and not a paraphrase or summary. However, the quote must still include—at the end of the passage—a parenthetical citation noting the source and page number.

Paraphrasing

This is when you use the basic meaning of an author's statement but change the words and structure of the sentence. For example, using Demko's quote above, you might paraphrase it in the following way:

Humans leave their mark wherever they go, even those places we have come to see as inhospitable or extreme (Demko 13).

Or you might write:

According to George Demko, former director of the United States Office of the Geographer, humans leave their mark wherever they go, even those places we have come to see as inhospitable or extreme (13).

Notice that you can't just change a few words or shuffle words around and still call it a paraphrase. If you do, it's considered plagiarism—even when you have a citation right next to it! In addition, many student writers assume that it is acceptable to paraphrase an entire paragraph as long as a citation is included at the end of the paragraph. However, this is not acceptable and is also considered plagiarism. After all, how would a reader know which ideas in the paragraph were those of the author and which were those of the student writer? Remember that all documentation styles aim for clarity and appropriate ownership of words and ideas.

Ideas

This is when you take the idea or information that the author provides but completely change the wording and structure of the sentence(s).

Although the conditions of a place vary widely, they do share one thing in common; it's rare to find a place that is not impacted in some way by humans (Demko 13).

Here you give credit for the information that is derived from your source, but you are really only summarizing that information rather than paraphrasing it. You might wonder why it is important to cite Demko's idea; after all, Demko's statement seems like common sense. However, this is Demko's idea, one derived from extensive experience in this field. Citing him is a way of properly crediting him for his work and insights. Citing him also contributes to your paper's credibility and persuasion. Finally, while the statement may seem to be one of general common sense, a careful reader could challenge you. Without extensive geographical knowledge of the world, how could one make such a statement without generalizing? Giving proper credit not only acknowledges the experts in a particular field, but it illustrates your understanding of their contributions.

6. **Include a References or Works Cited Page.** A References or Works Cited page lists the sources that you have cited in your paper. Only sources that show up in the body of the paper should be listed on this page. (If you don't use and cite a source in the body of your paper, it can't be listed in the Works Cited).

   Conversely, all the sources that you use in the body of your paper must be listed here. (You can't cite a source in the paper then forget to include it on the Works Cited page). Because you are only giving a small amount of information about each source within the paper (like last name of author and page number), the Works Cited or References page is where the reader can find the full bibliographic information about each source. Remember that there are plenty of reference guides to help you with this. To illustrate how a source might be listed, according to MLA style, here's the source used in the examples above:

   Demko, George J., with Jerome Agel and Eugene Boe. *Why in the World: Adventures in Geography.* NY: Doubleday, 1992.

Final Advice

It's important to understand what plagiarism is and how to avoid it. Academic dishonesty is taken very seriously at CCV. It can result in failed assignments or courses and even suspension or dismissal for more than one incident. However, plagiarism doesn't have to happen. By asking questions and paying attention to the "rules" associated with citing sources, anyone can avoid making a costly mistake.

What kinds of behaviors might be considered academic dishonesty?

Plagiarism is a form of academic dishonesty. It is the presentation of the language, ideas, or thoughts of another person as one's own work in the preparation of a paper, laboratory report, oral presentation, or any other type of presentation. While this list is not meant to be exhaustive or complete, here are specific examples of behaviors that are considered **academically dishonest:**

- Buying or downloading for free a paper, assignment, or other work from a Web site service and submitting it as your own;

- Copying all or part of a classmate's assignment, paper, discussion posting, exam, or other work and submitting at as your own;

- Copying material from a Web site, article, book, interview, or other source and submitting it as part of your own work without appropriately citing the source;

- Using material from a Web site, article, book, interview, or other source and submitting it in an oral or visual presentation without appropriately acknowledging the source to the audience;

- Using material from sources that you have put into your own words but have not acknowledged through appropriately citing those sources;

- Arranging for someone inside or outside of the class to complete all or part of your work for you;

- Arranging for someone inside or outside of a class to pose as you for the purposes of submitting work, meeting a class requirement, or participating in class activities;

- Conferring with other students or using notes and/or sources to complete an exam or other assignment when an instructor has not allowed for it;

- Using a cellphone, computer, or other electronic device to download material for use in a quiz, assessment, exam, or other situation when it is not allowed;

- Creating false material, data, research, sources, or other information in order to support assertions in a paper, lab report, or other academic work.

*J*anette Shaffer is associate library director at Community College of
Vermont.

Information Literacy

Janette Shaffer

Information literacy is one of the graduation standards the VSC
requires you to meet before you receive a degree from CCV. Your information literacy skills will be assessed through successful completion of a
final paper in the capstone course, Seminar in Educational Inquiry. As an
information literate person you will

- recognize when information is needed;

- know where and how to discover needed information;

- critically evaluate and synthesize information;

- confidently use a variety of tools to find, modify, and assimilate information; and

- use information ethically and legally.

If we don't assess your information literacy skills until you're about
to graduate, why are we introducing information literacy in this
Dimensions course?

Practicing information literacy skills in your first semester seminar
will provide you with a crucial foundation for a successful academic
career, workplace preparation, and global citizenship. After the first
semester seminar you will have the tools needed to navigate the infinite
amount of information available to you.

In Dimensions, you will learn how to search for relevant sources in
the "fastest growing new medium of all time," the Internet ("How Much
Information? 2003"). You will be able to evaluate Internet entries for credibility and reliability, and confidently choose and apply your sources.

Dimensions will also introduce you to the best source of information available to you as a CCV student: the Hartness Library. You will discover "ways to unearth a library's treasures [to] enhance your writing, boost your presentation skills, help you plan your career, and enable you to continue learning for the rest of your life" (Ellis, 322).

Starting to build your information literacy skills early on in your studies will enhance your subsequent learning and life experience. You will be a confident contributor to your learning community and a competent participant in your environment.

Works Cited

Ellis, Dave. *Becoming a Master Student.* 11th ed. New York: Houghton Mifflin Company, 2006.

"How Much Information? 2003." 2003. 28 April, 2008. http://21cif.imsa.edu/resources/difcore/index.html

*A*bigail Witherspoon is the pseudonym of an American author who writes *about her experiences working for a ghost writing service that pens term papers for students.*

This Pen for Hire
On grinding out papers for college students

Abigail Witherspoon

I am an academic call girl. I write college kids' papers for a living. Term papers, book reports, senior theses, take-home exams. My "specialties": art history and sociology, international relations and comparative literature, English, psychology, "communications," Western philosophy (ancient and contemporary), structural anthropology, film history, evolutionary biology, waste management and disposal, media studies, and pre-Confederation Canadian history. I throw around allusions to Caspar Weinberger and Alger Hiss, Sacco and Vanzetti, Haldeman and Ehrlichman, Joel Steinberg and Baby M. The teaching assistants eat it up. I can do simple English or advanced jargon. Like other types of prostitutes, I am, professionally, very accommodating.

I used to tell myself I'd do this work only for a month or two, until I found something else. But the official unemployment rate in this large Canadian city where I live is almost 10 percent, and even if it were easy to find a job, I'm American, and therefore legally prohibited from receiving a paycheck. So each day I walk up the stairs of a rotting old industrial building to an office with a sign on the window: TAILORMADE ESSAYS, WRITING AND RESEARCH. The owner, whom I'll call Matthew, claims that he started the business for ghostwriters, speechwriters, and closet biographers, and only gradually moved into academic work as a sideline. But even Grace, the oldest surviving writer on Tailormade's staff, can't remember anybody ever writing much other than homework for students at one university or another.

This is a good city for Tailormade. Next door is the city's university and its tens of thousands of students, a school that was once somewhat better when not all of its computer-registered classes numbered in the hundreds. Orders come in from Vancouver, Calgary, Winnipeg. There are plenty of essay services in the States, of course; they advertise in campus newspapers and the back pages of music magazines. Some of the big ones have toll-free phone numbers. They're sprinkled all over: California, Florida, New Jersey. But we still get American business too. Orders come in here from Michigan, Vermont, Pennsylvania; from Illinois, Wisconsin, upstate New York, sometimes California; from Harvard, Cornell, and Brown. They come in from teachers' colleges, from people calling themselves "gifted students" (usually teenagers at boarding schools), and, once in a while, from the snazzy places some of our customers apparently vacation with their divorced dads, like Paris.

Matthew runs the business with his wife, Sylvia. Or maybe she is his ex-wife, nobody's exactly sure. When you call Tailormade—it's now in the phone book—you hear Sylvia say that Tailormade is Canada's foremost essay service; that our very qualified writers handle most academic subjects; and that we are fast, efficient, and completely confidential. Sylvia speaks loudly and slowly and clearly, especially to Asian customers. She is convinced that everyone who phones the office will be Asian, just as she's convinced that all Asians drive white Mercedes or black BMWs with cellular phones in them. From my personal experience, I find the Asian customers at least more likely to have done the assigned reading.

Matthew and Sylvia are oddly complementary. Matthew, gentle and fumbly, calls out mechanically, "Thank you, sir, ma'am, come again" after each departing back slinking down the hall. Sylvia asks the Chinese customers loudly, "SIMPLE ENGLISH?" She tells the uncertain, "Well, don't show up here till you know what you want," and demands of the dissatisfied, "Whaddya mean you didn't like it? You ordered it, din'cha?"

This afternoon, October 10, I'm here to hand in a paper and fight it out with the other writers for more assignments. Some of us are legal, some aren't. Some have mortgages and cars, some don't. All of us are hungry. The office is jammed, since it's almost time for midterms. Tailormade does a brisk business from October to May, except for January. The chairs are full of customers studiously filling out order forms. You can always tell who is a student and who is a writer. The students are dressed elegantly and with precision; the writers wear ripped concert T-shirts or stained denim jackets with white undershirts peeking out. The students wear mousse and hair gel and nail polish and Tony Lama western boots and Tourneau watches and just the right amount of makeup. They smell of Escape, Polo for men, and gum. The writers smell of sweat, house pets, and crushed cigarettes. Four of the other writers are lolling in their chairs and fidgeting; work usually isn't assigned until all the order forms have been filled out, unless somebody requests a topic difficult to fill. Then Matthew will call out like an auctioneer: "Root Causes of the Ukrainian Famine? Second year? Anyone? Grace?" or "J. S. Mill's Brand of Humane Utilitarianism? Third year? Henry, that for you?" as some customer hovers in front of the desk, eyes straight ahead. Someone else in the room might idly remark that he or she took that course back in freshman year and it was a "gut" or a "real bird."

I suspect that each of us in the Tailormade stable of hacks sorts out the customers differently: into liberal-arts students and business students; into those that at least do the reading and those that don't bother; into those that have trouble writing academic English and those that just don't care about school; into those that do their assignments in other subjects and those that farm every last one of them out to us; into the struggling and inept versus the rich, lazy, and stupid. But for Matthew and Sylvia, the clientele are divisible, even before cash versus credit card, or paid-up versus owing, into Asian customers and non-Asian ones. There's been an influx of wealthy immigrants from Hong Kong in recent years, fleeing annexation. Matthew and Sylvia seem to resent their presence and, particularly, their money. Yet they know that it's precisely this pool of customers—who have limited written English language skills but possess education, sophistication, ambition, cash, and parents leaning hard on them for good grades—that keeps the business going.

When I hand in my twelve pages on "The Role of Market Factors in the Development of the Eighteenth-Century Fur Trade," Matthew tells me, "This lady's been patiently waiting without complaining." I must be very late. Turning to the client, he picks up one of my sheets and waves it. "At least it's a nice bib," he points out to her. "Look at that." Although I wasn't provided with any books for this essay, I managed to supply an extensive bibliography. I can't remember what I put on it.

I'm still waiting for an assignment. In fact, all the writers are still waiting. We often wait at the bar around the corner; Tailormade has its own table there, permanently reserved. But we all have to get ourselves to the office eventually to pick up assignments. Grace, the oldest writer and by now, probably, the best, sits sorrowfully by the window, her long gray hair falling into her lap and her head jammed into her turtleneck, on her thin face a look of permanent tragedy. Grace gets up at three in the morning to work; she never forgets a name, a fact, or an assignment; she has a deep, strange love for Japanese history and in ten years here has probably hatched enough pages and research for several doctoral dissertations in that field. Elliott, another writer, reclines near the door, his little dog asleep under his chair. He uses the dog as an icebreaker with the clients, especially young women. He is six and a half feet tall and from somewhere far up in the lunar landscape of northern Ontario. He has a huge head of blond hair down to his eyes and pants as tight as a rock star's. Elliott is the business writer. He specializes in finance, investment, management, and economics. He lives out of a suitcase; he and the little dog, perhaps practicing fiscal restraint, seem to stay with one of a series of girlfriends. When the relationship comes to an end, Elliott and the little dog wind up back in the office, where they sleep in the fax room and Elliott cranks out essays on his laptop. Henry and Russell, two other writers, twist around, changing position, the way travelers do when they're trying to nap on airport lounge chairs. They both look a little like El Greco saints, although perhaps it just seems that way to me because lately I've been doing a lot of art history papers. They both have long skinny legs, long thin white nervous twiddling hands, long thin faces with two weeks' worth of unintentional beard. Henry points out how good Russell looks, and we all agree. Russell is forty. He has a new girlfriend half his age who has, he says, provided a spiritual reawakening. Before he met her, Russell drank so much and held it so badly that he had the distinction of being the only staff member to be banned from the bar around the corner for life. Henry, by contrast, looks terrible. He's always sick, emaciated, coughing, but he invariably manages to meet his deadlines, to make his page quotas, and to show up on time. We used to have another writer on staff, older even than Russell or Grace, who smoked a pipe, nodded a lot, and never said anything. He was a professor who'd been fired from some school, we were never really sure where. Eventually, he went AWOL and started an essay-writing service of his own. He's now Tailormade's main competition. The only other competitors, apparently, worked out of a hot-dog stand parked next to a campus bookstore. Nobody knows whether they're open anymore.

In general, there is a furtiveness about the way we writers talk to one another, the way we socialize. In the office, we're a little like people who know each other from A.A. meetings or rough trade bars encountering each other on a Monday morning at the photocopy machine. It's not because we're competing for work. It's not even because some of us are illegal and everyone else knows it. It is, if anything, collective embarrassment. We know a lot more than Matthew and Sylvia do. They sit dumbly as we bullshit with the clients about their subjects and assignments ("Ah, introductory psychology! The evolution of psychotherapy is a fascinating topic . . . ever read a guy called Russell Jacoby?") in order to impress them and get them to ask for us. This must be the equivalent of the harlots' competitive bordello promenade. But we work for Matthew and Sylvia. They have the sense to pit us against each other, and it works. We can correct their pronunciation of "Goethe" and they don't care. They know it makes no difference. I suspect they have never been farther away than Niagara Falls; neither of them may have even finished high school. It doesn't matter. The laugh's on us, of course: they own the business.

OCTOBER 12, 1994. A tall gangly kid comes in for a twenty-page senior history essay about the ancient local jail. It involves research among primary sources in the provincial archives, and I spend a week there, going page by page through the faded brown script of the warden's prison logbooks of the 1830s. Agitators are being executed for "high treason" or "banished from the realm," which, I assume, means being deported. Once in a while there's a seductive joy to a project. You forget that you've undertaken it for money, that it isn't yours.

Most of the time, though, all I think about is the number of pages done, the number to go. Tailormade charges twenty dollars Canadian a page for first- and second-year course assignments, twenty-two a page for third- and fourth-year assignments, twenty-four for "technical, scientific, and advanced" topics. "Technical, scientific, and advanced" can mean nuclear physics, as it does in September when there is no business. Or it can mean anything Matthew and Sylvia want it to, as it does in March. Most major spring-term essays are due when final exams begin, in April, and so in March kids are practically lined up in the office taking numbers and spilling out into the hall. The writers get half, in cash: ten and eleven bucks a page; twelve for the technical, scientific, and advanced.

There's one other charge: if the client doesn't bring in her or his own books, except in September and January, she or he is "dinged," charged an extra two dollars a page for research. When the writers get an assignment, we ask if there are books. If there are, it saves us time, but we have to lug them home, and often they're the wrong books. If there are no books, we have to go to the libraries and research the paper ourselves. "Client wants twelve pages on clinical social work intervention," Matthew and Sylvia might tell us. "She has a reading list but no books. I think we can ding her." "He wants a book report on something called *Gravity's Rainbow?* Doesn't have the book, though. I'm gonna ding him."

OCTOBER 13. I am assigned a paper on the French philosopher Michel Foucault. The client has been dinged; I have to find some books. Foucault's *Discipline and Punish* and *Madness and Civilization* are hot properties in the public library system. They are not to be found anywhere. Perhaps this is because professors think Foucault is a hot property, too; he's all over everyone's syllabus.

I warn the client about this in the office. "If you don't find anything by the guy, call me," he says. He gives me his home phone number. "Only, *please* don't say you're from the essay service. Say you're . . . a classmate of mine." I promise to be discreet. Most of the clients get scared when you call them at home; most never give out their numbers. I don't blame them.

It was different, though, when I was a university student in the early 1980s. I wasn't aware of anyone who bought his or her homework anywhere, although it must have happened. It was about that time that Tailormade was putting up signs on the telephone poles outside the university's main classroom buildings. It advertised just outside the huge central library as well as outside the libraries of three or four smaller schools a few minutes' drive away. This burst of entrepreneurial confidence almost led to the service's undoing. In a spectacular cooperative sting operation among the security departments of the various schools, the office was raided. This event has become a sort of fearsome myth at Tailormade, discussed not unlike the way Syrians might occasionally mention the Israeli raid on Entebbe. Matthew and Sylvia were hauled off to court and a dozen or so clients were thrown out of their respective universities. Matthew and Sylvia, however, must have hired the right lawyer: they were allowed to reopen, provided that they stayed away from campuses and that they stamped every page of every essay TAILORMADE ESSAY SERVICE: FOR RESEARCH PURPOSES ONLY. Now the clients take the stamped essays home, retype them, and print them out on high-end laser printers much better than ours. If the client is obnoxious, complains, or is considered a whiner, each typewritten page will be stamped in the middle. If the client is steady and has good credit, each page will be stamped in the margin so that the stamp can be whited out and the pages photocopied.

By the time Tailormade reopened, I had moved back to this country after some years at home in the States. I had no money and no prospects of a legal job. I came in, handed Matthew a résumé, spent a couple of weeks on probationary trial, and then began a serious career as a hack. "What are your specialties?" Matthew had asked me. I told him I'd majored in history and political science as an undergraduate. Over time, as my financial situation grew worse, my "specialties" grew to include everything except math, accounting, economics, and the hard sciences.

OCTOBER 23. Three weeks ago I was assigned an essay on the establishment and growth of political action committees among the Christian right. I am earnest about this one; I actually overprepare. I want to document, with carefully muted horror, the world of Paul Laxalt and direct mail, the arm-twisting of members of Congress on the school prayer issue. My contempt for the client was mixed with pity: he knew not how much he was missing. Only afterward do I realize that after doing an essay I take seriously, I still expect, as in college, to get something back with a mark on it, as a reward or at least as an acknowledgment. I hear nothing, of course. I feel oddly let down. I'm certain it got the client an A. Today, the same client stops in to order something else and helpfully points out what he thinks I could have done to improve the essay I'd written for him.

OCTOBER 25. This summer, a woman wanted me to write about how aboriginal peoples' systems of law and justice were better developed than those of conquering colonials. I took books with titles like *The Treaties of Canada with the Indians of Manitoba and the North-West Territories, 1880* to the beach. After finishing the client's reading material, I still had no idea what aboriginal peoples thought about law or anything else; she had given me only books about the conquering colonials. So the paper went on, for twenty-odd pages, about the conquering colonials. Now she wants me to rewrite it. The time I will spend on this second version waters my pay down to about a dollar an hour.

NOVEMBER 8. I will not go into any of the university's libraries. I will not risk running into anyone I know, anyone who might think I'm one of those perpetual graduate students who never finished their dissertations and drift pathetically around university libraries like the undead, frightening the undergraduates. It would be as bad to be thought one of these lifelong grad students as to be suspected of being what I am. So I use the public libraries, usually the one closest to my apartment, on my street corner. It's a community library, with three wonderful librarians, three daily newspapers, and remarkably few books. If I haven't been given the books already, if the client has been dinged and I have to do research on my own, I come here. I have my favorite chair. The librarians assume I am a "mature" and "continuing" community college student, and make kind chitchat with me.

Sometimes, when I can't find any of the sources listed in the library's computer and don't have time to go to a real library, I use books barely appropriate for the essay: books for "young adults," which means twelve-year-olds, or books I have lying around my apartment—like Jane Jacobs's *The Death and Life of Great American Cities*, H. D. F. Kitto's *The Greeks*, Eduardo Galeano's *Open Veins of Latin America*, Roy Medvedev's book on Stalin or T. H. White's on John Kennedy, books by J. K. Galbraith, Lewis Mumford, Christopher Lasch, Erich Fromm. Books somewhere between the classic and the old chestnut; terrific books, yet with no relation to the topic at hand. But they're good for the odd quote and name-drop, and they can pad a bibliography. Sometimes I can't get away with this, though, and then I have no choice but to go back to an actual place of research, like the archives.

The archives are, in fact, a difficult place for me. They are full of oak tables, clicking laptops, whirring microfiche readers, and self-assured middle-aged men working with pretty young women whose hair is pinned up in nineteenth-century styles. Perhaps some of them are lovers, but certainly all of them are graduate students with their profs. I, by contrast, am a virtual student, a simulacrum.

NOVEMBER 16. I have also been pulling at least one or two all-nighters a week for three weeks now. They're very much like the all-nighters I did as an undergraduate. I eat licorice nibs for energy and drink molehill coffee for caffeine. You make molehill coffee by pouring an entire half cup of coffee grounds, the finer the better, in a number 4 paper filter, one filter per cup. At midnight the razzy voice of Tom Waits is temporarily replaced by the BBC news hour. It would be great to be able to speak just like the BBC newscaster, Somebody hyphen-Jones. If I sounded like that I'm sure I would be able to get credit, somehow, for writing about the birth of the Carolingian Renaissance, or the displacement of the samurai in Tokugawa times, or the inadequacies of the Treaty of Versailles.

I know by experience that if I start writing at midnight I can time my output: first page by the BBC's second news summary, second page by the financial news on the half hour, third page finished by the time they read the rugby scores. Except that the first page, the one with the thesis paragraph in it, is the hardest to write, and it clocks in at well over fifteen minutes.

At two-thirty I hit a wall. The molehill coffee still hasn't kicked in yet, or else it did and I didn't notice, and now it's worn off, or else I've just built up a fatal tolerance to the stuff, like a crack addict. I begin to fall asleep in my chair, even with my headphones on. I turn up the music and blast it through the headphones. This works for the time being. I plug along. I can't really remember what I said in my thesis paragraph, but I am not going to worry about it. The client wants fifteen pages, and when I find myself on the fourteenth I'll read the thing over and brace myself, if I have to, for a bow-out. Bow-outs, like legal fine print, allow you to dart gracefully out of the large ambitious thesis statement you've started the essay with: "The topic of bird evolution is an enormous one; I have been able to touch on just one or two interesting controversies within it." "Space does not permit a detailed discussion of all the internal contradictions within Sri Lanka's postcolonial history." And so on. Nine and a half pages down. Five and a half to go. I can still barely remember what I said in my thesis statement. I can barely remember what this paper is *about*. I want to put my head down for a minute on the keyboard, but God only knows what it would end up typing.

NOVEMBER 18. Things are picking up for Christmas vacation; everything, it seems, is due December 5 or December 15. The essay order form asks, "Subject & Level," "Topic," "No. of Pages," "Footnotes," "Bibliography," and then a couple of lines marked "Additional Information," by far the most common of which is "Simple English." As the year rolls on, we hacks will all, out of annoyance, laziness, or just boredom, start unsimplifying this simple English; by April it will approach the mega-watt vocabulary and tortured syntax of the Frankfurt School. But people hand these papers in and don't get caught, people who have difficulty speaking complete sentences in English; perhaps this is because classes and even tutorials are so big they never have to speak. But in December we're all still on pretty good behavior, simple instead of spiteful. I've just handed in an assignment in "Simple English," a paper titled "Mozart's Friendship with Joseph and Johann Michael Haydn and Its Impact on Mozart's Chamber Music." It reads, in part:

> Mozart was undeniably original. He was never derivative. That was part of his genius. So were the Haydn brothers. All of them were totally unique.

The little library on my corner didn't have much on Mozart or the Haydn brothers. As a result, one of the items in my bibliography is a child's book with a cardboard pop-up of a doughy-looking little Mozart, in a funky pigtail and knee breeches, standing proudly beside a harpsichord.

NOVEMBER 22. I'm assigned an overnight rush essay on the causes of the English Civil War. It may sound perverse, but I love rush essays. We get paid a dollar more a page (two for technical, scientific, and advanced), and if it's lousy we can always say, "Well, you wanted it in a hurry." Although I majored in history, I never took any courses on the English Civil War; I figured, wrongly, that Shakespeare's histories would take care of that. Now I find myself reading the books I took out from the little corner library, not for quotes, or to form an opinion on the roots, germination, feeding, and watering of the war, but just to find out what the hell went on. I find out enough to write five pages. It takes me all night.

NOVEMBER 23. I am handing in something entitled "Sri Lanka: A Study in Ethnic Division and Caste Co-optation," which Sylvia assigned me, over the phone, a week ago. "The girl says to tell you that *she's* Sri Lankan." Last year I wrote a senior sociology thesis on "The Italian-Canadian Family: Bedrock of Tradition or Agent of Change?" With that one I heard, "The girl says to tell you that *she's* Italian." I wanted to ask Sylvia if the client knew I wasn't, but I was afraid she'd interpret that as meaning I didn't want the work and she'd give it to someone else.

DECEMBER 2. Occasionally there is an assignment the writers fight for. This week somebody—not me—gets to take home *Fanny Hill* and *Lady Chatterley's Lover*, and get paid for it. I guess some kids really, *really* hate to read.

DECEMBER 5. A bad assignment: unnecessarily obscure, pedantic, pointless. Certain courses seem to consist of teaching kids the use of jargon as though it were a substitute for writing or thinking well. Often there is an implied pressure to agree with the assigned book. And many are simply impossible to understand; I often take home a textbook or a sheaf of photocopies for an assignment and see, next to a phrase such as "responsible acceptance of the control dimension," long strings of tiny

Chinese characters in ballpoint pen. No wonder the students find the assignments incomprehensible; they are incomprehensible to me.

DECEMBER 8. I hand in a paper on Machiavelli. "How'd it go?" asked the client, a boy in a leather bomber jacket reading John Grisham. I begin to go on about how great one of the books was, a revisionist biography called *Machiavelli in Hell*. I am hoping, with my scholarly enthusiasm, to make the client feel particularly stupid. "It's an amazing book," I tell him. "It makes a case for Machiavelli actually being kind of a liberal humanist instead of the cynical guy everybody always thinks he was—amazing." "That's good," the kid says. "I'm glad you're enjoying yourself on my tab. Did you answer the essay question the way you were supposed to?"

DECEMBER 16. Every so often clients come in with an opinion they want us to replicate. The freshman sociology and political science essays are already starting to rain in: a deluge of "Show why immigrants are a dead weight on the economy and take jobs away from us"; "Show why most social programs will become too expensive for an aging population"; "Show why gun control can be interpreted as an infringement on civil rights"; "Show the Pacific Rim's single-handed assault on North American economies." I ignore them. I write, depending on my mood, about the INS's unequal criteria for refugee status, or the movie *Roger and Me*, or the NRA's political clout. For instance, there is today's assignment: to describe Locke's influence, as an Enlightenment figure, on our own time. I think this is baloney. I talk about how the postwar military-industrial complex proves that God really did give the world, whatever Locke thought, to the covetous and contentious instead of to the industrious and the rational. No one's ever complained about finding my opinion in a paper instead of their own. Now I realize this isn't because I've persuaded anybody of anything. It's just laziness: there are some customers who actually retype their stamped essays without bothering to read them.

DECEMBER 27. During Christmas vacation, friends of mine invite me to a party. Some people will be there whom we know from college; they are in the process of becoming successful, even making it big. It will be important to project confidence, the illusion of fulfilling my abandoned early promise. "What do I say," I ask my friends, "when somebody asks me what I do for a living?"

"Tell them you're a writer."

My friend Lisa sticks by me loyally all evening. When people ask me, "What is it you do?" Lisa answers for me quickly: "She's a writer."

"Oh, what is it you write?"

"*Essays,*" I say, spitefully, drunkenly. Lisa thinks fast.

"Articles," she says. "She writes articles, on Sri Lanka, and Machiavelli, and the English Civil War."

"Isn't *that* interesting," they say, leaving us for the guacamole.

JANUARY 10, 1995. School has been back in session for a week now. The only work that is in are essays from the education students. I hate these assignments. I have trouble manipulating the self-encapsulated second language in which teaching students seem compelled to write. But it's after Christmas, and I'm broke. Education assignments all involve writing up our customers' encounters in their "practicum." Teaching students work several times a week as assistant teachers in grade school classrooms; instead of getting paid for this work, they pay tuition for it. Unfortunately, these expensive practice sessions don't seem to go well. My first such assignment was to write "reflections" on a "lesson plan" for a seventh-grade English class. The teaching student had given me some notes, and I had to translate these into the pedagogical jargon used in her textbooks. The idea seems to be that you have to say, as obscurely as possible, what you did with your seventh-grade kids and what you think about what you did:

> Preliminary Lesson Formulations: My objectives were to integrate lesson content with methodology to expand students' receptiveness and responsiveness to the material and to one another by teaching them how to disagree with one another in a constructive way. The class will draw up a T-chart covering "Disagreeing in an Agreeable Way," roughly in the manner of Bennett et al. Check for understanding. When the students discuss this, they are encouraged to listen to one another's language carefully and "correct" it if the wording is unhelpful, negative, or destructive. I shared my objectives with the class by asking them to read a fable and then divide into pairs and decide together what the moral was. Clearly, this is the "Think-Pair-Share" technique, as detailed in Bennett et al. The three strategies in use, then, are: 1) pair and sharing; 2) group discussion of the fable with mind-mapping; 3) group discussion of ways of disagreement. The teacher, modeling, divides the board in two with a line.

"Pair and share" seemed to mean "find a partner." I had no idea what "mind-mapping" or a "T-chart" was supposed to be. And come to think of it, after reading the fable, I had no idea what the moral was.

JANUARY 18. Somebody is applying to the graduate program in family therapy at some university somewhere and wants us to write the application. "She's my friend," said the young woman sitting across from Matthew at the desk. "She wants to start her own private practice as a therapist, right? So she can buy a house, right? And if you're a psychiatrist you have to go all the way through med school, right? So she's given me some notes for you about her here—she only needs one credit for her B.A. in psychology, and she volunteered at a shelter one summer. She wants you to tell them all that. Maybe make up some other things."

"See," Matthew tells me after she leaves. "If you ever go to one of those therapists, that's something you should think about."

JANUARY 20. When I first started this work, friends of mine would try to comfort me by telling me it would teach me to write better. Actually, academic prostitution, just like any other kind, seems to bring with it diseases, afflictions, vices, and bad habits. There is, for instance, the art of pretending you've read a book you haven't. It's just like every speed-reading course ever offered by the Learning Annex: read the introduction, where the writer outlines what he's going to say, and the conclusion, where he repeats what he's said.

> In his book *The Technological Society,* Jacques Ellul begins by defining the technical simply as the search for efficiency. He claims, however, that technique itself is subdivided into three categories: the social, the organizational, and the economic.

This is all on the book's *first four pages.* Sometimes—often—I find myself eating up as much space as possible. There are several ways to do this. One is to reproduce lengthy, paragraph-long quotes in full; another is to ramble on about your own apparently passionate opinion on something. Or you start talking about the United States and what a handbasket it's going to hell in. This is equally useful, for different reasons, on either side of the border. You can ask rhetorical questions to obsessive excess. ("Can Ellul present the technical in such a reductionist way? Can he really define technique in such a way? And is it really valid to distinguish between the social and the organizational?" etc.) And there's always the art of name-dropping as a way to fill pages and convince the teaching assistant that your client has read *something*, even if it wasn't what was on the syllabus.

> Certainly, as writers from Eduardo Galeano to Andre Gunder Frank to Noam Chomsky to Philip Agee to Allan Frankovich to Ernesto Laclau document, the CIA has long propped up the United Fruit Company.

At least you can make the client feel stupid. It's the third week of January, my apartment is cold, and I am bitter.

FEBRUARY 8. I'm learning, as the environmentalists tell us, to reuse and recycle. It's easier when I adapt a paper, with minor changes, on the same topic for different classes, or when I use the same paper for the same class again the following year. I've never worried much about a recycled essay being recognized: the pay for teaching assistants is low enough, and the burnout rate high enough, that the odds are substantially against the same person reading and grading papers for the same course two years in a row. Some topics just seem to beg for recycling: freshmen are forever being asked to mull over the roles of determinism, hubris, and moral responsibility in the Oedipus cycle; sociology and philosophy majors, the ethics of abortion. There are essays on shantytowns in developing countries, export-oriented economies in developing countries, structural adjustment in developing countries, and one only has to make the obvious case that the three are interrelated to be able to extend the possibilities for parts of essays in any of those three categories to resurface magically within another. Other essays can be recycled with just a little tinkering to surmount minor differences in topic or in emphasis: for instance, "Italian Fascists in North America," to which "The Italian-Canadian Family" lends itself nicely; "Taboo-Breaking in Racine and Ford," which re-emerges, after minor cosmetic surgery, as "Master-Slave Relationships in Ford and Racine: What They Tell Us About Lust, Fate, and Obligation." And so on.

FEBRUARY 15. I'm sitting on the floor with a pile of old magazines, cutting out pictures of Oreo cookies and Wendy's burgers. This is Andy's essay. It's not an essay, actually, it's a food bingo chart. I have to find a large sheet of cardboard, divide it into squares, and glue on pictures of what is recognizably food. Andy is another education student: he wants to teach junior kindergarten, and his assignment is, apparently, to teach the little tots where food comes from, or what it is, or that advertising is a vital component of each of the four basic food groups, or something. I come into Tailormade with food bingo under my arm. I've gotten some strange looks on the subway. It nets me twenty-five bucks.

MARCH 7. I was supposed to turn in an essay today, one I don't have. I fell asleep at the keyboard last night and accidentally slept through the whole night, headphones and all.

MARCH 16. There's a regular customer whose course load would be appropriate for the résumé of a U.N. secretary general. She's taking several courses on developing economies, including one referred to by other clients in the same class as "Third World Women." And one on the history of black Americans from Reconstruction to the present. I wrote her a twenty-five-page history of the early years of the civil-rights movement. She was sitting in the office when I handed it in. "Interesting course, isn't it?" she asked. She requested me again. I wrote her a paper on Costa Rica, one on dowry murders in India, one on the black leader W. E. B. Du Bois. "It's a great course, isn't it?" she asked me when she got the paper on dowry murders. "He seems like a fascinating guy," she said the day she collected W. E. B. Du Bois. "Somebody told me he wound up in *Ghana.*" Today I take a shortcut across the university campus on my way to the essay service and see her with a group of other students. I make a direct beeline for her and I smile. I watch her blanch, look around, try to decide whether to pretend not to know me, decide that maybe that isn't a good idea. She gives me a stricken look and a big toothy grin.

MARCH 26. One day I'm given five pages on the Treaty of Versailles. Last year at the same time, I was assigned a paper on the same topic. A memorable paper. Two days after I turned it in, there was a camera crew outside. It turned out to be the local cable station for kids, doing an "exposé" on cheating. We taped it when it came on. It featured kids sitting in shadow, faces obscured, *60 Minutes* style.

"There she is, the little rat," Sylvia glowered at the time. The pretty young fake client handed my paper to some professor sitting behind a desk and asked, "What do you think about this? Is it better or worse than what you would normally get? Would you assume that it was a real paper or one that had been bought?"

"Well . . . it's a *credible* paper," said the professor. "I mean, one *wouldn't* think it was . . . *synthetic* unless one had reason to."

"What kind of grade would you give it?"

"Oh, I'd give it . . . a B minus."

"Please." I was really offended. Elliott comforted me. "Well, he has to say that. Now that he knows it's ours, he can't admit it's an A paper even if he wants to."

We all sat tight and waited for every professor within fifty miles to call us, threatening death. But professors don't watch cable shows for teenagers; neither do ambitious young teaching assistants. Instead, the show turned out to be a free advertising bonanza. Soon the phone rang off the hook with kids calling up and asking, "You mean, like, you can write my term paper for me if I pay you?"

APRIL 16. Today, working on a paper I was reminded that there *are* good professors. They're the ones who either convince the kids the course content is inherently interesting and get them to work hard on the assignments or who figure out ways to make the assignments, at least, creative events to enjoy. But students with shaky language skills falter at surprises, even good ones; lazy students farm the assignments out no matter what they are. Such assignments are oddly comforting for me: I can almost pretend the two of us are talking over the clients' heads. When I'm alone in my room, in front of the computer and between the headphones, it's hard not to want to write something good for myself and maybe even for the imaginary absentee professor or appreciative T. A., something that will last. But when I'm standing in the crowded Tailormade office, next to someone elegant and young and in eight hundred bucks' worth of calfskin leather, someone who not only has never heard of John Stuart Mill and never read *Othello* but doesn't even know he hasn't, doesn't even mind that he hasn't, and doesn't even care that he hasn't, the urge to make something that will last somehow vanishes.

APRIL 28. The semester is almost at an end. Exams have started; the essays have all been handed in. Elliott and Russell begin their summer jobs as bike couriers. Henry, like me, is illegal; but he confides to me that he's had enough. "You can only do so much of this," he says. I know, I tell him. I know.

*F*rederick Douglas (1817?–1895) was born into slavery in Talbot County, Maryland. He escaped slavery in 1838 to become the leading Negro in the antislavery movement and, after the Civil War, in the fight for Negro rights. He wrote three autobiographies, at different stages of his life. He was famous as an antislavery orator and, during the Civil War, helped recruit Negro soldiers and served as an advisor to Abraham Lincoln. After the war he remained active in the fight to secure and protect the rights of Negroes.

Learning to Read and Write

Frederick Douglass

I lived in Master Hugh's family about seven years. During this time, I succeeded in learning to read and write. In accomplishing this, I was compelled to resort to various stratagems. I had no regular teacher. My mistress, who kindly commenced to instruct me, had, in compliance with the advice and direction of her husband, not only ceased to instruct, but had set her face against my being instructed by any one else. It is due, however, to my mistress to say of her, that she did not adopt this course of treatment immediately. She at first lacked the depravity indispensable to shutting me up in mental darkness. It was at least necessary for her to have some training in the exercise of irresponsible power, to make her equal to the task of treating me as though I were a brute.

My mistress was, as I have said, a kind and tender-hearted woman; and in the simplicity of her soul she commenced, when I first went to live with her, to treat me as she supposed one human being ought to treat another. In entering upon the duties of a slaveholder, she did not seem to perceive that I sustained to her the relation of a mere chattel, and that for her to treat me as a human being was not only wrong, but dangerously so. Slavery proved as injurious to her as it did to me. When I went there, she was a pious, warm, and tender-hearted woman. There was no sorrow or suffering for which she had not a tear. She had bread for the hungry, clothes for the naked, and comfort for every mourner that came within her reach. Slavery soon proved its ability to divest her of these heavenly qualities. Under its influence, the tender heart became stone, and the lamb-like disposition gave way to one of tiger-like fierceness. The first step in her downward course was in her ceasing to instruct me. She now commenced to practise her husband's precepts. She finally became even more violent in her opposition than her husband himself. She was not satisfied with simply doing as well as he had commanded; she seemed anxious to do better. Nothing seemed to make her more angry than to see me with a newspaper. She seemed to think that here lay the danger. I have had her rush at me with a face made all up of fury, and snatch from me a newspaper, in a manner that fully revealed her apprehension. She was an apt woman; and a little experience soon demonstrated, to her satisfaction, that education and slavery were incompatible with each other.

From this time I was most narrowly watched. If I was in a separate room any considerable length of time, I was sure to be suspected of having a book, and was at once called to give an account of myself. All this, however, was too late. The first step had been taken. Mistress, in teaching me the alphabet, had given me the *inch*, and no precaution could prevent me from taking the *ell*.

The plan which I adopted, and the one by which I was most successful, was that of making friends of all the little white boys whom I met in the street. As many of these as I could, I converted into teachers. With their kindly aid, obtained at different times and in different places, I finally succeeded in learning to read. When I was sent on errands, I always took my book with me, and by doing one part of my errand quickly I found time to get a lesson before my return. I used also to carry bread with me, enough of which was always in the house, and to which I was always welcome; for I was much better off in this regard than many of the poor white children in our neighborhood. This bread I used to bestow upon the hungry little urchins, who, in return, would give me that more valuable bread of knowledge. I am strongly tempted to give the names of two or three of those little boys, as a testimonial of the gratitude and affection I bear them; but prudence forbids;—not that it would injure me, but it might embarrass them; for it is almost an unpardonable offence to teach slaves to read in this Christian country. It is enough to say of the dear little fellows, that they lived on Philpot Street, very near Durgin and Bailey's shipyard. I used to talk this matter of slavery over with them. I would sometimes say to them, I wished I could be as free as they would be when they got to be men. "You will be free as soon as you are twenty-one, *but I am a slave for life!* Have not I as good a right to be free as you have?" These words used to trouble them; they would express for me the liveliest sympathy, and console me with the hope that something would occur by which I might be free.

I was now about twelve years old, and the thought of being *a slave for life* began to bear heavily upon my heart. Just about this time, I got hold of a book entitled "The Columbian Orator." Every opportunity I got, I used to read this book. Among much of other interesting matter, I found in it a dialogue between a master and his slave. The slave was represented as having run away from his master three times. The dialogue represented the conversation which took place between them, when the slave was retaken the third time. In this dialogue, the whole argument in behalf of slavery was brought forward by the master, all of which was disposed of by the slave. The slave was made to say some very smart as well as impressive things in reply to his master—things which had the desired though unexpected effect; for the conversation resulted in the voluntary emancipation of the slave on the part of the master.

In the same book, I met with one of Sheridan's mighty speeches on and in behalf of Catholic emancipation. These were choice documents to me. I read them over and over again with unabated interest. They gave tongue to interesting thoughts of my own soul, which had frequently flashed through my mind, and died away for want of utterance. The moral which I gained from the dialogue was the power of truth over the conscience of even a slaveholder. What I got from Sheridan was a bold denunciation of slavery, and a powerful vindication of human rights. The reading of these documents enabled me to utter my thoughts, and to meet the arguments brought forward to sustain slavery; but while they relieved me of one difficulty, they brought another even more painful than the one of which I was relieved. The more I read, the more I was led to abhor and detest my enslavers. I could regard them in no other light than a band of successful robbers, who had left their homes, and gone to Africa, and stolen us from our homes, and in a strange land reduced us to slavery. I loathed them as being the meanest as well as the most wicked of men. As I read and contemplated the subject, behold! that very discontentment which Master Hugh had predicted would follow my learning to read had already come, to torment and sting my soul to unutterable anguish. As I writhed under it, I would at times feel that learning to read had been a curse rather than a blessing. It had given me a view of my wretched condition, without the remedy. It opened my eyes to the horrible pit, but to no ladder upon which to get out. In moments of agony, I envied my fellow-slaves for their stupidity. I have often wished myself a beast. I preferred the condition of the meanest reptile to my own. Any thing, no matter what, to get rid of thinking! It was this everlasting thinking of my condition that tormented me. There was no getting rid of it. It was pressed upon me by every object within sight or hearing, animate or inanimate. The silver trump of freedom had roused my soul to eternal wakefulness. Freedom now appeared, to disappear no more forever. It was heard in every sound, and seen in every thing. It was ever present to torment me with a sense of my wretched condition. I saw nothing without seeing it, I heard nothing without hearing it, and felt nothing without feeling it. It looked from every star, it smiled in every calm, breathed in every wind, and moved in every storm.

I often found myself regretting my own existence, and wishing myself dead; and but for the hope of being free, I have no doubt but that I should have killed myself, or done something for which I should have been killed. While in this state of mind, I was eager to hear anyone speak of slavery. I was a ready listener. Every little while, I could hear something about the abolitionists. It was some time before I found what the word meant. It was always used in such connections to make it an interesting word to me. If a slave ran away and succeeded in getting clear; or if a slave killed his master, set fire to a barn, or did anything wrong in the mind of a slaveholder, it was spoken of as the fruit of *abolition*. Hearing the word in this connection very often, I set about learning what it meant. The dictionary afforded me little or no help. I found it was "the act of abolishing;" but then I did not know what was to be abolished. Here I was perplexed. I did not dare to ask any one about its meaning, for I was satisfied that it was something they wanted me to know very little about. After a patient waiting, I got one of our city papers, containing an account of the number of petitions from the north, praying for the abolition of slavery in the District of Columbia, and of the slave trade between the States. From this time I understood the words *abolition* and *abolitionist*, and always drew near when that word was spoken, expecting to hear something of importance to myself and fellow-slaves. The light broke in upon me by degrees. I went one day down on the wharf of Mr. Waters; and seeing two Irishmen unloading a scow of stone, I went, unasked, and helped them. When we had finished, one of them came to me and asked me if I were a slave. I told him I was. He asked, "Are ye a slave for life?" I told him that I was. The good Irishman seemed to be deeply affected by the statement. He said to the other that it was a pity so fine a fellow as myself should be a slave for life. He said it was a shame to hold me. They both advised me to run away to the north; that I should find friends there, and that I should be free. I pretended not to be interested in what they said, and treated them as if I did not understand them; for I feared they might be treacherous. White men have been known to encourage slaves to escape, and then, to get the reward, catch them and return them to their masters. I was afraid that these seemingly good men might use me so; but I nevertheless remembered their advice, and from that time I resolved to run away. I looked forward to a time at which it would be safe for me to escape. I was too young to think of doing so immediately; besides, I wished to learn how to write, as I might have occasion to write my own pass. I consoled myself with the hope that I should one day find a good chance. Meanwhile, I would learn to write.

The idea as to how I might learn to write was suggested to me by being in Durgin and Bailey's ship-yard, and frequently seeing the ship carpenters, after hewing, and getting a piece of timber ready for use, write on the timber the name of that part of the ship for which it was intended. When a piece of timber was intended for the larboard side, it would be marked thus—"L." When a piece was for the starboard side, it would be marked thus—"S." A piece for the larboard side forward, would be marked thus—"L. F." When a piece was for starboard side forward, it would be marked thus—"S. F." For larboard aft, it would be marked thus—"L. A." For starboard aft, it would be marked thus—"S. A." I soon learned the names of these letters, and for what they were intended when placed upon a piece of timber in the shipyard. I immediately commenced copying them, and in a short time was able to make the four letters named. After that, when I met with any boy who I knew could write, I would tell him I could write as well as he. The next word would be, "I don't believe you. Let me see you try it." I would then make the letters which I had been so fortunate as to learn, and ask him to beat that. In this way I got a good many lessons in writing, which it is quite possible I should never have gotten in any other way. During this time, my copy-book was the board fence, brick wall, and pavement; my pen and ink was a lump of chalk. With these, I learned mainly how to write. I then commenced and continued copying the Italics in Webster's Spelling Book, until I could make them all without looking on the book. By this time, my little Master Thomas had gone to school, and learned how to write, and had written over a number of copy-books. These had been brought home, and shown to some of our near neighbors, and then laid aside. My mistress used to go to class meeting at the Wilk Street meeting-house every Monday afternoon, and leave me to take care of the house. When left thus, I used to spend the time in writing in the spaces left in Master Thomas's copy-book, copying what he had written. I continued to do this until I could write a hand very similar to that of Master Thomas. Thus, after a long, tedious effort for years, I finally succeeded in learning how to write.

*R*ichard Wright (1908–1960) was the first black author of a best seller, Native
Son (1940). He was born near Natchez, Mississippi. He had a difficult life
including extreme poverty and an education that did not go beyond junior high.
Black Boy, an autobiographical work, is considered his best work. His writing
affirms the dignity and humanity of society's outcasts and indicts those who have
cast them out.

The Library Card

Richard Wright

One morning I arrived early at work and went into the bank lobby
where the Negro porter was mopping. I stood at a counter and picked up
the Memphis *Commercial Appeal* and began my free reading of the press.
I came finally to the editorial page and saw an article dealing with one H.
L. Mencken. I knew by hearsay that he was the editor of the *American
Mercury*, but aside from that I knew nothing about him. The article was a
furious denunciation of Mencken, concluding with one, hot, short sentence: Mencken is a fool.

I wondered what on earth this Mencken had done to call down upon
him the scorn of the South. The only people I had ever heard denounced
in the South were Negroes, and this man was not a Negro. Then what
ideas did Mencken hold that made a newspaper like the *Commercial
Appeal* castigate him publicly? Undoubtedly he must be advocating ideas
that the South did not like. Were there, then, people other than Negroes
who criticized the South? I knew that during the Civil War the South had
hated northern whites, but I had not encountered such hate during my
life. Knowing no more of Mencken than I did at that moment, I felt a
vague sympathy for him. Had not the South, which had assigned me the
role of a non-man, cast at him its hardest words?

Now, how could I find out about this Mencken? There was a huge
library near the riverfront, but I knew that Negroes were not allowed to
patronize its shelves any more than they were the parks and playgrounds
of the city. I had gone into the library several times to get books for the
white men on the job. Which of them would now help me to get books?
And how could I read them without causing concern to the white men with
whom I worked? I had so far been successful in hiding thoughts and feelings from them, but I knew that I would create hostility if I went about
this business of reading in a clumsy way.

I weighed the personalities of the men on the job. There was Don, a Jew; but I distrusted him. His position was not much better than mine and I knew that he was uneasy and insecure; he had always treated me in an offhand, bantering way that barely concealed his contempt. I was afraid to ask him to help me to get books; his frantic desire to demonstrate a racial solidarity with the whites against Negroes might make him betray me.

Then how about the boss? No, he was a Baptist and I had the suspicion that he would not be quite able to comprehend why a black boy would want to read Mencken. There were other white men on the job whose attitudes showed clearly that they were Kluxers or sympathizers, and they were out of the question.

There remained only one man whose attitude did not fit into an anti-Negro category, for I had heard the white men refer to him as a "Pope lover." He was an Irish Catholic and was hated by the white Southerners. I knew that he read books, because I had got him volumes from the library several times. Since he, too, was an object of hatred, I felt that he might refuse me but would hardly betray me. I hesitated, weighing and balancing the imponderable realities.

One morning I paused before the Catholic fellow's desk.

"I want to ask you a favor," I whispered to him.

"What is it?"

"I want to read. I can't get books from the library. I wonder if you'd let me use your card?"

He looked at me suspiciously.

"My card is full most of the time," he said.

"I see," I said and waited, posing my question silently.

"You're not trying to get me into trouble, are you, boy?" he asked, staring at me.

"Oh, no, sir."

"What book do you want?"

"A book by H. L. Mencken."

"Which one?"

"I don't know. Has he written more than one?"

"He has written several."

"I didn't know that."

"What makes you want to read Mencken?"

"Oh, I just saw his name in the newspaper," I said.

"It's good of you to want to read," he said. "But you ought to read the right things."

I said nothing. Would he want to supervise my reading?

"Let me think," he said. "I'll figure out something."

I turned from him and he called me back. He stared at me quizzically.

"Richard, don't mention this to the other white men," he said.

"I understand," I said. "I won't say a word."

A few days later he called me to him.

"I've got a card in my wife's name," he said. "Here's mine."

"Thank you, Sir."

"Do you think you can manage it?"

"I'll manage fine," I said.

"If they suspect you, you'll get in trouble," he said.

"I'll write the same kind of notes to the library that you wrote when you sent me for books," I told him. "I'll sign your name."

He laughed.

"Go ahead. Let me see what you get," he said.

That afternoon I addressed myself to forging a note. Now, what were the names of books written by H. L. Mencken? I did not know any of them. I finally wrote what I thought would be a foolproof note: *Dear Madam: Will you please let this nigger boy*—I used the word "nigger" to make the librarian feel that I could not possibly be the author of the note—*have some books by H. L. Mencken?* I forged the white man's name.

I entered the library as I had always done when on errands for whites, but I felt that I would somehow slip up and betray myself. I doffed my hat, stood a respectful distance from the desk, looked as unbookish as possible, and waited for the white patrons to be taken care of. When the desk was clear of people, I still waited. The white librarian looked at me.

"What do you want, boy?"

As though I did not possess the power of speech, I stepped forward and simply handed her the forged note, not parting my lips.

"What books by Mencken does he want?" she asked.

"I don't know, ma'am," I said, avoiding her eyes.

"Who gave you this card?"

"Mr. Falk," I said.

"Where is he?"

"He's at work, at the M——Optical Company," I said. "I've been in here for him before."

"I remember," the woman said. "But he never wrote notes like this."

Oh, God, she's suspicious. Perhaps she would not let me have the books? If she had turned her back at that moment, I would have ducked out the door and never gone back. Then I thought of a bold idea.

"You can call him up, ma'am," I said, my heart pounding.

"You're not using these books, are you?" she asked pointedly.

"Oh, no, ma'am. I can't read."

"I don't know what he wants by Mencken," she said under her breath.

I knew now that I had won; she was thinking of other things and the race question had gone out of her mind. She went to the shelves. Once or twice she looked over her shoulder at me, as though she was still doubtful. Finally she came forward with two books in her hand.

"I'm sending him two books," she said. "But tell Mr. Falk to come in next time, or send me the names of the books he wants. I don't know what he wants to read."

I said nothing. She stamped the card and handed me the books. Not daring to glance at them, I went out of the library, fearing that the woman would call me back for further questioning. A block away from the library I opened one of the books and read a title: *A Book of Prefaces*. I was nearing my nineteenth birthday and I did not know how to pronounce the word "preface." I thumbed the pages and saw strange words and strange names. I shook my head, disappointed, looked at the other book; it was called *Prejudices*. I knew what that word meant; I had heard it all my life. And right off I was on guard against Mencken's books. Why would a man want to call a book *Prejudices?* The word was so stained with all my memories of racial hate that I could not conceive of anybody using it for a title. Perhaps I had made a mistake about Mencken? A man who had prejudices must be wrong.

When I showed the books to Mr. Falk, he looked at me and frowned.

"That librarian might telephone you," I warned him.

"That's all right," he said. "But when you're through reading those books, I want you to tell me what you get out of them."

That night in my rented room, while letting the hot water run over my can of pork and beans in the sink, I opened *A Book of Prefaces* and began to read. I was jarred and shocked by the style, the clear, clean, sweeping sentences. Why did he write like that? And how did one write like that? I pictured the man as a raging demon, slashing with his pen, consumed with hate, denouncing everything American, extolling everything European or German, laughing at the weaknesses of people, mocking God, authority. What was this? I stood up, trying to realize what reality lay behind the meaning of the words. . . . Yes, this man was fighting, fighting with words. He was using words as a weapon, using them as one would use a club. Could words be weapons? Well, yes, for here they were. Then, maybe, perhaps, I could use them as a weapon? No. It frightened me. I read on and what amazed me was not what he said, but how on earth anybody had the courage to say it.

Occasionally I glanced up to reassure myself that I was alone in the room. Who were these men about whom Mencken was talking so passionately? Who was Anatole France? Joseph Conrad? Sinclair Lewis, Sherwood Anderson, Dostoevski, George Moore, Gustave Flaubert, Maupassant, Tolstoy, Frank Harris, Mark Twain, Thomas Hardy, Arnold Bennett, Stephen Crane, Zola, Norris, Gorky, Bergson, Ibsen, Balzac, Bernard Shaw, Dumas, Poe, Thomas Mann, O. Henry, Dreiser, H. G. Wells, Gogol, T. S. Eliot, Gide, Baudelaire, Edgar Lee Masters, Stendhal, Turgenev, Huneker, Nietzsche, and scores of others? Were these men real? Did they exist or had they existed? And how did one pronounce their names?

I ran across many words whose meanings I did not know, and I either looked them up in a dictionary or, before I had a chance to do that, encountered the word in a context that made its meaning clear. But what strange world was this? I concluded the book with the conviction that I had somehow overlooked something terribly important in life. I had once tried to write, had once reveled in feeling, had let my crude imagination roam, but the impulse to dream had been slowly beaten out of me by experience. Now it surged up again and I hungered for books, new ways of looking and seeing. It was not a matter of believing or disbelieving what I read, but of feeling something new, of being affected by something that made the look of the world different.

As dawn broke I ate my pork and beans, feeling dopey, sleepy. I went to work, but the mood of the book would not die; it lingered, coloring everything I saw, heard, did. I now felt that I knew what the white men were feeling. Merely because I had read a book that had spoken of how they lived and thought, I identified myself with that book. I felt vaguely guilty. Would I, filled with bookish notions, act in a manner that would make the whites dislike me?

I forged more notes and my trips to the library became more frequent. Reading grew into a passion. My first serious novel was Sinclair Lewis's *Main Street*. It made me see my boss, Mr. Gerald, and identify him as an American type. I would smile when I saw him lugging his golf bags into the office. I had always felt a vast distance separating me from the boss, and now I felt closer to him, though still distant. I felt now that I knew him, that I could feel the very limits of his narrow life. And this had happened because I had read a novel about a mythical man called George F. Babbitt.

The plots and stories in the novels did not interest me so much as the point of view revealed. I gave myself over to each novel without reserve, without trying to criticize it; it was enough for me to see and feel something different. And for me, everything was something different. Reading was like a drug, a dope. The novels created moods in which I lived for days. But I could not conquer my sense of guilt, my feeling that the white men around me knew that I was changing, that I had begun to regard them differently.

Whenever I brought a book to the job, I wrapped it in newspaper—a habit that was to persist for years in other cities and under other circumstances. But some of the white men pried into my packages when I was absent and they questioned me.

"Boy, what are you reading those books for?"

"Oh, I don't know, sir."

"That's deep stuff you're reading, boy."

"I'm just killing time, sir."

"You'll addle your brains if you don't watch out."

I read Dreiser's *Jennie Gerhardt* and *Sister Carrie* and they revived in me a vivid sense of my mother's suffering; I was overwhelmed. I grew silent, wondering about the life around me. It would have been impossible for me to have told anyone what I derived from these novels, for it was nothing less than a sense of life itself. All my life had shaped me for the realism, the naturalism of the modern novel, and I could not read enough of them.

Steeped in new moods and ideas, I bought a ream of paper and tried to write; but nothing would come, or what did come was flat beyond telling. I discovered that more than desire and feeling were necessary to write and I dropped the idea. Yet I still wondered how it was possible to know people sufficiently to write about them? Could I ever learn about life and people? To me, with my vast ignorance, my Jim Crow station in life, it seemed a task impossible of achievement. I now knew what being a Negro meant. I could endure the hunger. I had learned to live with hate. But to feel that there were feelings denied me, that the very breath of life itself was beyond my reach, that more than anything else hurt, wounded me. I had a new hunger.

In buoying me up, reading also cast me down, made me see what was possible, what I had missed. My tension returned, new, terrible, bitter, surging, almost too great to be contained. I no longer *felt* that the world about me was hostile, killing; I *knew* it. A million times I asked myself what I could do to save myself, and there were no answers. I seemed forever condemned, ringed by walls.

I did not discuss my reading with Mr. Falk, who had lent me his library card; it would have meant talking about myself and that would have been too painful. I smiled each day, fighting desperately to maintain my old behavior, to keep my disposition seemingly sunny. But some of the white men discerned that I had begun to brood.

"Wake up there, boy!" Mr. Olin said one day.

"Sir!" I answered for the lack of a better word.

"You act like you've stolen something," he said.

I laughed in the way I knew he expected me to laugh, but I resolved to be more conscious of myself, to watch my every act, to guard and hide the new knowledge that was dawning within me.

If I went north, would it be possible for me to build a new life then? But how could a man build a life upon vague, unformed yearnings? I wanted to write and I did not even know the English language. I bought English grammars and found them dull. I felt that I was getting a better sense of the language from novels than from grammars. I read hard, discarding a writer as soon as I felt that I had grasped his point of view. At night the printed page stood before my eyes in sleep.

Mrs. Moss, my landlady, asked me one Sunday morning:

"Son, what is this you keep on reading?"

"Oh, nothing. Just novels."

"What you get out of 'em?"

"I'm just killing time," I said.

"I hope you know your own mind," she said in a tone which implied that she doubted if I had a mind.

I knew of no Negroes who read the books I liked and I wondered if any Negroes ever thought of them. I knew that there were Negro doctors, lawyers, newspapermen, but I never saw any of them. When I read a Negro newspaper I never caught the faintest echo of my preoccupation in its pages. I felt trapped and occasionally, for a few days, I would stop reading. But a vague hunger would come over me for books, books that opened up new avenues of feeling and seeing, and again I would forge another note to the white librarian. Again I would read and wonder as only the naive and unlettered can read and wonder, feeling that I carried a secret, criminal burden about with me each day.

That winter my mother and brother came and we set up housekeeping, buying furniture on the installment plan, being cheated and yet knowing no way to avoid it. I began to eat warm food and to my surprise found the regular meals enabled me to read faster. I may have lived through many illnesses and survived them, never suspecting that I was ill. My brother obtained a job and we began to save toward the trip north, plotting our time, setting tentative dates for departure. I told none of the white men on the job that I was planning to go north: I knew that the moment they felt I was thinking of the North they would change toward me. It would have made them feel that I did not like the life I was living, and because my life was completely conditioned by what they said or did, it would have been tantamount to challenging them.

I could calculate my chances for life in the South as a Negro fairly clearly now.

I could fight the southern whites by organizing with other Negroes, as my grandfather had done. But I knew that I could never win that way; there were many whites and there were but few blacks. They were strong and we were weak. Outright black rebellion could never win. If I fought openly I would die and I did not want to die. News of lynchings were frequent.

I could submit and live the life of a genial slave, but that was impossible. All of my life had shaped me to live by my own feelings, and thoughts. I could make up to Bess and marry her and inherit the house. But that, too, would be the life of a slave; if I did that, I would crush to death something within me, and I would hate myself as much as I knew the whites already hated those who had submitted. Neither could I ever willingly present myself to be kicked, as Shorty had done. I would rather have died than do that.

I could drain off my restlessness by fighting with Shorty and Harrison. I had seen many Negroes solve the problem of being black by transferring their hatred of themselves to others with a black skin and fighting them. I would have to be cold to do that, and I was not cold and I could never be.

I could, of course, forget what I had read, thrust the whites out of my mind, forget them; and find release from anxiety and longing in sex and alcohol. But the memory of how my father had conducted himself made that course repugnant. If I did not want others to violate my life, how could I voluntarily violate it myself?

I had no hope whatever of being a professional man. Not only had I been so conditioned that I did not desire it, but the fulfillment of such an ambition was beyond my capabilities. Well-to-do Negroes lived in a world that was almost as alien to me as the world inhabited by whites.

What, then, was there? I held my life in my mind, in my consciousness each day, feeling at times that I would stumble and drop it, spill it forever. My reading had created a vast sense of distance between me and the world in which I lived and tried to make a living, and that sense of distance was increasing each day. My days and nights were one long, quiet, continuously contained dream of terror, tension, and anxiety. I wondered how long I could bear it.

Section Two:

Journals, Memoirs, First-Person Accounts

*M*artha Martin *was the pseudonym of the wife of a gold prospector in Alaska. Her diary was discovered by a book editor in the 1950s; while it was not dated, it was probably written in the 1920s. In this excerpt, Martin shares how, injured and stranded alone in the Alaskan wilds, she gives birth to her baby. Some controversy exists, regarding the authenticity of the story.*

from O Rugged Land of Gold

Martha Martin

I killed a sea otter today. I actually did kill a sea otter. I killed him with the ax, dragged him home, and skinned him. I took his liver out, and ate part of it. I'm going to eat the rest of it, and his heart, too. His liver was quite large, bigger than a deer's, and it had more lobes to it. It was very good liver, and I enjoyed it.

Most of today was devoted to the sea otter; getting the hide off was a real task. It's a lovely skin, the softest, silkiest, thickest fur I have ever seen. I am going to make a robe for my baby out of the beautiful fur. My darling child may be born in a lowly cabin, but she shall be wrapped in one of the earth's most costly furs.

It was such a splendid piece of luck. Lucky in more ways than one. The otter might have killed me, although I have never heard of such a thing.

This morning I went to the woods to gather a load of limbs. As I was coming home with them, I saw the tide was nearly out, and I thought I'd walk over to the bar and take a look at the boat . . . I was going along, swinging the ax in my left hand, managing the crutch with the right hand, . . . not thinking of anything in particular, when right beside me I heard a bark. It was like a dog bark; not a bow-wow bark, more of a yip. I looked around and saw a huge creature reared up on its haunches. I saw its white teeth.

Without thinking, I swung the ax at the side of its head, saw it hit, felt the jar in my arm, heard the thud. As I swung the ax, I turned and tried to run. I was so terrified the thing would nab me from behind that I could hardly move. I glanced over my shoulder to see how close it was. It hadn't budged from where it dropped . . .

I got down on my knees and examined it from one end to the other. First off, I noticed the lovely fur. I took off my glove and ran my fingers through the nice silky coat. I decided right then I would have the skin. I saw it as a baby blanket . . .

It is very much against the law to kill a sea otter. Right now I don't care a rap for law. Id like to have a picture of a game warden who could arrest me now. I am safe enough from the law, and I think I always will be. Under the circumstances I doubt if any judge would send me to jail for what I have done . . .

I dragged my kill home, and was a long time doing so. I'll bet the creature weighed a hundred pounds. I worked and worked, rested, pulled, and dragged, rested some more, and by and by I reached the cabin with my prize . . .

I decided to skin it exactly the way the men do a deer. I have watched them many times, but I never helped or paid much attention. I didn't know very much about skinning a furbearing animal when I went to work on that creature. How I wished I had an Indian squaw to instruct and help me . . .

The head was a mess, so I just cut the skin at the neck line and let the head fur go. I chopped off the feet and threw them in the stove. After I got the legs and sides skinned, I turned the otter on his belly and worked the skin off his back down to the tail. I had more trouble with that tail than I did with all the rest of the animal, I wanted it for a neckpiece, and I tried to get the bony tail out without slitting the skin. It can't be done . . .

My hands got awful cold examining the innards, rather smelly, too. I had let the fire go down, and there wasn't enough hot water for me to scrub properly. I made up the fire, washed a little, and then sat down to rest and gloat over my wonderful sea-otter fur . . .

I woke up in the night, and felt rested, so I got up, lit the carbide lamp, and sat here writing all about my sea otter.

I had planned to work on my otter skin today, but when I looked out this morning I saw Old Nick was flaunting a plume [a sign that a cold wind was coming up] . . . I put all my energy into gathering wood and left the skin alone . . .

Goodness, I have lots of work to do before I am ready for my little darling. I must get the fur finished for her. I am determined my child shall have a priceless gift . . .

I've begun scraping off the fat from my otter skin, and it's about half done. I have learned a few things about scraping skins: they scrape better when they are stretched tight over the end of a block of wood, and the fat comes off easier when it is cold. Another thing, when a skin looks scraped, it still has lots of fat on it. I know I'll have to go over the whole hide at least twice . . .

At last I have finished scraping the otter skin. It is all very nicely done, and not one single hole did I cut in it . . . I am going to scrub it well in lots of warm soapy water . . .

Goodness me, I have more chores than a farmer . . .

Hurray! My otter skin is nailed to the door. It's the biggest thing— much bigger than I thought it was. It nearly covers the whole door . . .

The wind still howls, swirls, and rages. It's awful cold, maybe ten below. All the peaks look like volcanoes with their great trailing plumes . . . I brought in some more wood today, but I didn't stay out long. It was too cold and windy . . .

While I was out in the cold, my breasts ached. They drew up and the nipples stuck out firm, and they ached. When I came in I examined them, and found they were swelling and have water in them, not milk, but clear water. Soon my child will be here, and I am not yet ready to receive her. So much to do and so little time . . .

I have decided to burn the floor. I'll cut the part I have already taken up, now, and save the rest for reserve. There are seven sills, all logs ten to twelve inches through, under the floor, which is nailed to them. If I can dig around them, saw them in two, pry them out, and cut them into blocks, they'll make a lot of fine wood. They are yellow cedar, and so is the puncheon . . .

The otter skin is a disappointment. It's as hard as a board, and I'm just sick about it. I might make it into a Robinson Crusoe umbrella, but it can never become an infant's robe in its present stiff state. I remember reading or hearing that the Eskimoes chew skins to make them soft. It would take a lot of chewing to make this big skin soft. I just can't chew it, and I won't even try.

The fur is lovely, and it smells clean. I put my face in it, and it's the softest thing I've ever touched. I do wish the skin wasn't so stiff. There must be some way I can fix it. Baby must have one present.

If we were home she would have many gifts—a ring, a silver cup with her name on it, a necklace, a silver spoon, a baby book, dresses with lace and ribbons, fine soft, knitted things. Even in this northland she would have gifts if anyone knew we were here . . .

I believe I have found a way to soften the otter skin. I doubled over a corner of it, and it didn't break as I thought it might, so I folded it some more. No breaks. I kept on folding and creasing it, and now it is no longer board-like; but it's still a very long way from being as soft as I want it to be.

I washed a few clothes today. I want clean things for the coming of my child. Surely she will be here soon. I am getting things ready to receive her, and I have done a lot of sewing. Tomorrow I will bathe and make myself presentable for a newborn child . . .

I made a birth cloth today from one of Don's union suits. It is all wool and should serve nicely to wrap a newborn child in . . .

I plan to use string raveled from a flour sack to tie the cord. I boiled a piece to make sure it is clean . . .

I've worked again on the fur, and I'm pleased with the result. I used a different system—pulled it back and forth around the bunk pole. I admire the fur more and more, and I want so much to get it soft enough to use for my baby . . .

The milk case is pretty well filled with baby things. Don's shaving soap is in one of the pockets. Shaving soap should be good for baby. It seems right to bathe my child with her father's shaving soap . . .

Only a few more days now until I will have a child in my arms.

I have been working and working at the otter skin, and I am making progress . . . A dozen times a day I pick it up, rub a part of it between my hands, brush it, hold it to my face, hold it at arm's length to admire it . . .

The wind has died away. It is very much warmer, and a haze covers the sky. I went wood gathering and was delighted with my outing. I saw twenty-six deer, and I brought some boughs for the ones who will pay me a friendly call . . . Two ravens came to eat the otter. I wonder how they knew it was there . . . Maybe they smelled it. My thrush never comes back, and I liked it so much. Those mean old jays—I really shouldn't feed them a crumb . . .

I baked bread, lots of it, far more than I need for myself. The deers are fond of bread, and I thought I'd have an extra amount on hand. Five of them came today to bum a handout, and I didn't disappoint them. I think all of them have been here several times before, but I can be sure of only one—Sammy with the mark on his throat. He is the tamest of the lot, and knows me. He even eats out of my hand . . .

I pounded up my cast and put it on the floor with the gravel. It was quite hard, much harder than I thought. If I had fallen, the cast would have given my arm good protection. Now that my arm is well, I haven't worn the cast for weeks. I don't use my crutch any more, either, but I'm not disposing of it yet . . .

I always think of the child as a girl. What if it's a boy? Oh, it couldn't be . . .

This awful deep snow and hard cold is going to kill off much of our wild life. Poor creatures, what a pity they can't all be like bears and sleep the winter through. But then, what would I do without my friendly bums to come around and ask for bread and lick their chops at me?

Since the baby came down to live in the lower part of my abdomen, I have been constipated, and I don't like it. I think it's the cause of my swollen ankles. I had absolutely nothing here to correct it, so I looked around to see what the wilderness might provide, and hit on the idea of eating seaweed. Certainly it can be called roughage . . . I went along the beach and gathered a mess . . . I picked it over well, washed it thoroughly, and ate quite a lot—ate it raw. It wasn't too awful, but I certainly don't like the stuff. It was very effective, almost more effective than I desired it to be. I was busy all day with the honey bucket . . .

The otter skin is getting to be as soft as I want it to be. I have invented another way to soften it. I made a small mallet and gently pound the folded fur over a block of wood . . .

The fur is finished, and it's exactly as I wished it to be. I am very proud of it. So soft and warm—such a lovely thing. I shall wrap my baby in it when she goes for her outings, and we will walk pridefully along the beach . . .

Snow seals every crack, so I only burn a little wood when there is no wind, and open the door for air.

I have bathed and washed my head. My hair has grown about three inches and is as curly as can be.[1] I like short hair because it's so easy to wash and dry. I think I may keep it short and never again be bothered with hairpins . . .

My body is heavy, and my movements are slow and not too definite. I am becoming clumsy and awkward. I don't like it. Maybe I should sit down and just twiddle my thumbs until Baby comes. I do hope she comes before I use up all this water and burn all my wood . . .

I brought a few branches and put a bouquet of cedar and hemlock boughs on my windowsill and placed the finest of Don's ore specimens on either side of it. The window has a nice look, as though a man and a woman lived here . . .

There was a little show of blood, and when I saw it I remembered my mother saying it was a sure sign that the child would be born soon . . .

I have never seen a child born. I always felt inadequate to help and was too modest to want to be a spectator. I have never seen anything born—not even a cat . . . I am no longer afraid, yet I do wish someone were with me to help me take care of the child . . .

[Martha's child was born after two days of labor, during which she cooked, cared for herself and wrote recollections of life with her husband to try "to order my thoughts, be calm, and not bother my head about all I don't know." Again, she found herself able to cope alone, to deliver the child, to rest, to tie the cord, cut it, and then deliver the afterbirth. And the next day she went on with her narrative.]

My darling little girl-child, after such a long and troublesome waiting I now have you in my arms. I am alone no more. I have my baby.

I went outside for a short walk on the beach today. It's the first time
I've been out since the baby came. The tide was nearly low, and there were
dozens of deer on the beach, maybe forty or fifty, maybe as many as a hundred . . . Poor things, they are starving . . . I just can't let all the deer starve.
I can cut a little brush, maybe enough to keep some of them alive . . .

Several of them followed me back to the cabin and begged for food.
I fed them a little, and promised more. I promised to bake lots of bread
and make a feast . . . It will be the christening feast for the baptism of
Donnas. I'll invite the deer to come share our joy and gladness and our
food . . .

Yesterday was lovely. A beautiful late winter day with a bright sun
and a warm southerly breeze. It was a perfect christening day . . . When
the deer saw me go for a little walk and heard me call to them, they came,
and all went well.

Donnas was dressed in all her finery and wrapped in the otter robe,
only her little face showing deep down in the fur . . .

"Donnas Martin, I baptize thee in the name of the Father, and of the
Son, and of the Holy Ghost. Amen."

I dipped the tips of my fingers in the water and signed my child with
the sign of the cross. Then I threw more bread morsels to our guests,
whose attention had begun to wander . . .

I held my baby close, wrapped well in her fur robe, loved her and
talked to her. It's wondrous good to talk. It's been so long since I've
talked to anyone . . . I told her all about us.

"I'm the queen," I told her, "and you are the little princess. The cabin
is our palace. None are here to dare dispute our word."

I told her the deer are our helpers and our friends, our subjects and
our comfort, and they will give us food and clothing according to our
needs. I told her of the birds, the little ptarmigan, the geese, ducks,
grouse, and the kindly owl; the prankish ravens and the lordly eagle.
Told her of the fishes, the clams, and the mussels. Told her of the mink
and the otter, and the great brown bear with his funny, furry cub. Told her
of the forest and of the things it will give us; of roots, stems, leaves, and
berries, and the fun of gathering them; of the majestic mountain uprising

behind us with a vein of gold-bearing ore coming straight from its heart. Told her that all these things were ours to have and to rule over and care for. . . .

This afternoon I went out and cut brush for the deer. I left baby alone in the cabin, explaining that it was my duty as reigning queen to provide for my subjects. I told her famine was now on our land and I must go cut brush . . .

When deer are hungry, they behave differently than when well fed. When a deer is feeling good, he will look up for his food, at least some of the time; but when he is weak with hunger he looks down all the time. There's lots of browse within reach if they would only stretch their necks to get it, but they act stupid, and don't seem to know anything about the food within their reach. Perhaps they are too weak to stretch up: maybe they get dizzy looking up . . .

Half an hour before dark seven gray arctic geese came in and settled on the beach almost in front of the cabin. They are either sick or exhausted, or maybe they're tame geese. I went out to look at them, being careful not to frighten them away. I was ready to duck back into the cabin at the first sign of alarm. They didn't seem alarmed, and I went quite close to them. I then gave them food, and they paid no attention to me. Why should wild geese act so? Has something happened to me since my baby came?

This is the last piece of usable paper. But that doesn't matter, for I no longer have such need to write. I have no problems to ponder through . . . I am not lonely any more; I have my baby for company . . .

Soon someone will come and find us here . . .

Maybe the Indians will come to their fish camp . . .

The Indians have come, good, good Indians. Shy, fat, smelly, friendly, kindhearted Indians.

Early this morning Donnas and I were out on the beach, she getting the benefit of the warm spring sun, and I putting the finishing touches on the bottom of my overturned dinghy. I looked up from my work and saw two Indian canoes near the far side of the Arm.

I rushed to the cabin, grabbed my gun, and fired call shots. I shouted and waved. The canoes turned and started toward my shore.

Hurriedly I made up the fire and set coffee water to boil. I brought out my baby's best clothes and got her into them in a jiffy. I ran outside and waved, saw I had time, rushed back and prettied myself up.

The cabin was already clean, and there were fresh blueberry blossoms on the windowsill and on the table. I shook out the otter skin to fluff the fur, wrapped Donnas in it, and went to the water's edge. There we awaited our guests.

Both canoes grounded at about the same time, and right in front of me. For a little while we just looked at each other. I was all trembly, and it was hard to behave with dignity. After what seemed a rather long time, I did manage to say, "Good morning."

"Hello." A breathing space, then another "Hello."

"I'm glad to see you." That came a little easier.

"You bet," was the reply, and following a pause, "By golly."

There was a consultation in Siwash.

"Not dead?"

"No, not dead."

So the conversation went on until I had told my story. No one made a move to get out of the canoes, and it occurred to me they might be waiting politely for an invitation. I hastened to extend one, ending with, "And come see my baby." I held her out toward them.

They piled out, nineteen of them. They didn't seem to see the baby, or me either. All eyes were on the otter skin. There was much Siwash talk, then the spokesman fingered the fur. "Against law. You go jail."

They all laughed.

"Where you get otter?"

I pointed to the spot on the beach where I had killed the animal, then I acted out the part. That seemed to loosen my tongue, and I talked a streak. The Indians laughed and laughed. They came and fingered the fur, stroked it, looked at the underside.

Then an old squaw said, "Pret-ty good." Splendid words of praise . . .

I knew these poor people needed all the fish they could catch, and I hated to ask them to take time out to do anything for me, yet I thought I had been here long enough, so I asked to be taken to Big Sleeve.

"You bet," was the quick answer. But the west wind was blowing, and it would increase until sundown. It would be better to go in the morning . . .

I was glad for a little more time in my cabin. I almost didn't want to leave at all, I was so mixed up. . . .

Note

[1] Martha had treated her scalp wounds with bacon grease, but mice nibbled at the grease while she slept and she cut her hair to the roots.

Sylvia Ashton-Warner (1908–1984) became famous as a teacher because of her books Teacher *and* Spinster, *which are based on diaries that she kept while she taught Maori children in her native New Zealand.*

from Teacher

Sylvia Ashton-Warner

When I teach people, I marry them. I found this out last year when I began the orchestra. To do what I wanted them to do they had to need to be like me. More than that. They had to be part of me. As the season progressed the lesson began to teach itself to me. I found that for good performances we had to be one thing. One organ. And physically they had to be near to each other and to me. We had to bundle into a heap round the piano. I say "we had to," but that's not it. They *did* pile up round me at the piano, irrespective of what I tried to make them do. However, I arranged their seating to face the audience and with a view to each child being visible; nevertheless, at the end of the song, there they would all be, married all over and round me.

Rules like the best sound coming from a throat or instrument when facing the auditorium were just walked over. Although I didn't learn that thing until I heard the . . . *saw* the youth club sing a lament . . . They were too shy to face the gathering, so instinctively, they turned inward into a ring, seeing only one another. As for me, I learned this particular lesson once and for all. I know it now.

Now where was I? I was talking marriage with my orchestra. I would never have learned this through any other medium but music, I'm sure. I've never learned it all this time teaching. But now that I do know it I see it in other areas. There is quietly occurring in my infant room a grand espousal. To bring them to do what I want them to do they come near me, I draw them near me, in body and in spirit. They don't know it but I do. They become part of me, like a lover. The approach, little different. The askance observation first, the acceptance next, then the gradual or quick coming, until in the complete procuration, there glows the harmony, the peace.

94

And what is the birth? From the orchestra it is music, and from the infant room it is work. A long, perpetuating, never-ending, transmuting birth, beginning its labor every morning and a rest between pains every evening.

Now that I see this as espousal the prickly, difficult, obscured way clears. It's all so simple.

Tall words. Wild words. Grand words. But there is an even deeper meaning beneath it all. It's integration of my living. And integration of theirs.

All the rules of love-making apply to these spiritual and intellectual fusions. There must be only two, for instance. As soon as another allegiance pushes in, the first union breaks apart. Love interferes with fidelities. I can't teach in the true essential medium when that approaching face turns away to another interest. I have tried in the past to do this, before I knew what I know now, but the answer was grating, discord, and even hatred. When love turns away, now, I don't follow it. I sit and suffer, unprotesting, until I feel the tread of another step. . . .

Integration. That fatal, vital word continues to press upward before the inner eye. Married to the life about you. However small or however big the social horizon. For the environment at hand has little bearing on the expansion of the mind and spirit. . . .

I'm glad to know this at last, that to teach I need first to espouse. . . .

I've got so much to say that I'm going to stop trying to say it. This is the last lot of this diary. The level of it is rising over my head.

Its purpose has already been fulfilled. I was lonely, professionally. I wanted gifted, intimate understanding . . .

Before I stop I'll try to cover the very vital and organic pattern of my professional life over the last weeks. It's always when things happen that we have no time to record them. But I'll try to give the picture, the conglomeration of imagery that has been banking up before the inner eye, waiting and pushing for expression. And the order will be its own. An order of emotional importance.

Stronger than any other image in the world behind is one of Mr. Tremaine in my infant room last week saying to me softly, "I want to hear you speak." Through everything else I hear this. Right through the Ballet on Thursday evening, the evening of his visit, I heard this. True, he had

brought with him Professor ——— from the chair of ——— and Dr. ———
from the chair of ——— at ——— University College to meet me, but it
was this modest sentence of Mr. Tremaine's that remains the strongest
thought within. The strongest sensation.

He kept from me who the visitors were. They had come to see my
Maori primer books. They got me talking, Mr. Tremaine did, and these
two men I lectured from the infant-room table with all the fire of conviction I had in me on the results of my recent experiments with the Key
Vocabulary. . . .

"The way," I reproved Mr. Tremaine at morning tea . . . "you come
out here and make me talk. You make me talk! I talk everyone down for
an hour, then feel ashamed of it afterwards!"

He smiled in enjoyment. "I always find," he told us, "that if I keep
quiet I learn something."

"Are you important?" I asked the visitors.

"Oh no, no!"

"Well, as long as I know. I would have passed you your tea first.
Anyway Mr. Tremaine, I like your technique of dropping important people
on us. If I knew they were coming I'd never be here!"

He roared at this and I wondered what for. Some secret interpretation
he had. But as he shook my hand goodbye in the porch I said, "I'm attacking Maori delinquency."

"Thank you for all the work you are doing," he replied. "And I
enjoyed listening to you."

That was the day I gave him my Maori Infant Reading Scheme. He
stood in the cold outside, so very big and tall in his greatcoat, turning
over the pages . . . "Look at this," he said tenderly. Ah, the simple rapture
of fulfilment at my work being understood that cold morning. What
unutterable reward for my labor.

Emily Carr (1871–1945) was a famous Canadian artist whose passion was painting the Canadian wilderness. She studied painting in San Francisco, London and Paris and then returned to her home in Victoria, British Colombia. She finally gained recognition for her art in her sixties. At that time she began to devote herself to writing, working on a diary she began when she was fifty-six. It was published under the title Hundreds and Thousands.

from Hundreds and Thousands

Emily Carr

November 23rd, 1930

Yesterday I went to town and bought this book to enter scraps in, not a diary of statistics and dates and decency of spelling and happenings but just to jot me down in, unvarnished me, old me at fifty-eight—old, old, old, in most ways and in others just a baby with so much to learn and not much time left here but maybe somewhere else. It seems to me it helps to write things and thoughts down. It makes the unworthy ones look more shamefaced and helps to place the better ones for sure in our minds. It sorts out jumbled up thoughts and helps to clarify them, and I want my thoughts clear and straight for my work.

I used to write diaries when I was young but if I put anything down that was under the skin I was in terror that someone would read it and ridicule me, so I always burnt them up before long. Once my big sister found and read something I wrote at the midnight of a new year. I was sorry about the old year, I had seemed to have failed so, and I had hopes for the new. But when she hurled my written thoughts at me I was angry and humbled and hurt and I burst smarting into the New Year and broke all my resolutions and didn't care. I burnt the diary and buried the thoughts and felt the world was a mean, sneaking place. I wonder why we are always sort of ashamed of our best parts and try to hide them. We don't mind ridicule of our "sillinesses" but of our "sobers," oh! Indians are the same and even dogs. They'll enjoy a joke with you, but ridicule of their "reals" is torment.

When I returned from the East in 1927, Lawren Harris and I exchanged a few letters about work. They were the first real exchanges of thought in regard to work I had ever experienced. They helped wonderfully. He made many things clear, and the unaccustomed putting down of my own thoughts in black and white helped me to clarify them and to find out my own aims and beliefs. Later, when I went East this Spring, I found he had shown some of my letters to others. That upset me. After that I could not write so freely. Perhaps it was silly, but I could not write my innermost thoughts if *anybody* was to read them, and the innermost thoughts are the only things that count in painting. I asked him not to. He saw my point and said he wouldn't. I trust him and can now gabble freely. Still, even so, I can't write too often, hence this jotting book for odd thoughts and feelings.

July 16th, 1933

Once I heard it stated and now I believe it to be true that there is no true art without religion. The artist himself may not think he is religious but if he is sincere his sincerity in itself is religion. If something other than the material did not speak to him, and if he did not have faith in that something and also in himself, he would not try to express it. Every artist I meet these days seems to me to leak out the fact that somewhere inside him he is groping religiously for something, some in one way, some in another, tip-toeing, stretching up, longing for something beyond what he sees or can reach.

I wonder will death be much lonelier than life. Life's an awfully lonesome affair. You can live close against other people yet your lives never touch. You come into the world alone and you go out of the world alone yet it seems to me you are more alone while living than even going and coming. Your mother loves you like the deuce while you are coming. Wrapped up there under her heart is perhaps the cosiest time in existence. Then she and you are one, companions. At death again hearts loosen and realities peep out, but all the intervening years of living something shuts you up in a "yourself shell." You can't break through and get out; nobody can break through and get in. If there was an instrument strong enough to break the "self shells" and let out the spirit it would be grand. . . .

July 23rd

Dreams do come true sometimes. Caravans ran round inside of my head from the time I was no-high and read children's stories in which gypsies figured. Periodically I had caravan fever, drew plans like covered express carts drawn by a fat white horse. After horses went and motors came in I quit caravan dreaming, engines in no way appealing to me and my purse too slim to consider one anyhow. So I contented myself with shanties for sketching outings, cabins, tents, log huts, houseboats, tool sheds, lighthouses—many strange quarters. Then one day, plop! into my very mouth, like a great sugar plum for sweetness, dropped the caravan.

There it sat, grey and lumbering like an elephant, by the roadside— "For sale." I looked her over, made an offer, and she is mine. Greater even than the surprise of finding her was the fact that *nobody* opposed the idea but rather backed it up. We towed her home in the dark and I sneaked out of bed at 5 o'clock the next morning to make sure she was really true and not just a grey dream. Sure enough, there she sat, her square ugliness bathed in the summer sunshine, and I sang in my heart.

Now she's just about fixed up. She has no innards, that is works, so I'll have to be hauled. I've chosen the spot, Goldstream Flats, a lovely place. I'm aching to be off but not yet as nobody wants to go with me. I've asked one or two. I thought it would be nice to have someone to enthuse to, just for the first trip. With one accord they all made excuses except Henry. Poor Henry, who has lived twenty years and only developed nine when sleeping-sickness overwhelmed him and arrested his progress, like a clock whose hands have stuck though it goes on ticking—Henry *wants* to go along.

July 27th

Oh, these mountains! They won't bulk up. They are thin and papery. They won't brood like great sitting hens, squatting immovable, unperturbed, staring, guarding their precious secrets till something happens. At 'em again, old girl, they're worth the big struggle.

July 28th

. . . I have wiped out the village at the foot of the mountain. Now I shall paint the little cowed hollow that the village sits in and maybe toss the huts in last of all. It is the mountain I *must* express, all else subservient to that great dominating strength and spirit brooding there.

August 12th

. . . I thought my mountain was coming this morning. It began to move, it was near to speaking, when suddenly it shifted, sulked, returned to obscurity, to smallness. It has eluded me again and sits there, mean, puny, dull. Why? Did I lower my ideal? Did I carelessly bungle, pandering to the material instead of to the spiritual? . . .

August 19th

My van elephant is now a reality. While she sat there in the lot she was only a dream shaping itself. She was bought so suddenly after long years of waiting. It is two months from the morning that I got out of bed at 5 A.M. to peep out of the studio window and see if she was really there in the lot beneath. Then came all the fixings, meat safe, dog boxes and monkey-proof corner. And when she was ready, equipped in full, the hauler came and said that it was impossible to get her out of the lot because she was too low, and he was horrid and I was mad. "Well," I said, "if the man brought her 3,370 miles across the Rockies, surely she can be taken twelve miles to Goldstream Flats." And she was, but not by that old fool. The third who inspected ventured. The family sat on the creature crates and watched the tugging, heaving and wrenching. Sweat and cussings poured! Poor rat Susie was aboard and must have got severely jerked. The lid was off her box when we got there but Susie sweetly asleep within.

Henry and I and the animals drove in the truck. Whew, it was hot at the wood yard! The jacking-up blocks weren't ready. Then we stopped for the tires to be winded. We lumbered right through Government Street. Mercy, it was hot! And the delays were so numerous I patted my wallet and wondered if she was fat enough but they only charged the original $3.50 agreed upon. I was so thrilled that I "coned" and "ginger-popped" the man liberally when we got to the pop shop on the Flats.

It wasn't the spot I had picked, but the Elephant found it to her liking. The Elephant is a grand sitter but a heavy traveller.

Henry went all to pieces when we got there, not a steady nerve in his body. He hopped and wiggled and shook and stuttered. I ran hither and thither getting blocks and bricks and stones to aid the man in hoisting the Elephant off her tires. It was almost 5 P.M. when he left. The Elephant had chosen a favourite cow spot and much raking was necessary. This was accomplished with the aid of a row of rake teeth absolutely devoid of a handle. Everyone on the Flats collected to see us unpack, the monkey, of course, being the centre of attraction. The tent fly tormented me but I got it stuck up at last unaided. I made up the beds and prepared supper. Black fell down among the great cedars before I was nearly out of the mess.

Neither of us slept. I could hear Henry groaning and tossing under the tent. The creatures were all in the van with me and very good. The monkey is housed in a hollow cedar tree, cuddled into its very heart. Surely I have at last found her a habitation she *cannot* wreck. She'd have made matchwood of the Elephant. I ship-shaped up next morning and we are spick and span, very comfortable and very happy. Henry's nerves torment and wrack him a little less. There's a great peace under these magnificent cedars and the endless water sings its endless sound not a stone's throw off. I've made a range to rival any "Monarch" or "Canada's Pride" ever invented. The ingredients are a piece of automobile frame, the leg of a stove, a pile of rocks, scraps of iron, tin and wire, and parts of a gridiron. It's a peach!

Last night we slept like babies. Each creature has dropped into its own niche. The spirit of freemasonry and intimacy among us all is superb. It's wonderful to watch the joy of the pups playing tag among the cedars. There is a delicious little breeze bumming among the leaves without bluster or vulgarity. Today I love life, so do the four dogs, the monkey and the rat. And poor Henry; this must make up to him a little for all that he hasn't got in life.

Last night when the pop shop was shut and everyone was in bed I slipped into a nondescript garment and tumbled into the river. It was wonderful. I lay down on the stones and let the water ripple over me, clear, soft water that made the skin of you feel like something namelessly exquisite, even my sixty-year-old skin. When I had rubbed down and was between the sheets in the Elephant's innards, I felt like a million dollars, only much cleaner and sweeter and nicer. The precious pups were asleep all round, and rat Susie, Woo just outside the window in her hollow cedar, Henry in the tent lean-to. The cedars and pines and river all whispered soothingly, and there was life, life, life in the soft blackness of the night.

Today is wonderful again. Henry has found companionship with the pop lady's small boys. They are playing ball, all laughing. . . .

August 31st

A wet day in camp. The rain pattered on the top of the Elephant all night. Mrs. "Pop Shop" and I went for our nightly dip in the river. It was cold and took courage and much squealing and knee-shaking. Neither of us has the pluck to exhibit the bulges of our fat before the youngsters, so we "mermaid" after dark. I dare not *run* back; the footing among the cedars is ribbed with big roots. One's feet must pick and one's eyes must peer through the dim obscurity of the great cedars and maples. Once inside the Elephant, scrubbed down with a hard brush and cuddled up to a hot bottle, I thought I loved the whole world, I felt so good. But last night as I stood in my nightie and cap, a male voice made a howl and a male head thrust into the van. Well, all the love and charity fled from my soul. I was red hot and demanded his wants. By this time the dogs were in an uproar and I couldn't hear his answer. Finally I caught, "Can I get any bread?" "No," I replied tartly, "the shop is shut out there." He disappeared in the night and then I felt a beast and ran to the door to offer him what I had in camp but he had vanished, swallowed up in the black night. I might have been more tolerant, but I hate my privacy being torn up by the roots. I thought of that one word "bread" every time I awoke. . . .

September 5th

It started to rain last night and has rained all day. I packed Henry off home because his shelter was too slim. Anyhow he has had two good weeks. I had spent all day rearranging the camp for rain and snugging it up. I moved the "Monarch" range up close in front of the awning. The great cedar hangs over it and sheds off the rain. Woo in its innards is dry and cosy. She loves her cedar home. The woods are delightful in the rain, heavily veiled in mystery. They are delicious to *all* the senses but most to the smell. An owl came and sat on my cedar beside the fire. How I love it when the wild creatures pal up that way! The van is cosy, come rain, come shine, and all is well. Now Henry is gone I hope to try and work. Perhaps it wasn't Henry; maybe it was me. I care much too much for creature comforts and keeping the camp cosy and tidy. It seems necessary, especially with all the creatures. Mrs. Giles, the nursery woman, said that when her small boys went home and reported that there was a lady in the Flats in a house on wheels, with four dogs, a monkey and a rat, and a hopping boy, she thought it must be a section of a circus or travelling show. They also reported that when they came into my camp I chased them all off with a broom. I believe I was considerably tormented that first morning. How different you sound when described to what you feel!

September 8th

. . . I had thought this place somehow incongruous, the immensity of the old trees here and there not holding with the rest but belonging to a different era, to the forest primeval. There is no second growth, no in-between. It is too great a jump from immensity to the littleness of scrub brush. Today I see that I am what Whitman would call "making pictures with reference to parts" not with reference to "ensemble." The individual mighty trees stagger me. I become engaged with the figures and not the sum and so I get no further with my reckoning of the total. Nothing stands alone; each is only a part. A picture must be a portrayal of relationships. . . .

September 14th

I have found winter grazing for the Elephant after much tramping. It has settled in to pour. Mrs. Hooper supped in my camp and by the fire we sat long, talking. There is a straight-from-the-shoulderness about her I like. She does what comes to her hand to help people—reared a worse than parentless girl, looked after and helped old poor sick women. Through her conversation (not boastfully) ran a thread of kindness and real usefulness. I feel wormy when I see what others do for people and I doing so little. I try to work honestly at my job of painting but I don't see that it does anyone any good. If I could only feel that my painting lifted someone or gave them joy, but I don't feel that. I enjoy my striving to express. Another drinks because he enjoys drinking or eats because he enjoys eating. It's all selfish.

The rain is thundering on the van top. The creatures are all folded down in sleep, the park blackly wrapped about in that dense dark. There is a solidity about the black night in this little valley, as if you could cut slices out of it and pile them up. Not a light anywhere. The stream gargles as if it had a perpetual sore throat. A car passes up on the Malahat highway with a swift flash of light on this and that up above us and is gone like an unreality.

September 16th

After living for a whole month, or thereabouts, in a caravan and then to return to a two-storey house with six rooms all to oneself makes one feel as if one had straddled the whole world. The Elephant is bedded down opposite the Four Mile House in a quiet pasture. It is hard to settle down. The house feels stuffy and oppressive but the garden is joyful . . .

I have uncovered "The Mountain." It makes me sick. I am heavy in spirit over my painting. It is so lacking. What's the use? Sometimes I could quit paint and take to charring. It must be fine to clean perfectly, to shine and polish and *know* that it could not be done better. In painting that never occurs. . . .

October 5th

Oh, that mountain! I'm dead beat tonight with struggling. I repainted almost the whole show. It's still a bad, horrid, awful, mean little tussock. No strength, nobility, solidarity. I've been looking at A. Y. Jackson's mountains in the C.N.R. Jasper Park folder. Four good colour prints but they do not impress me. Now *I* could not do one tenth as well but somehow I don't *want* to do mountains like that. Shut up, me! Are you jealous and ungenerous? I don't think it is that.

October 6th

My mountain is dead. As soon as she has dried, I'll bury her under a decent layer of white paint and top her off with another picture. But I haven't done with the old lady; far from it. She's sprawling over a new clean canvas, her germ lives and is sprouting vigorously. My inner self said, "Start again and profit by your experience." Oh, if I could only make her throb into life, a living, moving mass of splendid power and volume!

October 17th

The mountain is finished, and the Brackendale landscape and the tree with moving background will be coffined tomorrow and away. They ought not to go out as pictures, finished. I feel them incomplete studies, just learners not show-ers. Will I ever paint a show-er, forgetting the paint and remembering the glory? I will not berate them. I have wrestled with them honestly, now I put them from me and push on to the next, carrying with me some bit of knowledge and growth acquired through them— on, up! Oh, the glory of growth, silent, mighty, persistent, inevitable! To awaken, to open up like a flower to the light of a fuller consciousness! I want to see and feel and expand, little book, you holder of my secrets.

December 12

Emily Carr, born Dec. 13, 1871, at Victoria B.C., 4 A.M., in a deep snow storm, tomorrow will be sixty-two. It is not all bad, this getting old, ripening. After the fruit has got its growth it should juice up and mellow. God forbid I should live long enough to ferment and rot and fall to the ground in a squash . . . .

April 6, 1934

. . . I'm a bit ashamed of being a little depressed again. Perhaps it is reading the autobiography of Alice B. Toklas—all the artists there in Paris, like all the artists in the East, jogging along, discussing, condemning, adoring, fighting, struggling, enthusing, *seeking* together, jostling each other, instead of solitude, no shelter, exposed to all the "winds" like a lone old tree with no others round to strengthen it against the buffets with no waving branches to help keep time. B-a-a-a-, old sheep, bleating for fellows. Don't you know better by now? It must be my fault somewhere, this repelling of mankind and at the same time rebelling at having no one to shake hands with but myself and the right hand weary of shaking the left. . . .

August 3rd

It's a long week since I told you anything, little book. Here's a secret first. Others might say it was silly. For the second time a soul has kissed my hand because of a picture of mine—once a man, once a woman. It makes one feel queer, half ashamed and very happy, that some thought you have expressed in paint has touched somebody. Today I sold a sketch and gave another, though of my very most recent. They always pick the newest and leave the old frowses. Ones glad, in a way, that the recentest should be approved above the older. It looks like progress. One would rather like to keep one's latest, but there's always the hope that there'll be better ones than the latest by and by, so scoot them off before they grow too drab. . . .

August 12th

I haven't one friend of my own age and generation. I wish I had. I don't know if it's my own fault. I haven't a *single thing* in common with them. They're all snarled up in grandchildren or W.A. or church teas or bridge or society. None of them like painting and they particularly dislike my kind of painting. It's awkward, this oil and water mixing. I have lots more in common with the young generation, but there you are. Twenty can't be expected to tolerate sixty in all things, and sixty gets bored stiff with twenty's eternal love affairs. Oh God, why did you make me a pelican and sit me down in a wilderness? These old maids of fifty to sixty, how dull they are, so self-centred, and the married women are absorbed in their husbands and families. Oh Lord, I thank Thee for the dogs and the monkey and the rat. I loafed all day. Next week I must step on the gas.

June 30th, 1935

The wind is roaring and it is cold. I revolted against wrestling with the campfire and shivering over breakfast in the open field, so I breakfast in the van. It is a day to cuddle down. Even the monkey pleaded to come back to her sleeping box, tuck her shawls about her and watch me. . . .

I did two sketches, large interiors, trying to unify the thought of the whole wood in the bit I was depicting. I did not make a good fist of it but I felt connections more than ever before. Only three more whole days of this absolute freedom and then I have to pack up and get back to the old routine, though it will be nice to get back to those two dear sisters who plod on, year in and year out, with never a break or pause in their monotonous lives. But it would not give *them* a spacious joy to sit at a little homemade table writing, with three sleeping pups on the bunk beside me, a monk at my shoulder and the zip and roar of the wind lifting the canvas and shivering the van so that you feel you are part and parcel of the storming yourself. That's living! You'd never get that feel in a solid house shut away securely from the living elements by a barricade!

Christmas eve, 1935

We have just had our present-giving at Alice's, just we three old girls. Alice's house was full of the smell of new bread. The loaves were piled on the kitchen table; the dining-room table was piled with parcels, things changing hands. This is our system and works well: we agree on a stated amount—it is small because our big giving is birthdays. Each of us buys something for ourselves to our own liking, goods amounting to the stated sums. We bring them along and Christmas Eve, with kissings and thankings, accept them from each other—homely, practical little wants, torch batteries, hearth brooms, coffee strainers, iron handles, etc. It's lots of fun. We lit four red candles in the window and drank ginger ale and ate Christmas cake and new bread and joked and discussed today and tomorrow and yesterday and compared tirednesses and rheumatics and rejoiced that Christmas came only once per year. We love each other, we three; with all our differences we are very close.

Christmas Day, 1935

. . . Two would-be art critics came to the studio. They were "pose-y," waved their paws describing sweeps and motions in my pictures, screwed their eyes, made monocles of their fists, discoursed on aesthetics, asked prices, and expounded on technique. One paints a little and teaches a lot, the other "aesthetics" with I do not quite know what aim. Both think women and their works beneath contempt but ask to come to the studio on every occasion. Why?

February 9th, 1936

. . . Lover's letters I destroyed years back; no other eye should see those. But there was a note, written forty years and more after the man had been my sweetheart and he loved me still. He married as he told me he should. He demanded more than I could have given; he demanded *worship*. He thought I made a great mistake in not marrying him. He ought to be glad I did not; he'd have found me a bitter mouthful and very indigestible and he would have bored me till my spirit died . . . .

April 16, 1937

. . . I have been thinking that I am a shirker. I have dodged publicity, hated write-ups and all that splutter. Well, that's all selfish conceit that embarrassed me. I have been forgetting Canada and forgetting women painters. It's them I ought to be upholding, nothing to do with puny me at all. Perhaps what brought it home was the last two lines of a crit in a Toronto paper: "Miss Carr is essentially Canadian, not by reason of her subject matter alone, but by her approach to it." I am glad of that. I am also glad that I am showing these men that women can hold up their end. The men resent a woman getting any honour in what they consider is essentially their field. Men painters mostly despise women painters. So I have decided to stop squirming, to throw any honour in with Canada and women. It is wonderful to feel the grandness of Canada in the raw, not because she is Canada but because she's something sublime that you were born into, some great rugged power that you are a part of.

December 13, 1937

Sixty-six years ago tonight I was hardly me. I was just a pink bundle snuggled in a blanket close to Mother. The north wind was bellowing round, tearing at everything. The snow was all drifted up on the little balcony outside Mother's window. The night before had been a disturbed one for everybody. Everything was quieted down tonight. The two-year-old Alice was deposed from her baby throne. The bigger girls were sprouting motherisms, all-over delighted with the new toy. Mother hardly realized yet that I was me and had set up an entity of my own. I wonder what

Father felt. I can't imagine him being half as interested as Mother. More
to Father's taste was a nice juicy steak served piping on the great pewter
hotwater dish. That made his eyes twinkle. I wonder if he ever cosseted
Mother up with a tender word or two after she'd been through a birth or
whether he was as rigid as ever, waiting for her to buck up and wait on
him. He ignored new babies until they were old enough to admire him,
old enough to have wills to break.

March 6, 1940

. . . I used to wonder what it would feel like to be sixty-eight. I have
seen four sisters reach sixty-eight and pass, but only by a few years. My
father set three score years and ten as his limit, reached it and died. I, too,
said that after the age of seventy a painter probably becomes poor and
had better quit, but I wanted to work till I was seventy. At sixty-four my
heart gave out but I was able to paint still and I learned to write. At sixty-
eight I had a stroke. Three months later I am thinking that I may work on
perhaps to seventy after all. I do not feel dead, and already I am writing
again a little.

I used to wonder how it would feel to be old. As a child I was very
devoted to old ladies. They seemed to me to have faded like flowers. I am
not half as patient with old women now that I am one. I am impatient of
their stupidity and their selfishness. They want still to occupy the centre
of the picture. They have had their day but they won't give place. They
grudge giving up. They won't face up to old age and accept its slowing
down of energy and strength. Some people call this sporty and think it
wonderful for Grannie to be as bobbish as a girl. There are plenty of girls
to act the part. Why can't the old lady pass grandly and grudgingly on,
an example, not a rival? Old age without religion must be ghastly, looking forward only to dust and extinction. I do not call myself religious. I
do not picture after-life in detail. I am content with "Eye hath not seen,
nor ear heard" . . . but I cannot imagine anything more hideous than feeling life decay, hurrying into a dark shut-off.

The days fill out. They are happy, contented days. I am nearer sixty-
nine than sixty-eight now, and a long way recovered from my stroke.
There is a lot of life in me yet. Maybe I shall go out into the woods sketching again, who knows? . . .

December 13th, 1940

. . . Life has been good and I have got a lot out of it, lots to remember and relive. I have liked life, perhaps the end more than the beginning. I was a happy-natured little girl but with a tragic streak, very vulnerable to hurt. I developed very late. Looking back is interesting. I can remember the exact spot and the exact time that so many things dawned on me. Particularly is this so in regard to my work. I know just when and where and how I first saw or comprehended certain steps in my painting development. Of late years my writing has shown me very many reasons for things. I do not resent old age and the slowing-down process. As a child I used to say to myself, "I shall go everywhere I can and see and do all I can so that I will have plenty to think about when I am old." I kept all the chinks between acts filled up by being interested in lots of odd things. I've had handy, active fingers and have made them work. I suppose the main force behind all this was my painting. That was the principal reason why I went to places, the reason why I drove ahead through the more interesting parts of life, to get time and money to push further into art, not the art of making pictures and becoming a great artist, but art to use as a means of expressing myself, putting into visibility what gripped me in nature.

February 21, 1941

. . . It is the ugliness of old age I hate. Being old is not bad if you keep away from mirrors, but broken-down feet, bent knees, peering eyes, rheumatic knuckles, withered skin, these are *ugly*, hard to tolerate with patience. I wish we could commune with our contemporaries about spiritual stuff. With death getting nearer it seems to get harder. We think of it often but rarely mention it, then only in stiff, unnatural words.

[The final entry of her diary:]

March 7 (1941)

Today Miss Austie took me for a drive round the park and to the Chinese cemetery. The sun was powerful, the Olympics strong, delicate blue, Mount Baker white. The cat bush is already green and the weeping willows round the lake droop with the weight of flowing life, but there are no leaves yet. Everything was splendid. The lend-lease bill has gone through in the States. The war is staggering. When you think of it you come to a stone wall. All private plans stop. The world has stopped; man has stopped. Everything holds its breath except spring. She bursts through as strong as ever. I gave the birds their mates and nests today. They are bursting their throats. Instinct bids them carry on. They fulfil their moment; carry on, carry on, carry on.

Carolina Maria de Jesus (1914–1977) was born in a small town in Brazil. She was forced to leave school at sixteen; after that she cleaned houses and lived, with her children, in extreme poverty. In order to keep from dwelling on the difficulties of her life, she wrote poems, novels, and plays, and also kept a diary which recorded the day-to-day life in the slums. Through a chance meeting with a journalist, Carolina de Jesus had her diaries published in newspapers and later in a book that became a best seller.

from Child of the Dark:
The Diary of Carolina Maria de Jesus

Carolina Maria de Jesus

July 15, 1955

The birthday of my daughter Vera Eunice. I wanted to buy a pair of shoes for her, but the price of food keeps us from realizing our desires. Actually we are slaves to the cost of living. I found a pair of shoes in the garbage, washed them, and patched them for her to wear. . . .

I was ill all day. I thought I had a cold. At night my chest pained me. I started to cough. I decided not to go out at night to look for paper. I searched for my son João. He was . . . near the market. A bus had knocked a boy into the sidewalk and a crowd gathered. João was in the middle of it all. I poked him a couple of times and within five minutes he was home.

I washed the children, put them to bed, then washed myself and went to bed. I waited until 11:00 for a certain someone. He didn't come. I took an aspirin and laid down again. When I awoke the sun was sliding in space. My daughter Vera Eunice said: "Go get some water, Mother!"

July 16

I got up and obeyed Vera Eunice. I went to get the water. I made coffee. I told the children that I didn't have any bread, that they would have to drink their coffee plain . . . I was feeling ill and decided to cure myself. I stuck my finger down my throat twice, vomited, and knew I was under the evil eye . . . I thought of the worrisome life that I led. Carrying paper,

111

washing clothes for the children, staying in the streets all day long. Yet I'm always lacking things, Vera doesn't have shoes and she doesn't like to go barefoot. For at least two years I've wanted to buy a meat grinder. And a sewing machine.

I came home and made lunch for the two boys. Rice, beans, and meat, and I'm going out to look for paper. I left the children, told them to play in the yard and not go into the street, because the terrible neighbors I have won't leave my children alone. I was feeling ill and wished I could lie down. But the poor don't rest nor are they permitted the pleasure of relaxation. I was nervous inside, cursing my luck. I collected two full sacks of paper. Afterward I went back and gathered up some scrap metal, some cans, and some kindling wood . . .

When I came home there was a crowd at my door. Children and women claiming José Carlos had thrown stones at their houses. They wanted me to punish him.

July 18

I got up at 7. Happy and content. Weariness would be here soon enough. . . .

Dona Silvia came to complain about my children. That they were badly educated. I don't look for defects in children. Neither in mine nor in others. I know that a child is not born with sense. When I speak with a child I use pleasant words. What infuriates me is that the parents come to my door to disrupt my rare moments of inner tranquillity. But when they upset me, I write. I know how to dominate my impulses. I only had two years of schooling, but I got enough to form my character. The only thing that does not exist in the favela is friendship. . . .

My kids are not kept alive by the church's bread. I take on all kinds of work to keep them. And those women have to beg or even steal. At night when they are begging I peacefully sit in my shack listening to Viennese waltzes. While their husbands break the boards of the shack, I and my children sleep peacefully. I don't envy the married women of the favelas who lead lives like Indian slaves.

I never got married and I'm not unhappy. Those who wanted to marry me were mean and the conditions they imposed on me horrible.

July 19

. . . When those female witches invade my shack, my children throw stones at them. The women scream:

"What uneducated brats!"

I reply:

"My children are defending me. You are ignorant and can't understand that. I'm going to write a book about the favela, and I'm going to tell everything that happened here. And everything that you do to me. I want to write a book, and you with these disgusting scenes are furnishing me with the material."

Silvia asked me to take her name out of my book. . . .

July 21

I woke with the voice of Dona Maria asking me if I wanted to buy bananas or lettuce . . . Then I went to wash clothes. While the clothes were bleaching I sat on the sidewalk and wrote. A man passed by and asked me:

"What are you writing?"

"All the cheating that the favela dwellers practice. Those human wrecks."

He said:

"Write it and give it to an editor so he can make revisions."

. . . I spent the rest of the afternoon writing. At 4:30 . . . I gave the children a bath and got ready to go out. I went out to pick up paper but I felt ill. I hurried because it was cold. When I got home it was 10:30. I turned on the radio, took a bath, and heated some food. I read a little. I don't know how to sleep without reading. I like to leaf through a book. The book is man's best invention so far.

July 27

. . . Senhor Gino came to ask me to go to his shack. That I am neglecting him. I answered: no!

I am writing a book to sell. I am hoping that with this money I can buy a place and leave the favela. I don't have time to go to anybody's house. Senhor Gino insisted. He told me:

"Just knock and I'll open the door."

But my heart didn't ask me to go to his room.

May 15, 1958

. . . I classify São Paulo this way: The Governor's Palace is the living room. The mayor's office is the dining room and the city is the garden. And the favela is the back yard where they throw the garbage.

May 19

. . . What our President Senhor Juscelino has in his favor is his voice. He sings like a bird and his voice is pleasant to the ears. And now the bird is living in a golden cage called Catete Palace. Be careful, little bird, that you don't lose this cage, because cats when they are hungry think of birds in cages. The *favelados* are the cats, and they are hungry. . . .

I washed the floor because I'm expecting a visit from a future deputy and he wants me to make some speeches for him. He says he wants to know the favelas and if he is elected he's going to abolish them.

The sky was the color of indigo, and I understood that I adore my Brazil. My glance went over to the trees . . . the leaves moved by themselves. I thought: they are applauding my gesture of love to my country. I went on looking for paper. . . .

May 20

. . . my children ran to tell me that they had found some macaroni in the garbage. As the food supply was low I cooked some of the macaroni with beans. And my son João said to me:

"Uh, huh. You told me you weren't going to eat any more things from the garbage."

It was the first time I had failed to keep my word. I said:

"I had faith in President Kubitschek."

"You had faith, and now you don't have it any more?"

"No, my son, democracy is losing its followers. In our country every-thing is weakening. The money is weak. Democracy is weak and the politicians are very weak. Everything that is weak dies one day."

The politicians know that I am a poetess. And that a poet will even face death when he sees his people oppressed.

June 1

. . . I haven't said anything about my dear mother. She was very good. She wanted me to study to be a teacher. It was the uncertainties of life that made it impossible for her to realize her dream. But she formed my char-acter, taught me to like the humble and the weak. That's why I have pity on the *favelados*. I know very well that there are contemptible people here, persons with perverted souls. Last night Amelia and her companion fought. She told him that he was with her only for the money she gave him. You only had to listen to Amelia's voice to know she enjoyed the argument. She had many children. Gave them all away. She has two boys at home that she doesn't want. She neglects children and collects men.

A man enters by the door. A child is the root of the heart. . . .

June 7

. . . When I was a girl my dream was to be a man to defend Brazil, because I read the history of Brazil and became aware that war existed. I read the masculine names of the defenders of the country, then I said to my mother:

"Why don't you make me become a man?"

She replied:

"If you walk under a rainbow, you'll become a man."

When a rainbow appeared I went running in its direction. But the rainbow was always a long way off. Just as the politicians are far from the people. I got tired and sat down. Afterward I started to cry. But the peo-ple must not get tired. They must not cry. They must fight to improve Brazil so that our children don't suffer as we are suffering. I returned and told my mother:

"The rainbow ran away from me."

June 23

I stopped at the butcher to buy a half kilo of beef . . . I was confused about the differences in prices. The butcher explained to me that filet was more expensive. I thought of the bad luck of the cow, the slave of man. Those that live in the woods eat vegetation, they like salt, but man doesn't give it because it's too expensive. After death they are divided, weighed, and selected. And they die when man wants them to. In life they give money to man. Their death enriches the man. Actually, the world is the way the whites want it. I'm not white, so I don't have anything to do with this disorganized world. . . .

June 24

When I returned to the favela I found Vera in the street. She tells me everything that goes on. She said the police had come to tell Paredão that his mother was dead.

She was a very good woman. Only she drank too much.

. . . Vera came to tell me there was a fight . . . It was Maria Mathias who was giving one of her hysterical spectaculars. A spectacular at the critical age. Only women and doctors will understand what I mean. . . .

July 30

I got 15 cruzeiros and went by the shoemaker to see if Vera's shoes were ready, because she complains when she has to go barefoot. They were, and she put on the shoes and began to smile. I stood watching my daughter's smile, because I myself don't know how to smile.

. . . I started thinking about the unfortunate children who, even being tiny, complain about their condition in the world. They say that Princess Margaret of England doesn't like being a Princess. Those are the breaks in life.

August 12

I left my bed at 6:30 and went to get water. There was a long line. The worst thing about it is that malice is the main subject. There was a Negress there who acted as if she'd been vaccinated by a phonograph needle. She talked about her daughter and son-in-law who were constantly fighting. And Dona Clara had to listen to it because she was the only one paying attention.

Lately it has become very difficult to get water, because the amount of people in the favela has doubled. And there is only one spigot.

September 8

Today I'm happy. I'm laughing without any reason. I'm singing. When I sing I make up the verses. I sing until I get tired of the song. Today I made this song:

> There is a voodoo curse on you
> And who did it, I know who.
> It was little Mary.
> The one you loved before.
> She said she loved you too
> But you showed her the door.

January 16, 1959

I went to the post office to take out the notebooks that returned from the United States. I came back to the favela as sad as if they had cut off one of my arms. *The Reader's Digest* returned my novels. The worst slap for those who write is the return of their works. . . .

May 6

At 9:30 the reporter appeared. I exclaimed:

"You said you would be here at 9:30 and not one minute late!"

He said that many people wanted to see him because they liked his articles. We got into a taxi. Vera was happy because she was in an automobile. We went to Arouche Square and the reporter started to photograph me. He took me to the São Paulo Academy of Letters. I sat in the doorway and put the sack of paper beside me. The janitor came and told me to get away from the door. He grabbed my sack. A sack that for me has an incalculable value, because I earn my daily bread with it. The reporter said that it was he who had told me to sit in the doorway. The janitor said that he wasn't allowed to let just anybody who wanted to sit in the front of the entrance.

We went to Seventh of April Street and the reporter bought a doll for Vera. I told the salesgirls that I had written a diary that was going to be published in *O Cruzeiro*.

June 8

When I got home and opened the door I found a note. I recognized the reporter's writing ... The note said that the article on me would come out on the 10th, in *O Cruzeiro*. That the book was going to be published. I filled with emotion.

Senhor Manuel arrived ...

"They earn money from your work and won't pay you. They're tricking you. You should never have given him the book."

I was not impressed with the skepticism of Senhor Manuel.

June 9

... I was reading stories to the children when there was a knock at the window. João said:

"Mama, there is a man here with glasses."

I went to see. It was Vera's father.

"Come in!"

"Where do you get in?"

"Go around front."

He came inside. He let his eyes wander around the shack.

He asked:

"Aren't you cold here? Doesn't it rain in?"

"It rains, but I'm used to it."

"You wrote me that the girl was ill, I came to see her. Thank you for the letters. I thank you because you promised to protect me and not reveal my name in your diary."

... He gave 100 cruzeiros. José Carlos thought that was very little, because he had other bills of 1,000.

June 10

. . . When João returned he said the story was out. I searched all my pockets for money. I had 13 cruzeiros. I lacked two. Senhor Luiz loaned them to me. And João went to get it. My heart was beating just like the springs in a watch. What would they write about me? When João came back with the magazine, I read it—"A Picture of the Favela in Carolina's diary."

I read the article and smiled. . . .

June 11

. . . I fed the children and sat on the bed to write. There was a knock at the door. I sent João to see who it was and shouted:

"Enter, black woman!"

"She isn't a black woman, Mama. It's a white woman and she has a copy of *O Cruzeiro* in her hands."

She came in. A very pretty blonde. She said that she had read the article in *O Cruzeiro* and wanted to take me to the *Díario da Noite* newspaper office to get help for me.

At the newspaper I got choked with emotion. The boss Senhor Antonio was on the third floor. He gave me a magazine to read. Afterward he went to get lunch for me, steak, potatoes and a salad. I was eating what I had dreamed about! I was in a pretty room.

Reality was much prettier than a dream.

. . . I am so happy! It feels as if my dirty life is now being washed.

July 13

. . . We went to a shoe shop and I bought a pair of shoes for Vera. When Senhor Manoel, a *nortista*, tried the shoes on her, she said:

"Shoes, please don't wear out! Because later Mama has to work hard to buy another pair, and I don't like to walk barefoot."

January 1, 1960

I got up at 5 and went to get water.

*A*nne Frank (1929–1944) was a young girl who, in her early teens, was forced into hiding for two years in Nazi-occupied Amsterdam, under the threat of discovery and annihilation in a death camp. The Diary of a Young Girl, written while she was in hiding, has been published in many languages and adapted for theatre and film.

from Anne Frank: The Diary of a Young Girl

Anne Frank

Sunday, 2 January, 1944

Dear Kitty,

This morning when I had nothing to do I turned over some of the pages of my diary and several times I came across letters dealing with the subject "Mummy" in such a hotheaded way that I was quite shocked, and asked myself: "Anne, is it really you who mentioned hate? Oh, Anne, how could you!" I remained sitting with the open page in my hand, and thought about it and how it came about that I should have been so brimful of rage and really so filled with such a thing as hate that I had to confide it all in you. I have been trying to understand the Anne of a year ago and to excuse her, because my conscience isn't clear as long as I leave you with these accusations, without being able to explain, on looking back, how it happened.

I suffer now—and suffered then—from moods which kept my head under water (so to speak) and only allowed me to see the things subjectively without enabling me to consider quietly the words of the other side, and to answer them as the words of one whom I, with my hotheaded temperament, had offended or made unhappy.

I hid myself within myself, I only considered myself and quietly wrote down all my joys, sorrows, and contempt in my diary. This diary is of great value to me, because it has become a book of memoirs in many places, but on a good many pages I could certainly put "past and done with."

I used to be furious with Mummy, and still am sometimes. It's true that she doesn't understand me, but I don't understand her either. She did love me very much and she was tender, but as she landed in so many unpleasant situations through me, and was nervous and irritable because of other worries and difficulties, it is certainly understandable that she snapped at me . . .

The period when I caused Mummy to shed tears is over. I have grown wiser and Mummy's nerves are not so much on edge. I usually keep my mouth shut if I get annoyed, and so does she, so we appear to get on much better together. I can't really love Mummy in a dependent childlike way—I just don't have that feeling.

I soothe my conscience now with the thought that it is better for hard words to be on paper than that Mummy should carry them in her heart.

Yours, Anne

Wednesday, 5 January, 1944

Dear Kitty,

I have two things to confess to you today, which will take a long time. But I must tell someone and you are the best one to tell, as I know that, come what may, you always keep a secret.

The first is about Mummy. You know that I've grumbled a lot about Mummy, yet still tried to be nice to her again. Now it is suddenly clear to me what she lacks. Mummy herself has told us that she looked upon us more as her friends than her daughters. Now that is all very fine, but still, a friend can't take a mother's place. I need my mother as an example which I can follow, I want to be able to respect her. I have the feeling that Margot thinks differently about these things and would never be able to understand what I've just told you. And Daddy avoids all arguments about Mummy.

I imagine a mother as a woman who, in the first place, shows great tact, especially towards her children when they reach our age, and who does not laugh at me if I cry about something—not pain, but other things—like "Mums" does . . .

The second is something that is very difficult to tell you, because it is about myself.

Yesterday I read an article about blushing by Sis Heyster. This article might have been addressed to me personally. Although I don't blush very easily, the other things in it certainly all fit me. She writes roughly something like this—that a girl in the years of puberty becomes quiet within and begins to think about the wonders that are happening to her body . . .

I think what is happening to me is so wonderful, and not only what can be seen on my body, but all that is taking place inside. I never discuss myself or any of these things with anybody; that is why I have to talk to myself about them.

Each time I have a period—and that has only been three times—I have the feeling that in spite of all the pain, unpleasantness, and nastiness, I have a sweet secret, and that is why, although it is nothing but a nuisance to me in a way, I always long for the time that I shall feel that secret within me again.

Sis Heyster also writes that girls of this age don't feel quite certain of themselves, and discover that they themselves are individuals with ideas, thoughts, and habits. After I came here, when I was just fourteen, I began to think about myself sooner than most girls, and to know that I am a "person." Sometimes, when I lie in bed at night, I have a terrible desire to feel my breasts and to listen to the quiet rhythmic beat of my heart.

I already had these kinds of feelings subconsciously before I came here, because I remember that once when I slept with a girl friend I had a strong desire to kiss her, and that I did so. I could not help being terribly inquisitive over her body, for she had always kept it hidden from me. I asked her whether, as a proof of our friendship, we should feel one another's breasts, but she refused. I go into ecstasies every time I see the naked figure of a woman, such as Venus, for example. It strikes me as so wonderful and exquisite that I have difficulty in stopping the tears rolling down my cheeks.

If only I had a girl friend!

Yours, Anne

Thursday, 6 January, 1944

Dear Kitty,

My longing to talk to someone became so intense that somehow or other I took it into my head to choose Peter.

Sometimes if I've been upstairs into Peter's room during the day, it always struck me as very snug, but because Peter is so retiring and would never turn anyone out who became a nuisance, I never dared stay long, because I was afraid he might think me a bore. I tried to think of an excuse to stay in his room and get him talking, without it being too noticeable, and my chance came yesterday. Peter has a mania for crossword puzzles at the moment and hardly does anything else. I helped him with them and we soon sat opposite each other at his little table, he on the chair and me on the divan.

It gave me a queer feeling each time I looked into his deep blue eyes, and he sat there with that mysterious laugh playing round his lips. I was able to read his inward thoughts. I could see on his face that look of help-lessness and uncertainty as to how to behave, and, at the same time, a trace of his sense of manhood. I noticed his shy manner and it made me feel very gentle; I couldn't refrain from meeting those dark eyes again and again, and with my whole heart I almost beseeched him: oh, tell me, what is going on inside you, oh, can't you look beyond this ridiculous chatter?

But the evening passed and nothing happened, except that I told him about blushing—naturally not what I have written, but just so that he would become more sure of himself as he grew older.

When I lay in bed and thought over the whole situation, I found it far from encouraging, and the idea that I should beg for Peter's patronage was simply repellent. One can do a lot to satisfy one's longings, which certainly sticks out in my case, for I have made up my mind to go and sit with Peter more often and to get him talking somehow or other.

Whatever you do, don't think I'm in love with Peter—not a bit of it! If the Van Daans had had a daughter instead of a son, I should have tried to make friends with her too. . . .

Sunday, 27 February, 1944

Dearest Kitty,

From early in the morning till late at night, I really do hardly any-thing else but think of Peter. I sleep with his image before my eyes, dream about him and he is still looking at me when I am awake . . .

But how and when will we finally reach each other? I don't know quite how long my common sense will keep this longing under control.

Yours, Anne

Thursday, 16 March, 1944

Dear Kitty,

The weather is lovely, superb, I can't describe it; I'm going up to the attic in a minute.

Now I know why I'm so much more restless than Peter. He has his own room where he can work, dream, think, and sleep. I am shoved about from one corner to another. I hardly spend any time in my "double" room and yet it's something I long for so much. That is the reason too why I so frequently escape to the attic. There, and with you, I can be myself for a while, just a little while . . .

Oh, it is so terribly difficult never to say anything to Peter, but I know that the first to begin must be he; there's so much I want to say and do, I've lived it all in my dreams, it is so hard to find that yet another day has gone by, and none of it comes true! Yes, Kitty, Anne is a crazy child, but I do live in crazy times and under still crazier circumstances.

But, still, the brightest spot of all is that at least I can write down my thoughts and feelings, otherwise I would be absolutely stifled! I wonder what Peter thinks about all these things? I keep hoping that I can talk about it to him one day. There must be something he has guessed about me, because he certainly can't love the outer Anne, which is the one he knows so far . . .

Friday, 28 April, 1944

. . . Oh Peter, what have you done to me? What do you want of me? Where will this lead us? . . . if I were older and he should ask me to marry him, what should I answer? Anne, be honest! You would not be able to marry him, but yet, it would be hard to let him go. Peter hasn't enough character yet . . . he is still a child in his heart of hearts . . .

Am I only fourteen? Am I really still a silly little schoolgirl? Am I really so inexperienced about everything? . . . I am afraid that in my longing I am giving myself too quickly. How, later on, can it ever go right with other boys? . . .

Sunday morning, 7 May, 1944

Dear Kitty,

Daddy and I had a long talk yesterday afternoon, I cried terribly and he joined in. Do you know what he said to me, Kitty? "I have received many letters in my life, but this is certainly the most unpleasant! You, Anne, who have received such love from your parents, you, who have parents who are always ready to help you, who have always defended you whatever it might be, can you talk of feeling no responsibility towards us? You feel wronged and deserted; no, Anne, you have done us a great injustice!"

. . . Oh, I have failed miserably; this is certainly the worst thing I've ever done in my life . . . Certainly, I have had a lot of unhappiness, but to accuse the good Pim, who had done and still does do everything for—no, that was too low for words . . .

I want to start at the beginning again and it can't be difficult, now that I have Peter . . . he loves me. I love him. I have my books, my story-book and my diary, not utterly stupid, have a cheerful temperament and want to have a good character! . . .

Monday, 8 May, 1944

. . . I can assure you I'm not at all keen of a narrow cramped existence like Mummy and Margot. I'd adore to go to Paris for a year and London for a year to learn the languages and study the history of art. Compare that with Margot, who wants to be a midwife in Palestine! I always long to see beautiful dresses and interesting people. . . .

Thursday, 11 May, 1944

. . . You've known for a long time that my greatest wish is to become a journalist someday and later on a famous writer . . . Whether I shall succeed or not, I cannot say, but my diary will be a great help. . . .

Friday, 19 May, 1944

. . . All goes well with Peter and me. The poor boy seems to need a little love even more than I do. He blushes every evening when he gets his good-night kiss and simply begs for another. . .

Friday, 9 June, 1944

. . . The whole of the Secret Annexe except Van Daan and Peter have read the trilogy *Hungarian Rhapsody* . . . It is a very interesting book, but in my opinion there is a bit too much about women in it . . .

Wednesday, 14 June, 1944

. . . Peter loves me not as a lover but as a friend and grows more affectionate every day . . . Peter is good and he's a darling, but still there's no denying that there's a lot about him that disappoints me . . . He lets me say a lot of things to him that he would never accept from his mother . . .

Both Peter and I have spent our most meditative years in the "Secret Annexe." We often discuss the future, the past, and the present, but . . . I still seem to miss the real thing and yet I know it's there.

Thursday, 6 July, 1944

Dear Kitty,

It strikes fear to my heart when Peter talks of later being a criminal, or of gambling; although it's meant as a joke, of course, it gives me the feeling that he's afraid of his own weakness . . .

We all live with the object of being happy; our lives are all different and yet the same . . . You must work and do good, not be lazy and gamble, if you wish to earn happiness. Laziness may *appear* attractive, but work *gives* satisfaction.

Poor boy, he's never known what it feels like to make other people happy, and I can't teach him that either . . .

Saturday, 15 July, 1944

. . . I have one outstanding trait in my character, which must strike anyone who knows me for any length of time, and that is my knowledge of myself. I can watch myself and my actions, just like an outsider. The Anne of every day I can face entirely without prejudice, without making excuses for her, and watch what's good and bad about her . . . I understand more and more how true Daddy's words were when he said: "All children must look after their own upbringing." Parents can only give good advice or put them on the right paths, but the final forming of a person's character lies in their own hands . . .

I ponder far more over Peter than Daddy. I know very well that I conquered him instead of him conquering me. I created an image of him in my mind, pictured him as a quiet, sensitive, lovable boy, who needed affection and friendship . . . I needed a living person to whom I could pour out my heart . . . it automatically developed into an intimacy which, on second thought, I don't think I ought to have allowed . . .

"For in its innermost depths youth is lonelier than old age." I read this saying in some book and I've always remembered it, and found it to be true . . .

Tuesday, 1 August, 1944

Dear Kitty,

"Little bundle of contradictions." That's how I ended my last letter and that's how I'm going to begin this one . . . What does contradiction mean? Like so many words, it can mean two things, contradiction from without and contradiction from within . . .

. . . I have, as it were, a dual personality. One half embodies my exuberant cheerfulness, making fun of everything, my high-spiritedness, and above all, the way I take everything lightly. This includes not taking offense at a flirtation, a kiss, an embrace, a dirty joke. This side is usually lying in wait and pushes away the other which is much better, deeper and purer. You must realize that no one knows Anne's better side and that's why most people find me so insufferable . . .

I'm awfully scared that everyone who knows me as I always am will discover that I have another side, a finer and better side. I'm afraid they'll laugh at me, think I'm ridiculous and sentimental, not take me seriously . . . Sometimes, if I really compel the good Anne to take the stage for a quarter of an hour, she simply shrivels up as soon as she has to speak, and lets Anne number one take over, and before I realize it, she has disappeared . . .

A voice sobs within me: 'There you are, that's what's become of you: you're uncharitable, you look supercilious and peevish, people dislike you and all because you won't listen . . ." Oh, I would like to listen, but it doesn't work; if I'm quiet and serious, everyone thinks it's a new comedy and then I have to get out of it by turning it into a joke, not to mention my own family, who are sure to think I'm ill, make me swallow pills for headaches and nerves, feel my neck and my head to see whether I'm running a temperature, ask if I'm constipated and criticize me for being in a bad mood. I can't keep that up: if I'm watched to that extent, I start by getting snappy, then unhappy, and finally I twist my heart round again, so that the bad is on the outside and the good is on the inside and keep on trying to find a way of becoming what I would so like to be, and I could be, if . . . there weren't any other people living in the world.

Yours, Anne

[This is the last entry. Three days later the occupants of the "Secret Annexe" were arrested. Eight months later Anne died in the concentration camp at Bergen-Belsen.]

*H*annah Senesh (1921–1944) was born in Hungary. In a diary that she kept *from the age of thirteen she recorded, first, her dreams of becoming a writer and later, events in her life after she left her family and moved to Palestine. There she became involved in a group of Palestinian soldiers trained to help Jews escape from Nazi occupied countries. She was captured, tortured, and killed for her efforts.*

from Hannah Senesh: Her Life and Diary

Hannah Senesh

November 2, 1940

I dream and plan as if there was nothing happening in the world, as if there was no war, no destruction, as if thousands upon thousands were not being killed daily; as if Germany, England, Italy, and Greece were not destroying each other. Only in our little country—which is also in danger and may yet find itself in the centre of hostilities—is there an illusion of peace and quiet. And I'm sitting here, thinking of the future. And what do I think about my personal future?

One of my most beautiful plans is to be a poultry farming instructor, to travel from one farm to the other, to visit settlements, to advise and to assist, to organize, to introduce record-keeping, to develop this branch of the economy. In the evenings I would conduct brief seminars for kibbutz members, teach them the important facets of the trade. And at the same time I would get to know the people, their way of life, and would be able to travel about the country.

My other plan is to instruct (seems I only want to teach) children in some sort of school. Perhaps in the institute at Shfeya, or in a regional agricultural school. The old dream is to combine agricultural work with child guidance and teaching.

My third plan—a plan I consider only rarely—has nothing to do with agriculture or children, but with writing . . . I want to write books, or plays, or I don't know what. Sometimes I think I have talent, and that it's sinful to waste or neglect it. Sometimes I think that if I really do have talent I'll eventually write without worrying about it, that if I feel the need of self-expression, the urge to write, I'll write. The important thing is to have a command of the language. I've made considerable progress during this first year in the Land, but I must do better.

And I've yet another plan. I'd like to live on a kibbutz. This can, however, be in conjunction with other plans. I'm quite sure I would fit in, if only the possibility of working at something that really interested me existed. . . .

February 25, 1941

It's time I wrote about Alex. Even though it's more "his" affair than something we share. Several things happened last month which I didn't write about, not only because I was busy working at the incubator, but also because I find it difficult to write about matters that aren't entirely clear to me, or about which I am undecided . . .

He recently told me he loves me, and asked me to marry him. I told him that although I respect and like him, I don't feel as he does. Nonetheless, I couldn't say this with absolute certainty, and the matter was left unresolved. He comes to see me as usual, but I asked him to wait a while before demanding a definite answer.

. . . The problem I now face is whether to marry a man "just like that," to disrupt my plans, give up my independence. Naturally, it's difficult not to be impressed and flattered by the love of a man of character, a man you respect and esteem. But this is still not love, and thus there is really no reason to continue.

April 12, 1941

Why am I so lonely? Not long ago I strolled through the moshav one evening. It was a fabulous, starry night. Small lights glittered in the lanes, and in the middle of the wide road. Sounds of music, songs, conversation, and laughter came from all around; and far, far in the distance I heard the barking of dogs. The houses seemed so distant; only the stars were near.

Suddenly I was gripped by fear. Where is life leading me? Will I always go on alone in the night, looking at the sparkling stars, thinking they are close? Will I be unable to hear the songs . . . the songs and the laughter around me? Will I fail to turn off the lonely road in order to enter the little houses? What must I choose? The weak lights, filtering through the chinks in the houses, or the distant light of the stars? Worst of all, when I'm among the stars I long for the small lights, and when I find my way into one of the little houses my soul yearns for the heavenly bodies. I'm filled with discontent, hesitancy, insecurity, anxiety, lack of confidence.

Sometimes I feel I am an emissary who has been entrusted with a mission. What this mission is—is not clear to me. (After all, everyone has a mission in life.) I feel I have a duty towards others, as if I were obligated to them. At times this appears to be all sheer nonsense, and I wonder why all this particular effort . . . and why particularly me?

January 8, 1943

. . . I've had a shattering week. I was suddenly struck by the idea of going to Hungary. I feel I must be there during these days in order to help organize youth immigration, and also to get my mother out. Although I'm quite aware how absurd the idea is, it still seems both feasible and necessary to me, so I'll get to work on it and carry it through. . . .

February 22, 1943

How strangely things work out. On January 8 I wrote a few words about the sudden idea that struck me. A few days ago a man from the Kibbutz Ma-agan, a member of the Palmach, visited the kibbutz and we chatted awhile. In the course of the conversation he told me that a Palmach unit was being organized to do—exactly what I felt then I wanted to do. I was truly astounded. The *identical* idea!

My answer, of course, was that I'm absolutely ready. . . .

September 19, 1943

I arrived in the Land four years ago. Immigrant House, Haifa. Everything was new, everything beautiful, everything a world of the future. Only one figure takes me back to the past: my mother at the railway station. Four years. I never would have believed the distance between us could ever be so great, so deep. Had I known . . . Or perhaps I knew but didn't dare to admit it.

. . . And now I stand before a new assignment again, one that demands great preparation for a difficult and responsible mission. Again a sense of transition coupled with strong emotions, aspirations, tensions. And the everlasting aloneness. Now it's clearer to me than ever that this has nothing to do with outside factors. There's a certain peculiarity within me, and a lack of sociability which keeps me away from people. This is especially difficult where it concerns men.

At times I think I love, or could love, someone. But . . . There are many objective "buts" in the way, and I lack the courage to overcome them . . . I am twenty-two years old, and I don't know how to be happy.

I wear a placid mask, and at times I say to myself, What is this? Is this how my life is going to unfold? It's no longer an external matter, but something within me. I have no complaints about life, really. I'm satisfied. I can't imagine a state in which I would be more content. On the contrary. And the assignment which lies ahead draws me on. But I forget how to laugh—to really laugh, heartily, as I once could with George while wrestling on the couch until we rolled off onto the floor—laughing about nothing but the joy of living, of being young and alive. Are hardship and loneliness to blame for the lack of that particular kind of joy? Or do I bear this sorrow from the time when—at the age of seven or eight—I stood beside my father's grave and began to write poems about the hardships in life? I feel I'm just chattering. However, this is necessary too. Amid essays, speeches, and silences, it's good to converse sometimes, even if only with oneself.

. . . I long for satisfying work. In the last four years I've done all kinds of work, not always out of conviction, always explaining to myself that it was all necessary, and never gaining any real satisfaction from it. I really wanted to be a teacher. If I had to decide today whether to emigrate to Palestine I'd do exactly as I did. . . .

In my life's chain of events nothing was accidental. Everything happened according to an inner need. I would have been miserable following a road other than the one I chose. No, perhaps this is an exaggeration. But had I chosen differently, I would not have been in harmony with myself. . . .

[Hannah wrote the following letter to her brother George to be given to him if she failed to return from her mission:]

December 25, 1943

Darling George!

Sometimes one writes letters one does not intend sending. Letters one must write without asking oneself, "I wonder whether this will ever reach its destination."

Day after tomorrow I am starting something new. Perhaps it's madness. Perhaps it's fantastic. Perhaps it's dangerous. Perhaps one in a hundred—or one in a thousand—pays with his life. Perhaps with less than his life, perhaps with more. Don't ask questions. You'll eventually know what it's about.

George, I must explain something to you. I must exonerate myself. I must prepare myself for that moment when you arrive inside the frontiers of the Land, waiting for that moment when, after six years, we will meet again, and you will ask, "Where is she?" and they'll abruptly answer, "She's not here."

I wonder, will you understand? I wonder, will you believe that it is more than a childish wish for adventure, more than youthful romanticism that attracted me? I wonder, will you feel that I could not do otherwise, that this was something I had to do?

There are events without which one's life becomes unimportant, a worthless toy; and there are times when one is commanded to do something, even at the price of one's life. . . .

*F*rances Anne Kemble (1809–1893) was an accomplished English actress and libertarian, who championed the rights of the working class. She married an American who later inherited his grandfather's plantations in the South that depended on slave labor. Horrified by the slaves' treatment and unable to do anything directly to help them, she kept a journal in which she recorded both what she witnessed and her feelings about it. This journal was later published in 1968, in both England and the U.S., as Journal of a Residence on a Georgian Plantation.

from Journal of a Residence on a Georgia Plantation in 1838–1839

Frances Anne Kemble

January, 1839

Dear Elizabeth,

. . . I must inform you of a curious conversation which took place between my little girl and the woman who performs for us the offices of chambermaid here—of course one of Mr. Butler's slaves. What suggested it to the child, or whence indeed she gathered her information, I know not; but children are made of eyes and ears, and nothing, however minute escapes their microscopic observation. She suddenly began addressing this woman.

"Mary, some persons are free and some are not (the woman made no reply). I am a free person (of a little more than three years old). I say, I am a free person, Mary—do you know that?"

"Yes, missis."

"Some persons are free and some are not—do you know that, Mary?"

"Yes, missis, here," was the reply; "I know it is so here, in this world."

Here my child's white nurse, my dear Margery, who had hitherto been silent, interfered, saying, "Oh, then you think it will not always be so?"

"Me hope not, missis."

I am afraid, Elizabeth, this woman actually imagines that there will be no slaves in heaven; isn't that preposterous, now, when, by the account of most of the Southerners, slavery itself must be heaven, or something uncommonly like it? Oh, if you could imagine how this title "Missis" addressed to me and to my children, shocks all my feelings! Several times I have exclaimed: "For God's sake do not call me that!" and only been awakened by the stupid amazement of the poor creatures I was address-ing to the perfect uselessness of my thus expostulating with them; once or twice, indeed, I have done more—I have explained to them, and they appeared to comprehend me well, that I have no ownership over them, for that I held such ownership sinful, and that, though I was the wife of the man who pretends to own them, I was, in truth, no more their mis-tress than they were mine. Some of them, I know, understood me, more of them did not. . . .

I forgot to tell you that in the hospital were several sick babies, whose mothers were permitted to suspend their field labor in order to nurse them. Upon addressing some remonstrances to one of these, who, besides having a sick child, was ill herself, about the horribly dirty condition of her baby, she assured me that it was impossible for them to keep their children clean; that they went out to work at daybreak, and did not get their tasks done till evening, and that then they were too tired and worn out to do anything but throw themselves down and sleep. This statement of hers I mentioned on my return from the hospital, and the overseer appeared extremely annoyed by it, and assured me repeatedly that it was not true. . . .

This morning I paid my second visit to the infirmary, and found there had been some faint attempt at sweeping and cleaning, in compliance with my entreaties. The poor woman Harriet, however, whose statement with regard to the impossibility of their attending properly to their chil-dren had been so vehemently denied by the overseer, was crying bitterly. I asked her what ailed her, when, more by signs and dumb show than words, she and old Rose informed me that Mr. O—— had flogged her that morning for having told me that the women had not time to keep their children clean. It is part of the regular duty of every overseer to visit the infirmary at least once a day, which he generally does in the morning, and Mr. O——'s visit had preceded mine but a short time only, or I might have been edified by seeing a man horsewhip a woman.

. . . I will tell you a story which has just formed an admirable illus-tration for my observation of all the miseries of which this accursed sys-tem of slavery is the cause, even under the best and most humane admin-istration of its laws and usages. Pray note it, my dear friend, for you will find, in the absence of all voluntary or even conscious cruelty on the part of the master, the best possible comment on a state of things which, without the slightest desire to injure and oppress, produces such intolerable results of injury and oppression.

We have, as a sort of under nursemaid and assistant of my dear M[argery], whose white complexion, as I wrote you, occasioned such indignation to my Southern fellow travelers, and such extreme perplexity to the poor slaves on our arrival here, a much more orthodox servant for these parts, a young woman named Psyche, but commonly called Sack, not a very graceful abbreviation of the divine heathen appellation. She cannot be much over twenty, has a very pretty figure, a graceful, gentle deportment, and a face which, but for its color (she is a dingy mulatto), would be pretty, and is extremely pleasing, from the perfect sweetness of its expression; she is always serious, not to say sad and silent, and has always an air of melancholy and timidity, that has frequently struck me very much, and would have made me think some special anxiety or sorrow must occasion it, but that God knows the whole condition of these wretched people naturally produces such a deportment, and there is no necessity to seek for special or peculiar causes to account for it. Just in proportion as I have found the slaves on this plantation intelligent and advanced beyond the general brutish level of the majority, I have observed this pathetic expression of countenance in them, a mixture of sadness and fear, the involuntary exhibition of the two feelings, which I suppose must be the predominant experience of their whole lives, regret and apprehension, not the less heavy, either of them, for being in some degree, vague and indefinite—a sense of incalculable past loss and injury, and a dread of incalculable future loss and injury.

I have never questioned Psyche as to her sadness, because, in the first place, as I tell you, it appears to me most natural, and is observable in all the slaves whose superior natural or acquired intelligence allows of their filling situations of trust or service about the house and family; and, though I cannot and will not refuse to hear any and every tale of suffering which these unfortunates bring to me, I am anxious to spare both myself and them the pain of vain appeals to me for redress and help, which, alas! it is too often utterly out of my power to give them. It is useless, and, indeed, worse than useless, that they should see my impotent indignation and unavailing pity, and hear expressions of compassion for them, and horror at their condition, which might only prove incentives to a hopeless resistance on their part to a system, under the hideous weight of whose oppression any individual or partial revolt must be annihilated and ground into the dust. Therefore, as I tell you, I asked Psyche no questions; but, to my great astonishment, the other day M[argery] asked me if I knew to whom Psyche belonged, as the poor woman had inquired of her with much hesitation and anguish if she could tell her who owned her and her children. She has two nice little children under six years old, whom she keeps as clean and tidy, and who are sad and as silent as herself. My astonishment at this question was, as you will readily believe, not small, and I forthwith sought out Psyche for an explanation. She was thrown into extreme perturbation at finding that her question had been referred to me, and it was some time before I could sufficiently reassure her to be able to comprehend, in the midst of her reiterated entreaties for pardon, and hopes that she had not offended me, that she did not know herself who owned her. She was, at one time, the property of Mr. K[ing], the former overseer, of whom I have already spoken to you, and who has just been paying Mr. [Butler] a visit. He, like several of his predecessors in the management, has contrived to make a fortune upon it (though it yearly decreases in value to the owners, but this is the inevitable course of things in the Southern states), and has purchased a plantation of his own in Alabama, I believe, or one of the Southwestern states. Whether she still belonged to Mr. K[ing] or not she did not know, and entreated me, if she did, to endeavor to persuade Mr. [Butler] to buy her. Now you must know that this poor woman is the wife of one of Mr. [Butler]'s slaves, a fine, intelligent, active, excellent young man, whose whole family are among some of the very best specimens of character and capacity on the estate. I was so astonished at the (to me) extraordinary state of things revealed by poor Sack's petition, that I could only tell her that I had supposed all the Negroes on the plantation were Mr. [Butler]'s property, but that I would certainly inquire, and find out for her, if I could, to whom she belonged, and if I could, endeavor to get Mr. [Butler] to purchase her, if she really was not his.

Now, E[lizabeth], just conceive for one moment the state of mind of this woman, believing herself to belong to a man who in a few days was going down to one of those abhorred and dreaded Southwestern states, and who would then compel her, with her poor little children, to leave her husband and the only home she had ever known, and all the ties of affection, relationship, and association of her former life, to follow him thither, in all human probability never again to behold any living creature that she had seen before; and this was so completely a matter of course that it was not even thought necessary to apprise her positively of the fact, and the only thing that interposed between her and this most miserable fate was the faint hope that Mr. [Butler] *might have* purchased her and her children. But if he had, if this great deliverance had been vouchsafed to her, the knowledge of it was not thought necessary; and with this deadly dread at her heart she was living day after day, waiting upon me and seeing me, with my husband beside me, and my children in my arms in blessed security, safe from all separation but the one reserved in God's great providence for all His creatures. Do you think I wondered any more at the woebegone expression of her countenance, or do you think it was easy for me to restrain within prudent and proper limits the expression of my feelings at such a state of things? And she had gone on from day to day enduring this agony, till I suppose its own intolerable pressure and M[argery]'s sweet countenance and gentle sympathizing voice and manner had constrained her to lay down this great burden of sorrow at our feet.

I did not see Mr. [Butler] until the evening; but, in the meantime, meeting Mr. O———, the overseer, with whom, as I believe I have already told you, we are living here, I asked him about Psyche, and who was her proprietor, when, to my infinite surprise, he told me that *he* had bought her and her children from Mr. K[ing], who had offered them to him, saying that they would be rather troublesome to him than otherwise down where he was going. "And so," said Mr. O———, "as I had no objection to investing a little money that way, I bought them." With a heart much lightened, I flew to tell poor Psyche the news, so that, at any rate, she might be relieved from the dread of any immediate separation from her husband. You can imagine better than I can tell you what her sensations were; but she still renewed her prayer that I would, if possible, induce Mr. [Butler] to purchase her, and I promised to do so.

Early the next morning, while I was still dressing, I was suddenly startled by hearing voices in loud tones in Mr. [Butler]'s dressing room, which adjoins my bedroom, and the noise increasing until there was an absolute cry of despair uttered by some man. I could restrain myself no longer, but opened the door of communication and saw Joe, the young man, poor Psyche's husband, raving almost in a state of frenzy, and in a voice broken with sobs and almost inarticulate with passion, reiterating his determination never to leave this plantation, never to go to Alabama, never to leave his old father and mother, his poor wife and children, and dashing his hat, which he was wringing like a cloth in his hands, upon the ground, he declared he would kill himself if he was compelled to follow Mr. K[ing]. I glanced from the poor wretch to Mr. [Butler], who was standing, leaning against a table with his arms folded, occasionally uttering a few words of counsel to his slave to be quiet and not fret, and not make fuss about what there was no help for. I retreated immediately from the horrid scene, breathless with surprise and dismay, and stood for some time in my own room, with my heart and temples throbbing to such a degree that I could hardly support myself. As soon as I recovered myself

I again sought Mr. O——, and inquired of him if he knew the cause of poor Joe's distress. He then told me that Mr. [Butler], who is highly pleased with Mr. K[ing]'s past administration of his property, wished, on his departure for his newly acquired slave plantation, to give him some token of his satisfaction, and *had made him a present* of the man Joe, who had just received the intelligence that he was to go down to Alabama with his new owner the next day, leaving father, mother, wife, and children behind. You will not wonder that the man required a little judicious soothing under such circumstances, and you will also, I hope, admire the humanity of the sale of his wife and children by the owner who was going to take him to Alabama, because *they* would be encumbrances rather than otherwise down there. If Mr. K[ing] did not do this after he knew that the man was his, then Mr. [Butler] gave him to be carried down to the South after his wife and children were sold to remain in Georgia. I do not know which was the real transaction, for I have not had the heart to ask; but you will easily imagine which of the two cases I prefer believing.

When I saw Mr. [Butler] after this most wretched story became known to me in all its details, I appealed to him, for his own soul's sake, not to commit so great a cruelty. Poor Joe's agony while remonstrating with his master was hardly greater than mine while arguing with him upon this bitter piece of inhumanity—how I cried, and how I adjured, and how all my sense of justice, and of mercy, and of pity for the poor wretch, and of wretchedness at finding myself implicated in such a state of things, broke in torrents of words from my lips and tears from my eyes! God knows such a sorrow at seeing anyone I belonged to commit such an act was indeed a new and terrible experience to me, and it seemed to me that I was imploring Mr. [Butler] to save himself more than to spare these wretches. He gave me no answer whatever, and I have since thought that the intemperate vehemence of my entreaties and expostulations perhaps deserved that he should leave me as he did without one single word of reply; and miserable enough I remained.

Toward evening, as I was sitting alone, my children having gone to bed, Mr. O—— came into the room. I had but one subject in my mind; I had not been able to eat for it. I could hardly sit still for the nervous distress which every thought of these poor people filled me with. As he sat down looking over some accounts, I said to him: "Have you seen Joe this afternoon, Mr. O——?" (I give you our conversation as it took place.)

"Yes, ma'am; he is a great deal happier than he was this morning."

"Why, how is that?" asked I, eagerly.

"Oh, he is not going to Alabama. Mr. K[ing] heard that he had kicked up a fuss about it" (being in despair at being torn from one's wife and children is called *kicking up a fuss*; this is a sample of overseer appreciation of human feelings), "and said that if the fellow wasn't willing to go with him, he did not wish to be bothered with any niggers down there who were to be troublesome, so he might stay behind."

"And does Psyche know this?"

"Yes, ma'am, I suppose so."

I drew a long breath; and whereas my needle had stumbled through the stuff I was sewing for an hour before, as if my fingers could not guide it, the regularity and rapidity of its evolutions were now quite edifying. The man was for the present safe, and I remained silently pondering his deliverance and the whole proceeding, and the conduct of everyone engaged in it, and, above all, Mr. [Butler]'s share in the transaction, and I think, for the first time, almost a sense of horrible personal responsibility and implication took hold of my mind, and I felt the weight of an unimagined guilt upon my conscience; and yet, God knows, this feeling of self-condemnation is very gratuitous on my part, since when I married Mr. [Butler] I knew nothing of these dreadful possessions of his, and even if I had I should have been much puzzled to have formed any idea of the state of things in which I now find myself plunged, together with those whose well-doing is as vital to me almost as my own.

With these agreeable reflections I went to bed. Mr. [Butler] said not a word to me upon the subject of these poor people all the next day, and in the meantime I became very impatient of this reserve on his part, because I was dying to prefer my request that he would purchase Psyche and her children, and so prevent any future separation between her and her husband, as I supposed he would not again attempt to make a present of Joe, at least to anyone who did not wish to be *bothered* with his wife and children. In the evening I was again with Mr. O—— alone in the strange, bare, wooden-walled sort of shanty which is our sitting room, and revolving in my mind the means of rescuing Psyche from her miserable suspense, a long chain of all my possessions, in the shape of bracelets, necklaces, brooches, earrings, etc., wound in glittering procession through my brain, with many hypothetical calculations of the value of each separate ornament, and the very doubtful probability of the amount of the whole being equal to the price of this poor creature and her children; and then the great power and privilege I had foregone of earning money by my own labor occurred to me, and I think, for the first time in my life, my past profession assumed an aspect that arrested my thoughts most seriously. For the last four years of my life that preceded my marriage I literally coined money, and never until this moment, I think, did I reflect on the great means of good, to myself and others, that I so gladly agreed to give up forever for a maintenance by the unpaid labor of slaves—people toiling not only unpaid, but under the bitter conditions the bare contemplation of which was then wringing my heart. You will not wonder that when, in the midst of such cogitations, I suddenly accosted Mr. O——, it was to this effect: "Mr. O——, I have a particular favor to beg of you. Promise me that you will never sell Psyche and her children without first letting me know of your intention to do so, and giving me the option of buying them."

Mr. O—— is a remarkably deliberate man, and squints, so that, when he has taken a little time in directing his eyes to you, you are still unpleasantly unaware of any result in which you are concerned; he laid down a book he was reading, and directed his head and one of his eyes toward me and answered: "Dear me, ma'am, I am very sorry—I have sold them."

My work fell down on the ground, and my mouth opened wide, but I could utter no sound, I was so dismayed and surprised; and he deliberately proceeded: "I didn't know, ma'am, you see, at all, that you entertained any idea of making an investment of that nature; for I'm sure, if I had, I would willingly have sold the woman to you; but I sold her and her children this morning to Mr. [Butler]."

My dear E[lizabeth], though [Mr. Butler] had resented my unmeasured upbraidings, you see they had not been without some good effect, and though he had, perhaps justly, punished my violent outbreak of indignation about the miserable scene I witnessed by not telling me of his humane purpose, he had bought these poor creatures, and so, I trust, secured them from any such misery in future. I jumped up and left Mr. O—— still speaking, and ran to find Mr. [Butler], to thank him for what he had done, and with that will now bid you good-by. Think, E[lizabeth], how it fares with slaves on plantations where there is no crazy Englishwoman to weep, and entreat, and implore, and upbraid for them, and no master willing to listen to such appeals.

My dearest Elizabeth, I write to you today (February 26) in great depression and distress. I have had a most painful conversation with Mr. Butler, who has declined receiving any of the people's petitions through me. Whether he is wearied with the number of these prayers and supplications, which he would escape but for me, as they probably would not venture to come so incessantly to him, and I, of course, feel bound to bring every one confided to me to him, or whether he has been annoyed at the number of pitiful and horrible stories of misery and oppression under the former rule of Mr. K[ing], which have come to my knowledge since I have been here, and the grief and indignation caused, but which cannot, by any means, always be done away with, though their expression may be silenced by his angry exclamations of: "Why do you listen to such stuff?" or "Why do you believe such trash? don't you know the niggers are all d——d liars?" etc., I do not know; but he desired me this morning to bring him no more complaints or requests of any sort, as the people had hitherto had no such advocate, and had done very well without, and I was only kept in an incessant state of excitement with all the falsehoods they "found they could make me believe." How well they have done without my advocacy, the conditions which I see with my own eyes, even more than their pitiful petitions, demonstrate; it is indeed true that the sufferings of those who come to me for redress, and, still more, the injustice done to the great majority who cannot, have filled my heart with bitterness and indignation that have overflowed my lips, till, I suppose Mr. [Butler] is weary of hearing what he has never heard before, the voice of passionate expostulation and importunate pleading against wrongs that he will not even acknowledge, and for creatures whose common humanity with his own I half think he does not believe, but I must return to the North, for my condition would be almost worse than theirs—condemned to hear and see so much wretchedness, not only without the means of alleviating it, but without permission even to represent it for alleviation; this is no place for me, since I was not born among slaves, and cannot bear to live among them.

Perhaps, after all, what he says is true: when I am gone they will fall back into the desperate uncomplaining habit of suffering, from which my coming among them, willing to hear and ready to help, has tempted them. He says that bringing their complaints to me, and the sight of my credulous commiseration, only tend to make them discontented and idle, and brings renewed chastisement upon them; and that so, instead of really befriending them, I am only preparing more suffering for them whenever I leave the place, and they can no more cry to me for help. And so I see nothing for it but to go and leave them to their fate; perhaps, too, he is afraid of the mere contagion of freedom which breathes from the very existence of those who are free; my way of speaking to the people, of treating them, or living with them, the appeals I make to their sense of truth, of duty, of self-respect, the infinite compassion and the human consideration I feel for them—all this, of course, makes my intercourse with them dangerously suggestive of relations far different from anything they have ever known; and, as Mr. O—— once almost hinted to me, my existence among slaves was an element of danger to the "institution." If I should go away, the human sympathy that I have felt for them will certainly never come near them again.

*P*hilip "Po" Bronson (1964–) is an American journalist and author best known for chronicling the technology boom of the 1990s, both in novels and articles published in "Wired" magazine and other technology-related publications. His first novel, Bombardiers, *was about bond-trading in San Francisco, and became an international best seller; in his novel* The First $20 Million Are Always the Hardest, *he wrote about technology start-up companies. His more recent bestseller,* What Shall I Do with My Life, *explores how different people address this universal life question.*

Introduction: Obvious Questions Don't Have Obvious Answers
From Your Fears Come Misconceptions

Po Bronson

We are all writing the story of our life. We want to know what it's "about," what are its themes and which theme is on the rise. We demand of it something deeper, or richer, or more substantive. We want to know where we're headed—not to spoil our own ending by ruining the surprise, but we want to ensure that when the ending comes, it won't be shallow. We will have done something. We will not have squandered our time here.

This book is about that urge, that need.

I began this project because I hit that point in my life. The television show I'd been writing for was canceled. The magazines I wrote for had thinned their pages. My longtime book editor had quit to pursue theater and film. I was out of work, I had a baby on the way (my first) and I was worried: how to be a good father, how to make money to support my family, and how to keep growing as a writer. I probably could have hustled up an assignment (the freelance writer's equivalent of following the advice "just go get a job") but I wasn't sure I should. I felt like the kinds of stories I'd been telling no longer worked. They no longer mapped the depth and drama of human life as I experienced it.

Looking for guidance and courage at this crossroads, I became intrigued by people who had unearthed their true calling, or at least those who were willing to try. Those who fought with the seduction of money, intensity, and novelty, but overcame their allure. Those who broke away from the chorus to learn the sound of their own voice. Nothing seemed more brave to me than facing up to one's own identity and filtering out the chatter that tells us to be someone we're not.

What might I learn from those who had confronted this question?

I decided on the simplest approach possible: I would express my curiosity to whoever would listen, trust this would provoke some leads, and travel the country tracking down the people whose stories spoke to me. I had no idea that sticking to this simple method would soon take me to so many places I'd never been, and far deeper into people's lives than I'd ever gone as a writer.

I hit on an incredible wellspring of honest sentiment. Complete strangers opened their lives and their homes to me, confessing feelings and events they hadn't revealed to their closest friends. This was at a time when we were losing our respect for corporate leaders, we no longer believed new technology would make our lives better, and the attack on our freedom made life precious and weighty. People were reassessing what mattered to them and what they believed in.

I heard some nine hundred stories, spent countless hours corresponding and on the phone, and came to know about seventy people closely. I spent time with them all in person, which was absolutely necessary. (About fifty are included in the book.) The word "interview" doesn't describe the emotional exchange that usually occurred. None were friends when I started, but most were by the time I was done. These were microwave friendships, forged with fast blasts of revelation and bonding, like those formed quickly in a freshman dorm, remembered for years. I let them cry in my arms. I slept on their couches. I sat in their musty attics, looking through old photo albums. We went running together. We traded secrets, I met their parents and held their children. I went to one's wedding. I became symbolically associated with their turning points. Many people described how much it helped them to have me listen; they talked their way into a greater understanding of what had transpired and why.

The people in this book are ordinary people. By that I mean they did not have available to them resources or character traits that gave them an uncommon advantage in pursuing a better life. Some have succeeded, many have not. They're not famous. Over half are parents. Over half participate actively in their church. They're a diverse assortment of ages and professions. Most (but not all) are educated, but a fair number earned that education later in life, as one step upward in their chosen transformation. A handful had spent years earning a high salary before they woke up to what their life was all about, but only a couple of them saved any of that money—most spent what they earned, just like anyone else, and as a result didn't have a safety net when they changed their life. Only two asked me not to use their real names. I've chosen stories that I hoped would encourage reflection and offer solace, not ones that merely entertained.

I was no expert. I had no credentials as a counselor or academic. I approached these people as merely "one of them." The events of my life had shredded any theories I used to have about how to address the question "What should I do with my life?" I had been humbled into admitting I knew nothing, and as I hit the road I was continuously humbled again by what some of these people had endured and the wisdom they seemed to radiate. I learned from them through inspiration and imitation. I also learned from the multiplicity of stories—by comparing how people talked and what language they invoked, certain patterns emerged, and I could place a story in the context of the larger picture.

I learned that it was in hard times that people usually changed the course of their life; in good times, they frequently only *talked* about change. Hard times forced them to overcome the doubts that normally gave them pause. It surprised me how often we hold ourselves back until we have no choice. So the people herein suffered layoffs, bankruptcies, divorces, evictions, illnesses, and the deaths of loved ones, and as a result they were as likely to stumble into a better life as they were to arrive there by reasoned planning. They made mistakes before summoning the courage to get it right. Their path called into question the notion that a calling is something you inherently know when you're young. Far from it. These people discovered in themselves gifts they rarely realized they had.

They spoke of fulfillment, not happiness. Very often they found fulfillment in living up to their moral responsibility to society—in finding some way to feel they were helping others, or at least connecting genuinely with others. In this sense, even though they were pursuing what they personally needed, they were learning selflessness. And while they had to fight hard to get what they loved, they also had to learn to love what they then got; while they scrapped for what was within their reach, they learned acceptance of events beyond their control. They did not find some Single Perfect Answer to the question; at some point it felt right enough that they made their choice, and the energy formerly spent casting about was now devoted to making their choice fruitful for as long as it might last. In every case, they found a place that was good for them. What I mean by that is, they found something that shaped their character in a positive way. Even if they didn't succeed wildly, the pursuit brought to the surface a trait that had been neglected. By no means have

I written about only the success stories. Many of the people I included were in midtransition, searching and hoping. This presented its own challenge, because they routinely asked for my counseling. This was always an uneasy role; usually, I handled this by telling other people's stories—"Here's what this person found, in a similar situation. . . . " In a few instances, I was not so passive when I sensed that my passivity—my listening mode—was being taken inappropriately as endorsement. I didn't want to be an accomplice to a wrong turn. So I cried to guide them by reminding them of their own stated resolutions. I didn't handle all these situations perfectly; I reveal these moments in the text to show my own fallibility.

People asked a great many questions that helped steer my research. Many of these questions were of the smart-aleck variety, merely intellectual/devil's advocate babble, but it was much more difficult and challenging to address those asked from the heart, by people stuck in the middle of it and honestly confused. Questions such as:

- Should I put my faith in mystical signs of destiny, or should my sense of "a right fit" be based on logical, practical reasons?

- When should I accept my lot, make peace with my ambition, and stop stressing out?

- Why do I feel guilty for thinking about this?

- Should I make money first, to fund my dream?

- How do I tell the difference between a curiosity and a passion?

- How do I weigh making myself a better person against external achievements?

- When do I need to change my situation, and when is it *me* that needs to change?

- What should I tell my parents, who worry about me?

- If I have a child, will my frustration over my work go away?

- What will it feel like when I get there? (How will I know I'm there?)

These were screamingly obvious questions, but it seemed they were almost so obvious that we hadn't publicly collected how we've learned to answer them—as if the answers should be obvious too, which they're not. Too often we're reticent about these issues. Talking about them can seem so fruitless, meanwhile inflaming anxiety and diverting us from the other things we have more control over, and can do. Yes, but it can also strengthen our resolve and shield us from distractions. I found that the biggest obstacle to answering the question this book poses is that people don't give themselves permission to take it seriously. At the risk of being fruitless, let this book be a safe place for a discussion.

This book does not research the history of its question. I don't quote experts, though I interviewed some, and I don't quote literature unless it was quoted to me by someone I wrote about. I didn't spend time in the library to write this book. Those sources of wisdom felt too abstract compared to the hard-earned record of those who actually took action, changed their life, and enjoyed or suffered the consequences.

Spending time with them affected me subtly. Afterward, I was always spent, and needed to recharge on the familiar patterns of my family, the writers' Grotto, and my soccer teams. I became hyperaware of what mattered to me and what was merely that week's noise intruding on my life. It stripped away some of the ways I had colored my past, and often I was visited by old friends in my dreams. I became more honest in person, less contrived in my writing. They helped me find my own story. They wanted to know how I'd come to be a writer, and how I'd recently become a husband (for the second time) and a father (for the first time). I'd never written about my own journey, never thought it was a story worth telling, but hearing their stories helped me tell my own in a way that it finally did have some oomph. To some it was inspiration, and to others it was kinship. *Okay, he gets it.*

My biggest surprise was how being a new dad folded into the book, and how I face this question now that I have a family. Writing hadn't come easily to me, and I've had to be very protective of my love for it. I was once so afraid that being a parent was incompatible with being a writer. The travel, the intense concentration. For years this fear had stopped me from mixing the two. Somehow, in a year in which our son, Luke, was born, and my wife, Michele, a molecular immunologist, was putting a drug through the FDA's approval process, I found the time and the room in my heart for this enormous project. I took my family with me whenever I could, which was most of the time. In his first year Luke went on seventeen trips of up to ten days in length, including weeks in London and Hong Kong, which he loved because it was hot. Now it seems like a miracle.

It's a far different book from what I originally envisioned. It reflects what I found, not what I predicted. I didn't write a single person's story until I had gotten to know two-thirds of them, and even then their meaning was just beginning to show itself. Nowhere is this more apparent than in the way I've arranged these stories. Since my method conveys how I'm implicitly suggesting we think about this question—and since figuring out how to do this didn't come easily—an explanation is probably necessary.

This book doesn't follow a conventional outline. Every week I sketched out another scenario for grouping these people's lives. Most people had fair claim to several groups. Too many never fit any. It was always clear that the benefits of categorization were outweighed by the harm in chopping their lives down to an anecdote.

I couldn't shake the urge to tame this question by shackling it with some orderly form. But the human soul resists taxonomy. What heals one person might harm another. Ultimately, I bowed down in respect. I recognized that my urge to classify was an attempt to make this journey easy or quick, and to strive for simplification demonstrated a hubris on my part, and a lack of appreciation for the blind winding road we must take. And once I'd done that, I finally found the right arrangement, a flow from story to story.

There are many very real stumbling blocks that prevent us from pursuing this question: *never enough money, never enough time.* We're aware of those constraints—they're right in front of us, every day. But we also have many psychological stumbling blocks that keep us from finding ourselves. Some of these are badly tangled misconceptions, some are deeply rooted fears. The two are related—like any prejudice, misconceptions get fabricated and sustained by fears. These psychological stumbling blocks are often less real than we imagine. By confronting them, we begin to see around all our obstacles, even the seemingly insurmountable ones. If you take care of these obstacles, you create an environment where the truth is invited into your life.

So this book is meant to unearth the psychological demons that haunt us. It's not organized by industry or personality type, and it's not a travelogue. It uses people's stories to demonstrate these misconceptions and fears, and shows how people are confronting them or have gotten past them. They're not meant to be read out of order, though there's no harm in that. They're meant to build on each other. Ideas and terminology brought up in earlier stories are invoked in subsequent ones, and the result is meant to resemble a rolling conversation, but one in which the ideas are continually reined in by dogged reality.

When people heard this book's title, the most common question I'd get asked was, "So is your book about life, or about careers?" And I'd laugh, and warn them not to get trapped by semantics, and answer, "It's about people who've dared to be honest with themselves."

*L*uther Standing Bear (1868?–1939) was born Ota K'te on the Pine Ridge Reservation in South Dakota, and was raised as a traditional Sioux. In the 1920s and 1930s he fought to improve conditions for Indians on the reservations, writing several books about Indian life and government policy. Luther Standing Bear worked as an assistant teacher at the government school on the Rosebud Reservation in South Dakota, owned a ranch, served as an assistant to a minister, traveled with Buffalo Bill's Wild West Show in Europe and became an actor and an activist in the Native American community in Los Angeles. He published four books, the first when he was more than fifty years old.

At Last I Kill a Buffalo

Luther Standing Bear

At last the day came when my father allowed me to go on a buffalo hunt with him. And what a proud boy I was!

Ever since I could remember my father had been teaching me the things that I should know and preparing me to be a good hunter. I had learned to make bows and to string them; and to make arrows and tip them with feathers. I knew how to ride my pony no matter how fast he would go, and I felt that I was brave and did not fear danger. All these things I had learned for just this day when father would allow me to go with him on a buffalo hunt. It was the event for which every Sioux boy eagerly waited. To ride side by side with the best hunters of the tribe, to hear the terrible noise of the great herds as they ran, and then to help to bring home the kill was the most thrilling day of any Indian boy's life. The only other event which could equal it would be the day I went for the first time on the warpath to meet the enemy and protect my tribe.

On the following early morning we were to start, so the evening was spent in preparation. Although the tipis were full of activity, there was no noise nor confusion outside. Always the evening before a buffalo hunt and when every one was usually in his tipi, an old man went around the circle of tipis calling, "I-ni-la," "I-ni-la," not loudly, but so every one could hear. The old man was saying, "Keep quiet," "Keep quiet." We all knew that the scouts had come in and reported buffalo near and that we must all keep the camp in stillness. It was not necessary for the old man to go into each tipi and explain to the men that tomorrow there would be a big hunt, as the buffalo were coming. He did not order the men to prepare their weapons and neither did he order the mothers to keep children from crying. The one word, "I-ni-la," was sufficient to bring quiet to the whole camp. That night there would be no calling or shouting from tipi to tipi and no child would cry aloud. Even the horses and dogs obeyed the command for quiet, and all night not a horse neighed and not a dog barked. The very presence of quiet was everywhere. Such is the orderliness of a Sioux camp that men, women, children, and animals seem to have a common understanding and sympathy. It is no mystery but natural that the Indian and his animals understand each other very well both with words and without words. There are words, however, that the Indian uses that are understood by both his horses and dogs. When on a hunt, if one of the warriors speaks the word "A-a-ah" rather quickly and sharply, every man, horse, and dog will stop instantly and listen. Not a move will be made by an animal until the men move or speak further. As long as the hunters listen, the animals will listen also.

The night preceding a buffalo hunt was always an exciting night, even though it was quiet in camp. There would be much talk in the tipis around the fires. There would be sharpening of arrows and of knives. New bowstrings would be made and quivers would be filled with arrows.

It was in the fall of the year and the evenings were cool as father and I sat by the fire and talked over the hunt. I was only eight years of age, and I know that father did not expect me to get a buffalo at all, but only to try perhaps for a small calf should I be able to get close enough to one. Nevertheless, I was greatly excited as I sat and watched father working in his easy, firm way.

I was wearing my buffalo-skin robe, the hair next to my body. Mother had made me a rawhide belt and this, wrapped around my waist, held my blanket on when I threw it off my shoulders. In the early morning I would wear it, for it would be cold. When it came time to shoot, I should not want my blanket but the belt would hold it in place.

You can picture me, I think, as I sat in the glow of the campfire, my little brown body bare to the waist watching, and listening intently to my father. My hair hung down my back and I wore moccasins and breechcloth of buckskin. To my belt was fastened a rawhide holster for my knife, for when I was eight years of age we had plenty of knives. I was proud to own a knife, and this night I remember I kept it on all night. Neither did I lay aside my bow, but went to sleep with it in my hand, thinking, I suppose, to be all the nearer ready in the morning when the start was made.

Father sharpened my steel points for me and also sharpened my knife. The whetstone was a long stone which was kept in a buckskin bag, and sometimes this stone went all over the camp; every tipi did not have one, so we shared this commodity with one another. I had as I remember about ten arrows, so when father was through sharpening them I put them in my rawhide quiver. I had a rawhide quirt, too, which I would wear fastened to my waist. As father worked, he knew I was watching him closely and listening whenever he spoke. By the time all preparations had been made, he had told me just how I was to act when I started out in the morning with the hunters.

We went to bed, my father hoping that tomorrow would be successful for him so that he could bring home some nice meat for the family and a hide for my mother to tan. I went to bed, but could not go to sleep at once, so filled was I with the wonderment and excitement of it all. The next day was to be a test for me. I was to prove to my father whether he was or was not justified in his pride in me. What would be the result of my training? Would I be brave if I faced danger and would father be proud of me? Though I did not know it that night I was to be tried for the strength of my manhood and my honesty in this hunt. Something happened that day which I remember above all things. It was a test of my real character and I am proud to say that I did not find myself weak, but made a decision that has been all these years a gratification to me.

The next morning the hunters were catching their horses about daybreak. I arose with my father and went out and caught my pony. I wanted to do whatever he did and show him that he did not have to tell me what to do. We brought our animals to the tipi and got our bows and arrows and mounted. From over the village came the hunters. Most of them were leading their running horses. These running horses were anxious for the hunt and came prancing, their ears straight up and their tails waving in the air. We were joined with perhaps a hundred or more riders, some of whom carried bows and arrows and some armed with guns.

The buffalo were reported to be about five or six miles away as we should count distance now. At that time we did not measure distance in miles. One camping distance was about ten miles, and these buffalo were said to be about one half camping distance away.

Some of the horses were to be left at a stopping-place just before the herd was reached. These horses were pack-animals which were taken along to carry extra blankets or weapons. They were trained to remain there until the hunters came for them. Though they were neither hobbled nor tied, they stood still during the shooting and noise of the chase.

My pony was a black one and a good runner. I felt very important as I rode along with the hunters and my father, the chief. I kept as close to him as I could.

Two men had been chosen to scout or to lead the party. These two men were in a sense policemen whose work it was to keep order. They carried large sticks of ash wood, something like a policeman's billy, though longer. They rode ahead of the party while the rest of us kept in a group close together. The leaders went ahead until they sighted the herd of grazing buffalo. Then they stopped and waited for the rest of us to ride up. We all rode slowly toward the herd, which on sight of us had come together, although they had been scattered here and there over the plain. When they saw us, they all ran close together as if at the command of a leader. We continued riding slowly toward the herd until one of the leaders shouted, "Ho-ka-he!" which means, "Ready, Go!" At that command every man started for the herd. I had been listening, too, and the minute the hunters started, I started also.

Away I went, my little pony putting all he had into the race. It was not long before I lost sight of father, but I kept going just the same. I threw my blanket back and the chill of the autumn morning struck my body, but I did not mind. On I went. It was wonderful to race over the ground with all these horsemen about me. There was no shouting, no noise of any kind except the pounding of the horses' feet. The herd was now running and had raised a cloud of dust. I felt no fear until we had entered this cloud of dust and I could see nothing about me—only hear the sound of feet. Where was father? Where was I going? On I rode through the cloud, for I knew I must keep going.

Then all at once I realized that I was in the midst of the buffalo, their dark bodies rushing all about me and their great heads moving up and down to the sound of their hoofs beating upon the earth. Then it was that fear overcame me and I leaned close down upon my little pony's body and clutched him tightly. I can never tell you how I felt toward my pony at that moment. All thought of shooting had left my mind. I was seized by blank fear. In a moment or so, however, my senses became clearer, and I could distinguish other sounds beside the clatter of feet. I could hear a shot now and then and I could see the buffalo beginning to break up into small bunches. I could not see father nor any of my companions yet, but my fear was vanishing and I was safe. I let my pony run. The buffalo looked too large for me to tackle, anyway, so I just kept going. The buffalo became more and more scattered. Pretty soon I saw a young calf that looked about my size. I remembered now what father had told me the night before as we sat about the fire. Those instructions were important for me now to follow.

I was still back of the calf, being unable to get alongside of him. I was anxious to get a shot, yet afraid to try, as I was still very nervous. While my pony was making all speed to come alongside, I chanced a shot and to my surprise my arrow landed. My second arrow glanced along the back of the animal and sped on between the horns, making only a slight wound. My third arrow hit a spot that made the running beast slow up in his gait. I shot a fourth arrow, and though it, too, landed it was not a fatal wound. It seemed to me that it was taking a lot of shots, and I was not proud of my marksmanship. I was glad, however, to see the animal going slower and I knew that one more shot would make me a hunter. My horse seemed to know his own importance. His two ears stood straight forward and it was not necessary for me to urge him to get closer to the buffalo. I was soon by the side of the buffalo and one more shot brought the chase to a close. I jumped from my pony, and as I stood by my fallen game, I looked all around wishing that the world could see. But I was alone. In my determination to stay by until I had won my buffalo, I had not noticed that I was far from every one else. No admiring friends were about, and as far as I could see I was on the plain alone. The herd of buffalo had completely disappeared. And as for father, much as I wished for him, he was out of sight and I had no idea where he was.

I stood and looked at the animal on the ground. I was happy. Every one must know that I, Ota K'te, had killed a buffalo. But it looked as if no one knew where I was, so no one was coming my way. I must then take something from this animal to show that I had killed it. I took all the arrows one by one from the body. As I took them out, it occurred to me that I had used five arrows. If I had been a skillful hunter, one arrow would have been sufficient, but I had used five. Here it was that temptation came to me. Why could I not take out two of the arrows and throw them away? No one would know, and then I should be more greatly admired and praised as a hunter. As it was, I knew that I should be praised by father and mother, but I wanted more. And so I was tempted to lie.

I was planning this as I took out my skinning knife that father had sharpened for me the night before. I skinned one side of the animal, but when it came to turning it over, I was too small. I was wondering what to do when I heard my father's voice calling, "To-ki-i-la-la-hu-wo," "Where are you?" I quickly jumped on my pony and rode to the top of a little hill near by. Father saw me and came to me at once. He was so pleased to see me and glad to know that I was safe. I knew that I could never lie to my father. He was too fond of me and I too proud of him. He had always told me to tell the truth. He wanted me to be an honest man, so I resolved then to tell the truth even if it took from me a little glory. He rode up to me with a glad expression on his face, expecting me to go back with him to his kill. As he came up, I said as calmly as I could, "Father, I have killed a buffalo." His smile changed to surprise and he asked me where my buffalo was. I pointed to it and we rode over to where it lay, partly skinned.

Father set to work to skin it for me. I had watched him do this many times and knew perfectly well how to do it myself, but I could not turn the animal over. There was a way to turn the head of the animal so that the body would be balanced on the back while being skinned. Father did this for me, while I helped all I could. When the hide was off, father put it on the pony's back with the hair side next to the pony. On this he arranged the meat so it would balance. Then he covered the meat carefully with the rest of the hide, so no dust would reach it while we traveled home. I rode home on top of the load.

I showed my father the arrows that I had used and just where the animal had been hit. He was very pleased and praised me over and over again. I felt more glad than ever that I had told the truth and I have never regretted it. I am more proud now that I told the truth than I am of killing the buffalo.

We then rode to where my father had killed a buffalo. There we stopped and prepared it for taking home. It was late afternoon when we got back to camp. No king ever rode in state who was more proud than I that day as I came into the village sitting high up on my load of buffalo meat. Mother had now two hunters in the family and I knew how she was going to make over me. It is not customary for Indian men to brag about their exploits and I had been taught that bragging was not nice. So I was very quiet, although I was bursting with pride. Always when arriving home I would run out to play, for I loved to be with the other boys, but this day I lingered about close to the tipi so I could hear the nice things that were said about me. It was soon all over camp that Ota K'te had killed a buffalo.

My father was so proud that he gave away a fine horse. He called an old man to our tipi to cry out the news to the rest of the people in camp. The old man stood at the door of our tipi and sang a song of praise to my father. The horse had been led up and I stood holding it by a rope. The old man who was doing the singing called the other old man who was to receive the horse as a present. He accepted the horse by coming up to me, holding out his hands to me, and saying, "Ha-ye," which means "Thank you." The old man went away very grateful for the horse.

That ended my first and last buffalo hunt. It lives only in my memory, for the days of the buffalo are over.

Malcom X (1925–1965) was born as Malcolm Little in Omaha, Nebraska, the seventh child of a Baptist minister and active member of Marcus Garvey's Universal Improvement Association. Later, Malcom X became a Black Muslim, was an assistant minister in Detroit, and founded Muslim temples throughout the United States. In 1964 he formed his own organization, the Organization of Afro-American Unity. This excerpt is taken from The Autobiography of Malcolm X.

Hair

Malcolm X

Shorty soon decided that my hair was finally long enough to be conked. He had promised to school me in how to beat the barbershop's three- and four-dollar price by making up congolene, and then conking ourselves.

I took the little list of ingredients he had printed out for me, and went to a grocery store, where I got a can of Red Devil lye, two eggs, and two medium-sized white potatoes. Then at a drugstore near the poolroom, I asked for a large jar of vaseline, a large bar of soap, a large-toothed comb and a fine-toothed comb, one of those rubber hoses with a metal spray-head, a rubber apron and a pair of gloves.

"Going to lay on that first conk?" the drugstore man asked me. I proudly told him, grinning, "Right!"

Shorty paid six dollars a week for a room in his cousin's shabby apartment. His cousin wasn't at home. "It's like the pad's mine, he spends so much time with his woman," Shorty said, "Now, you watch me—"

He peeled the potatoes and thin-sliced them into a quart-sized Mason fruit jar, then started stirring them with a wooden spoon as he gradually poured in a little over half the can of lye. "Never use a metal spoon; the lye will turn it black," he told me.

A jelly-like, starchy-looking glop resulted from the lye and potatoes, and Shorty broke in the two eggs, stirring real fast—his own conk and dark face bent down close. The congolene turned pale-yellowish. "Feel the jar," Shorty said. I cupped my hand against the outside, and snatched it away. "Damn right, it's hot, that's the lye," he said. "So you know it's going to burn when I comb it in—it burns *bad*. But the longer you can stand it, the straighter the hair."

He made me sit down, and he tied the string of the new rubber apron tightly around my neck, and combed up my bush of hair. Then, from the big vaseline jar, he took a handful and massaged it hard all through my hair and into the scalp. He also thickly vaselined my neck, ears and forehead. "When I get to washing out your head, be sure to tell me anywhere you feel any little stinging," Shorty warned me, washing his hands, then pulling on the rubber gloves, and tying on his own rubber apron. "You always got to remember that any congolene left in burns a sore into your head."

The congolene just felt warm when Shorty started combing it in. But then my head caught fire.

I gritted my teeth and tried to pull the sides of the kitchen table together. The comb felt as if it was raking my skin off.

My eyes watered, my nose was running. I couldn't stand it any longer; I bolted to the washbasin. I was cursing Shorty with every name I could think of when he got the spray going and started soap-lathering my head.

He lathered and spray-rinsed, lathered and spray-rinsed, maybe ten or twelve times, each time gradually closing the hot-water faucet, until the rinse was cold, and that helped some.

"You feel any stinging spots?"

"No." I managed to say. My knees were trembling.

"Sit back down, then. I think we got it all out okay."

The flame came back as Shorty, with a thick towel, started drying my head, rubbing hard. *"Easy, man, easy"* I kept shouting.

"The first time's always worst. You get used to it better before long. You took it real good, homeboy. You got a good conk."

When Shorty let me stand up and see in the mirror, my hair hung down in limp, damp strings. My scalp still flamed, but not as badly; I could bear it. He draped the towel around my shoulders, over my rubber apron, and began again vaselining my hair.

I could feel him combing, straight back, first the big comb, then the fine-tooth one.

Then, he was using a razor, very delicately, on the back of my neck. Then, finally, shaping the sideburns.

My first view in the mirror blotted out the hurting. I'd seen some pretty conks, but when it's the first time, on your *own* head, the transformation, after the lifetime of kinks, is staggering.

The mirror reflected Shorty behind me. We both were grinning and sweating. And on top of my head was this thick, smooth sheen of shining red hair—real red—as straight as any white man's.

How ridiculous I was! Stupid enough to stand there simply lost in admiration of my hair now looking "white," reflected in the mirror in Shorty's room. I vowed that I'd never again be without a conk, and I never was for many years.

This was my first really big step toward self-degradation: when I endured all of that pain, literally burning my flesh to have it look like white man's hair. I had joined that multitude of Negro men and women in America who are brainwashed into believing that the black people are "inferior"—and white people "superior"—that they will even violate and mutilate their God-created bodies to try to look "pretty" by white standards.

Sherman Alexie (1966–) is a Spokane Coeur D'Alene Indian from Wellpinit, Washington. His poems and stories are direct and concise, revolving around common situations that reflect his experience on the Spokane Indian Reservation. His works include The Lone Ranger and Tonto Fistfight in Heaven, *which is a collection of related short stories, and* The Absolutely True Diary of a Part-Time Indian, *a novel.*

Indian Education

Sherman Alexie

First Grade

My hair was too short and my U.S. Government glasses were horn-rimmed, ugly, and all that first winter in school, the other Indian boys chased me from one corner of the playground to the other. They pushed me down, buried me in the snow until I couldn't breathe, thought I'd never breathe again.

They stole my glasses and threw them over my head, around my out-stretched hands, just beyond my reach, until someone tripped me and sent me falling again, facedown in the snow.

I was always falling down; my Indian name was Junior Falls Down. Sometimes it was Bloody Nose or Steal-His-Lunch. Once, it was Cries-Like-a-White-Boy, even though none of us had seen a white boy cry.

Then it was a Friday morning recess and Frenchy SiJohn threw snowballs at me while the rest of the Indian boys tortured some other *top-yogh-yaught* kid, another weakling. But Frenchy was confident enough to torment me all by himself, and most days I would have let him.

But the little warrior in me roared to life that day and knocked Frenchy to the ground, held his head against the snow, and punched him so hard that my knuckles and the snow made symmetrical bruises on his face. He almost looked like he was wearing war paint.

But he wasn't the warrior. I was. And I chanted *It's a good day to die, it's a good day to die,* all the way down to the principal's office.

Second Grade

Betty Towle, missionary teacher, redheaded and so ugly that no one ever had a puppy crush on her, made me stay in for recess fourteen days straight.

"Tell me you're sorry," she said.

"Sorry for what?" I asked.

"Everything," she said and made me stand straight for fifteen minutes, eagle-armed with books in each hand. One was a math book; the other was English. But all I learned was that gravity can be painful.

For Halloween I drew a picture of her riding a broom with a scrawny cat on the back. She said that her God would never forgive me for that.

Once, she gave the class a spelling test but set me aside and gave me a test designed for junior high students. When I spelled all the words right, she crumpled up the paper and made me eat it.

"You'll learn respect," she said.

She sent a letter home with me that told my parents to either cut my braids or keep me home from class. My parents came in the next day and dragged their braids across Betty Towle's desk.

"Indians, indians, indians." She said it without capitalization. She called me "indian, indian, indian."

And I said, *Yes, I am. I am Indian. Indian, I am.*

Third Grade

My traditional Native American art career began and ended with my very first portrait: *Stick Indian Taking a Piss in My Backyard.*

As I circulated the original print around the classroom, Mrs. Schluter intercepted and confiscated my art.

Censorship, I might cry now. *Freedom of expression,* I would write in editorials to the tribal newspaper.

In third grade, though, I stood alone in the corner, faced the wall, and waited for the punishment to end.

I'm still waiting.

Fourth Grade

"You should be a doctor when you grow up," Mr. Schluter told me, even though his wife, the third grade teacher, thought I was crazy beyond my years. My eyes always looked like I had just hit-and-run someone.

"Guilty," she said. "You always look guilty."

"Why should I be a doctor?" I asked Mr. Schluter.

"So you can come back and help the tribe. So you can heal people."

That was the year my father drank a gallon of vodka a day and the same year that my mother started two hundred different quilts but never finished any. They sat in separate, dark places in our HUD house and wept savagely.

I ran home after school, heard their Indian tears, and looked in the mirror. *Doctor Victor,* I called myself, invented an education, talked to my reflection *Doctor Victor to the emergency room.*

Fifth Grade

I picked up a basketball for the first time and made my first shot. No. I missed my first shot, missed the basket completely, and the ball landed in the dirt and sawdust, sat there just like I had sat there only minutes before.

But it felt good, that ball in my hands, all those possibilities and angles. It was mathematics, geometry. It was beautiful.

At that same moment, my cousin Steven Ford sniffed rubber cement from a paper bag and leaned back on the merry-go-round. His ears rang, his mouth was dry, and everyone seemed so far away.

But it felt good, that buzz in his head, all those colors and noises. It was chemistry, biology. It was beautiful.

Oh, do you remember those sweet, almost innocent choices that the Indian boys were forced to make?

Sixth Grade

Randy, the new Indian kid from the white town of Springdale, got into a fight an hour after he first walked into the reservation school.

Stevie Flett called him out, called him a squawman, called him a pussy, and called him a punk.

Randy and Stevie, and the rest of the Indian boys, walked out into the playground.

"Throw the first punch," Stevie said as they squared off.

"No," Randy said.

"Throw the first punch," Stevie said again.

"No," Randy said again.

"Throw the first punch!" Stevie said for the third time, and Randy reared back and pitched a knuckle fastball that broke Stevie's nose.

We all stood there in silence, in awe.

That was Randy; my soon-to-be first and best friend, who taught me the most valuable lesson about living in the white world: *Always throw the first punch.*

Seventh Grade

I leaned through the basement window of the HUD house and kissed the white girl who would later be raped by her foster-parent father, who was also white. They both lived on the reservation, though, and when the headlines and stories filled the papers later, not one word was made of their color.

Just Indians being Indians, someone must have said somewhere and they were wrong.

But on the day I leaned through the basement window of the HUD house and kissed the white girl, I felt the good-byes I was saying to my entire tribe. I held my lips tight against her lips, a dry, clumsy, and ultimately stupid kiss.

But I was saying good-bye to my tribe, to all the Indian girls and women I might have loved, to all the Indian men who might have called me cousin, even brother.

I kissed that white girl and when I opened my eyes, she was gone from the reservation, and when I opened my eyes, I was gone from the reservation, living in a farm town where a beautiful white girl asked my name.

"Junior Polatkin," I said, and she laughed.

After that, no one spoke to me for another five hundred years.

Eighth Grade

At the farm town junior high, in the boys' bathroom, I could hear voices from the girls' bathroom, nervous whispers of anorexia and bulimia. I could hear the white girls' forced vomiting, a sound so familiar and natural to me after years of listening to my father's hangovers.

"Give me your lunch if you're just going to throw it up," I said to one of those girls once.

I sat back and watched them grow skinny from self-pity.

Back on the reservation, my mother stood in line to get us commodities. We carried them home, happy to have food, and opened the canned beef that even the dogs wouldn't eat.

But we ate it day after day and grew skinny from self-pity.

There is more than one way to starve.

Ninth Grade

At the farm town high school dance, after a basketball game in an overheated gym where I had scored twenty-seven points and pulled down thirteen rebounds, I passed out during a slow song.

As my white friends revived me and prepared to take me to the emergency room where doctors would later diagnose my diabetes, the Chicano teacher ran up to us.

"Hey," he said. "What's that boy been drinking? I know all about these Indian kids. They start drinking real young."

Sharing dark skin doesn't necessarily make two men brothers.

Tenth Grade

I passed the written test easily and nearly flunked the driving, but still received my Washington State driver's license on the same day that Wally Jim killed himself by driving his car into a pine tree.

No traces of alcohol in his blood, good job, wife and two kids.

"Why'd he do it?" asked a white Washington State trooper.

All the Indians shrugged their shoulders, looked down at the ground.

"Don't know," we all said, but when we look in the mirror, see the history of our tribe in our eyes, taste failure in the tap water, and shake with old tears, we understand completely.

Believe me, everything looks like a noose if you stare at it long enough.

Eleventh Grade

Last night I missed two free throws which would have won the game against the best team in the state. The farm town high school I play for is nicknamed the "Indians," and I'm probably the only actual Indian ever to play for a team with such a mascot.

This morning I pick up the sports page and read the headline: INDIANS LOSE AGAIN.

Go ahead and tell me none of this is supposed to hurt me very much.

Twelfth Grade

I walk down the aisle, valedictorian of this farm town high school, and my cap doesn't fit because I've grown my hair longer than it's ever been. Later, I stand as the school board chairman recites my awards, accomplishments, and scholarships.

I try to remain stoic for the photographers as I look toward the future.

Back home on the reservation, my former classmates graduate: a few can't read, one or two are just given attendance diplomas, most look forward to the parties. The bright students are shaken, frightened, because they don't know what comes next.

They smile for the photographer as they look back toward tradition.

The tribal newspaper runs my photograph and the photograph of my former classmates side by side.

Postscript: Class Reunion

Victor said, "Why should we organize a reservation high school reunion? My graduating class has a reunion every weekend at the Powwow Tavern."

*M*aya Angelou (1928–) was born in St. Louis and spent her early years in California and Arkansas. She has worked as a cook, a streetcar conductor, a television screenwriter, and an actress, but is best known as a writer, poet and public speaker. This excerpt is taken from I Know Why the Caged Bird Sings.

Graduation

Maya Angelou

The children in Stamps trembled visibly with anticipation. Some adults were excited too, but to be certain the whole young population had come down with graduation epidemic. Large classes were graduating from both the grammar school and the high school. Even those who were years removed from their own day of glorious release were anxious to help with preparations as a kind of dry run. The junior students who were moving into the vacating classes' chairs were tradition-bound to show their talents for leadership and management. They strutted through the school and around the campus exerting pressure on the lower grades. Their authority was so new that occasionally if they pressed a little too hard it had to be overlooked. After all, next term was coming, and it never hurt a sixth grader to have a play sister in the eighth grade, or a tenth-year student to be able to call a twelfth grader Bubba. So all was endured in a spirit of shared understanding. But the graduating classes themselves were the nobility. Like travelers with exotic destinations on their minds, the graduates were remarkably forgetful. They came to school without their books, or tablets or even pencils. Volunteers fell over themselves to secure replacements for the missing equipment. When accepted, the willing workers might or might not be thanked, and it was of no importance to the pregraduation rites. Even teachers were respectful of the now quiet and aging seniors, and tended to speak to them, if not as equals, as beings only slightly lower than themselves. After tests were returned and grades given, the student body, which acted like an extended family, knew who did well, who excelled, and what piteous ones had failed.

Unlike the white high school, Lafayette County Training School distinguished itself by having neither lawn, nor hedges, nor tennis court, nor climbing ivy. Its two buildings (main classrooms, the grade school and home economics) were set on a dirt hill with no fence to limit either its boundaries or those of bordering farms. There was a large expanse to the left of the school which was used alternately as a baseball diamond or a basketball court. Rusty hoops on the swaying poles represented the permanent recreational equipment, although bats and balls could be borrowed from the P.E. teacher if the borrower was qualified and if the diamond wasn't occupied.

Over this rocky area relieved by a few shady tall persimmon trees the graduating class walked. The girls often held hands and no longer bothered to speak to the lower students. There was a sadness about them, as if this old world was not their home and they were bound for higher ground. The boys, on the other hand, had become more friendly, more outgoing. A decided change from the closed attitude they projected while studying for finals. Now they seemed not ready to give up the old school, the familiar paths and classrooms. Only a small percentage would be continuing on to college—one of the South's A & M (agricultural and mechanical) schools, which trained Negro youths to be carpenters, farmers, handymen, masons, maids, cooks and baby nurses. Their future rode heavily on their shoulders, and blinded them to the collective joy that had pervaded the lives of the boys and girls in the grammar school graduating class.

Parents who could afford it had ordered new shoes and ready-made clothes for themselves from Sears and Roebuck or Montgomery Ward. They also engaged the best seamstresses to make the floating graduating dresses and to cut down secondhand pants which would be pressed to a military slickness for the important event.

Oh, it was important, all right. Whitefolks would attend the ceremony, and two or three would speak of God and home, and the Southern way of life, and Mrs. Parsons, the principal's wife, would play the graduation march while the lower-grade graduates paraded down the aisles and took their seats below the platform. The high school seniors would wait in empty classrooms to make their dramatic entrance.

In the Store I was the person of the moment. The birthday girl. The center. Bailey had graduated the year before, although to do so he had to forfeit all pleasures to make up for his time lost in Baton Rouge.

My class was wearing butter-yellow piqué dresses, and Momma launched out on mine. She smocked the yoke into tiny crisscrossing puckers, then shirred the rest of the bodice. Her dark fingers ducked in and out of the lemony cloth as she embroidered raised daisies around the hem. Before she considered herself finished she had added a crocheted cuff on the puff sleeves, and a pointy crocheted collar.

I was going to be lovely. A walking model of all the various styles of fine hand sewing and it didn't worry me that I was only twelve years old and merely graduating from the eighth grade. Besides, many teachers in Arkansas Negro schools had only that diploma and were licensed to impart wisdom.

The days had become longer and more noticeable. The faded beige of former times had been replaced with strong and sure colors. I began to see my classmates' clothes, their skin tones, and the dust that waved off pussy willows. Clouds that lazed across the sky were objects of great concern to me. Their shiftier shapes might have held a message that in my new happiness and with a little bit of time I'd soon decipher. During that period I looked at the arch of heaven so religiously my neck kept a steady ache. I had taken to smiling more often, and my jaws hurt from the unaccustomed activity. Between the two physical sore spots, I suppose I could have been uncomfortable, but that was not the case. As a member of the winning team (the graduating class of 1940) I had outdistanced unpleasant sensations by miles. I was headed for the freedom of open fields.

Youth and social approval allied themselves with me and we trammeled memories of slights and insults. The wind of our swift passage remodeled my features. Lost tears were pounded to mud and then to dust. Years of withdrawal were brushed aside and left behind, as hanging ropes of parasitic moss.

My work alone had awarded me a top place and I was going to be one of the first called in the graduating ceremonies. On the classroom blackboard, as well as on the bulletin board in the auditorium, there were blue stars and white stars and red stars. No absences, no tardinesses, and my academic work was among the best of the year. I could say the preamble to the Constitution even faster than Bailey. We timed ourselves often: "We the people of the United States in order to form a more perfect union . . ." I had memorized the Presidents of the United States from Washington to Roosevelt in chronological as well as alphabetical order.

My hair pleased me too. Gradually the black mass had lengthened and thickened, so that it kept at last to its braided pattern, and I didn't have to yank my scalp off when I tried to comb it.

Louise and I had rehearsed the exercises until we tired out ourselves. Henry Reed was class valedictorian. He was a small, very black boy with hooded eyes, a long, broad nose and an oddly shaped head. I had admired him for years because each term he and I vied for the best grades in our class. Most often he bested me, but instead of being disappointed I was pleased that we shared top places between us. Like many Southern

Black children, he lived with his grandmother, who was as strict as Momma and as kind as she knew how to be. He was courteous, respectful and soft-spoken to elders, but on the playground he chose to play the roughest games. I admired him. Anyone, I reckoned, sufficiently afraid or sufficiently dull could be polite. But to be able to operate at a top level with both adults and children was admirable.

His valedictory speech was entitled "To Be or Not To Be." The rigid tenth-grade teacher had helped him to write it. He'd been working on the dramatic stresses for months.

The weeks until graduation were filled with heady activities. A group of small children were to be presented in a play about buttercups and daisies and bunny rabbits. They could be heard throughout the building practicing their hops and their little songs that sounded like silver bells. The older girls (nongraduates, of course) were assigned the task of making refreshments for the night's festivities. A tangy scent of ginger, cinnamon, nutmeg and chocolate wafted around the home economics building as the budding cooks made samples for themselves and their teachers.

In every corner of the workshop, axes and saws split fresh timber as the woodshop boys made sets and stage scenery. Only the graduates were left out of the general bustle. We were free to sit in the library at the back of the building or look in quite detachedly, naturally, on the measures being taken for our event.

Even the minister preached on graduation the Sunday before. His subject was, "Let your light so shine that men will see your good works and praise your Father, Who is in Heaven." Although the sermon was purported to be addressed to us, he used the occasion to speak to backsliders, gamblers, and general ne'er-do-wells. But since he had called our names at the beginning of the service we were mollified.

Among Negroes the tradition was to give presents to children going only from one grade to another. How much more important this was when the person was graduating at the top of the class. Uncle Willie and Momma had sent away for a Mickey Mouse watch like Bailey's. Louise gave me four embroidered handkerchiefs. (I gave her three crocheted doilies.) Mrs. Sneed, the minister's wife, made me an underskirt to wear for graduation, and nearly every customer gave me a nickel or maybe even a dime with the instruction "Keep on moving to high ground," or some such encouragement.

Amazingly the great day finally dawned and I was out of bed before I knew it. I threw open the back door to see it more clearly, but Momma said, "Sister, come away from that door and put your robe on."

I hoped the memory of that morning would never leave me. Sunlight was itself still young, and the day had none of the insistence maturity would bring it in a few hours. In my robe and barefoot in the backyard, under cover of going to see about my new beans, I gave myself up to the gentle warmth and thanked God that no matter what evil I had done in my life He had allowed me to live to see this day. Somewhere in my fatalism I had expected to die, accidentally, and never have the chance to walk up the stairs in the auditorium and gracefully receive my hard-earned diploma. Out of God's merciful bosom I had won reprieve.

Bailey came out in his robe and gave me a box wrapped in Christmas paper. He said he had saved his money for months to pay for it. It felt like a box of chocolates, but I knew Bailey wouldn't save money to buy candy when we had all we could want under our noses.

He was as proud of the gift as I. It was a soft-leather-bound copy of a collection of poems by Edgar Allan Poe, or, as Bailey and I called him, "Eap." I turned to "Annabel Lee" and we walked up and down the garden rows, the cool dirt between our toes, reciting the beautifully sad lines.

Momma made a Sunday breakfast although it was only Friday. After we finished the blessing, I opened my eyes to find the watch on my plate. It was a dream of a day. Everything went smoothly and to my credit, I didn't have to be reminded or scolded for anything. Near evening I was too jittery to attend to chores, so Bailey volunteered to do all before his bath.

Days before, we had made a sign for the Store and as we turned out the lights Momma hung the cardboard over the doorknob. It read clearly: CLOSED. GRADUATION.

My dress fitted perfectly and everyone said that I looked like a sunbeam in it. On the hill, going toward the school, Bailey walked behind with Uncle Willie, who muttered, "Go on, Ju." He wanted him to walk ahead with us because it embarrassed him to have to walk so slowly. Bailey said he'd let the ladies walk together, and the men would bring up the rear. We all laughed, nicely.

Little children dashed by out of the dark like fireflies. Their crepe-paper dresses and butterfly wings were not made for running and we heard more than one rip, dryly, and the regretful "uh uh" that followed.

The school blazed without gaiety. The windows seemed cold and unfriendly from the lower hill. A sense of ill-fated timing crept over me, and if Momma hadn't reached for my hand I would have drifted back to Bailey and Uncle Willie, and possibly beyond. She made a few slow jokes about my feet getting cold, and tugged me along to the now-strange building.

Around the front steps, assurance came back. There were my fellow "greats," the graduating class. Hair brushed back, legs oiled, new dresses and pressed pleats, fresh pocket handkerchiefs and little handbags, all homesewn. Oh, we were up to snuff, all right. I joined my comrades and didn't even see my family go in to find seats in the crowded auditorium.

The school band struck up a march and all classes filed in as had been rehearsed. We stood in front of our seats, as assigned, and on a signal from the choir director, we sat. No sooner had this been accomplished than the band started to play the national anthem. We rose again and sang the song, after which we recited the pledge of allegiance. We remained standing for a brief minute before the choir director and the principal signaled to us, rather desperately I thought, to take our seats. The command was so unusual that our carefully rehearsed and smooth-running machine was thrown off. For a full minute we fumbled for our chairs and bumped into each other awkwardly. Habits change or solidify under pressure, so in our state of nervous tension we had been ready to follow our usual assembly pattern: the American National Anthem, then the pledge of allegiance, then the song every Black person I knew called the Negro National Anthem. All done in the same key, with the same passion and most often standing on the same foot.

Finding my seat at last, I was overcome with a presentiment of worse things to come. Something unrehearsed, unplanned, was going to happen, and we were going to be made to look bad. I distinctly remember being explicit in the choice of pronoun. It was "we," the graduating class, the unit, that concerned me then.

The principal welcomed "parents and friends" and asked the Baptist minister to lead us in prayer. His invocation was brief and punchy, and for a second I thought we were getting back on the high road to right action. When the principal came back to the dais, however, his voice had changed. Sounds always affected me profoundly and the principal's voice was one of my favorites. During assembly it melted and lowed weakly into the audience. It had not been in my plan to listen to him, but my curiosity was piqued and I straightened up to give him my attention.

He was talking about Booker T. Washington, our "late great leader," who said we can be as close as the fingers on the hand, etc. . . . Then he said a few vague things about friendship and the friendship of kindly people to those less fortunate than themselves. With that his voice nearly faded, thin, away. Like a river diminishing to a stream and then to a trickle. But he cleared his throat and said, "Our speaker tonight, who is also our friend, came from Texarkana to deliver the commencement address, but due to the irregularity of the train schedule, he's going to, as they say, 'speak and run.'" He said that we understood and wanted the man to know that we were most grateful for the time he was able to give us and then something about how we were willing always to adjust to another's program, and without more ado—"I give you Mr. Edward Donleavy."

Not one but two white men came through the door offstage. The shorter one walked to the speaker's platform, and the tall one moved over to the center seat and sat down. But that was our principal's seat, and already occupied. The dislodged gentleman bounced around for a long breath or two before the Baptist minister gave him his chair, then with more dignity than the situation deserved, the minister walked off the stage.

Donleavy looked at the audience once (on reflection, I'm sure that he wanted only to reassure himself that we were really there), adjusted his glasses and began to read from a sheaf of papers.

He was glad "to be here and to see the work going on just as it was in the other schools."

At the first "Amen" from the audience I willed the offender to immediate death by choking on the word. But Amen's and Yes, sir's began to fall around the room like rain through a ragged umbrella.

He told us of the wonderful changes we children in Stamps had in store. The Central School (naturally, the white school was Central) had already been granted improvements that would be in use in the fall. A well-known artist was coming from Little Rock to teach art to them. They were going to have the newest microscopes and chemistry equipment for their laboratory. Mr. Donleavy didn't leave us long in the dark over who made these improvements available to Central High. Nor were we to be ignored in the general betterment scheme he had in mind.

He said that he had pointed out to people at a very high level that one of the first-line football tacklers at Arkansas Agricultural and Mechanical College had graduated from good old Lafayette County Training School. Here fewer Amen's were heard. Those few that did break through lay dully in the air with the heaviness of habit.

He went on to praise us. He went on to say how he had bragged that "one of the best basketball players at Fisk sank his first ball right here at Lafayette County Training School."

The white kids were going to have a chance to become Galileos and Madame Curies and Edisons and Gauguins, and our boys (the girls weren't even in on it) would try to be Jesse Owenses and Joe Louises.

Owens and the Brown Bomber were great heroes in our world, but what school official in the white-goddom of Little Rock had the right to decide that those two men must be our only heroes? Who decided that for Henry Reed to become a scientist he had to work like George Washington Carver, as a bootblack, to buy a lousy microscope? Bailey was obviously always going to be too small to be an athlete, so which concrete angel glued to what country seat had decided that if my brother wanted to become a lawyer he had to first pay penance for his skin by picking cotton and hoeing corn and studying correspondence books at night for twenty years?

The man's dead words fell like bricks around the auditorium and too many settled in my belly. Constrained by hard-learned manners I couldn't look behind me, but to my left and right the proud graduating class of 1940 had dropped their heads. Every girl in my row had found something new to do with her handkerchief. Some folded the tiny squares into love knots, some into triangles, but most were wadding them, then pressing them flat on their yellow laps.

On the dais, the ancient tragedy was being replayed. Professor Parsons sat, a sculptor's reject, rigid. His large, heavy body seemed devoid of will or willingness, and his eyes said he was no longer with us. The other teachers examined the flag (which was draped stage right) or their notes, or the windows which opened on our now-famous playing diamond.

Graduation, the hush-hush magic time of frills and gifts and congratulations and diplomas, was finished for me before my name was called. The accomplishment was nothing. The meticulous maps, drawn in three colors of ink, learning and spelling decasyllabic words, memorizing the whole of *The Rape of Lucrece*—it was nothing. Donleavy had exposed us.

We were maids and farmers, handymen and washerwomen, and anything higher that we aspired to was farcical and presumptuous. Then I wished that Gabriel Prosser and Nat Turner had killed all whitefolks in their beds and that Abraham Lincoln had been assassinated before the signing of the Emancipation Proclamation, and that Harriet Tubman had been killed by that blow on her head and Christopher Columbus had drowned in the *Santa Maria*.

It was awful to be Negro and have no control over my life. It was brutal to be young and already trained to sit quietly and listen to charges brought against my color and no chance of defense. We should all be dead. I thought I should like to see us all dead, one on top of the other. A pyramid of flesh with the whitefolks on the bottom, as the broad base, then the Indians with their silly tomahawks and teepees and wigwams and treaties, the Negroes with their mops and recipes and cotton sacks and spirituals sticking out of their mouths. The Dutch children should all stumble in their wooden shoes and break their necks. The French should choke to death on the Louisiana Purchase (1803) while silkworms ate all the Chinese with their stupid pigtails. As a species, we were an abomination. All of us.

Donleavy was running for election, and assured our parents that if he won we could count on having the only colored paved playing field in that part of Arkansas. Also—he never looked up to acknowledge the grunts of acceptance—also, we were bound to get some new equipment for the home economics building and the workshop.

He finished, and since there was no need to give any more than the most perfunctory thank-you's, he nodded to the men on the stage, and the tall white man who was never introduced joined him at the door. They left with the attitude that now they were off to something really important. (The graduation ceremonies at Lafayette County Training school had been a mere preliminary.)

The ugliness they left was palpable. An uninvited guest who wouldn't leave. The choir was summoned and sang a modern arrangement of "Onward, Christian Soldiers," with new words pertaining to graduates seeking their place in the world. But it didn't work. Elouise, the daughter of the Baptist minister, recited "Invictus," and I could have cried at the impertinence of "I am the master of my fate, I am the captain of my soul."

My name had lost its ring of familiarity and I had to be nudged to go and receive my diploma. All my preparations had fled. I neither marched up to the stage like a conquering Amazon, nor did I look in the audience for Bailey's nod of approval. Marguerite Johnson, I heard the name again, my honors were read, there were noises in the audience of appreciation, and I took my place on the stage as rehearsed.

I thought about colors I hated: ecru, puce, lavender, beige and black.

There was shuffling and rustling around me, then Henry Reed was giving his valedictory address, "To Be or Not to Be." Hadn't he heard the whitefolks? We couldn't *be*, so the question was a waste of time. Henry's voice came out clear and strong. I feared to look at him. Hadn't he got the message? There was no "nobler in the mind" for Negroes because the world didn't think we had minds, and they let us know it. "Outrageous fortune"? Now, that was a joke. When the ceremony was over I had to tell Henry Reed some things. That is, if I still cared. Not "rub," Henry, "erase." "Ah, there's the erase." Us.

Henry had been a good student in elocution. His voice rose on tides of promise and fell on waves of warnings. The English teacher had helped him to create a sermon winging through Hamlet's soliloquy. To be a man, a doer, a builder, a leader, or to be a tool, an unfunny joke, a crush-er of funky toadstools. I marveled that Henry could go through with the speech as if we had a choice.

I had been listening and silently rebutting each sentence with my eyes closed; then there was a hush, which in an audience warns that something unplanned is happening. I looked up and saw Henry Reed, the conservative, the proper, the A student, turn his back to the audience and turn to us (the proud graduating class of 1940) and sing, nearly speaking,

> Lift ev'ry voice and sing
> Till earth and heaven ring
> Ring with the harmonies of Liberty . . .

It was the poem written by James Weldon Johnson. It was the music com-posed by J. Rosamond Johnson. It was the Negro National Anthem. Out of habit we were singing it.

Our mothers and fathers stood in the dark hall and joined the hymn of encouragement. A kindergarten teacher led the small children onto the stage and the buttercups and daisies and bunny rabbits marked time and tried to follow:

> Stony the road we trod
> Bitter the chastening rod
> Felt in the days when hope, unborn, had died.
> Yet with a steady beat
> Have not our weary feet
> Come to the place for which our fathers sighed?

Every child I knew had learned that song with his ABC's and along with "Jesus Loves Me This I Know." But I personally had never heard it before. Never heard the words, despite the thousands of times I had sung them. Never thought they had anything to do with me.

On the other hand, the words of Patrick Henry had made such an impression on me that I had been able to stretch myself tall and trembling and say, "I know not what course others may take, but as for me, give me liberty or give me death."

And now I heard, really for the first time:

We have come over a way that with tears has been watered,
We have come, treading our path through the blood of the slaughtered.

While echoes of the song shivered in the air, Henry Reed bowed his head, said "Thank you," and returned to his place in the line. The tears that slipped down many faces were not wiped away in shame.

We were on top again. As always, again. We survived. The depths had been icy and dark, but now a bright sun spoke to our souls. I was no longer simply a member of the proud graduating class of 1940; I was a proud member of the wonderful, beautiful Negro race.

Oh, Black known and unknown poets, how often have your auctioned pains sustained us? Who will compute the lonely nights made less lonely by your songs, or the empty pots made less tragic by your tales?

If we were a people much given to revealing secrets, we might raise monuments and sacrifice to the memories of our poets, but slavery cured us of that weakness. It may be enough, however, to have it said that we survive in exact relationship to the dedication of our poets (include preachers, musicians and blues singers).

Marta Salinas has published stories in California Living *and the* Los Angeles Herald Examiner. *She is an environmental activist and a writer.*

The Scholarship Jacket

Marta Salinas

The small Texas school that I attended carried out a tradition every year during the eighth grade graduation: a beautiful gold and green jacket, the school colors, was awarded to the class valedictorian, the student who had maintained the highest grades for eight years. The scholarship jacket had a big gold S on the left front side, and the winner's name was written in gold letters on the pocket.

My oldest sister Rosie had won the jacket a few years back, and I fully expected to win also. I was fourteen and in the eighth grade. I had been a straight A student since the first grade, and the last year I had looked forward to owning that jacket. My father was a farm laborer who couldn't earn enough money to feed eight children, so when I was six I was given to my grandparents to raise. We couldn't participate in sports at school because there were registration fees, uniform costs, and trips out of town; so even though we were quite agile and athletic, there would never be a sports school jacket for us. This one, the scholarship jacket, was our only chance.

In May, close to graduation, spring fever struck, and no one paid any attention in class; instead we stared out the windows and at each other, wanting to speed up the last few weeks of school. I despaired every time I looked in the mirror. Pencil thin, not a curve anywhere, I was called "Beanpole" and "String Bean," and I knew that's what I looked like. A flat chest, no hips, and a brain, that's what I had. That really isn't much for a fourteen-year-old to work with, I thought, as I absentmindedly wandered from my history class to the gym. Another hour of sweating in basketball and displaying my toothpick legs was coming up. Then I remembered my P.E. shorts were still in a bag under my desk where I'd forgotten them. I had to walk all the way back and get them. Coach Thompson was a real bear if anyone wasn't dressed for P.E. She had said I was a good forward and once she even tried to talk Grandma into letting me join the team. Grandma, of course, said no.

I was almost back at my classroom door when I heard angry voices and arguing. I stopped. I didn't mean to eavesdrop; I just hesitated, not knowing what to do. I needed those shorts and I was going to be late, but I didn't want to interrupt an argument between my teachers. I recognized the voices: Mr. Schmidt, my history teacher, and Mr. Boone, my math teacher. They seemed to be arguing about me. I couldn't believe it. I still remember the shock that rooted me flat against the wall as if I were trying to blend in with the graffiti written there.

"I refuse to do it! I don't care who her father is, her grades don't even begin to compare to Martha's. I won't lie or falsify records. Martha has a straight A plus average and you know it." That was Mr. Schmidt and he sounded very angry. Mr. Boone's voice sounded calm and quiet.

"Look, Joann's father is not only on the Board, he owns the only store in town; we could say it was a close tie and—"

The pounding in my ears drowned out the rest of the words, only a word here and there filtered through. ". . . Martha is Mexican. . . . resign. . . . won't do it. . . ." Mr. Schmidt came rushing out, and luckily for me went down the opposite way toward the auditorium, so he didn't see me. Shaking, I waited a few minutes and then went in and grabbed my bag and fled from the room. Mr. Boone looked up when I came in but didn't say anything. To this day I don't remember if I got in trouble in P.E. for being late or how I made it through the rest of the afternoon. I went home very sad and cried into my pillow that night so Grandmother wouldn't hear me. It seemed a cruel coincidence that I had overheard that conversation.

The next day when the principal called me into his office, I knew what it would be about. He looked uncomfortable and unhappy. I decided I wasn't going to make it any easier for him so I looked him straight in the eye. He looked away and fidgeted with the papers on his desk.

"Martha," he said, "there's been a change in policy this year regarding the scholarship jacket. As you know, it has always been free." He cleared his throat and continued. "This year the Board decided to charge fifteen dollars—which still won't cover the complete cost of the jacket."

I stared at him in shock and a small sound of dismay escaped my throat. I hadn't expected this. He still avoided looking in my eyes.

"So if you are unable to pay the fifteen dollars for the jacket, it will be given to the next one in line."

Standing with all the dignity I could muster; I said, "I'll speak to my grandfather about it, sir, and let you know tomorrow." I cried on the walk home from the bus stop. The dirt road was a quarter of a mile from the highway, so by the time I got home, my eyes were red and puffy.

"Where's Grandpa?" I asked Grandma, looking down at the floor so she wouldn't ask me why I'd been crying. She was sewing on a quilt and didn't look up.

"I think he's out back working in the bean field."

I went outside and looked out at the fields. There he was. I could see him walking between the rows, his body bent over the little plants, hoe in hand. I walked slowly out to him, trying to think how I could best ask him for the money. There was a cool breeze blowing and a sweet smell of mesquite in the air, but I didn't appreciate it. I kicked at a dirt clod. I wanted that jacket so much. It was more than just being a valedictorian and giving a little thank you speech for the jacket on graduation night. It represented eight years of hard work and expectation. I knew I had to be honest with Grandpa; it was my only chance. He saw me and looked up.

He waited for me to speak. I cleared my throat nervously and clasped my hands behind my back so he wouldn't see them shaking. "Grandpa, I have a big favor to ask you," I said in Spanish, the only language he knew. He still waited silently. I tried again. "Grandpa, this year the principal said the scholarship jacket is not going to be free. It's going to cost fifteen dollars and I have to take the money in tomorrow, otherwise it'll be given to someone else." The last words came out in an eager rush. Grandpa straightened up tiredly and leaned his chin on the hoe handle. He looked out over the field that was filled with the tiny green bean plants. I waited, desperately hoping he'd say I could have the money.

He turned to me and asked quietly, "What does a scholarship jacket mean?"

I answered quickly; maybe there was a chance. "It means you've earned it by having the highest grades for eight years and that's why they're giving it to you." Too late I realized the significance of my words. Grandpa knew that I understood it was not a matter of money. It wasn't that. He went back to hoeing the weeds that sprang up between the delicate little bean plants. It was a time-consuming job; sometimes the small shoots were right next to each other. Finally he spoke again.

"Then if you pay for it, Marta, it's not a scholarship jacket, is it? Tell your principal I will not pay the fifteen dollars."

I walked back to the house and locked myself in the bathroom for a long time. I was angry with Grandfather even though I knew he was right, and I was angry with the Board, whoever they were. Why did they have to change the rules just when it was my turn to win the jacket?

It was a very sad and withdrawn girl who dragged into the principal's office the next day. This time he did look me in the eyes.

"What did your grandfather say?"

I sat very straight in my chair.

"He said to tell you he won't pay the fifteen dollars."

The principal muttered something I couldn't understand under his breath, and walked over to the window. He stood looking out at something outside. He looked bigger than usual when he stood up; he was a tall gaunt man with gray hair, and I watched the back of his head while I waited for him to speak.

"Why?" he finally asked. "Your grandfather has the money. Doesn't he own a small bean farm?"

I looked at him, forcing my eyes to stay dry. "He said if I had to pay for it, then it wouldn't be a scholarship jacket," I said and stood up to leave. "I guess you'll just have to give it to Joann." I hadn't meant to say that; it had just slipped out. I was almost to the door when he stopped me.

"Martha—wait."

I turned and looked at him, waiting. What did he want now? I could feel my heart pounding. Something bitter and vile tasting was coming up in my mouth; I was afraid I was going to be sick. I didn't need any sympathy speeches. He sighed loudly and went back to his big desk. He looked at me, biting his lip, as if thinking.

"Okay, damn it. We'll make an exception in your case. I'll tell the Board, you'll get your jacket."

I could hardly believe it. I spoke in a trembling rush. "Oh, thank you, sir!" Suddenly I felt great. I didn't know about adrenaline in those days, but I knew something was pumping through me, making me feel as tall as the sky. I wanted to yell, jump, run the mile, do something. I ran out so I could cry in the hall where there was no one to see me. At the end of the day, Mr. Schmidt winked at me and said, "I hear you're getting a scholarship jacket this year."

His face looked as happy and innocent as a baby's, but I knew better. Without answering I gave him a quick hug and ran to the bus. I cried on the walk home again, but this time because I was so happy. I couldn't wait to tell Grandpa and ran straight to the field. I joined him in the row where he was working and without saying anything I crouched down and started pulling up the weeds with my hands. Grandpa worked alongside me for a few minutes, but he didn't ask what had happened. After I had a little pile of weeds between the rows, I stood up and faced him.

"The principal said he's making an exception for me, Grandpa, and I'm getting the jacket after all. That's after I told him what you said."

Grandpa didn't say anything, he just gave me a pat on the shoulder and a smile. He pulled out the crumpled red handkerchief that he always carried in his back pocket and wiped the sweat off his forehead.

"Better go see if your grandmother needs any help with supper."

I gave him a big grin. He didn't fool me. I skipped and ran back to the house whistling some silly tune.

*R*ichard Rodriguez (1944–) was born in San Francisco and holds degrees *from both Stanford and Columbia Universities. His writing, including his 1981 book* Hunger of Memory: The Education of Richard Rodriguez, *depicts the struggles of living between two cultures: his Spanish-speaking family of origin and the dominant culture of the United States. In* Los Pobres, *Rodriguez' summer job gives him the opportunity to reflect on his own personal identity, and how that might differ from others' experiences.*

Los Pobres

Richard Rodriguez

It was at Stanford, one day near the end of my senior year, that a friend told me about a summer construction job he knew was available. I was quickly alert. Desire uncoiled within me. My friend said that he knew I had been looking for summer employment. He knew I needed some money. Almost apologetically he explained: It was something I probably wouldn't be interested in, but a friend of his, a contractor, needed someone for the summer to do menial jobs. There would be lots of shoveling and raking and sweeping. Nothing too hard. But nothing more interesting either. Still, the pay would be good. Did I want it? Or did I know someone who did?

I did. Yes, I said, surprised to hear myself say it.

In the weeks following, friends cautioned that I had no idea how hard physical labor really is. ("You only *think* you know what it is like to shovel for eight hours straight.") Their objections seemed to me challenges. They resolved the issue. I became happy with my plan. I decided, however, not to tell my parents. I wouldn't tell my mother because I could guess her worried reaction. I would tell my father only after the summer was over, when I could announce that, after all, I did know what "real work" is like.

The day I met the contractor (a Princeton graduate, it turned out), he asked me whether I had done any physical labor before. "In high school, during the summer," I lied. And although he seemed to regard me with skepticism, he decided to give me a try. Several days later, expectant, I arrived at my first construction site. I would take off my shirt to the sun. And at last grasp desired sensation. No longer afraid. At last become like a *bracero.* "We need those tree stumps out of here by tomorrow," the contractor said. I started to work.

I labored with excitement that first morning—and all the days after. The work was harder than I could have expected. But it was never as tedious as my friends had warned me it would be. There was too much physical pleasure in the labor. Especially early in the day, I would be most alert to the sensations of movement and straining. Beginning around seven each morning (when the air was still damp but the scent of weeds and dry earth anticipated the heat of the sun), I would feel my body resist the first thrusts of the shovel. My arms, tightened by sleep, would gradually loosen; after only several minutes, sweat would gather in beads on my forehead and then—a short while later—I would feel my chest silky with sweat in the breeze. I would return to my work. A nervous spark of pain would fly up my arm and settle to burn like an ember in the thick of my shoulder. An hour, two passed. Three. My whole body would assume regular movements. Even later in the day, my enthusiasm for primitive sensation would survive the heat and the dust and the insects pricking my back. I would strain wildly for sensation as the day came to a close. At three-thirty, quitting time, I would stand upright and slowly let my head fall back, luxuriating in the feeling of tightness relieved.

Some of the men working nearby would watch me and laugh. Two or three of the older men took the trouble to teach me the right way to use a pick, the correct way to shovel. "You're doing it wrong, too fucking hard," one man scolded. Then proceeded so show me—what persons who work with their bodies all their lives quickly learn—the most economical way to use one's body in labor.

"Don't make your back do so much work," he instructed. I stood impatiently listening, half listening, vaguely watching, then noticed his work-thickened fingers clutching the shovel. I was annoyed. I wanted to tell him that I enjoyed shoveling the wrong way. And I didn't want to learn the right way. I wasn't afraid of back pain. I liked the way my body felt sore at the end of the day.

I was about to, but, as it turned out, I didn't say a thing. Rather it was at that moment I realized that I was fooling myself if I expected a few weeks of labor to gain me admission to the world of the laborer. I would not learn in three months what my father had meant by "real work." I was not bound to this job; I could imagine its rapid conclusion. For me the sensations of exertion and fatigue could be savored. For my father or uncle, working at comparable jobs when they were my age, such sensations were to be feared. Fatigue took a different toll on their bodies—and minds.

It was, I know, a simple insight. But it was with this realization that I took my first step that summer toward realizing something even more important about the "worker." In the company of carpenters, electricians, plumbers, and painters at lunch, I would often sit quietly, observant. I was not shy in such company. I felt easy, pleased by the knowledge that I was casually accepted, my presence taken for granted by men (exotics) who worked with their hands. Some days the younger men would talk and talk about sex, and they would howl at women who drove by in cars. Other days the talk at lunchtime was subdued; men gathered in separate groups. It depended on who was around. There were rough, good-natured workers. Others were quiet. The more I remember that summer, the more I realize that there was no single *type* of worker. I am embarrassed to say I had not expected such diversity. I certainly had not expected to meet, for example, a plumber who was an abstract painter in his off hours and admired the work of Mark Rothko. Nor did I expect to meet so many workers with college diplomas. (They were the ones who were not surprised that I intended to enter graduate school in the fall.) I suppose what I really want to say here is painfully obvious, but I must say it nevertheless: The men of that summer were middle-class Americans. They certainly didn't constitute an oppressed society. Carefully completing their work sheets; talking about the fortunes of local football teams; planning Las Vegas vacations; comparing the gas mileage of various makes of campers—they were not *los pobres* my mother had spoken about.

On two occasions, the contractor hired a group of Mexican aliens. They were employed to cut down some trees and haul off debris. In all, there were six men of varying age. The youngest in his late twenties; the oldest (his father?) perhaps sixty years old. They came and they left in a single old truck. Anonymous men. They were never introduced to the other men at the site. Immediately upon their arrival, they would follow the contractor's directions, start working—rarely resting—seemingly driven by a fatalistic sense that work which had to be done was best done as quickly as possible.

I watched them sometimes. Perhaps they watched me. The only time I saw them pay me much notice was one day at lunchtime when I was laughing with the other men. The Mexicans sat apart when they ate, just as they worked by themselves. Quiet I rarely heard them say much to each other. All I could hear were their voices calling out sharply to one another, giving directions. Otherwise, when they stood briefly resting, they talked among themselves in voices too hard to overhear.

The contractor knew enough Spanish, and the Mexicans—or at least the oldest of them, their spokesman—seemed to know enough English to communicate. But because I was around, the contractor decided one day to make me his translator. (He assumed I could speak Spanish.) I did what I was told. Shyly I went over to tell the Mexicans that the patrón wanted them to do something else before they left for the day. As I started to speak, I was afraid with my old fear that I would be unable to pronounce the Spanish words. But it was a simple instruction I had to convey. I could say it in phrases.

The dark sweating faces turned toward me as I spoke. They stopped their work to hear me. Each nodded in response. I stood there. I wanted to say something more. But what could I say in Spanish, even if I could have pronounced the words right? Perhaps I just wanted to engage in small talk, to be assured of their confidence, our familiarity. I thought for a moment to ask them where in Mexico they were from. Something like that. And maybe I wanted to tell them (a lie, if need be) that my parents were from the same part of Mexico.

I stood there.

Their faces watched me. The eyes of the man directly in front of me moved slowly over my shoulder, and I turned to follow his glance toward *el patrón* some distance away. For a moment I felt swept up by that glance into the Mexicans' company. But then I heard one of them returning to work. And then the others went back to work. I left them without saying anything more.

When they had finished, the contractor went over to pay them in cash. (He later told me that he paid them collectively—"for the job," though he wouldn't tell me their wages. He said something quickly about the good rate of exchange "in their own country.") I can still hear the loudly confident voice he used with the Mexicans. It was the sound of the *gringo* I had heard as a very young boy. And I can still hear the quiet, indistinct sounds of the Mexican, the oldest who replied. At hearing that voice I was sad for the Mexicans. Depressed by their vulnerability. Angry at myself. The adventure of the summer seemed suddenly ludicrous. I would not shorten the distance I felt from *los pobres* with a few weeks of physical labor. I would not become like them. They were different from me. . . .

In the end, my father was right—though perhaps he did not know how right or why—to say that I would never know what real work is. I will never know what he felt at his last factory job. If tomorrow I worked at some kind of factory, it would go differently for me. My long education would favor me. I could act as a public person—able to defend my interests, to unionize, to petition, to speak up—to challenge and demand. (I will never know what real work is.) I will never know what the Mexicans knew, gathering their shovels and ladders and saws.

Their silence stays with me now. The wages those Mexicans received for their labor were only a measure of their disadvantaged condition. Their silence is more telling. They lack a public identity. They remain profoundly alien. Persons apart. People lacking a union obviously, people without grounds. They depend upon the relative good will or fairness of their employers each day. For such people, lacking a better alternative, it is not such an unreasonable risk.

Their silence stays with me. I have taken these many words to describe its impact. Only: the quiet. Something uncanny about it. Its compliance. Vulnerability. Pathos. As I heard their truck rumbling away, I shuddered, my face mirrored with sweat. I had finally come face to face with *los pobres*.

James Earl "Jimmy" Carter, Jr. (1924–) was the thirty-ninth president of the United States (1977 to 1981), and a recipient of the Nobel Peace Prize in 2002 for his work in human rights and seeking peaceful solutions to conflicts around the world. Both Jimmy Carter and his wife Rosalynn Smith Carter (1928–) are key figures in the Habitat for Humanity project, and both received the Presidential Medal of Freedom in 1999 from President Bill Clinton.

Working with Our Hands

Jimmy Carter and Rosalynn Carter

"Working with Our Hands," from the book *Everything to Gain*, is former President Jimmy Carter and his wife Rosalynn's first-person account of their volunteer work with such groups as Habitat for Humanity, which builds housing for homeless people. In this segment the Carters discuss the circumstances that led to their decision to work with Habitat for Humanity and what they learned from their experiences about the problems of housing for poor people. The paragraphs that begin with "J" are Jimmy Carter's comments, and those that begin with "R" ore Rosalynn Carter's.

When it comes to giving, some folks will stop at nothing.

Jimmy Townsend

J. We planned to leave home on the Saturday before Labor Day, 1984, ride all night on the bus, and arrive in New York City Sunday afternoon. Under a program called Habitat for Humanity we were going to help renovate an old, dilapidated building in the Lower East Side and turn it into nineteen apartments for poor families.

On a previous trip to New York I had gone to the building on Sixth Street with a group of young Habitat volunteers. We had to push our way inside through piles of trash and debris and climb laboriously from one floor to another where stairs would one day be built. The place was a haven for drifters, drug dealers and addicts, some of whom had been building fires on top of the trash for warmth and cooking. Many of the ceiling joists were burned in two, and the floors had collapsed in places. From the top three stories we could look up and see the clouds and the blue sky.

My heart went out to the few young people responsible for the project. They were ambitious and determined, but I learned that they had very few specific plans and no means in sight to achieve the goals they had set for themselves. On the spur of the moment and half in jest I said, "I'll have to come back and do some volunteer carpenter work!"

By the time I returned home, Millard Fuller, the president and founder of Habitat, had already heard about my offer, and he called to thank me! He suggested that a few others might be willing to go with me and Rosalynn sometime during the summer. Rosalynn, too? I hadn't volunteered her for the task, and I didn't know whether I really wanted to go or not.

A trip to the big city to work for a week in the sweltering heat of July was not a very attractive proposition. And volunteers, if we could get them, would have to pay for their own transportation and food, carry their own tools, and stay in crowded bunk rooms that had been offered by an old church near the Lincoln Tunnel. There was no information about what our specific tasks would be, and most of the group that we might recruit probably would never have used a saw, mixed mortar, laid a brick, put up a stud, or used a hammer except to hang a picture on the wall.

However, after a few weeks we thought we might have enough prospects to fill a small van—including several professional carpenters, a member of the Americus City Council, a motel owner, a college professor and his new bride—and the list kept growing. It wasn't long before we had enough volunteers to fill a large bus, and we even turned down additional people who wanted to make the trip. Rosalynn's reaction had been: "I don't want to ride a bus all the way to New York!" She seemed to be excited about the trip, though. It would be an adventure of a different type for us, involving no speeches, no letters to write, no major problems to solve, no deep thinking—it would be only manual labor, which might be fun for a change and, she said, a real challenge.

So now the volunteers and I were on our way. The first day of work would be Monday, on which Rosalynn already had a long-standing speaking engagement for the morning. She would have to fly to New York and join us late in the afternoon. The truth is that if she had not had a previous engagement, I think she would have invented one. She felt that strongly about the long bus ride, which was necessary because many of the volunteers couldn't afford to take a week off from work and also spend the money required for airfare.

The trip turned out to be quite an experience. It was a tiring twenty-five-hour journey, with stops only for meals and a Sunday-morning worship service—but it was an exhilarating twenty-five hours. We sang and told stories, and there developed among us a camaraderie that comes from being somewhat set apart from others, joined together in a common and, we were sure, worthwhile cause. Many in the bus had never visited New York or seen any city larger than Atlanta, and the newness, excitement and uncertainty about what lay ahead gave us a feeling of adventure.

When we arrived at the site on Sunday afternoon, one look at the bare shell of a building—six stories high with no windows, no doors, no roof, and burned and collapsing floors and ceilings—instantly dampened our spirits. It looked much worse and more fragile now with the structure more fully exposed than it had been in April, when it was full of trash. Our hearts sank. And the loudest dissents were from the few professional builders in the group. "It can't be done," they said in chorus. "If this building has been purchased already, we need to tear it down and start from scratch. There is no way it can ever be made livable." To describe their reaction as despair would be an understatement. They were discouraged almost to the point of resentment that anyone—they all looked at me—could have thought of bringing them so far to be part of an absolute fiasco. There was almost total silence as we made the trip to the church where we would be staying.

During supper I invited the most experienced carpenters to sit with me, and asked each of them to describe a possible approach to be followed *if* we should go on with the job. Soon they were competing with each other to outline the best plan for how our group could be divided into teams, which tasks had to be performed first, what additional materials we would need, and how much might be accomplished while we were in New York. Finally, exhausted from the trip and still mostly discouraged, we all went to bed—or the first time in two days.

Even the narrow and cramped bunk beds didn't prevent our getting a good night's sleep, and early the next morning we piled into the bus again and drove to the old building. Everyone was grim as doubts returned, but no one expressed them. Instead, we all did our best to maintain an atmosphere of confidence. Seven or eight workers were assigned to each floor and the roof, each group under the supervision of someone with experience in construction. Then, donning hard hats, we went to work.

It was dirty, dusty, gritty work, and dangerous for those attempting to rebuild the roof and replace the large structural timbers in the upper floors. Soon we had to put on goggles and masks because of the thick dust that was sifting down from above and billowing up from below, where the remaining debris was being loaded into wheelbarrows and hauled away. It was a long, hard day, but we went back to the church in the late afternoon with a sense of fulfillment, for after only one day with fifty of us there we could begin to see that we could make a difference.

R. There is great satisfaction in being able to "make a difference" for someone who needs help. The tiredness that comes from any physical activity is all worthwhile, and the spirit sometimes soars. Working with Habitat has been that kind of experience for us. Of all the activities we have undertaken since leaving the White House, it is certainly one of the most inspiring. To help build a home for people who have never lived in a decent place and never dreamed of owning a home of their own can bring both a lot of joy and an emotional response. One has only to have had the experience to know what it means—to the one who is giving time and energy and to the one who is receiving the new home. Soon after we began our work with Habitat, we asked Tom Hall, who had come to the international headquarters for brief volunteer service and had already stayed five years, "Why do you keep on staying?" His answer was, "I see the faces of those who receive the homes." We have seen the faces too.

Habitat for Humanity is only one of many worthwhile programs in which anyone with a little time and inclination can perform challenging and useful work. There are so many people in trouble, so many needs right around us. We can find programs to help the poor, the elderly, the handicapped, the imprisoned, the mentally ill, alcoholics, and drug addicts, to name a few. So many of our young people need a helping hand, as do our hospitals, our libraries, art museums, and schools. There is something that every single one of us can do, even the busiest of younger people, but we in the "second half" of our lives often have more time for getting involved. And especially with our life span lengthening and the chances of good health so great, there is an additional stage of life after work when we can devote more of our time to voluntary service. And when we do, as one speaker at a national conference for retirees said, "Everyone benefits. The talents, wisdom and energy of our retirees are badly needed by our communities . . . and retirees who are active and involved have a new sense of self-worth, a source of daily enrichment, the aging process is slowed." That, we think, appeals to all of us!

Helping others can be surprisingly easy, since there is so much that needs to be done. The hard part comes in choosing what to do and getting started, making the first effort at something different. Once the initiative is taken we often find that we can do things we never thought we could.

J. Even Rosalynn, who often ventures into the unknown, was sure she would only be cleaning up around the work site on our Habitat trip to New York, or carrying tools and light supplies, or maybe even helping with meals for the other volunteers. To her amazement, she was soon doing a multitude of carpenter's jobs, and doing them well.

R. I arrived in New York somewhat anxious about what I would be doing. I went first to the church and everyone was there, having returned from the first full day of work. I was taken to the fourth floor and shown a bottom bunk in a dormitory-type room that I would be sharing with six other women. Though dinner was being served in the basement, many of the women were still upstairs. I soon learned why. There was one bathroom and more than twenty women! Some still had on their dirty work clothes, and their hair was stiff with plaster dust. Listening to them relate the stories of the day and the disbelief at the work conditions, I was even less sure about what I was in for.

Next morning I put on jeans and a Habitat T-shirt and prepared for my first day on the job. When we arrived at the site, I was assigned to the second story. Jimmy was the foreman of this level and had decided that the best thing we could do during the week would be to get down a good solid floor. It was a tall order. Many of the joists had to be replaced or shored up, and most of the floor was gone. To do any work we had to walk on plywood laid across what supporting beams were left.

I was first assigned, along with two other women, to clean up the floor that still remained in one corner of the back section. We scraped up layers of old glue and paint and patches of linoleum that were stuck to it, removed nails that were sticking up, and had made it perfectly smooth, when one of the men came over with a sheet of plywood and said, "Nail it down." Nail it down: Before we left home I had told Jimmy that I would do anything but hammer. I didn't think I could use a hammer and I didn't want to use a hammer. We nailed it down! At first it took me fifteen or twenty strokes for each nail; but before the week was over I could drive one in with only four or five strokes!

The next day Jimmy made me foreman of the back half of the second floor, which would eventually be two apartments. And with three other women and an occasional male volunteer, before the week was over we had laid the subfloor and the floor in our entire section—and with a great feeling of accomplishment. We had learned to leave a nail's width of space between the sheets of plywood we put down so that they could expand without buckling, to measure the spaces accurately, and to use a power saw to cut the plywood to fit the spaces. We were pleased and proud. The last day when we were racing against the clock to get our section finished, we had one piece of flooring left to put in place. It was in an awkward spot that fit around a brick chimney and tapered off at one end. We measured it, sawed the wood, held our breath, and dropped it in place. It was perfect! "A perfect fit!" We screamed, "We did it! We did it!"

Jimmy came running from the front of the building: "What's the matter? Who's hurt?" When he saw what we had done, even he was impressed—and we all signed our names to that one piece of flooring on the second floor in a new apartment in a New York City slum.

Brenda Peterson (1950–) is an essayist, novelist, and reporter. Born in the High Sierras of the Pacific Northwest and raised in a national forest, she is the author of several books related to nature and spirituality. In Nature and Other Mothers: Reflections on the Feminine in Everyday Life, *Peterson focuses on the connections of women and nature.*

The Sacredness of Chores

Brenda Peterson

One bright May morning, my arms piled high with clean, freshly folded laundry, I walked up to my housemate and dear friend's room and discovered that she'd taken her life. B. J. lay on that pale green carpet as if fallen from a great height, one hand outstretched. I did not see the gun gleaming like a dark fist at her temple as I knelt down to grab her wrist Not dead, I thought, teeth chattering, just hurt. I had never seen anyone so hurt. Fumbling with her wrist, I finally felt a thready pulse against my forefinger—but it was only my own heart beating. I was so cold. Never have I felt that bone-deep shiver and chill. Her body was warm with sunlight, even though its own inner warmth was gone.

Then I saw her face, the eyelids darkly swollen, shut. From her nose and mouth ran congealed rushes of blood, a red so brilliant and dense that I remembered my sister saying that she'd once watched a heart explode on the operating table as she assisted a surgery, that it bloomed upward from the body like a rose bursting open. For a moment I jumped up, then fell right down, legs buckling. I again took B. J.'s hand, thinking somehow my touch might spare her the sight of herself.

But it was I who needed sparing. Alongside B. J.'s dead body, I knelt on all fours and howled until suddenly I heard a far-off accompaniment. It was a *thud-thud* not of footsteps up the stairs but of something from deep within the bowels of the house itself. I listened, head cocked like an animal, listening with my eyes. And only after a time did I recognize the spin of the dryer. Then the thumping stopped and a piercing buzz began. It summoned me, this shrill signal, to stand upright, to leave the dead, to go downstairs and open the dryer door. More clean clothes tumbled into my arms, and I buried my face in the warm, fragrant cotton and colorful flannel. And because I could not carry B. J.'s body alone, because she no longer carried herself I bunched her clean laundry against my chest and called for help. Then I carefully folded every sock and cotton camisole, every blouse and nightgown until the sirens stopped at my door.

It was so breathtakingly swift, so complete, B. J.'s leave-taking of her body, of her son and family and friends; and, though in my mind some part of me will always be howling on all fours in fury and grief over her brutal abandonment, there also lingers with me these six years later the exact weight and clean smell of her laundry.

After sharing domestic chores for six months, B. J. and I had struck a bargain: I did laundry and vacuumed she did dishes and dusting. We shared scouring bathrooms, cooking, and the yard work, which was a kind of desultory dance between dandelions and an ancient push mower that mangled more than it trimmed. On the afternoon of B. J.'s death, I found myself sitting absolutely still in the kitchen. I stared at the bright haze of sunlight off Lake Washington, the silly burble of my coffee cheerful on the stove, the whir of the fridge, its rhythm loud and labored. I thought of the food inside this stupid, square, and noisy box—*Let it all rot and die!* At the same moment I remembered dully. *I should defrost that fridge.* It had been on my list of chores for the day, right after the laundry.

My morning list for that May day had read:

1) Finish Chapter 10

2) Laundry

3) Defrost fridge

4) Meet P. N. in the market (check for rhubarb)

I gazed at the little list, and it seemed so earnest, so busy, so foolish. What did defrosting fridges, making a strawberry-rhubarb pie, or even finishing a chapter have to do with anything when all the while I'd scribbled that list my friend had been dead upstairs? The coroner said she'd died deep in the night while I lay down the hall sleeping, practicing for my own death.

I looked despairingly down at my clothes and realized I was still in my pajamas, the ones I'd bought in imitation of Lauren Bacall, the ones I'd rolled up at wrist and ankle, the ones, I realized now that must also be washed clean. It was only when I threw my pajamas in the washer, slathered Cheer on the load, and turned on the churning machine that I found myself crying, kneeling on the cold cement floor and at last lamenting. It was safe enough to sob—the world had not stopped spinning, just as this washing machine spun and spun its little load through all its warm, delicate cycles.

This is how my friends found me. First, Paula, who arrived and busied herself during all the unexpected official paperwork of death by mowing the lawn furiously up and down outside as if her precise patterns in the scraggly grass could bring order back to my little yard, my small world. Two days later, when I decided to leave this house, my friends Laura and Susan came heroically armed with buckets, Fantastik, and huge, brightly colored sponges to scrub and scour and spend hours on their hands and knees, a final cleansing of B. J.'s room, a kind of womanly worship. I put Alberta Hunter on the stereo, and we all got down on the floor, crying and cleaning. As we left the house for the last time, it shone in the sun, welcoming. Others would live here and wake up to the lapping lake, the coffee, fresh laundry. This house was again ready for life, life abundant.

Those mundane tasks that sunny May ten years ago have forever changed my sense of daily life. Those simple chores, both solitary and in the company of other women, were my first comfort in what was also my first death. The smell of Comet is forever linked with consolation, the spin of a dryer with survival, the syncopated chant of women scrubbing with the racial memory of reverence.

"Cleaning is incantation, physical prayer," says a friend who is an artist. "You create a small and ordered sacred place that has been touched a thousand times by your hands. Its a ritual of caring."

"The actual cleaning is sometimes secondary to the mental housekeeping that takes place," adds my friend Rebecca, who has always made her living with her hands, either gardening or massaging. "Cleaning your house is like pruning a tree. The house and the tree are both alive. You take care of the debris first, then stand back to look at the true form—and that clarity, that original vision is what happens in the mind."

Stevie Smith, the British poet, commented that she dreamt up some of her best poems while "Hoovering." I have also opted for the vacuuming chores in my own household because the *rush* and *whoosh* of the Kirby, its solid paths on the thick carpet tell me where I've been, where I am, and exactly where I want to go.

All of us claim territory. Traditionally, the masculine way is to mark territory by scent, by song, by a boast, a show of power, a pile of weapons: "This is mine, do not enter or you'll reckon with me!" The feminine claiming is perhaps a fierce physical possessing of the space by adorning home with spells, magic, or brightly waving scarves in trees, as do the aborigines, who put powerful altars near their hearths both for worship and to summon protective guardian spirits.

In my current household, upon hearing that our rental home was to be scrutinized by potential buyers, my two housemates and I broke all real estate rules by staying home and doing our Saturday morning chores. While the house buyers perused, I maneuvered the noisiest vacuum this side of Seattle; one housemate ran the dishwasher and slung wet laundry everywhere, like so many volunteer scarecrow troops; my other housemate followed the harried home buyers from room to room wielding a defending dust mop. She actually sprayed the real estate agent with her lemon Pledge. Such was the territorial claiming of womanly warriors—and no prospective buyers have yet to make an offer these five months later.

Cleaning has long been women's work. For years women have borne the archetype of body, darkness, the erotic, the unclean, the Earth. This association has often imprisoned women in the home and trapped men in the world. Thus, leaving the home is traditionally associated with the heroic explorer, the powerful "man of the world," while the housework is seen as trivial, timid, uninspired, menial labor left to servants. But we are all in service to our homes, as well as our homeland of Earth.

For years environmentalists have been educating us to recognize that the whole wide world *is* our home; we cannot leave the world, or transcend it, or truly throw anything away. We must learn to be here. If women claim the world the way they already have their homes and if men claim their homes as fervently as they have the world, what might we create?

But instead of men and women creating their own homes, more and more people are leaving the home chores and ritual cleanings to hired hands. Are there some deep losses we all might incur from not cleaning up after ourselves? I suspect that doing our own chores is everyone's calling, no matter what our other important jobs. There is some sacredness in this daily, thoughtful, and very grounding housework that we cannot afford to lose if we are to be whole, integrated.

"Just getting down on my hands and knees and scouring the bathroom is like cleaning my soul," says a male friend. He adds with a laugh, "it shines—not necessarily my soul—but that white porcelain. And I feel new, like I've forgiven myself something."

Another of my men friends tells of his mother's death. When she, a meticulous cleaner, died, he stayed on alone in her house for three days and put everything right and tidy. "I felt very close to my mother then," he says. "After all, she had taught me how to clean."

Chores are a child's first work, though they are often presented in the form of play. Girls play house, and boys spend hours running toy trucks over miniature mud mountains. Before we even teach children to speak, we instruct them in their separate chores, and so we shape the world, the future. Somewhere along the line, society quit expecting boys to clean up their rooms, insisting they order the outside world instead. If I were a man, I would feel this as a loss, a wisdom and honor denied me and my home.

Among my friends, no matter their living situation, cleaning is a crucial issue. Perhaps it is simply the symbol of how we treat what we love. Some people clean like Lady Macbeth—"Out, damned spot!" Others dean haphazardly, or methodically, earnestly or devotedly. One of my housemates, Lynette Sue, cleans as a way of understanding and organizing her life. From room to room she goes, sighing with satisfaction, as under her broom and dust rag and window-washing squeegee the world must give way to her scrutiny, her vision of a higher order suggested by perfectly folded sheets and a piano that looks spit shined. She is particularly imperious in the bathroom, being a microbiologist and knowing well that those telltale bits of black mold on the shower ceiling are unhealthy organisms. I teasingly beg her, "Don't take me to Comet-witz," when she suggests my upstairs bathroom looks like a biologist's field trip, "*not* cleaning concentration camp!" But I have found, under her diligence, a luxury that nothing except lounging in a hot sparkling clean bathtub can give me.

Cleaning can be an art. I've often spent a Saturday morning dancing on the freeway of love right in the middle of my living room with Aretha and a vacuum. I admit to practicing arcane rites of exorcism as deep as psychoanalysis by simply cutting up ex-lovers' clothes to use as rags for those deep-down, won't-go-away cleaning jobs like stains on a rug, on a heart. Most recently cleaning came to my rescue when I received the final galley proofs for my novel in the mail with the dire red rubber stamp: RETURN: 36-HOUR PROOF. What did I do with only three days to read and correct my entire book? I spent the first day and a half in a frenzy of old-fashioned, whirlwind spring cleaning that shook the spiders from the rafters and my soul. The book was a breeze after my walk-in winter closet.

When we clean up after ourselves, whether it's a spilled jar, a broken chair, a disorganized study, or a death, we can see and reflect upon our own life and perhaps envision a new way that won't be so broken, so violent, so unconscious. By cleaning up our own homes we take responsibility for ourselves and for preserving what we love. But if our attitude is "my kingdom is not of this world," then there is a disturbing possibility that we'll finally do away with the world rather than clean it or ourselves. The feminine attitude of getting down on our hands and knees to scour—and at the most primitive level look at what needs cleaning—deserves our attention. For in this gesture of bended knees is some humility, some meditation, some time to recognize the first foundation of our homes.

It was a simple washing machine and dryer that got me to my knees that day my friend died—in horror, in mourning, in surrender not to death but to survival. It was a homing instinct that grounded me and made me want to stay on. To this day I have a ritual of running the washer and dryer while I am in my study at work. There is no more comforting sound to me than the spinning of that washer or dryer. It is the whole world spinning in there, cleansing itself and me.

As long as the washer and dryer spin, I tell myself, I am safe and those I love may choose to keep living alongside me. For there is laundry to be done and so many chores—chores of the living. There is so much to be remembered under the dust of our old contempt for cleaning up after ourselves, picking up our own socks. There is much to be swept away and shined bright and scrubbed down to its deepest, most illuminating level. Think of all the chores we have yet to do, quietly and on our knees—because home is holy.

*onald Hall (1928–) is an American poet and the fourteenth U.S. Poet
Laureate. He often writes about rural life in his native New England and
the value of work in ordinary life. Regarded as a master poet (he has published
fifteen books of poetry), Hall advocates the art of revision, and believes that writing is as much a craft as a means of expression.*

Life Work

Donald Hall

When I hear talk about "the work ethic" I puke. CEOs talk about it,
whose annual salaries average one hundred and thirty times their workers' wages. Whatever the phrase purports to describe, it is not an ethic; it
is not an idea of work's value or a moral dictate but a feeling or tone connected to work, and it is temperamental and cultural. Studs Terkel's
stonemason has it, and his line-worker does not; instead, the line-worker
has a work anger, or a work malevolence, which is entirely appropriate.
Mind you, the stonemason works alone with his hands solving problems
that change with every stone. He does something that he can look at and
put his name to. He can measure what he has done in walls and buildings
not in units of the same thing, like so many Chevrolet Impalas or so many
distributor cap linings. Shades of John Ruskin. I no more have a work
ethic than I have self-discipline. I have so many pages a day, so many
books and essays.

Visiting my mother in Connecticut, I sit beside her recliner and she
asks what I am up to. I tell her about *Life Work.* "I think your book will be
inspirational to people," she responds; she has been building me up since
I was born; but she has her own ego: "When I look around this house,"
she goes on, "I see so much that I have made. Drapes, curtains, bed-
spreads, most of the quilts. Not the blankets of course. Lace for the pil-
lowcases." She points to the drapes in the sunroom where she lives waking and sleeping. "I made those drapes in 1938 and the edges are all
worn. I hope they live longer than I do." After a moment she says, "I *know*
the upstairs drapes need washing but I *can't.*" In fact she cannot mount
the stairs to see that they are dirty but she knows it well enough. Then she
goes back to thinking of a life's work, shaped into objects throughout this
house. "They are *mine,*" she says.

All winter I find Jane standing by the dining-room windows looking into the secluded garden she has made behind the house; all winter she plans next summer's back garden. On mild days in March she begins cleaning the garden patch for the better days coming; when we hear that the temperature will drop below freezing again—March, April, even May—she covers or recovers bulbs and emerging snowdrops with mulch from last year's leaves. Snowdrops, daffodils, tulips, roses, peonies, hollyhocks, lilies. All summer she works every day that it does not rain, and sometimes she works in rain. She works on poems early at her desk, when the garden is wet with dew, or she might not write at all in summer. By nine-thirty or ten she is outside armed with spoons and spades, trimming and feeding, helping and preparing. On late warm evenings of June and July, only darkness forces her inside. She gardens twelve hours a day, some days.

And her flowers reward her work by their magnificence: peonies whiter than the idea of white and as big as basketballs; hollyhocks seven feet tall with a blossom delicately peach-pink. People swerve and slow down driving by, if they are flower people; we fear accidents.

I call it work and so does Jane although it is voluntary and produces no revenue—except when, in bare cold November or a rainy stretch of June, Jane writes a poem or an essay out of her gardening. Her garden is work because it is a devotion undertaken with passion and conviction; because it absorbs her; because it is a task or unrelenting quest which cannot be satisfied. True gardening is atavistic and represents or embodies or fulfills the centuries or millennia that her ancestors (all of our ancestors) spent working in dirt. Our forefathers and foremothers farmed not for pleasure but to stay alive or to satisfy the Squire, to survive on leavings from milord's table or to lay up sheepswool and turnips to sustain themselves through the snows of winter. Whatever the source or motive for their work, the hymns of dirt-work continue their chorus below the level of our consciousness.

As we look back across millennia, we see a social structure that is largely agricultural. Although many males from fourteen to fifty fight in the emperor's army or climb the rigging of the emperor's ships, the remaining males together with children and women plough, dig, plant seed, carry water, weed, and harvest. Thus in the suburbs we rake leaves together; thus we trim the forsythia; thus we arrange a sprinkler on the suburban lawn, edge the grass neatly against the sidewalk, mow, and mulch. If we could look from outer space down on North America on an August Saturday, we would watch a suburban nation of farmers tending tiny plots. Canceling time, or standing at a telescope further out in space, we would watch multitudes in 1000 B.C. growing wheat in Mesopotamia. In the city apartment when we raise African violets in the window we plant wheat beside the Nile. In Connecticut the millionaire in his modern house with a swimming pool spends one day a week driving his tractor— he could hire it done a thousand times over—to mow the smooth acres of his estate. He is never so happy—not playing bridge that night drinking Chivas, not reading the *Journal* over coffee or estimating his net worth at the market's close—as he is while he bumps over lawn on his Farmall, master of his lands gathering his weekly harvest.

Who is worst-off, for work, in human history? When I read Studs Terkel's *Working* I choose our nomadic Mexican farm laborers, laboring in the fields from early childhood until death, days sometimes elongated to seventeen hours. When I read Richard Henry Dana's *Two Years Before the Mast* I switch to sailors in nineteenth century merchant fleets: They never spent more than four hours in bed and usually worked a sixteen-hour day (longer in danger; and don't forget the danger) often seven days a week, away from land for months and from home for years at a time. Then I think of the soldier, legionary or hoplite marching all night to fight at dawn, hardtack and salt beef and what you can loot. I have not mentioned slavery, and the history of humanity is the history of slavery. Mind you, in some cultures or historical eras slaves were better off than gentleman soldiers. But the chattel slavery of the Americans, perpetuated until late in the Christian era, I propose as the nineteenth century's equivalent to Hitler's and Stalin's exterminations. Or read *Das Kapital*—or any objective history of the same period—and compare the labors of miners or factory workers in England—often women and children—with labors of the felaheen in the Old Kingdom.

Work is what we do to feed ourselves and keep ourselves warm. Some hunter-gatherers, in a fortunate climate with fortunate vegetation, can work twelve hours a week—leaving the rest of their time for love-making, magic, religion, gossip, games, and drinking the local brew. Watching television ads during sports events, I note that we aspire to the condition of this hunter-gatherer. D. H. Lawrence wrote that "for some mysterious or obvious reason, the modern woman and the modern man hate physical work," and "The dream of every man is that in the end he shall have to work no more." When there is work in the TV advertisement, it is something done quickly—and the reward is drinking beer. Do we want a house? A house goes up in twenty seconds in a crafted sequence of thirty shots; we watch the house rise as we watch a flower open when the camera takes a frame every four hours over two days.

These work-ads remind me of my dreams of gardening, which never included a sore back, in which I never dropped a hoe or misplaced a trowel; in television ads no one is tired, and no one is old. The hunting-gathering TV young, all slim and beautiful and energetic, gather to drink and dance and flirt at the Silver Bullet, aka the Earthly Paradise. We understand that centuries of offstage labor, not to mention evolution and history and civilization and the opposable thumb, have brought us to this time and moment of sexual leisure. We also understand the hunting-gathering young must have a life-expectancy like a slave's in a Hittite galley, because nobody here is as old as twenty-seven.

Lawrence writing seventy years ago foresaw the Silver Bullet. "It means, apart from the few necessary hours of highly paid and congenial labor, that men and women shall have nothing to do except enjoy themselves. No beastly housework for the women, no beastly homework for the men. Free! free to enjoy themselves. More films, more motor-cars, more dances, more golf, more tennis and more getting completely away from yourself. And the goal of life is enjoyment."

Baudelaire on the other hand claimed that work was less boring than amusing yourself. Surely I agree, but not everyone does: Enjoyment in the shape of golf absorbed my father as his work did not; work and its anxiety *engaged* him—but worry and dread do not characterize the absorbedness that Gurchuran Das described. Golf was an engaging pastime, and the atavistic sources of sport are as dear as the origins of lawn-care: not agriculture but warfare.

Pastimes are always atavistic and they will not do for a life's structure. When work is utterly disagreeable, and week awaits weekend, our delight in recreation reveals our misery. The Silver Bullet, like the touch football game that precedes it, is the house of wretchedness. The goal of life is enjoyment? It depends on the quality of the joy; elsewhere Lawrence wrote, "It seems as if the great aim and purpose in human life were to bring all life into the human consciousness. And this is the final meaning of work: the extension of human consciousness." We understand: Not everyone can work to extend the consciousness of others. For most of us, the exercise of freedom—doing what we like doing—may best extend our own.

But the goal is worthy: As Swami Vivekananda says: "work like a *master* and not as a *slave*; work incessantly, but do not do slave's work. Do you not see how everybody works? Nobody can be altogether at rest; ninety-nine percent of mankind work like slaves, and the result is misery; it is all selfish work. Work through freedom! Work through love!"

When I hung around baseball's major leagues, talking to ballplayers, I discovered to my glee that ballplayers talked about work, just as poets do, in opposite ways. I brag about six hundred drafts of "Another Elegy"; John Ashbery, on the other hand—confronted with having written a poem in twenty minutes when he was an undergraduate—answers, "Yes. I took longer then." Half the athletes told me that working at baseball is silly; hell, just go out there and have fun . . . The other half said (and wholly believed) that they lacked any natural ability, that they accomplished their success by dint of practice, preparation, hard work, and virtue. In *The Boys of Summer* Roger Kahn remembered how George "Shotgun" Shuba—who hit line drives for the old Dodgers—told him of arduous practice all winter, convinced that only hard labor allowed him to play baseball. (If I had practiced twelve hours a day, at my physical peak, I would never have hit a line drive off a major league pitch.) Roger Kahn kept telling him, "But you're a natural," until Shuba finally reared up and contradicted him: "You talk like a sportswriter. In the winters, for fifteen years after loading potatoes or anything else, even when I was in the majors, I'd swing at the clump six hundred times." Shuba hung a ball of string from the ceiling of his basement and swung a bat at it: "after sixty I'd make an X. Ten Xs and I had my six hundred swings. Then I could go to bed. . . . I swung a 44-ounce bat 600 times a night, 4,200 times a week, 47,200 swings every winter."

In spring training of 1992, Roger Clemens showed up in excellent physical shape, and then stepped up his preparations. On Florida days when he went five innings, he ran a mile and a half *before* pitching. He explained that he was toughening himself for late in the season, or even late in a game when he had to pitch tired. Between innings, in Winter Haven, he left the mound not to rest in the dugout but to do sit-ups; or he recruited a coach to throw him pick-ups—low ground balls which he fielded first on one side and then on the other. Asked why he worked so hard he answered, "People write articles about how you're *blessed* with the right arm . . . That might be true, for some people, but I had to work to get where I'm at."

*L*inda Hogan (1947–) *is a descendant of the Chicasaw Nation, but instead of growing up on a reservation, she moved often with her military family. Hogan is a poet, storyteller, and writer of novels and short stories. An environmentalist, Hogan focuses on environmental, holistic, and feminist themes, often drawing on her Native American ancestry.*

Waking Up the Rake

Linda Hogan

In the still dark mornings, my grandmother would rise up from her bed and put wood in the stove. When the fire began to burn, she would sit in front of its warmth and let down her hair. It had never been cut and it knotted down in two long braids. When I was fortunate enough to be there, in those red Oklahoma mornings, I would wake up with her, stand behind her chair, and pull the brush through the long strands of her hair. It cascaded down her back, down over the chair, and touched the floor.

We were the old and the new, bound together in front of the snapping fire, woven like a lifetime's tangled growth of hair. I saw my future in her body and face, and her past was alive in me. We were morning people, and in all of earth's mornings the new intertwines with the old. Even new, a day itself is ancient, old with earth's habit of turning over and over again.

Years later, I was sick, and I went to a traditional healer. The healer was dark and thin and radiant. The first night I was there, she also lit a fire. We sat before it, smelling the juniper smoke. She asked me to tell her everything, my life spoken in words, a case history of living, with its dreams and losses, the scars and wounds we all bear from being in the world. She smoked me with cedar smoke, wrapped a sheet around me, and put me to bed, gently, like a mother caring for her child.

The next morning she nudged me awake and took me outside to pray. We faced east where the sun was beginning its journey on our side of earth.

The following morning in red dawn, we went outside and prayed. The sun was a full orange eye rising up the air. The morning after that we did the same, and on Sunday we did likewise.

203

The next time I visited her it was a year later, and again we went through the same prayers, standing outside facing the early sun. On the last morning I was there, she left for her job in town. Before leaving, she said, "Our work is our altar."

Those words have remained with me.

Now I am a disciple of birds. The birds that I mean are eagles, owls, and hawks. I clean cages at the Birds of Prey Rehabilitation Foundation. It is the work I wanted to do, in order to spend time inside the gentle presence of the birds.

There is a Sufi saying that goes something like this: "Yes, worship God, go to church, sing praises, but first tie your camel to the post." This cleaning is the work of tying the camel to a post.

I pick up the carcasses and skin of rats, mice, and of rabbits. Some of them have been turned inside out by the sharp-beaked eaters, so that the leathery flesh becomes a delicately veined coat for the inner fur. It is a boneyard. I rake the smooth fragments of bones. Sometimes there is a leg or shank of deer to be picked up.

In this boneyard the still-red vertebrae lie on the ground beside an open rib cage. The remains of a rabbit, a small intestinal casing, holds excrement like beads in a necklace. And there are the clean, oval pellets the birds spit out, filled with fur, bone fragments, and, now and then, a delicate sharp claw that looks as if it were woven inside. A feather, light and soft, floats down a current of air, and it is also picked up.

Over time, the narrow human perspective from which we view things expands. A deer carcass begins to look beautiful and rich in its torn redness, the muscle and bone exposed in the shape life took on for a while as it walked through meadows and drank at creeks.

And the bone fragments have their own stark beauty, the clean white jaw bones with ivory teeth small as the head of a pin still in them. I think of medieval physicians trying to learn about our private, hidden bodies by cutting open the stolen dead and finding the splendor inside, the grace of every red organ, and the smooth, gleaming bone.

This work is an apprenticeship, and the birds are the teachers. Sweet-eyed barn owls, such taskmasters, asking us to be still and slow and to move in time with their rhythms, not our own. The short-eared owls with their startling yellow eyes require the full presence of a human. The marsh hawks, behind their branches, watch our every move.

There is a silence needed here before a person enters the bordered world the birds inhabit, so we stop and compose ourselves before entering their doors, and we listen to the musical calls of the eagles, the sound of wings in air, the way their feet with sharp claws, many larger than our own hands, grab hold of a perch. Then we know we are ready to enter, and they are ready for us.

The most difficult task the birds demand is that we learn to be equal to them, to feel our way into an intelligence that is different from our own. A friend, awed at the thought of working with eagles, said, "Imagine knowing an eagle." I answered her honestly, "It isn't so much that we know the eagles. It's that they know us."

And they know that we are apart from them, that as humans we have somehow fallen from our animal grace, and because of that we maintain a distance from them, though it is not always a distance of heart. The places we inhabit, even sharing a common earth, must remain distinct and separate. It was our presence that brought most of them here in the first place, nearly all of them injured in a clash with the human world. They have been shot, or hit by cars, trapped in leg hold traps, poisoned, ensnared in wire fences. To ensure their survival, they must remember us as the enemies that we are. We are the embodiment of a paradox; we are the wounders and we are the healers.

There are human lessons to be learned here, in the work. Fritjof Capra wrote: "Doing work that has to be done over and over again helps us recognize the natural cycles of growth and decay, of birth and death, and thus become aware of the dynamic order of the universe." And it is true, in whatever we do, the brushing of hair, the cleaning of cages, we begin to see the larger order of things. In this place, there is a constant coming to terms with both the sacred place life occupies, and with death. Like one of those early physicians who discovered the strange, inner secrets of our human bodies, I'm filled with awe at the very presence of life, not just the birds, but a horse contained in its living fur, a dog alive and running. What a marvel it is, the fine shape life takes in all of us. It is equally marvelous that life is quickly turned back to the earth-colored ants and the soft white maggots that are time's best and closest companions. To sit with the eagles and their flute-like songs, listening to the longer flute of wind sweep through the lush grasslands, is to begin to know the natural laws that exist apart from our own written ones.

One of those laws, that we carry deep inside us, is intuition. It is lodged in a place even the grave-robbing doctors could not discover. It's a blood-written code that directs us through life. The founder of this healing center, Sigrid Ueblacker, depends on this inner knowing. She watches, listens, and feels her way to an understanding of each eagle and owl. This vision, as I call it, directs her own daily work at healing the injured birds and returning them to the wild.

"Sweep the snow away," she tells me. "The Swainson's hawks should be in Argentina this time of year and should not have to stand in the snow."

I sweep.

And that is in the winter when the hands ache from the cold, and the water freezes solid and has to be broken out for the birds, fresh buckets carried over icy earth from the well. In summer, it's another story. After only a few hours the food begins to move again, as if resurrected to life. A rabbit shifts a bit. A mouse turns. You could say that they have been resurrected, only with a life other than the one that left them. The moving skin swarms with flies and their offspring, ants, and a few wasps, busy at their own daily labor.

Even aside from the expected rewards for this work, such as seeing an eagle healed and winging across the sky it fell from, there are others. An occasional snake, beautiful and sleek, finds its way into the cage one day, eats a mouse and is too fat to leave, so we watch its long muscular life stretched out in the tall grasses. Or, another summer day, taking branches to be burned with a pile of wood near the little creek, a large turtle with a dark and shining shell slips soundlessly into the water, its presence a reminder of all the lives beyond these that occupy us.

One green morning, an orphaned owl perches nervously above me while I clean. Its downy feathers are roughed out. It appears to be twice its size as it clacks its beak at me, warning me: stay back. Then, fearing me the way we want it to, it bolts off the perch and flies, landing by accident onto the wooden end of my rake, before it sees that a human is an extension of the tool, and it flies again to a safer place, while I return to raking.

The word *rake* means to gather or heap up, to smooth the broken ground. And that's what this work is, all of it, the smoothing over of broken ground, the healing of the severed trust we humans hold with earth. We gather it back together again with great care, take the broken pieces and fragments and return them to the sky. It is work at the borderland between species, at the boundary between injury and healing.

There is an art to raking, a very fine art, one with rhythm in it, and life. On the days I do it well, the rake wakes up. Wood that came from dark dense forests seems to return to life. The water that rose up through the rings of that wood, the minerals of earth mined upward by the burrowing tree roots, all come alive. My own fragile hand touches the wood, a hand full of my own life, including that which rose each morning early to watch the sun return from the other side of the planet. Over time, these hands will smooth the rake's wooden handle down to a sheen.

Raking. It is a labor round and complete, smooth and new as an egg, and the rounding seasons of the world revolving in time and space. All things, even our own heartbeats and sweat, are in it, part of it. And that work, that watching the turning over of life, becomes a road into what is essential. Work is the country of hands, and they want to live there in the dailiness of it, the repetition that is time's language of prayer, a common tongue. Everything is there, in that language, in the humblest of labor. The rake wakes up and the healing is in it. The shadows of leaves that once fell beneath the tree the handle came from are in that labor, and the rabbits that passed this way, on the altar of our work. And when the rake wakes up, all earth's gods are reborn and they dance and sing in the dusty air around us.

*R*ita Henley Jensen *is founder and editor in chief of Women's eNews, a daily news service covering issues of concern to women. A survivor of domestic violence and former welfare mother, Jensen earned degrees from Ohio State University and Columbia Graduate School of Journalism. She has received numerous journalism awards, and was named one of the hundred most influential women in New York by the* New York Daily News.

Welfare

Rita Henley Jensen

I am a woman. A white woman, once poor but no longer. I am not lazy, never was. I am a middle-aged woman, with two grown daughters. I was a welfare mother, one of those women society considers less than nothing.

I should have applied for Aid to Families with Dependent Children when I was 18 years old, pregnant with my first child, and living with a boyfriend who slapped me around. But I didn't.

I remember talking it over at the time with a friend. I lived in the neighborhood that surrounds the vast Columbus campus of Ohio State University. Students, faculty, hangers-on, hippies, runaways, and recent émigrés from Kentucky lived side by side in the area's relatively inexpensive housing. I was a runaway.

On a particularly warm midsummer's day, I stood on High Street, directly across from the campus' main entrance, with an older, more sophisticated friend, wondering what to do with my life. With my swollen belly, all hope of my being able to cross the street and enroll in the university had evaporated. Now, I was seeking advice about how merely to survive, to escape the assaults and still be able to care for my child.

My friend knew of no place I could go, nowhere I could turn, no one else I could ask. I remember saying in a tone of resignation, "I can't apply for welfare." Instead of disagreeing with me, she nodded, acknowledging our mutual belief that taking beatings was better than taking handouts. Being "on the dole" meant you deserved only contempt.

In August 1965, I married my attacker.

Six years later, I left him and applied for assistance. My children were 18 months and five and a half years old. I had waited much too long. Within a year, I crossed High Street to go to Ohio State. I graduated in four years and moved to New York City to attend Columbia University's Graduate School of Journalism. I have worked as a journalist for 18 years now. My life on welfare was very hard—there were times when I didn't have enough food for the three of us. But I was able to get an education while on welfare. It is hardly likely that a woman on AFDC today would be allowed to do what I did, to go to school and develop the kind of skills that enabled me to make a better life for myself and my children.

This past summer, I attended a conference in Chicago on feminist legal theory. During the presentation of a paper related to gender and property rights, the speaker mentioned as an aside that when one says "welfare mother" the listener hears "black welfare mother." A discussion ensued about the underlying racism until someone declared that the solution was easy: all that had to be done was have the women in the room bring to the attention of the media the fact that white women make up the largest percentage of welfare recipients. At this point, I stood, took a deep breath, stepped out of my professional guise, and informed the crowd that I was a former welfare mother. Looking at my white hair, blue eyes, and freckled Irish skin, some laughed; others gasped—despite having just acknowledged that someone like me was, in fact, a "typical" welfare mother.

Occasionally I do this. Speak up. Identify myself as one of "them." I do so reluctantly because welfare mothers are a lightning rod for race hatred, class prejudice, and misogyny. Yet I am aware that as long as welfare is viewed as an *African American* woman's issue, instead of a *woman's* issue—whether that woman be white, African American, Asian, Latina, or Native American—those in power can continue to exploit our country's racism to weaken and even eliminate public support for the programs that help low-income mothers and their children.

I didn't have the guts to stand up during a 1974 reception for Ohio state legislators. The party's hostess was a leader of the Columbus chapter of the National Organization for Women and she had opened up her suburban home so that representatives of many of the state's progressive organizations could lobby in an informal setting for an increase in the state's welfare allotment for families. I was invited as a representative of the campus area's single mothers' support group. In the living room, I came across a state senator in a just-slightly-too-warm-and-friendly state induced by the potent combination of free booze and a crowd of women. He quickly decided I looked like a good person to amuse with one of his favorite jokes. "You want to know how a welfare mother can prevent getting pregnant?" he asked, giggling. "She can just take two aspirin—and put them between her knees," he roared, as he bent down to place his Scotch glass between his own, by way of demonstration. I drifted away.

I finally did gather up my courage to speak out. It was in a classroom during my junior year. I was enrolled in a course on the economics of public policy because I wanted to understand why the state of Ohio thought it desirable to provide me and my two kids with only $204 per month—59 percent of what even the state itself said a family of three needed to live.

For my required oral presentation, I chose "Aid to Families with Dependent Children." I cited the fact that approximately two thirds of all the poor families in the country were white; I noted that most welfare families consisted of one parent and two children. As an audiovisual aid, I brought my own two kids along. My voice quavered a bit as I delivered my intro: I stood with my arms around my children and said, "We are a typical AFDC family."

My classmates had not one question when I finished. I don't believe anyone even bothered to ask the kids' names or ages.

If I were giving this talk today, I would hold up a picture of us back then and say we still represent typical welfare recipients. The statistics I would cite to back up that statement have been refined since the 1970s and now include "Hispanic" as a category. In 1992, 38.9 percent of all welfare mothers were white, 37.2 percent were black, 17.8 percent were "Hispanic," 2.8 percent were Asian, and 1.4 percent were Native American.

My report, however, would focus on the dramatic and unrelenting reduction in resources available to low-income mothers in the last two decades.

Fact: In 1970, the average monthly benefit for a family of three was $178. Not much, but consider that as a result of inflation, that $178 would be approximately $680 today. And then consider that the average monthly payment today is only about $414. That's the way it's been for more than two decades: the cost of living goes up (by the states' own accounting, the cost of rent, food, and utilities for a family of three has doubled), but the real value of welfare payments keeps going down.

Fact: The 1968 Work Incentive Program (the government called it WIN; we called it WIP) required that all unemployed adult recipients sign up for job training or employment once their children turned six.

The age has now been lowered to three, and states may go as low as age one. What that means is you won't be able to attend and finish college while on welfare. (In most states a college education isn't considered job training, even though experts claim most of us will need college degrees to compete in the workplace of the twenty-first century.)

Fact: Forty-two percent of welfare recipients will be on welfare less than two years during their entire lifetime, and an additional 33 percent will spend between two and eight years on welfare. The statistics haven't changed much over the years: women still use welfare to support their families when their children are small.

In 1974, I ended my talk with this joke: A welfare mother went into the drugstore and bought a can of deodorant. I explained that it was funny because everyone knew that welfare mothers could not afford "extras" like personal hygiene products. My joke today would be: A welfare mother believed that if elected public officials understood these facts, they would not campaign to cut her family's benefits.

The idea that government representatives care about welfare mothers is as ridiculous to me now as the idea back then that I would waste my limited funds on deodorant. It is much clearer to me today what the basic functions of welfare public policy are at this moment in U.S. history.

By making war on welfare recipients, political leaders can turn the public's attention away from the government's redistribution of wealth to the wealthy. Recent studies show that the United States has become the most economically stratified of industrial nations. In fact, Federal Reserve figures reveal that the richest 1 percent of American households—each with a minimum net worth of $2.3 million—control nearly 40 percent of the wealth, while in Britain, the richest 1 percent of the population controls about 18 percent of the wealth. In the mid-1970s, both countries were on a par: the richest 1 percent controlled 20 percent of the wealth. President Reagan was the master of this verbal shell game. He told stories of welfare queens and then presided over the looting of the nation's savings and loans by wealthy white men.

Without a doubt, the current urgency for tax cuts and spending reductions can be explained by the fact that President Clinton tried to shift the balance slightly in 1992 and the wealthy ended up paying 16 percent more in taxes the following year, by one estimate.

The purpose of this antiwelfare oratory and the campaigns against sex education, abortion rights, and aid to teenage mothers is to ensure a constant supply of young women as desperate and ashamed as I was.

Young women willing to take a job at any wage rate, willing to tolerate the most abusive relationships with men, and unable to enter the gates leading to higher education.

To accomplish their goals, political leaders continually call for reforms that include demands that welfare recipients work, that teenagers don't have sex, and that welfare mothers stop giving birth (but don't have abortions). Each "reform" addresses the nation's racial and sexual stereotypes: taking care of one's own children is not work; welfare mothers are unemployed, promiscuous, and poorly motivated; and unless the government holds their feet to the fire, these women will live on welfare for years, as will their children and their children's children.

This type of demagoguery has been common throughout our history. What sets the present era apart is the nearly across-the-board cooperation of the media. The national news magazines, the most prestigious daily newspapers, the highly regarded broadcast news outlets, as well as the supermarket tabloids and talk-radio hosts, have generally abandoned the notion that one of their missions is to sometimes comfort the afflicted and afflict the comfortable. Instead, they too often reprint politicians' statements unchallenged, provide charts comparing one party's recommendations to another's without really questioning those recommendations, and illustrate story after story, newscast after newscast, with a visual of an African American woman (because we all know they're the only ones on welfare) living in an urban housing project (because that's where all welfare recipients live) who has been on welfare for years.

When *U.S. News & World Report* did a major story on welfare reform this year, it featured large photographs of eight welfare recipients, seven of whom were women of color: six African Americans and one Latina or Native American (the text does not state her ethnicity). Describing the inability of welfare mothers to hold jobs (they are "hobbled not only by their lack of experience but also by their casual attitudes toward punctuality, dress, and coworkers"), the article offers the "excuse" given by one mother for not taking a 3 P.M. to 11 P.M. shift: "I wouldn't get to see my kids," she told the reporter. You can't win for losing—should she take that 3-to-11 job and her unsupervised kids get in trouble, you can be sure some conservative would happily leap on her as an example of one of those poor women who are bad mothers and whose kids should be in orphanages.

Why don't the media ever find a white woman from Ohio or Iowa or Wisconsin, a victim of domestic violence, leaving the father of her two children to make a new start? Or a Latina mother like the one living in my current neighborhood, who has one child and does not make enough as a home health care attendant to pay for her family's health insurance? Or a Native American woman living on a reservation, creating crafts for pennies that will be sold by others for dollars?

Besides reinforcing stereotypes about the personal failings of welfare recipients, when my colleagues write in-depth pieces about life on welfare they invariably concentrate on describing welfare mothers' difficulties with the world at large: addictions, lack of transportation, dangerous neighbors, and, most recently, shiftless boyfriends who begin beating them when they do get jobs—as if this phenomenon were limited to relationships between couples with low incomes.

I wonder why no journalist I have stumbled across, no matter how well meaning, has communicated what I believe is the central reality of most women's lives on welfare: they believe all the stereotypes too and they are ashamed of being on welfare. They eat, breathe, sleep, and clothe themselves with shame.

Most reporting on welfare never penetrates the surface, and the nature of the relationship between the welfare system and the woman receiving help is never explored. Like me, many women fleeing physical abuse must make the welfare department their first stop after seeking an order of protection. Studies are scarce, but some recent ones of women in welfare-to-work programs across the U.S. estimate that anywhere from half to three fourths of participants are, or have been, in abusive relationships. And surveys of some homeless shelters indicate that half of the women living in them are on the run from a violent mate.

But if welfare is the means of escape, it is also the institutionalization of the dynamic of battering. My husband was the source of my and my children's daily bread and of daily physical and psychological attacks. On welfare, I was free of the beatings, but the assaults on my self-esteem were still frequent and powerful, mimicking the behavior of a typical batterer.

As he pounds away, threatening to kill the woman and children he claims to love, the abuser often accuses his victims of lying, laziness, and infidelity. Many times, he threatens to snatch the children away from their mother in order to protect them from her supposed incompetence, her laziness, dishonesty, and sexual escapades.

On welfare, just as with my husband, I had to prove every statement was not a lie. Everything had to be documented: how many children I had, how much I paid for rent, fuel, transportation, electricity, child care, and so forth. It went so far as to require that at every "redetermination of need" interview (every six months), I had to produce the originals of my children's birth certificates, which were duly photocopied over and over again. Since birth certificates do not change, the procedure was a subtle and constant reminder that nothing I said was accepted as truth. Ever.

But this is a petty example. The more significant one was the suspicion that my attendance at Ohio State University was probably a crime. Throughout my college years, I regularly reported that I was attending OSU. Since the WIN limit at that time was age six and my youngest daughter was two when I started, I was allowed to finish my undergraduate years without having to report to some job training program that would have prepared me for a minimum-wage job. However, my caseworker and I shared an intuitive belief that something just had to be wrong about this. How could I be living on welfare and going to college? Outrageous! Each day I awoke feeling as if I were in a race, that I had to complete my degree before I was charged with a felony.

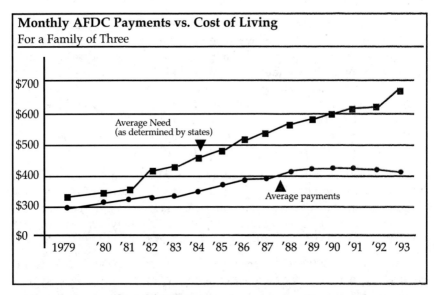

Monthly AFDC Payments vs. Cost of Living
For a Family of Three

As a matter of fact, I remember hearing, a short time after I graduated, that a group of welfare mothers attending college in Ohio were charged with food stamp fraud, apparently for not reporting their scholarships as additional income.

Batterers frequently lie to their victims—it's a power thing. Caseworkers do too. For example, when I moved to New York to attend graduate school and applied for assistance, I asked my intake worker whether I could apply for emergency food stamps. She told me there was no emergency food program. The kids and I scraped by, but that statement was false. I was unaware of it until welfare rights advocates successfully sued the agency for denying applicants emergency food assistance. In another case, when someone gave me a ten-year-old Opel so I could keep my first (very low paying) reporting job, my caseworker informed me in writing that mere possession of a car made me ineligible for welfare. (I appealed and won. The caseworker was apparently confused by the fact that although I was not allowed to have any assets, I did need the car to get to work. She also assumed a used car had to have some value. Not this one.)

Then there's the issue of sexual possessiveness: states rarely grant assistance to families with fathers still in the home. And as for feeling threatened about losing custody, throughout the time I was on welfare, I knew that if I stumbled at all, my children could be taken away from me. It is widely understood that any neighbor can call the authorities about a welfare mother, making a charge of neglect, and that mother, since she is less than nothing, might not be able to prove her competency. I had a close call once. I had been hospitalized for ten days and a friend took care of my children. After my return home, however, I was still weak. I would doze off on the sofa while the kids were awake—one time it happened when they were outside playing on the sidewalk. A neighbor, seeing them there unattended, immediately called the child welfare agency, which sent someone out to question me and to look inside my refrigerator to see if I had any food. Luckily, that day I did.

Ultimately, leaving an abusive relationship and applying for welfare is a little like leaving solitary confinement to become part of a prison's general population. It's better, but you are still incarcerated.

None of this is ever discussed in the context of welfare reform. The idiot state legislator, the prosecutor in Ohio who brought the charges against welfare mothers years ago, Bill Clinton, and Newt Gingrich all continue to play the race and sex card by hollering for welfare reform. They continue to exploit and feed the public's ignorance about and antipathy toward welfare mothers to propel their own careers. Sadly, journalists permit them to do so, perhaps for the same reason.

Lost in all this are the lives of thousands of women impoverished by virtue of their willingness to assume the responsibility of raising their children. An ex-boyfriend used to say that observing my struggle was a little like watching someone standing in a room, with arms upraised to prevent the ceiling from pressing in on her. He wondered just how long I could prevent the collapse.

Today, welfare mothers have even less opportunity than I did. Their talent, brains, luck, and resourcefulness are ignored. Each new rule, regulation, and reform makes it even more unlikely that they can use the time they are on welfare to do as I did: cross the High Streets in their cities and towns, and realize their ambitions. Each new rule makes it more likely that they will only be able to train for a minimum-wage job that will never allow them to support their families.

So no, I don't think all we have to do is get the facts to the media. I think we have to raise hell any way we can.

Our goal is simple: never again should there be a young woman, standing in front of the gates that lead to a better future, afraid to enter because she believes she must instead choose poverty and battery.

Section Three:
Poetry and Drama

*M*artín Espada (1957–) is a poet and professor at the University of Massachusetts–Amherst, where he teaches creative writing and literature. He has published thirteen books, and garnered numerous awards. In 1996, he won the American Book Award for his collection Imagine the Angels of Bread.

Jorge the Church Janitor Finally Quits

Martín Espada

No one asks
where I am from,
I must be
from the country of janitors,

I have always mopped this floor.
Honduras, you are a squatter's camp
outside the city
of their understanding.

No one can speak
my name,
I host the fiesta
of the bathroom,
stirring the toilet
Like a punchbowl.
The Spanish music of my name
is lost
when the guests complain
about toilet paper.

What they say
must be true:
I am smart,
but I have a bad attitude.

No one knows
that I quit tonight,
maybe the mop
will push on without me,
sniffing along the floor
like a crazy squid
with stringy gray tentacles.
They will call it Jorge.

*P*hilip Levine (1928–) is a poet and professor who was born and educated in Detroit, Michigan. His work has earned national recognition—including the National Book Critics Circle Award, the American Book Award, the National Book Award, and the Pulitzer Prize. Many of his poems are beautifully drawn portraits of working-class life.

What Work Is

Philip Levine

We stand in the rain in a long line
waiting at Ford Highland Park. For work.
You know what work is—if you're
old enough to read this you know what
work is, although you may not do it.
Forget you. This is about waiting,
shifting from one foot to another.
Feeling the light rain failing like mist
into your hair, blurring your vision
until you think you see your own brother
ahead of you, maybe ten places.
You rub your glasses with your fingers,
and of course it's someone else's brother,
narrower across the shoulders than
yours but with the same sad slouch, the grin
that does not hide the stubbornness,
the sad refusal to give in to
rain, to the hours wasted waiting,
to the knowledge that somewhere ahead
a man is waiting who will say, "No,
we're not hiring today," for any
reason he wants. You love your brother,
now suddenly you can hardly stand
the love flooding you for your brother,
who's not beside you or behind or
ahead because he's home trying to
sleep off a miserable night shift
at Cadillac so he can get up
before noon to study his German.

Works eight hours a night so he can sing
Wagner, the opera you hate most,
the worst music ever invented.
How long has it been since you told him
you loved him, held his wide shoulders,
opened your eyes wide and said those words,
and maybe kissed his cheek? You've never
done something so simple, so obvious,
not because you're too young or too dumb,
not because you're jealous or even mean
or incapable of crying in
the presence of another man, no,
just because you don't know what work is.

Emily Warn is the author of three books of poetry, including her latest book, Shadow Architect. A former Stegner Fellow at Stanford, she has taught creative writing at Lynchburg College in Lynchburg, Virginia, and is currently the editor for the Poetry Foundation Web site.

Vagrant

Emily Warn

Locust leaves fall
in the empty city park,
thickly, as if a crow pounds
the podium of the top branches.
Soon rains. Soon wake to darkness.
But today the light resembles California.
I'm stripped to my t-shirt,
enjoying the leaves sift down
with the same pleasure
the boy across the street must feel
pulling his jeans from the line,
burying his face in their smell,
asking, *What are we going to do today, Mother?*

A job application sits on my desk.
A whole day to fill it. I can't.
Instead I invent questions.
Why do pigeons have red feet?
What percentage of a day's sunlight
do locust leaves absorb?
How can I believe in ambition
when the man on the city stairs
whose wife kicked him out needs to talk?
And the wild ripe grapes need to be eaten?
And my shadow wants to walk, admiring
how it flattens against buildings and stripes trees.

Besides, turning the compost this morning,
I broke a spider web that I promised to fix.
A decade—at least—to weave a web
whose vacancies let wind and rain pour through,
yet snag the occasional fly.

*F*rancis LaFlesche (Zhogaxe) (1857–1932) was an important anthropologist and writer. He not only studied and wrote about his native Omaha culture, but he also contributed greatly to the scholarship regarding the Osage culture. He captured in sound some of the last remaining songs and dances of the Osage, a semi-nomadic Siouan people who inhabited what is now Missouri and Arkansas until they were forced to relocate to Kansas by traveling the infamous Trail of Tears.

Planting Song

Osage Song
Translated by Dr. Francis La Flesche

I have made a footprint, a sacred one.
I have made a footprint, through it the blades push upward.
I have made a footprint, through it the blades radiate.
I have made a footprint, over it the blades float in the wind.
I have made a footprint, over it the ears lean toward one another.
I have made a footprint, over it I bend the stalk to pluck the ears.
I have made a footprint, over it the blossoms lie gray.
I have made a footprint, smoke arises from my house.
I have made a footprint, there is cheer in my house.
I have made a footprint, I live in the light of day.

*R*ita Frances Dove (1952–) is a poet, scholar, professor, and writer. In 1987 she was awarded the Pulitzer Prize for Thomas and Beulah, a collection of poems drawn from the lives of her grandparents. In 1993 she became the first African-American and youngest recipient to be named as Poet Laureate of the United States. She has won numerous awards, honorary degrees, and prizes for her work.

Daystar

Rita Dove

She wanted a little room for thinking:
but she saw diapers steaming on the line,
a doll slumped behind the door.

So she lugged a chair behind the garage
to sit out the children's naps.

Sometimes there were things to watch—
the pinched armor of a vanished cricket,
a floating maple leaf. Other days
she stared until she was assured
when she closed her eyes
she'd see only her own vivid blood.

She had an hour, at best, before Liza appeared
pouting from the top of the stairs.
And just *what* was mother doing
out back with the field mice? Why.

building a palace. Later
that night when Thomas rolled over and
lurched into her, she would open her eyes
and think of the place that was hers
for an hour—where
she was nothing,
pure nothing, in the middle of the day.

Elizabeth Alexander (1962–) is a poet, writer, and professor. She currently teaches at Yale University, but has also served as a fellow at the Radcliffe Institute for Advanced Study at Harvard University. She has published four books of poetry, including American Sublime, *which was a finalist for the 2005 Pulitzer Award.*

Blues

Elizabeth Alexander

I am lazy, the laziest
girl in the world. I sleep during
the day when I want to, 'til
my face is creased and swollen,
'til my lips are dry and hot. I
eat as I please: cookies and milk
after lunch, butter and sour cream
on my baked potato, foods that
slothful people eat, that turn
yellow and opaque beneath the skin.
Sometimes come dinnertime Sunday
I am still in my nightgown, the one
with the lace trim listing because
I have not mended it. Many days
I do not exercise, only
consider it, then rub my curdy
belly and lie down. Even
my poems are lazy. I use
syllabics instead of iambs,
prefer slant to the gong of full rhyme,
write briefly while others go
for pages. And yesterday,
for example, I did not work at all!
I got in my car and I drove
to factory outlet stores, purchased
stockings and panties and socks
with my father's money.

To think, in childhood I missed only
one day of school per year. I went
to ballet class four days a week
at four-forty-five and on
Saturdays, beginning always
with plie, ending with curtsy.
To think, I knew only industry,
the industry of my race
and of immigrants, the radio
tuned always to the station
that said, Line up your summer
job months in advance. Work hard
and do not shame your family,
who worked hard to give you what you have.
There is no sin but sloth. Burn
to a wick and keep moving.

I avoided sleep for years,
up at night replaying
evening news stories about
nearby jailbreaks, fat people
who ate fried chicken and woke up
dead. In sleep I am looking
for poems in the shape of open
V's of birds flying in formation,
or open arms saying, I forgive you, all.

*W*alt Whitman (1818–1892) is widely viewed as the father of American poetry. His major work, Leaves of Grass, was influential in launching an entirely new type of poetry, one which captured the fresh and natural rhythms of common speech. His work also conveys a kind of optimism or exuberance for life, and was criticized at times for its frank and evocative approach to sexuality.

I Hear America Singing

Walt Whitman

I HEAR America singing, the varied carols I hear;
Those of mechanics—each one singing his, as it should be, blithe and
    strong;
The carpenter singing his, as he measures his plank or beam,
The mason singing his, as he makes ready for work, or leaves off work;
The boatman singing what belongs to him in his boat—the deckhand
    singing on the steamboat deck;
The shoemaker singing as he sits on his bench—the hatter singing as he
    stands;
The wood-cutter's song—the ploughboy's, on his way in the morning, or
    at the noon intermission, or at sundown;
The delicious singing of the mother—or of the young wife at work—or of
    the girl sewing or washing—Each singing what belongs to her,
    and to none else;
The day what belongs to the day—At night, the party of young fellows,
    robust, friendly,
Singing, with open mouths, their strong melodious songs.

*A*drienne Rich (1929–) is a poet and writer who has earned numerous awards *for her work, including the National Medal of Arts which she refused on political grounds. At the age of twenty-one, she published her first book as part of the Yale Series of Younger Poets prize. From there, she has gone on to publish more than twenty books of poetry and non-fiction. In much of her work, Rich explores political and feminist themes with passion and eloquence.*

Prospective Immigrants Please Note

Adrienne Rich

Either you will
go through this door
or you will not go through.

If you go through
there is always the risk
of remembering your name.

Things look at you doubly
and you must look back
and let them happen.

If you do not go through
it is possible
to live worthily

to maintain your attitudes
to hold your position
to die bravely

but much will blind you,
much will evade you,
at what cost who knows?

The door itself
makes no promises.
It is only a door.

Marge Piercy (1936–) is a poet, novelist, essayist, and playwright. The first in her family to attend college, she studied at the University of Michigan and won several of the University's Hopwood Awards for her writing. A prolific writer, she has published more than a dozen novels, more than a dozen collections of poetry, numerous essays, and a recent memoir. Integrated throughout her work is a deep and abiding interest in feminism and various social issues.

To Be of Use

Marge Piercy

The people I love the best
jump into work head first
without dallying in the shallows
and swim off with sure strokes almost out of sight.
They seem to become natives of that element,
the black sleek heads of seals
bouncing like half-submerged balls.

I love people who harness themselves, an ox to a heavy cart,
who pull like water buffalo, with massive patience,
who strain in the mud and the muck to move things forward,
who do what has to be done, again and again.

I want to be with people who submerge
in the task, who go into the fields to harvest
and work in a row and pass the bags along,
who stand in the line and haul in their places,
who are not parlor generals and field deserters
but move in a common rhythm
when the food must come in or the fire be put out.

The work of the world is common as mud.
Botched, it smears the hands, crumbles to dust.
But the thing worth doing well done
has a shape that satisfies, clean and evident.
Greek amphoras for wine or oil,
Hopi vases that held corn, are put in museums,

but you know they were made to be used.
The pitcher cries for water to carry
and a person for work that is real.

Seamus Heaney (1939–) was born in County Derry, Ireland, and spent his first years on his father's farm. He began publishing his poetry while enrolled at the Queen's University of Belfast. Since then, he has published more than forty books. He has taught at the University of California–Berkeley, Oxford University, and Harvard University among others. In 1995 he was awarded the Nobel Prize in Literature.

Digging

Seamus Heaney
1966

Between my finger and my thumb
The squat pen rests; snug as a gun.

Under my window, a clean rasping sound
When the spade sinks into gravelly ground:
My father, digging. I look down

Till his straining rump among the flowerbeds
Bends low, comes up twenty years away
Stooping in rhythm through potato drills
Where he was digging.

The coarse boot nestled on the lug, the shaft
Against the inside knee was levered firmly.
He rooted out tall tops, buried the bright edge deep
To scatter new potatoes that we picked
Loving their cool hardness in our hands.

By god, the old man could handle a spade.
Just like his old man.

My grandfather cut more turf in a day
Than any other man on Toner's bog.
Once I carried him milk in a bottle
Corked sloppily with paper. He straightened up
To drink it, then fell to right away
Nicking and slicing neatly, heaving sods
Over his shoulder, going down and down
For the good turf. Digging.

The cold smell of potato mould, the squelch and slap
Of soggy peat, the curt cuts of an edge
Through living roots awaken in my head.
But I've no spade to follow men like them.

Between my finger and my thumb
The squat pen rests.
I'll dig with it.

*P*hilip Larkin (1922–1985) is commonly regarded as one of the most important British poets of the latter twentieth century. He was educated and worked as a university librarian, but he was perhaps most influential as a writer and critic. His poems are known for their candor and plain-spoken quality, their curmudgeonly and even dour look at life. At its best, Larkin's work is bitingly sharp and precise.

Toads

Philip Larkin

Why should I let the toad *work*
   Squat on my life?
Can't I use my wit as a pitchfork
   And drive the brute off?

Six days of the week it soils
   With its sickening poison—
Just for paying a few bills!
   That's out of proportion.

Lots of folk live on their wits:
   Lecturers, lispers,
Losels, loblolly-men, louts—
   They don't end as paupers;

Lots of folk live up lanes
   With fires in a bucket,
Eat windfalls and tinned sardines—
   They seem to like it.

Their nippers have got bare feet,
   Their unspeakable wives
Are skinny as whippets—and yet
   No one actually *starves.*

Ah, were I courageous enough
   To shout *Stuff your pension!*
But I know, all too well, that's the stuff
   That dreams are made on:

For something sufficiently toad-like
   Squats in me, too;

Its hunkers are heavy as hard luck,
   And cold as snow,

And will never allow me to blarney
   My way to getting
The fame and the girl and the money
   All at one sitting.

I don't say, one bodies the other
   One's spiritual truth;
But I do say it's hard to lose either,
   When you have both.

Toads Revisited

Philip Larkin

Walking around in the park
Should feel better than work:
The lake, the sunshine,
The grass to lie on,

Blurred playground noises
Beyond black-stockinged nurses—
Not a bad place to be.
Yet it doesn't suit me,

Being one of the men
You meet of an afternoon:
Palsied old step-takers,
Hare-eyed clerks with the jitters,

Waxed-fleshed out-patients
Still vague from accidents,
And characters in long coats
Deep in the litter-baskets—

All dodging the toad work
By being stupid or weak.
Think of being them!
Hearing the hours chime,

Watching the bread delivered,
The sun by clouds covered,
The children going home;
Think of being them,

Turning over their failures
By some bed of lobelias,
Nowhere to go but indoors,
No friends but empty chairs—

No, give me my in-tray,
My loaf-haired secretary,
My shall-I-keep-the-call-in-Sir:
What else can I answer,

When the lights come on at four
At the end of another year?
Give me your arm, old toad;
Help me down Cemetery Road.

*R*obert Hayden (1913–1980) was an American poet and professor. Raised in a poor neighborhood in Detroit and shuffled between foster parents and his own estranged parents, Hayden went on to attend a local college and then begin work in the Federal Writer's Project on black history and culture. In 1940 he published his first book, but it was during the 1960s when his work gained a wide following. In 1976, he became the first black American to serve as Consultant in Poetry to the Library of Congress, which would later be called Poet Laureate.

Those Winter Sundays

Robert Hayden

Sundays too my father got up early
and put his clothes on in the blueblack cold,
then with cracked hands that ached
from labor in the weekday weather made
banked fires blaze. No one ever thanked him.

I'd wake and hear the cold splintering, breaking.
When the rooms were warm, he'd call,
and slowly I would rise and dress,
fearing the chronic angers of that house,

Speaking indifferently to him,
who had driven out the cold
and polished my good shoes as well.
What did I know, what did I know
of love's austere and lonely offices?

Coming Close

Philip Levine

Take this quiet woman, she has been
standing before a polishing wheel
for over three hours, and she lacks
twenty minutes before she can take
a lunch break. Is she a woman?
Consider the arms as they press
the long brass tube against the buffer,
they are striated along the triceps,
the three heads of which clearly show.
Consider the fine dusting of dark down
above the upper lip, and the beads
of sweat that run from under the red
kerchief across the brow and are wiped
away with a blackening wrist band
in one odd motion a child might make
to say No! No! You must come closer
to find out, you must hang your tie
and jacket in one of the lockers
in favor of a black smock, you must
be prepared to spend shift after shift
hauling off the metal trays of stock,
bowing first, knees bent for a purchase,
then lifting with a gasp, the first word
of tenderness between the two of you,
then you must bring new trays of dull,
unpolished tubes. You must feed her,
as they say in the language of the place.
Make no mistake, the place has a language,

239

and if by some luck the power were cut,
the wheel slowed to a stop so that you
suddenly saw it was not a solid object
but so many separate bristles forming
in motion a perfect circle, she would turn
to you and say, "Why?" Not the old *why*
of *why must I spend five nights a week?*
Just, "Why?" Even if by some magic
you knew, you wouldn't dare speak
for fear of her laughter, which now
you have anyway as she places the five
tapering fingers of her filthy hand
on the arm of your white shirt to mark
you for your own, now and forever.

The Token Woman

Marge Piercy

The token woman gleams like a gold molar in a toothless mouth.

The token woman arrives like a milkbottle on the stoop
coming full and departing emptied.

The token woman carries a bouquet of hothouse celery
and a stenographer's pad: she will take
the minutes, perk the coffee, smile
like a plastic daisy and put out
the black cat of her sensuous anger
to howl on the fence all night.

A fertility god serves a season
then is ritually dismembered.
Yet the name, the function live on:
so she finds the shopping lists
of exiled women in her coat pockets.

The token woman stands on the Square of the Immaculate
Exception blessing pigeons from a blue pedestal.
The token woman falls like a melon seed
on the cement: why has she no star shaped yellow flowers?
The token woman is placed like a scarecrow
in the longhaired corn: her muscles are wooden.
Why does she ride into battle on a clothes horse?
The token woman is a sandbag plugging
    the levee: shall the river
call her sister as the flood waters rage?
The token woman is a black Chicana fluent in Chinese
who has borne 1.2 babies

(not on the premises, no childcare provided),
owns a PhD, will teach freshmen English
for a decade and bleach your laundry
with tears, silent as a china egg.
Your department orders her from a taxidermist's catalog
and she comes luxuriously stuffed with goosedown
able to double as a sleeping
or punching bag.

Another woman can never join her,
help her, sister her, tickle her
but only replace her to become her
unless we make common cause
unless she grows out, one finger of a hand,
the entering wedge, the runner
from the bed of rampant peppermint
as it invades the next clipped turf
of the putting green.

Julia Dinsmore is an author and speaker on issues regarding poverty and justice. She grew up in Minneapolis, Minnesota, learning first-hand what it was to be poor. As an adult, she found herself once again living in poverty and, in a moment of "heart ache," crafted a poem which would make its way into numerous schools, community newsletters, and even the floor of the United States Senate.

My Name Is Not "Those People"

Julia Dinsmore

My name is not "Those People."
I am a loving woman, a mother in pain, giving birth to the future,
where my babies have the same chance to thrive as anyone.

My name is not "Inadequate."
I did not make my husband leave—he chose to,
and chooses not to pay child support.
Truth is thought, there isn't a job base for all
fathers to support their families.
While society turns its head, my children pay the price.

My name is not "Problem and Case to Be Managed."
I am a capable human being and citizen, not a client.
The social service system can never replace the compassion
and concern of loving Grandparents, Aunts, Uncles, Fathers,
Cousins, Community—all the bonded people who need to be
but are not present to bring children forward to their potential.

My name is not "Lazy, Dependent Welfare Mother."
If the unwaged work of parenting, homemaking and community building
was factored into the Gross National Product, my work would have
untold value. And I wonder why my middle-class sisters whose husbands
support them to raise their children are glorified—and they don't get
called lazy and dependent.

My name is not "Ignorant, Dumb or Uneducated."
I live with an income of $621 with $169 in food stamps.
Rent is $585. That leaves $36 a month to live on. I am such a genius at
surviving that I could balance the state budget in an hour.

Never mind that there is a lack of living-wage jobs.
Never mind that it is impossible to be the sole emotional, social and economic support to a family.
Never mind that parents are losing their children to the gangs, drugs, stealing, prostitution, social workers, kidnapping, the streets, the predator.
Forget about putting money into schools—just build more prisons.

My name is not "Lay Down and Die Quietly."
My love is powerful and my urge to keep my children alive will never stop. All children need homes and people who love them. They need safety and the chance to be the people they were born to be.

The wind will stop before I let my children become a statistic.
Before you give in to the urge to blame me,
the blames that lets us go blind and unknowing into
the isolation that disconnects us, take another look.
Don't go away.
For I am not the problem, but the solution.
And . . . My name is not "Those People."

*M*ary Oliver (1935–) is a poet, professor, and essayist who has written over *twenty-five books since 1963, most of them poetry collections, but she has also published a fair number of prose pieces, including a widely acclaimed hand-book for poets. Her work, prominent in contemporary American poetry, has been especially popular among those readers seeking to find solace in and connection with the natural world. Among her many awards, Oliver won the Pulitzer Prize for Poetry in 1984.*

The Journey

Mary Oliver

One day you finally knew
what you had to do, and began,
though the voices around you
kept shouting
their bad advice—
though the whole house
began to tremble
and you felt the old tug
at your ankles.
"Mend my life!"
each voice cried.
But you didn't stop.
You knew what you had to do,
though the wind pried
with its stiff fingers
at the very foundations,
though their melancholy
was terrible.
It was already late
enough, and a wild night,
and the road full of fallen
branches and stones.
But little by little,
as you left their voices behind,
the stars began to burn
through the sheets of clouds,
and there was a new voice
which you slowly

recognized as your own,
that kept you company
as you strode deeper and deeper
into the world,
determined to do
the only thing you could do—
determined to save
the only life you could save.

The Summer Day

Mary Oliver

Who made the world?
Who made the swan, and the black bear?
Who made the grasshopper?
This grasshopper, I mean—
the one who has flung herself out of the grass,
the one who is eating sugar out of my hand,
who is moving her jaws back and forth instead of up and down,
who is gazing around with her enormous and complicated eyes.
Now she lifts her pale forearms and thoroughly washes her face.
Now she snaps her wings open, and floats away.

I don't know exactly what a prayer is.
I do know how to pay attention, how to fall down
into the grass, how to kneel down in the grass,
how to be idle and blessed, how to stroll through the fields,
which is what I have been doing all day.
Tell me, what else should I have done?
Doesn't everything die at last, and too soon?
Tell me, what is it you plan to do
with your one wild and precious life?

Jane Flanders (1939 or 1940–2001) was the author of four poetry collections including her first volume, Leaving and Coming Back, *which was published in 1980 after years of working at home raising a family. Besides winning several awards for her work, Flanders also taught poetry at Sarah Lawrence College's Center for Continuing Education. After her death in 2001, her husband discovered a vast number of unpublished poems, many from the years preceding her first book, and these were made available posthumously in* Sudden Plenty.

The House That Fear Built: Warsaw, 1943

Jane Flanders

"The purpose of poetry is to remind us how difficult it is to remain just one person, for our house is open, there are no keys is the doors."

—Czeslaw Milosz

I am the boy with his hands raised over his head
in Warsaw.

I am the soldier whose rifle is trained
on the boy with his hands raised over his head
in Warsaw.

I am the woman with lowered gaze
who fears the soldier whose rifle is trained
on the boy with his hands raised over his head
in Warsaw.

I am the man in the overcoat
who loves the woman with lowered gaze
who fears the soldier whose rifle is trained
on the boy with his hands raised over his head
in Warsaw.

I am the stranger who photographs
the man in the overcoat
who loves the woman with lowered gaze
who fears the soldier whose rifle is trained
on the boy with his hands raised over his head
in Warsaw.

248

The crowd, of which I am each part, moves on
beneath my window, for I am the crone too
who shakes her sheets
over every street in the world
muttering
What's this? What's this?

*A*rthur Miller (1915–2005) was an important American playwright who wrote one of the most famous plays of the twentieth century, Death of a Salesman, for which he won a Pulitzer Prize in 1949. Born and raised in New York, Miller studied to become a journalist, though he began writing scripts for the radio when he emerged from college. After Death of a Salesman, which brought him international recognition, Miller went on to write numerous plays and scripts, including The Crucible, an allegory set during the time of the Salem witch trials.

from Death of a Salesman

Arthur Miller

Requiem

Charley. It's getting dark, Linda.

Linda doesn't react. She stares at the grave.

Biff. How about it, Mom? Better get some rest, heh? They'll be closing the gate soon.

Linda makes no move. Pause.

Happy (deeply angered). He had no right to do that. There was no necessity for it. We would've helped him.

Charley (grunting). Hmmm.

Biff. Come along, Mom.

Linda. Why didn't anyone come?

Charley. It was a very nice funeral.

Linda. But where are all the people he knew? Maybe they blame him.

Charley. Naa. It's a rough world, Linda. They wouldn't blame him.

Linda. I can't understand it. At this time especially. First time in thirty-five years we were just about free and clear. He only needed a little salary. He was even finished with the dentist.

Charley. No man only needs a little salary.

Linda. I can't understand it.

Biff. There were a lot of nice days. When he'd come home from a trip; or on Sundays, making the stoop; finishing the cellar; putting on the new porch; when he built the extra bathroom; and put up the garage. You know something, Charley, there's more of him in that front stoop than in all the sales he ever made.

Charley. Yeah. He was a happy man with a batch of cement.

Linda. He was so wonderful with his hands.

Biff. He had the wrong dreams. All, all, wrong.

Happy (almost ready to fight Biff). Don't say that!

Biff. He never knew who he was.

Charley (stopping Happy's movement and reply; to Biff). Nobody dast blame this man. You don't understand: Willy was a salesman. And for a salesman, there is no rock bottom to the life. He don't put a bolt to a nut, he don't tell you the law or give you medicine. He's a man way out there in the blue, riding on a smile and a shoeshine. And when they start not smiling back—that's an earthquake. And then you get yourself a couple of spots on your hat, and you're finished. Nobody dast blame this man. A salesman is got to dream, boy. It comes with the territory.

Biff. Charley, the man didn't know who he was.

Happy (infuriated). Don't say that!

Biff. Why don't you come with me, Happy'?

Happy. I'm not licked that easily. I'm staying right in this city, and I'm gonna beat this racket! *(He looks at Biff, his chin set.)* The Loman Brothers!

Biff. I know who I am, kid.

Happy. All right, boy. I'm gonna show you and everybody else that Willy Loman did not die in vain. He had a good dream. It's the only dream you can have—to come out number-one man. He fought it out here, and this is where I'm gonna win it for him.

Biff (with a hopeless glance at Happy, bends toward his mother). Let's go, Mom.

Linda. I'll be with you in a minute. Go on, Charley. *(He hesitates.)* I want to, just for a minute. I never had a chance to say good-by.

Charley moves away, followed by Happy. Biff remains a slight distance up and left of Linda. She sits there, summoning herself. The flute begins, not far away, playing behind her speech.

Linda. Forgive me, dear. I can't cry. I don't know what it is, but I can't cry. I don't understand it. Why did you ever do that? Help me, Willy, I can't cry. It seems to me that you're just on another trip. I keep expecting you. Willy, dear, I can't cry. Why did you do it? I search and search and I search, and I can't understand it, Willy. I made the last payment on the house today. Today, dear. And there'll be nobody home. *(A sob rises in her throat.)* We're free and clear. *(Sobbing more fully, released.)* We're free. *(Biff comes slowly toward her.)* We're free . . . We're free . . .

Biff lifts her to her feet and moves out up right with her in his arms. Linda sobs quietly. Bernard and Charley come together and follow them, followed by Happy. Only the music of the flute is left on the darkening stage as over the house the hard towers of the apartment buildings rise into sharp focus, and the curtain falls.

Section Four:
Short Fiction

Kate Chopin (1951–1904) was an American writer, born into a prosperous St. Louis family. She later married a French-Creole businessman, lived in New Orleans and had six children. After the death of her husband, Chopin returned to St. Louis and began to write fiction. Many of her writings are realistic tales of Creole and Cajun life, published in the 1890s.

The Story of an Hour

Kate Chopin

Knowing that Mrs. Mallard was afflicted with a heart trouble, great care was taken to break to her as gently as possible the news of her husband's death.

It was her sister Josephine who told her, in broken sentences, veiled hints that revealed in half concealing. Her husband's friend Richards was there, too, near her. It was he who had been in the newspaper office when intelligence of the railroad disaster was received, with Brently Mallard's name leading the list of "killed." He had only taken the time to assure himself of its truth by a second telegram, and had hastened to forestall any less careful, less tender friend in bearing the sad message.

She did not hear the story as many women have heard the same, with a paralyzed inability to accept its significance. She wept at once, with sudden, wild abandonment, in her sister's arms. When the storm of grief had spent itself she went away to her room alone. She would have no one follow her.

There stood, facing the open window, a comfortable, roomy arm-chair. Into this she sank, pressed down by a physical exhaustion that haunted her body and seemed to reach into her soul.

She could see in the open square before her house the tops of trees that were all aquiver with the new spring life. The delicious breath of rain was in the air. In the street below a peddler was crying his wares. The notes of a distant song which some one was singing reached her faintly, and countless sparrows were twittering in the eaves.

There were patches of blue sky showing here and there through the clouds that had met and piled above the other in the west facing her window.

She sat with her head thrown back upon the cushion of the chair quite motionless, except when a sob came up into her throat and shook her, as a child who has cried itself to sleep continues to sob in its dreams.

She was young, with a fair, calm face, whose lines bespoke repression and even a certain strength. But now there was a dull stare in her eyes, whose gaze was fixed away off yonder on one of those patches of blue sky. It was not a glance of reflection, but rather indicated a suspension of intelligent thought.

There was something coming to her and she was waiting for it, fearfully. What was it? She did not know; it was too subtle and elusive to name. But she felt it, creeping out of the sky, reaching toward her through the sounds, the scents, the color that filled the air.

Now her bosom rose and fell tumultuously. She was beginning to recognize this thing that was approaching to possess her, and she was striving to beat it back with her will—as powerless as her two white slender hands would have been.

When she abandoned herself a little whispered word escaped her slightly parted lips. She said it over and over under her breath; "Free, free, free!" The vacant stare and the look of terror that had followed it went from her eyes. They stayed keen and bright. Her pulses beat fast, and the coursing blood warmed and relaxed every inch of her body.

She did not stop to ask if it were not a monstrous joy that held her. A clear and exalted perception enabled her to dismiss the suggestion as trivial.

She knew that she would weep again when she saw the kind, tender hands folded in death; the face that had never looked save with love upon her, fixed and gray and dead. But she saw beyond that bitter moment a long procession of years to come that would belong to her absolutely. And she opened and spread her arms out to them in welcome.

There would be no one to live for her during those coming years; she would live for herself. There would be no powerful will bending her in that blind persistence with which men and women believe they have a right to impose a private will upon a fellow creature. A kind intention or a cruel intention made the act seem no less a crime as she looked upon it in that brief moment of illumination.

And yet she had loved him—sometimes. Often she had not. What did it matter! What could love, the unsolved mystery, count for in face of this possession of self-assertion which she suddenly recognized as the strongest impulse of her being.

"Free! Body and soul free!" she kept whispering.

Josephine was kneeling before the closed door with her lips to the keyhole, imploring for admission. "Louise, open the door! I beg; open the door—you will make yourself ill. What are you doing, Louise? For heaven's sake open the door."

"Go away. I am not making myself ill." No; she was drinking in a very elixir of life through that open window.

Her fancy was running riot along those days ahead of her. Spring days, and summer days, and all sorts of days that would be her own. She breathed a quick prayer that life might be long. It was only yesterday she had thought with a shudder that life might be long.

She arose at length and opened the door to her sister's importunities. There was a feverish triumph in her eyes, and she carried herself unwittingly like a goddess of Victory. She clasped her sister's waist, and together they descended the stairs. Richards stood waiting for them at the bottom.

Someone was opening the front door with a latchkey. It was Brently Mallard who entered, a little travel-stained, composedly carrying his gripsack and umbrella. He had been far from the scene of the accident, and did not even know there had been one. He stood amazed at Josephine's piercing cry; at Richards' quick motion to screen him from the view of his wife.

But Richards was too late.

When the doctors came they said she had died of heart disease—of joy that kills.

Charlotte Perkins Gilman (1860–1935) was a prolific writer and dedicated social reformer, who is best known for her short story, "The Yellow Wallpaper," which may have been based, in part, on her own experiences with post-partum depression. Gilman wrote poems, short stories, novels and thousands of nonfiction pieces. She wrote and edited her own magazine and lectured across the country on social issues of the time, including those related to women's lives.

The Yellow Wallpaper

Charlotte Perkins Gilman

It is very seldom that mere ordinary people like John and myself secure ancestral halls for the summer.

A colonial mansion, a hereditary estate, I would say a haunted house, and reach the height of romantic felicity—but that would be asking too much of fate!

Still I will proudly declare that there is something queer about it.

Else, why should it be let so cheaply? And why have stood so long untenanted?

John laughs at me, of course, but one expects that in marriage.

John is practical in the extreme. He has no patience with faith, an intense horror of superstitions, and he scoffs openly at any talk of things not to be felt and seen and put down in figures.

John is a physician, and *perhaps*—(I would not say it to a living soul, of course, but this is dead paper and a great relief to my mind)—*perhaps* that is one reason I do not get well faster.

You see he does not believe I am sick!

And what can one do?

If a physician of high standing, and one's own husband, assures friends and relatives that there is really nothing the matter with one but temporary nervous depression—a slight hysterical tendency—what is one to do?

My brother is also a physician, and also of high standing, and he says the same thing.

So I take phosphates or phosphites—whichever it is, and tonics, and journeys, and air, and exercise, and am absolutely forbidden to "work" until I am well again.

Personally, I disagree with their ideas.

Personally, I believe that congenial work, with excitement and change, would do me good.

But what is one to do?

I did write for a while in spite of them; but it *does* exhaust me a good deal—having to be so sly about it, or else meet with heavy opposition.

I sometimes fancy that in my condition if I had less opposition and more society and stimulus—but John says the very worst thing I can do is to think about my condition, and I confess it always makes me feel bad.

So I will let it alone and talk about the house.

The most beautiful place. It is quite alone, standing well back from the road, quite three miles from the village. It makes me think of English places that you read about, for there are hedges and walls and gates that lock, and lots of separate little houses for the gardeners and people.

There is a *delicious* garden! I never saw such a garden—large and shady, full of box-bordered paths, and lined with long grape-covered arbors with seats under them.

There were greenhouses, too, but they are all broken now.

There was some legal trouble, I believe, something about the heirs and co-heirs; anyhow, the place has been empty for years.

That spoils my ghostliness, I am afraid, but I don't care—there is something strange about the house—I can feel it.

I even said so to John one moonlight evening, but he said what I felt was a *draught*, and shut the window.

I get unreasonably angry with John sometimes. I'm sure I never used to be so sensitive. I think it is due to this nervous condition.

But John says if I feel so, I shall neglect proper self-control; so I take pains to control myself—before him, at least, and that makes me very tired.

I don't like our room a bit. I wanted one downstairs that opened on the piazza and had roses all over the window, and such pretty old-fashioned chintz hangings! But John would not hear of it.

He said there was only one window and not room for two beds, and no near room for him if he took another.

He is very careful and loving, and hardly lets me stir without special direction.

I have a schedule prescription for each hour in the day; he takes all care from me, and so I feel basely ungrateful not to value it more.

He said we came here solely on my account, that I was to have perfect rest and all the air I could get. "Your exercise depends on your strength, my dear," said he, "and your food somewhat on your appetite; but air you can absorb all the time." So we took the nursery at the top of the house.

It is a big, airy room, the whole floor nearly, with windows that look all ways, and air and sunshine galore. It was nursery first and then playroom and gymnasium, I should judge; for the windows are barred for little children, and there are rings and things in the walls.

The paint and paper look as if a boys' school had used it. It is stripped off—the paper—in great patches all around the head of my bed, about as far as I can reach, and in a great place on the other side of the room low down. I never saw a worse paper in my life.

One of those sprawling flamboyant patterns committing every artistic sin.

It is dull enough to confuse the eye in following, pronounced enough to constantly irritate and provoke study, and when you follow the lame uncertain curves for a little distance they suddenly commit suicide—plunge off at outrageous angles, destroy themselves in unheard of contradictions.

The color is repellent, almost revolting; a smoldering unclean yellow, strangely faded by the slow-turning sunlight.

It is a dull yet lurid orange in some places, a sickly sulphur tint in others.

No wonder the children hated it! I should hate it myself if I had to live in this room long.

There comes John, and I must put this away,—he hates to have me write a word.

We have been here two weeks, and I haven't felt like writing before, since that first day.

I am sitting by the window now, up in this atrocious nursery, and there is nothing to hinder my writing as much as I please, save lack of strength.

John is away all day, and even some nights when his cases are serious.

I am glad my case is not serious!

But these nervous troubles are dreadfully depressing.

John does not know how much I really suffer. He knows there is no *reason* to suffer, and that satisfies him.

Of course it is only nervousness. It does weigh on me so not to do my duty in any way!

I meant to be such a help to John, such a real rest and comfort, and here I am a comparative burden already!

Nobody would believe what an effort it is to do what little I am able—to dress and entertain, and order things.

It is fortunate Mary is so good with the baby. Such a dear baby!

And yet I *cannot* be with him, it makes me so nervous.

I suppose John never was nervous in his life. He laughs at me so about this wallpaper!

At first he meant to repaper the room, but afterwards he said that I was letting it get the better of me, and that nothing was worse for a nervous patient than to give way to such fancies.

He said that after the wallpaper was changed it would be the heavy bedstead, and then the barred windows, and then that gate at the head of the stairs, and so on.

"You know the place is doing you good," he said, "and really, dear, I don't care to renovate the house just for a three months' rental."

"Then do let us go downstairs," I said, "there are such pretty rooms there."

Then he took me in his arms and called me a blessed little goose, and said he would go down to the cellar, if I wished, and have it whitewashed into the bargain.

But he is right enough about the beds and windows and things.

It is an airy and comfortable room as any one need wish, and, of course, I would not be so silly as to make him uncomfortable just for a whim.

I'm really getting quite fond of the big room, all but that horrid paper.

Out of one window I can see the garden, those mysterious deepshaded arbors, the riotous old-fashioned flowers, and bushes and gnarly trees.

Out of another I get a lovely view of the bay and a little private wharf belonging to the estate. There is a beautiful shaded lane that runs down there from the house. I always fancy I see people walking in these numerous paths and arbors, but John has cautioned me not to give way to fancy in the least. He says that with my imaginative power and habit of story-making, a nervous weakness like mine is sure to lead to all manner of excited fancies, and that I ought to use my will and good sense to check the tendency. So I try.

I think sometimes that if I were only well enough to write a little it would relieve the press of ideas and rest me.

But I find I get tired when I try.

It is so discouraging not to have any advice and companionship about my work. When I get really well, John says we will ask Cousin Henry and Julia down for a long visit; but he says he would as soon put fireworks in my pillow-case as to let me have those stimulating people about now.

I wish I could get well faster.

But I must not think about that. This paper looks to me as if it *knew* what a vicious influence it had!

There is a recurrent spot where the pattern lolls like a broken neck and two bulbous eyes stare at you upside down.

I get positively angry with the impertinence of it and the everlastingness. Up and down and sideways they crawl, and those absurd, unblinking eyes are everywhere. There is one place where two breadths didn't match, and the eyes go all up and down the line, one a little higher than the other.

I never saw so much expression in an inanimate thing before, and we all know how much expression they have! I used to lie awake as a child and get more entertainment and terror out of blank walls and plain furniture than most children could find in a toy store.

I remember what a kindly wink the knobs of our big, old bureau used to have, and there was one chair that always seemed like a strong friend.

I used to feel that if any of the other things looked too fierce I could always hop into that chair and be safe.

The furniture in this room is no worse than inharmonious, however, for we had to bring it all from downstairs. I suppose when this was used as a playroom they had to take the nursery things out, and no wonder! I never saw such ravages as the children have made here.

The wallpaper, as I said before, is torn off in spots, and it sticketh closer than a brother—they must have had perseverance as well as hatred.

Then the floor is scratched and gouged and splintered, the plaster itself is dug out here and there, and this great heavy bed which is all we found in the room, looks as if it had been through the wars.

But I don't mind it a bit—only the paper.

There comes John's sister. Such a dear girl as she is, and so careful of me! I must not let her find me writing.

She is a perfect and enthusiastic housekeeper, and hopes for no better profession. I verily believe she thinks it is the writing which made me sick!

But I can write when she is out, and see her a long way off from these windows.

There is one that commands the road, a lovely shaded winding road, and one that just looks off over the country. A lovely country, too, full of great elms and velvet meadows.

This wallpaper has a kind of sub-pattern in a different shade, a particularly irritating one, for you can only see it in certain lights, and not clearly then.

But in the places where it isn't faded and where the sun is just so—I can see a strange, provoking, formless sort of figure, that seems to skulk about behind that silly and conspicuous front design.

There's sister on the stairs!

Well, the Fourth of July is over! The people are all gone and I am tired out. John thought it might do me good to see a little company, so we just had mother and Nellie and the children down for a week.

Of course I didn't do a thing. Jennie sees to everything now.

But it tired me all the same.

John says if I don't pick up faster he shall send me to Weir Mitchell in the fall.

But I don't want to go there at all. I had a friend who was in his hands once, and she says he is just like John and my brother, only more so!

Besides, it is such an undertaking to go so far.

I don't feel as if it was worth while to turn my hand over for anything, and I'm getting dreadfully fretful and querulous.

I cry at nothing, and cry most of the time.

Of course I don't when John is here, or anybody else, but when I am alone.

And I am alone a good deal just now. John is kept in town very often by serious cases, and Jennie is good and lets me alone when I want her to.

So I walk a little in the garden or down that lovely lane, sit on the porch under the roses, and lie down up here a good deal.

I'm getting really fond of the room in spite of the wallpaper. Perhaps *because* of the wallpaper.

It dwells in the mind so!

I lie here on this great immovable bed—it is nailed down, I believe—and follow that pattern about by the hour. It is good as gymnastics, I assure you. I start, we'll say, at the bottom, down in the corner over there where it has not been touched, and I determine for the thousandth time that I will follow that pointless pattern to some sort of conclusion.

I know a little of the principle of design, and I know this thing was not arranged on any laws of radiation, or alternation, or repetition, or symmetry, or anything else that I ever heard of.

It is repeated, of course, by the breadths, but not otherwise.

Looked at in one way each breadth stands alone, the bloated curves and flourishes—a kind of "debased Romanesque" with *delirium tremens*—go waddling up and down in isolated columns of fatuity.

But, on the other hand, they connect diagonally, and the sprawling outlines run off in great slanting waves of optic horror, like a lot of wallowing seaweeds in full chase.

The whole thing goes horizontally, too, at least it seems so, and I exhaust myself in trying to distinguish the order of its going in that direction.

They have used a horizontal breadth for a frieze, and that adds wonderfully to the confusion.

There is one end of the room where it is almost intact, and there, when the crosslights fade and the low sun shines directly upon it, I can almost fancy radiation after all—the interminable grotesques seem to form around a common centre and rush of headlong plunges of equal distraction.

It makes me tired to follow it. I will take a nap I guess.

I don't know why I should write this.

I don't want to.

I don't feel able.

And I know John would think it absurd. But I must say what I feel and think in some way—it is such a relief!

But the effort is getting to be greater than the relief.

Half the time now I am awfully lazy, and lie down ever so much.

John says I mustn't lose my strength, and has me take cod liver oil and lots of tonics and things, to say nothing of ale and wine and rare meat.

Dear John! He loves me very dearly, and hates to have me sick. I tried to have a real earnest reasonable talk with him the other day, and tell him how I wish he would let me go and make a visit to Cousin Henry and Julia.

But he said I wasn't able to go, nor able to stand it after I got there; and I did not make out a very good case for myself, for I was crying before I had finished.

It is getting to be a great effort for me to think straight. Just this nervous weakness I suppose.

And dear John gathered me up in his arms, and just carried me upstairs and laid me on the bed, and sat by me and read to me till it tired my head.

He said I was his darling and his comfort and all he had, and that I must take care of myself for his sake, and keep well.

He says no one but myself can help me out of it, that I must use my will and self-control and not let any silly fancies run away with me.

There's one comfort, the baby is well and happy, and does not have to occupy this nursery with the horrid wallpaper.

If we had not used it, that blessed child would have! What a fortunate escape. Why, I wouldn't have a child of mine, an impressionable little thing, live in such a room for worlds.

I never thought of it before, but it is lucky that John kept me here after all, I can stand it so much easier than a baby, you see.

Of course I never mention it to them any more—I am too wise—but I keep watch of it all the same.

There are things in that paper that nobody knows but me, or ever will.

Behind that outside pattern the dim shapes get clearer every day.

It is always the same shape, only very numerous.

And it is like a woman stooping down and creeping about behind that pattern. I don't like it a bit. I wonder—I begin to think—I wish John would take me away from here!

It is so hard to talk with John about my case, because he is so wise, and because he loves me so.

But I tried it last night.

It was moonlight. The moon shines in all around just as the sun does.

I hate to see it sometimes, it creeps so slowly, and always comes in by one window or another.

John was asleep and I hated to waken him, so I kept still and watched the moonlight on that undulating wallpaper till I felt creepy.

The faint figure behind seemed to shake the pattern, just as if she wanted to get out.

I got up softly and went to feel and see if the paper *did* move, and when I came back John was awake.

"What is it, little girl?" he said. "Don't go walking about like that—you'll get cold."

I thought it was a good time to talk, so I told him that I really was not gaining here, and that I wished he would take me away.

"Why darling!" said he, "our lease will be up in three weeks, and I can't see how to leave before."

"The repairs are not done at home, and I cannot possibly leave town just now. Of course if you were in any danger, I could and would, but you really are better, dear, whether you can see it or not. I am a doctor, dear, and I know. You are gaining flesh and color, your appetite is better, I feel really much easier about you."

"I don't weigh a bit more," said I, "nor as much; and my appetite may be better in the evening when you are here, but it is worse in the morning when you are away!"

"Bless her little heart!" said he with a big hug, "she shall be as sick as she pleases! But now let's improve the shining hours by going to sleep, and talk about it in the morning!"

"And you won't go away?" I asked gloomily.

"Why, how can I dear? It is only three weeks more and then we will take a nice little trip of a few days while Jennie is getting the house ready. Really dear you are better!"

"Better in body perhaps—" I began, and stopped short, for he sat up straight and looked at me with such a stern, reproachful look that I could not say another word.

"My darling," said he, "I beg of you, for my sake and for our child's sake, as well as for your own, that you will never for one instant let that idea enter your mind! There is nothing so dangerous, so fascinating, to a temperament like yours. It is a false and foolish fancy. Can you not trust me as a physician when I tell you so?"

So of course I said no more on that score, and we went to sleep before long. He thought I was asleep first, but I wasn't, and lay there for hours trying to decide whether that front pattern and the back pattern really did move together or separately.

On a pattern like this, by daylight, there is a lack of sequence, a defiance of law, that is a constant irritant to a normal mind.

The color is hideous enough, and unreliable enough, and infuriating enough, but the pattern is torturing.

You think you have mastered it, but just as you get well underway in following, it turns a back-somersault and there you are. It slaps you in the face, knocks you down, and tramples upon you. It is like a bad dream.

The outside pattern is a florid arabesque, reminding one of a fungus. If you can imagine a toadstool in joints, an interminable string of toadstools, budding and sprouting in endless convolutions—why, that is something like it.

That is, sometimes!

There is one marked peculiarity about this paper, a thing nobody seems to notice but myself, and that is that it changes as the light changes.

When the sun shoots in through the east window—I always watch for that first long, straight ray—it changes so quickly that I never can quite believe it.

That is why I watch it always.

By moonlight—the moon shines in all night when there is a moon—I wouldn't know it was the same paper.

At night in any kind of light, in twilight, candle light, lamplight, and worst of all by moonlight, it becomes bars! The outside pattern I mean, and the woman behind it is as plain as can be.

I didn't realize for a long time what the thing was that showed behind, that dim sub-pattern, but I am quite sure it is a woman.

By daylight she is subdued, quiet. I fancy it is the pattern that keeps her so still. It is so puzzling. It keeps me quiet by the hour.

I lie down ever so much now. John says it is good for me, and to sleep all I can.

Indeed he started the habit by making me lie down for an hour after each meal.

It is a very bad habit I am convinced, for you see I don't sleep.

And that cultivates deceit, for I don't tell them I'm awake—O no!

The fact is I am getting a little afraid of John.

He seems very queer sometimes, and even Jennie has an inexplicable look.

It strikes me occasionally, just as a scientific hypothesis—that perhaps it is the paper!

I have watched John when he did not know I was looking, and come into the room suddenly on the most innocent excuses, and I've caught him several times *looking at the paper!* And Jennie too. I caught Jennie with her hand on it once.

She didn't know I was in the room, and when I asked her in a quiet, a very quiet voice, with the most restrained manner possible, what she was doing with the paper—she turned around as if she had been caught stealing, and looked quite angry—asked me why I should frighten her so!

Then she said that the paper stained everything it touched, that she had found yellow smooches on all my clothes and John's, and she wished we would be more careful!

Did not that sound innocent? But I know she was studying that pattern, and I am determined that nobody shall find it out but myself!

Life is very much more exciting now than it used to be. You see I have something more to expect, to look forward to, to watch. I really do eat better, and am more quiet than I was.

John is so pleased to see me improve! He laughed a little the other day, and said I seemed to be flourishing in spite of my wallpaper.

I turned it off with a laugh. I had no intention of telling him it was *because* of the wallpaper—he would make fun of me. He might even want to take me away.

I don't want to leave now until I have found it out. There is a week more, and I think that will be enough.

I'm feeling ever so much better! I don't sleep much at night, for it is so interesting to watch development; but I sleep a good deal in the daytime.

In the daytime it is tiresome and perplexing.

There are always new shoots on the fungus, and new shades of yellow all over it. I cannot keep count of them, though I have tried conscientiously.

It is the strangest yellow, that wallpaper! It makes me think of all the yellow things I ever saw—not beautiful ones like buttercups, but old foul, bad yellow things.

But there is something else about that paper—the smell! I noticed it the moment we came into the room, but with so much air and sun it was not bad. No we have had a week of fog and rain, and whether the windows are open or not, the smell is here.

It creeps all over the house.

I find it hovering in the dining room, skulking in the parlor, hiding in the hall, lying in wait for me on the stairs.

It gets into my hair.

Even when I go to ride, if I turn my head suddenly and surprise it—there is that smell!

Such a peculiar odor, too! I have spent hours in trying to analyze it, to find what it smelled like.

It is not bad—at first, and very gentle, but quite the subtlest, most enduring odor I ever met.

In this damp weather it is awful, I wake up in the night and find it hanging over me.

It used to disturb me at first. I thought seriously of burning the house—to reach the smell.

But now I am used to it. The only thing I can think of that it is like the color of the paper! A yellow smell.

There is a very funny mark on this wall, low down, near the mop-board. A streak that runs round the room. It goes behind every piece of furniture, except the bed, a long, straight, even *smooch*, as if it had been rubbed over and over.

I wonder how it was done and who did it, and what they did it for. Round and round and round—round and round and round—it makes me dizzy!

I really have discovered something at last.

Through watching so much at night, when it changes so, I have finally found out.

The front pattern *does* move—and no wonder! The woman behind shakes it!

Sometimes I think there are a great many women behind, and sometimes only one, and she crawls around fast, and her crawling shakes it all over.

Then in the very bright spots she keeps still, and in the very shady spots she just takes hold of the bars and shakes them hard.

And she is all the time trying to climb through. But nobody could climb through that pattern—it strangles so; I think that is why it has so many heads.

They get through, and then the pattern strangles them off and turns them upside down, and makes their eyes white!

If those heads were covered or taken off it would not be half so bad.

I think that woman gets out in the daytime!

And I'll tell you why—privately—I've seen her!

I can see her out of every one of my windows!

It is the same woman, I know, for she is always creeping, and most women do not creep by daylight.

I see her on that long road under the trees, creeping along, and when a carriage comes she hides under the blackberry vines.

I don't blame her a bit. It must be very humiliating to be caught creeping by daylight!

I always lock the door when I creep by daylight. I can't do it at night, for I know John would suspect something at once.

And John is so queer now, that I don't want to irritate him. I wish he would take another room! Besides, I don't want anybody to get that woman out at night but myself.

I often wonder if I could see her out of all the windows at once.

But, turn as fast as I can, I can only see out of one at one time.

And though I always see her, she may be able to creep faster than I can turn!

I have watched her sometimes away off in the open country, creeping as fast as a cloud shadow in a high wind.

If only the top pattern could be gotten off from the under one! I mean to try it, little by little.

I have found out another funny thing, but I shan't tell it this time! It does not do to trust people too much.

There are only two more days to get this paper off, and I believe John is beginning to notice. I don't like the look in his eyes.

And I heard him ask Jennie a lot of professional questions about me. She had a very good report to give.

She said I slept a good deal in the daytime.

John knows I don't sleep very well at night, for all I'm so quiet!

He asked me all sorts of questions, too, and pretended to be very loving and kind.

As if I couldn't see through him!

Still, I don't wonder he acts so, sleeping under this paper for three months.

It only interests me, but I feel sure John and Jennie are secretly affected by it.

Hurrah! This is the last day, but it is enough. John is to stay in town over night, and won't be out until this evening.

Jennie wanted to sleep with me—the sly thing! but I told her I should undoubtedly rest better for a night all alone.

That was clever, for really I wasn't alone a bit! As soon as it was moonlight and that poor thing began to crawl and shake the pattern, I got up and ran to help her.

I pulled and she shook, I shook and she pulled, and before morning we had peeled off yards of that paper.

A strip about as high as my head and half around the room.

And then when the sun came and that awful pattern began to laugh at me, I declared I would finish it today!

We go away tomorrow, and they are moving all my furniture down again to leave things as they were before.

Jennie looked at the wall in amazement, but I told her merrily that I did it out of pure spite at the vicious thing.

She laughed and said she wouldn't mind doing it herself, but I must not get tired.

How she betrayed herself that time!

But I am here, and no person touches this paper but me—not *alive!*

She tried to get me out of the room—it was too patent! But I said it was so quiet and empty and clean now that I believe I would lie down again and sleep all I could; and not to wake me even for dinner—I would call when I woke.

So now she is gone, and the servants are gone, and the things are gone, and there is nothing left but that great bedstead nailed down, with the canvas mattress we found on it.

We shall sleep downstairs tonight, and take the boat home tomorrow.

I quite enjoy the room, now it is bare again.

How those children did tear about here!

This bedstead is fairly gnawed!

But I must get to work.

I have locked the door and thrown the key down into the front path.

I don't want to go out, and I don't want to have anybody come in, till John comes.

I want to astonish him.

I've got a rope up here that even Jennie did not find. If that woman does get out, and tries to get away, I can tie her!

But I forgot I could not reach far without anything to stand on!

This bed will *not* move!

I tried to lift and push it until I was lame, and then I got so angry I bit off a little piece at one corner—but it hurt my teeth.

Then I peeled off all the paper I could reach standing on the floor. It sticks horribly and the pattern just enjoys it! All those strangled heads and bulbous eyes and waddling fungus growths just shriek with derision!

I am getting angry enough to do something desperate. To jump out of the window would be admirable exercise, but the bars are too strong even to try.

Besides I wouldn't do it. Of course not, I know well enough that a step like that is improper and might be misconstrued.

I don't like to look out of the windows even—there are so many of those creeping women, and they creep so fast.

I wonder if they all come out of that wallpaper as I did?

But I am securely fastened now by my well-hidden rope—you don't get *me* out in the road there!

I suppose I shall have to get back behind the pattern when it comes night, and that is hard!

It is so pleasant to be out in this great room and creep around as I please!

I don't want to go outside. I won't, even if Jennie asks me to.

For outside you have to creep on the ground, and everything is green instead of yellow.

But here I can creep smoothly on the floor, and my shoulder just fits in that long smooch around the wall, so I cannot lose my way.

Why there's John at the door!

It is no use, young man, you can't open it!

How he does call and pound!

Now he's crying for an axe.

It would be a shame to break down that beautiful door!

"John dear!" said I in the gentlest voice, "the key is down by the front steps, under a plantain leaf!"

That silenced him for a few moments.

Then he said—very quietly indeed, "Open the door, my darling!"

"I can't," said I. "The key is down by the front door under a plantain leaf!"

And then I said it again, several times, very gently and slowly, and said it so often that he had to go and see, and he got it of course, and came in. He stopped short by the door.

"What is the matter?" he cried. "For God's sake, what are you doing!"

I kept on creeping just the same, but I looked at him over my shoulder.

"I've got out at last," said I, "in spite of you and Jane. And I've pulled off most of the paper, so you can't put me back!"

Now why should that man have fainted? But he did, and right across my path by the wall, so that I had to creep over him every time!

Shirley Jackson (1919–1965) was an American writer who often wrote tales involving psychological disturbance or the supernatural. Jackson didn't receive national attention until 1948, when the New Yorker *published "The Lottery." In 1962, Jackson had a nervous breakdown. She later resumed writing, but died before her novel,* Come Along with Me, *was published. Stanley Edgar Hyman, her huband, wrote after her death: "If she uses the resources of supernatural terror, it was to provide metaphors for the all-too-real terrors of the natural."*

The Lottery

Shirley Jackson

The morning of June 27 was clear and sunny, with the fresh warmth of a full-summer day; the flowers were blossoming profusely and the grass was richly green.

The people of the village began to gather in the square, between the post office and the bank, around ten o'clock; in some towns there were so many people that the lottery took two days and had to be started on June 26th, but in this village, where there were only about three hundred people, the whole lottery took less than two hours, so it could begin at ten o'clock in the morning and still be through in time to allow the villagers to get home for noon dinner.

The children assembled first, of course. School was recently over for the summer, and the feeling of liberty sat uneasily on most of them; they tended to gather together quietly for a while before they broke into boisterous play, and their talk was still of the classroom and the teacher, of books and reprimands. Bobby Martin had already stuffed his pockets full of stones, and the other boys soon followed his example, selecting the smoothest and roundest stones; Bobby and Harry Jones and Dickie Delacroix—the villagers pronounced this name "Dellacroy"—eventually made a great pile of stones in one corner of the square and guarded it against the raids of the other boys. The girls stood aside, talking among themselves, looking over their shoulders at the boys, and the very small children rolled in the dust or clung to the hands of their older brothers or sisters.

Soon the men began to gather, surveying their own children, speaking of planting and rain, tractors and taxes. They stood together, away from the pile of stones in the corner, and their jokes were quiet and they smiled rather than laughed. The women, wearing faded house dresses and sweaters, came shortly after their menfolk. They greeted one another and exchanged bits of gossip as they went to join their husbands. Soon the women, standing by their husbands, began to call their children, and the children came reluctantly, having to be called four or five times. Bobby Martin ducked under his mother's grasping hand and ran, laughing, back to the pile of stones. His father spoke up sharply, and Bobby came quickly and took his place between his father and his oldest brother.

The lottery was conducted—as were the square dances, the teenage club, the Halloween program—by Mr. Summers, who had time and energy to devote to civic activities. He was a round-faced, jovial man and he ran the coal business, and people were sorry for him, because he had no children and his wife was a scold. When he arrived in the square, carrying the black wooden box, there was a murmur of conversation among the villagers and he waved and called, "Little late today, folks." The postmaster, Mr. Graves, followed him, carrying a three-legged stool, and the stool was put in the center of the square and Mr. Summers set the black box down on it. The villagers kept their distance, leaving a space between themselves and the stool, and when Mr. Summers said, "Some of you fellows want to give me a hand?" there was a hesitation before two men, Mr. Martin and his oldest son, Baxter, came forward to hold the box steady on the stool while Mr. Summers stirred up the papers inside it.

The original paraphernalia for the lottery had been lost long ago, and the black box now resting on the stool had been put into use even before Old Man Warner, the oldest man in town, was born. Mr. Summers spoke frequently to the villagers about making a new box, but no one liked to upset even as much tradition as was represented by the black box. There was a story that the present box had been made with some pieces of the box that had preceded it, the one that had been constructed when the first people settled down to make a village here. Every year, after the lottery, Mr. Summers began talking again about a new box, but every year the subject was allowed to fade off without anything's being done. The black box grew shabbier each year; by now it was no longer completely black but splintered badly along one side to show the original wood color, and in some places faded or stained.

Mr. Martin and his oldest son, Baxter, held the black box securely on the stool until Mr. Summers had stirred the papers thoroughly with his hand. Because so much of the ritual had been forgotten or discarded, Mr. Summers had been successful in having slips of paper substituted for the chips of wood that had been used for generations. Chips of wood, Mr. Summers had argued, had been all very well when the village was tiny, but now that the population was more than three hundred and likely to keep on growing, it was necessary to use something that would fit more easily into the black box. The night before the lottery, Mr. Summers and Mr. Graves made up the slips of paper and put them in the box, and it was then taken to the safe of Mr. Summers's coal company and locked up until Mr. Summers was ready to take it to the square next morning. The rest of the year, the box was put away, sometimes one place, sometimes another; it had spent one year in Mr. Grave's barn and another year underfoot in the post office, and sometimes it was set on a shelf in the Martin grocery and left there.

There was a great deal of fussing to be done before Mr. Summers declared the lottery open. There were lists to make up—of heads of families, heads of households in each family, members of each household in each family. There was the proper swearing-in of Mr. Summers by the postmaster, as the official of the lottery; at one time, some people remembered, there had been a recital of some sort, performed by the official of the lottery, a perfunctory, tuneless chant that had been rattled off duly each year; some people believed that the official of the lottery used to stand just so when he said or sang it, others believed that he was supposed to walk among the people, but years and years ago this part of the ritual had been allowed to lapse. There had been, also, a ritual salute, which the official of the lottery had had to use in addressing each person who came up to draw from the box, but this also had changed with time, until now it was felt necessary only for the official to speak to each person approaching. Mr. Summers was very good at all this; in his clean white shirt and blue jeans, with one hand resting carelessly on the black box, he seemed very proper and important as he talked interminably to Mr. Graves and the Martins.

Just as Mr. Summers finally left off talking and turned to the assembled villagers, Mrs. Hutchinson came hurriedly along the path to the square, her sweater thrown over her shoulders, and slid into place in the back of the crowd. "Clean forgot what day it was," she said to Mrs. Delacroix, who stood next to her, and they both laughed softly. "Thought my old man was out back stacking wood," Mrs. Hutchinson went on, "and then I looked out the window and the kids were gone, and then I remembered it was the twenty-seventh and came a-running." She dried her hands on her apron, and Mrs. Delacroix said, "You're in time, though. They're still talking away up there."

Mrs. Hutchinson craned her neck to see through the crowd and found her husband and children standing near the front. She tapped Mrs. Delacroix on the arm as a farewell and began to make her way through the crowd. The people separated good humoredly to let her through; two or three people said, in voices just loud enough to be heard across the crowd, "Here comes your Missus, Hutchinson," and "Bill, she made it after all." Mrs. Hutchinson said, grinning, "Wouldn't have me leave m'dishes in the sink, now would you, Joe?" and soft laughter ran through the crowd as the people stirred back into position after Mrs. Hutchinson's arrival.

"Well, now," Mr. Summers said soberly, "guess we better get started, get this over with, so's we can go back to work. Anybody ain't here?"

"Dunbar," several people said. "Dunbar, Dunbar."

Mr. Summers consulted his list. "Clyde Dunbar," he said. "That's right. He's broke his leg, hasn't he? Who's drawing for him?"

"Me, I guess," a woman said, and Mr. Summers turned to look at her. "Wife draws for her husband," Mr. Summers said. "Don't you have a grown boy to do it for you, Janey?" Although Mr. Summers and everyone else in the village knew the answer perfectly well, it was the business of the official of the lottery to ask such questions formally. Mr. Summers waited with an expression of polite interest while Mrs. Dunbar answered.

"Horace's not but sixteen yet," Mrs. Dunbar said regretfully. "Guess I gotta fill in for the old man this year."

"Right," Mr. Summers said. He made a note on the list he was holding. Then he asked, "Watson boy drawing this year?"

A tall boy in the crowd raised his hand. "Here," he said. "I'm drawing for m'mother and me." He blinked his eyes nervously and ducked his head as several voices in the crowd said things like "Good fellow, Jack," and "Glad to see your mother's got a man to do it."

"Well," Mr. Summers said, "guess that's everyone. Old Man Warner make it?"

"Here," a voice said, and Mr. Summers nodded.

A sudden hush fell on the crowd as Mr. Summers cleared his throat and looked at the list. "All ready?" he called. "Now, I'll read the names—heads of families first—and the men come up and take a paper out of the box. Keep the paper folded in your hand without looking at it until everyone has a turn. Everything clear?

The people had done it so many times that they only half listened to the directions; most of them were quiet, wetting their lips, not looking around. Then Mr. Summers raised one hand high and said, "Adams." A man disengaged himself from the crowd and came forward. "Hi, Steve," Mr. Summers said, and Mr. Adams said, "Hi, Joe." They grinned at one another humorlessly and nervously. Then Mr. Adams reached into the black box and took out a folded paper. He held it firmly by one corner as he turned and went hastily back to his place in the crowd, where he stood a little apart from his family, not looking down at his hand.

"Allen," Mr. Summers said. "Anderson. . . . Bentham."

"Seems like there's no time at all between lotteries any more," Mrs. Delacroix said to Mrs. Graves in the back row. "Seems like we got through with the last one only last week."

"Time sure goes fast," Mrs. Graves said.

"Clark. . . . Delacroix."

"There goes my old man," Mrs. Delacroix said. She held her breath while her husband went forward.

"Dunbar," Mr. Summers said, and Mrs. Dunbar went steadily to the box while one of the women said, "Go on, Janey," and another said, "There she goes."

"We're next," Mrs. Graves said. She watched while Mr. Graves came around from the side of the box, greeted Mr. Summers gravely, and selected a slip of paper from the box. By now, all through the crowd there were men holding the small folded papers in their large hands, turning them over and over nervously. Mrs. Dunbar and her two sons stood together, Mrs. Dunbar holding the slip of paper.

"Harburt. . . . Hutchinson."

"Get up there, Bill," Mrs. Hutchinson said, and the people near her laughed.

"Jones."

"They do say," Mr. Adams said to Old Man Warner, who stood next to him, "that over in the north village they're talking of giving up the lottery."

Old Man Warner snorted. "Pack of crazy fools," he said. "Listening to the young folks, nothing's good enough for *them*. Next thing you know, they'll be wanting to go back to living in caves, nobody work any more, live *that* way for a while. Used to be a saying about 'Lottery in June, corn be heavy soon.' First thing you know, we'd all be eating stewed chickweed and acorns. There's *always* been a lottery," he added petulantly. "Bad enough to see young Joe Summers up there joking with everybody."

"Some places have already quit lotteries," Mrs. Adams said.

"Nothing but trouble in *that*," Old Man Warner said stoutly. "Pack of young fools."

"Martin." And Bobby Martin watched his father go forward. "Overdyke. . . . Percy."

"I wish they'd hurry," Mrs. Dunbar said to her older son. "I wish they'd hurry."

"They're almost through," her son said.

"You get ready to run tell Dad," Mrs. Dunbar said.

Mr. Summers called his own name and then stepped forward precisely and selected a slip from the box. Then he called, "Warner."

"Seventy-seventh year I been in the lottery," Old Man Warner said as he went through the crowd. "Seventy-seventh time."

"Watson." The tall boy came awkwardly through the crowd. Someone said, "Don't be nervous, Jack," and Mr. Summers said, "Take your time, son."

"Zanini."

After that, there was a long pause, a breathless pause, until Mr. Summers, holding his slip of paper in the air, said, "All right, fellows." For a minute, no one moved, and then all the slips of paper were opened. Suddenly, all the women began to speak at once, saying, "Who is it?" "Who's got it?" "Is it the Dunbars?" "Is it the Watsons?" Then the voices began to say, "It's Hutchinson. It's Bill." "Bill Hutchinson's got it."

"Go tell your father," Mrs. Dunbar said to her older son.

People began to look around to see the Hutchinsons. Bill Hutchinson was standing quiet, staring down at the paper in his hand. Suddenly, Tessie Hutchinson shouted to Mr. Summers, "You didn't give him time enough to take any paper he wanted! I saw you. It wasn't fair!"

"Be a good sport, Tessie," Mrs. Delacroix called, and Mrs. Graves said, "All of us took the same chance."

"Shut up, Tessie," Bill Hutchinson said.

"Well, everyone," Mr. Summers said, "that was done pretty fast, and now we've got to be hurrying a little more to get done in time." He consulted his next list. "Bill," he said, "you draw for the Hutchinson family. You got any other households in the Hutchinsons?"

"There's Don and Eva," Mrs. Hutchinson yelled. "Make *them* take their chance!"

"Daughters draw with their husbands' families, Tessie," Mr. Summers said gently. "You know that as well as anyone else."

"It wasn't fair," Tessie said.

"I guess not, Joe," Bill Hutchinson said regretfully. "My daughter draws with her husband's family, that's only fair. And I've got no other family except the kids."

"Then, as far as drawing for families is concerned, it's you," Mr. Summers said in explanation, "and as far as drawing for households is concerned, that's you, too. Right?"

"Right," Bill Hutchinson said.

"How many kids, Bill?" Mr. Summers asked formally.

"Three," Bill Hutchinson said. "There's Bill, Jr., and Nancy, and little Dave. And Tessie and me."

"All right, then," Mr. Summers said. "Harry, you got their tickets back?"

Mr. Graves nodded and held up the slips of paper. "Put them in the box then," Mr. Summers directed. "Take Bill's and put it in."

"I think we ought to start over," Mrs. Hutchinson said, as quietly as she could. "I tell you it wasn't *fair*. You didn't give him time enough to choose. *Every*body saw that."

Mr. Graves had selected the five slips and put them in the box, and he dropped all the papers but those onto the ground, where the breeze caught them and lifted them off.

"Listen, everybody," Mrs. Hutchinson was saying to the people around her.

"Ready, Bill?" Mr. Summers asked, and Bill Hutchinson, with one quick glance around at his wife and children, nodded.

"Remember," Mr. Summers said, "take the slips and keep them folded until each person has taken one. Harry, you help little Dave." Mr. Graves took the hand of the little boy, who came willingly with him up to the box. "Take a paper out of the box, Davy," Mr. Summers. Davy put his hand into the box and laughed.

"Take just *one* paper," Mr. Summers said. "Harry, you hold it for him." Mr. Graves took the child's hand and removed the folded paper from the tight fist and held it while little Dave stood next to him and looked up at him wonderingly.

"Nancy next," Mr. Summers said. Nancy was twelve, and her school friends breathed heavily as she went forward, switching her skirt, and took a slip daintily from the box. "Bill, Jr." Mr. Summers, and Billy, his face red and his feet over-large, nearly knocked the box over as he got a paper out. "Tessie," Mr. Summers said. She hesitated for a minute, looking around defiantly, and then set her lips and went up to the box. She snatched a paper out and held it behind her.

"Bill," Mr. Summers said, and Bill Hutchinson reached into the box and felt around, bringing his hand out at last with the slip of paper in it.

The crowd was quiet. A girl whispered, "I hope it's not Nancy," and the sound of the whisper reached the edges of the crowd.

"It's not the way it used to be," Old Man Warner said clearly. "People ain't the way they used to be."

"All right," Mr. Summers said. "Open the papers. Harry, you open little Dave's."

Mr. Graves opened the slip of paper and there was a general sigh through the crowd as he held it up and everyone could see that it was blank. Nancy and Bill, Jr., opened theirs at the same time, and both beamed and laughed, turning around to the crowd and holding their slips of paper above their heads.

"Tessie," Mr. Summers said. There was a pause, and then Mr. Summers looked at Bill Hutchinson, and Bill unfolded his paper and showed it. It was blank.

"It's Tessie," Mr. Summers said, and his voice was hushed. "Show us her paper, Bill."

Bill Hutchinson went over to his wife and forced the slip of paper out of her hand. It had a black spot on it, the black spot Mr. Summers had made the night before with the heavy pencil in the coal-company office. Bill Hutchinson held it up, and there was a stir in the crowd.

"All right, folks," Mr. Summers said, "let's finish quickly."

Although the villagers had forgotten the ritual and lost the original black box, they still remembered to use stones. The pile of stones the boys had made earlier was ready; there were stones on the ground with the blowing scraps of paper that had come out of the box. Mrs. Delacroix selected a stone so large she had to pick it up with both hands and turned to Mrs. Dunbar. "Come on," she said. "Hurry up."

Mrs. Dunbar had small stones in both hands, and she said, gasping for breath, "I can't run at all. You'll have to go ahead and I'll catch up with you."

The children had stones already, and someone gave little Davy Hutchinson a few pebbles.

Tessie Hutchinson was in the center of a cleared space by now and she held her hands out desperately as the villagers moved in on her. "It isn't fair," she said. A stone hit her on the side of the head.

Old Man Warner was saying, "Come on, come on, everyone." Steve Adams was in the front of the crowd of villagers, with Mrs. Graves beside him.

"It isn't fair, it isn't right," Mrs. Hutchinson screamed, and then they were upon her.

A lbert Maltz (1908–1985) was a dramatist, novelist, and scenarist, born in Brooklyn. After graduation from Columbia and study at the Yale Drama School, he began writing plays. His works focus on political strife—the struggles of the common working man. In 1938 he won the O. Henry Award for "The Happiest Man on Earth," a short story published in Harper's Magazine.

The Happiest Man on Earth

Albert Maltz

Jesse felt ready to weep. He had been sitting in the shanty waiting for Tom to appear, grateful for the chance to rest his injured foot, quietly, joyously anticipating the moment when Tom would say, "Why of course, Jesse, you can start whenever you're ready!"

For two weeks he had been pushing himself, from Kansas City, Missouri, to Tulsa, Oklahoma, through nights of rain and a week of scorching sun, without sleep or a decent meal, sustained by the vision of that one moment. And then Tom had come into the office. He had come in quickly, holding a sheaf of papers in his hand; he had glanced at Jesse only casually, it was true—but long enough. He had not known him. He had turned away. . . . And Tom Brackett was his brother-in-law.

Was it his clothes? Jesse knew he looked terrible. He had tried to spruce up at a drinking fountain in the park, but even that had gone badly; in his excitement he had cut himself shaving, an ugly gash down the side of his cheek. And nothing could get the red gumbo dust out of his suit even though he'd slapped himself till both arms were worn out. . . . Or was it just that he *had* changed so much?

True, they hadn't seen each other for five years; but Tom looked five years older, that was all. He was still Tom. God! was *he* so different?

Brackett finished his telephone call. He leaned back in his swivel chair and glanced over at Jesse with small, clear blue eyes that were suspicious and unfriendly. He was a heavy, paunchy man of forty-five, auburn-haired, rather dour looking; his face was meaty, his features pronounced and forceful, his nose somewhat bulbous and reddish-hued at the tip. He looked like a solid, decent, capable business man who was commander of his local branch of the American Legion—which he was. He surveyed Jesse with cold indifference, manifestly unwilling to spend

283

time on him. Even the way he chewed his toothpick seemed contemptuous to Jesse.

"Yes?" Brackett said suddenly. "What do you want?"

His voice was decent enough, Jesse admitted. He had expected it to be worse. He moved up to the wooden counter that partitioned the shanty. He thrust a hand nervously through his tangled hair.

"I guess you don't recognize me, Tom," he said falteringly, "I'm Jesse Fulton."

"Huh?" Brackett said. That was all.

"Yes, I am, and Ella sends her love."

Brackett rose and walked over to the counter until they were face to face. He surveyed Fulton incredulously, trying to measure the resemblance to his brother-in-law as he remembered him. This man was tall, about thirty. That fitted! He had straight good features and a lank erect body. That was right too. But the face was too gaunt, the body too spiny under the baggy clothes for him to be sure. His brother-in-law had been a solid, strong young man with muscle and beef to him. It was like looking at a faded, badly taken photograph and trying to recognize the subject: the resemblance was there but the difference was tremendous. He searched the eyes. They at least seemed definitely familiar, gray, with a curiously shy but decent look in them. He had liked that about Fulton.

Jesse stood quiet. Inside he was seething. Brackett was like a man examining a piece of broken-down horse flesh; there was a look of pure pity in his eyes. It made Jesse furious. He knew he wasn't as far gone as all that.

"Yes, I believe you are," Brackett said finally, "but you sure have changed."

"By God, it's five years, ain't it?" Jesse said resentfully. "You only saw me a couple of times anyway." Then, to himself, with his lips locked together, in mingled vehemence and shame, What if I have changed? Don't everybody? I ain't no corpse.

"You was solid looking," Brackett continued softly, in the same tone of incredulous wonder. "You lost weight, I guess?"

Jesse kept silent. He needed Brackett too much to risk antagonizing him. But it was only by deliberate effort that he could keep from boiling over. The pause lengthened, became painful. Brackett flushed. "Jiminy Christmas, excuse me," he burst out in apology. He jerked the counter up.

"Come in. Take a seat. Good God, boy"—he grasped Jesse's hand and shook it—"I *am* glad to see you; don't think anything else! You just looked so peaked."

"It's all right," Jesse murmured. He sat down, thrusting his hand through his curly, tangled hair.

"Why are you limping?"

"I stepped on a stone; it jagged a hole through my shoe." Jesse pulled his feet back under the chair. He was ashamed of his shoes. They had come from the Relief originally, and two weeks on the road had about finished them. All morning, with a kind of delicious, foolish solemnity, he had been vowing to himself that before anything else, before even a suit of clothes, he was going to buy himself a brand new strong pair of shoes.

Brackett kept his eyes off Jesse's feet. He knew what was bothering the boy and it filled his heart with pity. The whole thing was appalling. He had never seen anyone who looked more down and out. His sister had been writing to him every week, but she hadn't told him they were as badly off as this.

"Well now, listen," Brackett began, "tell me things. How's Ella?"

"Oh, she's pretty good," Jesse replied absently. He had a soft, pleasing, rather shy voice that went with his soft gray eyes. He was worrying over how to get started.

"And the kids?'

"Oh, they're fine. . . . Well, you know," Jesse added, becoming more attentive. "The young one has to wear a brace. He can't run around, you know. But he's smart. He draws pictures and he does things, you know."

"Yes," Brackett said. "That's good." He hesitated. There was a moment's silence. Jesse fidgeted in his chair. Now that the time had arrived, he felt awkward. Brackett leaned forward and put his hand on Jesse's knee. "Ella didn't tell me things were so bad for you, Jesse. I might have helped."

"Well, goodness," Jesse returned softly, "you been having your own troubles, ain't you?"

"Yes." Brackett leaned back. His ruddy face became mournful and darkly bitter. "You know I lost my hardware shop?"

"Well sure, of course," Jesse answered, surprised. "You wrote us. That's what I mean."

"I forgot," Brackett said. "I keep on being surprised over it myself. Not that it was worth much," he added bitterly. "It was running down hill for three years. I guess I just wanted it because it was mine." He laughed pointlessly, without mirth. "Well tell me about yourself," he asked. "What happened to the job you had?"

Jesse burst out abruptly, with agitation, "Let it wait, Tom, I got something on my mind."

"It ain't you and Ella?" Brackett interrupted anxiously.

"Why no!" Jesse sat back. "Why however did you come to think that? Why Ella and me," he stopped, laughing. "Why, Tom, I'm just crazy about Ella. Why she's just wonderful. She's just my whole life, Tom."

"Excuse me. Forget it." Brackett chuckled uncomfortably, turned away. The naked intensity of the youth's burst of love had upset him. It made him wish savagely that he could do something for them. They were both too decent to have had it so hard. Ella was like this boy too, shy and a little soft.

"Tom, listen," Jesse said, "I come here on purpose." He thrust his hand through his hair. "I want you to help me."

"Damn it, boy," Brackett groaned. He had been expecting this. "I can't much. I only get thirty-five a week and I'm damn grateful for it."

"Sure, I know," Jesse emphasized excitedly. He was feeling once again the wild delicious agitation that had possessed him in the early hours of the morning. "I know you can't help us with money! But we met a man who works for you! He was in our city! He said you could give me a job!"

"Who said?"

"Oh, why didn't you tell me?" Jesse burst out reproachfully. "Why as soon as I heard it I started out. For two weeks now I been pushing ahead like crazy."

Brackett groaned aloud. "You come walking from Kansas City in two weeks so I could give you a job?"

"Sure, Tom, of course. What else could I do?"

"God Almighty, there ain't no jobs, Jesse! It's a slack season. And you don't know this oil business. It's special. I got my Legion friends here but they couldn't do nothing now. Don't you think I'd ask for you as soon as there was a chance?"

Jesse felt stunned. The hope of the last two weeks seemed rolling up into a ball of agony in his stomach. Then, frantically, he cried, "But listen, this man said *you* could hire! He *told* me! He drives trucks for you! He said you *always* need men!"

"Oh! . . . You mean *my* department?" Brackett said in a low voice.

"Yes, Tom. That's it!"

"Oh, no, you don't want to work in my department," Brackett told him in the same low voice. "You don't know what it is."

"Yes, I do," Jesse insisted. "He told me all about it, Tom. You're a dispatcher, ain't you? You send the dynamite trucks out?"

"Who was the man, Jesse?"

"Everett, Everett, I think."

"Egbert? Man about my size?" Brackett asked slowly.

"Yes Egbert. He wasn't a phony, was he?"

Brackett laughed. For the second time his laughter was without mirth. "No, he wasn't a phony." Then, in a changed voice: "Jiminy, boy, you should have asked me before you trekked all the way down here."

"Oh, I didn't want to," Jesse explained with naive cunning. "I knew you'd say 'no.' He told me it was risky work, Tom. But I don't care."

Brackett locked his fingers together. His solid, meaty face became very hard. "I'm going to say 'no' anyway, Jesse."

Jesse cried out. It had not occurred to him that Brackett would not agree. It had seemed as though reaching Tulsa were the only problem he had to face. "Oh, no," he begged, "You can't. Ain't there any jobs, Tom?"

"Sure, there's jobs. There's even Egbert's job if you want it."

"He's quit?"

"He's dead!"

"Oh!"

"On the job, Jesse. Last night if you want to know."

"Oh!" . . . Then, "I don't care!"

"Now you listen to me," Brackett said. "I'll tell you a few things that you should have asked before you started out. It ain't dynamite you drive. They don't use anything as safe as dynamite in drilling oil wells. They wish they could, but they can't. It's nitroglycerin! Soup!"

"But I know," Jesse told him reassuringly. "He advised me, Tom. You don't have to think I don't know."

"Shut up a minute," Brackett ordered angrily. "Listen! You just have to *look* at this soup and it blows! You know how they transport it? In a can that's shaped like this, see, like a fan? That's to give room for compartments, because each compartment has to be lined with rubber. That's the only way you can even think of handling it."

"Listen, Tom—"

"Now wait a minute, Jesse. For God's sake just put your mind to this. I know you had your heart set on a job, but you've got to understand. This stuff goes only in special trucks! At night! They got to follow a special route! They can't go through any city! If they lay over, it's got to be in a special garage! Don't you see what that means? Don't that tell you how dangerous it is?"

"I'll drive careful," Jesse said. "I know how to handle a truck. I'll drive slow."

Brackett groaned. "Do you think Egbert didn't drive careful or know how to handle a truck?"

"Tom," Jesse said earnestly, "you can't scare me. I got my mind fixed on only one thing: Egbert said he was getting a dollar a mile. He was making five to six hundred dollars a month for a half a month's work, he said. Can I get the same?"

"Sure, you can get the same," Brackett told him savagely. "A dollar a mile. It's easy. But why do you think the company has to pay so much? It's easy—until you run over a stone that your headlights didn't pick out, like Egbert did. Or get a blowout! Or get something in your eye, so the wheel twists and you jar the truck! Or any other God damn thing nobody ever knows! We can't ask Egbert what happened to him. There's no truck to give any evidence. There's no corpse. There's nothing! Maybe tomorrow somebody'll find a piece of twisted steel way off in a cornfield. But we never find the driver. Not even a finger nail. All we know is that he don't come in on schedule. Then we wait for the police to call us. You know what happened last night? Something went wrong on the bridge. Maybe Egbert was nervous. Maybe he brushed the side with his fender. Only there's no bridge any more. No truck. No Egbert. Do you understand now? That's what you get for your God damn dollar a mile!"

There was a moment of silence. Jesse sat twisting his long thin hands. His mouth was sagging open, his face was agonized. Then he shut his eyes and spoke softly. "I don't care about that, Tom. You told me. Now you got to be good to me and give me the job."

Brackett slapped the palm of his hand down on his desk. "No!"

"Listen, Tom," Jesse said softly, "you just don't understand." He opened his eyes. They were filled with tears. They made Brackett turn away. "Just look at me, Tom. Don't that tell you enough? What did you think of me when you first saw me? You thought: 'Why don't that bum go away and stop panhandling?' Didn't you, Tom? Tom, I just can't live like this any more. I got to be able to walk down the street with my head up."

"You're crazy," Brackett muttered. "Every year there's one out of five drivers gets killed. That's the average. What's worth that?"

"Is my life worth anything now? We're just starving at home, Tom. They ain't put us back on relief yet."

"Then you should have told me," Brackett exclaimed harshly. "It's your own damn fault. A man has no right to have false pride when his family ain't eating. I'll borrow some money and we'll telegraph it to Ella. Then you go home and get back on relief."

"And then what?"

"And then wait, God damn it! You're no old man. You got no right to throw your life away. Sometime you'll get a job."

"No!" Jesse jumped up. "No. I believed that too. But I don't now," he cried passionately. "I ain't getting a job no more than you're getting your hardware store back. I lost my skill, Tom. Linotyping is skilled work. I'm rusty now. I've been six years on relief. The only work I've had is pick and shovel. When I got that job this spring I was supposed to be an A-1 man. But I wasn't. And they got new machines now. As soon as the slack started they let me out."

"So what?" Brackett said harshly. "Ain't there other jobs?"

"How do I know?" Jesse replied. "There ain't been one for six years. I'd even be afraid to take one now. It's been too hard waiting so many weeks to get back on relief."

"Well you got to have some courage," Brackett shouted. "You've got to keep up hope."

"I got all the courage you want," Jesse retorted vehemently, "but no, I ain't got no hope. The hope has dried up in me in six years' waiting. You're the only hope I got."

"You're crazy," Brackett muttered. "I won't do it. For God's sake think of Ella for a minute."

"Don't you *know* I'm thinking about her?" Jesse asked softly. He plucked at Brackett's sleeve. "That's what decided me, Tom." His voice became muted into a hushed pained whisper. "The night Egbert was at our house I looked at Ella like I'd seen her for the first time. She *ain't pretty any more, Tom!*" Brackett jerked his head and moved away. Jesse followed him, taking a deep, sobbing breath. "Don't that tell you, Tom? Ella was like a little doll or something, you remember. I couldn't walk down the street without somebody turning to look at her. She ain't twenty-nine yet, Tom, and she ain't pretty no more."

Brackett sat down with his shoulders hunched up wearily. He gripped his hands together and sat leaning forward, staring at the floor.

Jesse stood over him, his gaunt face flushed with emotion, almost unpleasant in its look of pleading and bitter humility. "I ain't done right for Ella, Tom. Ella deserved better. This is the only chance I see in my whole life to do something for her. I've just been a failure."

"Don't talk nonsense," Brackett commented, without rancor. "You ain't a failure. No more than me. There's millions of men in the identical situation. It's just the depression, or the recession, or the God damn New Deal, or . . . !" He swore and lapsed into silence.

"Oh, no," Jesse corrected him, in a knowing, sorrowful tone, "those things maybe excuse other men. But not me. It was up to me to do better. This is my own fault!"

"Oh, beans!" Brackett said. "It's more sun spots than it's you!"

Jesse's face turned an unhealthy mottled red. It looked swollen. "Well, I don't care," he cried wildly. "I don't care! You got to give me this! I got to lift my head up. I went through one stretch of hell but I can't go through another. You want me to keep looking at my little boy's legs and tell myself if I had a job he wouldn't be like that? Every time he walks he says to me, 'I got soft bones from the rickets and you give it to me because you didn't feed me right.' Jesus Christ, Tom, you think I'm going to sit there and watch him like that another six years?"

Brackett leaped to his feet. "So what if you do?" he shouted. "You say you're thinking about Ella. How's she going to like it when you get killed?"

"Maybe I won't," Jesse pleaded. "I've got to have some luck some-time."

"That's what they all think," Brackett replied scornfully. "When you take this job your luck is a question mark. The only thing certain is that sooner or later you get killed."

"Okay then," Jesse shouted back. "Then I do! But meanwhile I got something, don't I? I can buy a pair of shoes. Look at me! I can buy a suit that don't say 'Relief' by the way it fits. I can smoke cigarettes. I can buy some candy for the kids. I can eat some myself. Yes, by God, I want to eat some candy. I want a glass of beer once a day. I want Ella dressed up. I want her to eat meat three times a week, four times maybe. I want to take my family to the movies."

Brackett sat down. "Oh, shut up," he said wearily.

"No," Jesse told him softly, passionately, "you can't get rid of me. Listen, Tom" he pleaded, "I got it all figured out. On six hundred a month look how much I can save! If I last only three months look how much it is—a thousand dollars—more! And maybe I'll last longer. Maybe a couple years. I can fix Ella up for life!"

"You said it," Brackett interposed. "I suppose you think she'll enjoy living when you're on a job like that?"

"I got it all figured out," Jesse answered excitedly. "She don't know, see? I tell her I make only forty. You put the rest in a bank account for her, Tom."

"Oh, shut up," Brackett said. "You think you'll be happy? Every minute, waking and sleeping, you'll be wondering if tomorrow you'll be dead. And the worst days will be your days off, when you're not driving. They have to give you every other day free to get your nerve back. And you lay around the house eating your heart out. That's how happy you'll be."

Jesse laughed. "I'll be happy, I'll be singing. Lord God, Tom, I'm going to feel *proud* of myself for the first time in seven years!"

"Oh, shut up, shut up," Brackett said.

The little shanty became silent. After a moment Jesse whispered: "You got to, Tom. You got to. You got to."

Again there was silence. Brackett raised both hands to his head, pressing the palms against his temples.

"Tom, Tom—" Jesse said.

Brackett sighed. "Oh God damn it," he said finally, "all right, I'll take you on, God help me." His voice was low, hoarse, infinitely weary. "If you're ready to drive tonight, you can drive tonight."

Jesse didn't answer. He couldn't. Brackett looked up, tears were running down Jesse's face. He was swallowing and trying to speak, but only making an absurd, gasping noise.

"I'll send a wire to Ella," Brackett said in the same hoarse, weary voice. "I'll tell her you got a job, and you'll send her fare in a couple of days. You'll have some money then—that is, if you last the week out, you jackass!"

Jesse only nodded. His heart felt so close to bursting that he pressed both hands against it, as though to hold it locked within his breast.

"Come back here at six o'clock," Brackett said. "Here's some money. Eat a good meal."

Thanks," Jesse whispered.

"Wait a minute." Brackett said. "Here's my address." He wrote it on a piece of paper. "Take any car going that way. Ask the conductor where to get off. Take a bath and get some sleep."

"Thanks," Jesse said. "Thanks, Tom."

"Oh, get out of here," Brackett said.

"Tom."

"What?"

"I just—" Jesse stopped. Brackett saw his face. The eyes were still glistening with tears, but the gaunt face was shining now, with a kind of fierce radiance.

Brackett turned away. "I'm busy," he said.

Jesse went out. The wet film blinded him but the whole world seemed to have turned golden. He limped slowly with the blood pounding his temples and a wild, incommunicable joy in his heart. "I'm the happiest man in the world," he whispered to himself. "I'm the happiest man on the whole earth."

Brackett sat watching till finally Jesse turned the corner of the alley and disappeared. Then he hunched himself over, with his head in his hands. His heart was beating painfully, like something old and clogged. He listened to it as it beat. He sat in desperate tranquillity, gripping his head in his hands.

Tillie Olsen (1912–2007) came of age during the Depression years. She worked in everyday jobs, writing in her spare time and working for social and economic causes. She married during WWII and had four children, not resuming her writing again until the 1950s. A high school dropout, Olsen went on to teach at major universities and received a number of fellowships and honorary degrees. Her work has been translated into twelve different languages and is celebrated across the globe.

I Stand Here Ironing

Tillie Olsen

I stand here ironing, and what you asked me moves tormented back and forth with the iron.

"I wish you would manage the time to come in and talk with me about your daughter. I'm sure you can help me understand her. She's a youngster who needs help and whom I'm deeply interested in helping."

"Who needs help." Even if I came, what good would it do. You think because I am her mother I have a key, or that in some way you could use me as a key? She has lived for nineteen years. There is all that life that has happened outside of me, beyond me.

And where is there time to remember, to sift, to weigh, to estimate, to total? I will start and there will be an interruption and I will have to gather it all together again. Or I will become engulfed with all I did or did not do, with what should have been and what cannot be helped.

She was a beautiful baby. The first and only one of our five that was beautiful at birth. You do not guess how new and uneasy her tenancy in her now-loveliness. You did not know her all those years she was thought homely, or see her pouring over her baby pictures, making me tell her over and over how beautiful she had been—and would be, I would tell her—and was now, to the seeing eye. But the seeing eyes were few or nonexistent. Including mine.

I nursed her. They feel that's important nowadays. I nursed all the children, but with her, with all the fierce rigidity of first motherhood, I did like the books then said. Though her cries battered me to trembling and my breasts ached with swollenness, I waited till the clock decreed.

Why do I put that first? I do not even know if it matters, or if it explains anything.

She was a beautiful baby. She blew shining bubbles of sound. She loved motion, loved light, loved color and music and textures. She would lie on the floor in her blue overalls patting the surface so hard in ecstasy her hands and feet would blur. She was a miracle to me, but when she was eight months old I had to leave her daytimes with the woman downstairs to whom she was no miracle at all, for I worked or looked for work and for Emily's father, who "could no longer endure" (he wrote in his good-bye note) "sharing want with us."

I was nineteen. It was the pre-relief, pre-WPA world of depression. I would start running as soon as I got off the streetcar, running up the stairs, the place smelling sour, and awake or asleep to startle awake, when she saw me she would break into a clogged weeping that could not be comforted, a weeping I can hear yet.

After awhile I found a job hashing at night so I could be with her days, and it was better. But it came to where I had to bring her to his family and leave her.

It took a long time to raise the money for her fare back. Then she got the chicken pox and I had to wait longer. When she finally came, I hardly knew her, walking quick and nervous like her father, looking like her father, thin, and dressed in a shoddy red that yellowed her skin and glared at the pockmarks. All the baby loveliness had gone.

She was two. Old enough for nursery school they said, and I did not know then what I know now—the fatigue of the long day, and the lacerations of group life in nurseries that are only parking places for children.

Except that it would have made no difference if I had known.

It was the only place there was. It was the only way we could be together, the only way I could hold a job.

And even without knowing, I knew. I knew that the teacher was evil because all these years it has curdled into my memory, the little boy hunched in the corner, her rasp, "why aren't you outside, because Alvin hits you? that's no reason, go out, scaredy." I knew Emily hated it even if she did not clutch and implore "don't go Mommy" like the other children, mornings.

She always had a reason why we should stay home. Momma, you look sick, Momma. I feel sick. Momma, the teachers aren't there today, they're sick. Momma, we can't go, there was a fire there last night. Momma, it's a holiday today, no school, they told me.

But never a direct protest, never rebellion. I think of our others in their three-, four-year-oldness—the explosions, the tempers, the denunciations, the demands—and I feel suddenly ill. I put the iron down. What in me demanded that goodness in her? And what was the cost, the cost to her of such goodness?

The old man living in the back once said in his gentle way: "You should smile at Emily more when you look at her." What was in my face when I looked at her? I loved her. There were all the acts of love.

It was only with the others I remembered what he said, and it was the face of joy, and not of care or tightness or worry I turned to them—too late for Emily. She does not smile easily, let alone almost always as her brothers and sisters do. Her face is closed and somber, but when she wants, how fluid. You must have seen it in her pantomimes, you spoke of her rare gift for comedy on the stage that rouses a laughter out of the audience so dear they applaud and applaud and do not want to let her go.

Where does it come from, that comedy? There was none of it in her when she came back to me that second time, after I had had to send her away again. She had a new daddy now to learn to love, and I think perhaps it was a better time.

Except when we left her alone nights, telling ourselves she was old enough.

"Can't you go some other time, Mommy, like tomorrow?" she would ask. "Will it be just a little while you'll be gone? Do you promise?"

The time we came back, the front door open, the clock on the floor in the hall. She rigid awake. "It wasn't just a little while. I didn't cry. Three times I called you, just three times, and then I ran downstairs to open the door so you could come faster. The clock talked loud. I threw it away, it scared me what it talked."

She said the clock talked loud again that night I went to the hospital to have Susan. She was delirious with the fever that comes before red measles, but she was fully conscious all the week I was gone and the week after we were home when she could not come near the new baby or me.

She did not get well. She stayed skeleton thin, not wanting to eat, and night after night she had nightmares. She would call for me, and I would rouse from exhaustion to sleepily call back: "You're all right, darling, go to sleep, it's just a dream," and if she still called, in a sterner voice, "now go to sleep, Emily, there's nothing to hurt you." Twice, only twice, when I had to get up for Susan anyhow, I went in to sit with her.

Now when it is too late (as if she would let me hold and comfort her like I do the others) I get up and go to her at once at her moan or restless stirring. "Are you awake, Emily? Can I get you something?" And the answer is always the same: "No, I'm all right, go back to sleep, Mother."

They persuaded me at the clinic to send her away to a convalescent home in the country where "she can have the kind of food and care you can't manage for her, and you'll be free to concentrate on the new baby." They still send children to that place. I see pictures on the society page of sleek young women planning affairs to raise money for it, or dancing at the affairs, or decorating Easter eggs or filling Christmas stockings for the children.

They never have a picture of the children so I do not know if the girls still wear those gigantic red bows and the ravaged looks on the every other Sunday when parents can come to visit "unless otherwise notified"—as we were notified the first six weeks.

Oh, it is a handsome place, green lawns and tall trees and fluted flower beds. High up on the balconies of each cottage the children stand, the girls in their red bows and white dresses, the boys in white suits and giant red ties. The parents stand below shrieking up to be heard and the children shriek down to be heard, and between them the invisible wall "Not To Be Contaminated by Parental Germs or Physical Affection."

There was a tiny girl who always stood hand in hand with Emily. Her parents never came. One visit she was gone. "They moved her to Rose College," Emily shouted in explanation. "They don't like you to love anybody here."

She wrote once a week, the labored kind of writing of a seven-year-old. "I am fine. How is the baby. If I write my letter nicely I will have a star. Love." There never was a star. We wrote every other day, letters she could never hold or keep but only hear read once. "We simply do not have room for children to keep any personal possessions," they patiently explained when we pieced one Sunday's shrieking together to plead how much it would mean to Emily, who loved so to keep things, to be allowed to keep her letters and cards.

Each visit she looked frailer. "She isn't eating," they told us.

(They had runny eggs for breakfast or mush with lumps, Emily said later, I'd hold it in my mouth and not swallow. Nothing ever tasted good, just when they had chicken.)

It took us eight months to get her released home, and only the fact that she gained back so little of her seven lost pounds convinced the social worker.

I used to try to hold her and love her after she came back, but her body would stay stiff, and after a while she'd push away. She ate little. Food sickened her, and I think much of life too. Oh, she had physical lightness and brightness, twinkling by on skates, bouncing like a ball up and down up and down over the jump rope, skimming over the hill; but these were momentary.

She fretted about her appearance, thin and dark and foreign-looking at a time when every little girl was supposed to look or thought she should look a chubby blonde replica of Shirley Temple. The doorbell sometimes rang for her, but no one seemed to come and play in the house or be a best friend. Maybe because we moved so much.

There was a boy she loved painfully through two school semesters. Months later she told me how she had taken pennies from my purse to buy him candy. "Licorice was his favorite and I brought him some every day, but he still liked Jennifer better'n me. Why, Mommy?" The kind of question for which there is no answer.

School was a worry to her. She was not glib or quick in a world where glibness and quickness were easily confused with ability to learn. To her overworked and exasperated teachers she was an overconscientious "slow learner" who kept trying to catch up and was absent entirely too often.

I let her be absent, though sometimes the illness was imaginary. How different from my now-strictness about attendance with the others. I wasn't working. We had a new baby, I was home anyhow. Sometimes, after Susan grew old enough, I would keep her home from school, too, to have them all together.

Mostly Emily had asthma, and her breathing, harsh and labored, would fill the house with a curiously tranquil sound. I would bring the two old dresser mirrors and her boxes of collections to her bed. She would select beads and single earrings, bottle tops and shells, dried flowers and pebbles, old postcards and scraps, all sorts of oddments; then she and Susan would play Kingdom, setting up landscapes and furniture, peopling them with action.

Those were the only times of peaceful companionship between her and Susan. I have edged away from it, that poisonous feeling between them, that terrible balancing of hurts and needs I had to do between the two, and did so badly, those earlier years.

Oh there were conflicts between the others too, each one human, needing, demanding, hurting, taking—but only between Emily and Susan, no, Emily toward Susan that corroding resentment. It seems so obvious on the surface, yet it is not obvious. Susan, the second child, Susan, golden- and curly-haired and chubby, quick and articulate and assured, everything in appearance and manner Emily was not; Susan, not able to resist Emily's precious things, losing or sometimes clumsily break-ing them; Susan telling jokes and riddles to company for applause while Emily sat silent (to say to me later: that was *my* riddle, Mother, I told it to Susan); Susan, who for all the five years' difference in age was just a year behind Emily in developing physically.

I am glad for that slow physical development that widened the dif-ference between her and her contemporaries, though she suffered over it. She was too vulnerable for that terrible world of youthful competition, of preening and parading, of constant measuring of yourself against every other, of envy, "If I had that copper hair," "If I had that skin. . . ." She tor-mented herself enough about not looking like the others, there was enough of the unsureness, the having to be conscious of words before you speak, the constant caring—what are they thinking of me? without hav-ing it all magnified by the merciless physical drives.

Ronnie is calling. He is wet and I change him. It is rare there is such a cry now. That time of motherhood is almost behind me when the ear is not one's own but must always be racked and listening for the child cry, the child call. We sit for a while and I hold him, looking out over the city spread in charcoal with its soft aisles of light. "*Shoogily*," he breathes and curls closer. I carry him back to bed, asleep. *Shoogily*. A funny word, a family word, inherited from Emily, invented by her to say: *comfort*.

In this and other ways she leaves her seal, I say aloud. And startled at my saying it. What do I mean? What did I start to gather together, to try and make coherent? I was at the terrible, growing years. War years. I do not remember them well. I was working, there were four smaller ones now, there was not time for her. She had to help be a mother, and a house-keeper, and shopper. She had to set her seal. Mornings of crisis and near hysteria trying to get lunches packed, hair combed, coats and shoes found, everyone to school or Child Care on time, the baby ready for transportation. And always the paper scribbled on by a smaller one, the book looked at by Susan then mislaid, the homework not done. Running out to that huge school where she was one, she was lost, she was a drop; suffering over the unpreparedness, stammering and unsure in her classes.

There was so little time left at night after the kids were bedded down. She would struggle over books, always eating (it was in those years she developed her enormous appetite that is legendary in our family) and I would be ironing, or preparing food for the next day, or writing V-mail to Bill, or tending the baby. Sometimes, to make me laugh, or out of her despair, she would imitate happenings or types at school.

I think I said once: "Why don't you do something like this in the school amateur show?" One morning she phoned me at work, hardly understandable through the weeping: "Mother, I did it. I won, I won; they gave me first prize; they clapped and clapped and wouldn't let me go."

Now suddenly she was Somebody, and as imprisoned in her difference as she had been in anonymity.

She began to be asked to perform at other high schools, even in colleges, then at city and statewide affairs. The first one we went to, I only recognized her that first moment when thin, shy, she almost drowned herself into the curtains. Then: Was this Emily? The control, the command, the convulsing and deadly clowning, the spell, then the roaring, stamping audience, unwilling to let this rare and precious laughter out of their lives.

Afterwards: You ought to do something about her with a gift like that—but without money or knowing how, what does one do? We have left it all to her, and a gift has as often been eddied inside, clogged and clotted, as been used and growing.

She is coming. She runs up the stairs two at a time with her light graceful step, and I know she is happy tonight. Whatever it was that occasioned your call did not happen today.

"Aren't you ever going to finish the ironing, Mother? Whistler painted his mother in a rocker. I'd have to paint mine standing over an ironing board." This is one of her communicative nights and she tells me everything and nothing as she fixes herself a plate of food out of the icebox.

She is so lovely. Why did you want me to come in at all? Why were you concerned? She will find her way.

She starts up the stairs to bed. "Don't get me up with the rest in the morning." "But I thought you were having midterms." "Oh, those," she comes back in, kisses me, and says quite lightly, "in a couple of years when we'll all be atom-dead they won't matter a bit."

She has said it before. She *believes* it. But because I have been dredging the past, and all that compounds a human being is so heavy and meaningful in me, I cannot endure it tonight.

I will never total it all. I will never come in to say: She was a child seldom smiled at. Her father left me before she was a year old. I had to work her first six years when there was work, or I sent her home and to his relatives. There were years she had care she hated. She was dark and thin and foreign-looking in a world where the prestige went to blondness and curly hair and dimples, she was slow where glibness was prized. She was a child of anxious, not proud, love. We were poor and could not afford for her the soil of easy growth. I was a young mother, I was a distracted mother. There were other children pushing up, demanding. Her younger sister seemed all that she was not. There were years she did not want me to touch her. She kept too much to herself, her life was such she had to keep too much in herself. My wisdom came too late. She has much to her and probably nothing will come of it. She is a child of her age, of depression, of war, of fear.

Let her be. So all that is in her will not bloom—but in how many does it? There is still enough left to live by. Only help her to know—help make it so there is cause for her to know—that she is more than this dress on the ironing board, helpless before the iron.

George Orwell (1903–1950), renowned British essayist and novelist, was born in India, and from 1922–1927, served as assistant superintendent at the India Imperial Palace in Burma. Later, Orwell adopted a socialist philosophy and lived in self-imposed poverty in Paris and London. After being wounded in the Spanish Civil War, he returned to England and gained fame for his novels Animal Farm *and* 1984, *which powerfully explore the themes of freedom and oppression.*

Shooting an Elephant

George Orwell

In Moulmein, in lower Burma, I was hated by large numbers of people—the only time in my life that I have been important enough for this to happen to me. I was sub-divisional police officer of the town, and in an aimless, petty kind of way anti-European feeling was very bitter. No one had the guts to raise a riot, but if a European woman went through the bazaars alone somebody would probably spit betel juice over her dress. As a police officer I was an obvious target and was baited whenever it seemed safe to do so. When a nimble Burman tripped me up on the football field and the referee (another Burman) looked the other way, the crowd yelled with hideous laughter. This happened more than once. In the end the sneering yellow faces of young men that met me everywhere, the insults hooted after me when I was at a safe distance, got badly on my nerves. The young Buddhist priests were the worst of all. There were several thousands of them in the town and none of them seemed to have anything to do except stand on street corners and jeer at Europeans.

All this was perplexing and upsetting. For at that time I had already made up my mind that imperialism was an evil thing and the sooner I chucked up my job and got out of it the better. Theoretically—and secretly, of course—I was all for the Burmese and all against their oppressors, the British. As for the job I was doing, I hated it more bitterly than I can perhaps make clear. In a job like that you see the dirty work of Empire at close quarters. The wretched prisoners huddling in the stinking cages of the lock-ups, the gray, cowed faces of the long-term convicts, the scarred buttocks of the men who had been flogged with bamboos—all these oppressed me with an intolerable sense of guilt. But I could get nothing into perspective. I was young and ill educated and I had had to think out my problems in the utter silence that is imposed on every Englishman in the East. I did not even know that the British Empire is dying, still less did I know that it is a great deal better than the younger empires that are going to supplant it. All I knew was that I was stuck between my hatred of the empire I served and my rage against the evil-spirited little beasts who tried to make my job impossible. With one part of my mind I thought of the British Raj as an unbreakable tyranny, as something clamped down, in *saecula saeculorum*, upon the will of prostrate peoples; with another part I thought that the greatest joy in the world would be to drive a bayonet into a Buddhist priest's guts. Feelings like these are the normal by-products of imperialism; ask any Anglo-Indian official, if you can catch him off duty.

One day something happened which in a roundabout way was enlightening. It was a tiny incident in itself; but it gave me a better glimpse than I had had before of the real nature of imperialism—the real motives for which despotic governments act. Early one morning the sub-inspector at a police station the other end of town rang me up on the 'phone and said that an elephant was ravaging the bazaar. Would I please come and do something about it? I did not know what I could do, but I wanted to see what was happening and I got on to a pony and started out. I took my rifle, an old .44 Winchester and much too small to kill an elephant, but I thought the noise might be useful *in terrorem*. Various Burmans stopped me on the way and told me about the elephant's doings. It was not, of course, a wild elephant, but a tame one which had gone "must." It had been chained up, as tame elephants always are when their attack of "must" is due, but on the previous night it had broken its chain and escaped. Its mahout, the only person who could manage it when it was in that state, had set out in pursuit, but had taken the wrong direction and was now twelve hours' journey away, and in the morning the elephant had suddenly reappeared in the town. The Burmese population had no weapons and were quite helpless against it. It had already destroyed somebody's bamboo hut, killed a cow and raided some fruit-stalls and devoured the stock; also it had met the municipal rubbish van and, when the driver jumped out and took to his heels, had turned the van over and inflicted violences upon it.

The Burmese sub-inspector and some Indian constables were waiting for me in the quarter where the elephant had been seen. It was a very poor quarter, a labyrinth of squalid bamboo huts, thatched with palm-leaf, winding all over a steep hillside. I remember that it was a cloudy, stuffy morning at the beginning of the rains. We began questioning the people as to where the elephant had gone and, as usual, failed to get any definite information. That is invariably the case in the East; a story always sounds clear enough at a distance, but the nearer you get to the scene of events the vaguer it becomes. Some of the people said that the elephant had gone in one direction, some said that he had gone in another, some professed not even to have heard of any elephant. I had almost made up my mind that the whole story was a pack of lies, when we heard yells a little distance away. There was a loud, scandalized cry of "Go away, child! Go away this instant!" and an old woman with a switch in her hand came round the corner of a hut, violently shooing away a crowd of naked children. Some more women followed, clicking their tongues and exclaiming; evidently there was something that the children ought not to have seen. I rounded the hut and saw a man's dead body sprawling in the mud. He was an Indian, a black Dravidian coolie, almost naked, and he could not have been dead many minutes. The people said that the elephant had come suddenly upon him round the corner of the hut, caught him with its trunk, put its foot on his back and ground him into the earth. This was the rainy season and the ground was soft, and his face had scored a trench a foot deep and a couple of yards long. He was lying on his belly with arms crucified and head sharply twisted to one side. His face was coated with mud, the eyes wide open, the teeth bared and grinning with an expression of unendurable agony. (Never tell me, by the way, that the dead look peaceful. Most of the corpses I have seen look devilish.) The friction of the great beast's foot had stripped the skin from his back as neatly as one skins a rabbit. As soon as I saw the dead man I sent an orderly to a friend's house nearby to borrow an elephant rifle. I had already sent back the pony, not wanting it to go mad with fright and throw me if it smelt the elephant.

The orderly came back in a few minutes with a rifle and five cartridges, and meanwhile some Burmans had arrived and told us that the elephant was in the paddy fields below, only a few hundred yards away. As I started forward practically the whole population of the quarter flocked out of the houses and followed me. They had seen the rifle and were all shouting excitedly that I was going to shoot the elephant. They had not shown much interest in the elephant when he was merely ravaging their homes, but it was different now that he was going to be shot. It was a bit of fun to them and it would be to an English crowd; besides they wanted the meat. It made me vaguely uneasy. I had no intention of shooting the elephant—I had merely sent for the rifle to defend myself if necessary—and it is always unnerving to have a crowd following you. I marched down the hill, looking and feeling a fool, with the rifle over my shoulder and an ever-growing army of people jostling at my heels. At the bottom, when you got away from the huts, there was a metalled road and beyond that a miry waste of paddy fields a thousand yards across, not yet ploughed but soggy from the first rains and dotted with coarse grass.

The elephant was standing eight yards from the road, his left side toward us. He took not the slightest notice of the crowd's approach. He was tearing up bunches of grass, beating them against his knees to clean them, and stuffing them into his mouth.

I had halted on the road. As soon as I saw the elephant I knew with perfect certainty that I ought not to shoot him. It is a serious matter to shoot a working elephant—it is comparable to destroying a huge and costly piece of machinery—and obviously one ought not to do it if it can be avoided. And at that distance, peacefully eating, the elephant looked no more dangerous than a cow. I thought then and I think now that his attack of "must" was already passing off; in which case he would merely wander harmlessly about until the mahout came back and caught him. Moreover, I did not in the least want to shoot him. I decided that I would watch him for a little while to make sure that he did not turn savage again, and then go home.

But at that moment I glanced round at the crowd that had followed me. It was an immense crowd, two thousand at the least and growing every minute. It blocked the road for a long distance on either side. I looked at the sea of yellow faces above the garish clothes—faces all happy and excited over this bit of fun, all certain that the elephant was going to be shot. They were watching me as they would watch a conjurer about to perform a trick. They did not like me, but with the magical rifle in my hands I was momentarily worth watching. And suddenly I realized that I should have to shoot the elephant after all. The people expected it of me and I had got to do it; I could feel their two thousand wills pressing me forward, irresistibly. And it was at this moment, as I stood there with the rifle in my hands, that I first grasped the hollowness, the futility of the white man's dominion in the East. Here was I, the white man with his gun, standing in front of the unarmed native crowd—seemingly the leading actor of the piece; but in reality I was only an absurd puppet pushed to and fro by the will of those yellow faces behind. I perceived in this moment that when the white man turns tyrant it is his own freedom he destroys. He becomes a sort of hollow, posing dummy, the conventionalized figure of a sahib. For it is the condition of his rule that he shall spend his life in trying to impress the "natives," and so in every crisis he has got to do what the "natives" expect of him. He wears a mask, and his face grows to fit it. I had to shoot the elephant. I had committed myself to doing it when I sent for the rifle. A sahib has got to act like a sahib; do definite things. To come all that way, rifle in hand, with two thousand people marching at my heels, and then to trail feebly away, having done nothing—no, that was impossible. The crowd would laugh at me. And my whole life, every white man's life in the East, was one long struggle not to be laughed at.

But I did not want to shoot the elephant. I watched him beating his bunch of grass against his knees with the preoccupied grandmotherly air that elephants have. It seemed to me that it would be murder to shoot him. At that age I was not squeamish about killing animals, but I had never shot an elephant and never wanted to. (Somehow it always seems worse to kill a *large* animal.) Besides, there was the beast's owner to be considered. Alive the elephant was worth at least a hundred pounds; dead, he would only be worth the value of his tusks, five pounds, possibly. But I had got to act quickly. I turned to some experienced-looking Burmans who had been there when we arrived, and asked them how the elephant had been behaving. They all said the same thing; he took no notice of you if you left him alone, but he might charge if you went too close to him.

It was perfectly clear to me what I ought to do. I ought to walk up to within, say, twenty-five yards of the elephant and test his behavior. If he charged, I could shoot; if he took no notice of me, it would be safe to leave him until the mahout came back. But also I knew that I was going to do no such thing. I was a poor shot with a rifle and the ground was soft mud into which one would sink at every step. If the elephant charged and I missed him, I should have about as much chance as a toad under a steamroller. But even then I was not thinking particularly of my own skin, only of the yellow faces behind. For at that moment, with the crowd watching me, I was not afraid in the ordinary sense, as I would have been if I had been alone. A white man mustn't be frightened in front of "natives"; and so, in general, he isn't frightened. The sole thought in my mind was that if anything went wrong those two thousand Burmans would see me pursued, caught, trampled on, and reduced to a grinning corpse like that Indian up the hill. And if that happened it was quite probable that some of them would laugh. That would never do. There was only one alternative. I shoved the cartridges into the magazine and lay down on the road to get a better aim.

The crowd grew very still, and a deep, low, happy sigh, as of people who see the theater curtain go up at last, breathed from innumerable throats. They were going to have their bit of fun after all. The rifle was a beautiful German thing with cross-hair sights. I did not then know that in shooting an elephant one would shoot to cut an imaginary bar running from ear-hole to ear-hole. I ought, therefore, as the elephant was sideways on, to have aimed straight at his ear-hole; actually I aimed several inches in front of this, thinking the brain would be further forward.

When I pulled the trigger I did not hear the bang or feel the kick—one never does when a shot goes home—but I heard the devilish roar of glee that went up from the crowd. In that instant, in too short a time, one would have thought, even for the bullet to get there, a mysterious, terrible change had come over the elephant. He neither stirred, nor fell, but every line of his body had altered. He looked suddenly stricken, shrunken, immensely old, as though the frightful impact of the bullet had paralyzed him without knocking him down. At last, after what seemed a long time—it might have been five seconds, I dare say—he sagged flabbily to his knees. His mouth slobbered. An enormous senility seemed to have settled upon him. One could have imagined him thousands of years old. I fired again into the same spot. At the second shot he did not collapse but climbed with desperate slowness to his feet and stood weakly upright, with legs sagging and head drooping. I fired a third time. That was the shot that did for him. You could see the agony of it jolt his whole body and knock the last remnant of strength from his legs. But in falling he seemed for a moment to rise, for as his hind legs collapsed beneath him he seemed to tower upward like a huge rock toppling, his trunk reaching skyward like a tree. He trumpeted, for the first and only time, and then down he came, his belly toward me, with a crash that seemed to shake the ground even where I lay.

I got up. The Burmans were already racing past me across the mud. It was obvious that the elephant would never rise again, but he was not dead. He was breathing very rhythmically with long rattling gasps, his great mound of a side painfully rising and falling. His mouth was wide open—I could see far down into caverns of pale pink throat. I waited a long time for him to die, but his breathing did not weaken. Finally I fired my two remaining shots into the spot where I thought his heart must be. The thick blood welled out of him like red velvet, but still he did not die. His body did not even jerk when the shots hit him, the tortured breathing continued without a pause. He was dying, very slowly and in great agony, but in some world remote from me where not even a bullet could damage him further. I felt that I had got to put an end to that dreadful noise. It seemed dreadful to see the great beast lying there, powerless to move and yet powerless to die, and not even to be able to finish him. I sent back for my small rifle and poured shot after shot into his heart and down his throat. They seemed to make no impression. The tortured gasps continued as steadily as the ticking of a clock.

In the end I could not stand it any longer and went away. I heard later that it took him half an hour to die. Burmans were bringing dahs and baskets even before I left, and I was told they had stripped his body almost to the bones by the afternoon.

Afterward, of course, there were endless discussions about the shooting of the elephant. The owner was furious, but he was only an Indian and could do nothing. Besides, legally I had done the right thing, for a mad elephant has to be killed, like a mad dog, if its owner fails to control it. Among the Europeans opinion was divided. The older men said I was right, the younger men said it was a damn shame to shoot an elephant for killing a coolie, because an elephant was worth more than any damn Coringhee coolie. And afterward I was very glad that the coolie had been killed; it put me legally in the right and it gave me sufficient pretext for shooting the elephant. I often wondered whether any of the others grasped that I had done it solely to avoid looking a fool.

Jean Rhys (1890–1979), novelist, was born in Dominica, the daughter of a doctor of Welsh descent, and came to England in 1907. She briefly attended the Perse School, Cambridge, and the Academy of Dramatic Art, then worked as a chorus girl and film extra, and, during the First World War, as a volunteer cook. In 1919 she left England to marry the first of three husbands, Jean Lenglet, and remained abroad for many years, living mainly in Paris, where she began to write and where much of her early work is set.

I Used to Live Here Once

Jean Rhys

She was standing by the river looking at the stepping stones and remembering each one. There was the round unsteady stone, the pointed one, the flat one in the middle—the safe stone where you could stand and look round. The next wasn't so safe for when the river was full the water flowed over it and even when it showed dry it was slippery. But after that it was easy and soon she was standing on the other side.

The road was much wider than it used to be but the work had been done carelessly. The felled trees had not been cleared away and the bushes looked trampled. Yet it was the same road and she walked along feeling extraordinarily happy.

It was a fine day, a blue day. The only thing was that the sky had a glassy look that she didn't remember. That was the only word she could think of. Glassy. She turned the corner, saw that what had been the old pavé[1] had been taken up, and there too the road was much wider, but it had the same unfinished look.

She came to the worn stone steps that led up to the house and her heart began to beat. The screw pine was gone, so was the mock summer house called the *ajoupa*, but the clove tree was still there and at the top of the steps the rough lawn stretched away, just as she remembered it. She stopped and looked towards the house that had been added to and painted white. It was strange to see a car standing in front of it.

There were two children under the big mango tree, a boy and a little girl, and she waved to them and called "Hello" but they didn't answer her or turn their heads. Very fair children, as Europeans born in the West Indies so often are: as if the white blood is asserting itself against all odds.

308

The grass was yellow in the hot sunlight as she walked towards them. When she was quite close she called again, shyly: "Hello." Then, "I used to live here once," she said.

Still they didn't answer. When she said for the third time "Hello" she was quite near them. Her arms went out instinctively with the longing to touch them.

It was the boy who turned. His gray eyes looked straight into hers. His expression didn't change. He said: "Hasn't it gone cold all of a sudden. D'you notice? Let's go in." "Yes, let's," said the girl.

Her arms fell to her sides as she watched them running across the grass to the house. That was the first time she knew.

Note

1   **pavé**   cobblestone pavement

A & P

John Updike

In walks these three girls in nothing but bathing suits. I'm in the third checkout slot, with my back to the door, so I don't see them until they're over by the bread. The one that caught my eye first was the one in the plaid green two-piece. She was a chunky kid, with a good tan and a sweet broad soft-looking can with those two crescents of white just under it, where the sun never seems to hit, at the top of the back of her legs. I stood there with my hand on a box of HiHo crackers trying to remember if I rang it up or not. I ring it up again and the customer starts giving me hell. She's one of these cash-register-watchers, a witch about fifty with rouge on her cheekbones and no eyebrows, and I know it made her day to trip me up. She'd been watching cash registers for fifty years and probably never seen a mistake before.

By the time I got her feathers smoothed and her goodies into a bag—she gives me a little snort in passing, if she'd been born at the right time they would have burned her over in Salem—by the time I get her on her way the girls had circled around the bread and were coming back, without a pushcart, back my way along the counters, in the aisle between the checkouts and the Special bins. They didn't even have shoes on. There was this chunky one, with the two-piece—it was bright green and the seams on the bra were still sharp and her belly was still pretty pale so I guessed she just got it (the suit)—there was this one, with one of those chubby berry-faces, the lips all bunched together under her nose, this one, and a tall one, with black hair that hadn't quite frizzed right, and one of these sunburns right across under the eyes, and a chin that was too long—you know, the kind of girl other girls think is very "striking" and "attractive" but never quite makes it, as they very well know, which is why they like her so much—and then the third one, that wasn't quite so tall.

310

She was the queen. She kind of led them around, the other two peeking around and making their shoulders round. She didn't look around, not this queen, she just walked straight on slowly, on these long white prima-donna legs. She came down a little hard on her heels, as if she didn't walk in her bare feet that much, putting down her heels and then letting the weight move along her toes as if she was testing the floor with every step, putting a little deliberate action into it. You never know for sure how girls' minds work (do they really think it's a mind in there or just a little buzz like a bee in a glass jar?) but you got the idea she had talked the other two into coming in here with her, and now she was showing them how to do it, walk slow and hold yourself straight.

She had on a kind of dirty pink—beige maybe, I don't know—bathing suit with a little nubble all over it and, what got me, the straps were down. They were off her shoulders looped loose around the cool tops of her arms, and I guess as a result the suit had slipped on her, so all around the top of the cloth there was this shining rim. If it hadn't been there you wouldn't have known there could have been anything whiter than those shoulders. With the straps pushed off, there was nothing between the top of the suit and the top of her head except just *her*, this clean bare plane of the top of her chest down from the shoulder bones like a dented sheet of metal tilted in the light. I mean, it was more than pretty.

She had sort of oaky hair that the sun and salt had bleached, done up in a bun that was unravelling, and a kind of prim face. Walking into the A & P with your straps down, I suppose it's the only kind of face you *can* have. She held her head so high her neck, coming up out of those white shoulders, looked kind of stretched, but I didn't mind. The longer her neck was, the more of her there was.

She must have felt in the corner of her eye me and over my shoulder Stokesie in the second slot watching, but she didn't tip. Not this queen. She kept her eyes moving across the racks, and stopped, and turned so slow it made my stomach rub the inside of my apron, and buzzed to the other two, who kind of huddled against her for relief, and then they all three of them went up the cat and dog food—breakfast cereal—macaroni—rice—raisins—seasonings—spreads—spaghetti—soft drinks—crackers—and—cookies aisle. From the third slot I look straight up this aisle to the meat counter, and I watched them all the way. The fat one with the tan sort of fumbled with the cookies, but on second thought she put the package back. The sheep pushing their carts down the aisle—the girls were walking against the usual traffic (not that we have one-way signs or anything)—were pretty hilarious. You could see them, when Queenie's white shoulders dawned on them, kind of jerk, or hop, or hiccup, but their eyes snapped back to their own baskets and on they pushed. I bet you could set off dynamite in the A & P and the people would by and large keep reaching and checking oatmeal off their lists and muttering "Let me see, there was a third thing, began with A, asparagus, no, ah, yes, applesauce!" or whatever it is they do mutter. But there was no doubt, this jiggled them. A few house slaves in pin curlers even look around after pushing their carts past to make sure what they had seen was correct.

You know, it's one thing to have a girl in a bathing suit down on the beach, where what with the glare nobody can look at each other much anyway, and another thing in the cool of the A & P, under the fluorescent lights, against all those stacked packages, with her feet paddling along naked over our checker-board green-and-cream rubber-tile floor.

"Oh, Daddy," Stokesie said beside me. "I feel so faint." "Darling," I said. "Hold me tight." Stokesie's married, with two babies chalked up on his fuselage already, but as far as I can tell that's the only difference. He's twenty-two, and I was nineteen this April.

"Is it done?" he, asks, the responsible married man finding his voice. I forgot to say he thinks he's going to be a manager some sunny day, maybe in 1990 when it's called the Great Alexandrov and Petrooshki Tea Company or something.

What he meant was, our town is five miles from a beach, with a big summer colony out on the Point, but we're right in the middle of town, and the women generally put on a shirt or shorts or something before they get out of the car into the street. And anyway these are usually women with six children and varicose veins mapping their legs and nobody, including them, could care less. As I say, we're right in the middle of town, and if you stand at our front doors you can see two banks and the Congregational church and the newspaper store and three real estate offices and about twenty-seven old freeloaders tearing up Central Street because the sewer broke again. It's not as if we're on the Cape; we're north of Boston and there's people in this town haven't seen the ocean for twenty years.

The girls had reached the meat counter and were asking McMahon something. He pointed, they pointed, and they shuffled out of sight behind a pyramid of Diet Delight peaches. All that was left for us to see was old McMahon patting his mouth and looking after them sizing up their joints. Poor kids, I began to feel sorry for them, they couldn't help it.

Now here comes the sad part of the story, at least my family says it's sad, but I don't think it's so sad myself. The store's pretty empty, it being Thursday afternoon, so there was nothing much to do except lean on the register and wait for the girls to show up again. The whole store was like a pinball machine and I didn't know which tunnel they'd come out of. After a while they come around out of the far aisle, around the light bulbs, records at discount of the Caribbean Six or Tony Martin Sings or some such gunk you wonder why they waste the wax on, sixpacks of candy bars, and plastic toys done up in cellophane that fall apart when a kid looks at them anyway. Around they come, Queenie still leading the way, and holding a little gray jar in her hand. Slots Three through Seven are unmanned and I could see her wondering between Stokes and me, but Stokesie with his usual luck draws an old party in baggy gray pants who stumbles up with four giant cans of pineapple juice (what do these bums *do* with all that pineapple juice? I've often asked myself) so the girls come to me. Queenie puts down the jar and I take it into my fingers icy cold. Kingfish Fancy Herring Snacks in Pure Sour Cream: 49¢. Now her hands are empty, not a ring or a bracelet, bare as God made them, and I wonder where the money's coming from. Still with the prim look she lifts a folded dollar bill out of the hollow at the center of her nubbled pink top. The jar went heavy in my hand. Really, I thought that was so cute.

Then everybody's luck begins to run out. Lengel comes in from haggling with a truck full of cabbages on the lot and is about to scuttle into the door marked MANAGER behind which he hides all day when the girls touch his eye. Lengel's pretty dreary, teaches Sunday school and the rest, but he doesn't miss that much. He comes over and says, "Girls, this isn't the beach."

Queenie blushes, though maybe it's just a brush of sunburn I was noticing for the first time, now that she was so close. "My mother asked me to pick up a jar of herring snacks." Her voice kind of startled me, the way voices do when you see the people first, coming out so flat and dumb yet kind of tony, too, the way it ticked over "pick up" and "snacks." All of a sudden I slid right down her voice into her living room. Her father and the other men were standing around in ice-cream coats and bow ties and the women were in sandals picking up herring snacks on toothpicks off a big glass plate and they were all holding drinks the color of water with olives and sprigs of mint in them. When my parents have somebody over they get lemonade and if it's a real racy affair Schlitz in tall glasses with "They'll Do It Every Time" cartoons stencilled on.

"That's all right," Lengel said. "But this isn't the beach." His repeating this struck me as funny, as if it had just occurred to him, and he had been thinking all these years the A & P was a great big dune and he was the head lifeguard. He didn't like my smiling—as I say he doesn't miss much—but he concentrates on giving the girls that sad Sunday-school-superintendent stare.

Queenie's blush is no sunburn now, and the plump one in plaid, that I liked better from the back—a real sweet can—pipes up, "We weren't doing any shopping. We just came in for the one thing."

"That makes no difference," Lengel tells her, and I could see from the way his eyes went that he hadn't noticed she was wearing a two-piece before. "We want you decently dressed when you come in here."

"We *are* decent," Queenie says suddenly, her lower lip pushing, getting sore now that she remembers her place, a place from which the crowd that runs the A & P must look pretty crummy. Fancy Herring Snacks flashed in her very blue eyes.

"Girls, I don't want to argue with you. After this come in here with your shoulders covered. It's our policy." He turns his back. That's policy for you. Policy is what the kingpins want. What the others want is juvenile delinquency.

All this while, the customers had been showing up with their carts but, you know, sheep, seeing a scene, they had all bunched up on Stokesie, who shook open a paper bag as gently as peeling a peach, not wanting to miss a word. I could feel in the silence everybody getting nervous, most of all Lengel, who asks me, "Sammy, have you rung up this purchase?"

I thought and said "No" but it wasn't about that I was thinking. I go through the punches, 4, 9, GROC, TOT—it's more complicated than you think and after you do it often enough, it begins to make a little song, that you hear words to, in my case "Hello (*bing*) there, you (*gung*) hap-py *pee*pul *splat*)!"— the *splat* being the drawer flying out. I uncrease the bill, tenderly as you may imagine, it just having come from between the two smoothest scoops of vanilla I had ever known there were, and pass a half and a penny into her narrow pink palm and nestle the herrings in a bag and twist its neck and hand it over, all the time thinking.

The girls, and who'd blame them, are in a hurry to get out, so I say "I quit" to Lengel quick enough for them to hear, hoping they'll stop and watch me, their unsuspected hero. They keep right on going, into the electric eye; the door flies open and they flicker across the lot to their car, Queenie and Plaid and Big Tall Goony-Goony (not that as raw material she was so bad), leaving me with Lengel and a kink in his eyebrow.

"Did you say something, Sammy?"

"I said I quit."

"I thought you did."

"You didn't have to embarrass them."

"It was they who were embarrassing us."

I started to say something that came out "Fiddle-de-doo." It's a saying of my grandmother's, and I know she would have been pleased.

"I don't think you know what you're saying," Lengel said.

"I know you don't," I said. "But I do." I pull the bow at the back of my apron and start shrugging it off my shoulders. A couple customers that had been heading for my slot begin to knock against each other, like scared pigs in a chute.

Lengel sighs and begins to look very patient and old and gray. He's been a friend of my parents for years. "Sammy, you don't want to do this to your Mom and Dad," he tells me. It's true, I don't. But it seems to me that once you begin a gesture it's fatal not to go through with it. I fold the apron, "Sammy" stitched in red on the pocket, and put it on the counter, and drop the bow tie on top of it. The bow tie is theirs, if you've ever wondered. "You'll feel this for the rest of your life," Lengel says, and I know that's true too, but remembering how he made that pretty girl blush makes me so scrunchy inside I punch the No Sale tab and the machine whirs "pee-pul" and the drawer slats out. One advantage to this scene taking place in summer, I can follow this up with a clean exit, there's no fumbling around getting your coat and galoshes. I just saunter into the electric eye in my white shirt that my mother ironed the night before, and the door heaves itself open, and outside the sunshine is skating around on the asphalt.

I look around for my girls, but they're gone, of course. There wasn't anybody but some young married screaming with her children about some candy they didn't get by the door of a powder-blue Falcon station wagon. Looking back in the big windows, over the bags of peat moss and aluminum lawn furniture stacked on the pavement, I could see Lengel in my place in the slot, checking the sheep through. His face was dark gray and his back stiff, as if he'd just had an injection of iron, and my stomach kind of fell as I felt how hard the world was going to be to me hereafter.

*A*lice Walker (1944–), the daughter of Georgia sharecroppers, attended *Spelman College and Sarah Lawrence. During the Civil Rights Era, she became involved in voter registration in Georgia and the welfare rights movement in New York. Walker has published poetry, essays, and fiction. Perhaps the best known of her works is* The Color Purple *(1982), which deals with the effects of racism and the resiliency of black women.*

Everyday Use

For Your Grandmama

Alice Walker

I will wait for her in the yard that Maggie and I made so clean and wavy yesterday afternoon. A yard like this is more comfortable that most people know. It is not just a yard. It is like an extended living room. When the hard clay is swept clean as a floor and the fine sand around the edges lined with tiny, irregular grooves anyone can come and sit and look up into the elm tree and wait for the breezes that never come inside the house.

Maggie will be nervous until after her sister goes: she will stand hopelessly in corners homely and ashamed of the burn scars down her arms and legs, eyeing her sister with a mixture of envy and awe. She thinks her sister has held life always in the palm of one hand, that "no" is a word the world never learned to say to her.

You've no doubt seen those TV shows where the child who has "made it" is confronted, as a surprise, by her own mother and father, tottering in weakly from backstage. (A pleasant surprise, of course: What would they do if parent and child came on the show only to curse out and insult each other?) On TV mother and child embrace and smile into each other's faces. Sometimes the mother and father weep, the child wraps them in her arms and leans across the table to tell how she would not have made it without their help. I have seen these programs.

Sometimes I dream a dream in which Dee and I are suddenly brought together on a TV program of this sort. Out of a dark and soft-seated limousine I am ushered into a bright room filled with many people. There I meet a smiling, gray, sporty man like Johnny Carson who shakes my hand and tells me what a fine girl I have. Then we are on the stage and

Dee is embracing me with tears in her eyes. She pins on my dress a large orchid, even though she has told me once that she thinks orchids are tacky flowers.

In real life I am a large, big-boned woman with rough, man-working hands. In the winter I wear flannel nightgowns to bed and overalls during the day. I can kill and clean a hog as mercilessly as a man. My fat keeps me hot in zero weather. I can work all day, breaking ice to get water for washing. I can eat pork liver cooked over the open fire minutes after it comes steaming from the hog. One winter I knocked a bull calf straight in the brain between the eyes with a sledge hammer and had the meat hung up to chill before nightfall. But of course all this does not show on television. I am the way my daughter would want me to be: a hundred pounds lighter, my skin like an uncooked barley pancake. My hair glistens in the hot bright lights. Johnny Carson has much to do to keep up with my quick and witty tongue.

But that is a mistake. I know it before I wake up. Who ever knew a Johnson with a quick tongue? Who can even imagine me looking a strange white man in the eye? It seems to me I have talked to them always with one foot raised in flight, with my head turned in whichever way is farthest from them. Dee, though. She would always look anyone in the eye. Hesitation was no part of her nature.

"How do I look, Mama?" Maggie says, showing just enough of her thin body enveloped in pink skirt and red blouse for me to know she's there, almost hidden by the door.

"Come out into the yard," I say.

Have you ever seen a lame animal, perhaps a dog run over by some careless person rich enough to own a car, sidle up to someone who is ignorant enough to be kind to him? That is the way my Maggie walks. She has been like this, chin on chest, eyes on ground, feet in shuffle, ever since the fire that burned the other house to the ground.

Dee is lighter than Maggie, with nicer hair and a fuller figure. She's a woman now, though sometimes I forget. How long ago was it that the other house burned? Ten, twelve years? Sometimes I can still hear the flames and feel Maggie's arm sticking to me, her hair smoking and her dress falling off her in little black papery flakes. Her eyes seemed stretched open, blazed open by the flames reflected in them. And Dee. I see her standing off under the sweet gum tree she used to dig gum out of; a look of concentration on her face as she watched the last dingy gray board of the house fall in toward the red-hot brick chimney. Why don't you do a dance around the ashes? I'd wanted to ask her. She had hated the house that much.

I used to think she hated Maggie, too. But that was before we raised the money, the church and me, to send her to Augusta to school. She used to read to us without pity; forcing words, lies, other folks' habits, whole lives upon us two, sitting trapped and ignorant underneath her voice. She washed us in a river of make-believe, burned us with a lot of knowledge we didn't necessarily need to know. Pressed us to her with the serious way she read, to shove us away at just the moment, like dimwits, we seemed about to understand.

Dee wanted nice things. A yellow organdy dress to wear to her graduation from high school; black pumps to match a green suit she'd made from an old suit somebody gave me. She was determined to stare down any disaster in her efforts. Her eyelids would not flicker for minutes at a time. Often I fought off the temptation to shake her. At sixteen she had a style of her own and knew what style was.

I never had an education myself. After second grade the school was closed down. Don't ask me why: in 1927 colored asked fewer questions than they do now. Sometimes Maggie reads to me. She stumbles along good-naturedly but can't see well. She knows she is not bright. Like good looks and money, quickness passed her by. She will marry John Thomas (who has mossy teeth in an earnest face) and then I'll be free to sit here and I guess just sing church songs to myself. Although I never was a good singer. Never could carry a tune. I was always better at a man's job. I used to love to milk till I was hoofed in the side in '49. Cows are soothing and slow and don't bother you, unless you try to milk them the wrong way.

I have deliberately turned my back on the house. It has three rooms, just like the one that burned, except the roof is tin; they don't make shingle roofs any more. There are no real windows, just some holes cut in the sides like the portholes in a ship, but not round and not square, with rawhide holding the shutters up on the outside. This house is in a pasture, too, like the other one. No doubt when Dee sees it she will want to tear it down. She wrote me once that no matter where we "choose" to live, she will manage to come see us. But she will never bring her friends. Maggie and I thought about this and Maggie asked me, "Mama, when did Dee ever *have* any friends?"

She had a few. Furtive boys in pink shirts hanging about on washday after school. Nervous girls who never laughed. Impressed with her they worshipped the well-turned phrase, the cute shape, the scalding humor that erupted like bubbles in lye. She read to them.

When she was courting Jimmy T she didn't have much time to pay to us, but turned all her faultfinding power on him. He *flew* to marry a cheap gal from a family of ignorant flashy people. She hardly had time to recompose herself.

When she comes I will meet—but there they are!

Maggie attempts to make a dash for the house, in her shuffling way, but I stay her with my hand. "Come back here," I say. And she stops and tries to dig a well in the sand with her toe.

It is hard to see them clearly through the strong sun. But even the first glimpse of leg out of the car tells me it is Dee. Her feet were always neat-looking as if God himself had shaped them with a certain style. From the other side of the car comes a short, stocky man. Hair is all over his head a foot long and hanging from his chin like a kinky mule tail. I hear Maggie suck in her breath. "Uhnnnh," is what it sounds like. Like when you see the wriggling end of a snake just in front of your foot on the road. "Uhnnnh."

Dee next. A dress down to the ground, in this hot weather. A dress so loud it hurts my eyes. There are yellows and oranges enough to throw back the light of the sun. I feel my whole face warming from the heat waves it throws out. Earrings, too, gold and hanging down to her shoulders. Bracelets dangling and making noises when she moves her arm up to shake the folds of the dress out of her armpits. The dress is loose and flows, and as she walks closer, I like it. I hear Maggie go "Uhnnnh" again. It is her sister's hair. It stands straight up like the wool on a sheep. It is black as night and around the edges are two long pigtails that rope about like small lizards disappearing behind her ears.

"Wa-su-zo-Tean-o!" she says, coming on in that gliding way the dress makes her move. The short stocky fellow with the hair to his navel is all grinning and he follows up with "Asalamalakim,[1] my mother and sister!" He moves to hug Maggie but she falls back, right up against the back of my chair. I feel her trembling there and when I look up I see the perspiration falling off her chin.

"Don't get up," says Dee. Since I am stout it takes something of a push. You can see me trying to move a second or two before I make it. She turns, showing white heels through her sandals, and goes back to the car. Out she peeks next with a Polaroid. She stoops down quickly and lines up picture after picture of me sitting there in front of the house with Maggie cowering behind me. She never takes a shot without making sure the house is included. When a cow comes nibbling around the edge of the yard she snaps it and me and Maggie and the house. Then she puts the Polaroid in the back seat of the car, and comes up and kisses me on the forehead.

Meanwhile Asalamalakim is going through the motions with Maggie's hand. Maggie's hand is as limp as a fish, and probably as cold, despite the sweat, and she keeps trying to pull it back. It looks like Asalamalakim wants to shake hands but wants to do it fancy. Or maybe he don't know how people shake hands. Anyhow, he soon gives up on Maggie.

"Well," I say. "Dee."

"No, Mama," she says. "Not 'Dee,' Wangero Leewanika Kemanjo!"

"What happened to 'Dee'?" I wanted to know.

"She's dead," Wangero said. "I couldn't bear it any longer being named after the people who oppress me."

"You know as well as me you was named after your aunt Dicie," I said. Dicie is my sister. She named Dee. We called her "Big Dee" after Dee was born.

"But who was she named after?" asked Wangero.

"I guess after Grandma Dee," I said.

"And who was she named after?" asked Wangero.

"Her mother," I said, and saw Wangero was getting tired. "That's about as far back as I can trace it, " I said. Though, in fact, I probably could have carried it back beyond the Civil War through the branches.

"Well," said Asalamalakim, "there you are."

"Uhnnnh," I heard Maggie say.

"There I was not," I said, "before 'Dicie' cropped up in our family, so why should I try to trace it that far back?"

He just stood there grinning, looking down on me like somebody inspecting a Model A car. Every once in a while he and Wangero sent eye signals over my head.

"How do you pronounce this name?" I asked.

"You don't have to call me by it if you don't want to," said Wangero.

"Why shouldn't I?" I asked. "If that's what you want us to call you, we'll call you."

"I know it might sound awkward at first," said Wangero.

"I'll get used to it," I said. "Ream it out again."

Well, soon we got the name out of the way. Asalamalakim had a name twice as long and three times as hard. After I tripped over it two or three times he told me to just call him Hakim-a-barber. I wanted to ask him was he a barber, but I didn't really think he was, so I didn't ask.

"You must belong to those beef-cattle peoples down the road," I said. They said "Asalamalakim" when they met you, too, but they didn't shake hands. Always too busy: feeding the cattle, fixing the fences, putting up salt-lick shelters, throwing down hay. When the white folks poisoned some of the herd the men stayed up all night with rifles in their hands. I walked a mile and a half just to see the sight.

Hakim-a-barber said, "I accept some of their doctrines, but farming and raising cattle is not my style." (They didn't tell me, and I didn't ask, whether Wangero [Dee] had really gone and married him.)

We sat down to eat and right away he said he didn't eat collards and pork was unclean. Wangero, though, went on through the chitlins and corn bread, the greens and everything else. She talked a blue streak over the sweet potatoes. Everything delighted her. Even the fact that we still used the benches her daddy made for the table when we couldn't afford to buy chairs.

"Oh, Mama!" she cried. Then turned to Hakim-a-barber. "I never knew how lovely these benches are. You can feel the rump prints," she said, running her hands underneath her and along the bench. Then she gave a sigh and her hand closed over Grandma Dee's butter dish. "That's it!" she said. "I knew there was something I wanted to ask you if I could have." She jumped up from the table and went over in the corner where the churn stood, the milk in its clabber by now. She looked at the churn and looked at it.

"This churn top is what I need," she said. "Didn't Uncle Buddy whittle it out of a tree you all used to have?"

"Yes," I said.

"Uh huh," she said happily. "And I want the dasher, too."

"Uncle Buddy whittle that, too?" asked the barber.

Dee (Wangero) looked up at me.

"Aunt Dee's first husband whittled the dash," said Maggie so low you almost couldn't hear her. "His name was Henry, but they called him Stash."

"Maggie's brain is like an elephant's," Wangero said, laughing. "I can use the churn top as a centerpiece for the alcove table," she said, sliding a plate over the churn, "and I'll think of something artistic to do with the dasher."

When she finished wrapping the dasher the handle stuck out. I took it for a moment in my hands. You didn't even have to look close to see where hands pushing the dasher up and down to make butter had left a kind of sink in the wood. In fact, there were a lot of small sinks; you could see where thumbs and fingers had sunk into the wood. It was beautiful light yellow wood, from a tree that grew in the yard where Big Dee and Stash had lived.

After dinner Dee (Wangero) went to the trunk at the foot of my bed and started rifling through it. Maggie hung back in the kitchen over the dishpan. Out came Wangero with two quilts. They had been pieced by Grandma Dee and then Big Dee and me had hung them on the quilt frames on the front porch and quilted them. One was in the Lone Star pattern. The other was Walk Around the Mountain. In both of them were scraps of dresses Grandma Dee had worn fifty and more years ago. Bits and pieces of Grandpa Jarrell's Paisley shirts. And one teeny faded blue piece, about the size of a penny matchbox, that was from Great Grandpa Ezra"s uniform that he wore in the Civil War.

"Mama," Wangero said sweet as a bird. "Can I have these old quilts?"

I heard something fall in the kitchen, and a minute later the kitchen door slammed.

"Why don't you take one or two of the others?" I asked "These old things was just done by me and Big Dee from some tops your grandma pieced before she died."

"No," said Wangero. "I don't want those. They are stitched around the borders by machine."

"That's make them last better," I said.

"That's not the point," said Wangero. "These are all pieces of dresses Grandma used to wear. She did all this stitching by hand. Imagine!" She held the quilts securely in her arms, stroking them.

"Some of the pieces, like those lavender ones, come from old clothes her mother handed down to her," I said, moving up to touch the quilts.

Dee (Wangero) moved back just enough so that I couldn't reach the quilts. They already belonged to her.

"Imagine!" she breathed again, clutching them closely to her bosom.

"The truth is," I said, "I promised to give them quilts to Maggie, for when she marries John Thomas."

She gasped like a bee had stung her.

"Maggie can't appreciate these quilts!" she said. "She'd probably be backward enough to put them to everyday use."

"I reckon she would," I said. "God knows I been saving 'em for long enough with nobody using 'em. I hope she will!" I didn't want to bring up how I had offered Dee (Wangero) a quilt when she went away to college. Then she told me they were old-fashioned, out of style.

"But they're *priceless!*" she was saying now, furiously; for she has a temper. "Maggie would put them on the bed in five years they'd be in rags. Less than that!"

"She can always make some more," I said. "Maggie knows how to quilt."

Dee (Wangero) looked at me with hatred. "You just will not understand. The point is these quilts, *these* quilts!"

"Well," I said, stumped. "What would *you* do with them?"

"Hang them," she said. As if that was the only thing you *could* do with quilts.

Maggie by now was standing in the door. I could almost hear the sound her feet made as they scraped over each other.

"She can have them, Mama," she said, like somebody used to never winning anything, or having anything reserved for her. "I can 'member Grandma Dee without the quilts."

I looked at her hard. She had filled her bottom lip with checkerberry snuff and it gave her face a kind of dopey, hangdog look. It was Grandma Dee and Big Dee who taught her how to quilt herself. She stood there with scarred hands hidden in the folds of her skirt. She looked at her sister with something like fear but she wasn't mad at her. This was Maggie's portion. This was the way she knew God to work.

When I looked at her like that something hit me in the top of my head and ran down to the soles of my feet. Just like when I'm in church and the spirit of God touches me and I get happy and shout. I did something I never had done before: hugged Maggie to me, then dragged her on into the room, snatched the quilts out of Miss Wangero's hands and dumped them into Maggie's lap. Maggie just sat there on my bed with her mouth open.

"Take one or two of the others," I said to Dee.

But she turned without a word and went out to Hakim-a-barber.

"You just don't understand," she said, as Maggie and I came out to the car.

"What don't I understand?" I wanted to know.

"Your heritage," she said. And then she turned to Maggie, kissed her, and said, "You ought to try to make something of yourself, too, Maggie. It's really a new day for us. But from the way you and Mama still live you'd never know it."

She put on some sunglasses that hid everything above the tip of her nose and her chin.

Maggie smiled; maybe at the sunglasses. But a real smile, not scared. After we watched the car dust settle I asked Maggie to bring me a dip of snuff. And then the two of us sat there just enjoying, until it was time to go in the house and go to bed.

Note

[1] A Muslim greeting sounded phonetically. Likewise, Wa-su-zo-Tean-o is an African greeting.

*R*eginald McKnight (1956–) was born in Germany and moved frequently due to his father's work in the Air Force. After serving in the Marine Corps himself, he attended Pikes Peak Community College in Colorado, eventually earning advanced degrees in English and teaching at various universities, most recently as professor of English at the University of Georgia. His writing focuses on issues of cultural heritage and identity for African-Americans since the civil rights era and has won several awards, including the O. Henry Award and Pushcart Prize.

Gettin to Be Like the Studs

Reginald McKnight

Louisiana's the kind of place that can get cold as hell, or hot as hell, or rain like hell, or windy as hell, but it's usually just hot and sweaty as hell. But that mornin it was cold and it put me in a bad mood. I really don't like this place a whole lot. Besides the crummy weather is the people. The people ain't very friendly and they talk too slow. We got stationed here about six months ago, but I ain't made many friends yet. It ain't like Lackland Air Base over in Texas where we come from. It sure is funny the way you can move somewheres else and people don't even look at you, but in the place you was before, you had lots of friends. This is the kind of place where you got to be real good in some kind of sport, or be real good lookin or like that. Over in Texas, where we was, the thing was for you to have a ghetto blaster and to be able to dance real good and wear nice clothes. I guess I dance pretty good. Not as bad as some guys. I still miss Texas. I wasn't real, real, real popular, but I did OK. To tell you the truth, though, I think I'll be makin more friends now. Now that I got rid of Lenny.

Lenny's a nigger, but for awhile he was my friend. The only friend-friend I've had here so far. Well, he wasn't my best friend or anything. We just usually set on the bus together and made faces and told jokes and junk. Sometimes on weekends we'd throw the ol pigskin around or ride bikes to the base exchange and buy models and stuff like that. We'd build tanks and planes and cars, all kinds. Lenny was pretty good at models. He showed me a lot of neat tricks with paint to make the models real realistic. I thought he was a pretty good guy, and he seemed pretty smart a lot of the time but he was in the slow classes like me. We never had any classes together, though. The only time I ever saw him in school was in the cafeteria, but I never set next to him there. He was the only coon in the whole school.

So anyway, when I walked over to the bus stop that mornin everything was all frosty over. The whole street looked like somebody'd gone berserk with about a hundred cans of fake snow. Everything was white as hell.

I got to the bus stop and there was ol Lenny standin there all by hisself. He really stood out against all that white frost. I guess he was standin there all by hisself cause all the other people out there was girls. He said he didn't like girls, but I knew he did. He was just chicken. He didn't want to get his butt kicked by Buck Tyler or Terry LaPort. Them two guys was the toughest in the whole school and they both hated Lenny's guts. They told him that if they even caught him lookin at any of the girls in school they'd bust his head open. They told him a couple of times, but all Lenny'd ever do was shake his head and say he didn't even like girls. He was such a coward. He wouldn't even admit he liked girls. Sometimes I wanted to bust his head too.

Anyway, I got to the bus stop and just sorta waved to Lenny but I went over and stood next to the girls. I didn't want no one to think I was queer for him or nothin. I like girls, but I'm not a stud like Buck or Terry, I guess. I figure with those guys around the girls didn't have much use for a guy like me. Buck and Terry are the toughest guys you ever seen. Buck's a hellified football player. Boy you shoulda seen how he played against Monroe Jr. Boy, he like to never stop runnin over them punks. He scored three touchdowns and he scored all the extra points. We beat the livin hell outa Monroe and just about everybody else we played. Terry's captain of the football team and also the quarterback, When he threw the ol pigskin the damn thing'd whistle.

Both these guys are always neck-and-neck for top scorer on the basketball team. And everybody at school says the baseball coach and the track coach, Mr. Deimus and Mr. Meno, are always fightin to get both of em on their teams. See, track and baseball go on at the same time. Girls fight over em too. They got all the chicks they can stand and they get away with just about anything they want at school. They're always pullin some crazy stuff in the cafeteria like puttin salt in somebody's milk or puttin ketchup on somebody's dessert, and stuff like that. Cracks me up. And you think anybody'd do anything about it? Hell no. Once Terry snatched my milk off my tray and drank it down in one gulp. Then he rubbed me on the head and said, "Now what you think a that, pencil neck?" I just looked at him with a mean-looking squint in my eyes, but real fakelike so he could tell I was just playin and wouldn't get mad, and I said, "Do that again, Terry, and I'll just have to buy you another one." Terry pinched me on the cheek and said, "I just bet you would, sweetheart." To be honest, I was a little pissed off by that cause Mom only gives us enough money for one milk a day, but it was pretty funny. At least I didn't say something like, "Duh, that's OK, Terry, I don't even like milk."

So, anyway, I set down on the bus and as usual ol black Lenny sets right down next to me. Boy goddam, I used to hate the way everybody'd hurry to crowd in them seats so they wouldn't have to set with him. And they all treated me like a leper cause I'd always end up settin next to him. Like it was my job or somethin. That's how I got to know Lenny so good. We'd talk all the way to school and we found out we liked a lot of the same things. After awhile, though, I got pretty tired of settin with the same guy all the time. Especially a colored guy. I tried to set next to ol Big Tim Long once, but he told me he had a real bad cold and that nobody could set next to him. At the next stop, though, Paul Bradford plunked right down next to Tim and Big Tim didn't say one word about havin no cold.

So Lenny sets next to me and right off he starts actin all stupid.

"Hi, Big Ears," he says.

"Oh, hi."

"Man, is it ever cold outside."

"Brilliant one, Sherlock."

"Hey, did you see that new guy sit on the girl's side?"

"Nope."

"Well, he sat next to Cindy Birdsong and she—"

"Everybody makes mistakes. Hey, Lenny, I sorta got this cold. Maybe you should set somewheres else. It's a pretty bad cold."

"A cold ain't gonna kill me, Ears." He was gettin on my nerves. I just couldn't stand to listen to him sometimes. His voice was always quiet like a sissy or somethin and he never cussed or called nobody down. Boy, he was nothin like Buck or Terry. When them guys cussed some fool, he stayed cussed. I remember once Buck called this ol Jewboy down so hard the son of a bitch cried like a baby. Sure, he coulda beat the living crap out of the boy, but when Buck cussed a guy out he didn't need no fisticuffs. This Jewboy, Martin Sharp, was trying to put the moves on Mary Chambeau, this seventh-grader who gots the biggest tits in school.

"What's this shit I hear about you trying to droop Mary Chambeau, Sharp?" Buck said to this guy in the locker room. Ol Sharp was standin there with nothin but his towel on him, and you know he wasn't lookin to fight nobody.

Buck's voice can crack like a whip. It's real deep. "What would she want with a Wiener schnitzel like you?" Sharp didn't say nothin. "You no-good, shit-for-breakfast, dog-lookin cockbite. You so much as look her way again and I'll knock you into next-goddam-week." Sharp's bottom lip started tremblin.

"She talked to me first," ol Jewboy says.

"I don't give a goddam if she proposed to you, Mr. Ziggy Heil. I don't wanna have to tell you twice."

"I don't have to do what you say, Buck."

Then Buck got real tight in Sharp's face, and both of em was all red and puffed up like they was ready to fight. Then Buck says real quiet like a guy in a movie, "If I have to tell you one more time, schnitzel-breath, I'll just rip off your head and yell down your fuckin lungs." And ol Jewboy starts tremblin like mad and tears start rollin down his cheeks. Buck just turns around, grins, and struts away. And you think ol Sharp talked to Mary Chambeau after that? But you gotta respect a guy like Sharp for at least standin up some to Buck. Lenny'd never even defend hisself when somebody cussed him. When I asked him why he was so nice to everybody he just gave me that stupid grin of his and says, "Well, you can't fight the whole world." Who's talkin about the whole world?

Well, like I was sayin, there I was, tryin to give him a shove outa my seat and hopefully outa my life, and all he says is, "I don't care if you got a cold. Besides, I don't get sick easy. And anyway, the only other seats are on the girl's side and I ain't sittin over there with them."

"Well why not?"

"You know why."

"Cause you're a faggot."

"You are if I am, elephant ears."

I almost decked him when he called me that. I didn't cause it really didn't bother me all that much if he did it when we wasn't around anyone else. Terry told me once that I shouldn't never let a nigger call me no names. Cept it really wasn't just a name. I mean, I really do have pretty big ears. Well, they really ain't all that big. Mom says my ears are prominent. Lenny's got real small ears and I used to call him Little Ears. Big Ears and Little Ears, that's what we'd call each other. A lot of guys at school call me Dumbo. Some girls too. I really don't like that at all, but Terry says they don't mean no harm. But when Lenny called me elephant ears I just got mad as hell and told him to shut up.

We rode along on the bus and everything was real quiet. Nobody said a word. Most people just stared real sleepylike out the windows. Frost was just sprayed all over the place. We passed by the orchard, and everything was all silvery. Even though all the trees in the orchard was fruit trees they all looked like Christmas trees in a way. With bulbs in all. Usually when it wasn't so cold you could smell the fruit and it made your mouth water even if you'd had a big breakfast. I remember when I first got here me and Lenny rode our bikes all the way out to the orchard. Boy, it's a hell of a long way out there by bike. There's a lot of hills out that way and by the time we got there we was beat as all get out.

We had a hell of a good time once we got out there. A hell of a pretty good time, anyway. It was funny, though, the way Lenny and me was hangin on the trees actin like monkeys. Lenny had a pear stuck in his teeth and he was makin monkey noises, hangin upside-down in that tree. I was whoopin and carryin on myself. I did have a peach in my mouth, but it was too green and tasted terrible. I got the idea to play Tarzan and I told Lenny he could be a native or a gorilla and I could fight him, but he said no. He said he didn't wanna be no damn native, cause in Tarzan movies natives always get the crap beat out em. Then he got sorta sad lookin. I felt sorry for him on account of what I said, but then he shouldn't be so damn sensitive.

He was lookin kinda hurt and sensitive when I told him to shut the hell up about my ears, but I was glad he was. I mean, I got tired of that son-of-a-bitch gettin all droopy and sad whenever you said two words about slaves or natives or how it's mainly niggers that brung crack and AIDS into the country and all that. But I guess I'd be embarrassed by all that too if I was colored. I looked at him out of the corner of my eye to see if he was mad at me. "Lenny," I says to him, "How's it feel bein the only colored guy in school?"

"I'm used to it," he said. "I don't really mind. It was like this when we were stationed in Nebraska. Besides . . . nobody really bothers me."

"Oh yeah? Well as for myself, I couldn't stand it."

"How come?"

"Cause I'd just want to be around my own kind." I was tryin to let him down easy. But he was too dumb to get my message. He just set there lookin out the window.

"Well," he said back, "what's so great about bein around your own kind?"

"I don't know. Cause you'd be a lot better off. Look, you're the only colored guy in the whole school. You can't have no girlfriends. The fellas wouldn't let you on none of the sports teams. Nobody sits by you at lunch. Hell, you don't even have a locker partner. Everybody calls you names, Lenny, and you let em. I myself couldn't stand it. I just couldn't stand it. If I was you I'd ask my folks to let me transfer to Washington over in downtown. I myself couldn't stand it, not being around my own kind."

He didn't say nothin for the longest time. He just set there and nodded his big black head. Then he looked up and stared me right in the eyes. He started talkin and his voice was real, real quiet. Quieter than I ever heard it. "So tell me something, Ears," he said. "How much goddam better off are you, man?" He said some more stuff, but I wasn't listenin. Couldn't stand that mousey voice of his no more.

The bus pulled up to the school and we got off. Everybody got off real zombielike. I hopped off the steps and walked away from Lenny as fast as I could. I tried to lose him in the crowd. I didn't run cause you can get in trouble for runnin on school grounds. But I was movin like a blue blaze and I figured I'd lost him. I stood in line and hoped I'd got my point across to him. But when I turned around, there he was standin right there behind me. I turned away real fast so no one could tell we was together, When I turned, though, I seen Buck's big, blond head way up to the front of the line. I thought he seen me too. I didn't want him to see me there next to Lenny. Lenny was standin there looking all dumb and niggery, and then he tapped me on the arm and said, "Well, only two more days of school and then it's Saturday, Ears." I didn't say nothin at first and then I turned around real fast and boy I let him have it.

"Why don't you quit followin me, dog."

He just looked at me and grinned. I guess he thought I was playin.

"Get the hell away from me," I said. "You always follow me around like a damn dog. Is that what you are, a damn, stupid dog? Ya dog." I had to say it loud enough so Buck could hear me. "Get away from me, dog. Ya act like a damn dog followin me around. Ya make me sick as hell."

I thought he was gonna hit me at first cause his eyes got real tight lookin, and for a second there I got a little scared. He had his fist all balled up and he looked like he wanted to kill me. Then he looked around him and all the people in line who heard me was howlin and barkin like dogs and laughin like a son of a bitch. Then Lenny's eyes got all sad and worried-lookin and I thought for sure he was gonna cry. But he just stood there, shakin like a leaf.

The bell rung and the line started movin for the door. I walked on but Lenny just stood there lookin stupid. I have to admit he did look pretty pitiful, like Jewboy Sharp. A few people were still makin dog noises at him, but he didn't do nothin. He just stood there, lookin down at his big feet. I guess everybody thought it was pretty funny. It was, in a way. When I got to the front door I turned around to see if I could see ol Lenny but he wasn't around nowhere. Then Buck come runnin up to me and slapped me on the shoulder. He was crackin up. "Damn, Dumbo," he said to me, "you sure did put that jig in his place, didn't you?"

"Yeah, I guess I did."

"You sure as hell did, Dumbo. I was pretty worried about you for awhile there, boy." He slapped me on the shoulder again and walked off into the buildin, lookin tough as all get out. I looked back to see ol Lenny, but he wasn't around. I tried like hell to be nice to him. I tried to shake him loose and not be too obvious about it. But Terry LaPort says you can't be too nice to them people. He said they got brains as small as golf balls inside skulls as hard as brick. I guess he's right.

Anyway, I felt pretty good about the whole thing. Cause even though I called him down and got him away from me for good, I think I was pretty decent about it. I mean, I didn't hit him or call him nigger which woulda really been hard on him.

He really would be better off with his own kind. Everybody is. Like me. I really ain't made no real friends yet, no friend-friends. But Buck and them says yo to me every now and then. They're pretty friendly when you get on their good side. I know them and me'll get real tight one day. Cause since I cussed out ol black Lenny, I'm gettin to be a hell of a lot more like the studs every day.

John Steinbeck (1902–1968) grew up in the agricultural area of California known as Salinas Valley, the setting for much of his writing. His work captures the needs, experiences, and strength of a range of characters, especially those of migrant workers, the poor, and social outcasts. Some of his most famous works include Tortilla Flat, Of Mice and Men, Cannery Row, *and* East of Eden.

The Chrysanthemums

John Steinbeck

The high gray-flannel fog of winter closed off the Salinas Valley from the sky and from all the rest of the world. On every side it sat like a lid on the mountains and made of the great valley a closed pot. On the broad, level land floor the gang plows bit deep and left the black earth shining like metal where the shares had cut. On the foothill ranches across the Salinas River, the yellow stubble fields seemed to be bathed in pale cold sunshine, but there was no sunshine in the valley now in December. The thick willow scrub along the river flamed with sharp and positive yellow leaves.

It was a time of quiet and of waiting. The air was cold and tender. A light wind blew up from the southwest so that the farmers were mildly hopeful of a good rain before long; but fog and rain do not go together.

Across the river, on Henry Allen's foothill ranch there was little work to be done, for the hay was cut and stored and the orchards were plowed up to receive the rain deeply when it should come. The cattle on the higher slopes were becoming shaggy and rough-coated.

Elisa Allen, working in her flower garden, looked down across the yard and saw Henry, her husband, talking to two men in business suits. The three of them stood by the tractor shed, each man with one foot on the side of the little Fordson. They smoked cigarettes and studied the machine as they talked.

Elisa watched them for a moment and then went back to her work. She was thirty-five. Her face was lean and strong and her eyes were as clear as water. Her figure looked blocked and heavy in her gardening costume, a man's black hat pulled down over her eyes, clodhopper shoes, a figured print dress almost completely covered by a big corduroy apron with four big pockets to hold the snips, the trowel and scratcher, the seeds and the knife she worked with. She wore heavy leather gloves to protect her hands while she worked.

She was cutting down the old year's chrysanthemum stalks with a pair of short and powerful scissors. She looked down toward the men by the tractor shed now and then. Her face was eager and mature and handsome; even her work with the scissors was over-eager, over-powerful. The chrysanthemum stems seemed too small and easy for her energy.

She brushed a cloud of hair out of her eyes with the back of her glove, and left a smudge of earth on her cheek in doing it. Behind her stood the neat white farm house with red geraniums close-banked around it as high as the windows. It was a hard-swept looking little house, with hard-polished windows, and a clean mud-mat on the front steps.

Elisa cast another glance toward the tractor shed. The strangers were getting into their Ford coupe. She took off a glove and put her strong fingers down into the forest of new green chrysanthemum sprouts that were growing around the old roots. She spread the leaves and looked down along the close-growing stems. No aphids were there, no sowbugs or snails or cutworms. Her terrier fingers destroyed such pests before they could get started.

Elisa started at the sound of her husband's voice. He had come near quietly, and he leaned over the wire fence that protected her flower garden from cattle and dogs and chickens.

"At it again," he said. "You've got a strong new crop coming."

Elisa straightened her back and pulled on the gardening glove again. "Yes. They'll be strong this coming year." In her tone and on her face there was a little smugness.

"You've got a gift with things," Henry observed. "Some of those yellow chrysanthemums you had this year were ten inches across. I wish you'd work out in the orchard and raise some apples that big."

Her eyes sharpened. "Maybe I could do it, too. I've a gift with things, all right. My mother had it. She could stick anything in the ground and make it grow. She said it was having planters hands that knew how to do it."

"Well, it sure works with flowers," he said.

"Henry, who were those men you were talking to?"

"Why, sure, that's what I came to tell you. They were from the Western Meat Company. I sold them those thirty head of three-year-old steers. Got nearly my own price, too."

"Good," she said. "Good for you."

"And I thought," he continued, "I thought how it's Saturday afternoon, and we might go into Salinas for dinner at a restaurant, and then to a picture show to celebrate, you see."

"Good," she repeated. "Oh, Yes. That will be good."

Henry put on his joking tone. "There's fights tonight. How'd you like to go to the fights?"

"Oh, no," she said breathlessly. "No; I wouldn't like fights."

"Just fooling, Elisa. We'll go to a movie. Let's see. It's two now. I'm going to take Scotty and bring down those steers from the hill. It'll take us maybe two hours. We'll go in town about five and have dinner at the Cominos Hotel. Like that?"

"Of course I'll like it. It's good to eat away from home."

"All right, then, I'll go get up a couple of horses."

She said, "I'll have plenty of time to transplant some of these sets, I guess."

She heard her husband calling Scotty down by the barn. And a little later she saw the two men ride up the pale yellow hillside in search of the steers.

There was a little square sandy bed kept for rooting the chrysanthemums. With her trowel she turned the soil over and over, and smoothed it and patted it firm. Then she dug ten parallel trenches to receive the sets. Back at the chrysanthemum bed she pulled out the little crisp shoots, trimmed off the leaves of each one with her scissors and laid it on a small orderly pile.

A squeak of wheels and plod of hoofs came from the road. Elisa looked up. The country road ran along the dense bank of willows and cottonwoods that bordered the river, and up this road came a curious vehicle, curiously drawn. It was an old spring-wagon, with a round canvas top on it like the cover of a prairie schooner. It was drawn by an old bay horse and a little gray-and-white burro. A big stubble-bearded man sat between the cover flaps and drove the crawling team. Underneath the wagon, between the hind wheels, a lean and rangy mongrel dog walked sedately. Words were painted on the canvas, in clumsy, crooked letters. "Pots, pans, knives, sisors, lawn mores, Fixed." Two rows of articles, and the triumphantly definitive "Fixed" below. The black paint had run down in little sharp points beneath each letter.

Elisa, squatting on the ground, watched to see the crazy, loose-jointed wagon pass by. But it didn't pass. It turned into the farm road in front of her house, crooked old wheels skirling and squeaking. The rangy dog darted from between the wheels and ran ahead. Instantly the two ranch shepherds flew out at him. Then all three stopped and with stiff and quivering tails, with taut straight legs, with ambassadorial dignity, they slowly circled, sniffing daintily. The caravan pulled up to Elisa's wire fence and stopped. Now the newcomer dog, feeling outnumbered, lowered his tail and retired under the wagon with raised hackles and bared teeth.

The man on the wagon seat called out, "That's a bad dog in a fight when he gets started."

Elisa laughed. "I see he is. How soon does he generally get started?"

The man caught up her laughter and echoed it heartily. "Sometimes not for weeks and weeks," he said. He climbed stiffly down, over the wheel. The horse and the donkey drooped like unwatered flowers.

Elisa saw that he was a very big man. Although his hair and beard were graying, he did not look old. His worn black suit was wrinkled and spotted with grease. The laughter had disappeared from his face and eyes the moment his laughing voice ceased. His eyes were dark, and they were full of the brooding that gets in the eyes of teamsters and of sailors. The calloused hands he rested on the wire fence were cracked, and every crack was a black line. He took off his battered hat.

"I'm off my general road, ma'am," he said. "Does this dirt road cut over across the river to the Los Angeles highway?"

Elisa stood up and shoved the thick scissors in her apron pocket. "Well, yes, it does, but it winds around and then fords the river. I don't think your team could pull through the sand."

He replied with some asperity, "It might surprise you what them beasts can pull through."

"When they get started?" she asked.

He smiled for a second. "Yes. When they get started."

"Well," said Elisa, "I think you'll save time if you go back to the Salinas road and pick up the highway there."

He drew a big finger down the chicken wire and made it sing. "I ain't in any hurry, ma'am. I go from Seattle to San Diego and back every year. Takes all my time. About six months each way. I aim to follow nice weather."

Elisa took off her gloves and stuffed them in the apron pocket with the scissors. She touched the under edge of her man's hat, searching for fugitive hairs. "That sounds like a nice kind of way to live," she said.

He leaned confidentially over the fence. "Maybe you noticed the writing on my wagon. I mend pots and sharpen knives and scissors. You got any of them things to do?"

"Oh, no," she said quickly. "Nothing like that." Her eyes hardened with resistance.

"Scissors is the worst thing," he explained. "Most people just ruin scissors trying to sharpen 'em, but I know how. I got a special tool. It's a little bobbit kind of thing, and patented. But it sure does the trick."

"No. My scissors are all sharp."

"All right, then. Take a pot," he continued earnestly, "a bent pot, or a pot with a hole. I can make it like new so you don't have to buy no new ones. That's a saving for you."

"No," she said shortly. "I tell you I have nothing like that for you to do."

His face fell to an exaggerated sadness. His voice took on a whining undertone. "I ain't had a thing to do today. Maybe I won't have no supper tonight. You see—I'm off my regular road. I know folks on the highway clear from Seattle to San Diego. They save their things for me to sharpen up because they know I do it so good and save them money."

"I'm sorry," Elisa said irritably. "I haven't anything for you to do."

His eyes left her face and fell to searching the ground. They roamed about until they came to the chrysanthemum bed where she had been working. "What's them plants, ma'am?"

The irritation and resistance melted from Elisa's face. "Oh, those are chrysanthemums, giant whites and yellows. I raise them every year, bigger than anybody around here."

"Kind of a long-stemmed flower? Looks like a quick puff of colored smoke?" he asked.

"That's it. What a nice way to describe them."

"They smell kind of nasty till you get used to them," he said.

"It's a good bitter smell," she retorted, "not nasty at all."

He changed his tone quickly. "I like the smell myself."

"I had ten-inch blooms this year," she said.

The man leaned farther over the fence. "Look. I know a lady down the road a piece, has got the nicest garden you ever seen. Got nearly every kind of flower but no chrysanthemums. Last time I was mending a copper-bottom washtub for her (that's a hard job but I do it good), she said to me, 'If you ever run acrost some nice chrysanthemums I wish you'd try to get me a few seeds.' That's what she told me."

Elisa's eyes grew alert and eager. "She couldn't have known much about chrysanthemums. You *can* raise them from seed, but it's much easier to root the little sprouts you see there."

"Oh," he said. "I s'pose I can't take none to her, then."

"Why yes you can," Elisa cried. "I can put some in damp sand, and you can carry them right along with you. They'll take root in the pot if you keep them damp. And then she can transplant them."

"She'd sure like to have some, ma'am. You say they're nice ones?"

"Beautiful," she said. "Oh, beautiful." Her eyes shone. She tore off the battered hat and shook out her dark pretty hair. "I'll put them in a flower pot, and you can take them right with you. Come into the yard."

While the man came through the picket gate Elisa ran excitedly along the geranium-bordered path to the back of the house. And she returned carrying a big red flower pot. The gloves were forgotten now. She kneeled on the ground by the starting bed and dug up the sandy soil with her fingers and scooped it into the bright new flower pot. Then she picked up the little pile of shoots she had prepared. With her strong fingers she pressed them into the sand and tamped around them with her knuckles. The man stood over her. "I'll tell you what to do," she said. "You remember so you can tell the lady."

"Yes, I'll try to remember."

"Well, look. These will take root in about a month. Then she must set them out, about a foot apart in good rich earth like this, see?" She lifted a handful of dark soil for him to took at. "They'll grow fast and tall. Now remember this: In July tell her to cut them down, about eight inches from the ground."

"Before they bloom?" he asked.

"Yes, before they bloom." Her face was tight with eagerness. "They'll grow right up again. About the last of September the buds will start."

She stopped and seemed perplexed. "It's the budding that takes the most care," she said hesitantly. "I don't know how to tell you." She looked deep into his eyes, searchingly. Her mouth opened a little, and she seemed to be listening. "I'll try to tell you," she said. "Did you ever hear of planting hands?"

"Can't say I have, ma'am."

"Well, I can only tell you what it feels like. It's when you're picking off the buds you don't want. Everything goes right down into your fingertips. You watch your fingers work. They do it themselves. You can feel how it is. They pick and pick the buds. They never make a mistake. They're with the plant. Do you see? Your fingers and the plant. You can feel that, right up your arm. They know. They never make a mistake. You can feel it. When you're like that you can't do anything wrong. Do you see that? Can you understand that?"

She was kneeling on the ground looking up at him. Her breast swelled passionately.

The man's eyes narrowed. He looked away self-consciously. "Maybe I know," he said. "Sometimes in the night in the wagon there—"

Elisa's voice grew husky. She broke in on him, "I've never lived as you do, but I know what you mean. When the night is dark—why, the stars are sharp-pointed, and there's quiet. Why, you rise up and up! Every pointed star gets driven into your body. It's like that. Hot and sharp and—lovely."

Kneeling there, her hand went out toward his legs in the greasy black trousers. Her hesitant fingers almost touched the cloth. Then her hand dropped to the ground. She crouched low like a fawning dog.

He said, "Its nice, just like you say. Only when you don't have no dinner, it ain't."

She stood up then, very straight, and her face was ashamed. She held the flower pot out to him and placed it gently in his arms. "Here. Put it in your wagon, on the seat, where you can watch it. Maybe I can find something for you to do."

At the back of the house she dug in the can pile and found two old and battered aluminum saucepans. She carried them back and gave them to him. "Here, maybe you can fix these."

His manner changed. He became professional. "Good as new I can fix them." At the back of his wagon he set a little anvil, and out of an oily tool box dug a small machine hammer. Elisa came through the gate to watch him while he pounded out the dents in the kettles. His mouth grew sure and knowing. At a difficult part of the work he sucked his underlip.

"You sleep right in the wagon?" Elisa asked.

"Right in the wagon, ma'am. Rain or shine I'm dry as a cow in there."

"It must be nice," she said. "It must be very nice. I wish women could do such things."

"It ain't the right kind of a life for a woman."

Her upper lip raised a little, showing her teeth. "How do you know? How can you tell?" she said.

"I don't know, ma'am," he protested. "Of course I don't know. Now here's your kettles, done. You don't have to buy no new ones."

"How much?"

"Oh, fifty cents'll do. I keep my prices down and my work good. That's why I have all them satisfied customers up and down the highway."

Elisa brought him a fifty-cent piece from the house and dropped it in his hand. "You might be surprised to have a rival some time. I can sharpen scissors, too. And I can beat the dents out of little pots. I could show you what a woman might do."

He put his hammer back in the oily box and shoved the little anvil out of sight. "It would be a lonely life for a woman, ma'am, and a scarey life, too, with animals creeping under the wagon all night." He climbed over the singletree, steadying himself with a hand on the burro's white rump. He settled himself in the seat, picked up the lines. "Thank you kindly, ma'am," he said. "I'll do like you told me; I'll go back and catch the Salinas road."

"Mind," she called, "if you're long in getting there, keep the sand damp."

"Sand, ma'am? . . . Sand? Oh, sure. You mean around the chrysanthemums. Sure I will." He clucked his tongue. The beasts leaned luxuriously into their collars. The mongrel dog took his place between the back wheels. The wagon turned and crawled out the entrance road and back the way it had come, along the river.

Elisa stood in front of her wire fence watching the slow progress of the caravan. Her shoulders were straight, her head thrown back, her eyes haft-closed, so that the scene came vaguely into them. Her lips moved silently, forming the words "Good-bye—good-bye." Then she whispered, "That's a bright direction. There's a glowing there." The sound of her whisper startled her. She shook herself free and looked about to see whether anyone had been listening. Only the dogs had heard. They lifted their heads toward her from their sleeping in the dust, and then stretched out their chins and settled asleep again. Elisa turned and ran hurriedly into the house.

In the kitchen she reached behind the stove and felt the water tank. It was full of hot water from the noonday cooking. In the bathroom she tore off her soiled clothes and flung them into the corner. And then she scrubbed herself with a little block of pumice, legs and thighs, loins and chest and arms, until her skin was scratched and red. When she had dried herself she stood in front of a mirror in her bedroom and looked at her body. She tightened her stomach and threw out her chest. She turned and looked over her shoulder at her back.

After a while she began to dress slowly. She put on her newest underclothing and her nicest stockings and the dress which was the symbol of her prettiness. She worked carefully on her hair, penciled her eyebrows and rouged her lips.

Before she was finished she heard the little thunder of hoofs and the shouts of Henry and his helper as they drove the red steers into the corral. She heard the gate bang shut and set herself for Henry's arrival.

His steps sounded on the porch. He entered the house calling, "Elisa, where are you?"

"In my room dressing. I'm not ready. There's hot water for your bath. Hurry up. It's getting late."

When she heard him splashing in the tub, Elisa laid his dark suit on the bed, and shirt and socks and tie beside it. She stood his polished shoes on the floor beside the bed. Then she went to the porch and sat primly and stiffly down. She looked toward the river road where the willow-line was still yellow with frosted leaves so that under the high gray fog they seemed a thin band of sunshine. This was the only color in the gray afternoon. She sat unmoved for a long time. Her eyes blinked rarely.

Henry came banging out of the door, shoving his tie inside his vest as he came. Elisa stiffened and her face grew tight. Henry stopped short and looked at her. "Why—why, Elisa. You look so nice!"

"Nice? You think I look nice? What do you mean by 'nice'?"

Henry blundered on. "I don't know. I mean you look different, strong and happy."

"I am strong? Yes, strong. What do you mean 'strong'?"

He looked bewildered. "You're playing some kind of a game," he said helplessly. "It's a kind of a play. You look strong enough to break a calf over your knee, happy enough to eat it like a watermelon."

For a second she lost her rigidity. "Henry! Don't talk like that. You didn't know what you said." She grew complete again. "I'm strong," she boasted. "I never knew before how strong."

Henry looked down toward the tractor shed, and when he brought his eyes back to her, they were his own again. "I'll get out the car. You can put on your coat while I'm starting."

Elisa went into the house. She heard him drive to the gate and idle down his motor, and then she took a long time to put on her hat. She pulled it here and pressed it there. When Henry turned the motor off she slipped into her coat and went out.

The little roadster bounced along on the dirt road by the river, raising the birds and driving rabbits into the brush. Two cranes flapped heavily over the willow-line and dropped into the riverbed.

Far ahead on the road Elisa saw a dark speck. She knew.

She tried not to look as they passed it, but her eyes would not obey. She whispered to herself sadly, "He might have thrown them off the road. That wouldn't have been much trouble, not very much. But he kept the pot," she explained. "He had to keep the pot. That's why he couldn't get them off the road."

The roadster turned a bend and she saw the caravan ahead. She swung full around her husband so she could not see the little covered wagon and the mismatched team as the car passed them.

In a moment it was over. The thing was done. She did not look back.

She said loudly, to be heard above the motor, "It will be good, tonight, a good dinner."

"Now you're changed again," Henry complained. He took one hand from the wheel and patted her knee. "I ought to take you in to dinner oftener. It would be good for both of us. We get so heavy out on the ranch."

"Henry," she asked, "could we have wine at dinner?"

"Sure we could. Say! That will be fine."

She was silent for a while; then she said, "Henry, at those prize fights, do the men hurt each other very much?"

"Sometimes a little, not often. Why?"

"Well, I've read how they break noses, and blood runs down their chests. I've read how the fighting gloves get heavy and soggy with blood."

He looked around at her. "What's the matter, Elisa? I didn't know you read things like that." He brought the car to a stop, then turned to the right over the Salinas River bridge.

"Do any women ever go to the fights ?" she asked.

"Oh, sure, some. What's the matter, Elisa? Do you want to go! I don't think you'd like it, but I'll take you if you really want to go."

She relaxed limply in the seat. "Oh, no. No. I don't want to go. I'm sure I don't." Her face was turned away from him. "It will be enough if we can have wine. It will be plenty." She turned up her coat collar so he could not see that she was crying weakly—like an old woman.

Isaac Babel (1894–1940) was born to a Jewish Russian family in Odessa, surviving a 1905 pogrom and overcoming quota restrictions on university entrance for Jewish students. His experiences in the 1st Cavalry Army in the Polish-Soviet War of 1920 form the basis of The Red Cavalry, *a short story collection that included "My First Goose." As his writings captured the horror and brutality of war and forced collectivization that he witnessed, he accumulated many enemies and was ultimately arrested, tortured, forced to confess to spying, and shot.*

My First Goose

Isaac Babel

Savitsky, Commander of the VI Division, rose when he saw me, and I wondered at the beauty of his giant's body. He rose, the purple of his riding breeches and the crimson of his little tilted cap and the decorations stuck on his chest cleaving the hut as a standard cleaves the sky. A smell of scent and the sickly sweet freshness of soap emanated from him. His long legs were like girls sheathed to the neck in shining riding boots.

He smiled at me, struck his riding whip on the table, and drew toward him an order that the Chief of Staff had just finished dictating. It was an order for Ivan Chesnokov to advance on Chugunov-Dobryvodka with the regiment entrusted to him, to make contact with the enemy and destroy the same.

"For which destruction," the Commander began to write, smearing the whole sheet, "I make this same Chesnokov entirely responsible, up to and including the supreme penalty, and will if necessary strike him down on the spot; which you, Chesnokov, who have been working with me at the front for some months now, cannot doubt."

The Commander signed the order with a flourish, tossed it to his orderlies and turned upon me gray eyes that danced with merriment.

I handed him a paper with my appointment to the Staff of the Division.

"Put it down in the Order of the Day," said the Commander. "Put him down for every satisfaction save the front one. Can you read and write?"

"Yes, I can read and write," I replied, envying the flower and iron of that youthfulness. "I graduated in law from St. Petersburg University."

"Oh, are you one of those grinds?" he laughed. "Specs on your nose, too! What a nasty little object! They've sent you along without making any enquiries; and this is a hot place for specs. Think you'll get on with us?"

"I'll get on all right," I answered, and went off to the village with the quartermaster to find a billet for the night.

The quartermaster carried my trunk on his shoulder. Before us stretched the village street. The dying sun, round and yellow as a pumpkin, was giving up its roseate ghost to the skies.

We went up to a hut painted over with garlands. The quartermaster stopped, and said suddenly, with a guilty smile:

"Nuisance with specs. Can't do anything to stop it, either. Not a life for the brainy type here. But you go and mess up a lady, and a good lady too, and you'll have the boys patting you on the back."

He hesitated, my little trunk on his shoulder; then he came quite close to me, only to dart away again despairingly and run to the nearest yard. Cossacks were sitting there, shaving one another.

"Here, you soldiers," said the quartermaster, setting my little trunk down on the ground. "Comrade Savitsky's orders are that you're to take this chap in your billets, so no nonsense about it, because the chap's been through a lot in the learning line."

The quartermaster, purple in the face, left us without looking back. I raised my hand to my cap and saluted the Cossacks. A lad with long straight flaxen hair and the handsome face of the Ryazan Cossacks went over to my little trunk and tossed it out at the gate. Then he turned his back on me and with remarkable skill emitted a series of shameful noises.

"To your guns—number double-zero!" an older Cossack shouted at him and burst out laughing. "Running fire!"

His guileless art exhausted, the lad made off. Then, crawling over the ground, I began to gather together the manuscripts and tattered garments that had fallen out of the trunk. I gathered them up and carried them to the other end of the yard. Near the hut, on a brick stove, stood a cauldron in which pork was cooking. The steam that rose from it was like the far-off smoke of home in the village, and it mingled hunger with desperate loneliness in my head. Then I covered my little broken trunk with hay, turning it into a pillow, and lay down on the ground to read in *Pravda* Lenin's speech at the Second Congress of the Comintern. The sun fell upon me from behind the toothed hillocks, the Cossacks trod on my feet, the lad made fun of me untiringly, the beloved lines came toward me along a thorny path and could not reach me. Then I put aside the paper and went out to the landlady, who was spinning on the porch.

"Landlady," I said, "I've got to eat."

The old woman raised to me the diffused whites of her purblind eyes and lowered them again.

"Comrade," she said, after a pause, "what with all this going on, I want to go and hang myself."

"Christ!" I muttered, and pushed the old woman in the chest with my fist. "You don't suppose I'm going to go into explanations with you, do you?"

And turning around I saw somebody's sword lying within reach. A severe-looking goose was waddling about the yard, inoffensively preening its feathers. I overtook it and pressed it to the ground. Its head cracked beneath my boot, cracked and emptied itself. The white neck lay stretched out in the dung, the wings twitched.

"Christ!" I said, digging into the goose with my sword. "Go and cook it for me, landlady."

Her blind eyes and glasses glistening the old woman picked up the slaughtered bird, wrapped it in her apron, and started to bear it off toward the kitchen.

"Comrade," she said to me, after a while, "I want to go and hang myself." And she closed the door behind her.

The Cossacks in the yard were already sitting around their cauldron. They sat motionless, stiff as heathen priests at a sacrifice, and had not looked at the goose.

"The lad's all right," one of them said, winking and scooping up the cabbage soup with his spoon.

The Cossacks commenced their supper with all the elegance and restraint of peasants who respect one another. And I wiped the sword with sand, went out at the gate, and came in again, depressed. Already the moon hung above the yard like a cheap earring.

"Hey, you," suddenly said Surovkov, an older Cossack. "Sit down and feed with us till your goose is done."

He produced a spare spoon from his boot and handed it to me. We supped up the cabbage soup they had made, and ate the pork.

"What's in the newspaper?" asked the flaxen-haired lad, making room for me.

"Lenin writes in the paper," I said, pulling out *Pravda*. "Lenin writes that there's a shortage of everything."

And loudly, like a triumphant man hard of hearing, I read Lenin's speech out to the Cossacks.

Evening wrapped about me the quickening moisture of its twilight sheets; evening laid a mother's hand upon my burning forehead. I read on and rejoiced, spying out exultingly the secret curve of Lenin's straight line.

"Truth tickles everyone's nostrils," said Surovkov, when I had come to the end. "The question is, how's it to be pulled from the heap. But he goes and strikes at it straight off like a hen pecking at a grain!"

This remark about Lenin was made by Surovkov, platoon commander of the Staff Squadron; after which we lay down to sleep in the hayloft. We slept, all six of us, beneath a wooden roof that let in the stars, warming one another, our legs intermingled. I dreamed: and in my dreams saw women. But my heart, stained with bloodshed, grated and brimmed over.

*F*lannery O'Connor (1925–1964) was born in Savannah, Georgia, and began her college education at the Georgia State College for Women. She earned an MFA from the University of Iowa. "Everything That Rises Must Converge" was published in 1965, the title story of her second short story collection.

Everything That Rises Must Converge

Flannery O'Connor

Her doctor had told Julian's mother that she must lose twenty pounds on account of her blood pressure, so on Wednesday nights Julian had to take her downtown on the bus for a reducing class at the Y. The reducing class was designed for working girls over fifty, who weighed from 165 to 200 pounds. His mother was one of the slimmer ones, but she said ladies did not tell their age or weight. She would not ride the buses by herself at night since they had been integrated, and because the reducing class was one of her few pleasures, necessary for her health, and *free*, she said Julian could at least put himself out to take her, considering all she did for him. Julian did not like to consider all she did for him, but every Wednesday night he braced himself and took her.

She was almost ready to go, standing before the hall mirror, putting on her hat, while he, his hands behind him, appeared pinned to the door frame, waiting like Saint Sebastian for the arrows to begin piercing him. The hat was new and had cost her seven dollars and a half. She kept saying, "Maybe I shouldn't have paid that for it. No, I shouldn't have. I'll take it off and return it tomorrow. I shouldn't have bought it."

Julian raised his eyes to heaven. "Yes, you should have bought it," he said. "Put it on and let's go." It was a hideous hat. A purple velvet flap came down on one side of it and stood up on the other; the rest of it was green and looked like a cushion with the stuffing out. He decided it was less comical than jaunty and pathetic. Everything that gave her pleasure was small and depressed him.

She lifted the hat one more time and set it down slowly on top of her head. Two wings of gray hair protruded on either side of her florid face, but her eyes, sky-blue, were as innocent and untouched by experience as they must have been when she was ten. Were it not that she was a widow who had struggled fiercely to feed and clothe and put him through school and who was supporting him still, "until he got on his feet," she might have been a little girl that he had to take to town. "It's all right, it's all right," he said. "Let's go." He opened door himself and started down the walk to get her going. The sky was a dying violet and the houses stood out darkly against it, bulbous liver-colored monstrosities of a uniform ugliness though no two were alike. Since this had been a fashionable neighborhood forty years ago, his mother persisted in thinking they did well to have an apartment in it. Each house had a narrow collar of dirt around it in which sat, usually, a grubby child. Julian walked with his hands in his pockets, his head down and thrust forward and his eyes glazed with the determination to make himself completely numb during the time he would be sacrificed to her pleasure.

The door closed and he turned to find the dumpy figure, surmounted by the atrocious hat, coming toward him. "Well," she said, "you only live once and paying a little more for it, I at least won't meet myself coming and going."

"Some day I'll start making money," Julian said gloomily—he knew he never would—"and you can have one of those jokes whenever you take the fit." But first they would move. He visualized a place where the nearest neighbors would be three miles away on either side.

"I think you're doing fine," she said, drawing on her gloves. "You've only been out of school a year. Rome wasn't built in a day."

She was one of the few members of the Y reducing class who arrived in hat and gloves and who had a son who had been to college. "It takes time," she said, "and the world is in such a mess. This hat looked better on me than any of the others, though when she brought it out I said, 'Take that thing back. I wouldn't have it on my head,' and she said, 'Now wait till you see it on,' and when she put it on me, I said, 'We-ull,' and she said, 'If you ask me, that hat does something for you and you do something for the hat, and besides,' she said, 'with that hat, you won't meet yourself coming and going.'"

Julian thought he could have stood his lot better if she had been self-ish, if she had been an old hag who drank and screamed at him. He walked along, saturated in depression, as if in the midst of his martyr-dom he had lost his faith. Catching sight of his long, hopeless, irritated face, she stopped suddenly with a grief-stricken look, and pulled back on his arm. "Wait on me," she said. "I'm going back to the house and take this thing off and tomorrow I'm going to return it. I was out of my head. I can pay the gas bill with that seven-fifty."

He caught her arm in a vicious grip. "You are not going to take it back," he said. "I like it."

"Well," she said, "I don't think I ought . . ."

"Shut up and enjoy it," he muttered, more depressed than ever.

"With the world in the mess it's in," she said, "it's a wonder we can enjoy anything. I tell you, the bottom rail is on the top."

Julian sighed.

"Of course," she said, "if you know who you are, you can go any-where." She said this every time he took her to the reducing class. "Most of them in it are not our kind of people," she said, "but I can be gracious to anybody. I know who I am."

"They don't give a damn for your graciousness," Julian said savagely. "Knowing who you are is good for one generation only. You haven't the foggiest idea where you stand now or who you are."

She stopped and allowed her eyes to flash at him. "I most certainly do know who I am," she said, "and if you don't know who you are, I'm ashamed of you."

"Oh hell," Julian said.

"Your great-grandfather was a former governor of this state," she said. "Your grandfather was a prosperous land-owner. Your grandmother was a Godhigh."

"Will you look around you," he said tensely, "and see where you are now?" and he swept his arm jerkily out to indicate the neighborhood, which the growing darkness at least made less dingy.

"You remain what you are," she said. "Your great-grand-father had a plantation and two hundred slaves."

"There are no more slaves," he said irritably.

"They were better off when they were," she said. He groaned to see that she was off on that topic. She rolled onto it every few days like a train on an open track. He knew every stop, every junction, every swamp along the way, and knew the exact point at which her conclusion would roil majestically into the station: "It's ridiculous. It's simply not realistic. They should rise, yes, but on their own side of the fence."

"Let's skip it," Julian said.

"The ones I feel sorry for," she said, "are the ones that are half white. They're tragic."

"Will you skip it?"

"Suppose we were half white. We would certainly have mixed feelings."

"I have mixed feelings now," he groaned.

"Well let's talk about something pleasant," she said. "I remember going to Grandpa's when I was a little girl. Then the house had double stairways that went up to what was really the second floor—all the cooking was done on the first. I used to like to stay down in the kitchen on account of the way the walls smelled. I would sit with my nose pressed against the plaster and take deep breaths. Actually the place belonged to the Godhighs but your grandfather Chestny paid the mortgage and saved it for them. They were in reduced circumstances," she said, "but reduced or not, they never forgot who they were."

"Doubtless that decayed mansion reminded them," Julian muttered. He never spoke of it without contempt or thought of it without longing. He had seen it once when he was a child before it had been sold. The double stairways had rotted and been torn down. Negroes were living in it. But it remained in his mind as his mother had known it. It appeared in his dreams regularly. He would stand on the wide porch, listening to the rustle of oak leaves, then wander through the high-ceilinged hall into the parlor that opened onto it and gaze at the worn rugs and faded draperies. It occurred to him that it was he, not she, who could have appreciated it. He preferred its threadbare elegance to anything he could name and it was because of it that all the neighborhoods they had lived in had been a torment to him—whereas she had hardly known the difference. She called her insensitivity "being adjustable."

"And I remember the old darky who was my nurse, Caroline. There was no better person in the world. I've always had a great respect for my colored friends," she said. "I'd do anything in the world for them and they'd . . ."

"Will you for God's sake get off that subject?" Julian said. When he got on a bus by himself, he made it a point to sit down beside a Negro, in reparation as it were for his mother's sins.

"You're mighty touchy tonight," she said. "Do you feel all right?"

"Yes I feel all right" he said. "Now lay off."

She pursed her lips. "Well, you certainly are in a vile humor," she observed "I just won't speak to you at all."

They had reached the bus stop. There was no bus in sight and Julian, his hands still jammed in his pockets and his head thrust forward, scowled down the empty street. The frustration of having to wait on the bus as well as ride on it began to creep up his neck like a hot hand. The presence of his mother was borne in upon him as she gave a pained sigh. He looked at her bleakly. She was holding herself very erect under the preposterous hat wearing it like a banner of her imaginary dignity. There was in him an evil urge to break her spirit. He suddenly unloosened his tie and pulled it off and put it in his pocket

She stiffened. "Why must you look like *that* when you take me to town?" she said. "Why must you deliberately embarrass me?"

"If you'll never learn where you are," he said, "you can at least learn where I am."

"You look like a thug," she said.

"Then I must be one" he murmured.

"I'll just go home" she said. "I will not bother you. If you can't do a little thing' like that for me . . ."

Rolling his eyes upward, he put his tie back on. "Restored to my class," he muttered. He thrust his face toward her and hissed, "True culture is in the mind, the *mind*," he said, and tapped his head, "the mind."

"It's in the heart," she said, "and in how you do things and how you do things is because of who you *are.*"

"Nobody in the damn bus cares who you are."

"I care who I am" she said icily.

The lighted bus appeared on top of the next hill and as it approached, they moved out into the street to meet it. He put his hand under her elbow and hoisted her up on the creaking step. She entered with a little smile, as if she were going into a drawing room where everyone had been waiting for her. While he put in the tokens, she sat down on one of the broad front seats for three which faced the aisle. A thin woman with protruding teeth and long yellow hair was sitting on the end of it. His mother moved up beside her and left room for Julian beside herself. He sat down and looked at the floor across the aisle where a pair of thin feet in red and white canvas sandals were planted.

His mother immediately began a general conversation meant to attract anyone who felt like talking. "Can it get any hotter?" she said and removed from her purse a folding fan, black with a Japanese scene on it, which she began to flutter before her.

"I reckon it might could," the woman with the protruding teeth said, "but I know for a fact my apartment couldn't get no hotter."

"It must get the afternoon sun, " his mother said. She sat forward and looked up and down the bus. It was half filled. Everybody was white. "I see we have the bus to ourselves," she said. Julian cringed.

"For a change," said the woman across the aisle, the owner of the red and white canvas sandals. "I come on one the other day and they were thick as fleas—up front and all through."

"The world is in a mess everywhere," his mother said. "I don't know how we've let it get in this fix."

"What gets my goat is all those boys from good families stealing automobile tires," the woman with the protruding teeth said. "I told my boy, I said you may not be rich but you been raised right and if I ever catch you in any such mess, they can send you on to the reformatory. Be exactly where you belong."

"Training tells," his mother said. "Is your boy in high school?"

"Ninth grade," the woman said.

"My son just finished college last year. He wants to write but he's selling typewriters until he gets started," his mother said.

The woman leaned forward and peered at Julian. He threw her such a malevolent look that she subsided against the seat. On the floor across the aisle there was an abandoned newspaper. He got up and got it and opened it out in front of him. His mother discreetly continued the conversation in a lower tone but the woman across the aisle said in a loud voice, "Well that's nice. Selling typewriters is close to writing. He can go right from one to the other."

"I tell him," his mother said, "that Rome wasn't built in a day."

Behind the newspaper Julian was withdrawing into the inner compartment of his mind where he spent most of his time. This was a kind of mental bubble in which he established himself when he could not bear to be a part of what was going on around him. From it he could see out and judge but in it he was safe from any kind of penetration from without. It was the only place where he felt free of the general idiocy of his fellows.

His mother had never entered it but from it he could see her with absolute clarity.

The old lady was clever enough and he thought that if she had started from any of the right premises, more might have been expected of her. She lived according to the laws of her own fantasy world outside of which he had never seen her set foot. The law of it was to sacrifice herself for him after she had first created the necessity to do so by making a mess of things. If he had permitted her sacrifices, it was only because her lack of foresight had made them necessary. All of her life had been a struggle to act like a Chestny and to give him everything she thought a Chestny ought to have without the goods a Chestny ought to have; but since, said she, it was fun to struggle, why complain? And when you had won, as she had won, what fun to look back on the hard times! He could not forgive her that she had enjoyed the struggle and that she thought *she* had won.

What she meant when she said she had won was that she had brought him up successfully and had sent him to college and that he had turned out so well—good looking (her teeth had gone unfilled so that his could be straightened), intelligent (he realized he was too intelligent to be a success), and with a future ahead of him (there was of course no future ahead of him). She excused his gloominess on the grounds that he was still growing up and his radical ideas on his lack of practical experience. She said he didn't yet know a thing about "life," that he hadn't even entered the real world—when already he was as disenchanted with it as a man of fifty.

The further irony of all this was that in spite of her, he had turned out so well. In spite of going to only a third-rate college, he had, on his own initiative, come out with a first-rate education; in spite of growing up dominated by a small mind, he had ended up with a large one; in spite of all her foolish views, he was free of prejudice and unafraid to face facts. Most miraculous of all, instead of being blinded by love for her as she was for him, he had cut himself emotionally free of her and could see her with complete objectivity. He was not dominated by his mother.

The bus stopped with a sudden jerk and shook him from his meditation. A woman from the back lurched forward with little steps and barely escaped falling in his newspaper as she righted herself. She got off and a large Negro got on. Julian kept his paper lowered to watch. It gave him a certain satisfaction to see injustice in daily operation. It confirmed his view that with a few exceptions there was no one worth knowing within a radius of three hundred miles. The Negro was well dressed and carried a briefcase. He looked around and then sat down on the other end of the seat where the woman with the red and white canvas sandals was sitting. He immediately unfolded a newspaper and obscured himself behind it. Julian's mother's elbow at once prodded insistently into his ribs. "Now you see why I won't ride on these buses by myself," she whispered.

The woman with the red and white canvas sandals had risen at the same time the Negro sat down and had gone farther back in the bus and taken the seat of the woman who had got off. His mother leaned forward and cast her an approving look.

Julian rose, crossed the aisle, and sat down in the place of the woman with the canvas sandals. From this position, he looked serenely across at his mother. Her face had turned an angry red. He stared at her, making his eyes the eyes of a stranger. He felt his tension suddenly lift as if he had openly declared war on her.

He would have liked to get in conversation with the Negro and to talk with him about art or politics or any subject that would be above the comprehension of those around them, but the man remained entrenched behind his paper. He was either ignoring the change of seating or had never noticed it. There was no way for Julian to convey his sympathy.

His mother kept her eyes fixed reproachfully on his face. The woman with the protruding teeth was looking at him avidly as if he were a type of monster new to her.

"Do you have a light?" he asked the Negro.

Without looking away from his paper, the man reached in his pocket and handed him a packet of matches.

"Thanks," Julian said. For a moment he held the matches foolishly. A **NO SMOKING** sign looked down upon him from over the door. This alone would not have deterred him; he had no cigarettes. He had quit smoking some months before because he could not afford it. "Sorry," he muttered and handed back the matches. The Negro lowered the paper and gave him an annoyed look. He took the matches and raised the paper again.

His mother continued to gaze at him but she did not take advantage of his momentary discomfort. Her eyes retained their battered look. Her face seemed to be unnaturally red, as if her blood pressure had risen. Julian allowed no glimmer of sympathy to show on his face. Having got the advantage, he wanted desperately to keep it and carry it through. He would have liked to teach her a lesson that would last her a while, but there seemed no way to continue the point. The Negro refused to come out from behind his paper.

Julian folded his arms and looked stolidly before him, facing her but as if he did not see her, as if he had ceased to recognize her existence. He visualized a scene in which, the bus having reached their stop, he would remain in his seat and when she said, "Aren't you going to get off?" he would look at her as at a stranger who had rashly addressed him. The corner they got off on was usually deserted, but it was well lighted and it would not hurt her to walk by herself the four blocks to the Y. He decided to wait until the time came and then decide whether or not he would let her get off by herself. He would have to be at the Y at ten to bring her back, but he could leave her wondering if he was going to show up. There was no reason for her to think she could always depend on him.

He retired again into the high-ceilinged room sparsely settled with large pieces of antique furniture. His soul expanded momentarily but then he became aware of his mother across from him and the vision shriveled. He studied her coldly. Her feet in little pumps dangled like a child's and did not quite reach the floor. She was training on him an exaggerated look of reproach. He felt completely detached from her. At that moment he could with pleasure have slapped her as he would have slapped a particularly obnoxious child in his charge.

He began to imagine various unlikely ways by which he could teach her a lesson. He might make friends with some distinguished Negro professor or lawyer and bring him home to spend the evening. He would be entirely justified but her blood pressure would rise to 300. He could not push her to the extent of making her have a stroke, and moreover, he had never been successful at making any Negro friends. He had tried to strike up an acquaintance on the bus with some of the better types, with ones that looked like professors or ministers or lawyers. One morning he had sat down next to a distinguished-looking dark brown man who had answered his questions with a sonorous solemnity but who had turned out to be an undertaker. Another day he had sat down beside a cigar-smoking Negro with a diamond ring on his finger, but after a few stilted pleasantries, the Negro had rung the buzzer and risen, slipping two lottery tickets into Julian's hand as he climbed over him to leave.

He imagined his mother lying desperately ill and his being able to secure only a Negro doctor for her. He toyed with that idea for a few minutes and then dropped it for a momentary vision of himself participating as a sympathizer in a sit-in demonstration. This was possible but he did not linger with it. Instead, he approached the ultimate horror. He brought home a beautiful suspiciously Negroid woman. Prepare yourself, he said. There is nothing you can do about it. This is the woman I've chosen. She's intelligent, dignified, even good, and she's suffered and she hasn't thought it *fun*. Now persecute us, go ahead and persecute us. Drive her out of here, but remember, you're driving me too. His eyes were narrowed and through the indignation he had generated, he saw his mother across the aisle, purple-faced, shrunken to the dwarf-like proportions of her moral nature, sitting like a mummy beneath the ridiculous banner of her hat.

He was tilted out of his fantasy again as the bus stopped. The door opened with a sucking hiss and out of the dark a large, gaily dressed, sullen-looking colored woman got on with a little boy. The child, who might have been four, had on a short plaid suit and a Tyrolean hat with a blue feather in it. Julian hoped that he would sit down beside him and that the woman would push in beside his mother. He could think of no better arrangement.

As she waited for her tokens, the woman was surveying the seating possibilities—he hoped with the idea of sitting where she was least wanted. There was something familiar-looking about her but Julian could not place what it was. She was a giant of a woman. Her face was set not only to meet opposition but to seek it out. The downward tilt of her large lower lip was like a warning sign: DON'T TAMPER WITH ME. Her bulging figure was encased in a green crepe dress and her feet overflowed in red shoes. She had on a hideous hat. A purple velvet flap came down on one side of it and stood up on the other; the rest of it was green and looked like a cushion with the stuffing out. She carried a mammoth red pocketbook that bulged throughout as if it were stuffed with rocks.

To Julian's disappointment, the little boy climbed up on the empty seat beside his mother. His mother lumped all children, black and white, into the common category, "cute," and she thought little Negroes were on the whole cuter than little white children. She smiled at the little boy as he climbed on the seat.

Meanwhile the woman was bearing down upon the empty seat beside Julian. To his annoyance, she squeezed herself into it. He saw his mother's face change as the woman settled herself next to him and he realized with satisfaction that this was more objectionable to her than it was to him. Her face seemed almost gray and there was a look of dull recognition in her eyes, as if suddenly she had sickened at some awful confrontation. Julian saw that it was because she and the woman had, in a sense, swapped sons. Though his mother would not realize the symbolic significance of this, she would feel it. His amusement showed plainly on his face.

The woman next to him muttered something unintelligible to herself. He was conscious of a kind of bristling next to him, a muted growling like that of an angry cat. He could not see anything but the red pocketbook upright on the bulging green thighs. He visualized the woman as she had stood waiting for her tokens—the ponderous figure, rising from the red shoes upward over the solid hips, the mammoth bosom, the haughty face, to the green and purple hat.

His eyes widened.

The vision of the two hats, identical, broke upon him with the radiance of a brilliant sunrise. His face was suddenly lit with joy. He could not believe that Fate had thrust upon his mother such a lesson. He gave a loud chuckle so that she would look at him and see that he saw. She turned her eyes on him slowly. The blue in them seemed to have turned a bruised purple. For a moment he had an uncomfortable sense of her innocence, but it lasted only a second before principle rescued him. Justice entitled him to laugh. His grin hardened until it said to her as plainly as if he were saying aloud: Your punishment exactly fits your pettiness. This should teach you a permanent lesson.

Her eyes shifted to the woman. She seemed unable to bear looking at him and to find the woman preferable. He became conscious again of the bristling presence at his side. The woman was rumbling like a volcano about to become active. His mother's mouth began to twitch slightly at one corner. With a sinking heart, he saw incipient signs of recovery on her face and realized that this was going to strike her suddenly as funny and was going to be no lesson at all. She kept her eyes on the woman and an amused smile came over her face as if the woman were a monkey that had stolen her hat. The little Negro was looking up at her with large fascinated eyes. He had been trying to attract her attention for some time.

"Carver!" the woman said suddenly. "Come heah!"

When he saw that the spotlight was on him at last, Carver drew his feet up and turned himself toward Julian's mother and giggled.

"Carver!" the woman said. "You heah me? Come heah!"

Carver slid down from the seat but remained squatting with his back against the base of it, his head turned slyly around toward Julian's mother, who was smiling at him. The woman reached a hand across the aisle and snatched him to her. He righted himself and hung backwards on her knees, grinning at Julian's mother. "Isn't he cute?" Julian's mother said to the woman with the protruding teeth.

"I reckon he is," the woman said without conviction.

The Negress yanked him upright but he eased out of her grip and shot across the aisle and scrambled, giggling wildly, onto the seat beside his love.

"I think he likes me," Julian's mother said, and smiled at the woman. It was the smile she used when she was being particularly gracious to an inferior. Julian saw everything lost. The lesson had rolled off her like rain on a roof.

The woman stood up and yanked the little boy off the seat as if she were snatching him from contagion. Julian could feel the rage in her at having no weapon like his mother's smile. She gave the child a sharp slap across his leg. He howled once and then thrust his head into her stomach and kicked his feet against her shins. "Be–have," she said vehemently.

The bus stopped and the Negro who had been reading the newspaper got off. The woman moved over and set the little boy down with a thump between herself and Julian. She held him firmly by the knee. In a moment he put his hands in front of his face and peeped at Julian's mother through his fingers.

"I see yoooooooo!" she said and put her hand in front of her face and peeped at him.

The woman slapped his hand down. "Quit yo' foolishness," she said, "before I knock the living Jesus out of you!"

Julian was thankful that the next stop was theirs. He reached up and pulled the cord. The woman reached up and pulled it at the same time. Oh my God, he thought. He had the terrible intuition that when they got off the bus together, his mother would open her purse and give the little boy a nickel. The gesture would be as natural to her as breathing. The bus stopped and the woman got up and lunged to the front, dragging the child, who wished to stay on, after her. Julian and his mother got up and followed. As they neared the door, Julian tried to relieve her of her pocketbook.

"No," she murmured, "I want to give the little boy a nickel."

"No!" Julian hissed. "No!"

She smiled down at the child and opened her bag. The bus door opened and the woman picked him up by the arm and descended with him, hanging at her hip. Once in the street she set him down and shook him.

Julian's mother had to close her purse while she got down the bus step but as soon as her feet were on the ground, she opened it again and began to rummage inside. "I can't find but a penny," she whispered, "but it looks like a new one."

"Don't do it!" Julian said fiercely between his teeth. There was a streetlight on the corner and she hurried to get under it so that she could better see into her pocketbook. The woman was heading off rapidly down the street with the child still hanging backward on her hand.

"Oh little boy!" Julian's mother called and took a few quick steps and caught up with them just beyond the lamppost. "Here's a bright new penny for you," and she held out the coin, which shone bronze in the dim light.

The huge woman turned and for a moment stood, her shoulders lifted and her face frozen with frustrated rage, and stared at Julian's mother. Then all at once she seemed to explode like a piece of machinery that had been given one ounce of pressure too much. Julian saw the black fist swing out with the red pocketbook. He shut his eyes and cringed as he heard the woman shout, "He don't take nobody's pennies!" When he opened his eyes, the woman was disappearing down the street with the little boy staring wide-eyed over her shoulder. Julian's mother was sitting on the sidewalk.

"I told you not to do that," Julian said angrily. "I told you not to do that!"

He stood over her for a minute, gritting his teeth. Her legs were stretched out in front of her and her hat was on her lap. He squatted down and looked her in the face. It was totally expressionless. "You got exactly what you deserved," he said. "Now get up."

He picked up her pocketbook and put what had fallen out back in it. He picked the hat up off her lap. The penny caught his eye on the sidewalk and he picked that up and let it drop before her eyes into the purse. Then he stood up and leaned over and held his hands out to pull her up. She remained immobile. He sighed. Rising above them on either side were black apartment buildings, marked with irregular rectangles of light. At the end of the block a man came out of a door and walked off in the opposite direction. "All right," he said, "suppose somebody happens by and wants to know why you're sitting on the sidewalk?"

She took the hand and, breathing hard, pulled heavily up on it and then stood for a moment, swaying slightly as if the spots of light in the darkness were circling around her. Her eyes, shadowed and confused, finally settled on his face. He did not try to conceal his irritation. "I hope this teaches you a lesson," he said. She leaned forward and her eyes raked his face. She seemed to be trying to determine his identity. Then, as if she found nothing familiar about him, she started off with a headlong movement in the wrong direction.

"Aren't you going on to the Y?" he asked.

"Home," she muttered.

"Well, are we walking?"

For answer she kept going. Julian followed along, his hands behind him. He saw no reason to let the lesson she had had go without backing it up with an explanation of its meaning. She might as well be made to understand what had happened to her. "Don't think that was just an uppity Negro woman," he said. "That was the whole colored race which will no longer take your condescending pennies. That was your black double. She can wear the same hat as you, and to be sure," he added gratuitously (because he thought it was funny), "it looked better on her than it did on you. What all this means," he said, "is that the old world is gone. The old manners are obsolete and your graciousness is not worth a damn." He thought bitterly of the house that had been lost for him. "You aren't who you think you are," he said.

She continued to plow ahead, paying no attention to him. Her hair had come undone on one side. She dropped her pocketbook and took no notice. He stooped and picked it up and handed it to her but she did not take it.

"You needn't act as if the world had come to an end," he said, "because it hasn't. From now on you've got to live in a new world and face a few realities for a change. Buck up," he said, "it won't kill you."

She was breathing fast.

"Let's wait on the bus," he said.

"Home," she said thickly.

"I hate to see you behave like this," he said. "Just like a child. I should be able to expect more of you." He decided to stop where he was and make her stop and wait for a bus. "I'm not going any farther," he said, stopping. "We're going on the bus."

She continued to go on as if she had not heard him. He took a few steps and caught her arm and stopped her. He looked into her face and caught his breath. He was looking into a face he had never seen before. "Tell Grandpa to come get me," she said.

He stared, stricken.

"Tell Caroline to come get me," she said.

Stunned, he let her go and she lurched forward again, walking as if one leg were shorter than the other. A tide of darkness seemed to be sweeping her from him. "Mother!" he cried. "Darling, sweetheart, wait!" Crumpling, she fell to the pavement. He dashed forward and fell at her side, crying, "Mamma, Mamma!" He turned her over. Her face was fiercely distorted. One eye, large and staring, moved slightly to the left as if it had become unmoored. The other remained fixed on him, raked his face again, found nothing and closed.

"Wait here, wait here!" he cried and jumped up and began to run for help toward a cluster of lights he saw in the distance ahead of him. "Help, help!" he shouted, but his voice was thin, scarcely a thread of sound. The lights drifted farther away the faster he ran and his feet moved numbly as if they carried him nowhere. The tide of darkness seemed to sweep him back to her, postponing from moment to moment his entry into the world of guilt and sorrow.

Section Five:
Essays and Non-Fiction

Jonathan Swift (1667–1745) was the child of English parents in Dublin. He attended Trinity College and ultimately received a M.A. from Oxford. He prepared to become an Anglican clergyman and was known for his strong religious and political satire. He is best known for his book Gulliver's Travels, *published in 1726, and this essay, "A Modest Proposal," published in 1729.*

A Modest Proposal
For Preventing the Children of Poor People in Ireland from Being a Burden to Their Parents or Country, and for Making Them Beneficial to the Public

Jonathan Swift

It is a melancholy object to those who walk through this great town or travel in the country, when they see the streets, the roads, and cabin doors, crowded with beggars of the female-sex, followed by three, four, or six children, all in rags and importuning every passenger for an alms. These mothers, instead of being able to work for their honest livelihood, are forced to employ all their time in strolling to beg sustenance for their helpless infants, who, as they grow up, either turn thieves for want of work, or leave their dear native country to fight for the Pretender in Spain, or sell themselves to the Barbadoes.

I think it is agreed by all parties that this prodigious number of children in the arms, or on the backs, or at the heels of their mothers, and frequently of their fathers, is in the present deplorable state of the kingdom a very great additional grievance; and therefore whoever could find out a fair, cheap, and easy method of making these children sound, useful members of the commonwealth would deserve so well of the public as to have his statue set up for a preserver of the nation.

But my intention is very far from being confined to provide only for the children of professed beggars; it is of a much greater extent, and shall take in the whole number of infants at a certain age who are born of parents in effect as little able to support them as those who demand our charity in the streets.

As to my own part, having turned my thoughts for many years upon this important subject, and maturely weighted the several schemes of other projectors, I have always found them grossly mistaken in their computation. It is true, a child just dropped from its dam may be supported by her milk for a solar year, with little other nourishment; at most not above the value of two shillings, which the mother may certainly get, or the value in scraps, by her lawful occupation of begging; and it is exactly at one year old that I propose to provide for them in such a manner as instead of being a charge upon their parents or the parish, or wanting food and raiment for the rest of their lives, they shall on the contrary contribute to the feeding, and partly to the clothing, of many thousands.

There is likewise another great advantage in my scheme, that it will prevent those voluntary abortions, and that horrid practice of women murdering their bastard children, alas, too frequent among us, sacrificing the poor innocent babes, I doubt, more to avoid the expense than the shame, which would move tears and pity in the most savage and inhuman breast.

The number of souls in this kingdom being usually reckoned one million and a half, of these I calculate there may be about two hundred thousand couples whose wives are breeders; from which number I subtract thirty thousand couples who are able to maintain their own children, although I apprehend there cannot be so many under the present distresses of the kingdom; but this being granted, there will remain an hundred and seventy thousand breeders. I again subtract fifty thousand for those women who miscarry, or whose children die by accident or disease within the year. There only remain an hundred and twenty thousand children of poor parents annually born. The question therefore is, how this number shall be reared and provided for, which, as I have already said, under the present situation of affairs, is utterly impossible by all the methods hitherto proposed. For we can neither employ them in handicraft or agriculture; we neither build houses (I mean in the country) nor cultivate land. They can very seldom pick up a livelihood by stealing till they arrive at six years old, except where they are of towardly parts; although I confess they learn the rudiments much earlier, during which time they can however be looked upon only as probationers, as I have been informed by a principal gentlemen in the county of Cavan, who protested to me that he never knew above one or two instances under the age of six, even in a part of the kingdom so renowned for the quickest proficiency in that art.

I am assured by our merchants that a boy or girl before twelve years old is no salable commodity; and even when they come to this age they will not yield above three pounds, or three pounds and half a crown at most on the Exchange; which cannot turn to account either to the parents or the kingdom, the charge of nutriment and rags having been at least four times that value.

I shall now therefore humbly propose my own thoughts, which I hope will not be liable to the least objection.

I have been assured by a very knowing American of my acquaintance in London, that a young healthy child well nursed is at a year old a most delicious, nourishing, and wholesome food, whether stewed, roasted, baked or boiled; and I make no doubt that it will equally serve in a fricassee or a ragout.

I do therefore humbly offer it to public consideration that of the hundred and twenty thousand children, already computed, twenty thousand may be reserved for breed, whereof only one fourth part to be males, which is more than we allow to sheep, black cattle, or swine; and my reason is that these children are seldom the fruits of marriage, a circumstance not much regarded by our savages, therefore one male will be sufficient to serve four females. That the remaining hundred thousand may at a year old be offered in sale to the persons of quality and fortune through the kingdom, always advising the mother to let them suck plentifully in the last month, so as to render them plump and fat for a good table. A child will make two dishes at an entertainment for friends; and when the family dines alone, the fore or hind quarter will make a reasonable dish, and seasoned with a little pepper or salt will be very good boiled on the fourth day, especially in winter.

I have reckoned upon a medium that a child just born will weigh twelve pounds, and in a solar year if tolerably nursed increaseth to twenty-eight pounds.

I grant this food will be somewhat dear, and therefore very proper for landlords, who, as they have already devoured most of the parents, seem to have the best title to the children.

Infant's flesh will be in season throughout the year, but more plentiful in March, and a little before and after. For we are told by a grave author, an eminent French physician, that fish being a prolific diet, there are more children born in Roman Catholic countries about nine months after Lent than at any other season: therefore, reckoning a year after Lent, the markets will be more glutted than usual, because the number of popish infants is at least three to one in this kingdom; and therefore it will have one other collateral advantage, by lessening the number of Papists among us.

I have already computed the charge of nursing a beggar's child (in which list I reckon all cottagers, laborers, and four fifths of the farmers) to be about two shillings per annum, rags included: and I believe no gentleman would repine to give ten shillings for the carcass of a good fat child, which, as I have said, will make four dishes of excellent nutritive meat, when he hath only some particular friend or his own family to dine with him. Thus the squire will learn to be a good landlord, and grow popular among the tenants; the mother will have eight shillings net profit, and be fit for work till she produces another child.

Those who are more thrifty (as I must confess the times require) may flay the carcass; the skin of which artificially dressed will make admirable gloves for ladies, and summer boots for fine gentlemen.

As to our city of Dublin, shambles may be appointed for this purpose in the most convenient parts of it, and butchers we may be assured will not be wanting; although I rather recommend buying the children alive, and dressing them hot from the knife as we do roasting pigs.

A very worthy person, a true lover of his country, and whose virtues I highly esteem, was lately pleased in discoursing on this matter to offer a refinement upon my scheme. He said that many gentlemen of this kingdom, having of late destroyed their deer, he conceived that the want of venison might be well supplied by the bodies of young lads and maidens, not exceeding fourteen years of age nor under twelve, so great a number of both sexes in every county being now ready to starve for want of work and service; and these to be disposed of by their parents, if alive, or otherwise by their nearest relations. But with due deference to so excellent a friend and so deserving a patriot, I cannot be altogether in his sentiments; for as to the males, my American acquaintance assured me from frequent experience that their flesh was generally tough and lean, like that of our schoolboys, by continual exercise, and their taste disagreeable; and to fatten them would not answer the charge. Then as to the females, it would, I think with humble submission, be a loss to the public, because they soon would become breeders themselves: and besides, it is not improbable that some scrupulous people might be apt to censure such a practice (although indeed very unjustly) as a little bordering upon cruelty; which, I confess, hath always been with me the strongest objection against any project, how well so ever intended.

But in order to justify my friend, he confessed that this expedient was put into his head by the famous Psalmanazar, a native of the island Formosa, who came from thence to London above twenty years ago, and in conversation told my friend that in his country when any young person happened to be put to death, the executioner sold the carcass to persons of quality as a prime dainty; and that in his time the body of a plump girl of fifteen, who was crucified for an attempt to poison the emperor, was sold to his Imperial Majesty's prime minister of state, and other great mandarins of the court, in joints from the gibbet, at four hundred crowns. Neither indeed can I deny that if the same use were made of several plump young girls in this town, who without one single groat to their fortunes cannot stir abroad without a chair, and appear at the playhouse and assemblies in foreign fineries which they never will pay for, the kingdom would not be the worse.

Some persons of a desponding spirit are in great concern about that vast number of poor people who are aged, diseased, or maimed, and I have been desired to employ my thoughts what course may be taken to ease the nation of so grievous an encumbrance. But I am not in the least pain upon that matter, because it is very well known that they are every day dying and rotting by cold and famine, and filth and vermin, as fast as can be reasonably expected. And as to the younger laborers, they are now in almost as hopeful a condition. They cannot get work, and consequently pine away for want of nourishment to a degree that if at any time they are accidentally hired to common labor, they have not strength to perform it; and thus the country and themselves are happily delivered from the evils to come.

I have too long digressed, and therefore shall return to my subject. I think the advantages by the proposal which I have made are obvious and many, as well as of the highest importance.

For first, as I have already observed, it would greatly lessen the number of Papists, with whom we are yearly overrun, being the principal breeders of the nation as well as our most dangerous enemies; and who stay at home on purpose to deliver the kingdom to the Pretender, hoping to take their advantage by the absence of so many good Protestants, who have chosen rather to leave their country than to stay at home and pay tithes against their conscience to an Episcopal curate.

Secondly, the poorer tenants will have something valuable of their own, which by law may be made liable to distress, and help to pay their landlord's rent, their corn and cattle being already seized and money a thing unknown.

Thirdly, whereas the maintenance of an hundred thousand children, from two years old and upwards, cannot be computed at less than ten shillings a piece per annum, the nation's stock will be thereby increased fifty thousand pounds per annum, besides the profit of a new dish introduced to the tables of all gentlemen of fortune in the kingdom who have any refinement in taste. And the money will circulate among ourselves, the goods being entirely of our own growth and manufacture.

Fourthly, the constant breeders, besides the gain of eight shillings sterling per annum by the sale of their children, will be rid of the charge of maintaining them after the first year.

Fifthly, this food would likewise bring great custom to taverns, where the vintners will certainly be so prudent as to procure the best receipts for dressing it to perfection, and consequently have their houses frequented by all the fine gentlemen, who justly value themselves upon their knowledge in good eating; and a skillful cook, who understands how to oblige his guests, will contrive to make it as expensive as they please.

Sixthly, this would be a great inducement to marriage, which all wise nations have either encouraged by rewards or enforced by laws and penalties. It would increase the care and tenderness of mothers toward their children, when they were sure of a settlement for life to the poor babes, provided in some sort by the public, to their annual profit instead of expense. We should see an honest emulation among the married women, which of them could bring the fattest child to the market. Men would become as fond of their wives during the time of their pregnancy as they are now of their mares in foal, their cows in calf, or sows when they are ready to farrow; nor offer to beat or kick them (as is too frequent a practice) for fear of a miscarriage.

Many other advantages might be enumerated. For instance, the addition of some thousand carcasses in our exportation of barreled beef, the propagation of swine's flesh, and improvement in the art of making good bacon, so much wanted among us by the great destruction of pigs, too frequent at our tables, which are no way comparable in taste or magnificence to a well-grown, fat yearling child, which roasted whole will make a considerable figure at a lord mayor's feast or any other public entertainment. But this and many others I omit, being studious of brevity.

Supposing that one thousand families in this city would be constant customers for infants' flesh, besides others who might have it at merry meetings, particularly weddings and christenings, I compute that Dublin would take off annually about twenty thousand carcasses, and the rest of the kingdom (where probably they will be sold somewhat cheaper) the remaining eighty thousand.

I can think of no one objection that will possibly be raised against this proposal, unless it should be urged that the number of people will be thereby much lessened in the kingdom. This I freely own, and it was indeed one principal design in offering it to the world. I desire the reader will observe, that I calculate my remedy for this one individual kingdom of Ireland and for no other that ever was, is, or I think ever can be upon earth. Therefore let no man talk to me of other expedients: of taxing our absentees at five shillings a pound: of using neither clothes nor household furniture except what is of our own growth and manufacture: of utterly rejecting the materials and instruments that promote foreign luxury: of curing the expensiveness of pride, vanity, idleness, and gaming in our women: of introducing a vein of parsimony, prudence, and temperance: of learning to love our country, in the want of which we differ even from Laplanders and the inhabitants of Topinamboo: of quitting our animosities and factions, nor acting any longer like the Jews, who were murdering one another at the very moment their city was taken: of being a little cautious not to sell our country and conscience for nothing: of teaching landlords to have at least one degree of mercy toward their tenants: lastly, of putting a spirit of honesty, industry, and skill into our shopkeepers; who, if a resolution could be now taken to buy only our native goods, would immediately unite to cheat and exact upon us in the price, the measure and the goodness, nor could ever yet be brought to make one fair proposal of just dealing, though often and earnestly invited to it.

Therefore I repeat, let no man talk to me of these and the like expedients, till he hath at least some glimpse of hope that there will ever be some hearty and sincere attempt to put them in practice.

But as to myself, having been wearied out for many years with offering vain, idle, visionary thoughts, and at length utterly despairing of success, I fortunately fell upon this proposal, which, as it is wholly new, so it hath something solid and real, of no expense and little trouble, full in our own power, and whereby we can incur no danger in disobliging England. For this kind of commodity will not bear exportation, the flesh being of too tender a consistence to admit a long continuance in salt, although perhaps I could name a country which would be glad to eat up our whole nation without it.

After all, I am not so violently bent upon my own opinion as to reject any offer proposed by wise men, which shall be found equally innocent, cheap, easy, and effectual. But before something of that kind shall be advanced in contradiction to my scheme, and offering a better, I desire the author or authors will be pleased maturely to consider two points. First, as things now stand, how they will be able to find food and raiment for an hundred thousand useless mouths and backs. And secondly, there being a round million of creatures in human figure throughout this kingdom, whose sole subsistence put into a common stock would leave them in debt two millions of pounds sterling, adding those who are beggars by profession to the bulk of farmers, cottagers, and laborers, with their wives and children who are beggars in effect; I desire those politicians who dislike my overture, and may perhaps be so bold to attempt an answer, that they will first ask the parents of these mortals whether they would not at this day think it a great happiness to have been sold for food at a year old in the manner I prescribe, and thereby have avoided such a perpetual scene of misfortunes as they have since gone through by the oppression of landlords, the impossibility of paying rent without money or trade, the want of common sustenance, with neither house nor clothes to cover them from the inclemencies of the weather, and the most inevitable prospect of entailing the like or greater miseries upon their breed forever.

I profess, in the sincerity of my heart, that I have not the least personal interest in endeavoring to promote this necessary work, having no other motive than the public good of my country, by advancing our trade, providing for infants, relieving the poor, and giving some pleasure to the rich. I have no children by which I can propose to get a single penny; the youngest being nine years old, and my wife past childbearing.

*B*ertrand Russell (1872–1970) was born in Wales to an aristocratic family. He had a keen academic interest in mathematics and philosophy; among his major works in these fields are Principia Mathematica *and* A History of Western Philosophy. *He was a strong advocate for nuclear disarmament, a critic of the Vietnam War, and was recognized as a scholar and public commentator worldwide. In 1950 he received the Nobel Prize in Literature.*

Work

Bertrand Russell

Whether work should be placed among the causes of happiness or among the causes of unhappiness may perhaps be regarded as a doubtful question. There is certainly much work which is exceedingly irksome, and an excess of work is always very painful. I think, however, that, provided work is not excessive in amount, even the dullest work is to most people less painful than idleness. There are in work all grades, from mere relief of tedium up to the profoundest delights, according to the nature of the work and the abilities of the worker. Most of the work that most people have to do is not in itself interesting, but even such work has certain great advantages. To begin with, it fills a good many hours of the day without the need of deciding what one shall do. Most people, when they are left free to fill their own time according to their own choice, are at a loss to think of anything sufficiently pleasant to be worth doing. And whatever they decide on, they are troubled by the feeling that something else would have been pleasanter. To be able to fill leisure intelligently is the last product of civilization, and at present very few people have reached this level. Moreover the exercise of choice is in itself tiresome. Except to people with unusual initiative it is positively agreeable to be told what to do at each hour of the day, provided the orders are not too unpleasant. Most of the idle rich suffer unspeakable boredom as the price of their freedom from drudgery. At times, they may find relief by hunting big game in Africa, or by flying round the world, but the number of such sensations is limited, especially after youth is past. Accordingly the more intelligent rich men work nearly as hard as if they were poor, while rich women for the most part keep themselves busy with innumerable trifles of whose earth-shaking importance they are firmly persuaded.

Work therefore is desirable, first and foremost, as a preventive of boredom, for the boredom that a man feels when he is doing necessary though uninteresting work is as nothing in comparison with the boredom that he feels when he has nothing to do with his days. With this advantage of work another is associated, namely that it makes holidays much more delicious when they come. Provided a man does not have to work so hard as to impair his vigor, he is likely to find far more zest in his free time than an idle man could possibly find.

The second advantage of most paid work and of some unpaid work is that it gives chances of success and opportunities for ambition. In most work success is measured by income, and while our capitalistic society continues, this is inevitable. It is only where the best work is concerned that this measure ceases to be the natural one to apply. The desire that men feel to increase their income is quite as much a desire for success as for the extra comforts that a higher income can procure. However dull work may be, it becomes bearable if it is a means of building up a reputation, whether in the world at large or only in one's own circle. Continuity of purpose is one of the most essential ingredients of happiness in the long run, and for most men this comes chiefly through their work. In this respect those women whose lives are occupied with housework are much less fortunate than men, or than women who work outside the home. The domesticated wife does not receive wages, has no means of bettering herself, is taken for granted by her husband (who sees practically nothing of what she does), and is valued by him not for her housework but for quite other qualities. Of course this does not apply to those women who are sufficiently well-to-do to make beautiful houses and beautiful gardens and become the envy of their neighbors; but such women are comparatively few, and for the great majority housework cannot bring as much satisfaction as work of other kinds brings to men and to professional women.

The satisfaction of killing time and of affording some outlet, however modest, for ambition, belongs to most work, and is sufficient to make even a man whose work is dull happier on the average than a man who has no work at all. But when work is interesting, it is capable of giving satisfaction of a far higher order than mere relief from tedium. The kinds of work in which there is some interest may be arranged in a hierarchy. I shall begin with those which are only mildly interesting and end with those that are worthy to absorb the whole energies of a great man.

Two chief elements make work interesting; first, the exercise of skill, and second, construction.

Every man who has acquired some unusual skill enjoys exercising it until it has become a matter of course, or until he can no longer improve himself. This motive to activity begins in early childhood: a boy who can stand on his head becomes reluctant to stand on his feet. A great deal of work gives the same pleasure that is to be derived from games of skill. The work of a lawyer or a politician must contain in a more delectable form a great deal of the same pleasure that is to be derived from playing bridge. Here of course there is not only the exercise of skill but the outwitting of a skilled opponent. Even where this competitive element is absent, however, the performance of difficult feats is agreeable. A man who can do stunts in an aeroplane finds the pleasure so great that for the sake of it he is willing to risk his life. Imagine that an able surgeon, in spite of the painful circumstances in which his work is done, derives satisfaction from the exquisite precision of his operations. The same kind of pleasure, though in a less intense form, is to be derived from a great deal of work of a humbler kind. All skilled work can be pleasurable, provided the skill required is either variable or capable of indefinite improvement. If these conditions are absent, it will cease to be interesting when a man has acquired his maximum skill. A man who runs three-mile races will cease to find pleasure in this occupation when he passes the age at which he can beat his own previous record. Fortunately there is a very considerable amount of work in which new circumstances call for new skill and a man can go on improving, at any rate until he has reached middle age. In some kinds of skilled work, such as politics, for example, it seems that men are at their best between sixty and seventy, the reason being that in such occupations a wide experience of other men is essential. For this reason successful politicians are apt to be happier at the age of seventy than any other men of equal age. Their only competitors in this respect are the men who are the heads of big businesses.

There is, however, another element possessed by the best work, which is even more important as a source of happiness than is the exercise of skill. This is the element of constructiveness. In some work, though by no means in most, something is built up which remains as a monument when the work is completed. We may distinguish construction from destruction by the following criterion. In construction the initial state of affairs is comparatively haphazard, while the final state of affairs embodies a purpose: in destruction the reverse is the case; the initial state of affairs embodies a purpose, while the final state of affairs is haphazard, that is to say, all that is intended by the destroyer is to produce a state of affairs which does not embody a certain purpose. This criterion applies in the most literal and obvious case, namely the construction and destruction of buildings. In constructing a building a previously made plan is carried out, whereas in destroying it no one decides exactly how the materials are to be when the demolition is complete. Destruction is of course necessary very often as a preliminary to subsequent construction; in that case it is part of a whole which is constructive. But not infrequently a man will engage in activities of which the purpose is destructive without regard to any construction that may come after. Frequently he will conceal this from himself by the belief that he is only sweeping away in order to build afresh, but it is generally possible to unmask this pretense, when it is a pretense, by asking him what the subsequent construction is to be. On this subject it will be found that he will speak vaguely and without enthusiasm, whereas on the preliminary destruction he has spoken precisely and with zest. This applies to not a few revolutionaries and militarists and other apostles of violence. They are actuated, usually without their own knowledge, by hatred: the destruction of what they hate is their real purpose, and they are comparatively indifferent to the question what is to come after it. Now I cannot deny that in the work of destruction as in the work of construction there may be joy. It is a fiercer joy, perhaps at moments more intense, but it is less profoundly satisfying, since the result is one in which little satisfaction is to be found. You kill your enemy, and when he is dead your occupation is gone, and the satisfaction that you derive from victory quickly fades. The work of construction, on the other hand, when completed is delightful to contemplate, and moreover is never so fully completed that there is nothing further to do about it. The most satisfactory purposes are those that lead on indefinitely from one success to another without ever coming to a dead end; and in this respect it will be found that construction is a greater source of happiness than destruction. Perhaps it would be more correct to say that those who find satisfaction in construction find in it greater satisfaction than the lovers of destruction can find in destruction, for if once you have become filled with hate you will not easily derive from construction the pleasure which another man would derive from it.

At the same time few things are so likely to cure the habit of hatred as the opportunity to do constructive work of an important kind.

The satisfaction to be derived from success in a great constructive enterprise is one of the most massive that life has to offer, although unfortunately in its highest forms it is open only to men of exceptional ability. Nothing can rob a man of the happiness of successful achievement in an important piece of work, unless it be the proof that after all his work was bad. There are many forms of such satisfaction. The man who by a scheme of irrigation has caused the wilderness to blossom like the rose enjoys it in one of its most tangible forms. The creation of an organization may be a work of supreme importance. So is the work of those few statesmen who have devoted their lives to producing order out of chaos, of whom Lenin is the supreme type in our day. The most obvious examples are artists and men of science. Shakespeare says of his verse: "So long as men can breathe, or eyes can see, so long lives this." And it cannot be doubted that the thought consoled him for misfortune. In his sonnets he maintains that the thought of his friend reconciled him to life, but I cannot help suspecting that the sonnets he wrote to his friend were even more effective for this purpose than the friend himself. Great artists and great men of science do work which is in itself delightful; while they are doing it, it secures them the respect of those whose respect is worth having, which gives them the most fundamental kind of power, namely power over men's thoughts and feelings. They have also the most solid reasons for thinking well of themselves. This combination of fortunate circumstances ought, one would think, to be enough to make any man happy. Nevertheless it is not so. Michael Angelo, for example, was a profoundly unhappy man, and maintained (not, I am sure, with truth) that he would not have troubled to produce works of art if he had not had to pay the debts of his impecunious relations. The power to produce great art is very often, though by no means always, associated with a temperamental unhappiness, so great that but for the joy which the artist derives from his work, he would be driven to suicide. We cannot, therefore, maintain that even the greatest work must make a man happy; we can only maintain that it must make him less unhappy. Men of science, however, are far less often temperamentally unhappy than artists are, and in the main the men who do great work in science are happy men, whose happiness is derived primarily from their work.

One of the causes of unhappiness among intellectuals in the present day is that so many of them, especially those whose skill is literary, find no opportunity for the independent exercise of their talents, but have to hire themselves out to rich corporations directed by Philistines, who insist upon their producing what they themselves regard as pernicious nonsense. If you were to inquire among journalists in either England or America whether they believed in the policy of the newspaper for which they worked, you would find, I believe, that only a small minority do so; the rest, for the sake of a livelihood, prostitute their skill to purposes which they believe to be harmful. Such work cannot bring any real satisfaction, and in the course of reconciling himself to the doing of it, a man has to make himself so cynical that he can no longer derive wholehearted satisfaction from anything whatever. I cannot condemn men who undertake work of this sort, since starvation is too serious an alternative, but I think that where it is possible to do work that is satisfactory to a man's constructive impulses without entirely starving, he will be well advised from the point of view of his own happiness if he chooses it in preference to work much more highly paid but not seeming to him worth doing on its own account. Without self-respect genuine happiness is scarcely possible. And the man who is ashamed of his work can hardly achieve self-respect.

The satisfaction of constructive work, though it may, as things are, be the privilege of a minority, can nevertheless be the privilege of a quite large minority. Any man who is his own master in his work can feel it; so can any man whose work appears to him useful and requires considerable skill. The production of satisfactory children is a difficult constructive work capable of affording profound satisfaction. Any woman who has achieved this can feel that as a result of her labor the world contains something of value which it would not otherwise contain.

Human beings differ profoundly in regard to the tendency to regard their lives as a whole. To some men it is natural to do so, and essential to happiness to be able to do so with some satisfaction. To others life is a series of detached incidents without directed movement and without unity. I think the former sort are more likely to achieve happiness than the latter, since they will gradually build up those circumstances from which they can derive contentment and self-respect, whereas the others will be blown about by the winds of circumstances now this way, now that, without ever arriving at any haven. The habit of viewing life as a whole is an essential part both of wisdom and of true morality, and is one of the things which ought to be encouraged in education. Consistent purpose is not enough to make life happy, but it is an almost indispensable condition of a happy life. And consistent purpose embodies itself mainly in work.

Perry Pascarella has worked in the field of leadership and worker motivation for over forty years. He was involved in the creation of the magazine Industry Week *and has authored seven books on leadership, among them* The New Achievers, *from which this selection is taken.*

What Happened to the Old Protestant Ethic?

Perry Pascarella

An individual comes to work to meet economic needs, belonging needs, the need to feel a sense of self-worth, the need to serve others, or the need for self-development and self-expression—any or all in their many shades. He or she may respond to different needs at different times. In earlier times, the reason for working was more clear-cut: economic necessity reinforced by a moral imperative.

The need to earn a living still drives people to seek a job, but work no longer seems to have that same transcendental connection for many Americans. It is impossible to measure the religious commitment of a society at any point in time and make a sound comparison with some time in the past; however, there is little doubt that religion is playing a lesser role in our public lives today than in early America and during the early years of industrialization. In the past two or three decades, the nation has become highly sensitized to any laws, regulations, or national policies—extant or proposed—that would bring church and state closer together. Religious beliefs, or the absence of them, are protected by barring discussion of religious or moral considerations in the official public arena.

Americans still consider themselves religious, however. Regardless of their church affiliation or nonaffiliation, regardless of the degree to which their daily lives are governed by transcendent considerations, they believe in a god, they say. In a study of American values done for the Connecticut Mutual Life Insurance Co., 94 percent of adults said they occasionally feel God loves them; 73 percent feel that frequently. Although only 44 percent of these people attend church regularly, 73 percent consider themselves "religious."

Other studies have shown, year after year, that over 90 percent of Americans believe in God but that fewer than 50 percent regularly attend worship services. There is little evidence, then, that most Americans are deeply and continuously influenced by the religious word. In fact, the analysts working on the Connecticut Mutual study call only one-fourth of the respondents "highly religious."

Religious commitment may no longer be the all-embracing force it once was, but the Connecticut Mutual report's authors conclude that it is still the "strongest predictor" of a person's satisfaction and involvement with his or her work. Of the most religious respondents to the survey, nearly all feel dedicated to their work while only two-thirds of the "least religious" feel that way.

Although religion may influence some people's attitudes toward work today, we are far from reaching a consensus on any of the troublesome questions that would be provided answers by a common ideology of work. There is little agreement about the relationship of work to life's purpose, of individual interests versus those of the community, or of working to perfect life here on earth versus relying on God's salvation. There is disagreement not only between "religious" and not-so-religious persons but even within the ranks of those with strong religious beliefs.

The effect of differing spiritual views on people's attitudes toward work was revealed in a survey done for the Continental Group. A high correlation appeared among those who engage in traditional religious activities, those who believe in giving a high priority to economic growth, and those who place a high priority on work that makes a contribution to society. We might call this the more traditional view of economic growth and the meaning of work. On the other hand, there is a growing number of people who favor more cautious economic growth and who give a high priority to preserving the earth's resources. People in this group are likely to regard themselves as "driven" individuals. They tend to be less content with their work situations and more aggressive in demanding that their expectations be met. We have, then, at least two work ethics shaping people's behavior. One leads its adherents to accept traditional work structures and rewards while the other leads to resistance.

Money and Morals

In early America there was an obvious need to work for one's economic survival and a dominant moral obligation to work as well. This obligation was the basis for what is referred to as the "Protestant ethic" or "Puritan ethic." The blend of economic necessity—for the individual and the community—and the moral force weaved its way through much of American history. In time, however, this fabric became unraveled. Why?

Two powerful and competing movements laid the ideological foundation for American life: the Reformation and the Enlightenment. Both were reactions against the traditional church. Both carried strong messages regarding the individual in relation to the universe, his work, and his wealth.

The Reformation began with Martin Luther (1483–1546) challenging the notion that individual salvation could be earned through good works as prescribed by the church. Salvation could come only through God's grace, said Luther. While the Roman Church had an "elect"—the priests—Luther and other Protestant leaders taught that the "elect" could be anyone. Anyone, but not all. John Calvin (1509–1564) said that those who would be granted salvation had already been predetermined. Material success, he allowed, is a sign that one has been designated by God for salvation.

Luther saw no particular virtue or evil in poverty. "God does not condemn the possession of wealth, but the evil use of it, that is, its use merely to satisfy one's selfish desire. . . ." Man is in the world to be of service to his fellow man and to God, said Luther. A person who conducts himself accordingly will not lose his heart to wealth and will use his riches for the good of all, he believed. He advanced the revolutionary concept of a worldly "calling"—the keystone of what was to become the Protestant work ethic. Prior to that, in the teachings of the Roman Church, the highest calling had been the monastic life of contemplation. But Luther's "calling" was to action in the secular world as an expression of brotherly love. ". . . this moral justification of worldly activity was one of the most important results of the Reformation," wrote Max Weber, the German sociologist, in his classic book *The Protestant Ethic and the Spirit of Capitalism.*

For many centuries, man had regarded work as a curse. For early Hebrews, it was atonement for original sin. For early Christians, "labor" or "toil" was not something to be pursued with all one's energies. But Luther and Calvin brought significance to work. They presented it as the bridge between heaven and earth.

Calvin went one step further in drawing man into worldly activity for spiritual purpose. He preached "maximum effort"; when a person produces more than he needs, said Calvin, this surplus should not be wasted on personal appetites. It should serve the glory of God by being reinvested to improve one's work and provide even greater surpluses for the glory of God. For centuries, Christianity had condemned profit-making; but early Protestantism supported a profound social and economic shift. Wealth had long been associated with oppressors; now it was taken as a sign that one was among God's elect.

Early Lutheranism and Calvinism coincided with secular, economic changes that were occurring in Europe. People were rising above the subsistence level. A middle class was developing. The "calling" to work justified a working class. The division of people into classes and occupations was, for Luther, the result of Divine Will. It is man's duty to persevere in his assigned place, he taught. Protestantism supported another aspect of the new economic system by discouraging wasteful consumption and the enjoyment of possessions. Calvin's concept of "maximum effort" laid a spiritual foundation for amassing capital. This powerful religious movement thus generated a high-production, high investment mentality. It made self-denial in production and consumption both ethically right and economically effective.

Self-Destructing Ethic

Two centuries after the thinking of Luther and Calvin had begun working their effect on society, John Wesley (1703–1791) foresaw the likely negative outcome of such expressions of faith. Religion, he said, will produce industry and frugality which will lead to riches; as riches increase, so will pride, anger, and desire. Religion thus brings on its own decay. It would be futile to try to prevent people from working and accumulating wealth, Wesley realized. His practical solution was to encourage them to do so and then to share their wealth so they would grow in grace.

Later, in young America, riches did indeed increase. Work and wealth became signs of respectability—a principal motivating force in people's lives. Religious forces drew people's attention to the secular life, but, in time, many lost sight of the treasures in heaven. Attempts to make the church of the saved visible in this world shifted people's concern from the hereafter to the here and now. Material success became an end in itself.

While Protestantism served early America well and laid the foundation for industrialization with its justification of work and investment, the industrial system eventually abused and then lost touch with that ethic. The notion of work as a spiritual calling fell out of sync with the mechanized work of mass production. The objective of work centered on economic gain, and even that was beyond the reach of many people.

Industrialization eventually eroded the certainty that work would bring success to the individual. Semiskilled workers, trapped in the mills of the nineteenth century, realized that no amount of hard work would lift them to wealth or self-improvement. Thus came the mounting negative feelings toward work and demands for more and more economic compensation in exchange for surrendering to such meaningless activity.

Work was no longer done for God's glorification; it took on a more utilitarian meaning. Ironically, what had been the foundation for industrialization was eventually eroded by it. American industry progressed, from that point, not on the work ethic but despite it. The Protestant ethic had taught people to work hard, save their money, and get their rewards in the future or the hereafter. But that message became perverted to a consumption ethic: "Work as little as possible, spend your money because it's shrinking in value, and demand your rewards now." By the 1960s, this trend culminated in the "me generation"—people devoted to self-gratification. The me-generation mentality affected more than just the youth of this country. Their parents had led the way in the scramble for houses, cars, appliances, and leisure-time goods; the youth merely expected more and then turned to new experiences when goods no longer satisfied their hunger.

Mixed Messages

The American brand of capitalism succeeded in creating such widespread prosperity relative to anything the world had ever seen that the imperative came to be one of consumption, not production. Demand for goods and services became the flywheel that kept the economic engine running fast and smooth. The spiritual dimension, meanwhile, faded as a justification for the accumulation of wealth. Whereas the Protestant view of work and wealth was once clear and present, it is now mixed at best. The individual seeking guidance in the Bible regarding those messages encounters some popular passages that admonish him to work and others that suggest that work is unimportant. For example, most Americans with any exposure to the New Testament will have heard Matt. 6:26—"Look at the birds of the air; they neither sow nor reap nor gather into barns, and yet your heavenly Father feeds them." The message seems to be: don't worry about working or storing up wealth. On the other hand, they may hear 2 Thess. 3:11–12—". . . we hear that some of you are living in idleness, mere busybodies, not doing any work. Now such persons we command and exhort in the Lord Jesus Christ to do their work in quietness and to earn their own living." And there is 1 Tim. 1:4—"If any would not work, neither should he eat."

Few verses are more widely known that those regarding the curse of wealth such as Matt. 19:23–24—". . . it will be very hard for rich people to enter the kingdom of heaven. Again I tell you, it is easier for a camel to go through the eye of a needle than for a rich man to enter the kingdom of God." Yet people may be led in the other direction by Matt. 25:29— "For to every person who has something, even more will be given, and he will have more than enough; but the person who has nothing, even the little that he has will be taken away from him."

Literal interpretations of selected passages from the New Testament do not necessarily convey the central message of Christianity. When people attempt to set guidelines for living and working in such a manner, they do not all arrive at the same conclusions. As a result, even those who are listening to "The Word" do not necessarily share a common ethic. In addition, biblical stories regarding wealth and poverty or servant and master seem hardly relevant to a society in which wealth is widespread and servant-master relationships have long since disappeared.

As John Wesley had feared, the Protestant ethic came to support an economic system that led to its own undoing. Today, our economic system is in danger of failing because it has no spiritual foundation despite the fact that many Americans assume a spiritual ethic is built into their political-economic system. After all, they believe, the United States is essentially a Christian nation.

A Christian Nation?

The nation's founders provided a philosophical base but not a religious one—especially not a specifically Christian one. Our founding fathers were influenced by Enlightenment thinking which matured in the eighteenth and nineteenth centuries. They believed that all men were created equal and that, given the proper material and social conditions, fully realized human beings would evolve. If our institutions would conform to "natural law," man would develop his natural perfection, according to this utopian line of thought.

Enlightenment thinking also meshed well with the rise of science. By the eighteenth century, man's view of nature was changing in the Western world. Nature was no longer mysterious and divine. It had been reduced to a scientific machine, and man's place was to master this machine to produce wealth. America's seemingly unbounded resources and new frontiers promised material gain and freedom for man to fully realize his potential far beyond what some of the earlier Enlightenment thinkers may ever have dreamed. Economic expansion became part of America's destiny.

The Declaration of Independence, signed a century and a half after the white man began to settle the land, is a most humanitarian document, but it is not a Christian document. Thomas Jefferson, Benjamin Franklin, and George Washington rank among the greatest statesmen of all time, but they were deists out of the Enlightenment fashion, allowing that supreme power had created the world but was no longer acting in its unfolding. The great document that launched America toward nationhood contains only three references to a divine being:

1. "equal station to which the Laws of Nature and of Nature's God entitle them"

2. "that they are endowed by their Creator"

3. "with a firm reliance on the protection of Divine Providence"

In its single reference to spiritual matters, our other great document, The Constitution, reads: "Congress shall make no law respecting an establishment of religion, or prohibiting the free exercise thereof." The reference was not made in the original articles, but added its the First Amendment! This nation, which so may citizens regarded as having built-in Christian values, was launched officially according to deist concepts but made no official recognition of a particular religion. We were given the foundation for a liberal society.

In time, the Protestant's concern for salvation gave way to the liberal's notion that society is perfectible. As man learned to read some of nature's laws, there seemed to be less need for divine intervention. Even Christians suspected that the Kingdom was coming on earth, that it was happening right here, and that one could be concerned with self-pursuits because "the system" would take care of thy neighbor. Moralists like Ben Franklin spoke of work and wealth in terms of usefulness rather than the Glory of God. Protestantism had begun to elevate the concept of wealth, and the pragmatism that developed in America raised it still higher. The old Protestant ethic was being secularized.

Rigid Rules

Eighteenth and nineteenth-century America did have a strong Christian thrust despite the lack of official direction. The churches that took root in this land of freedom did not allow man to follow nature's laws, despite the intentions of the founding fathers. Quite the contrary! The early Protestants were no longer subject to the rule of the priests, but they lived under strict rules for daily conduct. Protestantism allowed everyone to be part of the "elect," but it enforced rigid rules for involvement in the secular world.

Early American churches left little room for the individual to fall victim to his wicked natural inclinations. "The core of Puritanism . . . was an intense moral zeal for the regulation of everyday conduct," says Daniel Bell. "Given the external dangers and psychological strains of living in a closed world, the individual had to be concerned not only with his own behavior but with the community." Spiritual values were central to people's lives and tied all the elements of life into a meaningful whole.

Despite the tight religious rules for social conduct, preoccupation with individual salvation sometimes justified a person's acquisitiveness at the expense of others rather than as a blessing to be shared with others. Thus there was a religious "justification" for the inhumanities of the early days of the Industrial Revolution. Max Weber discussed the development of a bourgeois ethic which permitted the businessman to pursue his financial interests, enjoy a supply of industrious workers, and assure himself that unequal economic distribution was the result of Divine Providence. By the twentieth century, increased prosperity and the attainment of greater economic and social equality had undermined the notion of high calling for both businessman and laborer. Even at the beginning of this century, Weber was able to note that the idea of duty in one's calling "prowls about in our lives like the ghost of dead religious beliefs."

Protestantism has carried within itself a fundamental conflict between individualism and community. When economic interests conflict with the central Christian message of love and sharing, some Protestants divorce their private life and their religion from their public activities. They focus on individual religious experiences. For some, this leads to concern for grace and being one of the "elect" and generates hostility rather than compassion for sinners. Martin Marty, in *Righteous Empire*, describes the division between personal and community concern. "Private" Protestantism, beginning especially in the early nineteenth century, stressed individual salvation and the moral life of the "saved." Its followers were concerned with conversion and reaffirmation of faith. They were out to save souls. "Public" Protestantism, on the other hand, was more concerned with social order and man's social role. Adherents worked for transformation of the world; they were out to save society.

In recent years, religion has become an internalized, private affair for many Americans. Following the peak of public party Protestantism in the 1960s, with its highly visible mobilization for civil rights and against war, the private side has returned to the fore. Perhaps, with the rise of big systems—government, business, and labor unions—the individual has seen little choice but to retreat inward.

The interplay of religion, social development, and economic growth over American history is much too complex to treat fully here. Cause and effect are not easily distinguished and invite oversimplification. We can safely conclude, however, that the underlying spiritual dimension to work and the predominant view of man have changed significantly over the past two centuries. As people turn inward, many find their work has no meaning. Although some embrace the more traditional, self-denial values that provide meaning for their work, far more find the contrast between what they believe they are and what the workplace expects of them too great to bear. They may rebel at the pressures that threaten to compress or extinguish their spirituality. The workplace is one of the principal places where they strike out against their loss of power and the fragmentation of their lives. The old Protestant ethic taught people to deny their selfish desires and work for greater social and spiritual glory, but denying oneself does not seem to make sense in an era of rational and scientific thinking. Many, including a significant portion of those in the ranks of traditional religions, embrace the humanist notion that man's highest goal is progress here on earth. Their concerns, whether personal or societal, are essentially secular.

Many of us stand naked with neither spiritual connection nor social agreement to give purpose to our work. In the late nineteenth century, we had regarded ourselves as the chosen nation. Less than a century later, the country which had fought World War II convinced that God was on its side waged a nonwar in Vietnam that it hoped God wouldn't hear about. Blood-letting in the ghettos and on the campuses revealed our inner conflicts and suggested that we were hypocrites who could no longer hide our selfish, inhumane, un-Christian tendencies. Scarcities and uncertainties have risen up to dampen our traditional eagerness to meet the future. Rather than striking at the heart of the problem, we expect to do little more than cope with an undesirable situation. We have given up the notion of the perfectibility of man. We try instead to fine-tune our institutions to compensate for our individual shortcomings. Our institutions are of less and less help in the struggle, however, because they were designed to serve an ethic of consumption rather than the earlier calling to work that opposed immediate gratification of desires. The early success of capitalism had been built, not on the "impulse to acquisition" but on the restraint of that impulse. But that discipline of worker and businessman has been lost.

While the old Protestant ethic or some vestige of it is still at work in some people's lives, it is not the predominant influence on attitudes toward work today. After centuries of its undoing there is little reason to expect a return to widespread acceptance of the old ethic. We should, instead, look to see if there is a new work ethic that can be articulated for our time. We should look, too, at why our organizations are failing to bring together the work that needs to be done and the needs that people could satisfy through work.

Pekka Himanen (1973–) is a Finnish philosopher and advisor to the Finnish government on living in the information society. He wrote The Hacker Ethic *with Linus Torvalds, creator of the Linux operating system, and Manuel Castells, a professor of sociology at the University of California–Berkely. The* Hacker Ethic *attempts to present a philosophical alternative to the concept of a "Protestant work ethic," originally described by German sociologist Max Weber (1864–1920) in his book* The Protestant Ethic and the Spirit of Capitalism, *an exploration of the impact of religion and culture on the economy.*

The Hacker Work Ethic

Pekka Himanen

Linus Torvalds says in his Prologue that, for the hacker, "the computer itself is entertainment," meaning that the hacker programs because he finds programming intrinsically interesting, exciting, and joyous.

The spirit behind other hackers' creations is very similar to this. Torvalds is not alone in describing his work with statements like "Linux hackers do something because they find it to be very interesting." For example, Vinton Cerf, who is sometimes called "the father of the Internet," comments on the fascination programming exerts: "There was something amazingly enticing about programming." Steve Wozniak, the person who built the first real personal computer, says forthrightly about his discovery of the wonders of programming: "It was just the most intriguing world." This is a general spirit: hackers program because programming challenges are of intrinsic *interest* to them. Problems related to programming arouse genuine curiosity in the hacker and make him eager to learn more.

The hacker is also *enthusiastic* about this interesting thing; it energizes him. From the MIT of the sixties onward, the classic hacker has emerged from sleep in the early afternoon to start programming with enthusiasm and has continued his efforts, deeply immersed in coding, into the wee hours of the morning. A good example of this is the way sixteen-year-old Irish hacker Sarah Flannery describes her work on the so-called Cayley-Purser encryption algorithm: "I had a great feeling of excitement. . . . I worked constantly for whole days on end, and it was exhilarating. There were times when I never wanted to stop."

Hacker activity is also *joyful*. It often has its roots in playful explorations. Torvalds has described, in messages on the Net, how Linux began to expand from small experiments with the computer he had just acquired. In the same messages, he has explained his motivation for developing Linux by simply stating that "it was/is fun working on it." Tim Berners-Lee, the man behind the Web, also describes how this creation began with experiments in linking what he called "play programs." Wozniak relates how many characteristics of the Apple computer "came from a game, and the fun features that were built in were only to do one pet project, which was to program . . . [a game called] Breakout and show it off at the club."

Flannery comments on how her work on the development of encryption technology evolved in the alternation between library study of theorems and the practice of exploratory programming: "With a particularly interesting theorem . . . I'd write a program to generate examples. . . . Whenever I programmed something I'd end up playing around for hours rather than getting back to plodding my way through the paper."

Sometimes this joyfulness shows in the hacker's "flesh life" as well. For example, Sandy Lerner is known not only for being one of the hackers behind the Internet routers but also for riding naked on horseback. Richard Stallman, the bearded and longhaired hacker guru, attends computer gatherings in a robe, and he exorcises commercial programs from the machines brought to him by his followers. Eric Raymond, a well-known defender of hacker culture, is also known for his playful lifestyle: a fan of live role-playing games, he roams the streets of his Pennsylvania hometown and the surrounding woods attired as an ancient sage, a Roman senator, or a seventeenth-century cavalier.

Raymond has also given a good summary of the general hacker spirit in his description of the Unix hackers' philosophy:

> To do the Unix philosophy right, you have to be loyal to excellence. You have to believe that software is a craft worth all the intelligence and passion you can muster. . . . Software design and implementation should be a joyous art, and a kind of high-level play. If this attitude seems preposterous or vaguely embarrassing to you, stop and think; ask yourself what you've forgotten. Why do you design software instead of doing something else to make money or pass the time? You must have thought software was worthy of your passions once. . . .
>
> To do the Unix philosophy right, you need to have (or recover) that attitude. You need to *care*. You need to *play*. You need to be willing to *explore*.

In summing up hacker activity's spirit, Raymond uses the word *passion*, which corresponds to Torvalds's *entertainment*, as he defined it in the Prologue. But Raymond's term is perhaps even more apt because, even though both words have associations that are not meant in this context, *passion* conveys more intuitively than *entertainment* the three levels described above—the dedication to an activity that is intrinsically interesting, inspiring, and joyous.

This passionate relationship to work is not an attitude found only among computer hackers. For example, the academic world can be seen as its much older predecessor. The attitude of passionate intellectual inquiry received similar expression nearly 2,500 years ago when Plato, founder of the first academy, said of philosophy, "Like light flashing forth when a fire is kindled, it is born in the soul and straightway nourishes itself."

The same attitude may also be found in any number of other spheres of life—among artists, artisans, and the "information professionals," from managers and engineers to media workers and designers, for example. It is not only the hackers' "jargon file" that emphasizes this general idea of being a hacker. At the first Hacker Conference in San Francisco in 1984, Burrell Smith, the hacker behind Apple's Macintosh computer, defined the term as follows: "Hackers can do almost anything and be a hacker. You can be a hacker carpenter. It's not necessarily high tech. I think it has to do with craftsmanship and caring about what you're doing." Raymond notes in his guide "How to Become a Hacker" that "there are people who apply the hacker attitude to other things [than software], like electronics and music—actually, you can find it at the highest levels of any science or art."

Looked at on this level, computer hackers can be understood as an excellent example of a more general work ethic—which we can give the name *the hacker work ethic*—gaining ground in our network society, in which the role of information professionals is expanding. But although we use a label coined by computer hackers to express this attitude, it is important to note that we could talk about it even without any reference to computer people. We are discussing a general social challenge that calls into question the Protestant work ethic that has long governed our lives and still maintains a powerful hold on us.

Let's see what type of long historical and strong societal forces the hacker work ethic, in this sense, faces. The familiar expression "Protestant work ethic" derives, of course, from Max Weber's famous essay *The Protestant Ethic and the Spirit of Capitalism* (1904–1905). Weber starts out by describing how the notion of work as a duty lies at the core of the capitalist spirit that arose in the sixteenth century: "This peculiar idea, so familiar to us today, but in reality so little a matter of course, of one's duty in a calling, is what is most characteristic of the social ethic of capitalistic culture, and is in a sense the fundamental basis of it. It is an obligation which the individual is supposed to feel and does feel towards the content of his professional activity, no matter in what it consists, in particular no matter whether it appears on the surface as a utilization of his personal powers, or only of his material possessions (as capital)." Weber goes on to say: "Not only is a developed sense of responsibility absolutely indispensable, but in general also an attitude which, at least during working hours, is freed from continual calculations of how the customary wage may be earned with a maximum of comfort and a minimum of exertion. Labour must, on the contrary, be performed as if it were an absolute end in itself, a calling."

Then Weber demonstrates how the other main force described in his essay, the work ethic taught by Protestants, which also arose in the sixteenth century, furthered these goals. The Protestant preacher Richard Baxter expressed that work ethic in its pure form: "It is for action that God maintaineth us and our activities; work is the moral as well as the natural end of power," and to say "I will pray and meditate [instead of working], is as if your servant should refuse his greatest work and tie himself to some lesser, easier part." God is not pleased to see people just meditating and praying—he wants them to do their job.

True to the capitalist spirit, Baxter advises employers to reinforce this idea in workers of wanting to do one's job as well as possible by making it a matter of conscience: "A truly godly servant will do all your service in obedience to God, as if God Himself had bid him do it." Baxter sums up this attitude by referring to labor as a "calling," a good expression of the three core attitudes of the Protestant work ethic: work must be seen as an end in itself, at work one must do one's part as well as possible, and work must be regarded as a duty, which must be done because it must be done.

While the hacker work ethic's precursor is in the academy, Weber says that the Protestant ethic's only historical precursor is in the monastery. And certainly, if we expand on Weber's comparison, we can see many similarities. In the sixth century, for example, Benedict's monastic rule required all monks to see the work assigned to them as their duty and warned work-shy brethren by noting that "idleness is the enemy of the soul." Monks were also not supposed to question the jobs they were given. Benedict's fifth-century predecessor John Cassian made this clear in his monastic rule by describing in admiring tones the obedience of a monk, named John, to his elder's order to roll a stone so large that no human being could move it:

Again, when some others were anxious to be edified by the example of his [John's] obedience, the elder called him and said: "John, run and roll that stone hither as quickly as possible;" and he forthwith, applying now his neck, and now his whole body, tried with all his might and main to roll an enormous stone which a great crowd of men would not be able to move, so that not only were his clothes saturated with sweat from his limbs, but the stone itself was wetted by his neck; in this too never weighing the impossibility of the command and deed, out of reverence for the old man and the unfeigned simplicity of his service, as he believed implicitly that the old man could not command him to do anything vain or without reason.

This Sisyphean straining epitomizes the idea, central to monastic thought, that one should not question the nature of one's work. Benedict's monastic rule even explained that the nature of the work did not matter because the highest purpose of work was not actually to get something done but to *humble* the worker's soul by making him do whatever he is told—a principle that seems to be still active in a great number of offices. In medieval times, this prototype for the Protestant work ethic existed only within the monasteries, and it did not influence the prevailing attitude of the church, much less that of society at large. It was only the Protestant Reformation that spread the monastic thinking to the world beyond the monastery walls.

However, Weber went on to emphasize that even though the spirit of capitalism found its essentially religious justification in the Protestant ethic, the latter soon emancipated itself from religion and began to operate according to its own laws. To use Weber's famous metaphor, it turned into a religiously neutral iron cage. This is an essential qualification. In our globalizing world, we should think of the term *Protestant ethic* in the same way we think of an expression such as *platonic love*. When we say that someone loves another person platonically, we do not mean that he is a Platonist— that is, an adherent of Plato's philosophy, metaphysics and all. We may attribute a platonic love relationship to a follower of any philosophy, religion, or culture. In the same way, we can speak of someone's "Protestant ethic" regardless of his or her faith or culture. Thus, a Japanese person, an atheist, or a devout Catholic may act—and often does act—in accordance with a Protestant ethic.

One need not look very far to realize how strong a force this Protestant ethic still is. Commonplace remarks like "I want to do my job well," or those made by employers in their little speeches at employee retirement parties about how a person "has always been an industrious/responsible/reliable/loyal worker" are the legacy of the Protestant ethic in that they make no demands on the nature of the work itself. The elevation of work to the status of the most important thing in life—at its extreme, a work addiction that leads to complete neglect of one's loved ones—is another symptom of the Protestant ethic. So is work done with clenched jaws and a responsibility-ridden attitude and the bad conscience many feel when they have to miss work due to ill health.

Seen in a larger historical context, this continued dominance of the Protestant ethic is not so surprising when we remember that even though our network society differs in many significant ways from its predecessor, the industrial society, its "new economy" does not involve a total break with the capitalism Weber describes; it is merely *a new kind of capitalism*. In *The Information Age*, Castells stresses that work, in the sense of labor, is not about to end, despite wild paradisiacal forecasts such as Jeremy Rifkin's *The End of Work*. We easily fall for this illusion that technological advances will, somehow, automatically, make our lives less work-centered—but if we just look at the empirical facts of the rise of the network society so far and project them into the future, we must agree with Castells on the nature of the prevailing pattern: "Work is, and will be for the foreseeable future, the nucleus of people's life." The network society itself does not question the Protestant ethic. Left to its own devices, the work-centered spirit easily continues to dominate within it.

Seen in this overall context, the radical nature of general hackerism consists of its proposing an alternative spirit for the network society—a spirit that finally questions the dominant Protestant ethic. In this context, we find the only sense in which all hackers are really crackers: they are trying to crack the lock of the iron cage.

The Purpose of Life

The displacement of the Protestant ethic will not happen overnight. It will take time, like all great cultural changes. The Protestant ethic is so deeply embedded in our present consciousness that it is often thought of as if it were just "human nature." Of course, it is not. Even a brief look at pre-Protestant attitudes toward work provides a healthy reminder of that fact. Both the Protestant and the hacker ethic are historically singular.

Richard Baxter's view of work was completely alien to the pre-Protestant church. Before the Reformation, clerics tended to devote time to questions such as "Is there life after death?" but none of them worried about whether there was *work* after life. Work did not belong among the church's highest ideals. God himself worked for six days and finally rested on the seventh. This was the highest goal for human beings as well: in Heaven, just as on Sundays, people would not have to work. Paradise was in, office was out. One might say that Christianity's original answer to the question "What is the purpose of life?" was: the purpose of life is Sunday.

This statement is not just a witticism. In the fifth century, Augustine compared our life quite literally to Friday, the day when, according to the teachings of the church, Adam and Eve sinned and Christ suffered on the cross. Augustine wrote that in Heaven we'll find a perennial Sunday, the day on which God rested and Christ ascended to Heaven: "That will truly be the greatest of Sabbaths; a Sabbath that has no evening." Life is just a long wait for the weekend.

Because the Church Fathers saw work as merely a consequence of the fall from grace, they also took very particular conceptual care in their descriptions of Adam's and Eve's activities in Paradise. Whatever Adam and Eve may have done there, it could not be seen as *work*. Augustine emphasizes that in Eden "praiseworthy work was not toilsome"—it was no more than a pleasant *hobby*.

The pre-Protestant churchmen understood work, "toil," as punishment. In medieval visionary literature that speaks to churchmen's images of Hell, the implements of labor fully reveal their true nature as instruments of torture: sinners are punished with hammers and other tools. What's more, according to these visions, there is in Hell an even more cruel torture than the directly inflicted physical one: perennial toil. When the devout brother Brendan saw, in the sixth century, a worker on his visit to the beyond, he immediately made the sign of the cross: he realized that he had arrived where all hope must be abandoned. Here is the narrator of his vision:

> When they had passed on further, about a stone's throw, they heard the noise of bellows blowing like thunder, and the beating of sledge hammers on the anvils and iron. Then St. Brendan armed himself all over his body with the sign of the Cross, saying, "O Lord Jesus Christ, deliver us from this sinister island." Soon one of the inhabitants appeared to do some work. He was hairy and hideous, blackened with fire and smoke. When he saw the servants of Christ near the island, he withdrew into his forge, crying aloud: "Woe! Woe! Woe!"

If you do not conduct yourself well in this life, the thinking went, you are condemned to work even in the next. And, even worse, that work, according to the pre-Protestant church, will be absolutely useless, meaningless to an extent you could never have imagined even on your worst working day on earth.

This theme crystallizes in the apotheosis of the pre-Protestant worldview, Dante's *Divine Comedy* (completed just before his death in 1321), in which sinners who have devoted their lives to money—both spendthrifts and misers—are doomed to push huge boulders around an eternal circle:

More shades were here than anywhere above,
and from both sides, to the sounds of their own screams,
straining their chests, they rolled enormous weights.

And when they met and clashed against each other
they turned to push the other way, one side
screaming, "Why hoard?," the other side, "Why waste?"

And so they moved back round the gloomy circle,
returning on both sides to opposite poles
to scream their shameful tune another time;

again they came to clash and turn and roll
forever in their semicircle joust.

Dante borrows this idea from Greek mythology. In Tartarus, where the very worst human beings were dispatched, the most severe punishment was meted out to greedy Sisyphus, who was doomed to endlessly push a big rock up to the top of a hill, from which it always rolled back down. Sunday always beckons to Sisyphus and the sinners in Dante's Inferno, but it never comes. They are condemned to an eternal Friday.

Considering this background, we can now gain a better understanding of how great a change in our attitude toward work the Protestant Reformation entailed. In allegorical terms, it moved life's center of gravity from Sunday to Friday. The Protestant ethic reoriented ideology so thoroughly that it even turned Heaven and Hell upside down. When work became an end in itself on earth, the clerics found it difficult to imagine Heaven as a place for mere time-wasting leisure, and work could no longer be seen as infernal punishment. Thus, reformed eighteenth-century cleric Johann Kasper Lavater explained that even in Heaven "we cannot be blessed without having occupations. To have an occupation means to have a calling, an office, a special, particular task to do." Baptist William Clarke Ulyat put it in a nutshell when he described Heaven at the beginning of the twentieth century: "practically it is a workshop."

The Protestant ethic proved so powerful that its work-centeredness permeated even our imagination. A great example of this is Daniel Defoe's *Robinson Crusoe* (1719), a novel written by a man trained as a Protestant preacher. Marooned on an abundant island, Crusoe does not take it easy; he works all the time. He is such an orthodox Protestant that he does not even take Sunday off, though he otherwise still observes the seven-day week. After saving an aborigine from his enemies, he aptly names him Friday, trains him in the Protestant ethic, and then praises him in a manner that perfectly describes that ethic's ideal worker: "Never man had a more faithful, loving, sincere servant, perfectly obliged and engaged; his very affections were ty'd to me, like those of a child to a father."

In Michel Tournier's twentieth-century satirical retelling of the novel, *Vendredi* (Friday), Friday's conversion to the Protestant ethic is still more total. Crusoe decides to put Friday to the test by giving him a task even more Sisyphean than what Cassian's monastic rule prescribed:

> I set him a task which in every prison in the world is held to be the most degrading of harassments—the task of digging a hole and filling it in with the contents of a second; then digging a third, and so on. He labored at this for an entire day, under a leaden sky and in heat like that of a furnace. . . . To say that Friday gave no sign of resenting this idiotic employment, is not enough. I have seldom seen him work with such good will.

Sisyphus has truly become a hero.

The Passionate Life

When the hacker ethic is placed in this large historical context, it is easy to see that this ethic—understood not just as the computer hackers' ethic but as a general social challenge—resembles the pre-Protestant ethic to a much greater degree than it does the Protestant one. In this sense, one could say that for hackers the purpose of life is closer to Sunday than to Friday. But, it is important to note, only closer: ultimately, the hacker ethic is not the same as the pre-Protestant work ethic, which envisions a paradise of life without doing anything. Hackers want to realize their passions, and they are ready to accept that the pursuit even of interesting tasks may not always be unmitigated bliss.

For hackers, *passion* describes the general tenor of their activity, though its fulfillment may not be sheer joyful play in all its aspects. Thus, Linus Torvalds has described his work on Linux as a combination of enjoyable hobby and serious work: "Linux has very much been a hobby (but a serious one: the best type)." Passionate and creative, hacking also entails hard work. Raymond says in his guide "How to Become a Hacker": "Being a hacker is lots of fun, but it's a kind of fun that takes a lot of effort." Such effort is needed in the creation of anything even just a little bit greater. If need be, hackers are also ready for the less interesting parts necessary for the creation of the whole. However, the meaningfulness of the whole gives even its more boring aspects worth. Raymond writes: "The hard work and dedication will become a kind of intense play rather than drudgery."

There's a difference between being permanently joyless and having found a passion in life for the realization of which one is also willing to take on less joyful but nonetheless necessary parts.

*E*ric Liu (1968–) was born in Poughkeepsie, NY, to Chinese parents who immigrated from Taiwan. He earned degrees from Yale University and Harvard Law School and served as a speechwriter to President Bill Clinton. His autobiography, The Accidental Asian: Notes of a Native Speaker (1998) explores his own identity and career as an American and Asian American.

A Chinaman's Chance:
Reflections on the American Dream

Eric Liu

A lot of people my age seem to think that the American Dream is dead. I think they're dead wrong.

Or at least only partly right. It is true that for those of us in our twenties and early thirties, job opportunities are scarce. There looms a real threat that we will be the first American generation to have a lower standard of living than our parents.

But what is it that we mean when we invoke the American Dream?

In the past, the American Dream was something that held people of all races, religions, and identities together. As James Comer has written, it represented a shared aspiration among all Americans—black, white, or any other color—"to provide well for themselves and their families as valued members of a democratic society." Now, all too often, it seems the American Dream means merely some guarantee of affluence, a birthright of wealth.

At a basic level, of course, the American Dream is about prosperity and the pursuit of material happiness. But to me, its meaning extends beyond such concerns. To me, the dream is not just about buying a bigger house than the one I grew up in or having shinier stuff now than I had as a kid. It also represents a sense of opportunity that binds generations together in commitment, so that the young inherit not only property but also perseverance, not only money but also a mission to make good on the strivings of their parents and grandparents.

The poet Robert Browning once wrote that "a man's reach must exceed his grasp—else what's a heaven for?" So it is in America. Every generation will strive, and often fail. Every generation will reach for success, and often miss the mark. But Americans rely as much on the next generation as on the next life to prove that such struggles and frustrations are not in vain. There may be temporary setbacks, cutbacks, recessions, depressions. But this is a nation of second chances. So long as there are young Americans who do not take what they have—or what they can do—for granted, progress is always possible.

My conception of the American Dream does not take progress for granted. But it does demand the *opportunity* to achieve progress—and values the opportunity as much as the achievement. I come at this question as the son of immigrants. I see just as clearly as anyone else the cracks in the idealist vision of fulfillment for all. But because my parents came here with virtually nothing, because they did build something, I see the enormous potential inherent in the ideal.

I happen still to believe in our national creed: freedom and opportunity, and our common responsibility to uphold them. This creed is what makes America unique. More than any demographic statistic or economic indicator, it animates the American Dream. It infuses our mundane struggles—to plan a career, do good work, get ahead—with purpose and possibility. It makes America the only country that could produce heroes like Colin Powell—heroes who rise from nothing, who overcome the odds.

I think of the sacrifices made by my own parents. I appreciate the hardship of the long road traveled by my father—one of whose first jobs in America was painting the yellow line down a South Dakota interstate—and by my mother—whose first job here was filing pay stubs for a New York restaurant. From such beginnings, they were able to build a comfortable life and provide me with a breadth of resources—through arts, travel, and an Ivy League education. It was an unspoken obligation for them to do so.

I think of my boss in my first job after college, on Capitol Hill. George is a smart, feisty, cigar-chomping, take-no-shit Greek-American. He is about fifteen years older than I, has different interests, a very different personality. But like me, he is the son of immigrants, and he would joke with me that the Greek-Chinese mafia was going to take over one day. He was only half joking. We'd worked harder, our parents doubly harder, than almost anyone else we knew. To people like George, talk of the withering of the American Dream seems foreign.

It's undeniable that principles like freedom and opportunity, no matter how dearly held, are not enough. They can inspire a multiracial March on Washington, but they can not bring black salaries in alignment with white salaries. They can draw wave after wave of immigrants here, but they can not provide them the means to get out of our ghettos and barrios and Chinatowns. They are not sufficient for fulfillment of the American Dream.

But they are necessary. They are vital. And not just to the children of immigrants. These ideals form the durable thread that weaves us all in union. Put another way, they are one of the few things that keep America from disintegrating into a loose confederation of zip codes and walled-in communities.

What alarms me is how many people my age look at our nation's ideals with a rising sense of irony. What good is such a creed if you are working for hourly wages in a deadend job? What value do such platitudes have if you live in an urban war zone? When the only apparent link between homeboys and housepainters and bike messengers and investment bankers is pop culture—MTV, the NBA, movies, dance music—then the social fabric is flimsy indeed.

My generation has come of age at a time when the country is fighting off bouts of defeatism and self-doubt, at a time when racism and social inequities seem not only persistent but intractable. At a time like this, the retreat to one's own kind is seen by more and more of my peers as an advance. And that retreat has given rise again to the notion that there are essential and irreconcilable differences among the races—a notion that was supposed to have disappeared from American discourse by the time my peers and I were born in the sixties.

Not long ago, for instance, my sister called me a "banana."

I was needling her about her passion for rap and hip-hop music. Every time I saw her, it seemed, she was jumping and twisting to Arrested Development or Chubb Rock or some other funky group. She joked that despite being the daughter of Chinese immigrants, she was indeed "black at heart." And then she added, light-heartedly, "You, on the other hand—well, you're basically a banana." Yellow on the outside, but white inside.

I protested, denied her charge vehemently. But it was too late. She was back to dancing. And I stood accused.

Ever since then, I have wondered what it means to be black, or white, or Asian "at heart"—particularly for my generation. Growing up, when other kids would ask whether I was Chinese or Korean or Japanese, I would reply, a little petulantly, "American." Assimilation can still be a sensitive subject. I recall reading about a Korean-born

Congressman who had gone out of his way to say that Asian-Americans should expect nothing special from him. He added that he was taking speech lessons "to get rid of this accent." I winced at his palpable self-hate. But then it hit me: Is this how my sister sees me?

There is no doubt that minorities like me can draw strength from our communities. But in today's environment, anything other than ostentatious tribal fealty is taken in some communities as a sign of moral weakness, a disappointing dilution of character. In times that demand ever-clearer thinking, it has become too easy for people to shut off their brains: "It's a black/Asian/Latino/white thing," says the variable T-shirt. "You wouldn't understand." Increasingly, we don't.

The civil-rights triumphs of the sixties and the cultural revolutions that followed made it possible for minorities to celebrate our diverse heritages. I can appreciate that. But I know, too, that the sixties—or at least, my generation's grainy, hazy vision of the decade—also bequeathed to young Americans a legacy of near-pathological race consciousness.

Today's culture of entitlement—and of race entitlement in particular—tells us plenty about what we get if we are black or white or female or male or old or young.

It is silent, though, on some other important issues. For instance: What do we "get" for being American? And just as importantly, What do we owe? These are questions around which young people like myself must tread carefully, since talk of common interests, civic culture, responsibility, and integration sounds a little too "white" for some people. To the new segregationists, the "American Dream" is like the old myth of the "Melting Pot": an oppressive fiction, an opiate for the unhappy colored masses.

How have we allowed our thinking about race to become so twisted? The formal obstacles and the hateful opposition to civil rights have long faded into memory. By most external measures, life for minorities is better than it was a quarter century ago. It would seem that the opportunities for tolerance and cooperation are commonplace. Why, then, are so many of my peers so cynical about our ability to get along with one another?

The reasons are frustratingly ambiguous. I got a glimpse of this when I was in college. It was late in my junior year, and as the editor of a campus magazine, I was sitting on a panel to discuss "The White Press at Yale: What Is to Be Done?" The assembly hall was packed, a diverse and noisy crowd. The air was heavy, nervously electric.

Why weren't there more stories about "minority issues" in the Yale *Daily News?* Why weren't there more stories on Africa in my magazine, the foreign affairs journal? How many "editors of color" served on the boards of each of the major publications? The questions were volleyed like artillery, one round after another, punctuated only by the applause of an audience spoiling for a fight. The questions were not at all unfair. But it seemed that no one—not even those of us on the panel who *were* people of color—could provide, in this context, satisfactory answers.

Toward the end of the discussion, I made a brief appeal for reason and moderation. And afterward, as students milled around restlessly, I was attacked: for my narrow-mindedness—How dare you suggest that Yale is not a fundamentally prejudiced place!—for my simplemindedness—Have you, too, been co-opted?

And for my betrayal—Are you just white inside?

My eyes were opened that uncomfortably warm early summer evening. Not only to the cynical posturing and the combustible opportunism of campus racial politics. But more importantly, to the larger question of identity—my identity—in America. Never mind that the aim of many of the loudest critics was to generate headlines in the very publications they denounced. In spite of themselves—against, it would seem, their true intentions—they got me to think about who I am.

In our society today, and especially among people of my generation, we are congealing into clots of narrow commonality. We stick with racial and religious comrades. This tribal consciousness-raising can be empowering for some. But while America was conceived in liberty—the liberty, for instance, to associate with whomever we like—it was never designed to be a mere collection of subcultures. We forget that there is in fact such a thing as a unique American identity that transcends our sundry tribes, sets, gangs, and cliques.

I have grappled, wittingly or not, with these questions of identity and allegiance all my life. When I was in my early teens, I would invite my buddies overnight to watch movies, play video games, and beat one another up. Before too long, my dad would come downstairs and start hamming it up—telling stories, asking gently nosy questions, making corny jokes, all with his distinct Chinese accent. I would stand back, quietly gauging everyone's reaction. Of course, the guys loved it. But I would feel uneasy.

What was then cause for discomfort is now a source of strength. Looking back on such episodes, I take pride in my father's accented

English; I feel awe at his courage to laugh loudly in a language not really his own.

It was around the same time that I decided that continued attendance at the community Chinese school on Sundays was uncool. There was no fanfare; I simply stopped going. As a child, I'd been too blissfully unaware to think of Chinese school as anything more than a weekly chore, with an annual festival (dumplings and spring rolls, games and prizes). But by the time I was a peer-pressured adolescent, Chinese school seemed like a badge of the woefully unassimilated. I turned my back on it.

Even as I write these words now, it feels as though I am revealing a long-held secret. I am proud that my ancestors—scholars, soldiers, farmers—came from one of the world's great civilizations. I am proud that my grandfather served in the Chinese Air Force. I am proud to speak even my clumsy brand of Mandarin, and I feel blessed to be able to think idiomatically in Chinese, a language so much richer in nuance and subtle poetry than English.

Belatedly, I appreciate the good fortune I've had to be the son of immigrants. As a kid, I could play Thomas Jefferson in the bicentennial school play one week and the next week play the poet Li Bai at the Chinese school festival. I could come home from an afternoon of teen slang at the mall and sit down to dinner for a rollicking conversation in our family's hybrid of Chinese and English. I understood, when I went over to visit friends, that my life was different. At the time, I just never fully appreciated how rich it was.

Yet I know that this pride in my heritage does not cross into prejudice against others. What it reflects is pride in what my country represents. That became clear to me when I went through Marine Corps Officer Candidates' School. During the summers after my sophomore and junior years of college, I volunteered for OCS, a grueling boot camp for potential officers in the swamps and foothills of Quantico, Virginia.

And once I arrived—standing 5'4", 135 pounds, bespectacled, a Chinese Ivy League Democrat—I was a target straight out of central casting. The wiry, raspy-voiced drill sergeant, though he was perhaps only an inch or two taller than I, called me "Little One" with as much venom as can be squeezed into such a moniker. He heaped verbal abuse on me, he laughed when I stumbled, he screamed when I hesitated. But he also never failed to remind me that just because I was a little shit didn't mean I shouldn't run farther, climb higher, think faster, hit harder than anyone else.

That was the funny thing about the Marine Corps. It is, ostensibly, one of the most conservative institutions in the United States. And yet, for those twelve weeks, it represented the kind of color-blind equality of opportunity that the rest of society struggles to match. I did not feel uncomfortable at OCS to be of Chinese descent. Indeed, I drew strength from it. My platoon was a veritable cross section of America: forty young men of all backgrounds, all regions, all races, all levels of intelligence and ability, displaced from our lives (if only for a few weeks) with nowhere else to go.

Going down the list of names—Courtemanche, Dougherty, Grella, Hunt, Liu, Reeves, Schwarzman, and so on—brought to mind a line from a World War II documentary I once saw, which went something like this: The reason why it seemed during the war that America was as good as the rest of the world put together was that America *was* the rest of the world put together.

Ultimately, I decided that the Marines was not what I wanted to do for four years and I did not accept the second lieutenant's commission. But I will never forget the day of the graduation parade: bright sunshine, brisk winds, the band playing Sousa as my company passed in review. As my mom and dad watched and photographed the parade from the rafters, I thought to myself: this is the American Dream in all its cheesy earnestness. I felt the thrill of truly being part of something larger and greater than myself.

I do know that American life is not all Sousa marches and flag-waving. I know that those with reactionary agendas often find it convenient to cloak their motives in the language of Americanism. The "American Party" was the name of a major nativist organization in the nineteenth century. "America First" is the siren song of the isolationists who would withdraw this country from the world and expel the world from this country. I know that our national immigration laws were once designed explicitly to cut off the influx from Asia.

I also know that discrimination is real. I am reminded of a gentle old man who, after Pearl Harbor, was stripped of his possessions without warning, taken from his home, and thrown into a Japanese internment camp. He survived, and by many measures has thrived, serving as a community leader and political activist. But I am reluctant to share with him my wide-eyed patriotism.

I know the bittersweet irony that my own father—a strong and optimistic man—would sometimes feel when he was alive. When he came across a comically lost cause—if the Yankees were behind 14–0 in the ninth, or if Dukakis was down ten points in the polls with a week left—he would often joke that the doomed party had "a Chinaman's chance" of success. It was one of those insensitive idioms of a generation ago, and it must have lodged in his impressionable young mind when he first came to America. It spoke of a perceived stacked deck.

I know, too, that for many other immigrants, the dream simply does not work out. Fae Myenne Ng, the author of *Bone*, writes about how her father ventured here from China under a false identity and arrived at Angel Island, the detention center outside the "Gold Mountain" of San Francisco. He got out, he labored, he struggled, and he suffered "a bitter no-luck life" in America. There was no glory. For him, Ng suggests, the journey was not worth it.

But it is precisely because I know these things that I want to prove that in the long run, over generations and across ethnicities, it *is* worth it. For the second-generation American, opportunity is obligation. I have seen and faced racism. I understand the dull pain of dreams deferred or unmet. But I believe still that there is so little stopping me from building the life that I want. I was given, through my parents' labors, the chance to bridge that gap between ideals and reality. Who am I to throw away that chance?

Plainly, I am subject to the criticism that I speak too much from my own experience. Not everyone can relate to the second-generation American story. When I have spoken like this with some friends, the issue has been my perspective. *What you say is fine for you. But unless you grew up where I did, unless you've had people avoid you because of the color of your skin, don't talk to me about common dreams.*

But are we then to be paralyzed? Is respect for different experiences supposed to obviate the possibility of shared aspirations? Does the diversity of life in America doom us to a fractured understanding of one another? The question is basic: Should the failure of this nation thus far to fulfill its stated ideals incapacitate its young people, or motivate us?

Our country was built on, and remains glued by, the idea that everybody deserves a fair shot and that we must work together to guarantee that opportunity—the original American Dream. It was this idea, in some inchoate form, that drew every immigrant here. It was this idea, however sullied by slavery and racism, that motivated the civil-rights movement. To write this idea off—even when its execution is spotty—to let American life descend into squabbles among separatist tribes would not just be sad. It would be a total mishandling of a legacy, the squandering of a great historical inheritance.

Mine must not be the first generation of Americans to lose America. Just as so many of our parents journeyed here to find their version of the American Dream, so must young Americans today journey across boundaries of race and class to rediscover one another. We are the first American generation to be born into an integrated society, and we are accustomed to more race mixing than any generation before us. We started open-minded, and it's not too late for us to stay that way.

Time is of the essence. For in our national political culture today, the watchwords seem to be *decline* and *end*. Apocalyptic visions and dark millennial predictions abound. The end of history. The end of progress. The end of equality. Even something as ostensibly positive as the end of the Cold War has a bittersweet tinge, because for the life of us, no one in America can get a handle on the big question, "What Next?"

For my generation, this fixation on endings is particularly enervating. One's twenties are supposed to be a time of widening horizons, of bright possibilities. Instead, America seems to have entered an era of limits. Whether it is the difficulty of finding jobs from some place other than a temp agency, or the mountains of debt that darken our future, the message to my peers is often that this nation's time has come and gone; let's bow out with grace and dignity.

A friend once observed that while the Chinese seek to adapt to nature and yield to circumstance, Americans seek to conquer both. She meant that as a criticism of America. But I interpreted her remark differently. I *do* believe that America is exceptional. And I believe it is up to my generation to revive that spirit, that sense that we do in fact have control over our own destiny—as individuals and as a nation.

If we are to reclaim a common destiny, we must also reach out to other generations for help. It was Franklin Roosevelt who said that while America can't always build the future for its youth, it can—and must—build its youth for the future. That commitment across generations is as central to the American Dream as any I have enunciated. We are linked, black and white, old and young, one and inseparable.

I know how my words sound. I am old enough to perceive my own naïveté but young enough still to cherish it. I realize that I am coming of age just as the American Dream is showing its age. Yet I still have faith in this country's unique destiny—to create generation after generation of hyphenates like me, to channel this new blood, this resilience and energy into an ever more vibrant future for *all* Americans.

And I want to prove—for my sake, for my father's sake, and for my country's sake—that a Chinaman's chance is as good as anyone else's.

*W*illiam Adler is a freelance writer living in Texas who has written for various *publications, including* Esquire *and* Rolling Stone. *Since publishing "A Job on the Line" in 2000 in* Mother Jones, *he has expanded the work to book length and published it as* Mollie's Job *in 2001.*

A Job on the Line

William M. Adler

After 34 years, Mollie James lost her place on the global assembly line. Now Balbina Duque holds her job in Mexico—and both women struggle to make ends meet.

At 3 o'clock on a warm June afternoon, the second of two wash-up bells rings for the final time. Mollie James stands hunched over the sink as she rinses her hands with industrial soap alongside her co-workers. She first came to work here, on the assembly line at Universal Manufacturing Company in Paterson, New Jersey, a few years after the factory opened in 1951. She was the first woman at the factory to run a stamping machine, the first to laminate steel. She was among the first female union stewards and among the first African American stewards; hers was a self-assured presence any grievant would want on their side. And now, after 34 years on the line—nearly two-thirds of her life—she is the last to go.

At the end of every other shift for more than three decades, Mollie and her fellow employees beat a quick path to the plant parking lot. On this day there is less sense of hurry. There are still children to feed, clothes to wash, bills to pay, errands to run, other jobs to race to. But as she and the others leave the washroom, no one seems pressed to leave. All about the plant entrance, and out in the lot, people stand in small clusters, like mourners at their own wake, talking, laughing, hugging, crying. Almost always Mollie James is outgoing and outspoken, her voice loud and assertive, her smile nicely lighted. At 59 she is a strong woman, her strength forged from a life of hard work and sacrifice, and faith in God. She is not one to betray her emotions, but this day is different. Her bearing has turned to reserve, her normally quick eyes dull and watery. Her working life is over, and that is the only life she has ever known.

Universal had always turned a tidy profit. Its signature product, ballasts that regulate the current in fluorescent lights, attracted attention only when the ballast failed—causing the light fixture to hum or flicker. In the mid-1980s, however, the locally owned company was twice swept up in the gale winds of Wall Street's merger mania. Twice within eight months Universal was sold, both times to firms headed by disciples of Michael Milken, the Street's reigning evil genius. Not long after the second sale, to a Los Angeles-based electrical components conglomerate called MagneTek, Inc., movers began pulling up the plant's massive machinery, much of which had been bolted to the floor when the factory opened.

Mollie had sensed what was happening in January 1989, the morning she came to work and noticed the hole in the floor. It wasn't a hole, really, in the sense of an opening; it was more of a void: a great yawning space of discolored concrete where just the afternoon before had sat a steel-stamping machine, a hulking piece of American industrial might. Before long, more holes appeared, each tracing the outline of the base of another machine, like chalk around a sidewalk corpse.

Now, on the last day, when there is no one left to say goodbye to, Mollie slumps behind the wheel of her rusting 1977 Dodge Charger and follows the procession out of the lot. It is not far, three miles or so, from the plant in Paterson's industrial Bunker Hill neighborhood to the three-story, three-family house she owns on the near East Side. Upon pulling into her customary space in the driveway, Mollie sits in the car a good long while, letting the heat of the summer afternoon settle her. By the time she fits the key into the back-door lock and begins climbing the three flights of stairs to her bedroom, she has stopped crying.

The machine that Mollie used to stamp steel for three decades makes its way south, past factories that Universal opened in Mississippi and Arkansas during the 1960s and 1970s to take advantage of cheaper labor and taxes, before arriving in Matamoros, Mexico, a booming border city just across the Rio Grande from Brownsville, Texas. On a blindingly blue morning, MagneTek executives from "corporate" in L.A. arrive for the gala ribbon cutting of the first MagneTek plant here. Plant manager Chuck Peeples, an affable Arkansas expatriate, leads the officials on a tour of the gleaming factory. Outfitted in natty going-native panama hats emblazoned with the company's royal-blue capital-M "power" logo, the MagneTek honchos parade past equipment ripped from the shopworn floor in Paterson, machinery now operated by a young, almost entirely female workforce. These women, primarily in their teens and 20s, have come north to Matamoros in search of work and a better future than the bleakness promised in the jobless farming towns of the interior.

Balbina Duque Granados found a job at MagneTek in 1993, after leaving her family's home in a picturesque but poor mountain village of central Mexico. Just out of her teens, she has an easy, dimpled smile and long black hair worn in a ponytail. With its comparatively low wages, endless supply of labor, lack of regulation, and proximity to the United States, Matamoros is a magnet for maquiladoras, the foreign-owned assembly plants that wed First World engineering with Third World working conditions. Balbina's probationary pay is slightly less than $26 a week, or about 65 cents an hour. It is difficult work, winding coils, repetitive and tiring and mind numbing, but it is a job she is thrilled to have—her "answered prayer." And although Balbina doesn't know it, it is not just any job. It is Mollie's job.

The job in which Mollie James once took great pride, the job that both fostered and repaid her loyalty by enabling her to rise above humble beginnings and provide for her family—that job does not now pay Balbina Duque a wage sufficient to live on. Embedded in that central fact, and in the intersecting lives and fates of the two women who held that single job, is a broader story about the fundamental changes currently remaking the economy—the ways in which "free trade" harms democracy, undermines stable businesses and communities, and exploits workers on both sides of the border, both ends of the global assembly line.

At a few minutes before 2 o'clock on a cold, pitch-black morning in November 1950, Mollie and her father, Lorenzo Brown, waited anxiously on the platform of the ornate World War I–era train station in Richmond, Virginia. The Browns were from Cartersville, 45 miles west, in the rolling farmland of central Virginia. Mollie was headed to Penn Station in Newark, New Jersey, to meet her fiance, Sam James, who would take her home, to Paterson, to her new life. She was dressed in her finest: a new navy-blue suit, new shoes, new hairdo. She carried nearly everything she owned in a half-dozen sky-blue suitcases her father had given her for the trip.

Mollie was traveling alone, but the "colored" train cars of the Silver Meteor, and indeed those of the other great northbound coaches—the Champion, the Florida Sunbeam, the Silver Comet—were full of Mollie Browns: black southerners crossing the Mason-Dixon Line, heading for the promised land. Mollie's intended was waiting at the station in his new, yellow, two-door Ford to take her to Paterson, a city of 140,000 residents some 15 miles west of New York City. Sam drove her home to the one-room apartment he rented for $20 a week above the flat where his sister and brother-in-law lived. Although the accommodations were far from luxurious—Mollie and Sam shared a kitchen and bath with other upstairs tenants—her new life seemed as bright as Sam's shiny car.

Paterson at precisely the middle of the 20th century was absolutely humming, filled with vibrant neighborhoods, a bustling downtown retail and cultural district, and above all, factories small and large, producing everything from textiles to machine tools to electrical components. "There were so many places to work, I could have five jobs in the same day," Mollie recalled years later. "And if I didn't like one, I could leave and get another, sure."

Mollie's new hometown was born of entrepreneurial dreamers and schemers. The city had been founded on the 16th anniversary of the Declaration of Independence, July 4, 1792, not as a municipality but as a business: the home of the country's first industrial corporation, the Society for Useful Manufactures. The grand plans of the society and its guiding light, Alexander Hamilton, ultimately failed, but Paterson established itself as a cradle of American industry. The city became renowned for its textile mills—silk, especially—and later for the union-busting tactics of its mill owners. During the 19th century, textile manufacturers in Paterson were responsible for what were probably the nation's first runaway shops, opening "annexes" in rural Pennsylvania to take advantage of workers who could be subjected to longer hours for half the wages paid in New Jersey. In 1913, the Industrial Workers of the World mobilized Paterson's 25,000 employees to walk away from their looms, effectively nailing shut the nation's silk-manufacturing center. Able to rely on their nonunion factories, mill owners refused to negotiate; starved into submission, the strikers were forced to return to work with neither gains in wages nor improved working conditions.

By the time the 19-year-old Mollie Brown arrived in Paterson, the economy was booming. Unemployment was low, wages high. In her first few years in town, Mollie ran through several jobs. "You'd just catch the bus and go from factory to factory and see who was hiring." Among her stops was a low-slung cement building in northeast Paterson. The sign out front said Universal Manufacturing Co. The owner himself, a gregarious man named Archie Sergy, showed her through the plant, explaining that the company made a part for fluorescent lights called a ballast. "They showed me how it was made, the whole assembly line. I learned there's a lot to it, a very lot." The starting salary was 90 cents an hour, but the company was about to implement a second shift, from 3 p.m. to midnight, that would pay an extra dime an hour. Those hours were ideal for Mollie. She and Sam had three children under the age of five and another on the way, and if she were to work nights and he days, the couple could care for the children without hiring a sitter. She accepted the job. "I hope you'll be here a long time," Sergy told her. "I hope we'll all be here a long time!"

By the early 1960s, Universal employed a workforce of some 1,200. Archie Sergy and his top managers continued to demonstrate a sincere interest in the welfare of their employees. "They never treated you as inferior, regardless of whether you cleaned the toilets or whatever your job was," Mollie says. "They'd walk up and down the line and talk to us, joke with us, sometimes have their sandwiches with us right there on the line . . . If you needed a home loan, they'd give it to you, and you could make arrangements to pay it back."

Sergy saw the world as an industrialist, not a financier, and he maintained a steely eyed focus on quality and customer service to the degree that it probably hurt profit margins. But his company was no social service agency; it venerated the bottom line as much as any self-respecting capitalist enterprise. Mollie and her co-workers enjoyed good wages and job security in large part because they belonged to Teamsters Local 945, which bargained for higher pay and better benefits. In 1963, determined to insulate Universal from threats of work stoppage, Sergy followed the tradition established by the early Paterson silk makers: He opened an annex, a Universal factory in the Deep South. The new plant was located in rural Mississippi, providing Sergy with a low-wage workforce as well as an ever-present threat of plant closing to quiet employees in Paterson.

That same year, strapped for operating capital and lacking a successor, Sergy also succumbed to the lure of Wall Street: He sold Universal to a New York–based conglomerate. Sergy remained as titular head of Universal, but outsiders controlled the economic destiny of the women and men who toiled there. This was most evidently revealed when Sergy announced to the employees in April 1968, seven months before his death, that the parent company itself had been swallowed whole by another conglomerate. "We're all working for a company out of Chicago," he said. "Who they are I have no idea."

Whether those who held the purse strings were faceless financiers from New York or Chicago or Los Angeles didn't matter much to Mollie James. Owners came and went, and the principal visible sign of each transition was a new company name on the payroll checks. So when word spread in early 1986 that an outfit called MagneTek was the new owner, Mollie took the news calmly. Surely some things would change— managers in, managers out, maybe—but she had no reason to question her job security. Although the company had added a second Southern plant, in Arkansas, Paterson was still the flagship. Mollie came to work for Universal—and stayed—because of the peace of mind that came from a secure job: a job she could raise a family on, buy a house, a car, borrow money against, count on for the future.

But right away Mollie could tell the future was darkening. Like the earlier owners, MagneTek was a faraway, far-flung holding company, but the previous management's hands-off, don't-fix-it-if-it-ain't-broke page was missing from its corporate manual. "It started the day our name disappeared from the building," she says. "Poof, no more Universal." By the end of 1988, not only had Universal's name vanished from the plant; its machines, too, were disappearing, torn from the floor like trees from their roots. "The movers came at night, like thieves, sometimes just taking one piece at a time," Mollie recalls. "We'd come in in the mornings and there'd be another hole in the floor."

The machinery had been used to make a large specialty ballast known as the HID, or High Intensity Discharge, the kind used in thousand-watt fixtures installed in outdoor stadiums. Paterson was the lone Universal plant manufacturing the HID; making its precision-wound coils required different training and equipment than the garden-variety 40-watt fluorescent ballast the two Southern plants pumped out by the tens of thousands daily.

If Paterson's workers were more sophisticated, they were also more costly. Mollie earned $7.91 an hour, 75 cents more than she would have earned in Mississippi and almost a dollar more than in Arkansas. But if the wages down South were low, they were not low enough. They were not the cheapest possible wages. They weren't as low as workers earned in Mexico, where the prevailing pay at the maquiladoras was less than $8 a day. And so, in the early months of 1988, the machines began disappearing, bound ultimately for Matamoros. "All we kept hearing was how good a job we were doing," Mollie says, "that we had nothing to worry about, that we'd always have work in Paterson."

The nightly bus to Matamoros would not roll through the depot nearest Balbina Duque's village until 9:15. It was only mid-morning, just a couple of hours since she'd said her goodbyes to the family, since she'd pressed her lips for the last time to her baby son's cheek and handed him to her mother. It was only mid-morning, and already Balbina could feel the tropical sun on her face, could feel her funds dwindling fast. She had started with 200 pesos, the equivalent of about $65, and now that she'd paid a man nearly $20 to taxi her the hour from Monte Bello, her mountain village—a place of clean and clear air, brilliant high-desert flowers, and almost surrealistically bright light—to the bus station in town, and now that she'd bought a couple of tamales from a sidewalk vendor and a one-way ticket to the border for $30, Balbina was down to less than $15.

Balbina had turned 20 only weeks earlier. She was leaving for Matamoros, 400 miles north, to look for work in the maquiladoras. She was torn about going, especially about having to leave behind her 18-month-old son, Iban. "If there were work here," Balbina said in Spanish during a visit home some years later, "everyone would stay."

There was nothing to keep them at home. Balbina's village comprised maybe 1,000 people living in a couple of hundred pastel-colored homes with thatched roofs. There was neither running water nor electricity. Much of Balbina's day was spent filling and refilling a water bucket from a central well down a hill and carrying it back on her head to use for bathing, laundry, washing dishes, cooking, and drinking. A typical day might require 24 trips to the well, a chore that claimed three to four hours beginning at first light.

The interminable, grueling days were not for Balbina. Monte Bello felt like a sentence from which she needed to escape. It was a place for "people too old to work or too young to work," she said. "For me there was nothing. If you do not work in the fields there is nothing else to do." She decided she would celebrate her 20th birthday with her family, and then, as soon as she had saved enough for the bus fare, would take off for the border, where the maquiladoras favor young women for their nimble fingers and compliant minds, and where a job in a maquila trumps any other employment options.

It was dark when Balbina finally boarded the bus. Heading north, through a vast valley of corn, Highway 85 was flat as a tortilla. With two seats to herself, Balbina was able to curl into a comfortable enough position, and sleep came at once. When the bus pulled into Matamoros at dawn, she had to rouse herself from a dream about her son. Meeting her at the central station on Canales Avenue was a distant aunt, who escorted her to a small dwelling in the liltingly named Colonia Vista Hermosa—Beautiful View. But there was little beauty in the colonia; it was wedged between a pungent, milky-white irrigation canal and the Finsa park, the massive industrial park where MagneTek and other foreign-owned maquiladoras employed most of the working-age residents of Vista Hermosa.

One morning, the second Friday of 1993, Balbina and her younger sister, Elsa, caught a ride downtown to the headquarters of the big maquiladora workers' union, the SJOI—the Spanish acronym for the Union of Industrial Workers and Day Laborers. Four times weekly, waves of several thousand applicants washed up at dawn at the SJOI offices, the de facto employment agency for the maquilas. All nonsalaried workers applied through its central hiring hall, women on Mondays and Fridays, men on Tuesdays and Thursdays.

It was not yet 7 o'clock, and Balbina and Elsa had already been in line for an hour, a line that snaked through the three-story building, past the armed guard at the door, and stretched outside for more than a block. By eight, they had squeezed and elbowed and prodded their way inside the assembly hall, a room roughly the size and ambience of a drafty old high-school gymnasium. Mounted fans whirred overhead, efficiently distributing the rank air and grime into all corners.

At 8:30, with no conspicuous signal that the cattle call was on the verge of starting, there was a near stampede toward the makeshift elevated stage at the front quadrant of the room. The entire room seemed like an aquarium, one rear corner of which had suddenly been tipped, causing its entire contents to flow into its diagonal. For the next few hours, Balbina, Elsa, and 1,600 other hopefuls would be crammed nose to shoulder, as close to the stage as possible, like groupies at a rock concert.

At 8:40, three union officials emerged from the anteroom beside the stage. Through a two-way mirror, they had been keeping an eye on the surging crowd while their clerks matched the day's maquila employment needs with the application forms on file. All morning long, the fax machines and phones in the union headquarters had been ringing with the day's specifications from the companies. One maquila, for instance, asked for 91 applicants, all of whom should be 16 (the legal minimum age) or older, with a secondary-school education and without "scheduling problems"—code for childless. All the maquilas favor youth, and some, MagneTek for one, insist on it. "No mayores de 27 años"—None older than 27—the company's director of industrial relations instructed in a faxed letter to the union. Women in their late teens and early 20s are considered in the prime of their working lives; a 31-year-old is unlikely to be hired, and a 35-year-old is considered a relic.

When the tally of the day's employment needs was deemed complete, the officials stepped onto the stage, and into the bedlam. Between them and the spirited throng were three steps cordoned by a thin chain, a flimsy plywood railing, and a bouncer the size of an offensive lineman, whose sartorial taste ran to late Elvis: a white shirt unbuttoned nearly the length of his heroic torso, a gold medallion dangling to his midsection, and a formidable, gleaming pompadour crowning a Frigidaire face and muttonchop sideburns.

Following a call to order on a tinny public-address system, a woman unceremoniously announced the day's available jobs. "We're calling workers for Deltronicos," she said, referring to the GM car-radio subsidiary, and then read a list of 50 names. The "lucky ones," as one disappointed applicant called them, made their way through a pair of swinging doors, where a fleet of old Loadstar school buses waited to transport them to the Finsa park for a job interview and medical screening with their prospective employer. If their luck held, they would then be hired for a 30-day probationary period at lower, "training" wages before attaining full-employee status.

The drill was repeated for each maquila until the day's hiring needs were met. Neither Balbina nor Elsa were among the lucky ones, but they knew that few are chosen on the first go-round; some they met had endured several months of twice-weekly trips to the hall. Each Monday and Friday over the next few weeks the Duques returned faithfully. In March, Balbina's prayers were finally answered. She was assigned to a third-shift coil-winding job at MagneTek. All she knew about the job was that her sister-in-law once worked in the same plant, a low-lying white building no more than 75 yards from her tiny house. What she did not know was that Mollie James once held that very job.

Balbina started work at MagneTek the same year President Clinton signed the North American Free Trade Agreement, designed in large part to hasten the spread of maquiladoras. The trade deal enables companies to take advantage of 700,000 workers at 1,800 plants all along the border in ways that would not be tolerated in the United States. When MagneTek first set up shop in Matamoros, employees worked six-day weeks in a stifling, poorly ventilated plant; speaking on the line or going to the bathroom was grounds for suspension.

Although the company has improved working conditions in the last few years, sexual harassment and discrimination remain a constant of factory life. Many female employees at MagneTek have firsthand stories to tell about sexism on the job. "When new girls come in," says a 31-year-old MagneTek retiree who asked not to be identified, "a supervisor gives them the eye and asks them to go for a walk." Balbina says she received similar propositions when she started work at Plant 1. "My supervisor asked if I wanted to work more overtime. I told him I did, but that I wouldn't go to a hotel with him to get it."

The other constant of factory life is low wages. Even when she works an eight-hour overtime shift, as she usually does two or three times a week, Balbina finds it impossible to make ends meet on a MagneTek salary. "No alcance," she says. It doesn't reach. For years she surmounted her weekly shortfall by pooling her income and expenses with Elsa. The sisters lived, like nearly all of their co-workers, "en montón"—in a heap: two adults and five children in two small rooms, the kitchen in front, the bedroom in the rear. Their shared three-family flat was a cement structure 45 feet by 15 feet by 10 feet high. Its corrugated metal roof doubled as the ceiling. There were cinder-block walls between the three units that stopped about a foot short of the ceiling, making for a pungent stew of sound and aroma when all three families were home.

The shadeless yard—of mud or dust, depending on the season—was fenced by chicken wire and a rickety gate, and served as an extension of the kitchen. The residents shared a clothesline, an outhouse, and a single spigot—the lone source of water. Balbina believes the water flowed from an open canal running near plants in the industrial park that manufacture pesticides or use toxic solvents. The water had to be boiled, of course; sometimes there was propane to do so, sometimes not.

The neighborhood, Vista Hermosa, exists in a commercial and municipal twilight zone. It sprang up to serve the maquiladoras, not the residents. There are several high-priced convenience stores in the colonia, but no full-fledged grocers, no place to buy meat. Nor is there a pharmacy or medical clinic. There is no police presence, and vandalism and petty theft are rampant. There is one school, an overcrowded kindergarten. Older students catch the same bus to school that drops off first-shift workers at the industrial park. "You have to adapt to the maquilas' routine," says a neighbor with school-age children, "because they're not going to adapt to ours."

The city mostly shuns residents because of the high cost and low return of providing them with services. "They have no money," says Andres Cuellar, the city historian of Matamoros, "so no city official accepts responsibility." But a former mayor offers a different explanation: Federal policy prevents the city from taxing the maquilas to improve the colonias. "We insisted before the federal government that we don't have the financial means to support the maquilas' growth," says Fernando Montemayor Lozano, mayor from 1987 until 1989. "Besides the salaries paid to Mexican workers, the maquiladora contribution is practically zero here." It was not until 1991 that running water was piped into the neighborhood (but not as yet into houses), and only in 1993 were the first houses wired for electricity. The roads remain unpaved and deeply rutted. Nor does the city provide trash pickup; Balbina and her neighbors burn their garbage in a nearby ditch.

Vista Hermosa breeds disease like it does mosquitoes. The lack of septic and sewage lines, potable water, and sanitation services puts the neighborhood at great risk for all manner of illnesses, from intestinal parasites to tuberculosis. But the gravest, most frightening threat comes not from the neighborhood, but from beyond the chain-link fence around the Finsa park. The fence, less than a football field away from Balbina's house, may divide the First and Third worlds, but it also unites them under a single toxic cloud. When the maquilas illegally dump toxic waste into irrigation canals, when a hot north wind blows the acrid smell of chapapote—pitch—from the MagneTek plant over its workers' homes, when runoff from a pesticide plant spills into a ditch, when chemical spills or leaks or explosions or fires erupt in the air, it doesn't take a Sierra Club member to understand the environmental wasteland the maquilas have created.

Nor does it take an epidemiologist to question the cause of an outbreak of anencephaly—babies born with either incomplete or missing brains and skulls. In one 36-hour period in the spring of 1991, three babies were born without brains at a single hospital across the river in Brownsville. Doctors soon learned of dozens of other anencephalic births in Brownsville and Matamoros. From 1989 to 1991, the rate of such defects for Brownsville was 10 times the U.S. average, or about 30 anencephalic births per 10,000 births. During the same years, there were 68 cases in Matamoros and 81 in Reynosa, a maquila site upriver.

Many who have studied the outbreak suspect it was due to industrial pollution unchecked by regulatory agencies in both countries. "These were atrocities committed by two uncaring governments," says Dr. Margaret Diaz, the occupational health specialist in Brownsville who detected the anencephaly cluster. "They are the product of years of neglect."

In a lawsuit filed in 1993, families of 28 children born with anencephaly or spina bifida—an incomplete closure of the spinal cord—blamed the outbreak on contamination from the Matamoros maquilas. The families sued 40 maquilas, including MagneTek, charging that the companies negligently handled "toxic compounds" and that the birth defects occurred after "exposure to toxins present in the local environment." The companies steadfastly denied wrongdoing, but internal memoranda documented that some plants released toxic emissions into the air in quantities impermissible in the United States. And trash sifted from the

Matamoros city dump established that the maquilas were burning their industrial waste there, rather than disposing of it in the United States, as required by law. One videotape made by an investigator for the families portrays the charred but clearly visible remains of a MagneTek rapid-start ballast. The companies eventually paid a total of $17 million to the stricken families and cleaned up their worst excesses.

Although MagneTek and other companies insist they are improving conditions both inside and outside their plants, wages remain at poverty levels. Rolando Gonzalez Barron, a maquila owner and former president of the Matamoros Maquila Association, points to an advertising supplement in the Brownsville Herald lauding companies for their financial contributions to Matamoros schools. "Take 'Adopt-a-School,'" he says. "We put sewerage and bathrooms in schools where little girls had to do their necessities outside."

What about paying a living wage so that the parents of those little girls could afford indoor plumbing themselves? "Yes," Gonzalez replies, "housing needs to be developed, but our main goal is to create value for our customers."

What about your employees? What is your obligation to them? "If a worker is not eating," Gonzalez says, sounding every bit the farmer discussing a plow horse, "he's not going to work for you. We need to meet at least the basic needs."

But the basic needs—"eating, housing, clothing," as Gonzalez puts it —are unmet, and the evidence is as obvious and irrefutable as the colonia in MagneTek's backyard, where Balbina and her neighbors wrestle every single day with ferociously difficult decisions: Should I work overtime or huddle with my children to keep them warm? Buy meat or medicine? Pay the light bill or the gas bill? She makes those decisions based on a daily salary of 58 pesos, the equivalent of $7.43. That's an hourly wage of 92 cents—roughly the same starting wage Mollie James earned nearly half a century before. And Balbina often makes those decisions after working a grueling double shift—from 3:30 in the afternoon until six the following morning, after which she arrives home in time to fix breakfast for her children, accompany her oldest to school, and squeeze in a few hours of sleep before heading back to the plant in the afternoon.

No alcance. It doesn't reach. Over and over one hears this. No alcance, but we make it reach. They make it reach by taking odd jobs, or by scavenging for recyclables at the Matamoros city dump—an otherworldly metropolis of its own covering 50 acres—or peddling wares in the plant during breaks and shift changes. "It's prohibited," Balbina says, "but the company looks the other way and almost everybody does it." There are the ubiquitous Avon ladies, as well as sellers of homemade candy, tamales and gorditas, clothes, marijuana. And some sell their bodies, living la doble vida—the double life of coil-winder by day and prostitute by night.

Balbina has yet to resort to a second job. Instead, she works overtime as often as possible and recently moved into a government-subsized house; it is more comfortable than the one she shared with her sister, but it is hers only as long as she keeps her job. She is 29, an advanced age for a maquiladora worker. She lives with her boyfriend, a fellow MagneTek employee, and they stagger their shifts so that one provides child care while the other is working. Still, even the small necessities remain out of reach. "I need a lock for the door," Balbina says one afternoon. "I don't need it now, but soon I will."

Why not now?

"There is nothing worth locking now," she replies.

Mollie James never again found full-time work. She received a severance payment, after taxes, of $3,171.66—about $93 for each of the 34 years she worked. She collected unemployment benefits for six months and then enrolled in a computer-repair school, receiving a certificate of completion and numerous don't-call-us responses to job inquiries. Late last year, at the age of 68, she took a part-time job as an attendant at a nursing home. For the remainder of her income, she depends on Social Security and the rent she collects from the three-family house she owns, as well as a monthly pension of $71.23 from her Teamsters local. "That's nothing," she says. "That doesn't even pay your telephone bill. It's gone before you know it."

Although Paterson is a tenacious city, it seems defined by what is gone. Its last heyday was during and after World War II, when entrepreneurs like Archie Sergy and migrants like Mollie James helped sustain the city as a proud symbol of industrial might. But the old factory district near the Great Falls has been in ruins for decades, and although a number of the ancient brick mills have been splendidly restored—as a museum, a hospital clinic, and housing for artists—Paterson today is thought of as one of those discarded American places, a city so squalid, so defeated, that few people who do not live or work in Paterson venture there.

Mollie James has spent a half-century in Paterson. She married and divorced there, raised four children, bought a house. She sunk deep roots, and would like nothing better than to see the seeds of renewal take sprout, but she is fed up with high taxes, crime, the unstable economy. Like many "up-South" blacks of retirement age, she thinks often about going home, to rural central Virginia, to the land she left as a teenager. She still owns her childhood home amid three wooded acres.

During a trip back home not long ago, Mollie visited the cemetery where her parents are buried. It is where she wishes to be buried as well. "They better not put me in no dirt up there in New Jersey," she says. "Bring me back home, brother."

Balbina, too, dreams of returning to her ancestral home, to the quiet and clear air of Monte Bello, where she could raise her children in a calm, safe place. But there is no work around Monte Bello for her, no future there for her children. She is more concerned with the immediate future of her job. In the last couple of years, MagneTek closed the two old Universal plants in Arkansas and Mississippi and transferred the bulk of those operations not to Matamoros, but 60 miles upriver to Reynosa, where the union is even weaker, the wages lower still. Now the talk in Matamoros is that the company will once again use the threat of a move, as it did first in Paterson and then in the Southern plants, as a lever for lower wages.

Balbina scoffs at the notion of transferring to Reynosa if the company relocates her job there. "What if they were to move again?" she asks. "Maybe to Juárez or Tijuana? What then? Do I chase my job all over the world?"

Lester Carl Thurow (1938–) received a Ph.D. in economics from Harvard University in 1964 and served as dean of the MIT Sloan School of Management. He has written numerous bestsellers on economic topics and has been a columnist for the New York Times, Boston Globe, USA Today, and Newsweek.

Why Women Are Paid Less than Men

Lester C. Thurow

In the 40 years from 1939 to 1979 white women who work full time have with monotonous regularity made slightly less than 60 percent as much as white men. Why?

Over the same time period, minorities have made substantial progress in catching up with whites, with minority women making even more progress than minority men. Black men now earn 72 percent as much as white men (up 16 percentage points since the mid-1950s) but black women earn 92 percent as much as white women. Hispanic men make 71 percent of what their white counterparts do, but Hispanic women make 82 percent as much as white women. As a result of their faster progress, fully employed black women make 75 percent as much as fully employed black men while Hispanic women earn 68 percent as much as Hispanic men.

This faster progress may, however, end when minority women finally catch up with white women. In the bible of the New Right, George Gilder's *Wealth and Poverty*, the 60 percent is just one of Mother Nature's constants like the speed of light or the force of gravity. Men are programmed to provide for their families economically while women are programmed to take care of their families emotionally and physically. As a result men put more effort into their jobs than women. The net result is a difference in work intensity that leads to that 40 percent gap in earnings. But there is no discrimination against women—only the biological facts of life.

The problem with this assertion is just that. It is an assertion with no evidence for it other than the fact that white women have made 60 percent as much as men for a long period of time.

"Discrimination against women" is an easy answer but it also has its problems as an adequate explanation. Why is discrimination against women not declining under the same social forces that are leading to a lessening of discrimination against minorities? In recent years women have made more use of the enforcement provisions of the Equal Employment Opportunities Commission and the courts than minorities. Why do the laws that prohibit discrimination against women and minorities work for minorities but not for women?

When men discriminate against women, they run into a problem. To discriminate against women is to discriminate against your own wife and to lower your own family income. To prevent women from working is to force men to work more.

When whites discriminate against blacks, they can at least think that they are raising their own incomes. When men discriminate against women they have to know that they are lowering their own family income and increasing their own work effort.

While discrimination undoubtedly explains part of the male-female earnings differential, one has to believe that men are monumentally stupid or irrational to explain all of the earnings gap in terms of discrimination. There must be something else going on.

Back in 1939 it was possible to attribute the earnings gap to large differences in educational attainments. But the educational gap between men and women has been eliminated since World War II. It is no longer possible to use education as an explanation for the lower earnings of women. Some observers have argued that women earn less money since they are less reliable workers who are more apt to leave the labor force. But it is difficult to maintain this position since women are less apt to quit one job to take another and as a result they tend to work as long, or longer, for any one employer. From any employer's perspective they are more reliable, not less reliable, than men.

Part of the answer is visible if you look at the lifetime earnings profile of men. Suppose that you were asked to predict which men in a group of 25-year-olds would become economically successful. At age 25 it is difficult to tell who will be economically successful and your predictions are apt to be highly inaccurate. But suppose that you were asked to predict which men in a group of 35-year-olds would become economically successful. If you are successful at age 35, you are very likely to remain successful for the rest of your life. If you have not become economically successful by age 35, you are very unlikely to do so later.

The decade between 25 and 35 is when men either succeed or fail. It is the decade when lawyers become partners in the good firms, when business managers make it onto the "fast track," when academics get tenure at good universities, and when blue collar workers find the job opportunities that lead to training opportunities and the skills that will generate high earnings. If there is any one decade when it pays to work hard and to be consistently in the labor force, it is the decade between 25 and 35. For those who succeed, earnings will rise rapidly. For those who fail, earnings will remain flat for the rest of their lives.

But the decade between 25 and 35 is precisely the decade when women are most apt to leave the labor force or become part-time workers to have children. When they do, the current system of promotion and skill acquisition will extract an enormous lifetime price.

This leaves essentially two avenues for equalizing male and female earnings. Families where women who wish to have successful careers, compete with men, and achieve the same earnings should alter their family plans and have their children either before 25 or after 35. Or society can attempt to alter the existing promotion and skill acquisition system so that there is a longer time period in which both men and women can attempt to successfully enter the labor force. Without some combination of these two factors, a substantial fraction of the male-female earnings differentials are apt to persist for the next 40 years, even if discrimination against women is eliminated.

Joanne B. Ciulla (1951–) has a Ph.D. in philosophy and teaches at the Jepson School of Leadership Studies at the University of Richmond. She has researched, written, and presented to audiences worldwide about issues of work, business leadership, and ethics. This excerpt is drawn from her 2000 book The Working Life.

Leisure and Consumption

Joanne B. Ciulla

Leisure is a special experience. It consists of activities that are freely chosen and good in themselves. Listening to music for pure enjoyment is one such pursuit. Aristotle believed that leisure was necessary for human happiness. Most people today think that we conduct business so that we can make money and buy things. And some trade time for leisure so that they can buy more things. Aristotle said we conduct business (or are "unleisurely") so that we can have leisure. Leisure brings out what is best and most distinctive about being human—our abilities to think, feel, reflect, create, and learn. We need leisure to develop wisdom.

The word for leisure in Greek is *skolé*; in Latin it is *otium*. In both languages the word for work is simply the negation of the word for leisure; *ascholi*a and *negotium* both mean "not leisure." This is also true in Spanish. Today *negocio*, the word for business, means "no leisure." Greek, Latin, and Spanish words compare work to leisure as if to say that leisure is the center of life. The English word leisure comes from the Latin *licere*, which means "to be permitted." Our language compares leisure to work as if to say that work is the norm of life and leisure is when we are "permitted" to stop working. The British essayist and self-confessed workaholic G. K. Chesterton wrote there are three parts to leisure: "The first is being allowed to do something. The second is being allowed to do anything and the third (and perhaps most rare and precious) is being allowed to do nothing."

In his book *Of Time, Work, and Leisure*, sociologist Sebastian de Grazia observed that although work can ennoble us, wear us down, or make us rich, it is leisure that perfects us as human beings. Writing in 1962, de Grazia applied Aristotle's notion of leisure to the twentieth century. He wrote, "Leisure and free time live in two different worlds. . . ." Free time refers to a special way of calculating a special kind of time. Leisure refers to a state of being, a condition of man." It is a frame of mind or attitude of imaginative people who love ideas. Until World War I, educated Virginians defined a Yankee as a person who didn't understand how to use his leisure. For de Grazia, leisure is a special intellectual state that few people are capable of having. It is more than simply organized activities, amusements, relaxation, and free time.

The idea that leisure is something that only a few people attain leaves us to wonder: Is leisure elitist, or do people like Aristotle and de Grazia take an elitist view of leisure? After all, who are they to make judgments on what is and is not leisure? Besides eating, sleeping, procreating, and getting ready for work, how we use our free time is a highly personal matter. Class, taste, income, education, and personal preference certainly influence what we choose to do. Just as there is a pecking order in work there is also one outside of it. Golfers look down on bowlers, tennis players look down on golfers, opera lovers sneer at soap opera fans, *New York Times* readers condescend to *National Enquirer* readers, Bloomingdale's shoppers scorn Wal-Mart shoppers. The prosperous and better-educated think (and have always thought) that their leisure pursuits are more enriching and self-fulfilling than those of the poor and the working class. But there are larger questions behind de Grazia's and Aristotle's discussions of leisure that get to the heart of how people experience life. Before we move to these questions, however, we need to look at the relationship of work to the way we spend our free time.

Work and Amusements

The Reformation, with its emphasis on work, did its best to make Sunday a boring day. Luther got rid of the saints and their holidays. The Protestants associated work with virtue and hence leisure with vice. In the Middle Ages holidays were times for music, dancing, and drinking, but later, in Protestant countries, they became days for silence and meditation. In the 1640s the Puritans, who dominated the British Parliament, banned all Christmas festivities and enjoyments, including plum pudding and mince pie. In our own times, starting in the 1980s all workers began to lose holidays and paid vacation time, and some managers began acting like Scrooge on Christmas. In 1986, when Christmas fell on a Thursday, 46 percent of employers gave workers Friday off. In 1997, when Christmas fell on a Thursday, only 36 percent did. Holidays are more than days off; they are supposed to be public celebrations. But the public can't celebrate together if most people are working.

According to de Grazia, businesspeople liked the idea of making Sunday a dismal bore because that would make work more desirable. If leisure were too rewarding and too much fun, people wouldn't want to go back to work. But the Protestants and employers were probably more concerned about amusements than leisure. *The Oxford English Dictionary* defines an amusement as a pleasurable occupation that distracts or diverts attention from something. Interestingly, it comes from the word *muse*, which in this context means to be "affected with astonishment" or to be put into a "stupid stare."

In the industrial era the English took legal measures to repress popular amusements in order to develop conduct suitable for work discipline. The Poor Law Amendment Act of 1834 wiped out the infrastructure of working-class entertainment. By restricting people to their parishes, the law effectively got rid of traveling balladeers, entertainers, and itinerant salesmen. The 1835 Highways Act forbade all street "nuisances," including soccer players, street entertainers, and traders. In the same year the Cruelty to Animals Act outlawed activities such as cockfights, but allowed fox hunting and other aristocratic pursuits. Working-class amusements moved off the streets and into pubs, which began providing various forms of entertainment to their customers. America never took such harsh legal measures except during the Prohibition years. Supporters of Prohibition argued that a shorter workweek would surely lead to more drinking.

At the turn of the century, employers opposed giving Saturday off because they claimed that their employees would only get into trouble. For example, in the early 1900s a Massachusetts firm required workers who were unwilling to attend church to stay indoors and "improve their time" by reading, writing, or performing other valuable duties. Mill owners of the time forbade drinking and gambling and justified the twelve-hour day and six-day week as means of keeping workers from vicious amusements. This was not a totally unfounded fear. As mentioned earlier, workers in the early industrial days of England often used their leisure time to drink, fight, and bet on animal contests, such as cockfights.

In early twentieth-century America, millions of workingmen spent their free time in bars and union clubs. There were more than ten thousand saloons in New York in 1900. In *Cheap Amusements*, Kathy Peiss estimates that workingmen in New York spent about 10 percent of their weekly income on personal expenses, the bulk of which were for beer and liquor, tobacco, and movie and theater tickets. An extensive study of workingmen's leisure found that married men spent half of their free time with their families. Workingmen felt that their work gave them a "right" to amusements after work—"I worked for someone else all day and now I deserve to have someone or something work to entertain me."

Married women did not start going out for entertainment in great numbers until after the invention of the nickelodeon in 1905. When young women found job opportunities outside domestic labor, they flocked to work in industry, department stores, and restaurants. Having grown up seeing their mothers work from dawn to dusk and observing domestic servants work twelve-to-fourteen-hour days, they too felt they had a "right" to outside entertainment. Workingwomen who loved to party were called "rowdy girls" in the Victorian era. They relished the freedom of going out with their friends, dancing, and socializing in mixed company. A manager from Macy's complained that young girls went out dancing on weeknights and came in exhausted for work the next day. Women also integrated amusements into their work. Female factory workers practiced the latest dance steps outside the factory during their breaks. Female cigar rollers insisted on having someone read the newspaper to them while they worked. Women became very protective of their work hours and filed grievances when asked to work overtime or when detained after closing time. Women workers were largely responsible for getting the workweek shortened for all workers. The more women worked by the clock outside the home the more they too felt entitled to a good time—something to distract them or take them away from work. Life became more segmented into bouts of uninterrupted work and bouts of amusement.

Not only did employers worry about the effects of workers' leisure on job performance, they had misgivings about what might happen when employees socialized together outside work. Union halls were just one form of association. Groupings of nonunion workers were also a threat because they gave employees ample time to bond and discuss working conditions and complaints, providing a fertile field for union organization.

In 1914 Henry Ford established a sociological department in his company. The department's mission was to supervise workers' lives so that they would be thrifty, industrious producers. They urged employees not to smoke and drink. Today's reformers who want to control sex and violence on TV, cigarettes, drugs, and alcohol face an uphill battle. If people like to engage in these activities during their free time, they will until they find—or the market offers them—alternatives they like more.

Television

Mass entertainment caters to passive leisure. One might even argue that television serves as a form of social control. The quality of "mass leisure" or amusements cannot vary too much from work, because if they did, the worker would have a difficult time adjusting to the worlds of work and leisure. Mass amusements provide relief from work without making the return to work unbearable. Again, if this sounds like leisure snobbery, consider this: How many people would want to work less so that they could watch more television? While it is true that some people might like to see their soap operas every day and others might wish they could have a day off to watch a World Series game, one rarely hears someone say, "Gee, I'd really like to have more time off to watch television." People wish for time off to build wood-strip canoes, travel, or spend time with their families, but *not* to watch more television (even if that's what they actually would do with time off). Herein lies the major difference between amusement and this more elevated idea of leisure. Mass entertainment we can pick up or drop at any time without longing or regret. It is enjoyable, but has no lingering meaning for most people. While many enjoy TV or miss it because they are used to having it on all the time, most people do not long for it.

Witold Rybczynski notes in *Waiting for the Weekend* that television is "voracious." Most Americans watch about three hours of television per day, or twenty-one hours per week. Rybczynski tells us that the only other pastime in history that engaged people for that many hours was reading, during the eighteenth century. He believes that one reason why people spend more time watching television than reading is that reading requires a short regular daily habit, whereas television can be watched at irregular intervals. Also, you have to remember or reread old parts of a book in order to remember the plot. With television, little mental effort is required from the viewer, and it is not necessary to remember the plot. Not only do continuing TV shows review the plot of the series, they also show previews of what is going to happen next in the show. Rybczynski remarks that there is generally so little mental involvement in TV watching that it should really be called TV *staring*. This makes it the perfect "amusement" or diversion from work—because it really is capable of putting us into a "stupid stare."

In contrast to amusement, leisure activities entail the same kind of sustainable involvement and satisfaction that people find in meaningful work. Leisure is usually an activity that requires reflection, learning, or the development of skill. Rybczynski argues that the weekend is not a place to escape work, but a place to create meaningful work and compensate for the lack of personal rewards on the job. But as we have seen, some people are either too tired or too busy for such leisure. Many want amusements that help them escape from work. There is nothing wrong with amusements like watching television, but there may be something wrong with work that so zaps us of our strength and resources that that's either all we feel like doing or all we can think of doing.

How Work Shapes Leisure

Marx believed that there was no such thing as human nature. Instead, people become what they are through what they do. Work not only creates the material world but it molds people from beings guided by animal instincts into conscious, self-directed, goal-oriented beings. When work is dull and mindless, it stifles the development of a person. Marx writes that such a person is only human in his animal functions (eating, sleeping, and procreating) and is an animal in his human functions (work and free time).

. . . [W]ork or lack of work can influence leisure in either a positive or a negative way. Research by sociologists confirms this view. Stanley Parker tells us that work shapes our free time because work is always in the back of our minds. When work is dull, tiresome, or stressful people are sometimes unable to do anything satisfying in their leisure. According to Parker, most sociological studies support the idea that people's leisure mirrors certain aspects of their work. These studies go back a long way. One from the early 1900s found that the workers who had the most menial and lowest-paid jobs spent the greatest amount of time in saloons, washing the workday away with beer. Sometimes those with exciting jobs demand exciting leisure and those with boring jobs settle for passive leisure. For example, a study in the late 1970s compared work and leisure across various occupational groups. It found that air traffic controllers, who had stressful and demanding jobs, expressed a greater preference for challenging leisure activities than did civil servants. A six-year longitudinal study of Swedish workers discovered that those whose jobs had become more passive took on more passive leisure, while those whose jobs had become more active took on more active leisure.

Some amusements resemble aspects of work. Parker uses the game of bingo as one such example. It is played in a large hall and the players sit at tables that are organized in rows. There is a caller and a "supervisor." Players mark off the letters and numbers called. They "work" through their card, and if all goes well they get paid. The supervisor designates certain periods for refreshments. There is no skill or personal challenge in the game. Playing bingo is similar to routine work. The activities themselves require little if any skill and have no intrinsic interest, and one cannot get better at them through practice (despite the fact that some gamblers believe that their "skill" improves over time). The excitement of bingo is the hope of a big payoff at the end. Bingo also allows for socializing, but that too is somewhat limited by the structure of the game.

Once leisure was regarded as a time for the amateur. The word *amateur* comes from the Latin *amator*, lover: *The Oxford English Dictionary* defines an amateur as "one who loves or is fond of something" or has a taste for something. The amateur cultivates a pastime because it is interesting and intrinsically rewarding and not for external rewards like money and fame. However, some prefer to take a professional approach to their leisure activities. This attitude may include buying expensive equipment, like the latest high-tech running shoes or experimental tennis racquets. With a *très* serious attitude and the best equipment, people "work" at their tennis game, take lessons, keep charts on their scores and times, and so on. Their leisure assumes the serious, no-nonsense attitude of work. This may be a continuation of one's attitude toward work or a longing for something not present at work, such as the desire to learn or get better at something. When such weekend warriors copy the dress or style of the professional, their leisure activity becomes a simulation of the pro's work. Often, what they lack in skill they make up for in equipment. For some, buying the equipment for a sport or hobby is as much fun as— if not more fun than—using it.

The content of leisure and work may also overlap in a positive way, especially when people like their work. Then we find the stockbroker who likes to gamble, the art teacher who likes to paint, the academic who enjoys lounging in a hammock reading journals. Some of us enjoy leisure activities that compensate for creativity, skills, or social interactions that we don't exercise or take part in at work. Examples of this abound: the office manager who paints with watercolors, the hospital administrator who does woodworking, the police officer who participates in a local theater group. Personality is also a factor in how people act at work and during leisure. The meticulous librarian collects stamps, the gregarious mailman heads up the community center basketball team. It takes a certain talent in life to separate work from leisure. Many get so overwhelmed by the physical and psychological strain of making a living that they are unable to pursue engaging leisure. For them, separation of work from life might be healthier than integration of work with life.

Trading Leisure for Consumption

In 1970 economist Steffan Linder published *The Harried Leisure Class*. In it he argued that in affluent societies, when people have to choose between more free time and more spending, most choose more spending. That is why he believed that an increase in income is not necessarily an increase in prosperity. In 1986, for example, Americans spent more than thirteen billion dollars on sports clothing, which meant that they traded 1.3 billion hours of potential leisure time for leisure clothing. Spending money takes time—time to make the money, time to shop, and time to enjoy the things the money buys, such as cabin cruisers, package tours, and the like. Americans not only have less vacation time than Europeans, but they spend three to four times as many hours shopping as Europeans do.

Consumption ties a tighter knot between work and free time than any of the schemes of reformers, employers, or governments. William H. Whyte was right to be concerned about the organization man's shallow roots in the community and deep roots in the organization. What he didn't calculate was the way that consumerism and credit reinforce the grip of work on people. Consumption creates a *need* to work even when the desire to work is weak. However, it can also make work feel more burdensome. The market tempts people with more leisure options than they can afford or have time to enjoy. We wish we didn't have to work so that we could enjoy what the market has to offer us in terms of toys, vacations, and other amusements—all of which cost money.

Even teenagers trade their leisure for consumption. In the past, teens often had to work to help their families or pay for college. Some still do, but now a growing number of middle-class teens work to buy luxury items for themselves. As we have seen, generations of Americans have encouraged young people to work, in the belief that it keeps them out of trouble and develops discipline. In a 1986 study, researchers Ellen Greenberger and Laurence Steinberg came to a radically different conclusion about work and teenagers. They found that teens often get into more trouble when they work too much than they do during free time. This is because they suffer the stress of work and school and they have the money to buy drugs and alcohol. But most interestingly, Greenberger and Steinberg also suggest that too much work not only interferes with teens' schoolwork but can cause an "adjusted blandness" at a time when they should be curious, imaginative, and combative. This "adjusted blandness" is exemplified by the routine "have a nice day" patter of counter workers in fast-food restaurants. Greenberger and Steinberg think that this is unhealthy.

At first their argument seems to go against the Protestant work ethic. But Greenberger and Steinberg maintain that instead of fostering respect for work, teenage employment often leads to increased cynicism about the ability of work to provide any personal satisfaction beyond a paycheck, since teens often work in menial jobs. They ask us to consider the image of a sixteen-year-old boy, who comes home from a long afternoon of work in a fast-food restaurant, downs a few beers, and thinks to himself, "People who work harder at their jobs than they have to are a little bit crazy." Work is "bogus"—you do the minimum necessary to get paid.

Other researchers believe that the social meaning of work determines whether work is good or bad for teens. In 1993 J. Schulenberg and J. G. Bachman found that teens suffered when they worked *only* for the money, for long periods of time, at boring jobs that were unconnected to future work. A study conducted by H. W. Marsh in 1991 indicated that when teens were working to save money for college, their grades improved, even when the teens had boring jobs. When teens worked to buy extras such as cars and CD players for themselves, their grades went down, regardless of the job. During the Depression era, similar studies showed the beneficial value of any kind of work for young people who contributed to the support of their families at a time of crisis. The young people gained self-confidence and a sense of efficacy from helping to care for their families.

These studies on teens offer an insight into how the meaning of work changes when teens conform to the demands of the workplace in order to conform to the desires elicited in the marketplace. Sometimes the reasons *why* we work are more important than the work we actually do. The experience of working to support a family or go to college may well be more satisfying than working for clothing and CD players, because the goals themselves are more lasting and meaningful. Nonetheless, many would still argue that it is better for young people to earn money to buy what they want than to have it given to them.

When teens substitute consumer goods for leisure, they get caught up in the work-and-spend pattern of their parents and something is lost. If they give up their free time so that they can make money to buy things, they don't have the leisure to discover what they like to do. They don't have the time to discover what activities they find intrinsically good. Far from fearing it (as parents and others in authority do), there is something to be said for doing nothing and hanging out with one's friends. While there may be the potential for trouble, there is also the potential to learn how to enjoy life on one's own terms and not those of the consumer market.

Critics of Consumerism

Of course, critics of consumerism and materialist values are legion. Somewhere in every major world religion is a warning about the dangers of the unfettered desire for material objects. We noted earlier that most of the seven deadly sins concern desire for material things. Nonetheless, many economists and businesspeople are cheered by the fact that consumer demand is insatiable. In *Social Limits to Growth*, Fred Hirsch wrote that the satisfaction that people derive from goods and services doesn't depend on their own consumption, but on the consumption of others, or "keeping up with the Joneses," which makes desire limitless. Juliet Schor's recent book *The Overspent American* picks up where Hirsch left off in his 1976 work. She argues that in the past our neighbors ("the Joneses") set the standard for what we wanted and thought we should buy. Today, she says, people often don't know their neighbors, and they compare what they own and want to own against the standards set by a wider range of people, such as those at work, on TV, in advertisements, and elsewhere. When we kept up with the Joneses, we kept up with people who had similar incomes. When we try to keep up with people at work or in the news, we may be trying to keep up with people who make many times more than we do. This draws one into a seamless cycle of spending, debt, and longer working hours. Schor tells us that people who had been sucked into this cycle, "increasingly looked to consumption to give satisfaction, even meaning to their lives."

Earlier we discussed David Riesman's observation, made in the 1950s, that Americans were becoming more other-directed, The other-directed person not only seeks affirmation from people but is driven by the material incentives of the market and the psychological incentives offered by employers. Riesman was right. It is ironic that we live in a free society that offers us choices, yet in spite of this, or perhaps because of this, much of our behavior is still determined by what others think we need and should want.

For Schor, consumption is largely connected to status. Social commentator Barbara Ehrenreich takes another tack. She believes that consumption is a form of compensation. She says that many middle-class people are disappointed with work and have jobs that give them no pleasure. In her book *Fear of Falling*, Ehrenreich argues that the middle class, unlike the working class, grew up expecting to have work that had intrinsic value. It wasn't that such jobs were scarce, but that they failed to pay enough to support the lifestyle that some people want. As a result of this, Ehrenreich tells us, "The would-be regional planner turned corporate lawyer, the would-be social worker turned banker, must compensate for abandoned dreams with spending." They bury themselves in increasing consumer demands and the pleasure that buying things brings them. Work, leisure, and consumerism lock us into a vicious circle. We work more to afford the things we want to buy, then we buy things and use our free time to compensate in some way for our hard work.

The "Customer" Is King!

People all over the world enjoy Coca-Cola, Big Macs, blue jeans, and VCRs. Consumer expenditures and replacement purchases rose during seventy of the eighty-four years between 1900 and 1984 as consumers continually switched to newer goods. From this fact, economist Stanley Lebergott argues that buying newer goods is a more "worthwhile experience" than sticking with the old. But why is buying something new more "worthwhile"? Sometimes newer products carry more prestige, work better, are more attractive, or have features that better suit our needs. However, this still doesn't explain why the act of buying something is a "worthwhile" or worth-our-time experience. Is the joy of buying something on a par with the joy of owning it? Not always. Schor tells us that people with "compulsive buying" disorder shop all the time, but easily lose interest in what they buy when they bring it home.

In her book *Consuming Passions*, Judith Williamson tells us that the marketplace consumes our passions and disarms them so that they are no longer threatening to the existing social order. Shopping is a hunt in which we attempt to get the best price and the best value. It makes us feel creative and in control as we buy the sweater we saw in Saks Fifth Avenue at a half-price sale at Lord & Taylor. Buying things cheers us up when we're down. A Saturday in the mall stimulates the senses with the sounds of people, the smells of food, and the abundant array of goods. In a consumer society, the desire for consumption is at least as important as consumption itself.

Money conceals many things, including how you earned it. As citizens we may be abused by the IRS, as parents we may be ignored by our children, as spouses we may be unappreciated, and as workers we may be powerless, but as customers we are sovereign. In the marketplace it doesn't matter who you are as long as you have cash, checks, or plastic. Almost anyone can decide, deliberate, express opinions, and make judgments about goods and services. Best of all, sales "associates" are paid to listen to customers and treat them with respect (despite numerous exceptions). The British used to say, "Americans give service without politeness and the British give politeness without service." Nowadays, especially under the influence of the "quality" movement in business, consumers demand

and often get both. If they don't, they can call for the employee's superior, yell, scream, and carry on in ways that would be unacceptable at home or at work. As customers we can have the feeling of being the boss. It's no wonder that the word *customer* has caught on in many new contexts. Organizations promise to treat their employees like customers because the customer is supposed to be "king" (or queen). Similarly, government agencies now refer to the people they serve as "customers" in the hope that civil servants will give "customers" better service than they gave citizens. Not only is it fun to buy things, but we expect to be treated with respect when we do it as "valued customers."

Consumerism picks up where the work ethic left off—or never took hold. Organizations no longer need to rely on people having a moral commitment to work. Shopping malls, debt, and the advertising industry whip everyone, even moody teenagers, into obedient workers and customers. If we have indeed traded freedom in the workplace for freedom in the marketplace, then one way to regain control is to restrict our freedom in the marketplace. Living below our means may not be as much fun as living above them, but it does allow more flexibility in deciding where we work and how much we work. Debt and desire tether us to a job that we hate and devour the time that we might spend doing something we like.

Intrinsic Rewards

The strongest defining feature of leisure is that it is intrinsically rewarding: we do something for the sake of doing it and because *we* like it. For those who have meaningful work, there is little qualitative difference between work and leisure. . . . [S]ome leisure activities would be less pleasurable if we had to do them for pay. A person who enjoys sewing might easily learn to hate it working as a professional seamstress. Sewing for your friends and family is different from sewing for the public. Freedom to start or stop doing something is a major element of leisure. So, for some, being paid to sew would take the fun out of it. For others being paid to sew might be their idea of meaningful work. The reason why leisure is important for everyone is that life would be barren if we could not spend time doing things just simply because we enjoyed them or found them rewarding. While some people dream of getting paid to do something that is intrinsically rewarding, researchers have found that paying people to do things that they would do without pay actually decreases their enjoyment of the activity.

In a field experiment, researchers Mark R. Lepper and David R. Greene observed nursery school children and determined what appeared to be each child's favorite play activity. They then rewarded the children every time they engaged in this activity. In a short time the children began to show less interest in the activity. Psychologist Edward Deci had performed similar experiments on adult subjects, who were asked to do enjoyable puzzles. They too appeared to find the task less interesting when they received external or extrinsic rewards for it. Deci called this the "overjustification effect." In other words, when you pay people to do something that they already find rewarding, they feel they are getting more than they should for doing it. To balance things out, people devalue the intrinsic reward and/or meaning of the task and focus more on the pay.

Even if it is not the case that we compensate for external rewards, Deci's experiment does tell us something about those unique and personal human experiences that we seek for no other purpose than personal gratification.

A simple story from Jewish folklore makes the same point as the research on intrinsic motivation. It goes like this: A Jewish tailor moved into a town in the American South. When the Ku Klux Klan heard about it they incited a group of local children to go and yell insulting names in front of his shop every day. On the first day that the children showed up, the tailor came out of his shop and said, "I will pay you each a quarter for every bad name you shout at me." They were delighted. The next day when the children showed up the tailor said, "I will pay you ten cents for every bad name that you call me." Many of the children complained, but grudgingly agreed. On the third day the tailor gave the children a nickel, and the day after he gave a penny. When the children came on the fifth day, the tailor said, "I am not going to pay you anymore." Whereupon the children grudgingly responded, "If you won't pay us, then we won't come and yell at you anymore."

By making the children's taunting into a business transaction, the wise tailor undercut their mean-spirited enjoyment. Once the children were paid to do what they liked, they no longer wanted to do it for fun as they had earlier. They felt they *deserved* to be paid.

Unless you block out the world around you (as many people do), it's difficult to enjoy leisure in a work- and consumer-oriented society that sometimes seems to be falling apart. Leisure is free, self-determined, reflective, and gratifying. It is what you really want to do, when you want to do it. Leisure doesn't cost money, it can be hanging out with friends or family, reading a novel, or just daydreaming. It is a time in which we do those things that are valuable to us and worth doing. Because leisure is a time when we are free, it is also a time when we are most ourselves. Without leisure we might lose track of who we are. Without leisure we may find it more difficult to make sense of our lives.

Henry David Thoreau (1817–1862) was born in Concord, Massachusetts, and attended Harvard University. A social and political activist as well as avid naturalist, he went to live in a self-built cabin on Walden Pond just a few miles from his family home and documented his experience and reflections on simple living in his masterpiece work, Walden *(1854). He is also well-known for his essay, "Civil Disobedience," (1849) in which he presents an argument for his refusal to pay his poll taxes as a means of moral opposition to slavery.*

from Walden: Conclusion

Henry David Thoreau

I left the woods for as good a reason as I went there. Perhaps it seemed to me that I had several more lives to live, and could not spare any more time for that one. It is remarkable how easily and insensibly we fall into a particular route, and make a beaten track for ourselves. I had not lived there a week before my feet wore a path from my door to the pond-side; and though it is Eve or six years since I trod it, it is still quite distinct. It is true, I fear, that others may have fallen into it, and so helped to keep it open. The surface of the earth is soft and impressible by the feet of men; and so with the paths which the mind travels. How worn and dusty, then, must be the Highways of the world, how deep the ruts of tradition and conformity! I did not wish to take a cabin passage, but rather to go before the mast and on the deck of the world, for there I could best see the moonlight amid the mountains. I do not wish to go below now.

Why level downward to our dullest perception always, and praise that as common sense? The commonest sense is the sense of men asleep, which they express by snoring. Sometimes we are inclined to class those who are once-and-a-half-witted with the half-witted, because we appreciate only a third part of their wit. Some would find fault with the morning-red, if they ever got up early enough. "They pretend," as I hear, "that the verses of Kabir have four different senses; illusion, spirit, intellect, and the exoteric doctrine of the Vedas"; but in this part of the world it is considered a ground for complaint if a man's writings admit of more than one interpretation. While England endeavors to cure the potato-rot, will not any endeavor to cure the brain-rot, which prevails so much more widely and fatally?

I do not suppose that I have attained to obscurity, but I should be proud if no more fatal fault were found with my pages on this score than was found with the Walden ice. Southern customers objected to its blue color, which is the evidence of its purity, as if it were muddy, and preferred the Cambridge ice, which is white, but tastes of weeds. The purity men love is like the mists which envelop the earth, and not like the azure ether beyond.

Some are dinning in our ears that we Americans, and moderns generally, are intellectual dwarfs compared with the ancients, or even the Elizabethan men. But what is that to the purpose? A living dog is better than a dead lion. Shall a man go and hang himself because he belongs to the race of pygmies, and not be the biggest pygmy that he can? Let every one mind his own business, and endeavor to be what he was made.

Why should we be in such desperate haste to succeed and in such desperate enterprises? If a man does not keep pace with his companions, perhaps it is because he hears a different drummer. Let him step to the music which he hears, however measured or far away. It is not important that he should mature as soon as an apple tree or an oak. Shall he turn his spring into summer? If the condition of things which we were made for is not yet, what were any reality which we can substitute? We will not be shipwrecked on a vain reality. Shall we with pains erect a heaven of blue glass over ourselves, though when it is done we shall be sure to gaze still at the true ethereal heaven far above, as if the former were not?

There was an artist in the city of Kouroo who was disposed to strive after perfection. One day it came into his mind to make a staff. Having considered that in an imperfect work time is an ingredient, but into a perfect work time does not enter, he said to himself, It shall be perfect in all respects, though I should do nothing else in my life. He proceeded instantly to the forest for wood, being resolved that it should not be made of unsuitable material; and as he searched for and rejected stick after stick, his friends gradually deserted him, for they grew old in their works and died, but he grew not older by a moment. His singleness of purpose and resolution, and his elevated piety, endowed him, without his knowledge, with perennial youth. As he made no compromise with Time, Time kept out of his way, and only sighed at a distance because he could not overcome him. Before he had found a stick in all respects suitable the city of Kouroo was a hoary ruin, and he sat on one of its mounds to peel the stick. Before he had given it the proper shape the dynasty of the Candahars was at an end, and with the point of the stick he wrote the name of the last of that race in the sand, and then resumed his work. By the time he had smoothed and polished the staff Kalpa was no longer the pole-star; and ere he had put on the ferule and the head adorned with precious stones, Brahma had awoke and slumbered many times. But why do I stay to mention these things? When the finishing stroke was put to his work, it suddenly expanded before the eyes of the astonished artist into the fairest of all the creations of Brahma. He had made a new system in making a staff, a world with full and fair proportions; in which, though the old cities and dynasties had passed away, fairer and more glorious ones had taken their places. And now he saw by the heap of shavings still fresh at his feet, that, for him and his work, the former lapse of time had been an illusion, and that no more time had elapsed than is required for a single scintillation from the brain of Brahma to fall on and inflame the tinder of a mortal brain. The material was pure, and his art was pure; how could the result be other than wonderful?

No face which we can give to a matter will stead us so well at last as the truth. This alone wears well. For the most part, we are not where we are, but in a false position. Through an infinity of our natures, we suppose a case, and put ourselves into it, and hence are in two cases at the same time, and it is doubly difficult to get out. In sane moments we regard only the facts, the case that is. Say what you have to say, not what you ought. Any truth is better than make-believe. Tom Hyde, the tinker, standing on the gallows, was asked if he had anything to say. "Tell the tailors," said he, "to remember to make a knot in their thread before they take the first stitch." His companion's prayer is forgotten.

However mean your life is, meet it and live it; do not shun it and call it hard names. It is not so bad as you are. It looks poorest when you are richest. The fault-finder will find faults even in paradise. Love your life, poor as it is. You may perhaps have some pleasant, thrilling, glorious hours, even in a poor-house. The setting sun is reflected from the windows of the almshouse as brightly as from the rich man's abode; the snow melts before its door as early in the spring. I do not see but a quiet mind may live as contentedly there, and have as cheering thoughts, as in a palace. The town's poor seem to me often to live the most independent lives of any. Maybe they are simply great enough to receive without misgiving. Most think that they are above being supported by the town; but it oftener happens that they are not above supporting themselves by dishonest means, which should be more disreputable. Cultivate poverty like a garden herb, like sage. Do not trouble yourself much to get new things, whether clothes or friends. Turn the old; return to them. Things do not change; we change. Sell your clothes and keep your thoughts. God will see that you do not want society. If I were confined to a corner of a garret all my days, like a spider, the world would be just as large to me while I had my thoughts about me. The philosopher said: "From an army of three divisions one can take away its general, and put it in disorder; from the man the most abject and vulgar one cannot take away his thought." Do not seek so anxiously to be developed, to subject yourself to many influences to be played on; it is all dissipation. Humility like darkness reveals the heavenly lights. The shadows of poverty and meanness gather around us, "and lo! creation widens to our view." We are often reminded that if there were bestowed on us the wealth of Croesus, our aims must still be the same, and our means essentially the same. Moreover, if you are restricted in your range by poverty, if you cannot buy books and news-papers, for instance, you are but confined to the most significant and vital experiences; you are compelled to deal with the material which yields the most sugar and the most starch. It is life near the bone where it is sweet-est. You are defended from being a trifler. No man loses ever on a lower level by magnanimity on a higher. Superfluous wealth can buy super-fluities only. Money is not required to buy one necessary of the soul.

I live in the angle of a leaden wall, into whose composition was poured a little alloy of bell-metal. Often, in the repose of my mid-day, there reaches my ears a confused *tintinnabulum* from without. It is the noise of my contemporaries. My neighbors tell me of their adventures with famous gentlemen and ladies, what notabilities they met at the dinner-table; but I am no more interested in such things than in the con-tents of the Daily Times. The interest and the conversation are about cos-tume and manners chiefly; but a goose is a goose still, dress it as you will. They tell me of California and Texas, of England and the Indies, of the Hon. Mr.——of Georgia or of Massachusetts, all transient and fleeting phenomena, till I am ready to leap from their court-yard like the Mameluke bey. I delight to come to my bearings,—not walk in procession with pomp and parade, in a conspicuous place, but to walk even with the Builder of the universe, if I may,—not to live in this restless, nervous, bustling, trivial Nineteenth Century, but stand or sit thoughtfully while it goes by. What are men celebrating? They are all on a committee of arrangements, and hourly expect a speech from somebody. God is only the president of the day, and Webster is his orator. I love to weigh, to set-tle, to gravitate toward that which most strongly and rightfully attracts me;—not hang by the beam of the scale and try to weigh less,—not sup-pose a case, but take the case that is; to travel the only path I can, and that on which no power can resist me. It affords me no satisfaction to com-merce to spring an arch before I have got a solid foundation. Let us not play at kittly-benders. There is a solid bottom everywhere. We read that the traveller asked the boy if the swamp before him had a hard bottom. The boy replied that it had. But presently the traveller's horse sank in up to the girths, and he observed to the boy, "I thought you said that this bog had a hard bottom." "So it has," answered the latter, "but you have not got half way to it yet." So it is with the bogs and quicksands of society; but he is an old boy that knows it. Only what is thought, said, or done at a certain rare coincidence is good. I would not be one of those who will foolishly drive a nail into mere lath and plastering; such a deed would keep me awake nights. Give me a hammer, and let me feel for the furring. Do not depend on the putty. Drive a nail home and clinch it so faithfully that you can wake up in the night and think of your work with satisfaction,—a work at which you would not be ashamed to invoke the Muse. So will help you God, and so only. Every nail driven should be as another rivet in the machine of the universe, you carrying on the work.

Rather than love, than money, than fame, give me truth. I sat at a table where were rich food and wine in abundance, and obsequious attendance, but sincerity and truth were not; and I went away hungry from the inhospitable board. The hospitality was as cold as the ices. I thought that there was no need of ice to freeze them. They talked to me of the age of the wine and the fame of the vintage; but I thought of an older, a newer, and purer wine, of a more glorious vintage, which they had not got, and could not buy. The style, the house and grounds and "entertainment" pass for nothing with me. I called on the king, but he made me wait in his hall, and conducted like a man incapacitated for hospitality. There was a man in my neighborhood who lived in a hollow tree. His manners were truly regal. I should have done better had I called on him.

How long shall we sit in our porticoes practising idle and musty virtues, which any work would make impertinent? As if one were to begin the day with long-suffering, and hire a man to hoe his potatoes; and in the afternoon go forth to practise Christian meekness and charity with goodness aforethought! Consider the China pride and stagnant self-complacency of mankind. This generation inclines a little to congratulate itself on being the last of an illustrious line; and in Boston and London and Paris and Rome, thinking of its long descent, it speaks of its progress in art and science and literature with satisfaction. There are the Records of the Philosophical Societies, and the public Eulogies of *Great Men!* It is the good Adam contemplating his own virtue. "Yes, we have done great deeds, and sung divine songs, which shall never die."—that is, as long as we can remember them. The learned societies and great men of Assyria,—where are they? What youthful philosophers and experimentalists we are! There is not one of my readers who has yet lived a whole human life. These may be but the spring months in the life of the race. If we have had the seven-years' itch, we have not seen the seventeen-year locust yet in Concord. We are acquainted with a mere pellicle of the globe on which we live. Most have not delved six feet beneath the surface, nor leaped as many above it. We know not where we are. Beside, we are sound asleep nearly half our time. Yet we esteem ourselves wise, and have an established order on the surface. Truly, we are deep thinkers, we are ambitious spirits! As I stand over the insect crawling amid the pine needles on the forest floor, and endeavoring to conceal itself from my sight, and ask myself why it will cherish those humble thoughts, and hide its head from me who might, perhaps, be its benefactor, and impart to its race some cheering information, I am reminded of the greater Benefactor and Intelligence that stands over me the human insect.

There is an incessant influx of novelty into the world, and yet we tolerate incredible dulness. I need only suggest what kind of sermons are still listened to in the most enlightened countries. There are such words as joy and sorrow, but they are only the burden of a psalm, sung with a nasal twang, while we believe in the ordinary and mean. We think that we can change our clothes only. It is said that the British Empire is very large and respectable, and that the United States are a first-rate power. We do not believe that a tide rises and falls behind every man which can float the British Empire like a chip, if he should ever harbor it in his mind. Who knows what sort of seventeen-year locust will next come out of the ground? The government of the world I live in was not framed, like that of Britain, in after-dinner conversations over the wine.

The life in us is like the water in the river. It may rise this year higher than man has ever known it, and flood the parched uplands; even this may be the eventful year, which will drown out all our muskrats. It was not always dry land where we dwell. I see far inland the banks which the stream anciently washed, before science began to record its freshets. Every one has heard the story which has gone the rounds of New England, of a strong and beautiful bug which came out of the dry leaf of an old table of apple-tree wood, which had stood in a farmer's kitchen for sixty years, first in Connecticut, and afterward in Massachusetts,—from an egg deposited in the living tree many years earlier still, as appeared by counting the annual layers beyond it; which was heard gnawing out for several weeks, hatched perchance by the heat of an urn. Who does not feel his faith in a resurrection and immortality strengthened by hearing of this? Who knows what beautiful and winged life, whose egg has been buried for ages under many concentric layers of woodenness in the dead dry life of society, deposited at first in the alburnum of the green and living tree, which has been gradually converted into the semblance of its well-seasoned tomb,—heard perchance gnawing out now for years by the astonished family of man, as they sat round the festive board,—may unexpectedly come forth from amidst society's most trivial and hand-selled furniture, to enjoy its perfect summer life at last!

I do not say that John or Jonathan will realize all this; but such is the character of that morrow which mere lapse of time can never make to dawn. The light which puts out our eyes is darkness to us. Only that day dawns to which we are awake. There is more day to dawn. The sun is but a morning star.

*B*arbara Brandt is a long-time organizer and social change activist from the Boston area. She has worked on projects ranging from solar energy, community gardening, to workplace conditions. This article was excerpted from a paper prerpared by the Shorter Hours Work-Time Group of Boston.

Less Is More:
A Call for Shorter Work Hours

Barbara Brandt

America is suffering from overwork. Too many of us are too busy, trying to squeeze more into each day while having less to show for it. Although our growing time crunch is often portrayed as a personal dilemma, it is in fact a major social problem that has reached crisis proportions over the past 20 years.

The simple fact is that Americans today—both women and men—are spending too much time at work, to the detriment of their homes, their families, their personal lives, and their communities. The American Dream promised that our individual hard work paired with the advances of modern technology would bring about the good life for all. Glorious visions of the leisure society were touted throughout the '50s and '60s. But now most people are working more than ever before, while still struggling to meet their economic commitments. Ironically, the many advances in technology, such as computers and fax machines, rather than reducing our workload, seem to have speeded up our lives at work. At the same time, technology has equipped us with "conveniences" like microwave ovens and frozen dinners that merely enable us to adopt a similar frantic pace in our home lives so we can cope with more hours at paid work.

A recent spate of articles in the mainstream media has focused on the new problems of overwork and lack of time. Unfortunately, overwork is often portrayed as a special problem of yuppies and professionals on the fast track. In reality, the unequal distribution of work and time in America today reflects the decline in both standard of living and quality of life for most Americans. Families whose members never see each other, women who work a double shift (first on the job, then at home), workers who need more flexible work schedules, and unemployed and underemployed people who need more work are all casualties of the crisis of overwork.

Americans often assume that overwork is an inevitable fact of life—like death and taxes. Yet a closer look at other times and other nations offers some startling surprises.

Anthropologists have observed that in pre-industrial (particularly hunting and gathering) societies, people generally spend 3 to 4 hours a day, 15 to 20 hours a week, doing the work necessary to maintain life.

The rest of the time is spent in socializing, partying, playing, story-telling, and artistic or religious activities. The ancient Romans celebrated 175 public festivals a year in which everyone participated, and people in the Middle Ages had at least 115.

In our era, almost every other industrialized nation (except Japan) has fewer annual working hours and longer vacations than the United States. This includes all of Western Europe, where many nations enjoy thriving economies and standards of living equal to or higher than ours. Jeremy Brecher and Tim Costello, writing in *Z Magazine* (Oct. 1990), note that "European unions during the 1980s made a powerful and largely successful push to cut working hours. In 1987 German metalworkers struck and won a 37.5-hour week; many are now winning a 35-hour week. In 1990, hundreds of thousands of British workers have won a 37-hour week."

In an article about work-time in the *Boston Globe*, Suzanne Gordon notes that workers in other industrialized countries "enjoy—as a statutory right—longer vacations [than in the U.S.] from the moment they enter the work force. In Canada, workers are legally entitled to two weeks off their first year on the job . . . . After two or three years of employment, most get three weeks of vacation. After 10 years, it's up to four, and by 20 years, Canadian workers are off for five weeks. In Germany, statutes guarantee 18 days minimum for everyone, but most workers get five or six weeks. The same is true in Scandinavian countries, and in France."

In contrast to the extreme American emphasis on productivity and commitment, which results in many workers, especially in professional-level jobs, not taking the vacations coming to them, Gordon notes that "In countries that are America's most successful competitors in the global marketplace, all working people, whether lawyers or teacher, CEOs or janitors, take the vacations to which they are entitled by law. 'No one in West Germany,' a West German embassy's officer explains, 'no matter how high up they are, would ever say they couldn't afford to take a vacation. Everyone takes their vacation.'"

And in Japan, where dedication to the job is legendary, Gordon notes that the Japanese themselves are beginning to consider their national workaholism a serious social problem leading to stress-related illnesses and even death. As a result, the Japanese government recently established a commission whose goal is to promote shorter working hours and more leisure time.

Most other industrialized nations also have better family-leave policies than the United States, and in a number of other countries workers benefit from innovative time-scheduling opportunities such as sabbaticals.

While the idea of a shorter workweek and longer vacations sounds appealing to most people, any movement to enact shorter work-time as a public policy will encounter surprising pockets of resistance, not just from business leaders but even from some workers. Perhaps the most formidable barrier to more free time for Americans is the widespread mindset that the 40-hour workweek, 8 hours a day, 5 days a week, 50 weeks a year, is a natural rhythm of the universe. This view is reinforced by the media's complete silence regarding the shorter work-time and more favorable vacation and family-leave policies of other countries. This lack of information, and our leaders' reluctance to suggest that the United States can learn from any other nation (except workaholic Japan) is one reason why more Americans don't identify overwork as a major problem or clamor for fewer hours and more vacation. Monika Bauerlein, a journalist originally from Germany now living in Minneapolis, exclaims, "I can't believe that people here aren't rioting in the streets over having only two weeks of vacation a year."

A second obstacle to launching a powerful shorter work-time movement is America's deeply ingrained work ethic, or its modern incarnation, the workaholic syndrome. The work ethic fosters the widely held belief that people's work is their most important activity and that people who do not work long and hard are lazy, unproductive, and worthless.

For many Americans today, paid work is not just a way to make money but is a crucial source of their self-worth. Many of us identify ourselves almost entirely by the kind of work we do. Work still has a powerful psychological and spiritual hold over our lives—and talk of shorter work-time may seem somehow morally suspicious.

Because we are so deeply a work-oriented society, leisure-time activities—such as play, relaxation, engaging in cultural and artistic pursuits, or just quiet contemplation and "doing nothing"—are not looked on as essential and worthwhile components of life. Of course, for the majority of working women who must work a second shift at home, much of the time spent outside of paid work is not leisure anyway. Also much of our non-work time is spent not just in personal renewal, but in building and maintaining essential social ties—with family, friends, and the larger community.

Today, as mothers and fathers spend more and more time on the job, we are beginning to recognize the deleterious effects—especially on our young people—of the breakdown of social ties and community in American life. But unfortunately, our nation reacts to these problems by calling for more paid professionals—more police, more psychiatrists, more experts—without recognizing the possibility that shorter work hours and more free time could enable us to do much of the necessary rebuilding and healing, with much more gratifying and longer-lasting results.

Of course, the stiffest opposition to cutting work hours comes not from citizens but from business. Employers are reluctant to alter the 8-hour day, 40-hour workweek, 50 weeks a year because it seems easier and more profitable for employers to hire fewer employees for longer hours rather than more employees—each of whom would also require health insurance and other benefits—with flexible schedules and work arrangements.

Harvard University economist Juliet B. Schor, who has been studying issues of work and leisure in America, reminds us that we cannot ignore the larger relationship between unemployment and overwork: While many of us work too much, others are unable to find paid work at all. Schor points out that "workers who work longer hours lose more income when they lose their jobs. The threat of job loss is an important determinant of management's power on the shop floor." A system that offers only two options—long work hours or unemployment—serves as both a carrot and a stick. Those lucky enough to get full-time jobs are bribed into docile compliance with the boss, while the spectre of unemployment always looms as the ultimate punishment for the unruly.

Some observers suggest that keeping people divided into "the employed" and "the unemployed" creates feelings of resentment and inferiority/superiority between the two groups, thus focusing their discontent and blame on each other rather than on the corporations and political fig-ures who actually dictate our nation's economic policies.

Our role as consumers contributes to keeping the average work week from falling. In an economic system in which addictive buying is the basis of corporate profits, working a full 40 hours or more each week for 50 weeks a year gives us just enough time to stumble home and dazedly—almost automatically—shop; but not enough time to think about deeper issues or to work effectively for social change. From the point of view of corporations and policymakers, shorter work-time may be bad for the economy, because people with enhanced free time may begin to find other things to do with it besides mindlessly buying products. It takes more free time to grow vegetables, cook meals from scratch, sew clothes, or repair broken items than it does to just buy these things at the mall.

Any serious proposal to give employed Americans a break by cutting into the eight-hour work day is certain to be met with anguished cries about international competitiveness. The United States seems gripped by the fear that our nation has lost its economic dominance, and pundits, policymakers and business leaders tell us that no sacrifice is too great if it puts America on top again.

As arguments like this are put forward (and we can expect them to increase in the years to come), we need to remember two things. First, even if America maintained its dominance (whatever that means) and the economy were booming again, this would be no guarantee that the gains—be they in wages, in employment opportunities, or in leisure—would be distributed equitably between upper management and every-one else. Second, the entire issue of competitiveness is suspect when it pits poorly treated workers in one country against poorly treated work-ers in another; and when the vast majority of economic power, anyway, is in the control of enormous multinational corporations that have no loy-alty to the people of any land.

Many people are experimenting with all sorts of ways to cope with grueling work schedules. Those with enough money use it to "buy time." They find child care, order take-out meals, and hire people to pick their children up from school and do the family shopping. Other options being pursued by both men and women include actively looking for good part-time jobs; sharing jobs; arranging more flexible work schedules; going into business for themselves; working at home; and scaling back on con-sumption in order to work fewer hours for lower pay. While these ideas work in some cases, they are often stymied by a lack of support from employers. and they aren't available to many people, especially those with lower incomes.

But perhaps the major shortcoming of all these individual responses is precisely that: They are individual. The problem of overwork is a broad problem of our economic system. It cannot be solved by just one individual. family, or business. Individual approaches ignore the many larger causes of the problem.

Annual Vacation Time (in weeks)		
agreement	By law	By bargaining
Austria	4	4–5
Denmark	—	5
Finland	5	5–6
France	5	5-6
Germany	3	4–6
Greece	4	
Ireland	3	4
Italy	—	4–6
Netherlands	3	4–5
Portugal	4	
Spain	5	5
Sweden	5	5–8
Switzerland	4	4–5
United States	—	2–4

Source: "Reduction of Working Time in Europe, European Industrial Relations Review, No. 127, August 1984: 9–13.

A number of solutions now discussed for the overwork crisis are actually steps in the wrong direction.

The conservative climate of the '80s and '90s has spawned a neo-traditional cultural movement that holds up the 1950s as a golden age from which we have unwisely strayed. Their simplistic solution to the complex set of social issues involved with overwork is to force women back into the home. While we all should support the right of any woman to freely choose home and family as her primary responsibility and source of fulfillment, we need to oppose social and economic policies that either seek to keep women at home or offer them only limited opportunity—low-paying, low-status, part-time jobs—outside the home. Such policies are not only unfair to women themselves, they are economically harmful to the many families supported by working women.

The idea of a four-day, 10-hour-a-day workweek has frequently been suggested as a superior alternative to the current five-day workweek. But this is no shortening of work hours, and it ignores the fact that many people who do paid work also need to care for home and family when they get home. Lengthening the workday would add considerably to the burden these people already carry.

Finally, we should be wary of programs supposedly aimed at helping working parents and their families when the ultimate outcome is to keep parents at work longer—day care for sick children and corporate day care centers open on weekends to accommodate parents who want to work extended hours, for example.

Now that public attention is beginning to take note of the mounting personal, economic, and social toll of overwork, it is time to treat overwork as a major political and social issue. To accomplish this, the Shorter Work-Time Group of Boston—a multicultural group of women's and labor activists—proposes a national campaign for shorter work hours that could foster a formidable alliance of unions, community groups, women's groups, and workers in all fields. To begin this campaign, we propose a 10-point plan that could help heal the problems of overwork in its many forms and enhance the quality of all our lives—at home, on the job, and in the community.

1. Establish a 6-hour day/30-hour week.

We propose that a 6-hour day / 30-hour week be made the new standard for "full-time work." This new policy would not only give America's workers more time to devote to our families, friends, and personal and community lives, but would also provide benefits to employers in increased efficiency and productivity, reduced accidents and absenteeism, improved morale, lower turnover, and retention of valuable employees.

So that workers do not suffer financially from reduction of their work-time, we also propose that any reduction in hours be accompanied by a corresponding increase in hourly income—that the six-hour day be compensated by what was formerly eight-hour pay. Since numerous studies have shown shortened workdays improve productivity, this would not be economically unrealistic.

2. Extend paid vacations for all American workers.

American workers should enjoy what their counterparts around the world take for granted—four to six weeks of paid vacation each year. Vacation should be based on overall years in the work force rather than tied to the number of years a person has been employed in a particular firm.

3. Improve family-leave policies.

The Family and Medical Leave Act, vetoed last year by President Bush, needs broad national support so that politicians would fear reprisals from an angry public if they did not support it. This bill would provide job security for people who have to leave work for extended periods in order to care for newborn children or seriously ill family members. Although it does not provide for pay during such leaves, paid leave should be an eventual goal.

4. Establish benefits for all workers.

At present, employers of part-time and temporary workers are not legally required to provide health insurance, vacations, pensions, or any other benefits. This is especially insidious because women and many low-income workers are most likely to hold part-time and temporary jobs. Congresswoman Pat Schroeder has introduced HR 2575, the Part-Time and Temporary Workers Protection Act, to rectify this situation at the national level.

5. Discourage overtime work.

Since overtime is detrimental to workers, their families, and the other workers it replaces, we would like to see it eliminated as much as possible. This can be done by mandating the elimination of compulsory overtime and raising the pay rate to double time for voluntary overtime.

6. Support alternative working arrangements.

We encourage business to increase flex-time and other innovative work-time arrangements that enable employees to better meet their personal and family needs.

7. Acknowledge workaholism as a social disorder.

In Japan, they even coined a word—*karoshi* (death from overwork)—to show this is a serious disease.

8. Promote awareness that our citizens and our nation as a whole will benefit from shorter work-time.

We need a public education campaign to raise public consciousness about the devastating effects that overwork is having on our health, our families, our communities, and especially on our young people. American workers must have more time to care for their families and restore their communities. This does not mean sending women back home. It means giving all people the time and resources to create their own solutions. If we had more time for ourselves, for example, we would probably see a wide variety of child-care options. In some families, women would do this exclusively; in others, women and men would share child-care responsibilities; some people would hire paid help; and others would develop cooperative or community-based programs for their children; many people would take advantage of a mix of options. The same would probably occur with regard to a wide range of family and community issues.

9. Look at how the issue of overwork influences the problems of underemployment and unemployment.

Because of increasing economic pressures, many corporations are developing a two-tier work force: a core of workers who enjoy good salaries, job security, and full benefits, and another group of lower paid part-time and temporary workers who have no benefits or job security.

10. Challenge the assertion that we have to enslave ourselves to our jobs in order to keep America competitive.

Germany, for example, has mandated shortened work hours, and clearly has not lost its competitive edge in the world economy.

Seth Godin (1960–) grew up in Buffalo, New York, and earned an under-graduate degree in computer science and philosophy from Tufts University and an MBA from Standford. He has written several business bestsellers, includ-ing an e-book, Unleashing the Ideavirus, *and maintains a personal blog at sethgodin.typepad.com.*

There Is No Correlation at All between Success and Hours Worked

Seth Godin

Situation report: Profits are off. The Dow can't decide if it should have five digits or four. The best and the brightest—as well as the slow-est and the lamest—are announcing layoffs more frequently than LaGuardia announces landings.

My recommendation: Relax. Don't work so hard. Take a little time off. Chill out!

To understand why this is the best advice for bosses and workers alike, you need to hear about the Kalihi-Palama Public Library in Honolulu, Hawaii.

The Kalihi-Palama Public Library is open until 5 P.M. most days. Years ago, when the only way to research stuff was by asking people (as opposed to using the Web), this was a vitally important fact to me and to many people on the East Coast. Why? Because in those days, if you hap-pened to find yourself working away on a proposal at 10 P.M. New York time, the library in Hawaii was still open. You could give them a call, and a librarian would happily answer your question, regardless of how obscure it was.

One of the least savory by-products of the new economy has been an almost complete disregard for sleep, family, and personal time. Macho companies marching toward IPOs pride themselves on the army of their totally committed employees, who are all too happy to endure sleepless nights and to take showers at the office.

When I was working on my first product launch about 15 years ago, a team of 40 of us stayed in the office all night and all day for about a month. We slept on the floor (when we slept at all) and only left the office for an occasional shower. And if I remember correctly, the showers were pretty occasional.

We made our deadline (just barely—we had to bribe the UPS man with champagne in order to get the last 100 units off of the assembly line) and saved the company. I remember the perverse pride we all took in our insane dedication. The camaraderie that we developed during those late nights lasts to this day.

But it almost cost me my girlfriend (I ended up marrying her, which is definitely the good news here), and it definitely cost me my health: I was sick for six months afterward.

If you're shaking your head in understanding or agreement, then we need to talk. There is no correlation at all between success and hours worked. People who run huge corporations, superpower governments, and insanely profitable, tiny proprietorships are all working fewer hours than you are. It's time to stop the madness and reset your internal clock.

I think the sleeplessness started when we moved off the farm. Sure, there are a few weeks a year of really long hours on a farm, when you had better get the crops in or they'll die. But there's a limited amount of stuff to harvest, and bringing in more sharecroppers and putting in longer hours isn't really going to pay off. Sooner or later, you run out of corn.

It wasn't that way in factories or in mines, however. That kind of grunt work-brunt work had a simple mantra: Work more, get more. You lived off the sweat of your brow, and the more your brow sweat, the more you got. Even better, getting your employees to work longer hours made you more money—without the sweat (at least not yours).

Understandably, the workers of the world united. They realized that while management got more, they really didn't. Hence, the 40-hour workweek.

Suddenly, in came the new economy, entrepreneurs, freelancers, free agents, speed to market, first-mover advantage, IPOs, and cutthroat competition in a winner-take-all world. The workers got their wish: They got to feel like owners, and all bets were off.

File this part of the new economy under the lesson, Be careful what you wish for, because you just might get it. Check your e-mail. There are people sending you messages at midnight or at 4 A.M. One of my closest friends regularly calls me from work at 9 A.M. my time, here in New York—which would be fine, except that she lives in California. The original Macintosh team may have gotten the finest massages and the best catering, but they worked like dogs for more than a year.

One company in Silicon Valley often schedules important strategy meetings at 6 P.M. Of course, by that time, most people are running late, so the meetings start at 7:30 or 8 P.M. That accomplishes a few things: First, only the really dedicated hard-liners show up. The folks who don't really care are at home hanging out with their family, cooking dinner. The true loyalists—at least, according to company culture—are at work. Second, everyone is tired and punchy, which ensures that crisp, analytical thinking will be in pretty short supply. And third and most important, even the diehards are beginning to think about going home, so there won't be much dissent unless the decision about to be made is really dumb or really important!

Of course, even if you're not at work, you stay in touch. You use your PDA to check your e-mail in a taxi. You make sure that your cell phone has a headset so you can talk while you're driving the family to the Grand Canyon for vacation.

For a while, it seemed as if all of this made sense. It seemed as if working longer hours made your company move faster and that moving faster made your company win.

Well, now that the NASDAQ has cooled off and we've seen that maybe, just maybe, the new economy is not a speed-to-market, first-mover advantage, IPO, winner-take-all world, it's time to reevaluate this work-ethic mind-set. But ironically, instead of getting us to challenge the myth of the grindstone, the NASDAQ hiccup has a lot of people too scared to act smart.

What's smart? The fact is, the companies that made good decisions a year ago or even five years ago are thriving today. Their stock may be down, but the companies are still on course.

Alas, among those that failed to make the right decisions, the strategy is apparently not to step back and start making the best decisions. Instead, the approach seems to be to work even harder, ignoring the fact that companies may be working hard on the wrong things!

Some folks think their boss, their boss's boss, or Wall Street wants to hear, "Well, we'll just keep our heads down and work even harder." Wrong! I think what's missing is people saying, "We learned from that mistake. Here are the smart decisions that are going to take us where we want to go now."

There's a huge difference between working in a mine or a factory and doing what you do for a living. In the old days, people made stuff. You don't make stuff. You make decisions.

And the thing about making decisions is that you don't make better decisions when you work longer hours. You don't write better code when you work longer hours. You don't create better business-development deals, make better sales pitches, or invent cooler interfaces when you work longer hours either.

Let's face it: The marathon culture of "I work harder than you do" is nothing but an excuse to avoid making the hard decisions.

Think about the last time you faced a deadline at work. Odds are, you made the deadline—but just barely. Now imagine that the deadline had been one day further away. You still would have made the deadline. Your work would have been just as good. And the words "just barely" would still be associated with the project.

It's an old saw, but it's still true in the new economy: Work expands to fill the time allotted for it.

If you allot 12 hours to work every day, you'll spend 12 hours. But are you going to make more decisions? Better decisions?

Let's do a little history exercise. Imagine five success stories of the past decade. Think of companies such as Cisco, Palm, Yahoo!, Starbucks, and JetBlue.

Now list the six decisions that each company made that turned it into a success. Are there six things that each one decided to do that transformed it from an ordinary company into an extraordinary success? There might even be fewer than six things.

Everything else these companies did around those decisions is just commentary. Yes, there were important operations happening to make those decisions valid. But those operations weren't the key to those companies' successes. As strategist Gary Hamel says, in the future, business-model innovation will be a key success factor.

And it's not just fancy corporate-strategy stuff. Great programmers know that 80% of a software project's success or failure is determined by the decisions made during the first four weeks of systems architecture. Get that part right, and you won't be fighting an uphill battle for the rest of the project.

Talk to any truly successful lawyer—the kind with great clients, a great reputation, and plenty of cash. You'll find that the secret of her success isn't pulling an all-nighter the night before a client meeting or a big trial. The secret is understanding the key issues and making decisions about how to act on them. Nobody ever hired a law firm because he was impressed with how well stapled the memos were.

Now think about your company. Are people so busy implementing, defending, building, and pulling all-nighters that they are shortchanging the time that they ought to be spending making decisions?

Take a look at the future. When you write your company's history two years from now, which decisions will have really mattered? What were the key moments that led you to create such a success?

Write them down. Post them on the wall. And work on them!

That's what you should spend your time on. Getting those decisions right is far more important than answering your 103rd e-mail message or hacking that last piece of code.

Situation report: At *Reader's Digest* in the 1950s, Lila Wallace used to walk from office to office and say, "It's a beautiful day. Turn off the lights and go home." And it was 4—P.M.! Maybe if you left the office once a week at 4 P.M., the decisions that you would make the next day would be a lot better. Go home. Have dinner with your family. You'll be glad you did.

My recommendation: If your current job environment is one where the only way to avoid getting fired is to work all the time, then hey, get fired. The unemployment rate is still only 4%, and if you're smart enough to be reading this magazine, well, there are plenty of jobs out there that reward you for being smart—not for digging the most coal.

*S*usan Headden (1956–) graduated from Ohio Wesleyan University and is an assistant mangaging editor for U.S. News & World Report. She won a Pulitzer Prize in 1991 for an investigative feature series on medical malpractice and has written on a variety of other topics, including sweatshop labor, in this selection.

Made in the U.S.A.

Susan Headden

The little girl looked wistfully past oily sewing machines that rumbled like jackhammers on a cracked concrete floor. Nearby, cut cloth was piled high as snowdrifts. Plaster fell in flakes from the peeling ceiling. Through a broken window, a lazy fan drew sooty air from a narrow alley. Inside, the temperature was 90 degrees and climbing. Not far from the girl, 20 men and women hunched over scarred tables, sewing 30-inch inseams on bright slacks. Each inseam took three seconds flat. The girl paid no attention. On her nest of finished skirts, she fastened buttons, her little fingers precise as machines. When she was finished with one skirt, the girl hung it up for shipment. Then she turned to the next one. The girl worked not in Jakarta or Santo Domingo; she worked in midtown Manhattan at a company called Meralva Fashion. On each skirt the little girl hung up, there was a label. It said, "Crafted with Pride in the U.S.A." The little girl was 10 years old.

Consumers have a host of reasons to "Buy American." In theory, purchasing goods made here prevents jobs from disappearing overseas. There is, too, the satisfaction of supporting a uniquely American standard of living, one built on a federal minimum wage of $4.25 an hour plus the time-honored guarantee of Social Security and a safety net of other hard-won benefits and protections. Today, in the heat of the debate over the North American Free Trade Agreement, many union members feel especially obliged to buy American. Consumers with no such allegiances find other reasons: American-made clothing is simply thought by many to be superior to foreign. "Made in the U.S.A." tags have been shown to increase sales by as much as 24 percent.

That's one side of the Made in the U.S.A. story; the other is more harrowing. A three-month investigation by *U.S. News* found that as many as half of all women's garments made in America are produced in whole or in part by factories that pay below minimum wage, flout federal safety laws and require workers to spend 60 hours or more at their sewing machines each week. Overtime is not paid. Insurance benefits are nonexistent. "You can't complain," says Juan Pineda, a Los Angeles garment worker, "or someone else will get your job."

"Loads of Money."

Sweatshop labor is nothing new, of course. But nearly a century after a fire at New York's Triangle Shirtwaist factory killed more than 140 women, sparking demands for sweeping workplace reforms, much of the $38 billion-a-year women's apparel business still relies heavily on sweatshop labor. While the most expensive women's clothing is manufactured abroad or in clean, well-lighted factories in this country, there are exceptions. For lower-priced clothing today, such exceptions are the rule: More often than not, these garments are produced in sweatshops.

Most Americans, in fact, have probably worn something that was produced by an underpaid worker in an illegal factory. Many such factories still turn out cheap, ill-made garments like the sweatshops of old. But other factories that violate basic federal labor laws also produce clothes for some of the biggest names in American fashion. There are Main Street labels like J. C. Penney, Sears, and Wal-Mart. Creations dreamed up by celebrity designers Bob Mackie and Victor Costa have been run up by law-breaking contractors, records show. So have shopping mall staples with labels like the Limited, Casual Corner, Guess, and Esprit. Even Patagonia, the outdoorwear company that donates 10 percent of its profits to environmental causes, has contracted with manufacturers that employ sweatshop labor. "It's across the board, and it's shocking," says Rolene Otero, head of the wage and hour division of the U.S. Labor Department office in Los Angeles. "And what really bothers me is that there is loads of money in this industry."

For all the big-money glitz at the retail level, however, the apparel industry has been under pressure for years from foreign imports, particularly from Asia. Over the past two decades, for example, employment in New York City's apparel industry has fallen from around 200,000 workers to fewer than 100,000.

Particularly for women's clothes, where fashions change quickly and production schedules can be murderous, even highly profitable clothing companies struggle to keep production costs and inventories as low as possible. For this reason, lawbreaking contractors can be appealing. Low

---

Where the Money Goes

A skirt from the Limited retails for **$54**. The contractor earns **$4.25** to sew the garment. Payments to laborers account for **$3** of that. A breakdown:

Waistband with facing:		72¢
Hem, skirt:		6¢
Hem, lining:		7¢
Serging, skirt:		14¢
Serging, lining:		4¢
Cutting threads:		5¢
Belt loops: (4)		10¢
Sewing belt loops on skirt: (4)		8¢
Zipper:		17¢
Pressing:		15¢
Ironing loops:	ea.	15¢

---

overhead and low capitalization costs allow sweatshop operators to underbid legitimate manufacturers. In the past decade, many have been driven out of business. "Manufacturers can't compete," says Joe Allen, a former Dallas manufacturer who lost business to illegal sweatshops, "when they don't have a level playing field."

Lost Revenues

Clothing company executives say they work hard to avoid dealing with illegal contractors and police the contractors they do use. "Our policy," says a statement prepared by the Limited clothing chain in response to inquiries from *U.S. News*, "is that each of our vendors must deliver their products in compliance with the law, under penalty of damages and the immediate termination of orders." Recently, when the Limited learned of one wage violation, it fired the manufacturer that had employed the offending contractor.

The *U.S. News* investigation was based on visits to garment factories in the leading manufacturing centers of New York, Los Angeles, and Dallas. The visits took place between July and October. The magazine interviewed dozens of contractors, garment workers and manufacturers' employees and reviewed 400 pages of documents obtained through the Freedom of Information Act. Principal findings:

- State and federal treasuries lose hundreds of millions of dollars in tax revenues each year to unscrupulous garment contractors who refuse to pay any taxes at all. Of the estimated 50,000 sewing contractors nationwide, fully a third are believed to operate with no licenses or permits; workers are paid in cash. According to an internal memorandum from the California Employment Development Department made available to *U.S. News*, Los Angeles County alone lost an estimated $120 million in tax revenues last year.

- Most producers of low-end clothing appear to be breaking wage and hour laws. Of the 83 garment factories inspected by the California Department of Labor during one week in October, 77 were cited for violations of wage, hour, and record-keeping laws. In a typical case, an employee of Alicia Munoz Fashions in West Los Angeles earned just 7 cents for every $32 cotton blouse she pressed. At that rate, she would have to press a garment every minute just to earn the $4.25 minimum wage.

- Many garment factories routinely violate health and safety laws, but local health departments and the federal Occupational Safety and Health Administration rarely inspect them. Problems documented time and again at illegal sewing factories visited during the *U.S. News* inquiry: blocked fire exits, rodent infestation, and unsanitary bathrooms and lunch areas. At Washmax, a garment-processing plant in South Central Los Angeles, workers were throwing new denim into vats of noxious chemicals used to give the jeans a stylishly faded look. Signs posted at Washmax warned that the chemicals used could cause birth defects; the workers wore no protective gear. Washmax was assessed a heavy fine. Federal safety inspectors say there are many more factories like Washmax, but they complain that they have neither the time nor the resources to inspect all of them.

- Penalties under the Fair Labor Standards Act, the benchmark law that establishes wage and hour standards, are clearly insufficient to deter employers intent on breaking the law. The law, passed in 1938, imposes no fines on a first offense for failure to keep records and no requirements to pay back wages in instances where employers are found to have cheated employees. Criminal prosecutions under the law are understandably rare. Example: In New York, a U.S. Labor Department investigator found that a clothing manufacturer had failed to keep records on employees and owed one employee $4,326 in overtime pay. The Labor Department's response? It issued the employer a pamphlet explaining federal labor laws and *asked* the employer to pay his employee's overtime wages. The man refused.

The Labor Department then suggested the employee sue the employer on his own.

The trade organizations that tout the "Made in the U.S.A." labels on clothing say they have no knowledge of the illegal practices associated with some of the goods that carry their labels. The Made in the U.S.A. Foundation, which encourages consumers to buy domestically made products, includes on its list of recommended labels four manufacturers— Guess Inc., Cherokee Group, Ocean Pacific Sunwear Ltd., and Rampage Clothing Co. All four have employed contractors cited for labor law violations. A spokesperson for the Made in the U.S.A. Foundation says the violations are news to her. "If something is made here," says Colleen Caine, "the company should be complying with laws. But you can't really tell by looking at the label." Robert Swift, the director of the Crafted with Pride in U.S.A. Council, which promotes U.S.-made apparel, says his organization simply can't keep tabs on conditions in factories that affix his label. "If I audited every use of the mark," Swift sighs, "I couldn't afford to do anything."

Cutting Corners

Fed by the recent influx of Asian immigrants, competition among contractors is fierce. In New York's Chinatown, 400 contractors vie for manufacturers' business. The manager of Meralva Fashion, who pays her employees minimum wage but was cited for child labor violations, says she takes manufacturers' work at any price. "If you don't," says Meralva's Odilis Santana, "they won't call you anymore." Jorge Grunauer, the manager of Alicia Munoz Fashions, in West Los Angeles, says he *has* to cut corners: "If I am an honest businessman in this industry, I might as well close the door."

The numbers tell the story. Grunauer produces a contract showing what his shop was paid for a cotton shorts-and-top ensemble sold by L.A. Basic. The outfit retails for $32; Alicia Munoz Fashions made it for $1.80. The margins are getting slimmer. "The same company that used to pay $2 for a blouse," Grunauer says, "now pays only $1.85 for the same blouse." Other contractors confirm this. A few years ago, the contract price of a basic dress retailing for $100 was $8, according to New York contractor Danny Tsai; today, it's $6.

While sewing contractors scramble just to survive—the average life of a sewing shop is estimated at 13 months—many manufacturers are doing nicely. The reason: There are many steps between the factory floor and the retailer's display case, and profit margins can double at each one.

PROMISED LAND

Life on $111 a Week

From their fifth-floor room in a gloomy tenement reeking of urine and cheap perfume, Maria Chun and Thomas Krische have a bird's-eye view of the sewing factory where they work. The couple trim threads there and press clothes. The hours are 7 A.M. to 7 P.M., and Maria and Thomas put in six days a week. Their take-home pay is $111. That's combined.

For Maria, 32, and Thomas, 38, America is the promised land. They traded their lives in war-torn Guatemala, temporarily leaving their children for Los Angeles and a chance at prosperity. In their tiny room across from their employer, however, prosperity has so far eluded the couple. For the room they must pay $400 a month. To help cover the rent, they share their cramped quarters with a boarder, another man.

Nine Cents a Piece

Like most garment workers, Maria Chun and Thomas Krische are paid by the piece. The law says piece rates must be such that workers can earn the federally established minimum wage of $4.25 an hour. Sweatshop piece rates are rarely so kind. From her pocket, Maria Chun pulls a scrap of paper that serves as the only record of her earnings. For classifying garments by size, pulling threads, and attaching tags, Maria earned 9 cents a piece one week not long ago. It didn't add up to $4.25 an hour.

Guess had estimated profits of $108 million last year on sales of $492 million. The Limited, a nationwide chain of women's specialty stores, earned net profits of $455 million in 1992 on sales of $7 billion.

Repeat Offenders

Manufacturers say they are not to blame for the actions of their contractors, yet the abuses are widespread—and repeated. Several manufacturers have contracted with as many as eight illegal sewing factories, recently investigated by the U.S. Department of Labor. Some manufacturers, moreover, write contracts at prices so low they effectively preclude suppliers from paying their employees the minimum wage. New York contractor Danny Yee says he has sewn slacks for as little as $1 a pair.

In recent months, the federal government has made some effort to hold manufacturers accountable for the transgressions of their contractors. The "hot goods" law gives the Labor Department authority to hold up

The story is hardly unique. At United China Sportswear in New York, two employees said they worked 48 hours straight a few weeks back in order to finish sewing 15,000 pairs of slacks. The factory got the job done in five days; normally it takes two weeks. "If you are too fast," says Sau Mui Chan, an employee of another New York shop, "the boss will cut the rate." Working the long hours she does makes Sau Mui Chan's back ache and her legs numb. Her stomach is constantly upset.

For all their hard work, garment workers often go weeks at a time without being paid. Often, contractors tell workers they have deducted taxes from their small paychecks; investigations have found contractors who simply pocketed the "tax money." There are many ways to rip off the powerless. Using a common scheme, a Los Angeles contractor, C & C Apparel, paid its workers in scrip. The scrip was redeemable only at the delicatessen next door—where the owner tacked on a 5 percent surcharge.

At home in their cramped room in Los Angeles, Maria Chun and Thomas Krische are taking classes, learning more about their rights under the law. They are also learning to speak English. The couple say they know insisting on their legal rights could one day get them fired. Yet it is something they feel they must do. Maria surveys their tiny room. Its walls are cracked and stained, its space shrunk by a privacy wall for their boarder. The divider is a bedsheet hung from a clothesline. On a table are snapshots of the couple's smiling children. Is Maria Chun glad she came to America? She ponders the question and shakes her head from side to side. Then she starts to cry.

goods for shipment until workers—whether they are employees of the manufacturer or one of its contractors—are properly paid. The Labor Department recently secured a $573,000 settlement against Guess after finding that its $60 jeans were being made in a Los Angeles sweatshop by workers who made less than $1 an hour. Z. Cavaricci, a $100 million-a-year manufacturer of expensive jeans, also settled with the Labor Department, agreeing to pay $43,700 for numerous labor violations by its contractors. Guess and Cavaricci said they had not been aware of the violations.

The list goes on. Four well-known clothing manufacturers are now under investigation for labor-law and other potential violations by their contractors. One of them is Cross Colours, the hip African-American-owned manufacturer that rode the rap craze to $90 million in sales last year and runs a foundation to keep inner-city kids in school. A Los Angeles garment worker who, like most, wished to remain anonymous says a Cross Colours contractor pays him about $3 an hour. Prices for

A NEW ABUSE

No Place Like Home

Marilyn Quayle chose one for the 1988 inaugural ball. Ivana Trump wore one to celebrate her arrival on the International Best-Dressed List. The label is Dallas-based Victor Costa, who has built a $50 million-a-year business making inexpensive knockoffs of couture designs. Costa boasts that he can copy a $100,000 Karl Lagerfeld gown for $1,000. What he does not say is that many of his dresses have been made in violation of U.S. labor laws.

In Dallas and other centers of the apparel trade, manufacturers like Costa are cutting costs by replacing some of their own workers with subcontractors who farm out their cut pieces to immigrants who sew the goods at home. The revival of industrial homework, which has been banned in the women's apparel industry since the 1940s, is creating a vast underground economy that regulators find nearly impossible to control.

Homework may sound harmless, but the reality is often grim, with entire families sewing long hours for low pay.

Violations

The Dallas manufacturer most frequently associated with contractors' home-sewing violations is also one of the country's largest. Jerell Inc., with $60 million in annual sales, makes moderate and better dresses and sportswear for such chains as J. C. Penney, Dillard's, and Nordstrom. In the past three years, according to documents obtained through the Freedom of Information Act, seven Jerell contractors have been cited for wage and hour violations. Jerell's president, Ed Veirling, says his company has fired one contractor and is trying to make sure others obey the law.

After years of neglecting the problem of home-sewing operations, the U.S. Department of Labor finally decided to crack down last year. It issued 35 injunctions in the Dallas area alone, including two that cited Costa and his contractor for using home sewers and paying workers just $2 an hour. While Costa had violated the law once before, however, neither he nor his contractors were fined. None of the other manufacturers cited by the Labor Department was required to pay employees the difference between their wages and the federal minimum wage. Indeed, inspections were so casual that investigators often failed even to interview workers, citing language barriers. Today, enforcement of labor laws in Texas remains so lax that the General Accounting Office has begun an investigation.

Cross Colours clothes range from $20 for a T-shirt to $800 for a leather jacket. Susan Maiorano, production manager for Cross Colours, says the company is working to bring its contractors into compliance.

Regulators rarely enforce the hot-goods law. For one thing, the U.S. Labor Department doesn't have nearly enough investigators. Under President Jimmy Carter, the department had 1,600 wage and hour inspectors to police 90 million workers. Under President Reagan, that number was slashed to 700. "As far as we are concerned," says Susan Cowell of the International Ladies' Garment Workers' Union, "under Ronald Reagan, the Department of Labor didn't even exist." Things are not much better now. Today, the Labor Department claims just 800 wage and hour inspectors, and the number is not expected to grow anytime soon.

Saving Jobs?

At the state level, resources are also tight. The New York State Apparel Industry Task Force, regarded as the fiercest watchdog in the apparel business, has just five inspectors to monitor 2,000 clothing factories. Once they cite a factory for a violation, the task force rarely reinspects to ensure continued compliance: There simply isn't enough time or manpower. "Workload problems," explains New York State Labor Commissioner John Hudac. Even the International Ladies' Garment Workers' Union, which has organized nearly 90 percent of the shops in New York's Chinatown, has proved a surprisingly ineffective foe of unscrupulous sweatshop operators. Several employees of unionized Chinatown shops say they are paid subminimum wages for more than 60 hours a week. "I never saw the union care about minimum wage," says contractor Danny Tsai. "Fifteen years ago, the worker made the same as he does today. The worker joins the union just for medical benefits." The ILGWU concedes there have been problems, but representatives blame workers who they say are afraid to complain about exploitative bosses.

Some contractors contend that if manufacturers forced them to comply with compensation laws, they would take their jobs overseas or to Mexico, where protections are few and workers earn less than in the United States. Already, most high-end women's clothing is made overseas. High-volume trendsetters like Liz Claiborne and DKNY, for instance, set the season's colors and styles, so they can afford the tariffs and time delays that overseas production involves. Classic menswear makers also have the luxury of shipping work abroad, since they bend little to the whims of fashion. But most retailers of womenswear are followers who, after seeing what the Liz Claibornes are selling, must have copycat goods on the shelves in as little as two weeks. Since garments made in Asia can't begin to meet those deadlines, most midprice women's manufacturers make their goods at home.

As abuses in the garment industry persist, consumers may well wonder how they can ensure that their clothes are made in accordance with the law. They probably can't. Short of making their own clothes, consumers can only rely on state and federal labor departments to hold producers accountable. Regulators are making some progress. In 1993, New York has levied $1.4 million in fines and California an estimated $4 million in fines; the U.S. Labor Department has assessed well over $2 million in back wages. Some California manufacturers have pledged to do better, citing an agreement that commits them to pay contractors enough so that they can pay their employees minimum wage and overtime. Still, says New York State Labor Commissioner Hudac, for the problems to stop, "retailers will have to scrutinize [the manufacturers]. They need to make it clear that they will do business only with those who obey the law."

Ending the sweatshop abuses on clothing Made in the U.S.A. probably wouldn't cost much: It's just a matter of increasing the margins a bit. "For a buck more per garment," says the U.S. Labor Department's Rolene Otero, "this whole problem could be solved."

Mary Scott is a reporter who has also worked with several companies on developing and implementing social and environmental programs. Howard Rothman has been a small business owner and writes and consults on the impact of technology and progressive management practices. Together they wrote a best-selling book, Companies with a Conscience: Intimate Portraits of Twelve Firms that Make a Difference, *from which the following portrait of Ben & Jerry's is taken.*

Ice Cream and Integrity

Mary Scott and Howard Rothman

Company name: Ben & Jerry's Homemade Inc.

Type of business: premium ice cream and frozen yogurt maker

Location: Waterbury, Springfield, and Rockingham, Vermont

Number of employees: 400

Year founded: 1978

It is seven-thirty on an unseasonably warm November morning in Vermont, and Ben Cohen wants orange juice. The kitchen in a quaint country inn where he has scheduled a breakfast meeting is not yet open for business, so Cohen decides to fend for himself. He searches through a few cabinets until he finds a glass, then roots through a walk-in refrigerator for the juice. "I need liquids," he says with a husky laugh. "Now."

Cohen, wearing scruffy sneakers and a T-shirt plastered with the image of a smiling sun, looks like the kind of guy who always pours his own beverages—and helps his breakfast companions do the same. He does not look like the cofounder and chief executive officer (CEO) of a $100 million food company that employs 400 people and draws more visitors than any other tourist attraction in the Green Mountain State. He also doesn't look like half the team that oversees ninety retail franchises and company-owned stores in three countries as well as a fledgling manufacturing and retailing operation in the Soviet Union.

Cohen still looks—with the exception of a little gray in his beard—and acts much as he did when he and partner Jerry Greenfield first opened an ice cream shop in an abandoned Vermont gas station in 1978.

Then both twenty-eight, they vowed to stay in business for one year. Their now phenomenally popular and successful company, Ben & Jerry's Homemade Inc., may have grown by leaps and bounds since that time, but Jerry and Ben themselves have remained true to their roots.

Cohen and Greenfield have created one of the most impressive examples of corporate responsibility that the business world has ever seen. At the same time their company was achieving an almost mythical status in the minds of ice cream lovers everywhere, the boyhood friends managed to keep treating their employees like family, purchase as many ingredients as possible from suppliers that adhere to their principles and philosophies, and support worthy causes and organizations in both their home state and around the world. They even created a nonprofit foundation to give away a full 7.5 percent of their company's pretax profits each year.

As becomes apparent to everyone they meet, Ben and Jerry also remained surprisingly free of pretensions. They're still "regular" guys who haven't strayed one iota from their sixties roots as they set about the task of building a very nineties company. Their hair may be a little sparser than it used to be, but it's never been trimmed to fit the standard corporate mold, and neither have they.

Their company has been faced with challenges and problems, though. Like any growing business, theirs has certainly had its ups and downs. But as an example of caring capitalism—as the duo refers to their overall corporate philosophy—Ben & Jerry's is hard to beat. The company produces an excellent product, helps its suppliers, aids its community, and supports its workers. It is precisely what it purports to be.

The same can be said about Jerry and Ben. The only thing different about the two old friends today, in fact, is their ability to now help more of the causes that they and their colleagues deem worthy of support. Unlike most of their peers in corporate America, their willingness and enthusiasm for such philanthropy never faded.

"In the past, people who consciously decided to go into business usually did so because they saw it as a way to make a lot of money. People who were motivated by social and humanitarian values tended not to go into business because they saw business as valueless," Cohen says, settling into his breakfast meeting with a glass of fresh orange juice. "But some of these people with strong social and humanitarian values—like Jerry and me—got into business by accident and were not sorted through that grid. So, through some quirk of fate, instead of ending up in a nonprofit social service agency, we happen to be trapped in a for-profit business."

Cohen laughs heartily once again and reiterates two quotes that his company has lived by since its first anniversary—which they commemorated by giving away free ice cream cones. One was from Jerry: "If it's not fun, why do it?" The other was from Ben: "Business has a responsibility to give back to the community." And even when it was hard to do so, Cohen now recalls, the two have diligently adhered to both of these tenets.

"I think it's always difficult to do anything right," he muses aloud. "It's like that song by Jethro Tull, 'Nothing is easy.' If what you are trying to do is produce the highest-quality ice cream, that's difficult. If you're trying to make a lot of money, that's difficult. And if you're trying to run your business in a way that benefits the community, that's difficult, too. But I don't think any of those things are difficult to the point of not being possible," he adds. "I think it's really just a matter of priorities."

At Home in Vermont

The town of Waterbury is just a blip on Vermont's Interstate 89, nestled in a scenic valley about halfway between the state's capital and its largest city. Despite its prime location, Waterbury has been essentially unremarkable for most of its lengthy history. It is home to a few shops and restaurants, a couple of country inns, the Vermont state police, and some spectacular views. But it wasn't until the arrival of Ben and Jerry—and the decision to locate their main ice cream plant as well as their corporate offices in this community of about eight thousand—that Waterbury really showed up on the map.

The 43,000-square-foot plant began operating in 1985, and faithful ice cream lovers from around the world have been flocking to it ever since. Suprised company officials admitted 41,000 visitors during the first six months after they opened their doors to tourists, but they got over their shock by 1991, when an even larger number walked through the plant every month during peak season. Some 220,000 took the tour that year, making Ben & Jerry's Homemade the number-one tourist attraction in this very tourist oriented state.

But visits were not the only thing that skyrocketed between the mid- and late 1980s. An employee named Mary, who had driven a Ben & Jerry's ice cream truck in 1982 and was later hired to organize the new tour program, recalls that there were only forty-two employees at the company when she came on board in 1986. The year before, sales were just $9 million. But the company then embarked on a rapid nationwide expansion, thanks to funds raised through a special stock offering open only to Vermont residents and a second traditional option for investors across the country. The employee ranks and the corporate revenues were soon to increase tenfold.

All of the activity that brought about such growth, however, was accomplished without the company's altering any of its counterculture business practices: Tons of ice cream and lots of money were still given away, traditional advertising was never employed, and a unique management style remained in force. Longtime employees, such as Mary—as well as newcomers like a woman named Sarah, who started in the gift shop in late 1990—attribute this to the purposeful vision of Cohen and Greenfield, who never deviated from the unorthodox path that they chose long before.

"For a while we were growing at about a hundred percent a year," recalls Cohen, who freely admits to being troubled by a pace that would delight most other business leaders. "Our outside sales were expanding faster than our internal organization and our infrastructure. We knew we were growing too fast. So we made a very conscious decision to slow our outward growth and devote a large amount of energy and resources to improving the quality of our organization—the way we work together as a team and the way we develop each of our employees."

The company, he continues, dramatically changed the way it did business—something that Ben & Jerry's remained able to do because of the way it was structured. Movement into new markets was slowed; expansion of franchised "scoop shops" was curtailed. These actions put the company back on track, Cohen notes, and growth then continued as an organized juggernaut that shows no sign of abating as the nineties wear on.

But none of this is really surprising when one considers the history of the company and the background of its founders, two boyhood friends from Merrick, New York. They first bonded together as outsiders (and lovers of food) in the seventh grade, when they couldn't run track as well as the others in their junior high school class. Neither could find their niche as young adults, either—Greenfield tried his hand as a lab technician while hoping to get into medical school; Cohen studied pottery, drove a taxi, and taught crafts—and their drift to Vermont was as aimless as their career paths.

But then serendipity: The two discovered a correspondence course in ice cream making that was offered by Penn State and only cost five dollars. They took it, Greenfield and Cohen often say, because they could afford it and because they liked ice cream. And after achieving a perfect score on the open-book final exam, the duo took a $12,000 investment ($4,000 of which was borrowed) and in 1978 opened their first scoop shop in the college town of Burlington.

Financial success didn't come overnight—it actually took about five years before the young company turned a profit—but notoriety was theirs right from the start. It came in part from their strongly flavored home-made concoctions with unusual names. For example, Dastardly Mash and New York Super Fudge Chunk. But it also came in part from the two owners, who endeared themselves to locals by working hard and plastering their images on the pint containers of their product that they soon began selling throughout the winter in order to keep the business going.

The Seeds of Giving

In the summer of 1991, Ben & Jerry's sponsored free "One World, One Heart" festivals in Chicago, San Francisco, and Stowe, Vermont. Each included performances by such popular musicians as Dr. John, David Bromberg, John Prine, and Carlos Santana. Each included family-oriented activities like Dye Your Own Tie Dye T-shirts and Ben & Jerry's New Vaudeville Light Circus Bus. Each included presentations by a group called 20/20 Vision, which aims to cut military spending and meet environmental and human needs, as well as free ice cream cones for attendees who wrote postcards or made videos on-site for their congressional representatives.

Each also included the dumping of a billion seeds of grass on festival grounds to point out the excesses of the U.S. military budget by illustrating how much a billion of something really is.

By all accounts, the festivals were a huge success. As many as 100,000 people attended in each location. Hundreds of shirts were tie dyed, and performances on the circus bus were viewed by hundreds more. Thousands of postcards and video messages were sent to Washington, and tons of grass seeds were scooped into recycled paper bags by festival goers who could not help but think about the relationship they had to the billions of dollars spent annually on America's war-making machinery.

"One of the nice things about becoming bigger is that you can throw bigger parties," Jerry and Ben said in the flier announcing each event. "This festival is a time to play and celebrate together—it's also an opportunity to take the first step in a sustained effort at working together for a more just world."

But this message and the medium that carried it were only the latest manifestations of a concern for their environment that Greenfield and Cohen have been espousing since their company's beginnings.

"When we first started, our only goal was to have our homemade ice cream parlor on the corner; we didn't plan on being anything larger than that," Cohen remembers. "And while we had strong feelings about wanting to be a business that benefited the community, we didn't know what that meant at the time. So on our first anniversary, we gave out free cones to everybody to celebrate our first year in business and our amazement that we hadn't gone bankrupt yet."

As the company evolved, so did Ben and Jerry's commitment to their constituents. They continued their annual cone giveaways and instituted free summer movies and a yearly fall festival. But, Cohen notes, "these things just came about organically. The movie series came about because we were located at a gas station that had a big white wall next to it and we figured it was a great place to put up chairs where the cars used to go. And after our first summer, we really wanted to thank our customers for patronizing us and allowing us to survive, so we started our Fall Down festivals, which were family days of fun and games held in the park across the street from our shop."

In addition, the company began donating a lot of ice cream to a variety of local community organizations. But it wasn't really difficult yet to juggle business and social concerns, because the company wasn't even making a profit.

Ben & Jerry's eventually reached the point where its balance sheets were written in black ink; however, in 1981 it opened its first franchise, and by 1983 it was distributing ice cream outside of Vermont. Fred "Chico" Lager, a local nightclub owner, was brought in as president. And the company was giving away more and more ice cream and money. Everything, in fact, looked terrific—for a while.

"Originally, Jerry and I were ice cream men working in this ice cream shop," Cohen says. "But then the business started to become more of a business, and we had a bunch of employees and were spending our time talking on the phone and writing letters and memos and hiring and firing. We turned to each other and realized we were no longer ice cream men; we were businessmen. Our immediate reaction was to sell the business, because we didn't want to be businessmen. But then I ran into this old restaurateur down in Brattleboro, and he convinced me to keep the business. He said that if there was something I didn't like, I should just change it. That really hadn't occurred to me before."

They decided to raise capital for expansion in a novel way: by offering residents of their adopted state a chance to buy a piece of their company. In 1984, they sponsored the first-ever Vermont in-state public stock offering with a low minimum buy of $126 to allow everyone in who wanted a chance to participate. The sale was advertised in the front section of local newspapers, and it eventually raised $750,000—enough to finance construction of their Waterbury plant. A traditional nationwide public offering in 1985 permitted the expansion to continue, and their evolving commitment to social issues also continued as their financial resources grew.

A Foundation for Success

"We knew the main thing business does is make money, and if we were going to give back to the community, we had to give away a whole bunch of money," Cohen says. "So that's what we started to do."

To keep this commitment viable—and to appease the legions of new stockholders who sometimes wanted Ben & Jerry's run more like the public company that it had become—the partners created the nonprofit Ben & Jerry's Foundation in 1985. Initially established through a donation of company stock, the foundation was designed to "support projects which are models for social change; projects infused with a spirit of generosity and hopefulness; projects which enhance people's quality of life; and projects which exhibit creative problem solving."

Some of the causes Ben and Jerry support are the Devastators, an all-children's Afro-Latin percussion band that works to combat drug abuse, AIDS, and homelessness; the Heifer Project, which provides agricultural animals to impoverished communities; Boston's Women's Institute for Housing and Economic Development; and the Worker Owned Network of Athens, Georgia.

Each year since, the company has kept the foundation alive by donating to it 7.5 percent of Ben & Jerry's pretax profits. Grant proposals are solicited that relate to children and families, disadvantaged groups, and the environment.

That, however, is only the beginning of the company's philanthropic efforts. A special Employee Community Fund—financed by half of all revenue taken in from the one dollar charged to each adult who takes the plant tour—is granted to nonprofit community and statewide groups in Vermont. Funding decisions are made by voluntary employee committees, and recipients range from the Association of Vermont Recyclers to a group of woodworkers who produce toys for underprivileged local youngsters.

Factory seconds are also either given away to community organizations in the state, donated to food banks, or sold by special arrangement in Vermont stores—with a portion of that income also donated to community organizations, such as libraries, recreation centers, and local fire and rescue squads. In 1990, these payments totaled nearly $210,000. According to estimates from an employee named Eloise, who handles the community relations program, the company gave away about eight thousand gallons of free ice cream in 1991 to approximately one thousand Vermont organizations that simply requested it.

"Every day I come to work I feel I'm making the world a better place," says plant manager Don "Mac" MacLaughlin. His sentiments, in one form or another, are commonly echoed at every level in the company.

Despite such solidly based good feelings and the charitable activity on which they are based, Jerry, Ben, and others in the company felt they weren't doing enough. So in 1988 they wrote a Statement of Mission that dedicated the firm "to the creation and demonstration of a new corporate concept of linked prosperity." It consisted of three interrelated parts: a product mission ("to make, distribute and sell the finest-quality all-natural ice cream. . . ."), a social mission ("to operate the company in a way that actively recognizes the central role that business plays in the structure of society by initiating innovative ways to improve the quality of life. . . ."), and an economic mission ("to operate the company on a sound financial basis. . . .").

But this, it seems, was still not enough for Ben & Jerry's. For even with this new mission and a foundation giving away maybe $300,000 a year, the partners noticed that they were flooded with requests for assistance that they simply could not fill.

"All of them were worthy causes," Cohen recalls, "and we realized we were never going to solve all the problems that we were looking to solve. Our contributions were just a drop in the bucket. We started thinking about why there were all these social needs that went unmet, and it didn't take long to realize that it was because 40 percent of the national budget was going to the military. So we came to the conclusion that if we were really going to help the community and meet these social needs, we had to use our power as a business to direct money out of the military and into human and environmental needs."

Fortuitously, at just about that time, the company was coming out with a chocolate-covered ice cream bar on a stick. It decided to call the product a Peace Pop and use the packaging to talk to customers about a new organization that Ben & Jerry's was helping to found called One Percent for Peace. The group would actively promote the idea of redirecting 1 percent of the U.S. military budget to peaceful and humanitarian activities, and the Peace Pop would represent the first attempt by Ben & Jerry's to use its packaging to advance a social cause.

The company has continued with this theme ever since, too, attaching various messages onto its pints—such as those about the disappearance of America's family farms and the destruction of the world's rain forests. And this led quite naturally into another innovative area that Ben & Jerry's has successfully pioneered: that of purchasing its raw materials in a way that aids both the environment and the individual causes it chooses to support.

Blueberries, Peaches, Nuts, and Brownies

Few people outside of Maine know that the state's Passamaquoddy Indians, a group that has long been excluded from economic prosperity, works hard at the business of harvesting and processing wild blueberries on their reservation. Ben & Jerry's found out, however, and in the summer of 1990 the company contracted to buy $330,000 worth of fresh berries for use in its Wild Maine Blueberry ice cream from them.

At the same time, Ben & Jerry's was buying Brazil and cashew nuts from the Amazon rain forest for its Rainforest Crunch ice cream, brownies prepared by homeless employees of Greyston Bakery for Chocolate Fudge Brownie ice cream, peaches grown by African-American farmers in Georgia for Fresh Georgia Peach ice cream, and dairy ingredients from the five-hundred-member St. Albans Cooperative in Vermont for every one of its products. Developing such relationships with suppliers that address unmet social needs has become just another aspect of Ben & Jerry's ongoing mission and another way to meet its unique "two-part bottom line."

"This act—just consciously sourcing our ingredients, even though it might cost us more than somewhere else—ends up bringing about a more positive benefit than probably all of the money that we give away through our foundation," Cohen believes.

"We now do this on every level," he continues, "because we made it an integral part of our bottom line. We tried to figure out why business tends to be valueless and uncaring and in the worst situations actually harmful to the community and exploitative to its workers and its environment. And we found that this is because the success of business is measured solely by the traditional bottom line—that is, by how much money is left at the end of the year."

So Jerry and Ben decided to change the way their company measured success. They developed an alternative "two-part bottom line" that assesses the year by how much money is left over as well as by how much the company has helped the community. It didn't work right away; managers felt that the two goals were mutually exclusive. But the founders convinced them to simply add a new variable to their purchasing decisions and taught them to pick vendors according to three factors (social benefit, price, and quality) rather than the usual two (price and quality).

And once they began, the task became easier. Along with food products, Ben & Jerry's applied this philosophy to the millions of dollars of office and building supplies it regularly purchased. It switched to an insurance company and a credit-card issuer that place their premiums and profits in low-income housing and other similar investments. And it initiated proactive programs, like one in Newark, New Jersey, where Ben & Jerry's ice cream carts are operated by a foundation that runs a food bank and works with homeless people.

"Just by choosing these vendors, we're benefiting those other causes," Cohen explains. "Our goal is to integrate a concern for the community in all of our day-to-day business decisions. So far, we've been successful in maybe ten to twenty-five percent, so we've got a ways to go. But the trend is there; each year we find more and more ways to integrate this concern into our activities."

This move, not surprisingly, is also manifested in the company's resource-management efforts. Its environmental programs manager leads companywide efforts to raise awareness of recycling options and find markets for recyclable materials. Its art department works with suppliers that use recycled paper and soybean-based inks. Solid waste, such as cardboard and plastic pails, are reused whenever possible. And the company has even developed an incredible Solar Aquatics Greenhouse at its main plant that successfully purifies the waste from dairy production by means of a natural ecosystem of flowers, fish, and compost.

Ben & Jerry's also concentrates on the direct development of a variety of social and family activities, such as its free summer festivals. Other sponsorships of this nature include the Giraffe Project, which identifies and supports people who "stick their necks out" by doing exceptional things for their communities; the annual Halloween parade in New York's Greenwich Village, which distributes proceeds to various causes; free performances of the *Nutcracker Suite* for needy youngsters in several cities; and traveling voter-registration drives.

These projects not only extend Ben & Jerry's considerable social reach still farther; they also serve as the primary marketing tool for a company that never places traditional advertising in traditional media. "Rather than spending $35,000 on a full-page glossy ad, we'd rather do something that our public will enjoy," says Holly Alves, the marketing director. This concept must work, too: Consumers across the country clamor for the product, and more than fifteen thousand unsolicited job applications are received at the firm's headquarters each year.

Working for a Living

In the main plant, Peter, the company's flavor designer, toils in a room labeled "alchemy lab"; his business card officially proclaims him "primal ice cream therapist." The cabinets in his work space are tagged "sour things," "sinful things," "magical elixir," "secret stuff," "cold metallic things," and "I don't know."

Full-color life-sized cutouts of James Dean, John Wayne, and other movie stars, each wearing the pastel hair covering that is required headgear in all food-preparation areas, adorn numerous offices throughout the organization. White trash cans, emblazoned with the black markings of dairy cows, are everywhere. Wild and crazy artwork personalizes practically every work area. And if all that weren't enough, an officially designated group called the Joy Gang regularly sponsors a variety of companywide events, including a miniature car derby and an Elvis look-alike contest.

Alves remembers how this penchant for institutionalized fun once left her with some explaining to do. Shortly after she joined the company in 1990, her mother came up to Vermont from her home on Philadelphia's Main Line to see Alves in her new surroundings. Ironically, it was on the same day that sixties activist/prankster Wavy Gravy was visiting the plant to announce a new flavor named in his honor. The guest of honor was dressed, as usual, in a tie-dyed clown outfit; employees were acting even loonier than usual, and many were walking around with paper bags on their heads. "My mother was wondering what I had gotten myself into," Alves recalls.

Alves, too, wondered at first whether she made the right decision to leave a six-figure salary and a penthouse on San Francisco's Russian Hill for a lower-paying position and a smaller house in the hills of Vermont. "I was nervous that the company wouldn't be what it was supposed to be," she says. "But I was pleasantly surprised to find that it was."

Not everyone fits into the wacky atmosphere and liberal philosophy promoted by Ben and Jerry, of course, and those who don't tend to exit quickly. Overall, however, the turnover rate is only 8 percent, and most of those who stay are passionately committed to the founders' ideas and ideals.

Not surprisingly, the company also treats its primarily young work force quite well. Usual benefits, like health, dental, and life insurance, are supplemented by progressive programs, such as maternity and paternity leaves, stock-purchase options, educational assistance, profit sharing based on longevity, free membership at health clubs, wellness programs (cholesterol, blood pressure, smoking cessation, and substance-abuse counseling), and on-site educational seminars (writing skills, management, and financial advice). Even more unique is the domestic-partner coverage, which extends applicable benefits to nonmarried and homosexual partners of employees. And then there is the right to take home up to three free pints of ice cream every day.

Still, according to an employee named Carol in the benefits administration department, "the philosophy and social mission helps keep people more than the benefits."

One area that has occasionally proven a problem in recent years, however, is the company's salary structure. Ben & Jerry's works on a so-called compressed salary ratio, which means that the highest-paid employee can not make more than seven times the lowest full-time wage. The range was recently increased from its previous five-to-one ratio, but this policy—a visible extension of the "linked prosperity" philosophy—has caused several high-level job candidates to turn down employment offers.

Still, Ben & Jerry's appears to be a truly great place to work. People are committed to the company and to each other. And for those who come on board, the salary program that caps even Jerry and Ben's annual compensation at less than $90,000 each is no deterrent.

"Money's not always the issue," notes plant manager Mac MacLaughlin, a former pro football player with fourteen years of management experience who bypassed several higher-paying offers when he chose to accept the job at Ben & Jerry's. "Sometimes in life you have to give something back."

Planning for the Future

At first glance, Ben & Jerry's looks a lot like other midsized companies. A communications coordinator keeps the burgeoning employee base informed about comings and goings. A manager of investor relations deals with Wall Street's growing interest. A human resources director manages personnel operations and employee development, while a quality assurance director plans and implements a company-wide program in quality control. But the similarities stop there. Look deeper and Ben & Jerry's structure is all its own.

The quality assurance director, for example, developed a Ben & Jerry's version of the currently popular Total Quality Management program that implores workers to "keep that euphoric feeling" by doing the "ten steps of the Improvement Boogie." The human resources director is a self-proclaimed jack-of-all-trades who arrived as a consultant in 1984, moves into jobs where he is needed, and wouldn't stick around if the company wasn't committed to its social mission. And the manager of investor relations, who grew up in Vermont and has a primary background in agriculture, rarely travels to New York, because "we don't want to hype the stock."

And then there is the communications coordinator. Part of her increasingly difficult job is to publish a monthly newsletter that informs the expanding work force about items of interest while also striving to be as irreverent and as entertaining as everything else the company does. The publication reports on important activities (e.g., the free summer festivals) and interesting phenomenon (the tattoos of employees). And sometimes it is dedicated to a seminal corporate event, such as the December 1990 retirement of popular company president "Chico" Lager. (This tribute included sarcastic reminiscences, old photos, and a series of artist's renderings detailing Lager's dramatic hair loss during his tenure.)

Keeping this type of wild and crazy attitude alive in a company growing as fast as this one is no easy task, but Ben and Jerry are both working hard to ensure that it is retained. Unless they are traveling, they come into the office every day. Cohen has moved into the media forefront as the official spokesperson and marketing guru. Greenfield has solidified his position as an employee cheerleader and is apt to be found on the plant floor in the middle of the night, working with the late shift as it packages ice cream on the assembly line.

Changes, though, are part of the game. New president Chuck Lacy has brought continuity to the organization (he was promoted from within) and solidified its professional direction, even if he doesn't have the emotional persona and acknowledged wit of his predecessor. The nationwide movement toward healthier, low-fat food prompted the introduction of several frozen yogurt flavors. And while the firm has barely adjusted to the opening of a second plant in Springfield, Vermont, and the relocation of its support offices to a building a few miles away from the main Waterbury plant, more construction is afoot: a $3 million distribution center was recently built in Rockingham and a $12 million manufacturing facility is planned for the town of St. Albans.

Financial gains continue at an almost staggering pace, too, despite the company's conscious effort to slow its growth. Sales increased 23 percent in 1989, 32 percent in 1990, and 30 percent in 1991, while Ben & Jerry's share of the national premium ice cream market grew from 23 percent to more than 31 percent during that time. And now that the company has moved its products into most major supermarket chains throughout the United States, future expansion will stem from the introduction of new products and their increased presence in independent grocery outlets across the country.

Moreover, the social side of Ben & Jerry's remains inseparable from the business side. Controversial stands are as common as ever: In 1990 alone the company officially opposed licensing of the Seabrook nuclear power plant in New Hampshire and military action in the Persian Gulf while supporting work-place rights for AIDS sufferers and a boycott of Salvadoran coffee. And the company's success, despite this penchant for unconventionality, continues to illustrate that even public corporations can make a profit while helping their communities.

Ben Cohen speaks of all this proudly, if not with more than a bit of awe, as he wraps up his early breakfast meeting on that uncommonly warm November morning in Vermont. It is time to point his well-worn sneakers toward company headquarters, where a meeting is scheduled for Ben & Jerry's board of directors. (Cohen is chairperson; Greenfield is assistant secretary.)

"When we started out, our only goal was to remain in business for a year at the old ice cream shop in that Burlington gas station," he notes, slipping on his jacket and heading toward the door. "We never had any idea that it would evolve into this."

*R*obert Bernard Reich (1946–) attended high school in New York and then Dartmouth College, Oxford University, and Yale Law School. He served as Secretary of Labor under President Clinton from 1993–1997. He is a frequent writer and political commentator on economic issues and has offered a broad perspective on the trends in the global economy and consequences for Americans for over two decades. His most recent book is Supercapitalism: The Transformation of Business, Democracy, and Everyday Life (2007).

The Global Economy:
Consequences for American Inequality

Robert B. Reich

Between 1978 and 1987, the poorest fifth of American families became 8 percent poorer, and the richest fifth became 13 percent richer. That leaves the poorest fifth with less than 5 percent of the nation's income and the richest fifth with more than 40 percent. This widening gap can't be blamed on the growth in single-parent lower-income families, which in fact slowed markedly after the late 1970s. Nor is it due mainly to the stingy social policy of the Reagan years. Granted, Food Stamp benefits have dropped in real terms by about 13 percent since 1981, and many states have failed to raise benefits for the poor and unemployed to keep up with inflation. But this doesn't come close to accounting for the growing inequality. Rather, the trend is connected to a profound change in the American economy as it merges with the global economy. And because the merging is far from complete, this trend will not stop of its own accord anytime soon.

It is significant that the growth of inequality shows up most strikingly among Americans who have jobs. Through most of the postwar era, the wages of Americans at different income levels rose at about the same pace. Although different workers occupied different steps on the escalator, everyone moved up together. In those days poverty was the condition of *jobless* Americans, and the major economic challenge was to create enough jobs for everyone. Once people were safely on the work force escalator, their problems were assumed to be over. Thus "full employment" became a liberal rallying cry, while conservatives fretted over the inflationary tendencies of a full-employment economy.

In recent years working Americans have been traveling on two escalators—one going up, the other going down. In 1987 the average hourly earnings of non-supervisory workers, adjusted for inflation, were lower than in any year since 1966. Middle-level managers fared much better, although their median real earnings were only slightly above the levels of the 1970s. Executives, however, did spectacularly well. In 1981 alone, CEOs of the hundred largest publicly held industrial corporations received raises averaging almost 12 percent The renumerations of lesser executives rose almost as much, and executives of smaller companies followed close behind.

Between 1978 and 1987, as the real earnings of unskilled workers were declining, the real incomes of workers in the securities industry (investment bankers, arbitrageurs, and brokers) rose 21 percent. Few investment bankers pocket anything near the $50 million lavished yearly upon the partners of Kohlberg, Kravis, Roberts & Company, or the $550 million commandeered last year by Michael Milken, but it is not unusual for a run-of-the-mill investment banker to bring home comfortably over a million dollars. Partners in America's largest corporate law firms are comparatively deprived, enjoying average yearly earnings of only $400,000 to $1.2 million.

Meanwhile, the number of impoverished *working* Americans climbed by nearly two million, or 23 percent, between 1978 and 1987. The number who worked full time and year round but were poor climbed faster, by 43 percent. Nearly 60 percent of the 20 million people who now fall below the Census Bureau's poverty line are from families with at least one member in full-time or part-time work.

The American economy, in short, is creating a wider range of earnings than at any other time is the postwar era. The most basic reason, put simply, is that America itself is ceasing to exist as a system of production and exchange separate from the rest of the world. One can no more meaningfully speak of an"American economy" than of a "Delaware economy." We are becoming but a region—albeit still a relatively wealthy region of a global economy, whose technologies, savings, and investments move effortlessly across borders, making it harder for individual nations to control their economic destinies.

By now Washington officials well understand that the nation's fiscal and monetary policies cannot be set without taking account of the savings that will slosh in or slosh out of the nation in consequence. Less understood is the speed and ease with which new technologies now spread across the globe, from computers in, say, San Jose, to satellite, and then back down to computers in Taiwan. (America's efforts to stop the Japanese from copying our commercial designs and the Soviets from copying our military designs are about equally doomed.) And we have yet to come to terms with the rise of the global corporation, whose managers, shareholders, and employees span the world. Our debates over the future of American jobs still focus on topics like the competitiveness of the American automobile industry or the future of American manufacturing. But these categories are increasingly irrelevant. They assume the existence of a separate American economy in which all the jobs associated with a particular industry, or even more generally with a particular sector, are bound together, facing a common fate.

New technologies of worldwide communication and transportation have redrawn the playing field. American industries no longer compete against Japanese or European industries. Rather, a company with headquarters in the United States, production facilities in Taiwan, and a marketing force spread across many nations competes with another, similarly ecumenical company. So when General Motors, say, is doing well, that probably is good news for a lot of executives in Detroit, and for GM shareholders across the globe, but it isn't necessarily good news for a lot of assembly-line workers in Detroit, because there may, in fact, be very few GM assembly-line workers in Detroit, or anywhere else in America. The welfare of assembly-line workers in Detroit may depend, instead, on the health of corporations based in Japan or Canada.

More to the point, even if those Canadian and Japanese corporations are doing well, these workers may be in trouble. For they are increasingly part of an international labor market, encompassing Asia, Africa, Western Europe—and perhaps, before long, Eastern Europe. Corporations can with relative ease relocate their production centers, and alter their international lines of communication and transportation accordingly, to take advantage of low wages. So American workers find themselves settling for low wages in order to hold on to their jobs. More and more, your "competitiveness" as a worker depends not on the fortunes of any American corporation, or of any American industry, but on what function you serve within the global economy. GM executives are becoming more "competitive" even as GM production workers become less so, because the functions that GM executives perform are more highly valued in the world market than the function that GM production workers perform.

In order to see in greater detail what is happening to American jobs, it helps to view the work Americans do in terms of functional categories that reflect the real competitive positions of workers in the global economy. Essentially, three broad categories are emerging. Call these symbolic-analytic services, routine production services, and routine personal services.

(1) *Symbolic-analytic services* are based on the manipulation of information: data, words, and oral and visual symbols. Symbolic analysis comprises some (but by no means all) of the work undertaken by people who call themselves lawyers, investment bankers, commercial bankers, management consultants, research scientists, academics. public-relations executives, real estate developers, and even a few creative accountants. Also: advertising and marketing specialists, art directors, design engineers, architects, writers and editors, musicians, and television and film producers. Some of the manipulations performed by symbolic analysts reveal ways of more efficiently deploying resources or shifting financial assets, or of otherwise saving time end energy. Other manipulations grab money from people who are too slow or naive to protect themselves by manipulation in response. Still others serve to entertain the recipients.

Most symbolic analysts work alone or in small teams. If they work with others, they often have partners rather than bosses or supervisors, and their yearly income is variable, depending on how much value they add to the business. Their work environments tend to be quiet and tastefully decorated, often within tall steel-and-glass buildings. They rarely come in direct contact with the ultimate beneficiaries of their work. When they are not analyzing, designing, or strategizing, they are in meetings or on the telephone—giving advice or making deals. Many of them spend inordinate time in jet planes and hotels. They are articulate and well groomed. The vast majority are white males.

Symbolic analysis now accounts for more that 40 percent of America's gross national product, and almost 20 percent of our jobs. Within what we still term our "manufacturing sector," symbolic-analytic jobs have been increasing at a rate almost three times that of total manufacturing employment in the United Slates, as routine manufacturing jobs have drifted overseas or been mastered by machines.

The services performed by America's symbolic analysts are in high demand around the world, regardless of whether the symbolic analysts provide them in person or transmit them via satellite and fiber-optic cable. The Japanese are buying up the insights and inventions of America's scientists and engineers (who are only too happy to sell them at a fat profit). The Europeans, meanwhile, are hiring our management consultants, business strategists, and investment bankers. Developing nations are hiring our civil and design engineers; and almost everyone is buying the output of our pop musicians, television stars, and film producers.

It is the same with the global corporation. The central offices of these sprawling entities, headquartered in America, are filled with symbolic analysts who manipulate information and then expose their insights via the corporation's far-flung enterprise. IBM doesn't export machines from the United States; it makes machines all over the globe, and services them on the spot. IBM world headquarters, in Armonk, New York, just exports strategic planning and related management services.

Thus has the standard of living of America's symbolic analysts risen. They increasingly find themselves part of a global labor market, not a national one. And because the United States has a highly developed economy, and an excellent university system, they find that the services they have to offer are quite scarce in the context of the whole world. So elementary laws of supply and demand ensure that their salaries are quite high.

These salaries are likely to go even higher in the years ahead, as the world market for symbolic analysis continues to grow. Foreigners are trying to learn these skills and techniques, to be sure, but they still have a long way to go. No other country does a better job of preparing its most fortunate citizens for symbolic analysis than does the United States. None has surpassed America in providing experience and training, often with entire regions specializing in one or another kind of symbolic analysis (New York and Chicago for finance, Los Angeles for music and film, the San Francisco Bay area and greater Boston for science and engineering). In this we can take pride. But for the second major category of American workers—the providers of routine production services—the laws of supply and demand don't bode well.

(2) *Routine production services* involve tasks that are repeated over and over, as one step in a sequence of steps for producing a finished product. Although we tend to associate these jobs with manufacturing, they are becoming common in the storage and retrieval of information. Banking, insurance, wholesaling, retailing, health care—all employ hordes of people who spend their days processing data, often putting information into computers or taking it out.

Most providers of routine production services work with many other people who do similar work within large, centralized facilities. They are overseen by supervisors, who in turn are monitored by more senior supervisors. They are usually paid an hourly wage. Their jobs are monotonous. Most of these people do not have a college education; they need only be able to take directions and, occasionally, undertake simple computations. Those who deal with metal are mostly white males; those who deal with fabrics or information tend to be female and/or minorities.

Decades ago, jobs like these were relatively well paid. Henry Ford gave his early production workers 5 dollars a day, a remarkable sum for the time, in the (correct) belief that they and their neighbors would be among the major buyers of Fords. But in recent years American providers of routine production services have found themselves in direct competition with millions of foreign workers, most of whom are eager to work for a fraction of the pay of American workers. Through the miracle of satellite transmission, even routine data-processing can now be undertaken in relatively poor nations, thousands of miles away from the skyscrapers where the data are finally used. This fact has given management-level symbolic analysts ever greater bargaining leverage. If routine producers living in America don't agree to reduce their wages, then the work will go abroad.

And it has. In 1950 routine production services constituted about 30 percent of our national product and well over half of American jobs. Today such services represent about 20 percent of national product and one-fourth of jobs. And the scattering of foreign-owned factories placed here to circumvent American protectionism isn't going to reverse the trend. So the standard of living of America's routine production workers will likely keep declining. The dynamics behind the wage concessions, plant closings, and union-busting that have become commonplace are not likely to change.

(3) *Routine personal services* also entail simple, repetitive work, but, unlike routine production services, they are provided in person. Their immediate objects are specific customers rather than streams of metal, fabric, or data. Included in this employment category are restaurant and hotel workers, barbers and beauticians, retail sales personnel, cabdrivers, household cleaners, daycare workers, hospital attendants and orderlies, truck drivers, and—among the fastest-growing of all—custodians and security guards.

Like production workers, providers of personal services are usually paid by the hour, are carefully supervised, and rarely have more than a high school education. But unlike people in the other two categories of work, these people are in direct contact with the ultimate beneficiaries of what they do. And the companies they work for are often small. In fact, some routine personal service workers turn entrepreneurial. (Most new businesses and new jobs in America come from this sector—now constituting about 20 percent of GNP and 30 percent of jobs.) Women and minorities make up the bulk of routine personal-service workers.

Apart from the small number who strike out on their own, these workers are paid poorly. They are sheltered from the direct effects of global competition, but not the indirect effects. They often compete with illegal aliens willing to work for low wages, or with former or would-be production workers who can't find well-paying production jobs, or with labor-saving machinery (automated tellers, self-service gas pumps, computerized cashiers) dreamed up by symbolic analysts in America and manufactured in Asia. And because they tend to be unskilled and dispersed among small businesses, personal-service workers rarely hire a union or a powerful lobby group to stand up for their interests. When the economy turns sour, they are among the first to feel the effects. These workers will continue to have jobs in the years ahead and may experience some small increase in real wages. They will have demographics on their side, as the American work force shrinks. But for all the foregoing reasons, the gap between their earnings and those of the symbolic analysts will continue to grow.

These three functional categories—symbolic analysis, routine production, and routine personal service—cover at least three out of four American jobs. The rest of the nation's work force consists mainly of government employees (including public school teachers), employees in regulated industries (like utility workers), anti-government-financed workers (engineers working on defense weapons systems), many of whom are sheltered from global competition. One further clarification: Some traditional job categories overlap with several functional categories. People called "secretaries," for example, include those who actually spend their time doing symbolic-analytic work closely allied to what their bosses do; those who do routine data entry or retrieval of a sort that will eventually be automated or done overseas; and those who provide routine personal services.

The important point is that workers in these three functional categories are coming to have a different competitive position in the world economy. Symbolic analysts hold a commanding position in an increasingly global labor market. Routine production workers hold a relatively weak position in an increasingly global labor market. Personal-service workers still find themselves in a national labor market, but for various reasons they suffer the indirect effects of competition from workers abroad.

How should we respond to these trends? One response is to accept them as inevitable consequences of change, but try to offset their polarizing effects through a truly progressive income tax, coupled with more generous income assistance—including health insurance—for poor working Americans. (For a start, we might reverse the extraordinarily regressive Social Security amendments of 1983, through which poor working Americans are now financing the federal budget deficit, often paying more in payroll taxes than than in income taxes.)

A more ambitious response would be to guard against class rigidities by ensuring that any talented American kid can become a symbolic victory analyst—regardless of family income or race. Here we see the upside of a globalizaed economy. Unlike America's old vertically integrated economy, whose white-collar jobs were necessarily limited in proportion to the number of blue-collar jobs beneath them, the global economy imposes no particular limit upon the number of Americans who can sell symbolic-analytic services. In principle, all of America's routine production workers could become symbolic analysts and let their old jobs drift overseas. In practice, of course, we can't even inch toward such a state anytime soon. Not even America's gifted but poor children can aspire to such jobs until the government spends substantially more than it does now to ensure excellent public schools in every city and region to which talented children can go, and ample financial help when they are ready to attend college.

Of course, it isn't clear that even under those circumstances there would be radical growth in the number of Americans who became research scientists, design engineers, musicians, management consultants, or (even if the world needed them) investment bankers and lawyers. So other responses are also needed. Perhaps the most ambitious would be to increase the number of Americans who could apply symbolic analysis to production and to personal services.

There is ample evidence, for example, that access to computerized information can enrich production jobs by enabling workers to alter the flow of materials and components in ways that generate new efficiencies. (Shoshana Zuboff's recent book *In the Age of the Smart Machine* carefully documents these possibilities.) Production workers who thus have broader responsibilities and more control over how production is organized cease to be "routine" workers—becoming, in effect, symbolic analysts at a level very close to the production process. The same transformation can occur in personal-service jobs. Consider, for example, the checkout clerk whose computer enables her to control inventory and decide when to reorder items from the factory.

The number of such technologically empowered jobs, of course, is limited by the ability of workers to learn on the job. That means a far greater number of Americans will need good health care (including prenatal and postnatal) and also a good grounding in mathematics, basic science, and reading and communicating. So once again, comfortably integrating the

American work force into the new world economy turns out to rest heavily on education.

Education and health care for poor children are apt to be costly. Since poorer working Americans, already under a heavy tax load, can't afford it, the cost would have to be borne by wealthier Americans—who also would have to bear the cost of any income redistribution plans designed to neutralize the polarizing domestic effects of a globalized economy. Thus a central question is the willingness of the more fortunate American citizens—especially symbolic analysts, who constitute the most fortunate fifth, with 40 percent of the nation's income—to bear the burden. But here lies a Catch-22. For as our economic fates diverge, the top fifth may be losing the sense of connectedness with the bottom fifth or even the bottom half, that would elicit such generosity.

The conservative tide that has swept the land during the last decade surely has many causes, but these economic fundamentals should not be discounted. It is now possible for the most fortunate fifth to sell their expertise directly in the global market, and thus maintain and enhance their standard of living and that of their children even as that of other Americans declines. There is less and less basis for a strong sense of interclass interdependence. Meanwhile, the fortunate fifth have also been able to insulate themselves from the less fortunate, by living in suburban enclaves far removed from the effects of of poverty. Neither patriotism nor altruism may be sufficient to overcome these realities. Yet without the active support of the fortunate fifth, it will be difficult to muster the political will necessary for change.

George Bush speaks eloquently of "a thousand points of light" and of the importance of generosity. But so far his administration has set a poor example. A minuscule sum has been budgeted for education, training, and health care for the poor. The president says we can't afford any more. Meanwhile, he pushes a reduction in the capital gains tax rate—another boon to the fortunate fifth.

On withdrawing from the presidential race of 1988, Paul Simon of Illinois said, "Americans instinctively know that we are one nation, one family, and when anyone in that family hurts, all of us hurt." Sadly, that is coming to be less and less the case.

Jobs
Skills Before Credentials

Robert B. Reich

Nearly 50 years ago, the specter of long-term mass joblessness unnerved America. World War II had ended in triumph but the outbreak of peace held its own perils. The Great Depression had been submerged by war rather than resolved, and there seemed little reason to believe that 1948 would look much different from 1938. The returning GIs, it was thought, must either displace the new workers who had run the wartime economy or else face unemployment themselves as the Depression set in again. It seemed perfectly plain, to experts and ordinary citizens alike, that prospects were grim for a huge number of American workers.

Yet this period of apparently well-founded pessimism gave way to an era of rapid growth and rising living standards. The transition was by no means painless. But the main story, still, is the enormous discrepancy between the fearful expectations of the postwar years and the positive turn that history actually took.

The explanation seems simple: Americans at the time had a vivid picture of imperiled old jobs and only dim inklings of better jobs to come. The economy's capacity to create new jobs simply exceeded the mind's capacity to imagine them.

Unnecessary Pessimism

We may be at such a juncture once again. Global competition, defense down-sizing, corporate restructuring and technological change have put many established jobs at risk. Even informed Americans despair that there will ever be enough good jobs for new entrants to the labor force or for displaced workers. Anxious voices—"Where are the jobs?" "Training for what?"—greet proposals to reform education and deliver competitive job skills.

The future, to be sure, is ultimately as unknowable in 1994 as it was in 1949. But we may be able to use the lessons of the past—as well as some modest advances in economic forecasting—to gain a degree of insight into the jobs of the future. A clearer view of employment prospects may prevent pessimism from undermining concrete measures that would make the good jobs of the future come faster and more surely for American workers.

All the evidence points to strong, long-term growth in demand for workers with problem-solving skills. In the Clinton administration's first 11 months, the economy created more than 1.6 million private-sector jobs. Over the past year, nearly half of the employment growth has been in managerial and professional jobs. The Bureau of Labor Statistics predicts that the number of jobs for technicians will grow 37% between 1990 and 2005.

Yet these familiar categories are only approximate labels for the skill-centered work that is emerging. Distinctions are eroding. The old hierarchy of mid-level managers, lower-level supervisors and low-skilled drones is blurring into a broad class of workplace problem-solvers. Expertise and authority seep away from the front office and are dispersed throughout the productive team. "Goods" and "services" are becoming less distinct, as more and more of the value of a product is embedded in related services delivered both before it is manufactured (design, programming, process engineering) and after it is sold (targeted distribution, customized installation, training in applications).

Credentialism is breaking down. Many of the fastest-growing good jobs—factory technician, data-processor—don't require a college degree. But as formal credentials become less essential, up-to-date skills become ever more crucial—even in jobs where the unskilled could formerly thrive.

Workers without skills, meanwhile, find their options shrinking. More than ever before, what you earn depends on what you learn. Americans without training beyond high school have suffered a continuing decline in earnings over the past 15 years. High-school dropouts have been hit even harder, with collapsing wage rates and rising unemployment.

Like comparable periods before, our current era of rapid economic change opens new opportunities. Every American can develop the skills to make it in the new economy. The winners won't be limited to college graduates. A recent study by economists Tom Kane and Cecilia Rouse found that every year of post-secondary training in universities or community colleges, and whether leading to a degree or not, boosts annual earning power by 5% to 10%. The good jobs of the future won't fit neatly into our current categories of "manager/managed" or "high-tech/low-tech."

Examples abound. There's a new kind of delivery truck driver equipped with a computer and modem in her cab, so she can time deliveries to exactly when customers need them, and then custom-assemble the complex machinery she's delivering. She shares little more than a job title with the trucker of 10 years ago. She's a high-skilled service technician, and she's making good money.

Throughout the economy, familiar-sounding jobs are becoming more demanding, and more rewarding, as job descriptions metamorphose. In 1990, just 18% of the functions in a typical Ford automobile were computer-controlled. In 1994, the proportion is 82%. This technological shift has profound consequences for the number and nature of good jobs. Auto mechanics skilled in computer diagnostics can command annual salaries ranging from $30,000 to $75,000. In the same way, assembly work is transformed, as a new kind of factory worker sits behind a computer, programming and reprogramming a robot that does the pulling and twisting that human beings used to do.

The bad news about our current juncture in economic history is real enough: More and more old jobs are imperiled by global economic integration and technological change. Fewer and fewer Americans can count on holding a single job throughout their careers, and the unskilled face worsening odds for sustainable prosperity.

Skills Pay Off

But the good news is equally real, if less obvious: The payoff to skills is surging. Technological evolution is spawning a profusion of good new jobs. Integrated, expanding global markets create many more opportunities than they close off. And the skills needed for many of these high-skill, high-wage jobs can be learned, often through two-year associate's degrees, apprenticeship programs and on-the-job training.

Hard questions remain. How do we ensure that the right kinds of training are available, at the right time, as Americans struggle with work-force transitions? How do we buffer the shock of change for workers who now depend on vulnerable jobs and industries? The Clinton administration is working hard to answer these questions.

But one question—"training for what?"—is easier to answer than it seems. The evidence shows that skills pay off. The evidence shows that American workers can learn. "Training for what?" For the high-skill work taking shape all around us today. America's economy is racing into the future. There is no excuse for leaving a single citizen behind.

Samantha Power (1970–) was born in Ireland and immigrated to the U.S. in 1979. She attended high school in Georgia and then Yale University and Harvard Law School. She covered the Yugoslav Wars as a journalist in the 1990s and her book, A Problem from Hell: America and the Age of Genocide, *from which this excerpt is taken, won the Pulitzer Prize for General Non-Fiction in 2003.*

Preface from A Problem from Hell: America and the Age of Genocide

Samantha Power

My introduction to Sidbela Zimic a nine-year-old Sarajevan, came unexpectedly one Sunday in June 1995. Several hours after hearing the familiar whistle and crash of a nearby shell, I traveled a few blocks to one of the neighborhood's once-formidable apartment houses. Its battered façade bore the signature pockmarks left from three years of shrapnel spray and gunfire. The building lacked windows, electricity, gas, and water. It was uninhabitable to all but Sarajevo's proud residents, who had no place else to go.

Sidbela's teenage sister was standing not far from the entrance to the apartment, dazed. A shallow pool of crimson lay beside her on the playground, where one blue slipper, two red slippers, and a jump rope with ice-cream-cone handles had been cast down. Bosnian police had covered the reddened spot of pavement with plastic wrapping that bore the cheery baby blue and white emblem of the United Nations.

Sidbela had been known in the neighborhood for her bookishness and her many "Miss" pageants. She and her playmates made the best of a childhood that constrained movement, crowning "Miss Apartment Building," "Miss Street Corner," and "Miss Neighborhood." On that still morning, Sidbela had begged her mother for five minutes of fresh air.

Mrs. Zimic was torn. A year and a half before, in February 1994, just two blocks from the family's home, a shell had landed in the main downtown market, tearing sixty-eight shoppers and vendors to bits. The graphic images from this massacre generated widespread American sympathy and galvanized President Bill Clinton and his NATO allies. They issued an unprecedented ultimatum, in which they threatened massive air strikes against the Bosnian Serbs if they resumed their bombardment of Sarajevo or continued what Clinton described as the "murder of innocents."

"No one should doubt NATO's resolve." Clinton warned. "Anyone," he said, repeating the word for effect, "*anyone* shelling Sarajevo must . . . be prepared to deal with the consequences."[1] In response to America's perceived commitment, Sarajevo's 280,000 residents gradually adjusted to life under NATO's imperfect but protective umbrella. After a few cautious months, they began trickling outside, strolling along the Miljacka River and rebuilding cafes with outdoor terraces. Young boys and girls bounded out of dank cellars and out of their parents' lines of vision to rediscover outdoor sports. Tasting childhood, they became greedy for sunlight and play. Their parents thanked the United States and heaped praise upon Americans who visited the Bosnian capital.

But American resolve soon wilted. Saving Bosnian lives was not deemed worth risking U.S. soldiers or challenging America's European allies who wanted to remain neutral. Clinton and his team shifted from the language of genocide to that of "tragedy" and "civil war," downplaying public expectations that there was anything the United States could do. Secretary of State Warren Christopher had never been enthusiastic about U.S. involvement in the Balkans. He had long appealed to context to ease the moral discomfort that arose from America's nonintervention. "It's really a tragic problem," Christopher said. "The hatred between all three groups—the Bosnians and the Serbs and the Croatians—is almost unbelievable. It's almost terrifying, and it's centuries old. That really is a problem from hell."[2] Within months of the market massacre, Clinton had adopted this mindset, treating Bosnia as *his* problem from hell—a problem he hoped would burn itself out, disappear from the front pages, and leave his presidency alone.

Serb nationalists took their cue. They understood that they were free to resume shelling Sarajevo and other Bosnian towns crammed with civilians. Parents were left battling their children and groping for inducements that might keep them indoors. Sidbela's father remembered, "I converted the washroom into a playroom. I bought the children Barbie dolls, Barbie cars, everything, just to keep them inside." But his precocious daughter had her way, pressing, "Daddy, please let me live my life. I can't stay at home all the time."

America's promises, which Serb gunners took seriously at first, bought Sarajevans a brief reprieve. But they also raised expectations among Bosnians that they were safe to live again. As it turned out, the brutality of Serb political, military, and paramilitary leaders would be met with condemnation but not with the promised military intervention.

On June 25, 1995, minutes after Sidbela kissed her mother on the cheek and flashed a triumphant smile, a Serb shell crashed into the playground where she, eleven-year-old Amina Pajevic, twelve-year-old Liljana Janjic, and five-year-old Maja Skoric were jumping rope. All were killed, raising the total number of children slaughtered in Bosnian territory during the war from 16,767 to 16,771.

If any event could have prepared a person to imagine evil, it should have been this one. I had been reporting from Bosnia for nearly two years at the time of the playground massacre. I had long since given up hope that the NATO jets that roared overhead every day would bomb the Serbs into ceasing their artillery assault on the besieged capital. And I had come to expect only the worst for Muslim civilians scattered throughout the country.

Yet when Bosnian Serb forces began attacking the so-called "safe area" of Srebrenica on July 6, 1995, ten days after I visited the grieving Zimic family, I was not especially alarmed. I thought that even the Bosnian Serbs would not dare to seize a patch of land under UN guard. On the evening of July 10, I casually dropped by the Associated Press house, which had become my adopted home for the summer because of its spirited reporters and its functional generator. When I arrived that night, I received a jolt. There was complete chaos around the phones. The Serb attack on Srebrenica that had been "deteriorating" for several days had suddenly "gone to hell." The Serbs were poised to take the town, and they had issued an ultimatum, demanding that the UN peacekeepers there surrender their weapons and equipment or face a barrage of shelling. Some 40,000 Muslim men, women, and children were in grave danger.

Although I had been slow to grasp the magnitude of the offensive, it was not too late to meet my American deadlines. A morning story in the *Washington Post* might shame U.S. policymakers into responding. So frantic were the other correspondents that it took me fifteen minutes to secure a free phone line. When I did, I reached Ed Cody, the *Post's* deputy foreign editor. I knew American readers had tired of bad news from the Balkans, but the stakes of this particular attack seemed colossal. Bosnian Serb general Ratko Mladic was not dabbling or using a petty landgrab to send a political signal; he was taking a huge chunk of internationally "protected" territory and challenging the world to stop him. I began spewing the facts to Cody as I understood them: "The Serbs are closing in on the Srebrenica safe area. The UN says tens of thousands of Muslim refugees have already poured into their base north of the town center. It's only a matter of hours before the Serbs take the whole pocket. This is a catastrophe in the making. A United Nations safe area is going to fall."

A new contributor to the *Post*, I had been advised that Cody, a veteran of carnage in the Middle East, would not be one to get easily rattled. In this instance he heard me out and then posed a few incisive questions—questions that led me to believe he had understood the severity of the crisis unfolding. Then he stunned me: "Well, from what you are telling me, even if things proceed, the Serbs are not going to take the town tonight." I grimaced in anticipation of his next sentence, which duly followed. "It sounds like *when* Srebrenica falls, we'll have a story."

I protested, but not strenuously. I was half sure the Serbs would back down and was reluctant to cry wolf. By the following afternoon, however Srebrenica had fallen, and the petrified inhabitants of the enclave were in the hands of General Mladic, a suspected war criminal known to have orchestrated the savage siege of Sarajevo.

I had worked in Sarajevo, where Serb snipers took target practice on bundled old ladies hauling canisters of filthy water across town and where picturesque parks had been transformed into cemeteries to accommodate the deluge of young arrivals. I had interviewed emaciated men who had dropped forty and fifty pounds and who bore permanent scars from their time in Serb concentration camps. And I had only recently covered the massacre of four schoolgirls. Yet despite my experiences, or perhaps because of them, I could only imagine what I had already witnessed. It never dawned on me that General Mladic would or could systematically execute every last Muslim man and boy in his custody.

A few days after Srebrenica fell, a colleague of mine telephoned from New York and said the Bosnian ambassador to the UN was claiming that the Bosnian Serbs had murdered more than 1,000 Muslim men from Srebrenica in a football stadium. It was not possible. "No," I said simply. My friend repeated the charge. "No," I said again, determined.

I was right. Mladic did not execute 1,000 men. He killed more than 7,000.

When I returned to the United States, Sidbela and Srebrenica stayed with me. I was chilled by the promise of protection that had drawn a child out of a basement and onto an exposed Sarajevan playground. I was haunted by the murder of Srebrenica's Muslim men and boys, my own failure to sound a proper early warning, and the outside world's refusal to intervene even once the men's peril had become obvious. I found myself flashing back to the many debates I had had with my colleagues about intervention. We had wondered aloud—at press briefings, on road trips, and in interviews with senior Bosnian and American officials—how the United States and its allies might have responded if the same crimes had been committed in a different place (the Balkans evoke age-old animosities and combustible tinderboxes), against different victims (most of the atrocities were committed against individuals of Muslim faith), or at a different time (the Soviet Union had just collapsed, no new world vision had yet replaced the old world order, and the United Nations had not oiled its rusty parts or rid itself of its anachronistic practices and assumptions). In 1996, with some distance from the field, I began exploring America's responses to previous cases of mass slaughter. It did not take long to discover that the American response to the Bosnia genocide was in fact the most robust of the century. The United States had never in its history intervened to stop genocide and had in fact rarely even made a point of condemning it as it occurred.

As I surveyed the major genocides of the twentieth century, a few stood out. In addition to the Bosnian Serbs' eradication of non-Serbs, I examined the Ottoman slaughter of the Armenians, the Nazi Holocaust, Pol Pot's terror in Cambodia, Saddam Hussein's destruction of Kurds in northern Iraq, and the Rwandan Hutus' systematic extermination of the Tutsi minority. Although the cases varied in scope and not all involved the intent to exterminate every last member of a group, each met the terms of the 1948 genocide convention and presented the United States with options for meaningful diplomatic, economic, legal, or military intervention. The crimes occurred in Europe, Asia, the Middle East, and Africa. The victims covered a spectrum of races and religions—they were Asian, African, Caucasian, Christian, Jewish, Buddhist, and Muslim. The perpetrators operated at different stages of American might: The Armenian genocide (1915–1916) was committed during World War I, before the United States had become a world leader. The Holocaust (1939–1945) took place just as the United States was moving into that role. The Cambodian (1975–1979) and Iraqi (1987–1988) genocides were perpetrated after the Holocaust but during the Cold War and after Vietnam. Bosnia (1992–1995) and Rwanda (1994) happened after the Cold War and while American supremacy and awareness of the "lessons" of the Holocaust were at their height. U.S. decisionmakers also brought a wide variety of backgrounds and foreign policy ideologies to the table. Every American president in office in the last three decades of the twentieth century—Nixon, Ford, Carter, Reagan, Bush, and Clinton—made decisions related to the prevention and suppression of genocide. Yet notwithstanding all the variety among cases and within U.S. administrations, the U.S. policy responses to genocide were astonishingly similar across time, geography, ideology, and geopolitical balance.

In order to understand U.S. responses to genocide, I interviewed more than 300 Americans who had a hand in shaping or influencing U.S. policy.* Most were officials of varying ranks at the White House, State Department, Pentagon, and Central Intelligence Agency (CIA). Some were lawmakers and staff members on Capitol Hill. Others were journalists who covered the carnage or nongovernmental advocates who attempted to ameliorate it. A grant from the Open Society Institute enabled me to travel to Bosnia, Cambodia, Kosovo, and Rwanda, where I spoke with victims, perpetrators, and bystanders. I also visited the international war crimes tribunal for the former Yugoslavia at The Hague in the Netherlands, as well the UN court for Rwanda, located in Arusha, Tanzania. Thanks to the National Security Archive, a nonprofit organization that uses the Freedom of Information Act to secure the release of classified U.S. documents, I was able to draw on hundreds of pages of newly available government records. This material provides a clearer picture than was previously discernible of the interplay among people, motives, and genocidal events.

People have explained U.S. failures to respond to specific genocides by claiming that the United States didn't know what was happening, that it knew but didn't care, or that regardless of what it knew, there was nothing useful to be done. I have found that in fact U.S. policymakers knew a great deal about the crimes being perpetrated. Some Americans cared and fought for action, making considerable personal and professional sacrifices. And the United States did have countless opportunities to mitigate and prevent slaughter. But time and again, decent men and women chose to look away. We have all been bystanders to genocide. The crucial question is why.

The answers seemed to lie in the critical decisions—and decisions not to decide—made before, during, and after the various genocides. In exploring a century of U.S. reactions to genocide, I asked: Were there early warnings that mass killing was set to commence? How seriously were the warnings taken? By whom? Was there any reason to believe the

---

*   Quotes that are not sourced in the notes are taken from these exclusive interviews, conducted between July 1993 and November 2001. I have introduced these quotations using the present tense (e.g., "Senator McGovern recalls . . .")

violence expected would be qualitatively or quantitatively different from the "run-of-the-mill" killings that were sadly typical of local warfare? Once the violence began, what classified or open intelligence was available? What constraints operated to impede diagnosis? How and when did U.S. officials recognize that genocide (and not merely war) was under way? Who inside or outside the U.S. government wanted to do what? What were the risks or costs? Who opposed them? Who prevailed? How did public opinion and elite opinion diverge? And finally, how were the U.S. responses, the genocides, and the Americans who urged intervention remembered later? In reconstructing a narrative of events, I have divided most of the cases into warning, recognition, response, and aftermath sections.

Contrary to any assumption I may have harbored while I traveled around the former Yugoslavia, the Bush and Clinton administrations' responses to atrocities in Bosnia were consistent with prior American responses to genocide. Early warnings of massive bloodshed proliferated. The spewing of inflammatory propaganda escalated. The massacres and deportations started. U.S. policymakers struggled to wrap their minds around the horrors. Refugee stories and press reports of atrocities became too numerous to deny. Few Americans at home pressed for intervention. A hopeful but passive and ultimately deadly American waiting game commenced. And genocide proceeded unimpeded by U.S. action and often emboldened by U.S. inaction.

The book's major findings can be summarized as follows:

- Despite graphic media coverage, American policymakers, journalists, and citizens are extremely slow to muster the imagination needed to reckon with evil. Ahead of the killings, they assume rational actors will not inflict seemingly gratuitous violence. They trust in good-faith negotiations and traditional diplomacy. Once the killings start, they assume that civilians who keep their heads down will be left alone. They urge cease-fires and donate humanitarian aid.

- It is in the realm of domestic politics that the battle to stop genocide is lost. American political leaders interpret society-wide silence as an indicator of public indifference. They reason that they will incur no costs if the United States remains uninvolved but will face steep risks if they engage. Potential sources of influence—lawmakers on Capitol Hill, editorial boards, nongovernmental groups, and ordinary constituents—do not generate political pressure sufficient to change the calculus of America's leaders.

- The U.S. government not only abstains from sending its troops, but it takes very few steps along a continuum of intervention to deter genocide.

- U.S. officials spin themselves (as well as the American public) about the nature of the violence in question and the likely impact of an American intervention. They render the bloodshed two-sided and inevitable, not genocidal. They insist that any proposed U.S. response will be futile. Indeed, it may even do more harm than good, bringing perverse consequences to the victims and jeopardizing other precious American moral or strategic interests.[3] They brand as "emotional" those U.S. officials who urge intervention and who make moral arguments in a system that speaks principally in the cold language of interests. They avoid use of the word "genocide." Thus, they can in good conscience favor stopping genocide in the abstract, while simultaneously opposing American involvement in the moment.

The sharpest challenge to the world of bystanders is posed by those who have refused to remain silent in the age of genocide. In each case a few Americans stood out by standing up. They did not lose sight of right and wrong, even as they were repeatedly steered to a "context" that others said precluded action. They refused to accept either that they could not influence U.S. policy or that the United States could not influence the killers. These individuals were not alone in their struggles, but they were not in crowded company either. By seeing what they tried to get done, we see what America could have done. We also see what we might ourselves have attempted. By seeing how and why they failed, we see what we as a nation let happen.

In 1915 Henry Morgenthau Sr., the U.S. ambassador in Constantinople, responded to Turkey's deportation and slaughter of its Armenian minority by urging Washington to condemn Turkey and pressure its wartime ally Germany. Morgenthau also defied diplomatic convention by personally protesting the atrocities, denouncing the regime, and raising money for humanitarian relief. He was joined by former president Theodore Roosevelt, who went a step further, calling on the administration of Woodrow Wilson to enter World War I and forcibly stop the slaughter. But the United States clung to its neutrality and insisted that Turkey's internal affairs were not its business. An estimated 1 million Armenians were murdered or died of disease and starvation during the genocide.

Raphael Lemkin, a Polish Jew and international lawyer, warned about Hitler's designs in the 1930s but was scoffed at. After finding refuge in the United States in 1941, he failed to win support for any measure to protect imperiled Jews. The Allies resisted denouncing Hitler's atrocities, granting refuge to Europe's Jewry, and bombing the railroad tracks to the Nazi concentration camps. Undaunted, Lemkin invented the word "genocide" and secured the passage of the first-ever United Nations human rights treaty, which was devoted to banning the new crime. Sadly, he lived to see the genocide convention rebuffed by the U.S. Senate. William Proxmire, the quixotic U.S. senator from Wisconsin, picked up where Lemkin left off and delivered 3,211 speeches on the Senate floor urging ratification of the UN treaty. After nineteen years of daily soliloquies, Proxmire did manage to get the Senate to accept the genocide convention, but the U.S. ratification was so laden with caveats that it carried next to no force.

A handful of U.S. diplomats and journalists in Cambodia warned of the depravity of a sinister band of Communist rebels known as the Khmer Rouge. They were derided by the American left for falling for anti-Communist propaganda, and they failed to influence a U.S. policy that could not contemplate engagement of any kind in Southeast Asia after Vietnam. Pol Pot's four-year reign left some 2 million Cambodians dead, but the massacres elicited barely a whimper from Washington, which maintained diplomatic recognition of the genocidal regime even after it had been overthrown.

Peter Gaibraith, a staff member of the Senate Foreign Relations Committee, drafted punishing legislation for his boss, Senator Claiborne Pell, that would have cut off U.S. agricultural and manufacturing credits to Saddam Hussein in retaliation for his 1987–1988 attempt to wipe out Iraq's rural Kurds. The sanctions package was defeated by a determined White House, State Department, and U.S. farm lobby, which were eager to maintain friendly ties and sell rice and wheat to Iraq. And so Hussein's regime received generous American financial support while it gassed and executed some 100,000 Kurds.

Romeo Dallaire, a Canadian major general who commanded UN peacekeeping forces in Rwanda in 1994, appealed for permission to disarm militias and to prevent the extermination of Rwanda's Tutsi three months before the genocide began. Denied this by his political masters at the United Nations, he watched corpses pile up around him as Washington led a successful effort so remove most of the peacekeepers under his command and then aggressively worked to block authorization of UN reinforcements. The United States refused to use its technology to jam radio broadcasts that were a crucial instrument in the coordination and perpetuation of the genocide. And even as, on average, 8,000

Rwandans were being butchered each day, the issue never became a priority for senior U.S. officials. Some 800,000 Rwandans were killed in 100 days.

A few diplomats at the State Department and several lawmakers on Capitol Hill relentlessly tried to convince an intransigent bureaucracy to bomb Serb ethnic cleansers in Bosnia. These men watched the sanitization of cables, the repackaging of the conflict as "intractable" and "ancient," and the maintenance of an arms embargo against Bosnia's outgunned Muslims. Several foreign service officers who quit the department in disgust then watched, from a no less frustrating perch outside the U.S. government, the fall of the Srebrenica safe area and the largest massacre in Europe in fifty years. Between 1992 and 1995, while the nightly news broadcast the Serb onslaught, some 200,000 Bosnians were killed. Only when U.S. military intervention came to feel unavoidable and Bob Dole, the Kansas Republican and Senate majority leader, had persuaded Congress to lift the arms embargo did U.S. policy change. By bringing the war in Bosnia home, Dole helped spur President Clinton to begin NATO bombing. By then, however, Bosnia's genocide had been largely completed, and a multi-ethnic state had been destroyed.

This book deliberately spotlights the response of *American* policymakers and citizens for several reasons. First, the United States' decisions to act or not to act have had a greater impact on the victims' fortunes than those of any other major power. Second, since World War II, the United States has had a tremendous capacity to curb genocide. It could have used its vast resources to do so without undermining U.S. security. Third, the United States has made an unusually pronounced commitment to Holocaust commemoration and education. The Holocaust Memorial Museum, which stands baldly on the Mall alongside the Lincoln Monument and the Jefferson Memorial and just yards from the Vietnam Wall Memorial, draws 5,500 visitors a day, or 2 million per year, almost double the number of visitors tallied annually by the White House. Fourth, in recent years American leaders, steeped in a new culture of Holocaust awareness, have repeatedly committed themselves to preventing the recurrence of genocide. In 1979 President Jimmy Carter declared that out of the memory of the Holocaust, "we must forge an unshakable oath with all civilized people that never again will the world stand silent, never again will the world fail to act in time to prevent this terrible crime of genocide."[4] Five years later, President Ronald Reagan, too, declared. "Like you, I say in a forthright voice, 'Never again!'[5] President George Bush Sr. joined the chorus in 1991. Speaking "as a World War II veteran, as an American, and now as President of the United States," Bush said his visit to Auschwitz had left him with "the determination, not just to remember, but also to act."[6] Before becoming president, candidate Clinton chided Bush over Bosnia. "If the horrors of the Holocaust taught us anything:' Clinton said, "it is the high cost of remaining silent and paralyzed in the face of genocide."[7] Once in office, at the opening of the Holocaust Museum, Clinton faulted America's inaction during World War II. "Even as our fragmentary awareness of crimes grew into indisputable facts, far too little was done," he said. "We must not permit that to happen again."[8] But the forward-looking, consoling refrain of "never again," a testament to America's can-do spirit, never grappled with the fact that the country had done nothing, practically or politically, to prepare itself to respond to genocide. The commitment proved hollow in the face of actual slaughter.

Before I began exploring America's relationship with genocide, I used to refer to U.S. policy toward Bosnia as a "failure." I have changed my mind. It is daunting to acknowledge, but this country's consistent policy of nonintervention in the face of genocide offers sad testimony not to a broken American political system but to one that is ruthlessly effective. The system, as it stands now, *is working.*[9] No U.S. president has ever made genocide prevention a priority, and no U.S. president has ever suffered politically for his indifference to its occurrence. It is thus no coincidence that genocide rages on.

Notes

1   "Statement by President Clinton Regarding Proposals to Deal with Situation in Bosnia," Federal News Service, February 9, 1994.

2   Warren Christopher on *Face the Nation*, CBS, March 28, 1993.

3   I borrow the categories of justification—futility, perversity, and jeopardy—from Albert O. Hirschman's *Rhetoric of Reaction: Perversity, Futility, Jeopardy* (Cambridge, Mass.: Belknap Press, 1991). Hirschman shows how those who oppose progressive reform tend to take issue not with the goals of the proposed measure but with its likely "unintended consequences." Officials and citizens who oppose action provide detailed accounts of all that can go wrong but rarely admit the possibility of success, of *desirable* unintended consequences, or of some negative consequences but an overall net positive gain.

4   "President's Commission on the Holocaust: Remarks on Receiving the Final Report of the Commission," September 27, 1979, *Public Papers of the Presidents of the United States: Jimmy Carter, 1979* (Washington, D.C.: GPO, 1979), p. 1773.

5   "Remarks at the International Convention of B'nai B'rith," September 6,1984, *Public Papers of the Presidents of the United States: Ronald Reagan, 1987* (Washington, D.C.: GPO, 1987), p. 1244.

6   "Remarks of President George Bush at the Simon Wiesenthal Dinner, Century Plaza Hotel, Los Angeles, California," Federal News Service, June 16, 1991.

7   Clifford Krauss, "U.S. Backs Away from Charge of Atrocities in Bosnia Camps," *New York Times*, August 5, 1992, p. A12.

8   "Remarks at the Dedication of the U.S. Holocaust Memorial Museum," April 22, 1993, *Public Papers of the Presidents of the United States: William J. Clinton, 1993* (Washington, D.C.: GPO, 1994), p. 479.

9   See Leslie Celb and Richard Betts, *The Irony of Vietnam: The System Worked* (Washington, D.C.: Brookings Institution, 1979).

*B*ruce Jentleson earned degrees from Cornell University and the London School of Economics and is currently a professor of public policy and political science at Duke University. He served as a senior foreign policy advisor to Vice President Al Gore during the 2000 presidential campaign and has written extensively about international relations and American foreign policy.

A Responsibility to Protect
The Defining Challenge for the Global Community

Bruce W. Jentleson

We live in an age that is dependent on a strong sense of global community. Despite this fact, many of our current problems trace back to how weak that unifying sense truly is. This theme is most tragic when it appears in the form of genocide, ethnic cleansings, and other manifestations of the deadly politics of identity. For all the vows that there would "never again" be another genocide, reality has too many times proven otherwise. Yet again, millions of people have been killed, maimed, raped, displaced, and otherwise victimized, while the international community —including the United States, the United Nations, and the European Union—continues to do too little, too late.

If we cannot turn the "never again" pledge from rhetoric to reality, how can we genuinely claim to be a global community? Time and again we have witnessed man's inhumanity at its basest, most venal, and most outrageous. But where is the outrage? It has not been coming from recent US administrations—not from George H. W. Bush over Bosnia, not from Bill Clinton over Rwanda, and not from George W. Bush over Darfur. It has not been coming from the United Nations, in which countless resolutions about being "seized with the matter" are approved and then become "seized up" when it comes to meaningful action. And outrage has certainly not been coming from the many countries that buy into invocations of state sovereignty with little regard for supposedly shared values and commitments, which are codified in the Universal Declaration of Human Rights and the Genocide Convention.

There is no doubt that breaking the vicious political cycle of identity is difficult. But it is possible. Bosnia and Rwanda were rife with missed opportunities—so, too, was Darfur. Breaking the cycle is necessary for tangible reasons, since these conflicts feed other conflicts, including terrorism. It is also necessary for less tangible, but deeply penetrating reasons. We must understand that our actions determine whether the legacy we leave to future generations is one of despair or one of hope.

Key Questions in the Policy Debate

Looking across key cases, we can identify five core questions that frame policy debates on genocide prevention and related humanitarian intervention. First, what are the driving forces behind ethnic conflict and genocide? Then, given existing tensions, when should military force be used? Why is such intervention justified, if ever, and who should decide when intervention should happen? Finally, what constitutes effective intervention?

Driving Forces? Many policymakers take the "primordialist" view of these conflicts and view them as the inevitable outcomes of fixed, inherited, and deeply antagonistic group identities. In this understanding, the end of the Cold War stripped away the constraining effects of the overlay of bipolar geopolitics. The implication is that historical hatreds, including those that Robert Kaplan has called the "Balkan ghosts," are restored to their "natural" states of conflict.

But while history shapes these conflicts, it does not determine them nearly to the extent that such theories suggest. A number of studies have shown that ethnic identities are much less fixed over time; as a result, the frequency and intensity of ethnic conflict vary more than primordialist theory claims. This point is made, albeit with some amount of hyperbole, in a statement by a Bosnian Muslim schoolteacher: "We never, until the war, thought of ourselves as Muslims. We were Yugoslavs. But when we began to be murdered because we are Muslims, things changed. The definition of who we are today has been determined by our killing."

Such killing was not a predetermined playing out of history. Instead, it was an intentional manipulation of history by Slobodan Milosevic to turn grievances and prejudices into hatred and murder. This was also the case in Rwanda and elsewhere. The driving dynamic has been more purposeful than primordial. It has resulted primarily from conscious calculations made by leaders and groups whose needs could be served by political violence. It is true, as William Faulkner once wrote, that "the past is never dead. It's not even past." But historical influence is one thing, and historical determinism is quite another.

When Military Force? Noninterventionism has largely served the post-WWII international system well. Constraints on the major powers helped maintain order and security. Protection for small countries and newly independent states buttressed self-determination, freedom, and justice. Force was to be a last resort, and its usage was highly restricted. But identity conflicts in Bosnia, Rwanda, and elsewhere have exposed deep and disturbing contradictions between the traditional noninterventionist regime and the norms of peace, justice, and humanitarianism that underlie the United Nations. These cases have shown that while force should never be a first resort, it should at times be an early, and not just a last, option. "There are situations in which a quick, early use of force may well be the best method," writes Harvard Professor Stanley Hoffmann, "and the only one capable of preventing a further aggravation of the [humanitarian] crisis." For if the threshold for intervention is that the bodies have already started to pile up, it can hardly be considered humanitarian. One can consider it perhaps less inhumane than not acting at all—but that is not exactly a high standard.

Justification for Intervention? To understand justifications for intervention or inaction, it is crucial to examine the debate over the rights and responsibilities of state sovereignty in an international community. The traditional concept that sovereignty is a right maintains that states have jurisdictional exclusivity within their own borders. This grants very limited legitimacy to other actors, such as states or international institutions to intervene in what would be considered domestic affairs. But since intrastate clashes have become the dominant and most lethal form of conflict, the international community cannot continue to readily accept invocations of state sovereignty as a barrier behind which aggression can hide. The UN Charter, stressed Secretary-General Kofi Annan, "was issued in the name of 'the people,' not the governments . . . It was never meant as a license for governments to trample on human rights and human dignity."

In reality, it was not so much that other states had a right to intervene, but rather that the international community had a "responsibility to protect." These distinctions may seem like semantics, but they make a crucial difference in legitimizing intervention in intrastate conflicts. In 2005, building on the important work of the semi-official International Commission on Intervention and State Sovereignty, the United Nations did adopt the "responsibility to protect" as a norm. It stated that "the principle of non-intervention in internal affairs cannot be used to protect genocidal acts or other atrocities." It then claimed to affirm "the collective international responsibility to protect populations from genocide, war crimes, ethnic cleansing and crimes against humanity." There was still, however, much equivocation in the text. What was even worse was that despite these adopted norms, there was still inaction in the first test case of Darfur.

Who Decides? The crucial issue here concerns the extent of the UN Security Council's authority in making humanitarian intervention decisions. Consensus is stronger on the idea of the UN Security Council as the preferred decision-maker, rather than the exclusive one. Limitations on UN decision-making can be seen during the Kosovo situation, in which Chinese and Russian opposition prevented Security Council action. While he did not endorse the US-NATO intervention, Secretary-General Annan did speak out against Security Council inaction in the face of "crimes against humanity," which he considered a "betray[al of] the very ideals that inspired the founding of the United Nations." For all their invocations of Serbian sovereignty, Russia and China were concerned that UN intervention in Kosovo would set a dangerous precedent for the international community's response to independence movements in Chechnya, Taiwan, and Tibet. On the other hand, international cooperation is still necessary. The Bush administration's decision to go to war in Iraq exposed the problems of essentially unilateral action. The Iraq war has had an immediate and adverse impact on international unity. It has also indirectly exacerbated suspicions about humanitarian justification for the general use of force.

Effective Intervention? Actually achieving stated goals has been an issue for the United Nations, the United States, and regional leaders such as the European Union and the African Union. Doctrinally, the fundamental dilemma over effective intervention concerns the strength and breadth of the political mandate and the extent to which outside actors should field forces that could do more than just manifest impartiality or provide limited force protection. In classical peacekeeping, when the strategy is supporting parties that already have agreed to peace, impartiality works well. But when the parties are still in conflict, nonaligned action can be quite dysfunctional. Impartiality means not coercing either side, irrespective of which one is doing more killing, seizing more territory, or committing more war crimes. Mandates limited to self-protection do little to provide security to populaces facing humanitarian threats. Along these same lines, one recent study of major 1990s cases showed that success is more likely when the intervening forces have a sufficiently robust mandate that sanctions use of the military force needed to protect the populace from further aggression.

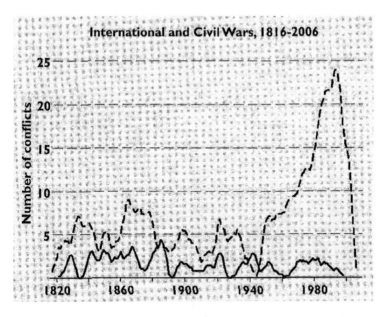

The two plots shown above represent the number of international and civil wars over the past two centuries. The data have been converted to five-year moving averages to emphasize trends over time. The number of international wars displays no clear pattern until recently, when it decreased. The number of civil wars, or intra-state conflicts, spiked dramatically near the end of the Cold War but has since seen a similarly rapid decline.

------ Inter-state

Intra-state

Darfur: Failing the Test Case

Darfur could have been the test case for turning "never again" from rhetoric into reality. But we are failing the test. Over 200,000 Darfurians have been killed. Thousands of women and young girls have been raped. Countless villages have been burnt or otherwise decimated. More than two million people are living in internal refugee camps or have been displaced across the border in Chad. Tragedy and genocide have happened yet again. This fact is shocking, but not surprising. Not one of the five core lessons has been taken to heart.

Yes, the Darfur conflict had deep historical roots. Darfurians are largely Muslim, and the main division has been between "Arabs" and "Africans." This is differentiated by skin color as well as by means of livelihood. The Arab Darfurians are primarily nomadic herders in need of grazing land, while the Africans are typically village-based farmers. Tensions were intensified by the devastating 1980s drought, which left the various tribal and religious groups competing for shrinking resources of water, grassland, and arable soil. While most accounts attribute the initial attacks to Darfurian rebel groups, the transformation from limited conflict with economic and ecological roots into mass killings was instigated by the purposeful Arabization policies of the Khartoum government. These policies targeted southern Christians as non-Muslims and Darfurians as Africans. They intensified and radicalized parts of the antigovernment insurgency, which increased the threat and dangers of this group.

Mostly, however, the insurgency provided an excuse for the government to team up with Arab tribesmen. They became known as the *janjaweed*, a name taken from an old epithet of "devils on horseback." Documents captured by the African Union peacekeeping force and reported by New York Times columnist Nicholas Kristof show the direct complicity of the Sudanese government. One document directed regional commanders and security officials to execute "all directives from the president of the republic" and thereby "change the demography of Darfur and make it void of African tribes . . . [by] killing, burning villages and farms, terrorizing people, confiscating property from members of African tribes and forcing them from Darfur."

Meanwhile, despite the UN's resolution on the responsibility to protect, the international community has done little. Anything that it has done has been too weak to be credible. It has continued to consider intervention as a last resort and has deferred to sovereignty as the right of states over the responsibility of international actors. This thinking has affected genocidal regimes such as those in Sudan. The Security Council has passed a number of resolutions, but they have been ineffectual and their deadlines not enforced. The message to aggressors is in the limits, not the scope, of such crimes. Aggressors know what they are doing. They understand that they are not complying with certain conditions and that they are not meeting certain deadlines.

Instead of complying with UN Security Council resolutions, the Sudanese government has continued financing the *janjaweed*. Indeed. Sudanese armed forces and law enforcement agencies themselves took part in rapes and gang rapes. Some in the international community claimed that they have sent a tough message, but the message was devoid of serious credibility. Instead, "the looming threat of complete lawlessness and anarchy draws nearer," Secretary-General Annan acknowledged in early 2006. The resolutions have been so devoid of credibility, in fact, that UN Special Envoy Jan Pronk stated, "The international response has been so ineffectual that people on the ground are just laughing."

Opposition from Russia and China was a main reason for the limits and weaknesses of the UN Security Council decisions on Darfur. Both of the countries' positions reflected Kosovo-like concerns over state sovereignty and economic interests. While Russia's ambassador dutifully deliberated in the Security Council, Russia was the seller of the military aircraft used to bomb villages in Darfur. China's opposition concerned Sudanese oil. As the supplier of six percent of China's oil needs and with projections very much on an upward curve, Sudan was integral to China's own geopolitical interest in global oil. China also had approximately US$3 billion invested in Sudans oil sector, had been awarded hundreds of millions of US dollars in additional contracts for the construction of pipelines and port facilities, and was the principal financer of a US$200 million hydroelectric plant.

US policy has shown some signs of focus and leadership on Darfur; but it has been uneven at best in its actual substance and follow-through. Secretary of State Condoleezza Rice made a dramatic visit to the region in July 2005, making it a point to meet with rape victims. Back home, though, the administration was slow to break the congressional deadlock over the Darfur Peace and Accountability Act. Some of this sloth was due to internal congressional issues and some to administration priorities. Bipartisan alliances such as those between Senators Barack Obama (D-Ill.) and Sam Brownback (R-Kan.) helped advance the legislation. The bill that finally passed did propose some targeted sanctions and provided some support for the African Union and UN peacekeeping forces, but it was only a partial measure and not a top White House priority.

The Darfur issue was less of a domestic US political problem than often is the case for humanitarian intervention. The Christian right, which had been very involved in the defense of Sudanese Christians in the South, was also weighing in on Darfur: "Just because you've signed a peace deal with the South," Franklin Graham, the son of Billy Graham, told a White House aide, "doesn't mean you can wash your hands of Darfur." On the left, various NGOs generated at least a degree of attention and action. These included the Genocide Intervention Network, started by socially entrepreneurial college students, and Genocide Watch, led by a former US State Department official. MySpace.com organized 20 benefit concerts that featured popular bands promoted on its website. Public opinion polls showed robust and broad support for strengthened

US leadership and tougher policies, though this support stopped short of the actual deployment of US ground forces.

The Rally to Stop Genocide, held April 30, 2006 in Washington DC, featured a range of speakers rarely found on the same podium. They included Richard Land, president of the Southern Baptist Convention; actor George Clooney; Holocaust survivor Elie Wiesel; and Paul Rusesabagina, made famous by the movie "Hotel Rwanda." Overall media attention was typically lacking, but at the very least, Nicholas Kristof began to make Darfur a recurring focus in his newspaper column.

To the extent that there has been some involvement, it has not been informed by the key lessons of effective intervention. The African Union is to be credited for intervening. But the mission was more than it could handle. It did not have the capacity to act, and it did not receive the assistance it needed from the United Nations, the United States, or Europe. Former US Assistant Secretary of State for Africa Susan Rice observed the perverse dynamic of "a conspiracy of absolution," in which "the African Union has absolved reluctant Western countries of any responsibility to consider sending their own troops," and for which the United States, the United Nations, and the European Union were "undoubtedly grateful." Even when the UN Security Council finally passed a resolution in August 2006 calling for a UN force to take over, it was yet again "seized with the matter" rhetoric that resulted in no real action.

The problem has had no shortage of ideas and alternatives. Numerous viable proposals for international action have been put forward throughout the crisis, but little has been done. Indeed, a whole series of proposals has come from just one NGO, the International Crisis Group (ICG). In March 2004, the ICG laid out a number of focused, feasible measures to toughen diplomacy. In August 2004, it laid out an "international action plan." In April, July, and October 2005, it presented updated versions. In March 2006 it called for a hand-off from the African Union Mission in Sudan to a UN peacekeeping force of double the size and with a more robust mission and mandate. Finally, in October 2006, it proposed further measures along the same lines. Despite these proposals, the international community has continued to squander opportunities for effective intervention. In acting as it did, the problems only intensified, and the details and nature of intervention became more complex.

The peace agreement reached in early May 2006 attracted some fanfare, but it quickly fell apart. After participating in the negotiations, Nigerian President Olusegun Obasanjo said with all-too-accurate foresight: "Unless the right spirit is there, the right attitude, this document will not be worth the paper its written on." Instead, as former US Assistant Secretary of State Cheryl Igiri warned in a November 2005 study, "The crisis in Darfur reveals that, despite all the promises since Rwanda that such a catastrophe would not be allowed to happen again, the international community still lacks the institutions, procedures and political unity to respond in a timely way. The global response to rapidly developing conflicts is still the same: painfully and tragically slow."

The Challenges of Achieving "Never Again"

Prevention of all mass killings is unrealistic. But prevention of more than what has been stopped in the past is not. To prevent any more mass killings, we need to provide better answers to the five core questions posed earlier.

First, political causality rather than historical determinism needs to be the analytic starting point for understanding the driving forces behind these conflicts. This moves the policy debate beyond "can anything at all be done?" to "what needs to be done?" Policy experience and various studies show that in Bosnia, Rwanda, and Darfur, the international community missed countless opportunities to limit, if not prevent, the exacerbation of these conflicts. If we yet again choose inaction or inadequate action, let us at least do it without the self-delusion of non-involvement. For when one party to the conflict concludes that the other cannot counter its aggression without international support, that party's choice to slaughter is indeed easier. US presidents and other world leaders need to make clear to their top aides and military and diplomatic establishments that they want to know what to do, not whether to act.

Second, the responsibility to protect needs to be further legitimized as a basis for abridging state sovereignty and intervening in intrastate conflicts. The Darfur case was the first major opportunity for the United Nations to demonstrate its commitment to this norm, and it has been showing quite the opposite. One does not have to buy into the Bush administration's tone and tenor, and especially not its contrarian objectives, to see that the United Nations puts its own credibility at risk when it says one thing and does another. For its part, especially given its unilateralist action in Iraq, the United States needs to stop manipulating high-minded humanitarian rationales for classically self-interested interventions. Those states and institutions that have power must uphold the legitimacy of the responsibility to protect. At the same time, states that restrict interventions in the name of principles such as sovereignty, which they use to preserve the freedom to be repressive and murderous within their own borders, need to be stripped of their cover stories.

Third, force cannot just be a last resort; it may need to be an early option. Until force can be used as something more than a last resort, we will continue to consign ourselves to picking up pieces of societies that have been torn asunder by mass deaths and other devastating destruction. As hard as conflict prevention is, post-conflict reconstruction is even harder. One study after another has shown the profound effects that these kinds of conflicts have on economies, inter-communal relations, and virtually all societal institutions.

Take a look at Somalia, which, as of early 2006, was on its fourteenth attempt since 1991 to reestablish a central government. Or look at Rwanda, which is still in the earliest phases of judicial and reconciliatory proceedings for war crimes that occurred over a decade ago. Failing states are enough of a problem, and failed ones are even worse. To be sure, all debates about the early use of force have been further complicated by the fallout from Iraq. However, as stressed earlier, dialogue on the threat of force as more than a last resort was already circulating before the Iraq war. There is a peace-through-strength logic here that is consistent with deterrence strategy as adapted to today's realities.

Fourth, on the decision-maker question, the UN Security Council should be the preferred, but not exclusive, source of legitimate authority. The Darfur case demonstrated the Security Council's limited functionality. This was due to the ability of major powers (China and Russia) to trump collective commitments. Other members (the US, the UK, and France) are also not exerting the political will necessary for concerted action. Yet from Iraq, we also recognize the dangers of the use of force and largely unilateral decision-making. Regional organizations provide a viable intermediate basis with potentially stronger claims to legitimacy than largely unilateral actors or ad hoc coalitions of the willing. The regional setup, however, can be complicated, especially if the Security Council explicitly opposes an action instead of simply not acting. But it is worth pondering which is worse for the international community: bypassing the Security Council or deferring to it as it does nothing to stop genocide.

Fifth, a greater capacity for humanitarian intervention must be created. Here there is already some progress. The 2005 Human Security Report heavily attributed the decline in the numbers and intensity of wars to the impacts of international preventive diplomacy and peace operations. The United Nations needs greater military intervention credibility and capacity. The only way to make such improvements is to take up the long-delayed issue of creating a standing UN military force that is geared toward peace operations. The African Union is to be credited for its effort in Darfur, although the setbacks it has faced point to the benefits of establishing a standing regional force. US strategy was shifting toward greater peace operations capacity in the latter part of the Clinton administration, but this was reversed during the Bush administration and undermined by the Iraq war. Recent Bush administration statements affirming the importance of peace operations are encouraging, but they are coming incredibly late. Finally, Europe also has a vital role to play, both through NATO and the European Union.

Meeting these five sets of challenges is a tall order. But it is still possible. Most of all, it is necessary. This is especially true if we are to have any chance of transforming the "never again" pledge from rhetoric into reality. Doing so is the only way for us to place credible worth in our efforts to become a true global community.

This selection was written by five leading experts in collaboration with United for a Fair Economy, a national nonpartisan organization based in Boston, Massachusetts, that works on reducing economic inequality. The work and writings of these five authors encompass the fields of social activism; public policy; economic justice; history; and African American, Latino, and Native American studies.

Overview:
The Roots of the Racial Wealth Divide

Meizhu Lui, Barbara Robles,
Betsy Leondar-Wright, Rose Brewer, Rebecca Adamson

Accumulating wealth—as distinct from making a big income—is key to your financial independence. It gives you control over assets, power to shape the corporate and political landscape, and the ability to ensure a prosperous future for your children and their heirs. . . . Wealth is used not just to pay the rent or buy groceries, but to create opportunities, to free you to pursue your dreams.

——Rev. Jesse Jackson, Sr., and Jesse Jackson, Jr.

For every dollar owned by the average white family in the United States, the average family of color has less than one dime. Why do people of color have so little wealth? Because for centuries, they were barred by law, by discrimination, and by violence from participating in government wealth-building programs that benefited white Americans. Understanding the roots of the racial wealth divide will lead to more understanding of racial inequalities in general and more understanding of how to reach equality.

What Is Wealth?

In this book, when we use the term "wealth," we mean economic assets. A family's net worth is their assets minus their debts, or what they own minus what they owe. Assets include houses and other real estate, cash, stocks and bonds, pension funds, businesses, and anything else that can be converted to cash, such as cars and works of art.

These are not the only kinds of wealth. Family, social, and community networks, education and skills, public infrastructure and a healthy environment, religion and spirituality: all these not only make us economically more secure, they help us feel well off in ways that money can't buy. But this book focuses on financial wealth, and the story of the government's role in influencing the racial wealth divide.

Our net worth is influenced by the net worth of our parents, grandparents, and earlier generations. Most private wealth in the United States was inherited. And even for people who do not inherit money after their parents' deaths, their family's education and social contacts and financial help from living relatives make a big difference.

The racial wealth gap has continued to grow (see Figure 1–1). From 1995 to 2001, according to the Federal Reserve Bank, the average family of color saw their net worth fall 7 percent, to $17,100 in just six years, while an average white family's net worth grew 37 percent, to $120,900, in the same period.

The gap in financial assets (cash, stocks, and bonds) is even greater, since most people of color's assets are invested in their home (see Figure 1–2).

Perception and Reality of Economic Inequality by Race

Explicit racial discrimination has been illegal since the Civil Rights laws of the 1960s, so many people now attribute racial differences in financial success entirely to individual behavior. White Americans in particular tend to believe that the playing field is now level. Every year Gallup takes a "minority rights and relations" poll that reveals ethnic differences in perceptions of opportunity. In the 2004 poll, 77 percent of white respondents and 69 percent of Latino respondents said they believe that African Americans have as good a chance as whites do to get any kind of job for which they are qualified. Only 41 percent of blacks felt the same.[1]

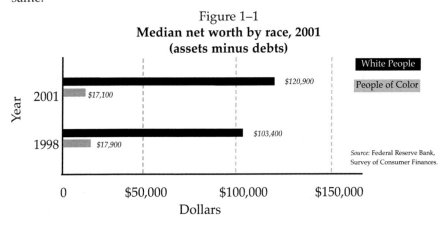

Figure 1–1
**Median net worth by race, 2001
(assets minus debts)**

Source: Federal Reserve Bank, Survey of Consumer Finances.

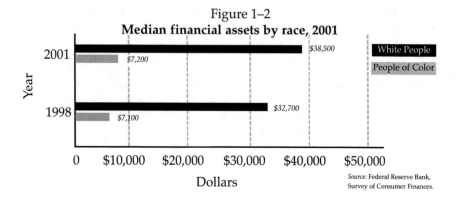

Figure 1–2
Median financial assets by race, 2001

Source: Federal Reserve Bank,
Survey of Consumer Finances.

A racially mixed group is gathered in a church basement for a workshop on the racial wealth divide. A trainer from United for a Fair Economy has just presented the facts that a typical white family has about $121,000 in assets, compared to the typical family of color, which has about $17,000 in assets.

In response, Ed, a middle-aged white man, raises his hand. "I hear what you are saying—that white people tend to have more money. But I don't like what you are imply-ing—that I should feel guilty about it. I swear, everything I have, I worked hard for."

Ed has a point. He says he studied hard in college, worked hard at every job, and saved steadily until he could buy a home. For the past several years, he and his wife have been contributing to a retirement account.

The trainers ask him who helped him become prosperous, and he says, "No one." When the discussion turns to affirmative action, he says he opposes racial preferences and government handouts.

But then the trainers lead the group in an exercise in which participants put mile-stones of their family's history on a giant timeline on the wall.

It turns out that Ed's great-great-grandfather got a farm in Nebraska through the Homestead Act—a program available only to whites.

His father, a World War II veteran, got a Veterans Administration mortgage and went to college on the G.I. Bill—programs that black G.I.s couldn't take full advantage of because of housing and education discrimination. Thanks to those boosts to earlier generations, Ed's college tuition as well as the down payment on his home could be paid by his parents.

It may be true that he studied hard, worked hard, saved—and so can claim some credit for his assets. But how much of the credit is his? How much is due to public investments in his family?

A Latina woman, Larisa, asks Ed, "What about me? I studied hard, worked hard, and saved just like you. But I didn't get the same rewards. Doesn't that mean your money comes partly from your race?" Ed admits that it does.

Not surprisingly, there's a similar division on the question of how much the government should try to improve the social and economic status of various groups. Sixty-eight percent of African Americans, 67 percent of Latinos, and only 32 percent of whites said government should play a major role.[2] Our explanation of the racial wealth gap has implications for the solutions we favor: individual failure implies individual responsibility for narrowing the gap, while structural causes require collective efforts for public solutions.

Depending on the particular question asked, between 40 percent and 60 percent of white Americans incorrectly believe that African Americans are doing as well as or better than white Americans in employment, income, education, and health care, according to a 2001 poll by the *Washington Post*, the Kaiser Family Foundation, and Harvard University.[3]

The comments of those polled are revealing. "It's good that the bad days are past and blacks have come up. As a whole, you don't hear about [problems] now as you used to. Now if something occurs, like a black guy being mistreated for a job or something, you hear about it," said Emily Reed of Russell, New York. "I think it's pretty even, but you'd never get blacks to admit it," said retiree Thomas Ripley of Belleville, Illinois. "It keeps the pressure on government for more programs."

Of course, individual effort does make a difference in financial success, compared to how the same individual would have fared without putting forth an effort. But Americans begin the race from different starting lines. Not only do well-off people, primarily whites, have significant head starts, but even many working-class whites have had modest advantages when compared with working class people of color, most of whom begin far behind whites' starting line.

Income is a short-term measure that shows the effects of education, effort, and talent, as well as the impacts of opportunity and discrimination, on the current generation. But differences in income are dwarfed by differences in wealth, which are far more likely to be affected by the policy environment of previous generations.

Higher incomes have been the primary focus ever the past forty years of economic justice activism. One reason is that assets can seem like a secondary concern for people who are incarcerated, homeless, or shut out of decent employment; advocacy has often been concentrated on the causes of people with the greatest need.

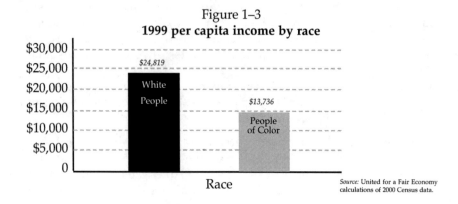

Figure 1–3
1999 per capita income by race

Source: United for a Fair Economy
calculations of 2000 Census data.

Figure 1–4
Home ownership rates, 2003

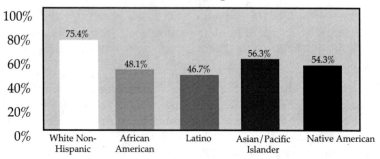

Source: U.S. Census Bureau, *Annual Statistics, 2003.*
Housing Vacancies and Homeownership, Table 20.

Getting into formerly all-white colleges and unions to win access to better paying jobs for people of color, affirmative action, welfare rights, living wage campaigns, and union drives have been worthy goals in the quest to boost the incomes of people of color from their low pre-Civil Rights Era levels. And these efforts have succeeded to some degree. African Americans' median family incomes have risen from $23,514 in 1968 (in 2002 dollars, adjusted for inflation) to $30,134 in 2004, though white incomes have risen even faster.[4] Black per capita income has more than doubled in those same years, as has white income.[5]

But focusing just on income misses much of the problem. People of color are more likely to be tossed on the waves of economic turmoil—and sometime drowned—because they don't have big enough asset security boats to help them stay afloat. Three-quarters of white people own their homes, while a slight majority of people of color are renters. In times of inflation, housing becomes easier to afford for homeowners with fixed mortgage rates, while renters see their housing costs rise. In times of recession or depression, those with savings accounts can better weather unemployment, while those without savings can be sunk into debt and deprivation. And in times of economic growth, those with assets can invest them or borrow against them to take advantage of business opportunities.

> *As the racial wealth divide workshop progressed, some of the participants seemed uncomfortable with the word "wealth."*
>
> *One young black man, Max, said, "I think part of what's wrong with this country is that everyone wants to be a millionaire. There's too much greed. What's wrong with just wanting to make a decent living?"*
>
> *A longtime community organizer, Kate, challenged the workshop's focus on assets, saying, "There's no point in programs for home ownership and savings accounts if people have low incomes and no health coverage."*

Income versus Wealth

Income feeds your stomach, but assets change your head. That is, you really do act differently when you have a cushion of assets so that you can strategize around important opportunities in life. When you are living from paycheck to paycheck you just think about how you're making the next day or the next week or the next month happen. But when you have a set of resources that allow you to think about your future in a positive way, you can strategize about the future, create and take advantage of opportunity. Otherwise you stay in the present.

Melvin Oliver, co-author of *Black Wealth, White Wealth*[6]

Income can change on a dime, but wealth changes over generations. Our lives are shaped by the wealth—or lack of wealth—of our parents, our grandparents, and our ancestors. As an estimated 80 percent of assets come from transfers from prior generations, the history of the financial situations of prior generations is a primary cause of the racial wealth gap.[7] Until government policy tackles disparities in wealth—not just income—and until it recognizes and compensates for its own responsibility for the racial wealth gap, the United States will never have racial or economic justice.

White people are much more likely to inherit money from deceased relatives than people of color. In *The Hidden Cost of Being African American*, Thomas Shapiro summarizes the research on racial differences in inheritance. One study he cites reports that one in four white families received an inheritance after a parent's death, averaging $144,652, while only one in twenty African American families inherited, with an average inheritance of $41,985. Another study found that as of 1989, one-third of white baby boomers stood to inherit more than $25,000, as opposed to one in twenty black baby boomers.

These numbers show that most white people do not receive any inheritances from deceased relatives' estates. But in interviewing black and white working-class families, Shapiro found that modest amounts of money passed down by living relatives were also far more common in white families than in black families. Whites who get such help often don't think of themselves as inheritors, but consider such transfers to be just a normal part of family life. Contributions to a down payment on a house and college tuition are the most common forms of family financial aid. Shapiro calls these "transformative assets," because they boost life-long prosperity and security. He estimates a national average of these transfers of $14,000.[8] About half of white families give this kind of head start to young adults, compared with about one in five black families.[9] He found that in white families, money flows from parents to children, while in black families money flows from adult children to their parents and other relatives.

Shapiro concludes:

> The real story of the meaning of race in modern America, however, must include a serious consideration of how one generation passes advantage and disadvantage to the next—how individuals' starting points are determined. While ending the old ways of outright exclusion, subjugation, segregation, custom, discrimination, racist ideology, and violence, our nation continues to reproduce racial inequality, racial hierarchy, and social injustice that is very real and formidable for those who experience it.[10]

Snapshot of the 1850s

Think back just a few generations to the 1850s. In that decade, the U.S. government treated people dramatically different based on their race, and the differences present then still affect us today.

For many whites, especially white men, the 1850s were a very exciting time.

- Gold had been discovered in California in 1849, and eighty thousand white men had moved there in search of their fortunes, many with government assistance. Only whites were eligible for California land claims, and many who didn't find gold became farmers.

- Slave owners were getting rich off of slave labor. The average South Carolina slave owner's income in 1850 was $565, more than ten times the $53 average earnings of all white residents of the state.

- White women—for centuries blocked from asset ownership—had recently taken a few small steps toward equal rights. The Women's Rights Convention at Seneca Falls had just happened, in 1848. Married white women had just won the right to own property in New York State.[11]

- Anti-immigrant and anti-Catholic groups such as the Know-Nothing Party won elections in the 1850s, but they were never a majority of any legislative body, and thus white immigrant groups, though poor and despised, never lost legal rights.

- Congress was discussing plans for distribution of millions of acres of western land to white people through what would become the 1862 Homestead Act.

But if you were a Native American, 1850 was the beginning of one of the most devastating decades in a devastating century.

- Throughout the 1850s, the U.S. Army waged battles over land against Indian tribes.

- In 1851, the Sioux tribe yielded all of Iowa to the United States.

- The state of California appropriated $1 million for bounties for Native American scalps in 1851. In 1853, the California Preemptive Act made all Indian lands available for white homesteaders.

- The Native American population of California fell from 310,000 in 1850 to less than 50,000 in 1855, mostly from diseases brought by the "49ers."

If you were African American in 1850, it seemed that slavery would never end.

- The Fugitive Slave Law, passed that year, made it a criminal offense to hide or assist runaway slaves. Slave catchers could search for escaped slaves even in free states.

- Congress passed the Compromise of 1850, which made the new state of California a free state and ended the slave trade in Washington, D.C., but allowed slavery by popular vote in the other territories that would become Arizona, Utah, Nevada, and New Mexico.

- Dred Scott, who had filed suit to win his freedom in 1847, was set free in 1850 by a St. Louis circuit court. But ten years later the Supreme Court overturned that precedent, ruling that African Americans weren't citizens and therefore couldn't file lawsuits.

- Free African Americans lost jobs to new immigrants. In 1830 most servants in New York City were black, but by 1850, 80 percent were Irish women.[12]

If your roots were in Latin America, the 1850s were a disasterous decade to live in what is now the United States.

- Mexico had lost half of its territory in 1848. In theory the Treaty of Guadalupe-Hidalgo proteced Mexican-American landowners. But in fact, one-third of these landowners became landless during the 1850s.

- The phrase "manifest destiny," coined a few years before, gained acceptance as a rationale to take much of North America from Mexico.

- A "Foreign Miner's Tax" was passed in California in 1850 to stop Mexicans from participating in the Gold Rush.[13] In 1852, it was extended to Chinese workers.

If you were Asian and immigrating to the United States around 1850, you found the country increasingly inhospitable.

- As several thousand Chinese men went to California in search of gold, special taxes, fees, and regulations were applied to prevent them from competing with white miners and business owners.

- In 1853, a court ruled that Chinese people weren't white, denying them many advantages of citizenship.

Snapshot of the 1950s

Now fast-forward a hundred years to the 1950s, within living memory for most Americans or their parents or grandparents. The racial wealth gap widened then, too.

If you were white, the postwar boom meant good jobs and moving to the suburbs.

- Thanks to the GI Bill a large number of white male veterans entered college after World War II; many entered professions or got management jobs in the rapidly growing corporate sector.

- More than a quarter of all white families shifted from renting to owning their homes in the twenty years after the war.

- The new suburbs grew with federal subsidies for roads, infrastructure, and mortgages, and they were almost entirely limited to white home buyers.

- The cold war and anticommunism put a chill on the political climate that silenced the voices of many who questioned racism and white advantages.

If you were African American, segregation still ruled.

- Hopes raised by the desegregation of the armed forced in 1948 and the integration of professional sports were dashed, as other employers continued to discriminate.

- Returning black veterans didn't get the same hero's welcome as white vets. Most black World War II vets found the GI Bill's educational benefits didn't work, except at historically black colleges, which were swamped with far more applicants than they could accommodate. And most colleges were segregated, in practice and in some cases by law.

- Rule by terror continued in the South. Fourteen-year-old Emmett Till was murdered in Mississippi in 1955.

- Less than 1 percent of all mortgages issued from 1930 to 1960 were issued to African Americans.

- In 1948 the Supreme Court banned the restrictive covenants that had limited white home sellers to white buyers. The Federal Housing Administration stopped subsidizing mortgages for homes with restrictive covenants in 1950. But banks, realtors, insurance companis, and white home owners continued to find ways to exclude African Americans from buying homes in white neighborhoods. Too many black families were limited to deteriorating urban ghettos.

If you were Asian American, the U.S. government was still hostile to your presence in the early 1950s.

- Asians were still unable to become naturalized citizens in 1950. Not until the McCarren-Walter Act was passed in 1952 were immigrants from Asia able to become citizens.[14]

- Japanese-Americans who lost property while in internment camps were awarded some reparations through the 1948 Evacuation Claims Act, but they got only about ten cents for every dollar lost.[15]

If you were Latino and living in the United States or its territories, you were more than likely living in poverty in the 1950s.

- Puerto Rico was a territory of the United States, and Puerto Ricans had one of the world's lowest incomes, only 40¢ per day in 1940.[16] Not surprisingly, by 1950 great numbers were moving to the mainland. They came to New York for low-wage factory jobs that disappeared shortly thereafter, leaving them with few opportunities by the end of the 1950s.

- Operation Bootstrap enacted in 1947 gave tax incentives for U.S. companies to set up shop on the island, thereby crowding out businesses owned by Puerto Ricans. More than one in eight Puerto Ricans was unemployed.

- Most Mexican Americans were landless laborers on land their parents and grandparents had owned.

- Mexicans were brought to the United States to fill labor shortages during the war, but in the mid-1950s hundreds of thousands were deported in Operation Wetback.

If you were Native American, you were struggling in 1950 to regain some of what your people had lost.

- There had been some progress for Indian tribes in recent decades. The Indian Reorganization Act of 1934 had allowed tribes to regain four million acres by 1950.

- But then, in 1953, Congress passed a tribal termination policy that ended federal recognition of and services for over a hundred tribes. The Klamath alone lost over 880,000 acres of timberland. The Menominee tribe went from prosperity to impoverishment after being terminated in 1954.

And in 2050?

When 2050 arrives, what will its snapshot look like? Will the rules of the economy still be tilted toward white people's prosperity? Will we maintain an economic order that fosters social divisions?

Or will our country have built a ladder of economic opportunity for Americans of all races to climb? Will we have given those held back for so long a boost to a higher rung? By 2050 a majority of our population will be people of color. Our nation's unity depends on our answers.

Why Not Just Fight Poverty?

Isn't the problem low income and assets, regardless of race? Why not just focus on ending poverty? Why focus specifically on the racial divide?

It's true that the racial wealth divide exists in the context of growing overall economic inequality, now at historic proportions not seen since 1929. And it's true that millions of white people are among those who have fallen backward over the last twenty-five years. More than one in six American children live in poverty, including one in eleven white children.[17] Many progressives of all races advocate organizing against poverty and economic insecurity generally—without highlighting the racial divide—to unite people against the excesses of the superrich.

Recent decades have been a great time for people whose income has come mostly from owning assets, with ten years of explosive growth in stock prices and tax cuts targeted at that group. By 2003, there were 2.27 million millionaires in the United States, up from 1.8 million in 1997.[18] Although major asset owners are disproportionately white, most whites depend on wages for their income. And wage earners did not share in the stock market growth of the 1980s and 1990s.

The wealthiest 1 percent of American families, who own a third of all U.S. wealth, saw their net worth grow by 63 percent, to an average of $12.6 million, from 1983 to 2001, and their financial wealth grow by 109 percent.[19] Meanwhile, the 40 percent with the lowest net worth saw their average wealth fall 44 percent in those same years, to $2,900.[20] Most of this was home equity, and their average financial net worth fell 46 percent to negative $10,000—in other words, more debt than financial assets.[21]

Wealth inequality gaps are much wider in the United States than in other industrialized countries.[22] While the average after tax income of the richest 1 percent tripled from 1979 to 2000, to $863,000, the bottom fifth only rose 9 percent, to $13,700, despite all the economic growth of those decades. The middle fifth gained just 15 percent, to $41,900.[23] The 2.8 million people in the richest 1 percent of American families had more after tax income in 2000 than the 110 million Americans in the lowest income four-tenths of the population.[24] CEO pay grew from 42 times median worker pay in 1980 to 431 times in 2004.[25]

Economic instability has grown among working people of all races. Almost forty-six million Americans lacked health coverage in 2004, and over seven million were counted as unemployed in August 2005.[26, 27] While the uninsured and the unemployed were disproportionately people of color, a majority of them were white. The trade policies, monetary policies, budget decisions, labor rights setbacks, and tax cuts of the last three decades benefited corporations and major asset owners and disadvantaged moderate and low-income people of all races.

One's impression of the wealth of the average white family depends on which definition of "average" is used. Using the mean, which divides the total wealth owned by the number of white people, distorts the picture by conflating ordinary families with the superrich elite. After all, if you average Bill Gates's assets with a Wal-Mart cashier's, they each have over $20 billion. But using the median—the family in the middle of the line if all white families were lined up in order of net worth (assets minus debts), about $121,000 in 2001—gives a more realistic picture of how little benefit white working families get from sharing a race with most of the superrich.

Whites who express resistance to the concept of the racial wealth divide are not necessarily racist but often are working-class people who can't see how government programs have benefited them. The term "white privilege" sometimes falls flat with white people who for reasons of class, gender, disability or age find themselves living lives that seem far from privileged. One-quarter of white families don't own a home, and more than one in twelve live below the poverty line. Those laid off in the recession of the early 2000s were disproportionately white men in high-tech industries, and they may never recover that lost ground in the new global high-tech economy. The growing economic insecurity faced by more and more white people also cries out for solutions.

The right wing takes advantage of the economic hardships of working and poor white people to recruit supporters for so-called color-blind policies. In 2003, Californians voted on and defeated Proposition 54, a referendum to prohibit public collection of racial information. The Center for Individual Rights has pressed lawsuits against affirmative action in several states. Their suit against the University of Michigan went to the U.S. Supreme Court with mixed results, affirming yet limiting the legality of race-based affirmative action programs.

At the crux of the argument over affirmative action is a historical debate about when discrimination against people of color ended, if ever. "Slavery was a long time ago," goes the argument against reparations for African Americans. And it is true that the best-known transfers of wealth from people of color to white people—taking land from Native Americans and Mexicans, as well as slavery—are no longer in living memory of the people in the United Stases today. The Civil Rights Movement tackled overt racial discrimination and won broad support for greater equality of opportunity, and the racial income gap and wealth gap shrank in those first post segregation decades.

So why not disregard race and simply work to eliminate poverty and economic insecurity for everyone?

Because this challenging economy presents more barriers for people of color than for white people. Because past effort to raise the floor left out most people of color. And therefore the goal of economic security for everyone won't be reached unless we intentionally tackle racism.

In what ways do people of color face more economic barriers than white people? Both outright discrimination and the costs of segregation block the advancement of people of color.

Discrimination

First, despite the denial by conservatives such as Dinesh D'Souza, author of *The End of Racism*, old-fashioned prejudice and discrimination have not gone away. A striking example was portrayed in the episode of ABC's *Primetime Live* in 1991 in which two young men, one black and one white and with similar credentials, moved to a new city.[28] While filmed by a secret camera, they applied for jobs, apartments, and car loans, and met very different receptions. The white young man was offered good deals and rapidly found a position, a home, and a car. The black man was told that apartments had been filled, was rejected for jobs, and was required to pay a higher down payment and interest rate on his car loan. People were rude to his face and security guards followed him around stores.

A 2003 study of job applications showed continuing employer discrimination. Researchers at the University of Chicago and the Massachusetts Institute of Technology sent fictitious responses to help-wanted ads, with either white-sounding names (Emily Walsh, Brendan Baker) or black sounding names (Lakisha Washington, Jamal Jones). Those with white-sounding names received 50 percent more invitations for an initial interview than applicants with black-sounding names. Black résumés weren't helped much by stronger credentials.[29] Similarly, a sociologist at Northwestern University sent white and black men with and without criminal records to job interviews, and found that white applicants with prison records were more likely to be hired than black applicants without one.[30]

The Costs of Segregation

Even when employers, landlords, and realtors aren't prejudiced and even when there is no outright discrimination, people of color still tend to be blocked by where they live and who they know from getting as much money as white people. Shapiro's research indicates that homes in neighborhoods that are more than 10 percent black have 16 percent less value compared with equivalent homes in overwhelmingly white neighborhoods.[31] Home ownership is worth, on average, $60,000 more to white families than to black families.[32] The asset accumulation method of millions of working-class and middle-class white people—buying a house and letting it appreciate in value until it's sold at retirement—continues to be impossible for most people of color.

Even low-income white people tend to have connections and advantages not available to their counterparts of color. White poor people spend a shorter time in poverty and suffer less extreme deprivation than poor people of color. A good example is a story Dalton Conley tells about growing up as one of the few white families in a poor black neighborhood. When the local school deteriorated, and his parents had no money to move or to send him to a private school, they contacted a friend on the other side of town who let them lie and use his address so Conley could get into a well-funded, high-quality school in that neighborhood.[33] Most of his black neighbors didn't have that option. He says that he likes to ask white people how they got their jobs. "Mostly people get their jobs through social networks and connections. Usually it's someone you know—your uncle in the next city or a friend of a friend who knows somebody in your industry. And that is how we get the foot in the door. Unfortunately, because most jobs in businesses are controlled or owned by whites, given the structure of ownership in America, that leads to the perpetuation of racial inequality in the labor market. Whites tend to hire whites because they get them through their personal networks, which tend to be white.[34]

But wouldn't universal solutions that reach every neighborhood, like single-payer, health care, a higher minimum wage, and public investment in affordable housing in fact disproportionately help people of color, while also helping whites in need? These universal solutions are indeed an important part of the answer, as the last chapter will elaborate. But too often universal remedies have been tilted in whites' favor, as with the Social Security Act and other New Deal legislation, which didn't mention race but still managed to give benefits almost entirely to white people in the 1930s and 1940s.

Imagine a first-time home-buyer program that helps two families, one white and one of color, with a lower down payment and a lower interest rate. The white family's "starter home" in a white neighborhood appreciates in value, enabling them to sell it and buy a bigger house in a neighborhood with better schools. Their next house appreciates in value, too, and they get a home equity loan against it to send their kids to college. By the time they retire, the mortgage is all paid off. They sell the house, buy a small senior apartment, and invest the difference to give them some income to supplement their social security. Home ownership has given them education and retirement as well as a place to live.

The family of color's house appreciates more slowly or not at all. With lower property values come lower property tax revenues for their city, and so their neighborhood schools are lower in quality. They are more likely to face prolonged unemployment and lose their home to foreclosure. But even if they are able to keep up with the mortgage payments, they can't turn their home into retirement income because there is no cheaper housing to move into. Banks are less likely to give them a home equity loan. Home ownership gave them little more than a place to live.

The first-time home-owner program staff probably thought of the program as colorblind, open to all races. Perhaps they even did extra outreach to make sure they reached people of color. But a program aimed at helping everyone equally ended up helping white people more.

Cultural practices of particular ethnic groups also become barriers with one size fits all white lenders, For example, Vietnamese families who have never incurred debt and pay all bills in cash are sometimes rejected as not credit worthy, and groups of Latino immigrants who pool their resources to start a business are evaluated as individuals instead of as a group.

The 1990s saw a proliferation of local asset-building initiatives, such as pilot Individual Development Account (IDA) programs, innovative approaches to private saving and home ownership, and small businesses that share equity broadly with employees. While these initiatives may help some people of color, without thinking through new initiatives so that they clearly address the racial dimension of wealth disparities, the racial gap may well remain constant.

Melvin Oliver and Thomas Shapiro, in their 1995 book, *Black Wealth/White Wealth*, found that differences in income, occupation, and education only accounted for about 29 percent of the difference between white and black families' assets in 1988; over 70 percent of the difference was related just to race.[35] They called this "the costs of being black," but it could also be called the benefit of being white.

The Underestimated Role of Government in Wealth Creation

"Help from the government" sounds like something poor people and seniors get, not working people or wealthy people. But in fact, all of us depend on public infrastructure such as roads, schools, and laws. And the process of building wealth depends on government programs like social security, Pell grants, subsidized mortgages, and farm loans—and in earlier centuries, land grants. All these have been more available to white people.

How we try to close the racial wealth gap depends on how we understand where assets come from. If we think well-off white people got their wealth only through individual ability and hard work, then the solution will be to urge low-income people of color to try harder. But if we also see how heavily white people have historically relied on government help to build assets, then we will support expanding assistance to all assetless Americans, and we will work for racial justice for those historically barred from wealth became of their race.

> At this point in the workshop, it's time to discuss the cause of the racial wealth gap. The trainer asks, "How do people get wealth?" Everyone calls out answers:
> "Marrying money!" The group laughs.
> "Hard work and saving, that's the only way that works."
> "If you're white, maybe. If you're black, forget it—you're not gonna get rich."
> "It's all who you know. You gotta have the connections."
> "Talent. If you're the best in the world at something."
> "Entrepreneurship. Starting a business that takes off."
> "Inheriting it. Most rich people got it from Daddy."
> The group falls silent, their list is complete.
> The trainer asks, "What about the government? Is there anything the government does that affects whether people have wealth?"
> There's silence in the room.
> Finally, one young woman, Susan, raises her hand and speaks tentatively.
> "Do you mean the lottery?"

Government racism has not been uniformly applied to all groups of color, but has been manifested through different mechanisms for different ethnic groups over the centuries. Native Americans were displaced from their land by force and then faced constantly changing conceptions of their status dreamed up in Washington, D.C. African Americans were enslaved and then kept at the bottom of the economy by legal segregation and violence. Conquest of Spanish-speaking countries, justified by the

Monroe Doctrine, turned Latinos into colonial subjects, both in their formerly independent lands and in the rest of the United States. Asian Americans have been treated as perpetual foreigners no matter how long they've been in the United States. One after the other, these groups were racialized, that is, made into a legal entity subordinate to white people.

Citizenship, as explored by Evelyn Nakano Glenn, is a government-granted status that opens the door to full membership in the society.[36] Citizenship rights ebbed and flowed for each race over the centuries, with all people of color and all women excluded at some times and places. In various ways, lesser political status meant exclusion from better jobs reserved for "free whites": for example, indentured servitude for Chinese immigrants and Native Americans in California in the 1850s, peonage for Mexican Americans, and of course slavery for African Americans.[37]

This book attempts to tell each of these distinct stories while also pointing out their commonalities in contrast to white Americans' experience. Though many white working-class and poor people, especially immigrants, have struggled with poverty and limited opportunity in the United States, never have they faced these kinds of official obstacles, and frequently the government has given them boosts to prosperity.

In stressing the role of government actions and inactions, we are not claiming that they are the only cause of the racial wealth divide. Ideology, culture, and economic systems are of course woven throughout the history of racial injustice in the United States as well. Government policy does not arise in a vacuum but is formed by voter attitudes and interests and by economic forces, and policy in turn influences beliefs and economic behavior. But as black scholar Adolph Reed Jr. said, "The role of the state is consistently underestimated" in analyzing racism.[38]

The economy is not an invisible hand that operates by its own natural laws. It's a human creation that embodies racial power differences, both caused by and causing discriminatory government policies and individual interactions.

The United States has an economic system based on private ownership and very limited public regulation and public services compared with other industrialized countries. This laissez-faire system did play a role in creating the racial wealth divide. Some scholars emphasize that wealthy white employers and investors always had excessive influence on creating policy in their own interest, despite the officially democratic political system. Manning Marable has said, "The U.S. state apparatus was created to facilitate the expansion and entrenchment of institutional racism in both slave and non-slaveholding states."[39] Theodore Allen documents the role of Virginia planters in steering the colonies and then the new United States away from more direct democracy.[40] William Julius Wilson tells the story of how, when black people were at last allowed to apply for every job, manufacturing jobs disappeared from the northern cities. Just as the ladder of upward mobility was opened to everyone, the ladder broke in half, with new service industries creating millions of nonunion, unstable "McJobs" to be filled by the workers at the bottom of the labor market, who because of historical racism were disproportionately people of color.[41]

In *Faded Dreams: The Politics and Economics of Race in America,* Martin Carnoy says that "every class politics implicitly takes a stand on issues of race," and it's not a coincidence that those disadvantaged by economic policies since the 1980s have been disproportionately people of color. Rather, antiworking-class policies were sold politically by framing them with racist rhetoric about underclass culture and "welfare queens."[42]

Racial inequality is also perpetuated through what Joe Feagin calls "racial oppressors in everyday practice."[43] Cultural, intellectual, religious, and psychological factors help racism permeate through the society.

But the most persistent racist ideologies tend to be those actively promoted by governments. For example, manifest destiny was the rationale for the Anglo conquest of western Native and Mexican lands.

Public policy represents institutionalized attitudes, for better or for worse. Just as segregation laws are institutionalized prejudice, antidiscrimination laws are institutionalized multicultural acceptance. Just as egalitarian whites couldn't legally act on their good attitudes under Jim Crow and antimiscegenation laws, bigoted whites can't legally act on their prejudice under affirmative action laws. The United States needs to institutionalize a multicultural vision of our society in which every group gets the resources and opportunities to thrive.

We see a complex interplay between economics, ideology, and government policies in forming the racial wealth gap. At key moments of U.S. history—after the Civil War, during the Great Depression, and during the turmoil of the 1960s—white Southern landowners and businessmen exerted political pressure to limit or reverse racial progress. Their motivations were presumably a combination of racist prejudice and economic self-interest. Since Southern congressmembers have always had more than their share of leadership roles, the federal government caved in to their pressure and weakened voting rights, the Social Security Act, and Great Society programs. A government not already saturated with institutional racism might have stood up to them.

> In the next part of the workshop, the trainer asks the group to list ways the government could narrow the racial wealth divide, and is surprised by the resistance she gets.
>
> A longtime black activist calls out, "We've tried that and we've been burned. You can't trust the government to do anything for people of color. We've got to rely on our own community development."
>
> A Native American college student and artist says, "Whatever the government does, there will still be misrepresentations of our people in movies and ads, and white people will still think we're not as good as them. You can't legislate positive images of people of color."
>
> The trainer widens the question to what anyone could do to narrow the racial wealth divide, and the discussion is off and running.

Similar stories can be found in other parts of the United States, keeping other racial groups at the bottom of the local economy. Southwestern growers in the 1940s successfully lobbied for a guest worker program to bring in short-term contract workers from Mexico, in violation of laws against peonage.[44] In Hawaii, sugar plantation owners influenced policy on who was allowed to immigrate there, and deliberately stirred up intergroup tensions by putting one Asian group over another as overseers.[45]

There's a circle of causation: economic interests foment prejudice; prejudiced people and self-interested campaign contributors elect racist politicians; racist politicians enact discriminatory policies that further white employers' interests.

However, the government's role is often ignored in popular images of racism. School curricula on the Civil War and for Black History Month often portray the federal government as the savior of black people, intervening on their behalf against slave owners and segregationist mobs. Its capitulations to white Southern racists are overlooked.

Martin Carnoy has seen three different common explanations for racial inequality, which he calls "individual responsibility," "pervasive racism," and "economic restructuring," and he thinks all three depoliticize racial inequality too much.[46] He thinks politics reinforced the economic and social conditions that impeded black progress.[47]

> A political explanation for changes in black progress is not a replacement for all other explanations. Rather, it makes otherwise rigid, depoliticized explanations rooted in racism, changing economic structures, and even individual responsibility more dynamic and coherent. A political explanation also suggests more hope for future improvement. How politics frames racial issues and how government policies treat these issues can be changed and changed more quickly than ingrained individual fears

about race or long-established business practices. . . . Politics is shaped by normative rules—how things should be, not how they are. Normative rules can, by their very nature, be shifted, and fairly quickly.[48]

Government Obstacles: Not Only Pre-1964

Legal discrimination was gradually chipped away at from the 1940s to the 1960s, culminating with the Civil Rights Laws. But traces of de jure (in law) discrimination lingered on. For example, the Federal Housing Administration (FHA) continued so exclude most people of color from subsidized mortgage programs, which was legal because the 1964 Civil Rights Act had specifically exempted federal mortgage insurance programs.[49] Enforcement of fair housing laws was so weak as to be almost nonexistent in the 1960s and 1970s.

Disparate treatment by the federal government has also been concealed in seemingly race-neutral policies, as the next five chapters will show. The federal mandate to aid family farms was interpreted by the Department of Agriculture as a mandate to aid *white* farmers. A 1980 class action lawsuit by North Carolina Black Farmers charged that the FHA discriminated in loans to farmers. The Equal Employment Opportunity Commission (EEOC) looked into the charges and found that they were true: white farmers got more help, quicker help, and help on easier terms than black farmers.[50]

President Reagan backed off from even the limited federal commitments to affirmative action and investments in communities of color that were made in the 1970s. Manning Marable describes the racist approach and widespread harm of the Reagan administrations this way:

Reagan's racial agenda was unambiguous to friend and foe alike. He opposed affirmative action, minority economic set-asides, and enforcement of equal employment opportunity regulations. . . . Reagan manipulated crude racist stereotypes in his standard speeches, such as images of "welfare" mothers abusing food stamps and other public assistance programs. Yet despite the deeply racist character of the "Reagan Revolution". . . its essential dynamics were driven by the political economy of capitalism. . . . Reaganism represented a fundamental departure from the liberal welfare state and Keynesian economic policies that had been followed to a great extent by both capitalist political parties. . . . Massive reductions in social programs across the board were mandated . . . 400,000 families were removed from federal and state welfare roles . . . the Department of Agriculture reduced the amount of food served to 26 million children at more than 94,000 schools across she country. Federal housing expenditures and special programs designed for low-income families virtually came to a halt. . . .The number of homeless Americans not surprisingly doubled during Reagan's tenure in office. Most other social programs, such as job training, community development agencies and cooperatives, and public health clinics were either eliminated completely or severely curtailed.[51]

Both the Clinton and Bush administrations have toughened bankruptcy, welfare, and social security rules under the rhetoric of "personal responsibility" and "the free market," but people of color have been disproportionately harmed. For example, the welfare reform law of 1996 was implemented more harshly for recipients of color than white recipients. White people leaving welfare are twice as likely as black and Latina people leaving welfare to receive transitional benefits like child care and transportation assistance.[52] Children of undocumented immigrants, even high school valedictorians whose parents have been paying taxes for decades, are barred from getting in-state tuition rates and public scholarships in many states, excluding some of them from higher education. The gains to people of color from government employment and antidiscrimination policies since the 1960s are counterbalanced by policies that boost white people and hold people of color back.

Everyone Would Benefit from Closing the Racial Wealth Gap

In the long run, white people also lose from policies that disadvantage people of color. The lower floor in the United States compared with western Europe, Canada, and other industrialized countries—below poverty minimum wage, weak social benefits, lack of guaranteed health care, poor education system—can be attributed to the racial divisions in the United States. The existence of a labor force with substandard wages enforced by racism has enabled employers to pay less to all workers. Undocumented immigrants are currently the most common group being used this way by unscrupulous employers. Public benefits like welfare and Medicaid are associated with people of color by politicians and media, thus weakening their support among white voters, and then poor whites also suffer when they are cut.

Our vision is not just success for a few, with people of color finally mirroring the class spectrum whites now have. We envision smaller inequality overall, real opportunity for all, and an economy with a higher floor. But within this fairer economy, people of color would be fully enfranchised, with as much economic security as white people. And that will only happen if boosts are given to help the targets of past discrimination accumulate wealth.

There is sometimes queasiness about wealth among progressives who critique the excessive, one-sided rewards to the owners of capital in this economic system. However, we make a distinction between asset ownership made lucrative by exploiting others on the one hand (such as rental housing with excessive rents or inadequate maintenance, or business ownership with low wages and no profit sharing), and basic assets that bring security on the other (such as home ownership and retirement accounts). Of course, there is an enormous gray area, and principled people can disagree about what constitutes exploitation. But it would be hard to argue that owning the home one lives in harms anyone else. It would be hard to argue that having a savings account or retirement account in a credit union or a bank committed to community reinvestment harms anyone else. By making a distinction between modest transformative assets and huge fortunes swollen by exploitation even the firmest critics of capitalism can get behind the goal of asset building for all.

Why These Five Racial Categories?

In the next five chapters, we tell the history of government obstacles to asset building for Native American, African American, Latino, and Asian American people, and of government boosts to asset building for white people.

We chose to divide the incredibly diverse population of the United Stases into these five ethnic groups because they are the largest groups to share a common history of racialization and to face common treatment by the United Stases government. We tell the histories of groups of color in the order that they began, to show how racism evolved from one group to the next.

Race is, of course, a social construct, not an absolute biological reality. Human beings share 99.9 percent identical DNA. If you look back far enough, all of us have ancestors who traveled the globe and intermingled; and before that we all share an original common ancestor in Africa. The people in the United States could be separated by "race," nationality, and ethnicity into two groups, four groups, eight groups, or a hundred groups, and reasons could be given for each clumping. The categories and words in common use have changed many times over the centuries, and they will change many times in the future.

But if the topic is government actions that affect assets, the five groupings in this book make historical sense. Native Americans of all tribes faced genocide and displacement. Latinos of all nationalities ended up in this country after the United States government invaded, dominated, and/or conquered their lands. Almost all African Americans are the descendants of slaves and of survivors of segregation and mob violence. Asian Americans of all nationalities have been treated as perpetual foreigners. And most European Americans of all ethnic groups have been treated (sometimes reluctantly) as citizens worthy of government assistance. Everyone's story—everyone's reasons for having the amount of assets they own—is different, but most of our ancestral stories fit into one of these five historical streams.

New policies based on race and nationality are still being enacted, such as the post–September 11 detention of over twelve hundred Arab and Muslim men without evidence of wrongdoing, and the registration required for immigrant men from only Muslim countries imposed in 2003. But we have chosen to focus on large groups with centuries-long histories of discrimination in the United States.

And these historical streams have affected each other. As Joe Feagin puts it,

> U.S. society is not a multiplicity of disconnected racisms directed at people of color. Instead, this U.S. society has a central white-supremacist core initially developed in the minds, ideologies, practices, and institutions of those calling themselves "whites" for destroying the indigenous societies and for exploiting African labor. This structure of racialized domination was later extended and adapted by the descendants of the founders for the oppressions of other non-European groups such as Asian and Latino Americans.[53]

Racial inequality used to be regarded as a black/white issue. In 1968, the Kerner Commission, a civil rights advisory board created by President Lyndon Johnson, warned that America was rapidly becoming "two nations," "black vs. white," "separate and unequal." In part, this framing was due to the invisibility of Native Americans, Latinos, and Asian Americans to oblivious white policy makers. But in truth, their numbers were much smaller then. In 1960, whites were 88.6 percent of those responding to the census, blacks, 10.5 percent, Asians, 0.5 percent, and Native Americans, 0.3 percent—almost the identical black and white percentages as in 1910.[54] Questions about Spanish language or Hispanic/Latino origins first appeared in 1970, when they were only about 4.5 percent of the respondents.[55]

Even when Melvin Oliver and Thomas Shapiro wrote their groundbreaking book *Black Wealth/ White Wealth* in 1995, the most recent census (widely criticized for undercounting people of color) showed Latino, Asian, and Native American people totaling only 13 percent together, compared with 12 percent black and 75 percent "non-Hispanic white" people.[56] But now it is clear that the United States is a multicultural country, and becoming more so as the global economy displaces more and more people. In 2000, for the first time, the U.S. Census allowed people to identify themselves as more than one race, and 2.4 percent took this multiracial option.[57] The 2000 census also found Latinos more numerous than non-Latino African Americans for the first time, 12.5 percent compared with 12.1 percent. Non-Latino whites had fallen to 69.1 percent, and the other categories had grown, with 0.7 percent American Indian, 3.6 percent Asian, 0.1 percent Native Hawaiian and Pacific Islander, and 5.5 percent "other."[58] In the South, where the historic dynamic has been between black and white, there has been a sudden increase in the population of Latinos. This has brought new attention to the historic racial dynamics among white, Chicano/Mexican American, and Native American people in the Southwest.

As a result of this multicultural trend and growing economic inequality, competition has heated up among communities of color for a slice of the pie. Misunderstandings and mythologies about each race have grown: it is hard to see what they have in common. Their stories are viewed as separate racisms—slavery, Indian genocide, Mexican conquest. In fact, all groups of color have faced the same racism expressed through different mechanisms. Manning Marable describes the issues among groups of color this way:

> With the growth of a more class-conscious black and Latino bourgeoisie, ironically a social product of affirmative action and civil rights gains, tensions between these two large communities of people of color [blacks and Latinos] began to grow. . . . The tragedy underlying this issue is that too little is done either by African American or Latino mainstream leaders who practice racial identity polities, to transcend parochialism and redefine their agendas on common ground. . . . While African Americans, Latinos and Asian Americans scramble over which group should control the mom-and-pop grocery store in their neighborhoods, almost no one questions the racist "redlining" policies of large banks that restrict access to capital to nearly all people of color. Black and Latino working people usually are not told by their race-conscious leaders and middle-class symbolic representatives that institutional racism has also frequently targeted Asian Americans throughout U.S. history. . . . We need to recognize that both perspectives of racial identity politics, which are frequently juxtaposed as integration/assimilation versus nationalist/separatism, are actually two different sides of the same ideological axis. . . . The ability to create a framework for multicultural democracy intergroup dialogue and interaction within and between the most progressive leaders, grassroots activists, intellectuals, and working people of these communities will determine the future of American society itself.[59]

And after September 11, anti-immigrant sentiment increased among U.S. citizens of all races. Now more than ever racial minorities need to recognize their commonalities in order to implement successful strategies to counter the conservative backlash and to wage the battle for full equality.

In 1903, W. E. B. DuBois named the color line as the key problem of the twentieth century. One century later, we face the same question. How it gets answered will determine our character as a nation. Do we continue to pay lip service to the ideals of our Constitution? Or will we practice what we preach, and truly become a beacon of democracy and equality? First, we must develop a shared understanding of the roots of the divisions, before we can understand how to overcome them. As the saying goes, You can't know where you're going if you don't know where you've been.

Notes

[1] Jones, Jeffrey, 2004.

[2] Ibid.

[3] Morin, 2001, A1.

[4] Muhammed, et al., 2004, 7.

[5] Ibid., 6.

[6] PBS, "Interview with Melvin Oliver," 2003.

[7] Shapiro, 2004, 60–61, citing a Kotilkoff-Summers study that estimates that as "much as 80 percent of family wealth derives not from savings but from transfers of money from generation to generation."

[8] Ibid., 63.

[9] Ibid., 64.

[10] Ibid., 8.

[11] Stanton, et al., 1889, 63–75.

[12] Takaki, 1993, 154, 156.

[13] Ibid., 195.

[14] Wong, 1995, 65.

[15] Reimers, 1989, 18.

[16] Amott and Matthaei, 1991, 270; Morales, 1986, 30.

[17] U.S. Census Bureau, Income, Poverty, and Health Insurance Coverage in the United States: 2004.

[18] Capgemini, 2004, 6.

[19] Computations from 1983 and 2001 Survey of Consumer Finances in Wolff, "Recent Trends in Wealth Ownership," 2004, pp. 30–31.

[20] Ibid., 31.

[21] Ibid., 12, 34.

22 Mishel et al., 2003, 413, Table 7.10.

23 Greenstein and Shapiro, 2003, 1–2.

24 Ibid., 2.

25 United for a Fair Economy, Executive Excess 2005, August 2005.

26 U.S. Census Bureau, *Income, Poverty, and Health Insurance Coverage in the United States:* 2004.

27 U.S. Bureau of Labor Statistics, Current Employment Statistics, Table A-1.

28 ABC News, 1991.

29 Muwakkil, 2003.

30 Ibid.

31 Shapiro, 2004, 121.

32 Ibid., 53.

33 PBS, "Interview with Dalton Conley," 2003.

34 Ibid.

35 Oliver and Shapiro, 1995, 169.

36 Glenn, 2002, 18–55.

37 Ibid., 68–69.

38 Reed, 2002.

39 Marable, 2000, 4.

40 Allen, 1997, passim.

41 Wilson, 1997, 39–46.

42 Carnoy, 1994, 53–55.

43 Feagin, 2000, Chapter 5.

44 Glenn, 2002, 238–239.

45 Ibid., 239.

46 Carnoy, 1994, 6–7.

47 Ibid., 10.

48 Ibid., 11.

49 Lipsitz, 1998, 27.

50 Gilbert and Eli, 2000, 164.

51 Marable, 2000, xxii–xxiii.

52 Applied Research Center, 2002, 19.

53 Feagin, 2000, 204.

54 U.S. Census Bureau, Population Division, Gibson, Campbell and Kay Jung, 2002, Table F-1. "Race and Hispanic Origin, for the United States and Historical Sections and Subsections of the United States: 1790 to 1900."

55 Ibid.

56   Ibid.
57   U.S. Census Bureau, 2000 Decennial Census, Table PCH-1.
58   Ibid.

Section Six:
Allegory of the Cave

*P*lato (428/7–348/7 B.C.) was a Greek philosopher, born into an aristocratic family. Plato, along with Socrates, his teacher, and Aristotle, his student, laid the foundations for Western philosophical thinking. Plato started the Academy, in Athens, which was the first institution of higher education in the western world. Many of Plato's writings survive, and the majority of them are in dialogue form, perhaps intended for public performance, or perhaps for presentation at the Academy. This translation is from Francis M. Cornford, published in 1941.

The Allegory of the Cave

Plato

The progress of the mind from the lowest state of unenlightenment to knowledge of the Good is now illustrated by the famous parable comparing the world of appearance to an underground Cave. In Empedocles' religious poem the powers which conduct the soul to its incarnation say, "We have come under this cavern's roof." The image was probably taken from mysteries held in caves or dark chambers representing the underworld, through which the candidates for initiation were led to the revelation of sacred objects in a blaze of light. The idea that the body is a prison-house, to which the soul is condemned for past misdeed, is attributed by Plato to the Orphics.

One moral of the allegory is drawn from the distress caused by a too sudden passage from darkness to light. The earlier warning against plunging untrained minds into the discussion of moral problems (498 A, p. 206), as the Sophists and Socrates himself had done, is reinforced by the picture of the dazed prisoner dragged out into the sunlight. Plato's ten years' course of pure mathematics is to habituate the intellect to abstract reasoning before moral ideas are called in question (537 E, ff., p. 259).

Next, said I, here is a parable to illustrate the degrees in which our nature may be enlightened or unenlightened. Imagine the condition of men living in a sort of cavernous chamber underground, with an entrance open to the light and a long passage all down the cave.[1] Here they have been from childhood, chained by the leg and also by the neck, so that they cannot move and can see only what is in front of them, because the chains will not let them turn their heads. At some distance higher up is the light of a fire burning behind them; and between the prisoners and the fire is a track[2] with a parapet built along it, like the screen at a puppet-show, which hides the performers while they show their puppets over the top.

I see, said he.

Now behind this parapet imagine persons carrying along various artificial objects, including figures of men and animals in wood or stone or other materials, which project above the parapet.

Naturally, some of these persons will be talking, others silent.[3]

It is a strange picture, he said, and a strange sort of prisoners.

Like ourselves, I replied; for in the first place prisoners so confined would have seen nothing of themselves or of one another except the shadows thrown by the fire-light on the wall of the Cave facing them, would they?

Not if all their lives they had been prevented from moving their heads.

And they would have seen as little of the objects carried past.

Of course.

Now, if they could talk to one another, would they not suppose that their words referred only to those passing shadows which they saw?[4]

Necessarily.

And suppose their prison had an echo from the wall facing them? When one of the people crossing behind them spoke, they could only suppose that the sound came from the shadow passing before their eyes.

No doubt.

In every way, then, such prisoners would recognize as reality nothing but the shadows of those artificial objects.[5]

Inevitably.

Now consider what would happen if their release from the chains and the healing of their unwisdom should come about in this way. Suppose one of them set free and forced suddenly to stand up, turn his head, and walk with eyes lifted to the light; all these movements would be painful, and he would be too dazzled to make out the objects whose shadows he had been used to see. What do you think he would say, if someone told him that what he had formerly seen was meaningless illusion, but now, being somewhat nearer to reality and turned towards more real objects, he was getting a truer view? Suppose further that he were

shown the various objects being carried by and were made to say, in reply
to questions, what each of them was. Would he not be perplexed and
believe the objects now shown him to be not so real as what he formerly
saw?[6]

Yes, not nearly so real.

And if he were forced to look at the fire-light itself, would not his
eyes ache, so that he would try to escape and turn back to the things
which he could see distinctly, convinced that they really were clearer than
these objects now being shown to him?

Yes.

And suppose someone were to drag him away forcibly up the steep
and rugged ascent and not let him go until he had hauled him out into
the sunlight, would he not suffer pain and vexation at such treatment,
and when he had come out into the light, find his eyes so full of its radiance that he could not see a single one of the things that he was now told
were real?

Certainly he would not see them all at once.

He would need, then, to grow accustomed before he could see things
in that upper world.[7] At first it would be easiest to make out shadows,
and then the images of men and things reflected in water, and later on the
things themselves. After that, it would be easier to watch the heavenly
bodies and the sky itself by night, looking at the light of the moon and
stars rather than the Sun and the Sun's light in the day-time.

Yes, surely.

Last of all, he would be able to look at the Sun and contemplate its
nature, not as it appears when reflected in water or any alien medium,
but as it is in itself in its own domain.

No doubt.

And now he would begin to draw the conclusion that it is the Sun
that produces the seasons and the course of the year and controls everything in the visible world, and moreover is in a way the cause of all that
he and his companions used to see.

Clearly he would come at last to that conclusion.

Then if he called to mind his fellow prisoners and what passed for
wisdom in his former dwelling-place, he would surely think himself
happy in the change and be sorry for them. They may have had a prac-

tice of honoring and commending one another, with prizes for the man who had the keenest eye for the passing shadows and the best memory for the order in which they followed or accompanied one another, so that he could make a good guess as to which was going to come next.[8] Would our released prisoner be likely to covet those prizes or to envy the men exalted to honor and power in the Cave? Would he not feel like Homer's Achilles, that he would far sooner "be on earth as a hired servant in the house of a landless man"[9] or endure anything rather than go back to his old beliefs and live in the old way?

Yes, he would prefer any fate to such a life.

Now imagine what would happen if he went down again to take his former seat in the Cave. Coming suddenly out of the sunlight, his eyes would be filled with darkness. He might be required once more to deliver his opinion on those shadows, in competition with the prisoners who had never been released, while his eyesight was still dim and unsteady; and it might take some time to become used to the darkness. They would laugh at him and say that he had gone up only to come back with his sight ruined; it was worth no one's while even to attempt the ascent. If they could lay hands on the man who was trying to set them free and lead them up, they would kill him.[10]

Yes, they would.

Every feature in this parable, my dear Glaucon, is meant to fit our earlier analysis. The prison dwelling corresponds to the region revealed to us through the sense of sight, and the fire-light within it to the power of the Sun. The ascent to see the things in the upper world you may take as standing for the upward journey of the soul into the region of the intelligible; then you will be in possession of what I surmise, since that is what you wish to be told. Heaven knows whether it is true; but this, at any rate, is how it appears to me. In the world of knowledge, the last thing to be perceived and only with great difficulty is the essential Form of Goodness. Once it is perceived, the conclusion must follow that, for all things, this is the cause of whatever is right and good; in the visible world it gives birth to light and to the lord of light, while it is itself sovereign in the intelligible world and the parent of intelligence and truth. Without having had a vision of this Form no one can act with wisdom, either in his own life or in matters of state.

So far as I can understand, I share your belief.

Then you may also agree that it is no wonder if those who have reached this height are reluctant to manage the affairs of men. Their souls long to spend all their time in that upper-world—naturally enough, if here once more our parable holds true. Nor, again, is it at all strange that one who comes from the contemplation of divine things to the miseries of human life should appear awkward and ridiculous when, with eyes still dazed and not yet accustomed to the darkness, he is compelled, in a law-court or elsewhere, to dispute about the shadows of justice or the images that cast those shadows, and to wrangle over the notions of what is right in the minds of men who have never beheld Justice itself.[11]

It is not at all strange.

No; a sensible man will remember that the eyes may be confused in two ways—by change from light to darkness or from darkness to light; and he will recognize that the same thing happens to the soul. When he sees it troubled and unable to discern anything clearly, instead of laughing thoughtlessly, he will ask whether, coming from a brighter existence, its unaccustomed vision is obscured by the darkness, in which case he will think its condition enviable and its life a happy one; or whether, emerging from the depths of ignorance, it is dazzled by excess of light. If so, he would rather feel sorry for it; or, if he were inclined to laugh, that would be less ridiculous than to laugh at the soul which has come down from the light.

That is a fair statement.

If this is true, then, we must conclude that education is not what it is said to be by some, who profess to put knowledge into a soul which does not possess it, as if they could put sight into blind eyes. On the contrary, our own account signifies that the soul of every man does possess the power of learning the truth and the organ to see it with; and that, just as one might have to turn the whole body round in order that the eye should see light instead of darkness, so the entire soul must be turned away from this changing world, until its eye can bear to contemplate reality and that supreme splendor which we have called the Good. Hence there may well be an art whose aim would be to effect this very thing, the conversion of the soul, in the readiest way; not to put the power of sight into the soul's eye, which already has it, but to ensure that, instead of looking in the wrong direction, it is turned the way it ought to be.

Yes, it may well be so.

It looks, then, as though wisdom were different from those ordinary virtues, as they are called, which are not far removed from bodily qualities, in that they can be produced by habituation and exercise in a soul which has not possessed them from the first. Wisdom, it seems, is certainly the virtue of some diviner faculty, which never loses its power, though its use for good or harm depends on the direction towards which it is turned. You must have noticed in dishonest men with a reputation for sagacity the shrewd glance of a narrow intelligence piercing the objects to which it is directed. There is nothing wrong with their power of vision, but it has been forced into the service of evil, so that the keener its sight, the more harm it works.

Quite true.

And yet if the growth of a nature like this had been pruned from earliest childhood, cleared of those clinging overgrowths which come of gluttony and all luxurious pleasure and, like leaden weights charged with affinity to this mortal world, hang upon the soul, bending its vision downwards; if, freed from these, the soul were turned round towards true reality, then this same power in these very men would see the truth as keenly as the objects it is turned to now.

Yes, very likely.

Is it not also likely, or indeed certain after what has been said, that a state can never be properly governed either by the uneducated who know nothing of truth or by men who are allowed to spend all their days in the pursuit of culture? The ignorant have no single mark before their eyes at which they must aim in all the conduct of their own lives and of affairs of state; and the others will not engage in action if they can help it, dreaming that, while still alive, they have been translated to the Islands of the Blest.

Quite true.

It is for us, then, as founders of commonwealth, to bring compulsion to bear on the noblest natures. They must be made to climb the ascent to the vision of Goodness, which we called the highest object of knowledge; and, when they have looked upon it long enough, they must not be allowed, as they now are, to remain on the heights, refusing to come down again to the prisoners or to take any part in their labors and rewards, however much or little these may be worth.

Shall we not be doing them an injustice, if we force on them a worse life than they might have?

You have forgotten again, my friend, that the law is not concerned to make any one class specially happy, but to ensure the welfare of the commonwealth as a whole. By persuasion or constraint it will unite the citizens in harmony, making them share whatever benefits each class can contribute to the common good; and its purpose in forming men of that spirit was not that each should be left to go his own way, but that they should be instrumental in binding the community into one.

True, I had forgotten.

You will see, then, Glaucon, that there will be no real injustice in compelling our philosophers to watch over and care for the other citizens. We can fairly tell them that their compeers in other states may quite reasonably refuse to collaborate: there they have sprung up, like a self-sown plant, in despite of their country's institutions; no one has fostered their growth, and they cannot be expected to show gratitude for a care they have never received. 'But,' we shall say, 'it is not so with you. We have brought you into existence for your country's sake as well as for your own, to be like leaders and king-bees in a hive; you have been better and more thoroughly educated than those others and hence you are more capable of playing your part both as men of thought and as men of action. you must go down, then, each in his turn, to live with the rest and let your eyes grow accustomed to the darkness. You will then see a thousand times better than those who live there always; you will recognize every image for what it is and know what it represents, because you have seen justice, beauty, and goodness in their reality; and so you and we shall find life in our commonwealth no mere dream, as it is in most existing states, where men live fighting one another about shadows and quarrelling for power, as if that were a great prize; whereas in truth government can be at its best and free from dissension only where the destined rulers are least desirous of holding office.'

Quite true.

Then will our pupils refuse to listen and to take their turns sharing in the work of the community, though they may live together for most of their time in a purer air?

No; it is a fair demand, and they are fair-minded men. No doubt unlike any ruler of the present day, they will think of holding power as an unavoidable necessity.

Yes, my friend; for the truth is that you can have a well-governed society only if you can discover for your future rulers a better way of life than being in office; then only will power be in the hands of men who are rich, not in gold, but in the wealth that brings happiness, a good and wise life. All goes wrong when starved for lack of anything good in their own lives, men turn to public affairs hoping to snatch from thence the happiness they hunger for. They set about fighting for power, and this internecine conflict ruins them and their country. The life of true philosophy is the only one that looks down upon office of state; and access to power must be confined to men who are not in love with it; other-wise rivals will start fighting. So whom else can you compel to undertake the guardianship of the commonwealth, if not those who, besides understanding best the principles of government, enjoy a nobler life than the politician's and look for rewards of a different kind?

There is indeed no other choice.

Notes

[1] The *length* of the "way in" (eisodos) to the chamber where the prisoners sit is an essential feature, explaining why no daylight reaches them.

[2] The track crosses the passage into the cave at right angles, and is *above* the parapet built along it.

[3] A modern Plato would compare his Cave to an underground cinema, where the audience watch the play of shadows thrown by the film passing before a light at their backs. The film itself is only an image of "real" things and events in the world outside the cinema. For the film Plato has to substitute the clumsier apparatus of part of the machinery, providing for the movement of the objects and the sounds whose echo the prisoners hear. The parapet prevents these persons' shadows from being cast on the wall of the Cave.

[4] Adam's text and interpretation. The prisoners, having seen nothing but shadows, cannot think their words refer to the objects carried past behind their backs. For them shadows (images) are the only realities.

[5] The state of mind called *eikasia* in the previous chapter.

[6] The first effect of Socratic questioning is perplexity. Cf. p. 8.

[7] Here is the moral—the need of habituation by mathematical study before discussing moral ideas and ascending through them to the form of the Good.

[8] The empirical politician, with no philosophic insight, but only a "knack of remembering what usually happens" (Gorg. 501 A). He has *eikasia* = conjecture as to what is likely (*eikos*).

[9] This verse (already quoted at 386 C, p. 76), being spoken by the ghost of Achilles, suggests that the Cave is comparable with Hades.

[10] An allusion to the fate of Socrates.

[11] In the *Gorgias* 486 A, Callicles, forecasting the trail of Socrates, taunts him with the philosopher's inability to defend himself in a court.

*B*enjamin Jowett published this translation of Plato's "The Allegory of the Cave" in 2002. How does this translation compare to the Cornford translation, which appears in the anthology just prior to these pages? Did you find one of the translations easier to read than the other? If the dialogue is set in ancient Greece, does the historical and cultural context of each translation differ?

2

The Allegory of the Cave

Plato

428–347 B.C.

(Socrates begins, addressing Glaucon)

And now, I said, let me show in a figure how far our nature is enlightened or unenlightened: Behold! human beings living in an underground den, which has a mouth open toward the light and reaching all along the den; here they have been from their childhood, and have their legs and necks chained so that they cannot move, and can only see before them, being prevented by the chains from turning round their heads. Above and behind them a fire is blazing at a distance, and between the fire and the prisoners there is a raised way; and you will see, if you look, a low wall built along the way, like the screen which marionette players have in front of them, over which they show the puppets.

I see.

And do you see, I said, men passing along the wall carrying all sorts of vessels, and statues and figures of animals made of wood and stone and various materials, which appear over the wall? Some of them are talking, others silent.

You have shown me a strange image, and they are strange prisoners.

Like ourselves, I replied; and they see only their own shadows, or the shadows of one another, which the fire throws on the opposite wall of the cave?

True, he said; how could they see anything but the shadows if they were never allowed to move their heads?

And of the objects which are being carried in like manner they would only see the shadows?

Yes, he said.

And if they were able to converse with one another, would they not suppose that they were naming what was actually before them?

Very true.

And suppose further that the prison had an echo which came from the other side, would they not be sure to fancy when one of the passers-by spoke that the voice which they heard came from the passing shadow?

No question, he replied.

To them, I said, the truth would be literally nothing but the shadows of the images.

That is certain.

And now look again, and see what will naturally follow if the prisoners are released and disabused of their error. At first, when any of them is liberated and compelled suddenly to stand up and turn his neck round and walk and look toward the light, he will suffer sharp pains; the glare will distress him, and he will be unable to see the realities of which in his former state he had seen the shadows; and then conceive someone saying to him, that what he saw before was an illusion, but that now, when he is approaching nearer to being and his eye is turned toward more real existence, he has a clearer vision—what will be his reply? And you may further imagine that his instructor is pointing to the objects as they pass and requiring him to name them—will he not be perplexed? Will he not fancy that the shadows which he formerly saw are truer than the objects which are now shown to him?

Far truer.

And if he is compelled to look straight at the light, will he not have a pain in his eyes which will make him turn away to take refuge in the objects of vision which he can see, and which he will conceive to be in reality clearer than the things which are now being shown to him?

True, he said.

And suppose once more, that he is reluctantly dragged up a steep and rugged ascent, and held fast until he is forced into the presence of the sun himself, is he not likely to be pained and irritated? When he approaches the light his eyes will be dazzled, and he will not be able to see anything at all of what are now called realities.

Not all in a moment, he said.

He will require to grow accustomed to the sight of the upper world. And first he will see the shadows best, next the reflections of men and other objects in the water, and then the objects themselves; then he will gaze upon the light of the moon and the stars and the spangled heaven; and he will see the sky and the stars by night better than the sun or the light of the sun by day?

Certainly.

Last of all he will be able to see the sun, and not mere reflections of him in the water, but he will see him in his own proper place, and not in another; and he will contemplate him as he is.

Certainly.

He will then proceed to argue that this is he who gives the season and the years, and is the guardian of all that is in the visible world, and in a certain way the cause of all things which he and his fellows have been accustomed to behold?

Clearly, he said, he would first see the sun and then reason about him.

And when he remembered his old habitation, and the wisdom of the den and his fellow prisoners, do you not suppose that he would felicitate himself on the change, and pity him?

Certainly, he would.

And if they were in the habit of conferring honors among themselves on those who were quickest to observe the passing shadows and to remark which of them went before, and which followed after, and which were together; and who were therefore best able to draw conclusions as to the future, do you think that he would care for such honors and glories, or envy the possessors of them? Would he not say with Homer, "Better to be the poor servant of a poor master," and to endure anything, rather than think as they do and live after their manner?

Yes, he said, I think that he would rather suffer anything than entertain these false notions and live in this miserable manner.

Imagine once more, I said, such a one coming suddenly out of the sun to be replaced in his old situation; would he not be certain to have his eyes full of darkness?

To be sure, he said.

And if there were a contest, and he had to compete in measuring the shadows with the prisoners who had never moved out of the den, while his sight was still weak, and before his eyes had become steady (and the time which would be needed to acquire this new habit of sight might be very considerable), would he not be ridiculous? Men would say of him that up he went and down he came without his eyes; and that it was better not even to think of ascending; and if anyone tried to loose another and lead him up to the light, let them only catch the offender, and they would put him to death.

No question, he said.

This entire allegory, I said, you may now append, dear Glaucon, to the previous argument; the prison-house is the world of sight, the light of the fire is the sun, and you will not misapprehend me if you interpret the journey upward to be the ascent of the soul into the intellectual world according to my poor belief, which, at your desire, I have expressed— whether rightly or wrongly, God knows. But, whether true or false, my opinion is that in the world of knowledge the idea of good appears last of all, and is seen only with an effort; and, when seen, is also inferred to be the universal author of all things beautiful and right, parent of light and of the lord of light in this visible world, and the immediate source of reason and truth in the intellectual; and that this is the power upon which he who would act rationally either in public or private life must have his eye fixed.

I agree, he said, as far as I am able to understand you.

Moreover, I said, you must not wonder that those who attain to this beatific vision are unwilling to descend to human affairs; for their souls are ever hastening into the upper world where they desire to dwell; which desire of theirs is very natural, if our allegory may be trusted.

Yes, very natural.

And is there anything surprising in one who passes from divine contemplations to the evil state of man, misbehaving himself in a ridiculous manner; if, while his eyes are blinking and before he has become accustomed to the surrounding darkness, he is compelled to fight in courts of law, or in other places, about the images or the shadows of images of justice, and is endeavoring to meet the conceptions of those who have never yet seen absolute justice?

Anything but surprising, he replied. Anyone who has common sense will remember that the bewilderments of the eyes are of two kinds, and arise from two causes, either from coming out of the light or from going into the light, which is true of the mind's eye, quite as much as of the bodily eye; and he who remembers this when he sees anyone whose vision is perplexed and weak, will not be too ready to laugh; he will first ask whether that soul of man has come out of the brighter life, and is unable to see because unaccustomed to the dark, or having turned from darkness to the day is dazzled by excess of light. And he will count the one happy in his condition and state of being, and he will pity the other; or, if he have a mind to laugh at the soul which comes from below into the light, there will be more reason in this than in the laugh which greets him who returns from above out of the light into the den.

That, he said, is a very just distinction.

But then, if I am right, certain professors of education must be wrong when they say that they can put a knowledge into the soul which was not there before, like sight into blind eyes.

They undoubtedly say this, he replied.

Whereas, our argument shows that the power and capacity of learning exists in the soul already; and that just as the eye was unable to turn from darkness to light without the whole body, so too the instrument of knowledge can only by the movement of the whole soul be turned from the world of becoming into that of being, and learn by degrees to endure the sight of being, and of the brightest and best of being, or, in other words, of the good.

Very true.

And must there not be some art which will effect conversion in the easiest and quickest manner; not implanting the faculty of sight, for that exists already, but has been turned in the wrong direction, and is looking away from the truth?

Yes, he said, such an art may be presumed.

And whereas the other so-called virtues of the soul seem to be akin to bodily qualities, for even when they are not originally innate they can be implanted later by habit and exercise, the virtue of wisdom more than anything else contains a divine element which always remains, and by this conversion is rendered useful and profitable; or, on the other hand, hurtful and useless. Did you never observe the narrow intelligence flashing from the keen eye of a clever rogue—how eager he is, how clearly his paltry soul sees the way to his end; he is the reverse of blind, but his keen eyesight is forced into the service of evil, and he is mischievous in proportion to his cleverness?

Very true, he said.

But what if there had been a circumcision of such natures in the days of their youth; and they had been severed from those sensual pleasures, such as eating and drinking, which, like leaden weights, were attached to them at their birth, and which drag them down and turn the vision of their souls upon the things that are below—if, I say, they had been released from these impediments and turned in the opposite direction, the very same faculty in them would have seen the truth as keenly as they see what their eyes are turned to now.

Very likely.

Yes, I said; and there is another thing which is likely, or rather a necessary inference from what has preceded, that neither the uneducated and uninformed of the truth, nor yet those who never make an end of their education, will be able ministers of the State; not the former, because they have no single aim of duty which is the rule of all their actions, private as well as public; nor the latter, because they will not act at all except upon compulsion, fancying that they are already dwelling apart in the islands of the blessed.1

Very true, he replied.

Then, I said, the business of us who are the founders of the State will be to compel the best minds to attain that knowledge which we have already shown to be the greatest of all—they must continue to ascend until they arrive at the good; but when they have ascended and seen enough we must not allow them to do as they do now.

What do you mean?

I mean that they remain in the upper world: but this must not be allowed; they must be made to descend again among the prisoners in the den, and partake of their labors and honors, whether they are worth having or not.

But is not this unjust? he said; ought we to give them a worse life, when they might have a better?

You have again forgotten, my friend, I said, the intention of the legislator, who did not aim at making any one class in the State happy above the rest; the happiness was to be in the whole State, and he held the citizens together by persuasion and necessity, making them benefactors of the State, and therefore benefactors of one another; to this end he created them, not to please themselves, but to be his instruments in binding up the State.

True, he said, I had forgotten.

Observe, Glaucon, that there will be no injustice in compelling our philosophers to have a care and providence of others; we shall explain to them that in other States, men of their class are not obliged to share in the toils of politics: and this is reasonable, for they grow up at their own sweet will, and the government would rather not have them. Being self-taught, they cannot be expected to show any gratitude for a culture which they have never received. But we have brought you into the world to be rulers of the hive, kings of yourselves and of the other citizens, and have educated you far better and more perfectly than they have been educated, and you are better able to share in the double duty. Wherefore each of you, when his turn comes, must go down to the general underground abode, and get the habit of seeing in the dark. When you have acquired the habit, you will see ten thousand times better than the inhabitants of the den, and you will know what the several images are, and what they represent, because you have seen the beautiful and just and good in their truth. And thus our State, which is also yours, will be a reality, and not a dream only, and will be administered in a spirit unlike that of other States, in which men fight with one another about shadows only and are distracted in the struggle for power, which in their eyes is a great good. Whereas the truth is that the State in which the rulers are most reluctant to govern is always the best and most quietly governed, and the State in which they are most eager, the worst.

Quite true, he replied.

And will our pupils, when they hear this, refuse to take their turn at the toils of State, when they are allowed to spend the greater part of their time with one another in the heavenly light?

Impossible, he answered; for they are just men, and the commands which we impose upon them are just; there can be no doubt that every one of them will take office as a stern necessity, and not after the fashion of our present rulers of State.

Yes, my friend, I said; and there lies the point. You must contrive for your future rulers another and a better life than that of a ruler, and then you may have a well ordered State; for only in the State which offers this, will they rule who are truly rich, not in silver and gold, but in virtue and wisdom, which are the true blessings of life. Whereas, if they go to the administration of public affairs, poor and hungering after their own private advantage, thinking that hence they are to snatch the chief good, order there can never be; for they will be fighting about office, and the civil and domestic broils which thus arise will be the ruin of the rulers themselves and of the whole State.

Most true, he replied.

And the only life which looks down upon the life of political ambition is that of true philosophy. Do you know of any other?

Indeed, I do not, he said.

And those who govern ought not to be lovers of the task? For, if they are, there will be rival lovers, and they will fight.

No question. Who, then, are those whom we shall compel to be guardians? Surely they will be the men who are wisest about affairs of State, and by whom the State is best administered, and who at the same time have other honors and another and a better life than that of politics?

They are the men, and I will choose them, he replied.

Note

1 "Islands of the Blessed": Plato's approximation of paradise, developed in Book X of *The Republic*.